Oracle User Productivity Kit 3.5

Build high-quality training simulations using Oracle UPK 3.5

Dirk Manuel

PACKT PUBLISHING

BIRMINGHAM - MUMBAI

Oracle User Productivity Kit 3.5

First published: September 2009

Production Reference: 2240909

Published by Packt Publishing Ltd.
32 Lincoln Road
Olton
Birmingham, B27 6PA, UK.

ISBN 978-1-849680-16-5

www.packtpub.com

Cover Image by Parag Kadam (paragvkadam@gmail.com)

Credits

Author
Dirk Manuel

Reviewer
Sjoerd De Vries

Acquisition Editor
James Lumden

Development Editor
Chaitanya Apte
John Antony

Technical Editor
Chaitanya Apte

Indexer
Monica Ajmera

Editorial Team Leader
Akshara Aware

Project Team Leader
Priya Mukherji

Project Coordinator
Ashwin Shetty

Proofreader
Chris Smith
Jeff Orloff
Lynda Sliwoski

Graphics
Nilesh R. Mohite

Production Coordinator
Aparna Bhagat
Shantanu Zagade

Cover Work
Aparna Bhagat

About the author

Dirk Manuel is a freelance documentation and training consultant, specializing in projects for the large-scale implementation of SAP. Dirk has been using UPK and its precursor OnDemand for five years, during which time he has developed hundreds of well-received simulations. Dirk has provided training on UPK and OnDemand to UPK developers in Europe, Asia Pacific, and the Americas.

Originally from the United Kingdom, Dirk has lived and worked in England, Germany, Belgium (twice), and Singapore, before settling in Houston, Texas.

Dirk has a B.Sc. (Hons.) in Computer Science, and a City & Guilds in the Communication of Technical Information. He is a Fellow of the Institute of Scientific and Technical Communicators (ISTC) and a Senior Member of the Society for Technical Communication (STC).

Acknowledgment

This book has been neither a labor of love nor a life's work. Being a Technical Writer by trade, documenting what I know is almost impossible to avoid. After being asked on several occasions if I could recommend a good book on UPK/OnDemand, and always having to reply that there simply weren't any books, good or bad, I decided to write my own.

This book is a distillation of five years' experience with UPK and OnDemand, and of teaching it to other developers.

I have seen many poor examples of simulations created using UPK or OnDemand, due primarily to a lack of knowledge on the part of the developers of the capabilities of UPK. My sole intention with this book is to show developers that it is not difficult to create truly impressive training simulations, with the correct knowledge and just a little effort.

I would like to thank the staff at Packt for their support, my long-standing client, ExxonMobil, for giving me the opportunity to learn so much about UPK and OnDemand, and the extremely knowledgeable Sjoerd De Vries, for doing such a great job on the technical review. I would also like to thank Seigun Kosabayashi and Yuki Iida for the Japanese texts, and Marc Wilms for the (*petit*) French.

About the reviewer

Sjoerd de Vries is a senior e-learning consultant and project manager for customers of SMS implementation engineers (`http://www.smsnet.nl`) in The Netherlands. In his work, he combines e-learning, documentation, and change management aspects to "engineers" in larger ERP and CRM software-implementation projects, for customers like SaraLee, Philip Morris, Ericsson, ExxonMobil, Hunter Douglas, ABN-AMRO, Dutch Ministry of Defense, and many others.

In these projects, the users of the software will have an important place in "learning by doing" and increasing performance support within their company. One of the preferred tools for almost 8 years is OnDemand software, currently renamed as Oracle's User Productivity Kit (UPK) as well as Knowledge Pathways (UPK Pro), also by Oracle.

As the first Dutch partner of OnDemand Software, SMS implementation engineers have implemented, trained, and supported OnDemand Software in Europe since 2001. Since 2004 the company also became a partner of Oracle to support the User Productivity Kit that was created by OnDemand Software to support Oracle implementations only. In 2008 OnDemand Software was acquired by Oracle and SMS implementation engineers became a Certified Partner of Oracle and also won the Best Partner Award.

The many years of experience in implementing, consulting, training, and content creation means that OnDemand and UPK have hardly any mysteries for Sjoerd. He became an appreciated and highly involved member of the OnDemand Software community (currently transitioned to the Oracle Support and LinkedIn communities about the UPK). At the last UPK Users' Conference in 2008, Sjoerd also won an "OSCA" award in an UPK contest. For his years of contribution to OnDemand and the later UPK, Sjoerd was asked to contribute to this book as a technical reviewer. Because sharing ideas and knowledge is his main job, he gladly cooperated and hopes that the readers of this book also will learn to like the UPK and understand its big advantage as a training and performance support tool.

Sjoerd has a Masters degree in Science and graduated after his study at the "Vrije Universiteit" in the Netherlands as a teacher (1st degree). After several jobs as a Biology teacher he joined SMS implementation engineers in 1998 and became an e-learning expert. Sjoerd is also chief editor of a Dutch web site for E-learning & Education.

Sjoerd is a real Dutch name and since it is often asked, it is pronounced as "shoe 'rd". Feel free to contact him via his company or LinkedIn.

LinkedIn: `http://www.linkedin.com/in/somdv`.

I would like to dedicate this book to my children, Finn, Freya, and Gil, who are the reason why I still do what I do (even if they have no idea what that is).

Table of Contents

Preface 1

Chapter 1: Oracle User Productivity Kit 7

What is UPK? 7

A brief history of UPK 8

Why use UPK? 8

Instructor-led training 10

Self-paced learning 11

How does UPK work? 11

Output formats 12

Online delivery 13

Documentation 17

Deciding how you will use UPK 19

Choosing delivery formats 19

Styles and standards 20

When to record 21

What to record 21

Summary 22

Chapter 2: Organizing your Library 23

Accessing the Library 24

Working in the Developer screen 25

Changing the screen layout 26

The Properties pane 26

The Broken Links pane 27

The Related Documents pane 28

Arranging panes on the screen 28

Changing the information displayed for objects 32

Working with Views 35

Choosing a structure for your Library 37
Creating folders 40
Changing the Library structure 40
Summary 41
Chapter 3: Recording a Simulation 43
How UPK captures a recording 43
Automatic recording 45
Capturing actions 46
Problematic actions 46
Planning your recording 47
Setting your content defaults 50
General options 50
Options for Bubble Text 52
Options for the Introduction/End Frames 55
Options for String Input 56
Our first recording 57
Creating an empty Topic 58
Recording an empty Topic 59
Recording a Topic immediately 59
The Recorder window 60
The Recorder window for automatic recording 62
Our sample exercise 62
Setting your Recorder options 64
Recording drag-and-drop activities 66
Summary 78
Chapter 4: Editing a Topic 79
Understanding the Topic Editor screen 80
The Screenshot pane 81
The Frame Structure pane 82
The Property Editor panes 86
Adjusting actions 87
The Action Properties pane 87
Working with mouse Actions 89
Adjusting Action Areas 90
Adjusting Bubble Text 92
Working with keyboard Actions 94
Working with string input Actions 98
Adjusting the string input action area 104
Adjusting the background color 105
Adjusting the font 107

Controlling what the user can enter 108
Case sensitivity and password fields 114
Changing the Bubble **115**
The Bubble Properties pane 115
Changing the Bubble format 116
Changing the Bubble pointer 116
Repositioning the Bubble 117
Changing the size of the Bubble 118
Adding an icon to a Bubble 118
Changing the Bubble Text 119
Template Text versus Custom Text 120
Using Custom Text 121
Choosing which texts are displayed 122
Formatting Bubble Text 123
Tagging Custom Text for different modes 124
Undo 127
Adjusting your recording **128**
Adding missing Frames 128
Inserting a No-context Frame 130
Replacing screenshots 131
Re-recording a Topic 134
Editing screenshots 136
Choosing an image editing application 136
Editing a screenshot 138
Deleting Frames 141
Summary **143**
Chapter 5: Building an Outline **145**
Outlines versus the Library **145**
Organizing your Topics **146**
Building an Outline **148**
Step 1: Creating an Outline 148
Step 2: Inserting Outline Elements into an Outline 151
Step 3: Inserting a Topic 152
Step 4: Inserting Topic placeholders 153
Adjusting the Outline 154
Summary **160**
Chapter 6: Publishing Your Content **161**
Pre-publication checks **162**
Checking your spelling 162
Changing your spelling options 166
Updating the Glossary links 168

Testing your content **168**
Previewing a Topic **170**
Publishing your content **171**
Publishing content—a generic approach 171
Published folder structure 179
Publishing for online use **180**
Creating a Player 180
Publishing options 181
Generated files 184
Example output 185
Creating an HTML Web Site 186
Publishing options 186
Generated files 186
Example output 187
Creating an LMS Package 191
Publishing options 192
Generated files 194
Example output 194
Creating Standalone Topic Files 195
Publishing options 195
Generated files 197
Example output 197
Publishing Documents **198**
Publishing a System Process document 199
Document Properties 199
Publishing options 201
Generated files 203
Example output 203
Publishing an Instructor Manual 205
Document Properties 205
Publishing options 205
Generated files 205
Example output 206
Publishing a Job Aid 207
Document Properties 207
Publishing options 207
Generated files 207
Example output 208
Publishing a Test Document 209
Document Properties 209
Publishing options 210
Generated files 210
Example output 210
Publishing an HP Quality Center test script 211
Document Properties 212
Publishing options 212

Generated files 213
Example output 213
Publishing a Training Guide 214
Document Properties 214
Publishing options 214
Generated files 214
Example output 214
Automatic publishing 216
Settings files 216
The command line command 216
Publishing via a batch job 218
Integrating published content into other environments 219
Integrating a Topic into a presentation 219
Integrating UPK into your application 223
What is context capturing, and what does it do? 224
SmartMatch and SmartHelp 229
Summary 230
Chapter 7: Version Management 233
Checking in a content object 234
UPK Workflow 235
Step 1: Selecting the content objects 237
Step 2: Confirming the scope of the check-in 237
Step 3: Specifying a reason for the change 239
Checking out a content object 240
Cancelling the check-out of a content object 241
Working with document versions 242
Displaying an earlier version 243
Reverting to an earlier version 243
Restoring a deleted document 245
Exporting and importing content 246
Exporting content objects 247
Importing content objects 249
Converting content from a previous version of UPK or OnDemand 252
Summary 256
Chapter 8: Allowing Alternatives 257
Adding Alternative Actions 257
Automatically capturing Alternative Actions 264
Alternative Paths and Branches 265
Adding an Alternative Path 266
Changing the end point of an Alternative Path 269
Deleting an Alternative Path 269

Inserting a Decision Frame 270
Inserting a Branch 273
Changing the order of paths 276
Deleting a decision path 277
Decision Frames in See It! mode 277
Decision Frames in Know It? mode 278
Stretching the envelope with Alternative Paths 278
Looping back 279
Automatically responding to user input 279
Summary 281
Chapter 9: Adding Value to Your Topics 283
Providing context through the use of Custom Text 284
The Start Frame 284
Introduction Text: Version differences 286
Action Frames 290
The End Frame 291
Explanation Frames 292
Copying and Pasting Frames 298
Putting Web Pages to good use 301
Using Web Pages in the Concept pane 302
Using images in Web Pages 306
Creating independent Web Pages 311
Using Web Pages in Topics 311
Linking via a hyperlink 312
Linking via an icon 314
Linking files through the use of Packages 316
Creating a Package 317
Adding files to a Package 318
Linking a Package into a content object 320
Linking to a URL 323
Using a Glossary 326
Creating a glossary 328
Assigning a Glossary to content objects 331
Regenerating the Glossary links 333
Updating Glossary links after updating the Glossary itself 333
Manually regenerating the Glossary links 335
Generating a stand-alone Glossary 336
Summary 338
Chapter 10: Adding Value in the Player 339
Working with roles 339
Defining your roles 340

Assigning roles to Topics 343
Selecting roles in the Player 345
Remembering a trainee's selection 348
Publishing for a role 349
Thinking beyond roles 352
Jump-in Points 352
Defining jump-in points 353
Selecting jump-in points in the Player 354
Facilitating effective searches 356
Using Keywords 357
Assigning Keywords to a Topic 357
Allowing trainees to change their Player options 359
Providing training on the Player 361
What to explain 362
How to train on the Player 362
Summary 364
Chapter 11: Incorporating Sound into Your Topics 365
Displaying sound properties for a Frame 365
Setting up your sound options 367
Recording sound files for Template Text 369
Locating the sound files in the Library 372
Recording custom text sound files 375
Importing and exporting sound files 377
Exporting sound files 377
Importing sound files 378
Deleting sound files 379
Publishing sound 380
Sound in the Player 382
Summary 382
Chapter 12: Configuring UPK 383
Configuring Template Text 383
Understanding the template file 387
The file header 387
The <Styles> section 388
The <Events> section 388
The <Classes> section 390
The <Defaults> section 392
The <Template> sections 392
The <Keynames> section 395
The <ShiftKeyPrefix> section 397
The <Instructions> section 397

Creating a custom template 402
Taking a copy of an existing template 402
Editing a custom template 403
Customizing the Template Text 404
Customizing the Template Text the "easy" way 406
Using your custom template 408
Using a custom template as the default template 408
Assigning a custom template to existing Topics 409
Defining a new object type 410
Customizing deployment packages 414
Understanding where the deployment formats are defined 415
Creating your own deployment category 417
Customizing the logo 419
Customizing an output style 422
Removing the ability to skip in Try It! mode 425
Customizing document formats 427
Copying an existing document format 427
Customizing the UPK settings 428
Changing a document's contents 434
Summary 440
Chapter 13: Localizing Your Content 441
Foreign-language templates 441
Supported languages 442
Foreign-language template format 444
Providing existing content in a foreign language 445
Taking a copy of the existing content 446
Using a foreign-language template 446
Using a foreign-language Deployment Package 448
Translating Custom Text 451
Exporting content for translation 451
Translating via XLIFF 457
Importing a translated file 459
Replacing screenshots with localized versions 463
Re-recording the sound files 466
Summary 466

Afterword **467**

Appendix A: Installing UPK 3.5 **469**

Installing the UPK developer environment **470**

Accessing UPK for the first time **478**

Accessing a stand-alone installation 478

Logging onto a UPK client 481

Installing the Topic Player **486**

Summary **490**

Appendix B: Object Types **491**

Index **497**

Preface

This book is a developer's guide to Oracle UPK version 3.5 (and its predecessor, OnDemand version 9.1, with which it shares 95% of its functionality). It covers all aspects of UPK's functionality, and explains how to get the most out of these features in order to build high-quality training exercises that will ensure the most effective knowledge transfer possible for your trainees.

Documentation on UPK has been (until the publication of this book) almost nonexistent (consisting solely of the *Content Development Guide* shipped with the software), and training is prohibitively expensive.

This book fills the documentation gap by providing developer-friendly, visually-appealing, and easy-to-read documentation on the core functionality of UPK. It fills the training gap by taking a guided approach to this functionality, introducing new concepts and functionality with each chapter, and building on the knowledge gained in the previous chapters. In this way, readers can start with the basics, and then progress to more advanced topics as they need them, rather than being presented with "everything you need to know" at once, in a dry and difficult-to-digest manner (as is the case with the Oracle-provided documentation).

Although it is primarily aimed at new or intermediate users, this book contains enough advanced information to keep all but the most hardcore of UPK developers happy. It includes tips on how to get the most out of UPK, suggestions on best practices for training material development with UPK, and advice on how to avoid some common mistakes.

What this book covers

This book provides a guided tour of UPK 3.5. Each chapter focuses on a specific task, based around specific functionality within UPK. Throughout the book, we will develop, and build on, a sample simulation, and use this to introduce, and explain, new functionality by applying this functionality to the sample simulation.

By chapter, this book covers the following topics:

Chapter 1, *An Introduction to UPK* provides a high-level overview of what UPK is, and what its main capabilities are.

Chapter 2, *Organizing your Library* provides a first look at the developer's working environment. It starts by explaining the various components of the Developer screen, and provides some basic navigation techniques. It then provides guidelines on how to choose a suitable folder structure for your Library, and explains how to implement the chosen structure.

Chapter 3, *Recording a simulation* explains how simulations are recorded in UPK, and provides instructions for creating the initial simulation that is built upon throughout the remainder of this book.

Chapter 4, *Editing a Topic* provides a comprehensive description of the functionality provided by the Topic Editor. It does this by editing the simulation recorded in the previous chapter, changing the Bubble Text, providing Custom Text, inserting missing Frames, and editing screenshots.

Chapter 5, *Building an Outline* introduces the concept of an Outline, and provides a full description of the capabilities of the Outline Editor. It explains the difference between Modules and Sections, and explains how best to use these to organize Topics into a structure suitable for presenting to the trainees.

Chapter 6, *Publishing Content* explains, how to preview and publish recorded Topics. It explains, with examples, the various online and document-based output formats, and provides instructions on how to generate each of them. This chapter also covers the quality assurance activities that should be carried out prior to publication, including spell-checking and testing. Finally, this chapter explains how to integrate UPK's output with other applications.

Chapter 7, *Version Management* is primarily aimed at developers working in a client/server environment. It explains the check-in and check-out functionality of UPK, including the version history, reverting to prior versions of content objects, and restoring deleted objects. The final sections of this chapter are applicable to both client/server installations and stand-alone installations, describing the importance of backups and explaining how to import and export content.

Chapter 8, *Allowing Alternatives* is concerned with expanding the usefulness of recorded simulations by providing Alternative Paths, along with Branches and Decision Frames. It also explains how to improve the realism of simulations by providing Alternative Actions, and explains how to capture these automatically.

Chapter 9, *Adding Value to Your Topics* is probably the single most important chapter in this book. It explains how to improve the quality of simulations by providing context through the use of Custom Text, and by using Explanation Frames, Web Pages and Packages. It also explains how to build and implement a Glossary.

Chapter 10, *Adding Value in the Player* explains the things that can be done to improve the quality of the trainees' interaction with the UPK Player. This includes using roles, jump-in points, and keywords. This chapter also explains how to prevent trainees from skipping through exercises without performing the required actions.

Chapter 11, *Incorporating Sound into your Topics* explains the auditory capabilities that UPK provides, and discusses how best to utilize these. It explains how to record new sound files, as well as how to import and export sound files.

Chapter 12, *Configuring UPK* covers the advanced topic of configuring UPK to meet your individual requirements. The chapter explains how to customize Template Text, and how to define new object types. It also explains how to customize the UPK player, and how to create a new document format.

Chapter 13, *Localizing Your Content* explains how to convert your recorded Topics into another language. This includes using local language texts, deploying content in local languages, translating custom text, and replacing screenshots with localized versions.

Appendix A, *Installing UPK* explains how to install the UPK developer environment, either as a stand-alone application, or as part of a client/server environment. It also explains how to install the UPK Standalone Topic Player.

Appendix B, *Object Types* provides a reference list of all of the predefined object types in UPK, and shows the template text that is generated for each of these using the Standard Template and the Microsoft Template.

Who this book is for

This book has been written with the following audiences in mind:

- **New users** of UPK, including those migrating from OnDemand to UPK, who want to understand the capabilities of UPK and how they can best utilize UPK to meet their training goals
- **Intermediate users** of UPK who want to improve the quality of their UPK training simulations
- **Experienced users** of UPK who want to learn how to customize UPK to better match their own requirements

Conventions

In this book, you will find a number of styles of text that distinguish between different kinds of information. Here are some examples of these styles, and an explanation of their meaning.

Code words in text are shown as follows: "We can include other contexts through the use of the `include` directive."

A block of code will be set as follows:

```
<Class Name="ROW_SELECT_BUTTON"
    ListName="Row selection button"
      DisplayName="row selection button"
        Gender="neutral">
  <Template Context="LClick1">
    <Text Sound="lclick1">Click on the</Text>
    <ObjectType />
    <Text Sound="lclick1b">for the</Text>
    <ObjectName />
    <Text>entry.</Text>
  </Template>
</Class>
```

When we wish to draw your attention to a particular part of a code block, the relevant lines or items will be shown in bold:

```
<Class Name="ROW_SELECT_BUTTON"
    ListName="Row selection button"
      DisplayName="row selection button"
        Gender="neutral">
  <Template Context="LClick1">
    <Text Sound="lclick1">Click on the</Text>
    <ObjectType />
    <Text Sound="lclick1b">for the</Text>
    <ObjectName />
    <Text>entry.</Text>
  </Template>
</Class>
```

New terms and **important words** are shown in bold. Words that you see on the screen, in menus or dialog boxes for example, appear in our text like this: "clicking the **Next** button moves you to the next screen".

[Warnings or important notes appear in a box like this.]

[Tips and tricks appear like this.]

Reader feedback

Feedback from our readers is always welcome. Let us know what you think about this book—what you liked or may have disliked. Reader feedback is important for us to develop titles that you really get the most out of.

To send us general feedback, simply drop an email to `feedback@packtpub.com`, and mention the book title in the subject of your message.

If there is a book that you need and would like to see us publish, please send us a note in the **SUGGEST A TITLE** form on `www.packtpub.com` or email `suggest@packtpub.com`.

If there is a topic that you have expertise in and you are interested in either writing or contributing to a book, see our author guide on `www.packtpub.com/authors`.

Customer support

Now that you are the proud owner of a Packt book, we have a number of things to help you to get the most from your purchase.

Downloading the example code for the book

Visit `http://www.packtpub.com/files/code/0165_Code.zip` to directly download the example code.

Errata

Although we have taken every care to ensure the accuracy of our contents, mistakes do happen. If you find a mistake in one of our books—maybe a mistake in text or code—we would be grateful if you would report this to us. By doing so, you can save other readers from frustration, and help us to improve subsequent versions of this book. If you find any errata, please report them by visiting `http://www.packtpub.com/support`, selecting your book, clicking on the **let us know** link, and entering the details of your errata. Once your errata are verified, your submission will be accepted and the errata added to any list of existing errata. Any existing errata can be viewed by selecting your title from `http://www.packtpub.com/support`.

Piracy

Piracy of copyright material on the Internet is an ongoing problem across all media. At Packt, we take the protection of our copyright and licenses very seriously. If you come across any illegal copies of our works in any form on the Internet, please provide us with the location address or website name immediately so that we can pursue a remedy.

Please contact us at `copyright@packtpub.com` with a link to the suspected pirated material.

We appreciate your help in protecting our authors, and our ability to bring you valuable content.

Questions

You can contact us at `questions@packtpub.com` if you are having a problem with any aspect of the book, and we will do our best to address it.

1
Oracle User Productivity Kit

The things we have to learn before we do them, we learn by doing them.

- Aristotle

In this first chapter, we will start with the absolute basics. We will look at what UPK is, and what it can do for us.

In this chapter, you will learn:

- What UPK is
- How UPK works and what it captures
- What are the formats in which UPK can generate its output
- What to consider when embarking upon a training project using UPK 3.5 or OnDemand 9.1

What is UPK?

UPK (User Productivity Kit) is a software application that can be used to create simulations of tasks performed in a software application for, use during training on that application. It can also generate various forms of **documentation**—such as job aids, test scripts, and business process procedures—based on these same recordings. UPK's deliverables can also be incorporated into an application's online help system to provide in-application performance support.

UPK does all of this by capturing a user's interaction with an application (typically, to perform a discrete business task), and then repurposing this information to create the various output formats.

UPK has found a strong market in large corporations for developing training material for large-scale software implementations. Although it is most commonly-used for providing training on enterprise-level software applications, such as those offered by Oracle, SAP, Siebel, JD Edwards, and so on, UPK can be used to record and publish simulations for any Windows-based application. However, the success with which UPK manages to capture the context of the user's interaction with these 'non-targeted' applications may vary.

A brief history of UPK

UPK is the latest incarnation of a product that has been around for over ten years. Starting as an offshoot from SAP Tutor (now itself called iTutor), UPK began life as OnDemand, which was developed and marketed by OnDemand Software. OnDemand Software was acquired by **Global Knowledge Software** (**GKS**), a division of Global Knowledge, Inc. In July 2008, GKS itself was acquired by Oracle Corporation. GKS was a long-time partner of Oracle, and OnDemand has been used extensively by Oracle and its customers for providing training on Oracle products.

As Oracle already had a product called **On Demand** (with a space), the decision was made to rename OnDemand to User Productivity Kit, or UPK. Concurrent with this, Oracle realigned the version numbering of UPK so that OnDemand version 9.1 was renumbered as UPK version 3.1. To confuse users even more, UPK 3.5.0 is, for all intents and purposes, a slightly enhanced version of OnDemand 9.1.7. This was the last official OnDemand release (and was itself released as UPK 3.1.7).

Oracle refers to "pre-takeover" versions of OnDemand as "UPK 2.x". I interpret "UPK 2.x" as referring to OnDemand version 8.x, and treat UPK 3.5 and OnDemand 9.1 as generally the same product, save some minor differences in functionality highlighted as such in this book.

Why use UPK?

Despite Oracle (and Global Knowledge before it) espousing the single-source document-creation capabilities of UPK, the primary use of UPK is for the creation of simulations for use in training. And for this, it can work very well—if the developer is willing to put in the effort.

Simulations are captured in the application for which the training is being developed. This means that the simulations have the "look and feel" of the actual system. When these simulations are executed, the trainee gets the impression that they are interacting with a real system, whereas in reality, they are working within the safe confines of a training tool.

An example of a UPK simulation screen is shown in the following screenshot:

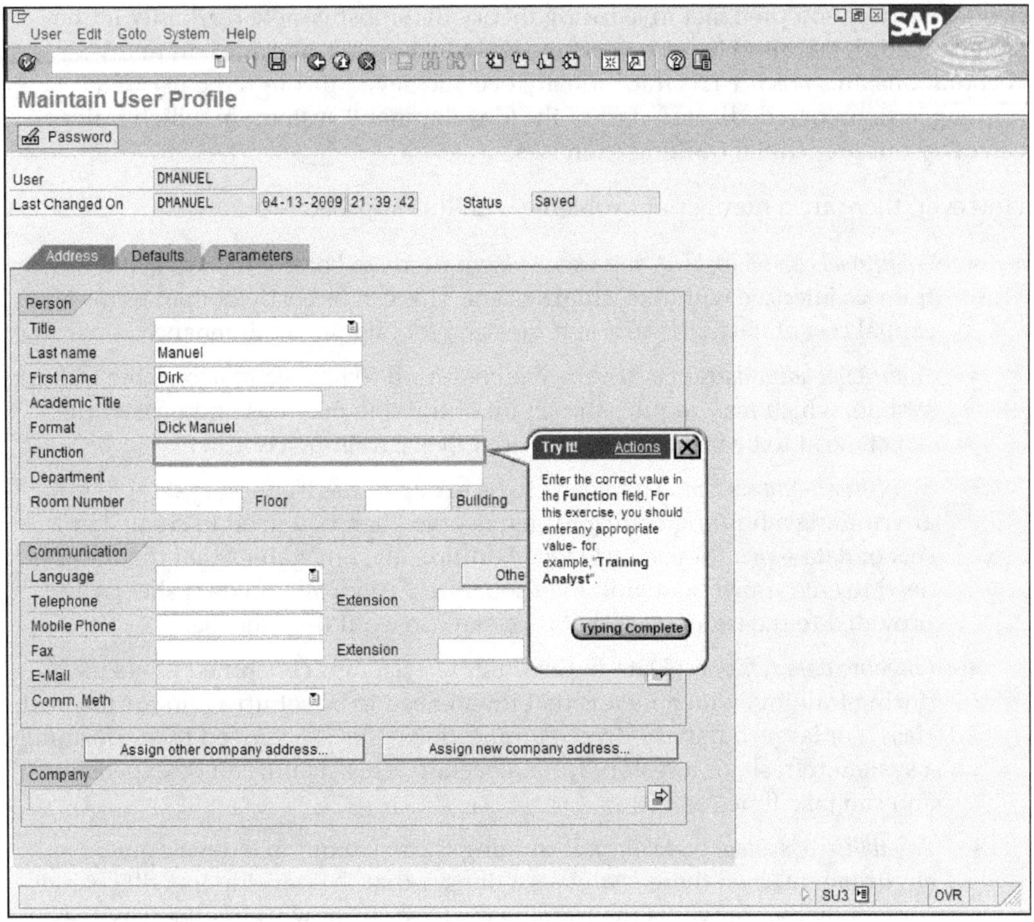

You will notice in this example that the simulation is played back in full screen, with the UPK-provided information overlaid on top if it. This information comprises a red rectangle indicating the area of the screen with which the user needs to interact, and a "bubble" that provides the user with instructions. The user types the specified information into the field indicated, just as they would with the actual system. Instead of interacting with SAP, they are in fact looking at a static screenprint and interacting with some clever JavaScript code that provides the "look and feel" of the system.

It is this actual "look and feel" that provides the greatest argument for using UPK.

Instructor-led training

It is a generally accepted fact in learning theory that most people (certainly in the sphere of adult learning) learn more effectively by *doing* (practicing). In many large corporations, this *practice* has traditionally been achieved through the use of a training system (or a dedicated part of the 'development' system) in which trainees can carry out predefined training exercises.

However, there are a number of problems with this approach:

- *Additional capital costs*: A separate system needs to be provided to avoid having trainees interfere with the actual system. This can be costly both in terms of the capital cost of the hardware, and the need for ongoing maintenance.
- *Additional administrative burden*: Trainees need to be able to access the training system, which may require the set up of training user IDs and passwords, which need to be reset before and after every training conduct.
- *Significant data set up*: Data needs to be set up in the training system. If you are running a training course for ten people, then you need to create ten sets of data—one for each trainee. Additionally, any values that the trainees need to enter must be maintained separately (typically on data sheets) and provided to the trainees so that they can carry out the exercise.
- *Ongoing data refreshes*: Data in the training system is consumed by its use during training, which means that it will need to be set up again for the next class. For large, database-driven applications, this is achieved by performing a system refresh, or a restore from a backup. This, again, can be expensive and can take time.
- *Possibility of system instability*: If training is carried out in a development environment, then there is always a danger that the developers will change something that prevents the training exercises from working the way they originally did. Nothing destroys user confidence in a new system than it "not working" during training.

UPK solves these problems by capturing what is effectively a snapshot of the application, using a single set of data. This recording is external to the application, which means that once it has been captured the system is no longer required. Trainees do not need to log onto the system, and it does not matter if the developers change anything—or even crash the system. Additionally, any information that the trainee requires regarding data values is built directly into the simulation, so there is no need for separate data sheets.

More importantly, because UPK generates a single, stand-alone simulation, every trainee can carry out the same simulation, at the same time, and see the same result. Furthermore, a trainee can carry out a single simulation multiple times and see exactly the same result every time. This is important, as it means that the trainee can return to a simulation after the course conduct (for example, when they are back in the office, performing the task for real) and see exactly what they saw during training, as a refresher.

Given this, UPK simulations are increasingly being seen as a good choice for providing exercises for classroom-based training. The classroom conduct still takes place, but instead of the instructor asking trainees to log on to the training system to carry out an exercise, they now ask the trainees to run a UPK exercise.

Self-paced learning

The fact that UPK simulations are self-contained, and do not rely on a system or instructor being available, means that they are well-suited to providing self-paced training (what used to be called computer-based training, before that term went out of vogue).

By placing all of the UPK output on a central server, or in a **Learning Management System (LMS)**, users can access the training simulations on their own, and receive training at their own desks at a time that suits them best.

However, it is important to understand that UPK does not instantly replace the need for a trainer. Yes, they can replace trainers, but doing so takes a significant amount of time. In a classroom environment, the trainer is there to explain an exercise, point out interesting information, and provide additional business-specific information. They add *context* to the mechanics of the key-strokes and mouse-clicks captured in the recording.

If the trainer is not present to provide this information, then it needs to be provided to the trainee through some other medium. Thankfully—as we shall see in this book—UPK works very well as this medium. But the information still needs to be entered into UPK so that the trainee has access to it.

How does UPK work?

It is a common misconception that UPK simulations are actual "recordings". UPK (and this book, on occasion) uses the term *recording*, and although this is probably the most apt term, it is important to understand that a UPK simulation is not a "recording" in the strict sense of the word. UPK does not capture "live-motion" actions in the way that Camtasia or other video capture software does. Sure, a UPK simulation may *look like* a recording when you play it back in **See It!** mode, but it isn't. What UPK captures when it "records" are screenshots and the actions that trigger the transition from one screenshot to the next.

For example, if you use UPK to create a simulation of someone entering a text string into an input field on a screen, UPK captures the following:

- A screenshot showing the field before any text has been entered into it
- The action of typing the text, along with the text itself, and the coordinates of the location on the screen where this text is entered
- A screenshot of the field after the text has been entered into it

In terms of the actual files (or *assets*) created for this simulation, there will be two `.png` files for the screenshots, and a snippet of JavaScript that defines the text and the coordinates. There is no `.wmf`, `.swf`, `.mp4`, or any other *movie-type* file.

When this simulation is played back (in See It! mode), UPK displays the first screenshot, displays the text on the screen one character at a time (so that it *looks* as though it is being typed), and then displays the second screenshot. Smoke and mirrors; that's all.

However, this simplicity has a couple of strong benefits. First, because the recordings consist purely of standard, browser-friendly assets (HTML files, `.png` images files, and JavaScript), the simulation can be played back in a simple web browser without the need for any add-ins, *codecs*, or proprietary players. Second, these assets all have very small individual file sizes, which means that they work well even over low-bandwidth connections.

But what is really clever is the way that UPK makes use of these assets. UPK allows exactly the same recording to be used to generate several different output formats, including four formats designed for online use, and six documentation formats.

Output formats

As stated above, UPK can provide output in four different formats designed for online use and six formats designed for printing. This seems to be pretty good value for money (ten-for-one), but it is important to understand that all of the output formats are generated from the same, single recording. This provides true single-sourcing, but it also means that, for example, a test document can (by default) only contain the same content as the training simulation, which can only contain same content as the business process procedure, and so on.

Unfortunately, what you want to teach a trainee during a classroom conduct (or in a self-paced training presentation) is not necessarily the same thing that you want described in your documentation. In training, you may want to look at certain scenarios. Maybe you want the trainee to hit a certain problem, and then explain how to overcome this. Maybe you want to take a bit more time and explain some related information on a screen, or point out how this ties in with that. In your documentation, and certainly for business process procedures (a.k.a. work steps, user procedures, work instructions, and so on), you are more likely to want to provide clear, concise instructions on how to do something the single, correct way.

So yes, UPK *can* generate documents, but this doesn't mean that you necessarily want to use them.

Online delivery

For online delivery, UPK provides four different output formats. These are all variations on the same theme: online simulations with which a trainee interacts. The four formats are:

- A **Player** format that provides access to a suite of simulations. The trainee can select a simulation from the list provided and run it in a number of modes (described below).
- An **LMS** package that provides the same suite of simulations as the Player, but in a format that is suitable for importing into an LMS. This package is AICC/SCORM-compliant, which means that a trainee's progress and scores can be tracked within the LMS.
- **Standalone Topic Files**, each of which provides a single-file version of a simulation. Trainees need a proprietary UPK Player to run simulations in this format.
- An HTML **Web Site** that provides simulations with limited interactivity, in a format suitable for displaying in a limited-functionality web browser, such as the browser on a mobile phone.

All of these formats are explained in greater detail in Chapter 6, *Publishing Content*. Because the Player format is the most commonly-used format, and because the other three modes are effectively variations on this, the Player format (only) is discussed in more detail in this chapter.

An example of the UPK Player is shown in the following screenshot:

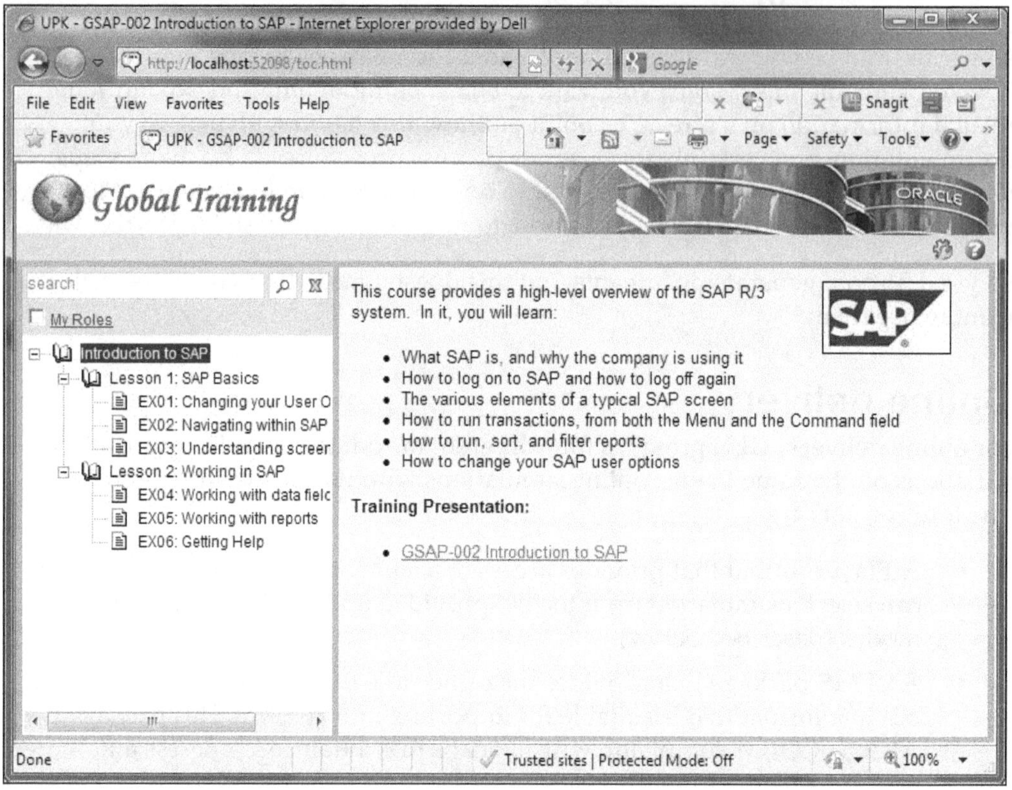

> This example shows the *finished product* of this book, using Web Pages, images, roles, hyperlinks, and a custom deployment format. If your first Player does not look like this, then don't worry; that's why this book was written—to get you there.

When a trainee selects a specific exercise from the list in the left-most pane of the Player, additional information about that exercise is displayed on the right-most side of the screen, along with option buttons for the five modes in which the exercise can be used (actually, four *playback* modes, and a single document format). An example of this exercise-level screen is shown in the following screenshot:

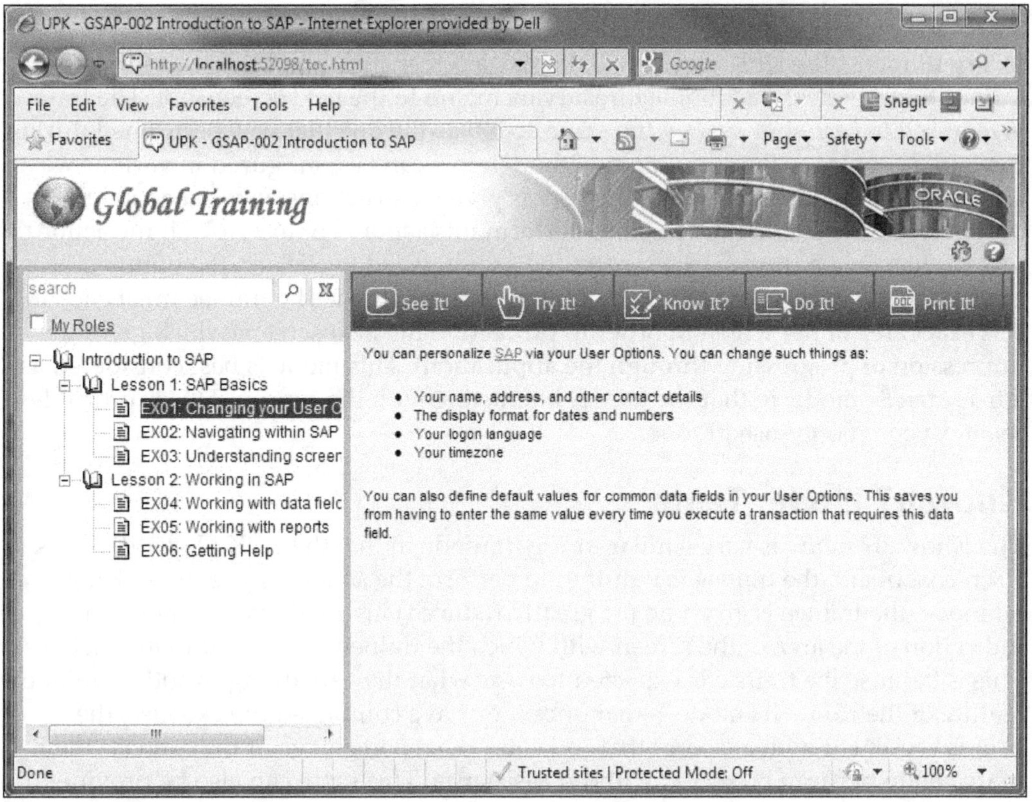

The five modes in which the training exercise can be 'experienced' are shown in the dark blue heading across the top of the lower-right portion of the screen. Each of these modes is explained separately, below.

See It! mode: Demonstrations

In **See It!** mode, the UPK player automatically displays the screenshots and carries out the required interactions. This *looks like* the playback of a video, and can be completely hands-free. This mode is best considered as a *demonstration* mode. When used in a classroom environment, the instructor would set this mode running and then provide additional commentary during the playback. Although this requires fairly close coordination between the instructor's speech and the playback, it does have the advantage (over the other modes) that the instructor does not need to interact with the simulation themselves, and can therefore better focus on the needs of the trainees.

Try It! mode: Exercises

In **Try It!** mode, the UPK player will display a screenshot, and then wait for the trainee to perform the action, before advancing on to the next screenshot. The trainee is required to carry out exactly the same action as the one that was performed during the initial capture of the simulation, although this can be configured in various ways, as we will see later in this book. The user is given instructions on what action to perform, and where on the screen to perform this action. For example, if the action was to click on a button on the screen, the user is asked to click on the button and the area of the screen containing the button is highlighted. The trainee must click in this exact area of the screen in order to proceed to the next screen (which gives the impression of progressing through the application). This mode is best considered as a true *exercise* mode, in that the user is interacting with the system. This is probably the most commonly-used mode.

Know It? mode: Tests

The **Know It?** mode is very similar to *Try It!* mode in that the UPK player displays a screenshot and the trainee is required to perform the action. However, in Know It? mode, the trainee is given no (or greatly reduced) instructions and there is no indication of the area of the screen with which the trainee is required to interact. This is because the trainee is expected to *know* what they are doing. Another unique feature of the Know It? mode is that once they have completed the exercise, the user is presented with a "score" that indicates what percentage of the exercise they managed to perform correctly, without assistance. This score can also be provided to an LMS, or some other system for monitoring trainee progress. This mode is therefore best thought of as a *test* (or verification) mode.

Do It! mode: Performance support

The **Do It!** mode differs from the other three playback modes in that it is specifically designed to provide assistance to users of the system (not trainees) while they are actually using the real system. With Do It! mode, the instructions for the actions are displayed in a help panel that floats above any other windows on the user's screen. The theory is that the user has the application open, and is working directly in it, with the UPK instructions being constantly visible at the same time. The truly clever part is that if the UPK system is configured to use *auto-advance*, as the user performs each action in the system, the UPK instructions will automatically advance to the next action. This way, the instructions keep pace with the user. If auto-advance is not configured, the user must manually move from one step to the next in the UPK simulation, although a keyboard shortcut can be used to do this from within the application itself, so that the user does not have to continually flip between the application and the UPK recording. This mode, therefore, is best thought of as *performance support* (or as providing an electronic performance support system, to use the latest buzzwords).

Print It!: Documentation

The fifth mode available through the Player is **Print It!**. This allows the trainee to print a hardcopy version of a simulation. This hardcopy is actually one of the (six) standard document formats discussed below—the developer can choose the format to use (for the entire Player) during publication. By default, this is the Job Aid, using the *Do It!* mode texts.

> **Version Difference**
> Print It! mode was introduced with UPK 3.5.0.

An understanding of the four playback modes is absolutely crucial when it comes to creating the simulation content, or specifically, when choosing the words to be used for describing (or not, depending on the mode) the actions that the trainee is required to carry out in the simulation. This is covered in detail in Chapter 4, *Editing a Topic*.

Documentation

As stated above, UPK can generate a number of different types of documentation. Again, these are all built from the same single recording, so the variation between them is extremely limited. Most of the uniqueness of a given document stems from a few small pieces of additional information that are entered outside of the actual recording, some minor formatting differences, and the display or suppression of certain elements of the recording.

The six available documents are explained below.

Training Guide

The Training Guide is effectively a hard-copy version of a training course for use by the trainee. Quite why they would want a two-dimensional printout when they have the full interactive version online is unclear. That said, some people like to receive handouts during training, and this will give them that. Additionally, because the Training Guide contains the full content of the simulation (all screenshots and all texts) it is useful for providing review copies of the training material to people who do not have access to the interactive, online version.

Instructor Manual

The Instructor Manual is, as the name suggests, designed to be a reference document for the instructor to use during a classroom conduct of a course. The content is the same as that of the Training Guide, with one additional (and optional) piece of information that the developer can provide in free-text form. The instructor may find it useful to refer to this document during demonstrations, or prior to the trainees carrying out the exercise, in order to familiarize themselves with the content of the simulation.

Job Aid

The Job Aid is a scaled-down version of the simulation. It does not include screenprints, and simply lists all of the actions as a single numbered list, formatted in a table. This format can be used as a 'quick reference'.

System Process Document

The System Process Document contains all of the actions carried out in the recording, including screenshots, plus some other developer-provided text describing the context of the process. The System Process Document is effectively a user procedure. This document format is sometimes referred to as a business process procedure, work instruction, job script, and so on.

> **Version Difference**
>
> Prior to UPK 3.5, the System Process Document was referred to as a **Business Process Document**, although the content of the document is identical in both cases.

Test Document

The Test Document provides the instructions from a simulation, but not the screenprints. It can also contain several additional pieces of information related to testing such as the purpose of the test, set-up instructions, expected time to complete, additional validation instructions, and so on. For each step in the procedure, the Test Document includes space to record the input (data entered or action taken), expected result, and whether the test (or step) was passed or failed.

HP Quality Center Test Script

The HP Quality Center Test Script format generates a Microsoft Excel file that is identical in format and content to those produced by HP Quality Center (previously known as Mercury TestDirector). Testers can record their results in this worksheet, and then load the worksheet back into HP Quality Center for testing progress monitoring.

Deciding how you will use UPK

Now that you understand what UPK *can* do for you, you need to think about exactly what you *want* it to do for you.

Choosing delivery formats

You need to decide whether you are going to use your simulations as an integral part of classroom training conducts, or will be providing your training as stand-alone deliverables suitable for self-paced learning. Or both.

If you only plan on using your exercises within a classroom environment, then you may be able to get by with providing less business context in your simulations because the trainer will be able to provide this context during the classroom conduct. However, if you do this you will be selling yourself short. There will undoubtedly come a time when your UPK exercises will be used for self-paced training, even if this is not the initial intention. Providing this capability up-front will save re-work in the long run.

If you will publish to any of the true interactive formats (Player, LMS, Standalone Topic Files), you need to decide which of the playback modes you will use. Editing Topics so that they will make sense in several different modes takes time—especially if you are using Custom Text extensively (which you should, if you want to provide *quality training*). If there are certain modes that you know you will never use, then you can save yourself some development time. However, bear in mind that the printed output formats can also make use of these playback modes, so you need to make sure that you develop your online content with these modes in mind, as well.

Consider which (if any) of the printed document formats you will use. As explained above, training is not the same as documentation. You can have high-quality, effective training simulations, but this does not necessarily mean that the documents generated from them will be as good.

Examine the available document formats and decide if you have a use for them. If you do not have a proven need for a document type, then do not generate it "just because you can". If you decide to use one of the document formats, then think about how these documents will be made available to the trainees or users. If you use only one document format, then you can provide access to this via the Print It! mode. If you provide more than one document format (which I'd question the need for, as they all provide basically the same information), decide how you will deliver these. If they are not immediately accessible to the people who need them, re-examine the wisdom of providing them at all.

UPK allows you to **tag** the text that is displayed to the users so that it appears only in specific modes. When you generate one of the document output formats, you need to tell UPK from which one of these (three) modes the text for the document should be taken. You should, therefore, make sure that text is tagged for the appropriate mode in the Topic so that when the document is generated from this mode, it includes the required text. Tagging text for different modes is described in Chapter 4, *Editing a Topic*.

Styles and standards

UPK does a very good job of ensuring consistency and adherence to styles and standards, via its built-in templates, which define the default texts shown in the yellow bubbles that are overlaid on the screenshots. One of the templates that it provides is even designed to be compatible with the terminology and formatting standards espoused by Microsoft's *Manual of Style for Technical Publications*.

You should check these default templates (Standard and Microsoft) to determine if they meet your in-house standards. If neither of them seems suitable, then you may want to consider creating your own template—or at least customizing one of the two provided templates to meet your requirements.

Over and above the Bubble Texts that are controlled by the template, you should develop your own style guide to specify the following things:

- The overall structure and content of your Outlines
- The information that should be provided in the Concepts pane
- The type of information that should be provided via Custom Text
- Whether icons should be used, and which ones should be used in which types of Frames and/or Bubbles
- Fonts for Bubble Text and fills for Bubbles
- Word choice for Custom Text
- Whether external documents should be incorporated into your output, and how
- Whether you want to use images, and the allowed size and formats of these

Don't worry if most of these terms do not mean anything to you yet; you will be intimately familiar with them by the end of this book.

Developing an unequivocal style guide, and then ensuring that all developers adhere to this for all simulations, will ensure that your training deliverables are seen as parts of a cohesive whole rather than "a bunch of stuff done by different people at different times".

When to record

You need to decide on the stage during the application development cycle at which you will capture your simulations. Ideally, your simulations should be captured in the final version of the system.

The whole point of simulations is that they should have the "look and feel" of the actual system. Specifically, they should match reality as closely as possible—there should be a willing suspension of disbelief on the part of the trainee that they are actually looking at static screenshots. This is a common fault with poor-quality UPK exercises: they do not allow for this suspension of disbelief because it is glaringly obvious that the trainee is not using an actual system. With a high-quality exercise, however, the trainee has the impression that they are using a "live" system. One of the common complaints that trainees have with training conducted using UPK simulations is that they would rather have a "real" system to play with. The easiest way to avoid such comments is by providing simulations that are as close to reality as possible.

That said, it is often impractical to wait until development for the entire application is complete before developing your training. Often, training development and application development will run in parallel. Fortunately, development is often gradual, with different parts of the application being completed over time (as opposed to nothing being ready until the whole thing is ready). You should therefore work closely with your development team to ensure that the training developers are informed as and when different pieces of the functionality are finalized, so that you can start developing training for these pieces, while the development teams work on the next piece of functionality.

What to record

Although you might think that *what* to record is obvious—just whatever the user will actually do—this is not necessarily the case. You need to think about whether you will demonstrate a specific scenario, or provide general instructions, or show everything that the user *can* do in the application (or transaction), regardless of whether they actually will do this.

You should also decide whether you want to teach only one way to do something, or will provide alternative actions and alternative paths (both of which are covered later in this book).

A useful technique when making these decisions is to produce a 'storyboard', or a simple flowchart of what screens you will go through in the application, what you will do on each screen, and how you will get from one screen to the next. Having this information available beforehand will save you from having to decide these things during the recording itself, and potentially missing things. Storyboards are also useful if you have less-experienced developers who perhaps need some more guidance for their recordings.

Summary

UPK captures a user's interactions with a software application. It can then generate a number of deliverables based on this recording. Some of these deliverables are more useful than others.

Before creating training deliverables using UPK, you should decide which of these deliverable formats you want to use. Although you can choose the required deliverables at the time of final publication, knowing which deliverable formats you want to use, and in what modes, will allow you to better focus your editing of the simulations.

2

Organizing your Library

In Chapter 1, we looked at what UPK is and how we can use it to develop quality training material. In this chapter, we get right down to business and start using UPK. However, before you can create content, you need to decide where you are going to store it, and this is in the **Library**. The Library is the main workspace in UPK. Content objects are created in, and exist within, the Library.

One of the key changes introduced with UPK 3.5 is the separation of the environment in which you—the developer—works, and the Player that the trainee sees. In OnDemand 8.7 and earlier, these were effectively one and the same, that is, the developers worked within a **Title**, which contained all of the **Topics** (the recorded simulations) for an application. These were then grouped into **Modules** and **Lessons**. Typically, one or more selected Modules from within this Title were published to a **Player**, which is what the trainee saw. This contained exactly the same (selected) Modules, Lessons, and Topics, organized in exactly the same structure as they did in the Title. Starting from OnDemand 9.1, developers work within a **Library** which will typically contain Topics for multiple applications. Topics are now organized via **Outlines**, and it is these Outlines that are used to create the Player packages. The way in which Topics are organized within an Outline need not bear any resemblance to the way in which the Topics are organized in the Library. In this chapter, we will look at the Library, and in Chapter 5, *Building an Outline* we will look at Outlines.

In this exercise, you will:

- Learn what the Library is and what it shows
- Understand the possibilities for organizing the Library
- Learn how to create folders in the Library, to organize your content

Accessing the Library

When you start UPK (other than for the very first time—see the note below), the **Start Screen** window is displayed. (Unless you deselect the **Show this screen at startup** option at the bottom of this window—see the comments after the following screenshot.) This window allows you to easily find the modules that you most recently accessed, and create outline elements and content elements. You can also choose to convert content from a prior version of UPK, or import content from another implementation of UPK. It also provides you with links to open the Library, or open a specific content object. An example of the **Start Screen** is displayed in the following screenshot:

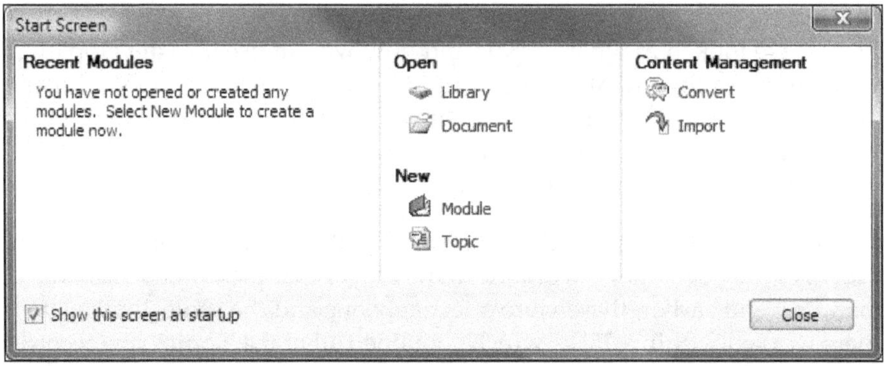

Note that you can prevent the **Start Screen** from being displayed whenever you start UPK by deselecting the **Show this screen at startup** option at the bottom of the dialog box. If you do this, then UPK will start up from the Library screen.

> The very first time that you access UPK you will be required to go through a few additional steps. These are explained in *Appendix A*.
>
> If you have access to multiple Libraries, you will also be prompted to select the Library that you want to access, via the *Profile Wizard*.

To access the Library, click on the **Library** link. The **Developer** screen is displayed, showing the selected Library. When you first install UPK and access the Library, it will be almost empty, as shown in the following screenshot:

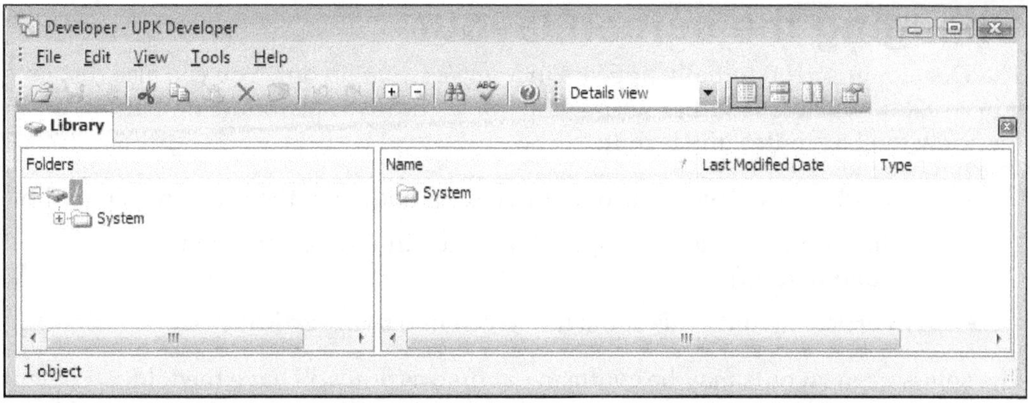

Note that if you are working in a client/server environment and are accessing an existing Library for the first time, you will see all of the content that you have been given access to. Also, bear in mind that different groups or projects within the same organization may have their own Libraries within the same implementation of UPK, so it is possible that the Library that you see does not reflect the entire content of the UPK server—just the content to which you have been given access.

Working in the Developer screen

The structure of the **Developer** screen will be familiar to Windows users, as it is conceptually very similar to Windows Explorer. It consists of two panes, the leftmost pane containing a hierarchical list of all folders in the Library (or the portion of the Library to which you have access), and the rightmost side listing the contents of the folder selected on the leftmost side. You will notice in the previous screenshot that the Library is actually shown on a tabbed page within the main screen. If you double-click on a content object on the right-hand side of the screen, it is opened in a new tab; the Library tab remains open. You can open several content objects at the same time and can switch between them by clicking on the appropriate tab. Actually, that's not *completely* true; Topics will always open in a separate window (the **Topic Editor**), but you can still switch between the **Topic Editor** and the **Developer** screen (and therefore any of the tabbed pages within it).

Changing the screen layout

The **Developer** screen initially appears in a *single screen* layout. You can also display it in a *split-screen* layout, either horizontally or vertically. The following buttons on the **View** toolbar control the layout:

- **Single view**: This is the default view, as shown in the previous screenshot
- **Horizontal layout**: This splits the screen into two, horizontally (top and bottom)
- **Vertical layout**: This splits the screen into two, vertically (left and right)

The split-screen layouts may be confusing at first, as you still have the folder/content panes within each split pane, and you will always have the same selection of tabbed pages in both split panes. However, you can select different tabs in each pane. Split screen is an extremely useful way of working when you are editing Outlines, as you can drag-and-drop Topics from the Library in one pane onto an Outline Element in the other. The split screen will come into its own in Chapter 5, *Building an Outline* when we go through Outlines in much more detail, including building an Outline via drag-and-drop.

The Properties pane

All content objects in the Library—Topics, Lessons, and Modules, as well as Web Pages and Packages, have a number of unique *attributes*. These attributes are maintained via the **Properties** pane, which can be displayed at any time by clicking on the **Properties** button ( ) from the **View** toolbar. Some of these attributes provide further information about the content object (such as the template used), whereas others define additional information that is used in different output formats.

Note that the **Properties** pane is independent of the split screen layouts - that is, you will only ever see one **Properties** pane. The attributes shown in it will be those that apply to the selected element in the *active* pane. An example of the **Developer** screen, using the *Horizontal* layout, and with the **Properties** pane displayed, is shown next (you can see that the buttons for these two options are selected, on the rightmost side of the **View** toolbar):

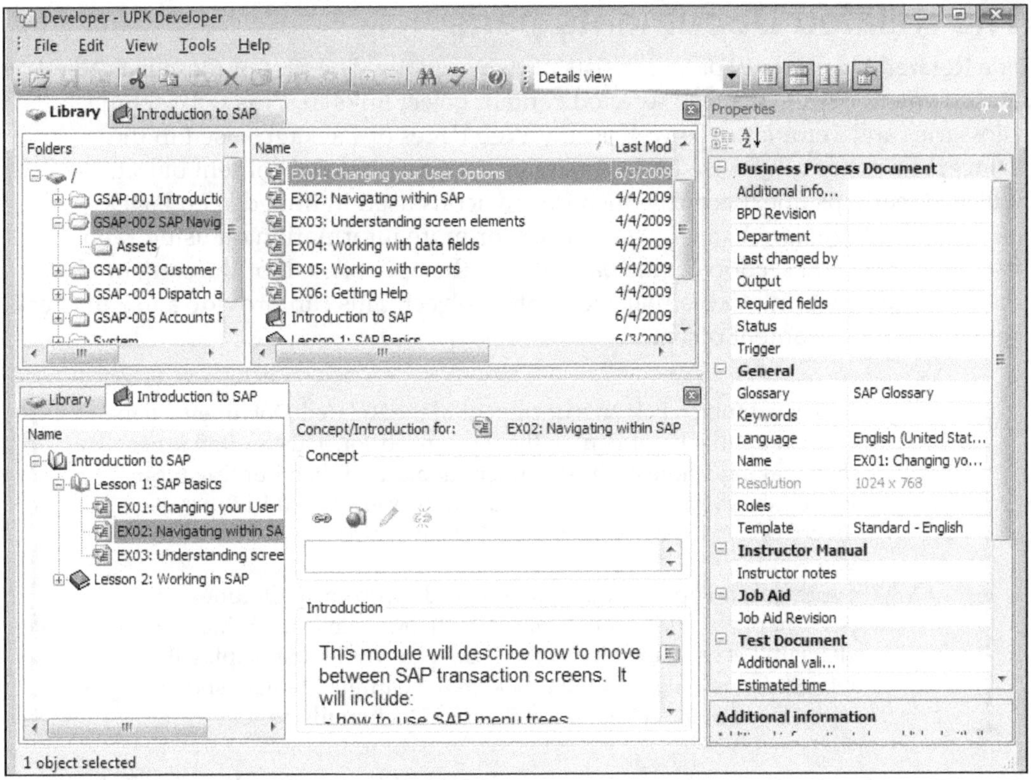

In this example above, there are two tabs open: The **Library**, and an Outline element (**Introduction to SAP**). Note that one of these is open in the upper frame, and the other is open in the lower pane. You will also note that the top frame is the *active* frame, so the details shown in the **Properties** pane are for the content object selected in this pane, and not the one selected in the lower split pane.

There are two more panes that can be displayed on the **Developer** screen. These are the **Broken Links** pane and the **Related Documents** pane. These are described individually, later in the chapter.

The Broken Links pane

The **Broken Links** pane lists all of the content objects to which the selected content object (or any of its related documents) were initially linked, but that have now disappeared. This will typically be because the linked content object has since been deleted, but could also be because the linked object has been created by another developer who has not yet checked that object in to the Library (assuming that you are working in a client/server environment). You should check for broken links periodically, and certainly before you publish your content.

The Related Documents pane

The **Related Documents** pane consists of two sections. The first of these lists all of the content objects that the selected content object links to. This will include Glossaries and Templates, as well as any Web Pages or Packages used in the **Concepts** pane or otherwise hyperlinked to from the selected content object. It will also, perhaps unexpectedly, include any icons used in linked Web Pages (see Chapter 9, *Adding Value to Your Topics* for more information on using Web Pages). The second section of this pane shows the opposite; all of the content objects in the Library that link to the selected content object. This can provide a useful check before deleting a content object.

> You can double-click on a document in the **Related Documents** pane to open up that document in the relevant editor. This is often faster than making a note of the document name, and then hunting for it in the Library (although the menu option **View | Find in Library**, described below, helps with the latter). It is also useful in cases when you want to preview a Topic, as this can only be done from an Outline (see Chapter 6, *Publishing Your Content*), but aren't sure which Outline element it is contained in. In this case, you would just display the related documents, and then click on the Outline Element shown in the *linked from* section of the **Related Documents** pane.

There is one more option that is worth mentioning at this point, although it doesn't really relate to the **Related Document** pane. If you click on any content object in an Outline and then select menu option **View | Find in Library**, UPK will switch to the Library view, open the folder within the Library in which the selected object is stored, and highlight the object by selecting it. This is extremely useful if you have linked a content object into an Outline Element, but cannot remember the folder within the Library in which it is stored.

Arranging panes on the screen

Let's look at how to arrange these three panes on the screen. Inexplicably, the **Related Documents** pane and the **Broken Links** pane do not have their own buttons as the **Properties** pane does. To display them, you need to select menu option **View | Related documents**, or **View | Broken links**, as appropriate. The following screenshot shows all three of the *sidebar* panes displayed and undocked:

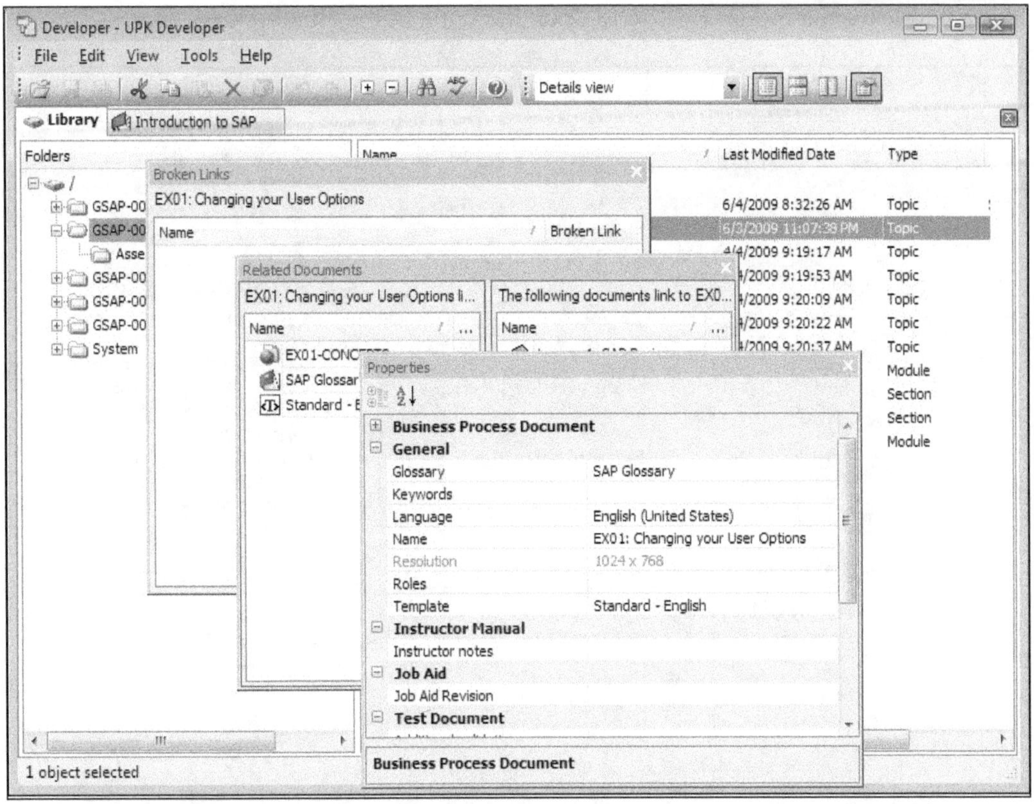

Any, or all of these three panes can be docked to any edge of the screen, as follows:

1. Click on the header of the pane that you want to dock.
2. Drag the pane towards the edge along which you want to dock it. As you start to drag the pane, a series of icons are displayed on the screen, one pointing to each edge, with a fifth icon appearing in the middle of the screen that features icons for all four edges.
3. To dock the pane against a particular edge, simply move the cursor over the icon (either on the perimeter of the screen or in the center) that is pointing to the required edge. Simply dragging the pane to the edge of the screen will not work. You must drag the cursor over one of the icons. As you do so, a shaded area appears on the screen, as shown in the following screenshot, showing where the pane will appear when it is docked.

4. Release the mouse button to dock the pane in the shaded area.

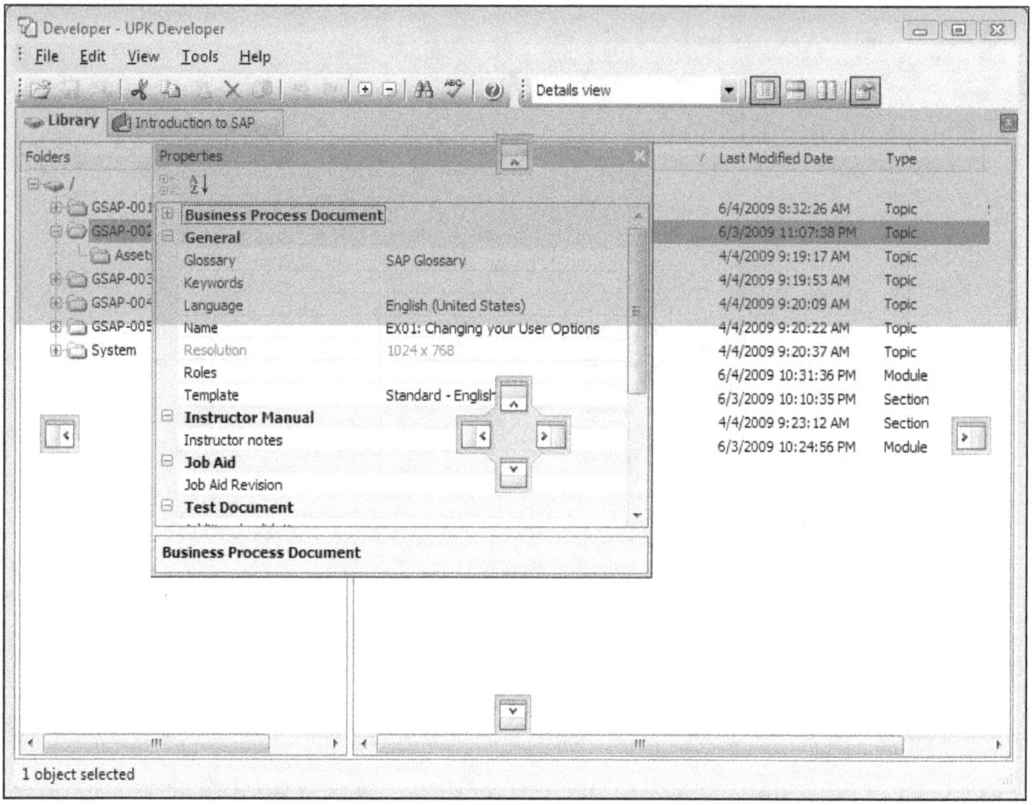

Although each pane can be docked independently, and all three can be docked separately against the same side, UPK also lets you dock all three panes together, in a single, tabbed pane. To do this, dock one pane, and then drag the next pane over the already-docked pane. When you do this, a "center" icon similar to the one in the previous screenshot is displayed. However, this time it has a further icon in the middle, as shown:

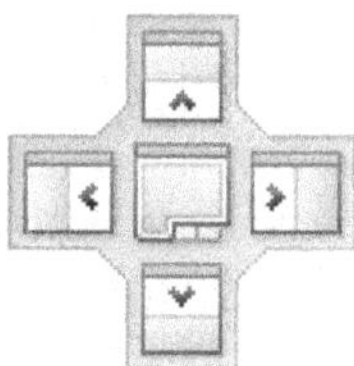

Drop the pane onto this new icon (in the middle of the group), and the pane will appear as a tabbed page within the existing docked pane, as shown in the next screenshot:

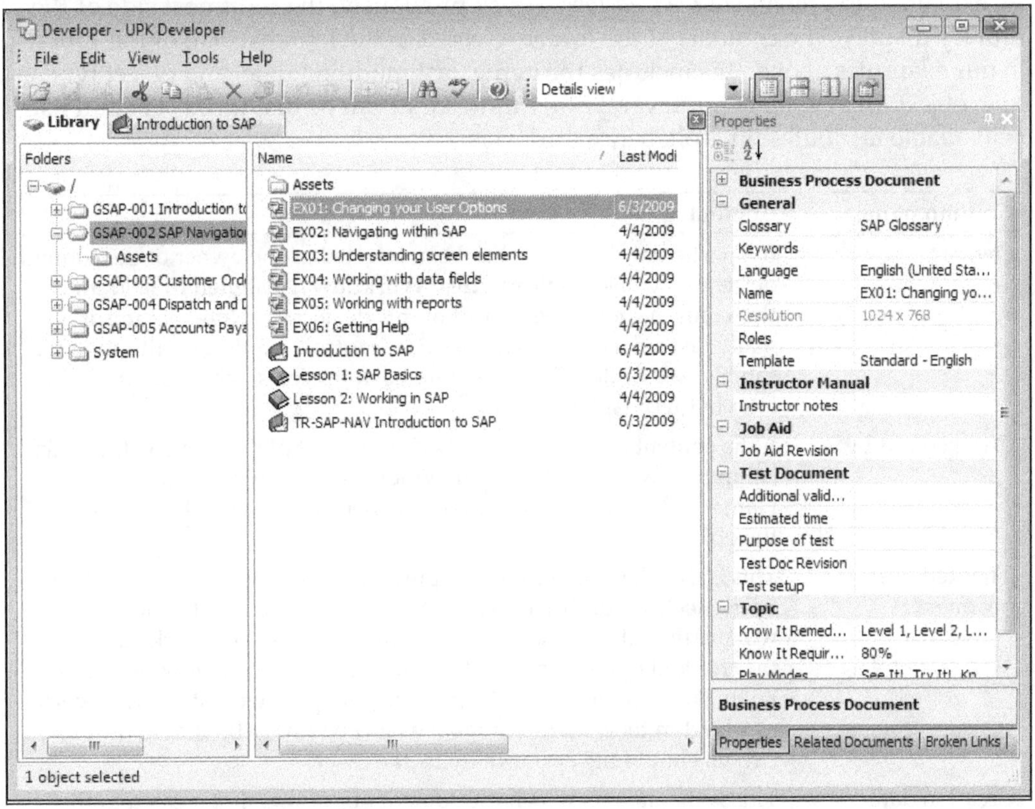

You can reorganize the order of the individual tabbed panes within the docked side pane, by dragging the tabs to the required position.

> You can hide the docked side pane by clicking on the thumb-tack in its title bar. The pane will then slide out of view, with only the tab names being displayed on the side of the screen. Hover the mouse over the tab names to slide the side pane out again.

Changing the information displayed for objects

As explained in *Working in the Developer screen* previously, the rightmost side of the **Library** displays the contents of the folder selected in the leftmost side of the **Library**. In our examples above, this includes the name, last modified date, and object type of each object. In fact, there are several other things that can be displayed. The full list of available attributes (in alphabetical order) is:

Column name	Content
Owner*	If a particular developer has been selected as the owner of the content object in the object's **Properties | Workflow | Assigned to** field, then this column shows the user id of this developer. Note that this is really just a fixed field—it does not "control" anything—although it can be used quite effectively with custom views, which are described later in this chapter.
Checked out by*	If the content object is currently checked out of the Library, then this column shows the user id (for Windows authentication, or Author Name for UPK authorization) of the person who has checked out the object.
Checked out hostname*	This is the identifier of the computer to which the content object has been checked out. Because objects are checked out to the developer's workstation, this is useful for determining on which workstation the checked out version can be found. This could be very useful to know if a developer is in the habit of changing workstations, and sees an object in their Library appear as locked under their own user id (which should never normally be the case).
Creation date	This is the date on which the content object was first created in the Library. Note that if you import content from another Library, or from a backup, then this date is the date that the content object was imported and not the original creation date.
Document ID	This is UPK's own internal 32-character identifier for a content object. This identifier is used (by UPK) in exported files (including translation files) and can be seen at few other places. Hopefully, you will never need this, but it is useful to know that it is there in case you do.
Frames	For Topics, this is the total number of Frames in the Topic. This is very useful for gauging the *size* of a Topic. Note that this count includes all Frame types and not just Action Frames.
Language	This is the language assigned to the content object. Note that this is only used for determining the spell-checker to use. It does not control the template that will be used, or the language in which the content will be published.

Column name	Content
Last modified by*	The user id of the person who last modified the content object.
Last modified date	The date and time on which the content object was last changed.
Link count	This provides the number of other content objects to which this object links. This corresponds to the number of objects listed in the *to* section of the **Related Documents** pane described above, and will always be at least 1 because every object must at least have a template attached to it.
Links to	The number of other content objects that link to this content object. This corresponds to the number of objects listed in the *from* section of the **Related Documents** pane described above.
Name	The display name of the content object. Note that this does not have to be unique—even within a single Library folder—because UPK uses its own 32-character identifier as the unique object reference. You will, however, find it much easier to differentiate between your objects if you use unique names.
Path	The full path of the folder in which the content object is located. As the path is easily-discernible from the leftmost pane of the **Library**, this is of negligible use (unless you are using a custom view in which case the hierarchical folder view is not displayed at all).
Roles	The names of the user Roles to which the content object has been assigned. Refer to Chapter 10, *Adding Value in the Player* for more information on Roles.
State*	The current "workflow state" of the object. Note that this is simply the content of the **Properties | Workflow | State** field. You can sort, filter, and publish content objects based on their State.
Type	The content object type. As the icon for the object type is always shown to the left of the **Name**, this is of limited use.
Version*	This is the version number of the object. The version number is a simple integer that is incremented by 1, each time the content object is checked into the Library. Refer to Chapter 7, *Version Management* for more information on versions.

Note that columns marked with an asterisk (*) are applicable only to a client/server environment. These columns will not be available in a stand-alone environment.

To add or remove columns from the display, right-click on any column header, and then select **Column Chooser** from the context menu. This will display the **Column Chooser** dialog box, as shown below:

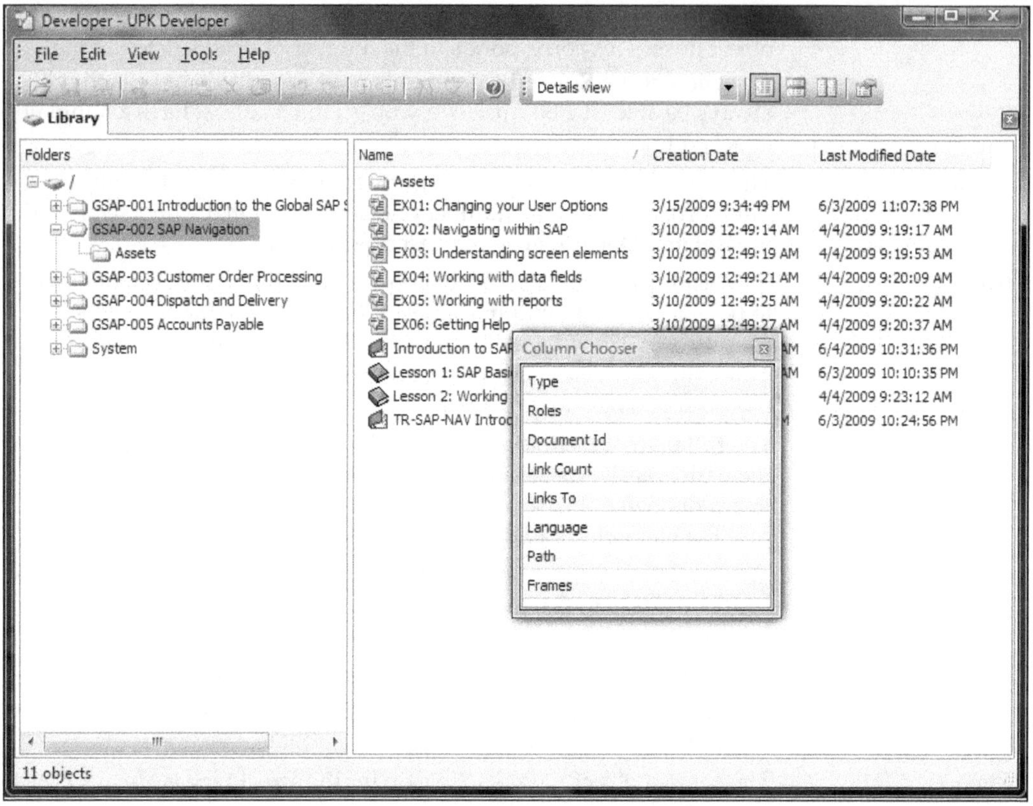

The **Column Chooser** dialog box lists all of the additional columns that are available, but are not currently displayed on the screen. To add a column to the display, click on the column name in the **Column Chooser** and drag this onto a column header in the rightmost section of the Library screen. The column will be added to the left of the column onto which you drop it. To remove a column, simply click on the column header in the object list, drag the column off the header bar, and drop it anywhere on the screen.

You can re-order the columns in the object list by dragging them into the required order within the header bar. You can also sort the object list according to any of the displayed columns simply by clicking on the column header. Successive clicks on a column header will alternate between sorting in ascending order and sorting in descending order. More advanced ordering, sorting, and even filtering options are available when maintaining **views**, as described in the next section of this chapter.

Working with Views

When you first access the Library, it will be displaying the **Details View**, which is the view described above. Although this is the view in which you will probably work most of the time, there are other views that are available, depending on the type of installation you are working in. The current **View** is specified in the **View** toolbar. You can select any other view via the **View** field's drop-down list button, as shown below:

If you are working in a client/server environment, then the following views are available. Each of these views provides a simple list of the objects—that is, the folder hierarchy is not provided.

- **Deleted documents**: This View lists all documents that have been deleted from the Library. Deleted documents will remain in the **Deleted documents** view until they are either restored by a developer, or purged by an Administrator. For more information on deleting and restoring documents, refer to Chapter 7, *Version Management*.
- **All by owner**: This view lists all content objects, grouped and sorted by the Owner of the content object. This view displays the columns **Owner**, **State**, **Checked Out By**, **Version**, and **Type**.
- **All by state**: This view lists all content objects, grouped and sorted by the current State of the content object. This view displays the columns **State**, **Owner**, **Checked Out By**, **Version**, and **Type**.
- **All checked out**: This view lists only content objects that are currently checked out by any developer, grouped and sorted according to the user id of the developer. This view displays the columns **Checked Out By**, **State**, **Last Modified Date**, **Version**, and **Type**.
- **Checked out to me**: This view lists only content objects that you (personally) currently have checked out, sorted according to the object's name. This view displays the columns **Checked Out By, Last Modified Date, Version, Type,** and **Checked Out Hostname**.
- **Owned by me**: This view lists only content objects that are owned by you, sorted according to the object's name. This view displays the columns **Owner, State, Checked Out By, Version**, and **Type**.

- **Lost documents**: This view identifies any content objects that have become "homeless" because the folder in which they were stored has become corrupted, or there is a problem with the folder's permission settings. You can select any of these lost documents and move them to the correct folder.

If you are working in a stand-alone environment, then you will only have the **Details** and **Lost documents** views available to you.

Creating a Custom View

In addition to the default views, in UPK 3.5, you can define your own Custom Views.

To define a Custom View, carry out the steps described below:

1. Select menu option **View | Manage Views**. The **Manage Views** dialog box is displayed, as shown in the following screenshot:

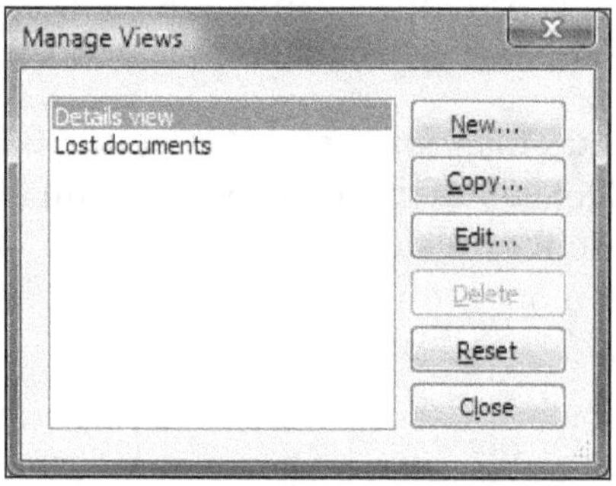

2. Click on **New**. The **View Editor** dialog box is displayed, as shown in the following screenshot:

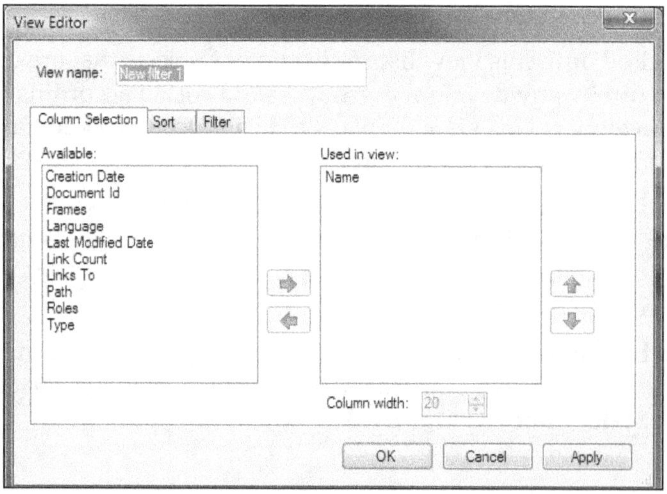

3. Enter a suitable name for your new Custom View in the **View name** field.
4. On the **Column Selection** tab, choose the columns that you want to appear in the view by selecting them and then clicking on the **Add** button. (You can also double-click on a column to add it to the *Used in view list*.) Use the **Up** and **Down** buttons to re-order the columns to the order in which you want them to be displayed (top to bottom in this list corresponds to left to right in the view left to right).
5. In the **Sort** tab, choose upto three columns on which to sort the view. Note that you can sort on any column, and not just the ones chosen in Step 4.
6. In the **Filter** tab, select any values on which you want certain columns to be filtered. Again, you can filter on any column, not just the ones chosen in Step 4.
7. Click on **OK** to return to the **Manage Views** dialog box.
8. Click on **Close** to close the **Manage Views** dialog box.

You can now select this new view from the **View** drop-down, as shown below.

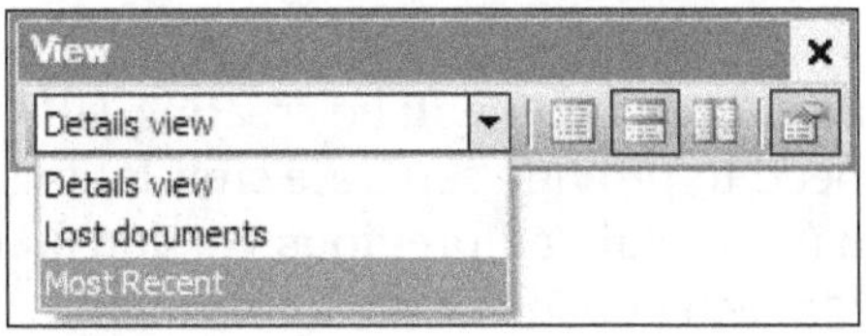

In this example, we have defined a new Custom view called **Most Recent**.

Choosing a structure for your Library

The Library initially contains only a single folder, `System`. Do not worry about what is in this folder at the moment—we will look at it in more detail in Chapter 12, *Configuring UPK*. What you do need to do now is decide on the overall structure of your Library. Basically, the Library is a set of nested folders that conceptually works in the same way as the folder structure you see in Windows Explorer or similar file management systems. It should, therefore, be a very familiar concept to you.

> Technically, content objects are not *stored* within this folder structure (or any folder structure). Instead, they are stored as objects in a database.

The difficulty for developers who are familiar with OnDemand Version 8.x and earlier is in divorcing the Outline (which is covered in more detail in Chapter 5, *Building an Outline*) from the Library. The Library is just a set of folders into which content is stored by the developers. The Outline organizes this content into a structure that the trainees will see. The Library does not necessarily bear any relation to the Outline. So the first thing that you need to decide is how you want to arrange your content for the benefit of the developer. As with Windows Explorer, there are an infinite number of possibilities, but some will make more sense than others. Some of the more commonly-used options are explained below:

- **Application-based structure:** If you (or all of the developers collectively) will be creating UPK simulations for a number of different applications, then you could choose to create a separate folder for each application and store all of the content for each application within its own folder.
- **Module-based structure**: With large ERP systems such as SAP, a company will typically implement several individual components of the ERP system. Here, it may be helpful to have separate folders for each functional area. So to use the example of SAP, you could have separate folders for `FI`, `MM`, `SD`, and so on.
- **Version-based structure:** If you will be creating UPK simulations for a single application, but need to provide separate simulations for different versions of the application (and retain all previous versions), then you could choose to have one folder for each version of the application.
- **Course-based structure**: Often, training programs will deliver a number of discrete training courses, possibly organized around the modules that the project is delivering, but more likely centered on the (business or system) roles of the users who are to be trained. Here, it may be sensible to organize the content into folders by course.
- **Content-based structure:** UPK recognizes several types of object, including the Module, Section, and Topic types of 'content', Web Pages, and Packages. These are explained in more detail in Chapter 9, *Adding Value to Your Topics*. You could, therefore, choose to store each type of content in its own folder.
- **Security-based structure:** In a client/server implementation of UPK 3.5.1, it is possible to define security for individual folders within a Library. In this case, you can choose to organize your content into folders based on who you want to be able to change those content objects.

In all likelihood, you will choose to have a hybrid structure. For example, you may choose to have separate folders per application, sub-folders below this for each course, and then further sub-folders for each type of content. Whatever approach you choose, just remember that this is entirely for the benefit of the developer(s)—do not think of the trainees, as they will never see the Library structure. Your sole objective should be to organize the content so that the developers can easily find what they are looking for when they need to change it.

For our sample Library structure, we will use a hybrid structure. At the highest level, we will use a course-based structure, with one folder per delivered course. This folder will be used to house all of the true content objects for our course: Modules, Sections, and Topics. Below this, we will have a separate directory that we will use to store all of the *assets* for the course—the Web Pages and Packages (which we will look at in Chapter 9, *Adding Value to Your Topics*). This will give us a structure as shown below:

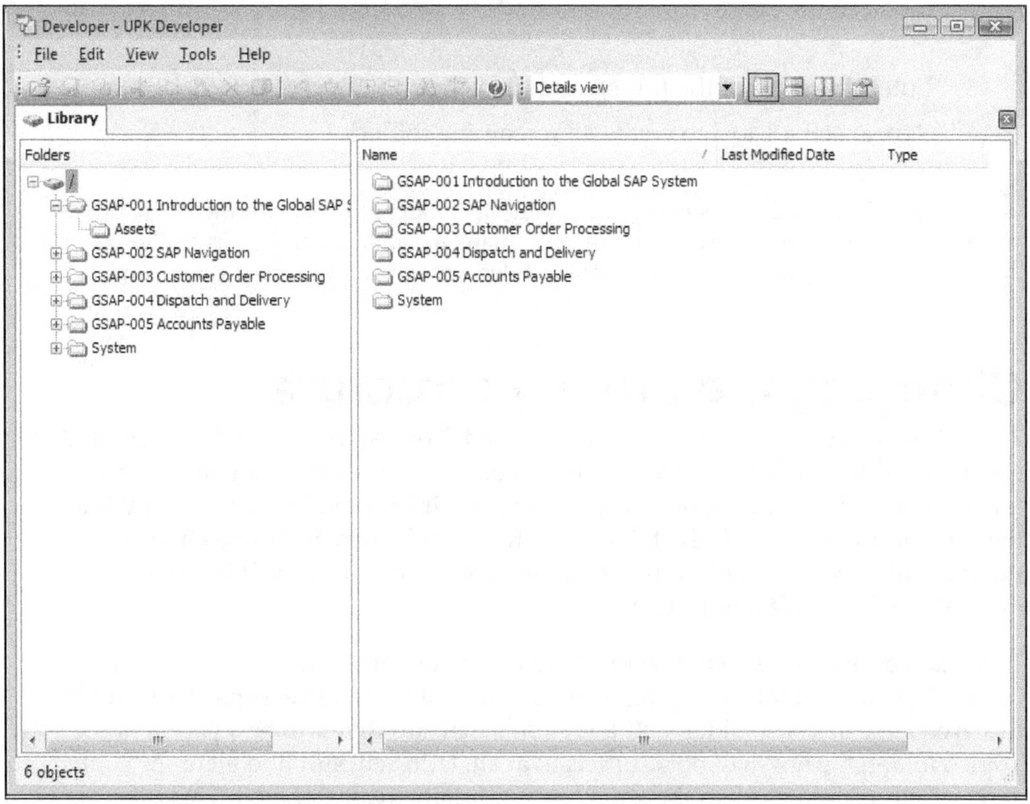

Creating folders

Now that you know how you want your Library structured, let's look at how to achieve this. To create a new folder, carry out the steps described below:

1. Click on the folder within which you want the new folder to be located. If this is the first folder that you are defining in your Library, then this will be the `root` folder, which is identified by a single slash (/).
2. Select menu option **File | New | Folder**. A dialog box is displayed, prompting you to specify a name for your new folder.

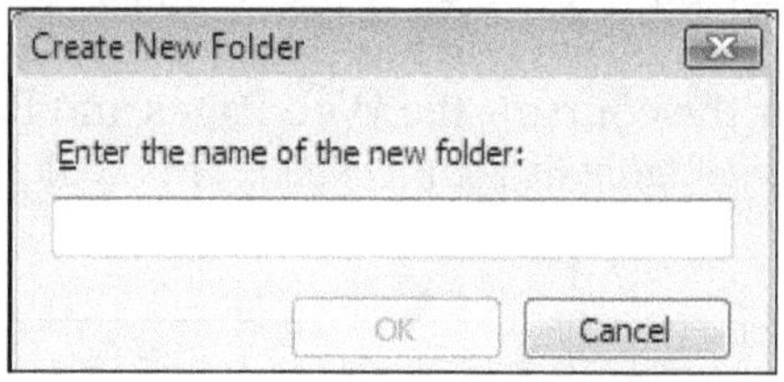

3. Enter the name of the folder, and then click on **OK**.
4. Repeat steps 1 to 3 to create all remaining folders.

> You can have as many levels of nested folder as you like—there is no limit (as there effectively was in OnDemand 8.7 and earlier, by virtue of only having a strict hierarchy of Modules, Lessons, and Titles within a Topic).

Changing the Library structure

The folder structure that you create is not fixed. You can rename folders (right-click on them and then select **Rename** from the context menu), move them around (via drag-and-drop or cut-and-paste), change their location in the hierarchy (move them up or down through the folder structure), and so on. So if you change your mind about how you want your content to be located within the Library (as you inevitably will), don't worry about it.

Any changes that you make to your Library will not affect any links that you have created in your content. For example, if you create a link from a Topic in one folder to a Web Page in a sub-folder, and then move that sub-folder to be a parent of the Topic's folder, the link will not be affected at all. UPK will still find all of the content, and everything will work in the way that you originally designed it. This is because UPK does not use the folder names or locations in any of the links. Instead, it uses its own unique (32-character) identifier for each content object (as described in the section *Displaying content information*, above).

> Actually, UPK does use the folder structure/location when identifying (for example) the Web Page attached to the Concepts pane of a Content Object. This is purely for your convenience (because it's easier to remember than a 32-character string). If, in this example, you move the Web Page to another folder, UPK will automatically update the folder reference.

Again, UPK can do this because the folder structure in the Library bears absolutely no reference to the structure that the trainee will see—as we shall see in Chapter 5, *Building an Outline*.

Summary

The **Library** is the primary interface through which you—the developer—will interact with all of the content in UPK. You create folders to house your content in the Library, and create content objects within these folders. The organization of the folders and their content does not impact or influence the structure in which these content objects will be arranged when they are presented to trainees.

The Library opens as a tabbed page within the **Developer** screen. The various editors within UPK will also open as tabbed pages within this same screen. You can split the **Developer** screen to show two different tabbed pages at the same time. Separate panes exist for key information about content objects. These include the **Properties** pane, the **Related Documents** pane, and the **Broken Links** pane. Each of these panes can be displayed, hidden, or docked, independently, as per your personal preferences.

3

Recording a Simulation

In the last chapter, we organized our Library. We are now ready to start recording the content to go into this Library. In doing so, we will take a close look at exactly what UPK is doing when it captures a recording. This understanding is essential if you intend to make any adjustments (and you should definitely count on having to adjust your recording!).

In this chapter, you will learn:

- What UPK captures during a recording
- How to record a simulation
- How to record drag-and-drop activities
- How to configure your recording options

How UPK captures a recording

Recording a simulation is a relatively simple activity, but before we jump into it, it is best that we understand exactly what UPK is doing when we record a simulation.

It is important to understand that UPK does not *record* activities, in the traditional sense of the word. It does not create a video of what you do (in the way that, say, Camtasia does). Instead, it captures screen prints and the actions performed to move between them.

Furthermore, UPK does not, by default, *automatically* capture these. You have to specifically tell it when to capture screen prints and actions by pressing the *Prt Scr* key (or other nominated key or key combination, see the *Setting your Recorder options* section).

> **Version Difference**
>
> Starting with UPK 3.5, you can set the Recorder to automatically record what you do without you having to press *Prt Scr* every time you want it to capture a new screenshot.

This requirement to tell the Recorder when to capture a screenshot is both bad and good. It's bad in that you have to remember to press *Prt Scr*, which can be distracting when you are trying to concentrate on what you are recording. But it is good in the sense that you only capture exactly the screenshots that you want. If an unexpected dialog box is displayed, then you simply don't press *Prt Scr*, and it is not captured (although you do need to be careful to ensure that the action is captured correctly; either that, or record the unexpected dialog box and then simply delete it from the recording, as we shall see in the next chapter).

When you press *Prt Scr*, UPK will take a screenshot of the screen as it appears when you pressed *Prt Scr*, and will capture the last action that you performed. This last action is effectively the thing that you did that caused the screen to look like it currently does (that is, as it looks in the screenshot that was captured). Often, this will be the key-press or mouse-click that moved you from the previous screen to the current screen, but it could also be the entry of a text string. Conceptually, therefore, UPK captures a set of action/screenshot pairs throughout a recording.

This *order of action then screenshot* is important. Each capture records the action that was carried out on the previous screen (that is, the screen to which the *previous* action/screenshot pair belongs), and a screenshot of the current screen (that is, the screen state once the action has been carried out). This is summarized in the following diagram, which shows what UPK captures for a simulation of the user entering a text string into an input field and then pressing *Enter*:

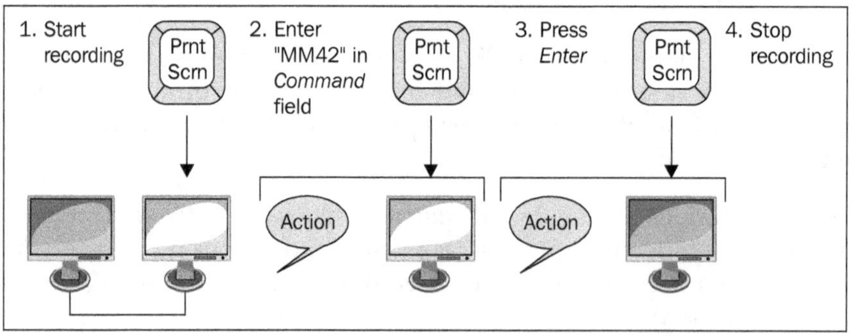

You will note, here, that we only performed two actions (the first one being the entry of the text string, and the second one being the key-press) but this has resulted in four screen prints being taken. Why? Because UPK will automatically insert a start screen and end screen and it uses the screenshots from the first and the last action screenshot pairs to do this. Note that they are shown grayed out in the previous diagram; they are grayed out in the actual recording as well.

Automatic recording

In version 3.5, UPK introduced the feature of automatic recording (much as RWD Productivity Pak/UPerform had been doing for years). If this feature is used, then you (the developer) only need to press *Prt Scr* twice—once to start the recording, and once to stop it. The Recorder will then automatically capture every mouse-click and key-press that you do. However, this comes with a large caveat; the recording will capture every time the screen changes, regardless of whether this is in response to a specific action that you want to record. This may or may not be what you want, but the chances are that you will need to do some cleanup of the recording to remove all of the unwanted screenshots.

That said, this option is extremely useful when you want to capture a demonstration by a **Subject Matter Expert** (**SME**). The SME will no doubt forget to press *Prt Scr*, resulting in (typically, critical) steps being missed out of the recording, or else find the Recorder pane distracting, or do something too fast for you to capture what they did. Here, you can just set the Recorder going, and leave them to it.

> There are some caveats to this approach. It is important that the Subject Matter Expert understands the limitations of automatic recording, and knows how to work around these. The main limitation is that pointing to an object will not automatically be recorded, so the SME should click on the object (and you will then need to change the action in the recording, which we explain in the next chapter). There are also limitations when using the clipboard (as SMEs have an annoying tendency to cut and paste data between windows), as explained below.

The automatic recording feature works well, and once you are comfortable with what the Recorder is capturing and understand what you will need to correct in this recording, you will probably use it most of the time. Within this book, however, we will use the manual recording option, partly because it gives us better control, and partly so that readers still using OnDemand 9.1 don't feel left out.

Capturing actions

It is important to understand that (with manual recording) UPK will only capture the last single action that you performed. For example, it can capture a single mouse-click, a single key-press, or a single text entry. So if you enter text in Field A, then enter text in Field B, and then press *Prt Scr*, your screenshot will show both Field A and Field B filled in, but the only action *captured* will be the entry of text into Field B (because this is the last action that you performed before pressing *Prt Scr*). If you then played back this recording, text would suddenly appear in Field A, without warning, when you are asked to enter the string in Field B.

For each action, UPK will capture the following things:

- The object against which the action was performed
- The action that was performed
- For text entry actions, the text that was entered

That's all. Nothing else. So it's not really that clever, after all! What *is* clever is the way that it uses this information, but we'll look at that later in this book.

Problematic actions

Although UPK will capture all of the (keyboard and mouse) actions that you perform, there are a few types of actions that cause problems. You should be aware of these before you start recording (assuming that you are recording manually, and not automatically).

- **Clipboard actions**: UPK uses the Windows clipboard to capture the screenshot. This means that whenever you press *Prt Scr*, UPK will lose the contents of the clipboard. If you need to record a copy-and-paste action then you should copy the content, press *Prt Scr*, re-copy the content, then paste, and then press *Prt Scr* again.
- **Changing text values**: If you need to record the changing of a text field, then you should record the complete entry of the text. For example, if you are changing a text field from "1234" to "1235" but do this (during recording) by selecting the last digit and pressing *5* on the keyboard, or by positioning the cursor at the end of the text string and pressing *Backspace* and then *5*, then UPK will only capture the action of entering "5". You should therefore select the entire text, overtype it with the full, new text, and capture this.

Planning your recording

Before recording a simulation, you should always plan out exactly what you want to record. This will save you the need to insert missing screenshots later, or re-record the exercise, because you forgot to capture a particular screen and/or action.

Bear in mind that the actual recording is only one step in the process of producing an effective simulation. It is worthwhile remembering the term PREP:

- Plan
- Record
- Edit
- Publish

As part of the Plan stage, consider sketching out the screens that you want to navigate to, and the actions that you want to perform on these screens. An example of a simple plan for the exercise captured later in this chapter is shown below:

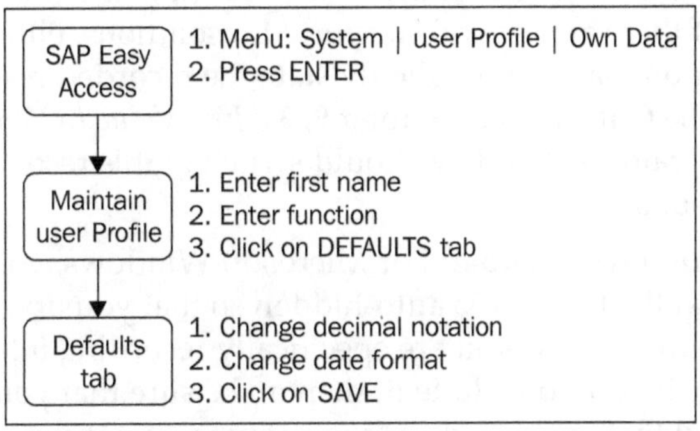

You should also make sure that any required data is available in the system. Bear in mind that the simulation should match reality as far as possible. This means that the screens should look exactly as they will when the end user sees them, that any data captured is correct and valid, and so on.

This, however, raises an interesting point regarding data in screenshots. You do want to use realistic data, but you would not normally want to include any data that could be considered sensitive or proprietary; for example, actual customers or vendors, invoices, pricing information, and so on. From this perspective, it may be wise to define a set of data that is to be used solely for training, using realistic, but entirely fictional, data.

Before recording a simulation, there are a number of things that you should do to prepare, or at least be aware of. Some of the things to watch out for are listed below:

- **Watch out for screen junk**: Make sure that there is no extraneous information on the screen. UPK will always capture full-screen images, so you may want to make sure that the application you are recording is in full-screen mode. If you do not record in full-screen mode, make sure that the application window stays in exactly the same position (to the nearest pixel) throughout the recording; otherwise, the playback will appear to "jump"'.
- **Set your screen to the correct resolution**: Set your screen to be the same resolution as the one to which your trainees screens will be set. For example, if your company's standard screen resolution is 1024x768 pixels, then make sure that you also record your simulations at this resolution. UPK will always display screens full-size, as it cannot scale them. If you record at a larger size than the user can display, the user will need to scroll around the screen to see it all. If you record at a smaller size, then the UPK Player will be centered on the screen and the surrounding area will be white, which will destroy the illusion of *reality*. If you do not know the resolution of the user's screens, or if there are several supported resolutions, either use the lowest common denominator, or explicitly state the recorded resolution up front (ideally, in the Outline, see Chapter 9, *Adding Value to Your Topics*) and advise your trainees that they should switch to this resolution for the best playback results.
- **Hide the Windows Taskbar**: For Microsoft Windows, you may want to ensure that the task bar is auto-hidden so that you do not capture it in the recording (unless you are specifically recording interactions with the task bar). If you do include it, then make sure that you only have the application(s) that you are recording running—your user's don't need to see that you have Gmail running, or that you're flipping between the application that you're recording and the CNN web site. Note that UPK will automatically "hide" itself, so your users will never see UPK in the Taskbar.
- **Close all other applications**: Close all applications apart from the one that you are recording, and UPK itself. You do not want unexpected interruptions—for example, by IM (Instant Messaging) clients, or other programs issuing alerts or pop-ups. Also, make sure that you have no other applications running that could interfere with the recording—especially screen capture applications, such as SnagIt, which also trap the *Prt Scr* key, and/or make use of the clipboard.

- **Remove any personalization**: Make sure that you are not using personalized display profiles or color settings. If the application that you are recording allows users to change (for example) their color profile, make sure that you record using the default color profile. If users access an application for the first time and see a color scheme different than the one they saw in training, they may become confused and/or concerned (really, I've seen it happen). If a user has customized their own profile, then the chances are that they are knowledgeable enough to realize that this explains the difference between what they saw in training and what they see in the actual application.
- **Watch out for session cookies**: When recording a simulation, try to capture screens as data-neutral as possible. Some applications will remember the last values used, and automatically use these for subsequent tasks (similar to session cookies). Remove any data that will not be auto-populated for a user the first time that they carry out the task in the "live" system. Similarly, remove all personal favorites, parameter defaults, and so on. Always ask yourself: "What would the user see if they are doing this for the first time?".
- **Record the complete task**: Related to this, try to record simulations from a neutral starting point, for example, the initial screen of an application (although it would probably be excessive to require the user to start or log on to the application every time). Unless you are providing something such as advanced troubleshooting exercises that start from the premise of "If you see this...", you should not just drop the user into the middle of a task; always explain to them how to get there.
- **Watch out for the cursor position**: When performing the actual recording, make sure that you pay attention to where the cursor is located. Although UPK will automatically hide the cursor itself, it will not automatically hide any ToolTip text that may be displayed. If you have screen objects that change appearance when you hover over them, make sure that the cursor is not hovering over them when you capture the screen print—especially if this is the object that they will be clicking on, as this would give them too much of a clue to the action (especially in *Know It?* mode).
- **Maintain data continuity**: If you record your simulation in more than one go, or if (when!) you have to re-capture screenshots, watch out for data continuity. For example, if you record a topic on one day, and then replace a few screens the next day, make sure that any timestamps shown on the screens are consistent, that any data used is consistent throughout, and so on. If anything is inconsistent, then this will be evident in the Player—it may only be a quick flash as the user navigates from one screenshot to the next, but again, it will ruin the illusion of reality.

- **Use realistic data**: Your simulations should look as close to reality as possible. This means that the data used in the simulations should, as much as possible, be realistic data. Avoid using customers called "Test Vendor", products called "Dummy", and so on. Try to use correct number ranges, document types, and so on. This will better facilitate the trainees transitioning their knowledge to the actual system. But on the other hand, you should make sure that you do not use any sensitive or confidential data (*realistic*, not necessarily *real*), such as actual customer names and addresses (unless, of course, you are recording a simulation on how to handle a specific customer). Although it may take longer to initially set up, it is worthwhile setting up (or having the data team set up for you) your own set of products, customers, and materials, that are only used in training.
- **Perform a test run before recording**: Finally, before you record a Topic, consider testing the activity before you go ahead and record it. Make sure that the application works as expected, and that you know what to capture. But be careful not to consume data that you will need for the actual recording.

Setting your content defaults

Before you record your first simulation, you should set up some defaults for your content. Although you can always change these things later, setting them up beforehand will save you some re-work when it comes to editing your Topic in the next chapter.

You access these defaults via menu option **Tools | Options**. There are 19 pages of options. We will look at all of these throughout this book, as needed. For now, we will just look at the options that will affect the content of your recording. These are under the **Content Defaults** category.

General options

You can define default values for your Topics' properties via the **General** options category. These are the values that are displayed in the *Properties* pane in the Library, which was discussed in Chapter 2, *Organizing Your Library*. The following screenshot shows these options:

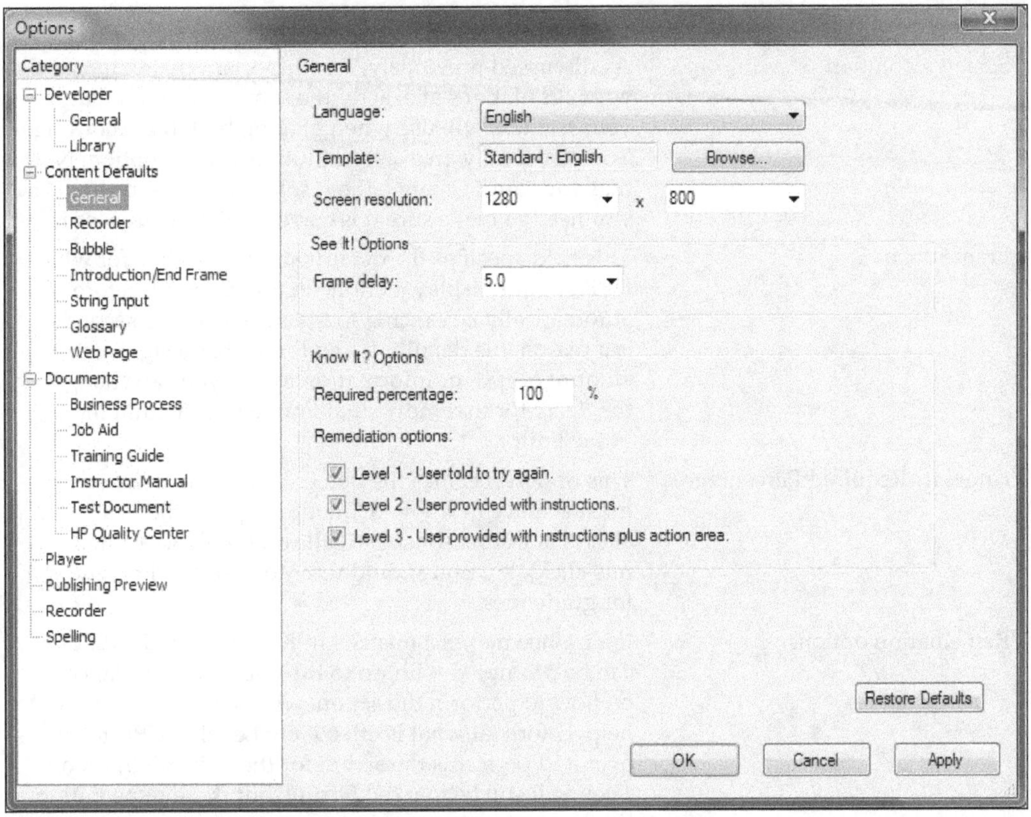

The following table describes the available options:

Option	Description
Language	This option specifies the language of the Template Text that will be used in the Bubbles, by default. This option is explained more fully in Chapter 12, *Localizing Your Content*. For now, leave it set to **English**.
Template	This option specifies the Template from which the Template Text will be taken (it is possible to have multiple templates for the same language; in fact, UPK ships with two separate Templates for each language). Templates are discussed in Chapter 11, *Configuring UPK*. For now, leave this option set to *Standard-English.*

Option	Description
Screen resolution	As discussed previously, it is important that you record your simulations at exactly the same resolution that your trainees will use when playing back the recording. You can specify an exact resolution via this option. Note that you cannot change the resolution of a recording, so you need to make sure it is correct before you record.
Frame delay	This field specifies the default amount of time for which UPK should display a Frame in *See It!* mode, before automatically advancing to the next screen. **5** seconds is a reasonable default. If any Frame has a significant amount of text, or information to see, you can change the delay for that individual Frame from within the Topic Editor.
Know It? Required Percentage	This option specifies the percentage that a trainee must achieve in Know It? mode to "pass" the "test". **80%** is not unreasonable (it allows for an occasional mis-click), but you should refer to your local practices for guidelines.
Remediation options	If a trainee makes a mistake in Know It? mode, they can be prompted with up to three levels of guidance on how to perform the action, with increasingly more help, before (at what is effectively Level 4) UPK takes over and performs the action for them, in *See It!* mode. They will still be marked wrong, but these remediation levels provide them with the opportunity to try again. It is usually sensible to provide all three levels of remediation.

Frame Delay

Setting a value of **0** will result in a much more "movie-like" playback, but the downside is that Decision Frames and Explanation Frames (both of which are explained in later chapters of this book) will not be displayed at all, so you will want to manually adjust these).

Options for Bubble Text

The options under the **Bubble** category allow you to define the defaults for your Bubbles (which are discussed more fully in Chapter 4, *Editing Your Topics*). The available options are shown in the next screenshot:

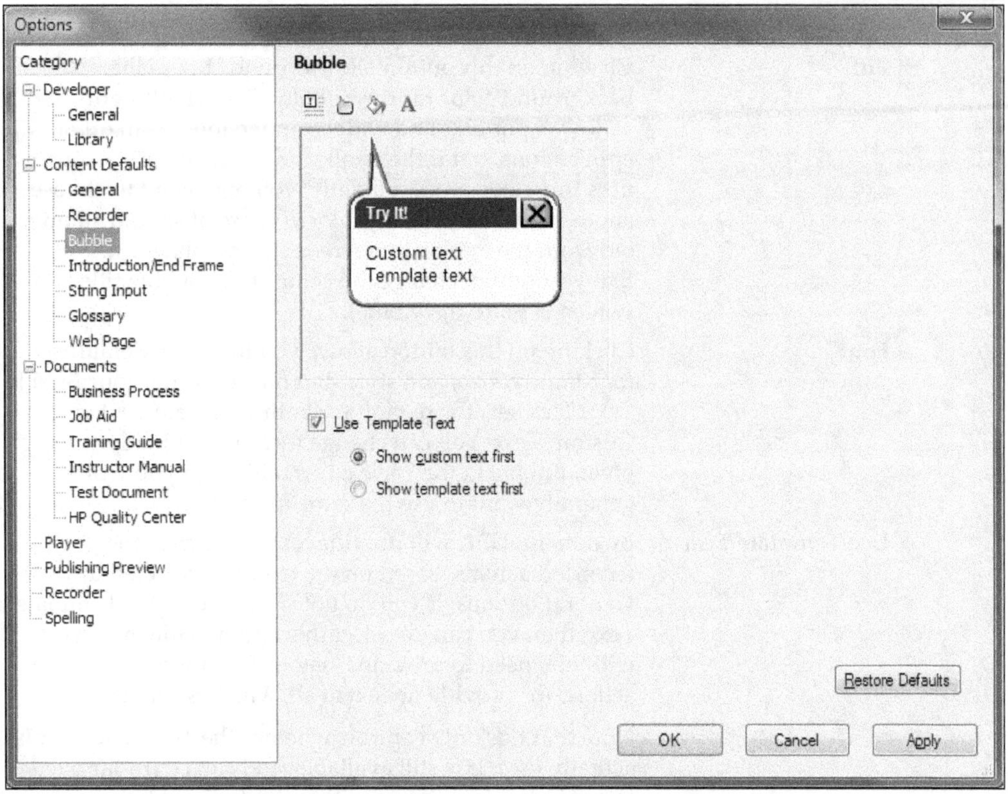

The table below describes the available options:

Option	Name	Description
	**Icon**	Clicking on this button allows you to choose an icon to display in each Bubble. These icons are discussed in Chapter 8, *Adding Value to Your Topic*. It is not recommended that you have an icon in every Bubble (let alone the same icon in every Bubble—there are 35 to choose from), so you should not normally use this option.
	**Bubble Pointer**	Clicking on this button allows you to choose a default position for the pointer on a Bubble. Pointers are discussed in Chapter 8, *Adding Value to Your Topic*. Unless you choose No pointer, it is unlikely that you will want to use a default for every Bubble. Just let UPK decide which position is best, based on the relative position of the Action Area.

Option	Name	Description
	**Fill**	Clicking on this button allows you to choose the background color for the Bubble. The default light yellow is popular and widely-understood from other applications, but if the application that you are recording uses this color predominantly, you may want to choose another color. Whatever color you use, it should stand out from the application screen during playback. Note that you cannot change the color of the Bubble title bar (which is set to navy blue).
	**Font**	Clicking on this button allows you to set the default font-family, size, and style (but not color) for your Bubble Text. This sets the default for both Template Text and Custom Text. You can change these individually for any given Bubble in the *Topic Editor*, although you would generally want to use the same for both.
	Use Template Text	By default, UPK will provide text to describe the recorded actions, based on the template selected in your **General** options. If you do not want to use this Template Text, then you can de-select this option. However, you will then need to provide Custom Text for all of your actions (or provide no text at all, which is unwise). Note that this only controls whether the Template Text is actually *used*. It is still available, and can be (re-)applied for an individual Frame within the *Topic Editor*. If you use Template Text then you can choose to have either the Template Text or the Custom Text displayed first. As discussed in Chapter 9, *Adding Value to Your Topics*, it is generally more useful to display the Custom Text first (this is the default in UPK 3.5, although in OnDemand 9.1 it was the other way round).

Options for the Introduction/End Frames

The **Introduction/End Frame** category allows you to change the background color and font for the Bubbles that are used on the Introduction (Start) Frame and the End Frame. The following screenshot shows the available options:

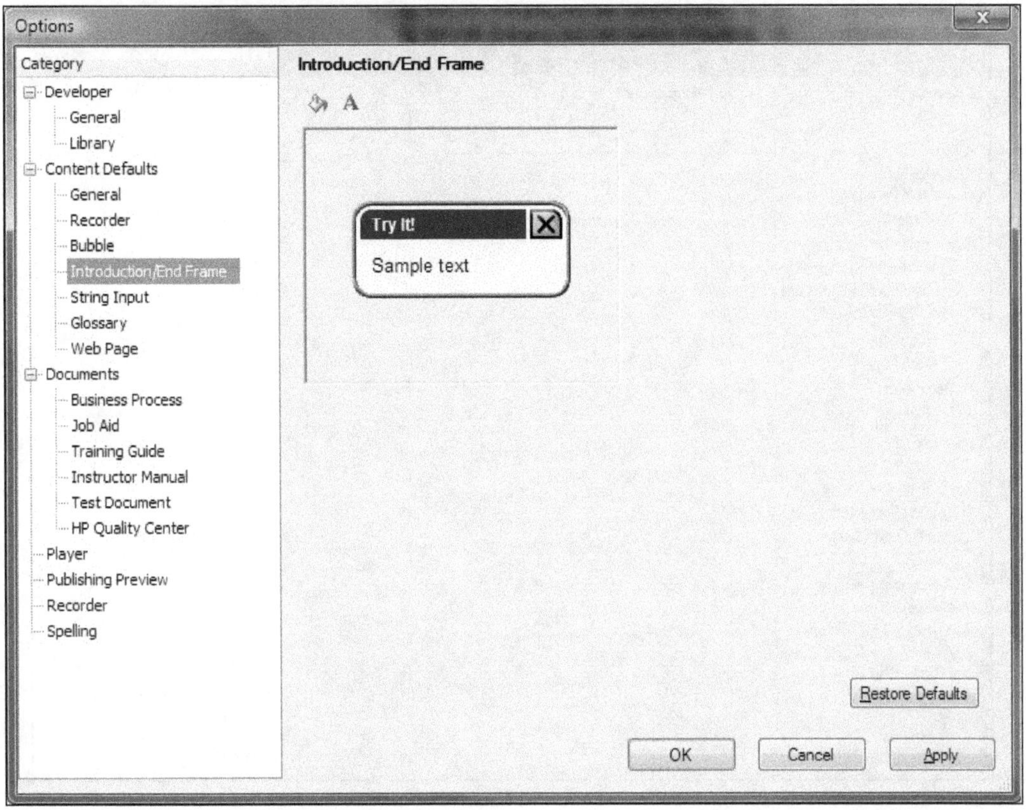

The buttons for these options, and their use, are the same as for the **Bubble** option, as described above. You would normally want to use the same values here as for Bubble Text, although if you want to draw particular attention to the Start Frame and the End Frame, then you could use a different format.

Options for String Input

The options under the **String Input** category allow you to change the options for string input actions. You should set these options carefully if you will be recording lots of string input actions in your application. The available options are shown in the next screenshot:

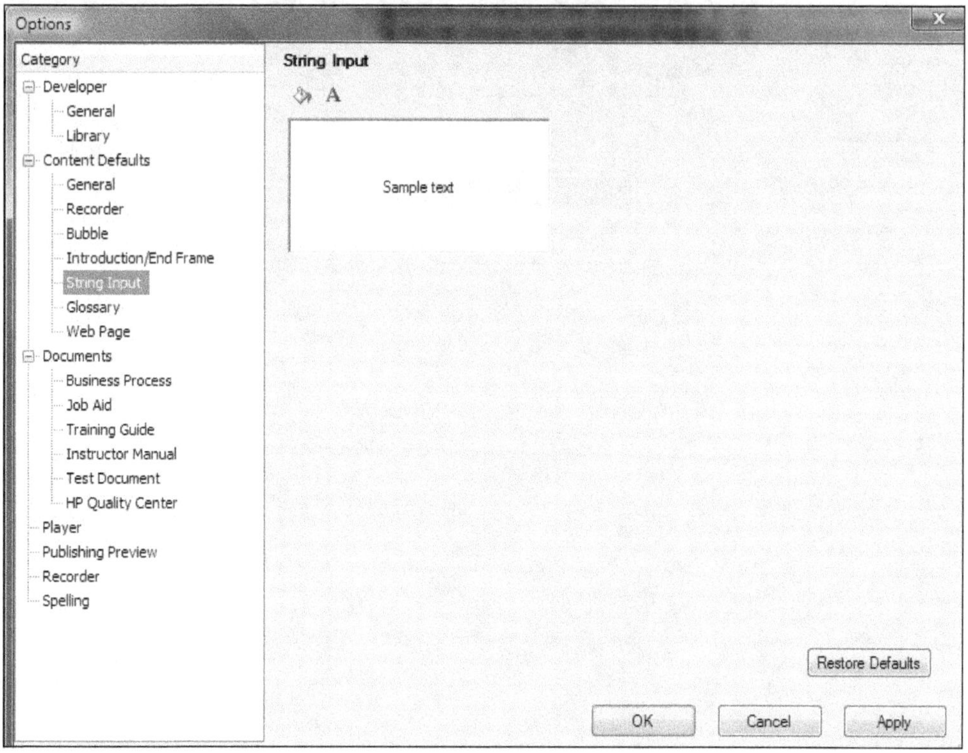

Again, the same two options (fill and font) are available as for the **Introduction/ End Frame**, and work as described for the Bubble option, above. Although here these options specify how string input is handled in the Player (or other online deployment format). In order to understand these, you need to understand how string input works.

When UPK plays back a string input Action, it overlays a text box onto the screenshot, at the point where the input field appears. This text box has a solid background. You may have expected this to be transparent, so that you could see the input field below it, but consider the case where the field contains an existing value that the trainee has to change—this would show through, too. You should therefore set the background of the text box to be exactly (and I cannot stress enough that this must be EXACTLY) the same as the background color of the input fields in the application that you are recording. This is white in many applications, but (for example) SAP uses a deep yellow background color on the active field, so when recording SAP, the background color of the string input field needs to be changed to match.

> Refer to Chapter 4, *Editing a Topic* for more information on the background colors and fonts used in common applications.

The same is true of the string input font. This must *exactly* match the font (face and size) that is used in your application for input fields. This may not always be the default **Microsoft Sans Serif 8pt**; SAP even has its own font: **Arial Monospaced for SAP**. You may be able to find out this information from the application itself, or you may need to use trial and error to find the correct one.

Our first recording

Now that we have set our defaults, let's go ahead and record our first simulation. We will record a very simple simulation that covers a variety of actions, including text entry, screen navigation, and some option selections. For the purposes of this exercise, our simulation will teach users how to change their user options in the SAP application. Do not worry if you do not use SAP. The actual application is irrelevant; what is important is how we capture the recording.

There are effectively two ways that you can record a new simulation. In the first method, you create and save an "empty" **Topic** element in an **Outline Element** and then perform the recording for this (now existing) Topic. As we will see in Chapter 6, *Publishing Content*, empty Topics are ignored when you publish an Outline, so there is no harm in pre-defining them.

> You may recall from Chapter 2, *Organizing your Library* that a **Topic** is the content object of the actual simulation. **Outline Elements** are content objects that are used to organize Topics into a structure for presentation to the trainees. These concepts are discussed in much more detail in Chapter 5, *Building an Outline*.

In the second method, you go directly into the Recorder, record your Topic, and then save it at the end of the recording. The first method is useful if you prefer to build an Outline with placeholders before you start your work. The second method is useful if you don't know the exact Outline in which the Topic will ultimately reside. Whichever method you use is up to you (and you can use one method for some Topics and the other method for other Topics, as you find convenient at the time). Both methods are explained below.

Creating an empty Topic

To create an empty Topic, as a placeholder, carry out the following steps.

1. Open the Outline Element into which you want the Topic to appear. For information on Outlines and Outline Elements, refer to Chapter 5, *Building an Outline.*
2. From the Outline Toolbar (again, see Chapter 5, *Building an Outline*), click on the Link New Topic button ( ). Alternatively, you can select menu option **Link | New Topic** (or press *Ctrl+T*).
3. A new Topic is inserted into the Outline Element. This will have an "empty Topic" icon ( ) and a name of **New Topic**. This Topic will inherit its basic properties (screen size, Template, and Glossary) from the Outline Element.
4. Over-type the Topic name with a suitable name for your Topic.

An example of an Outline Element showing an empty Topic is shown in the screenshot below.

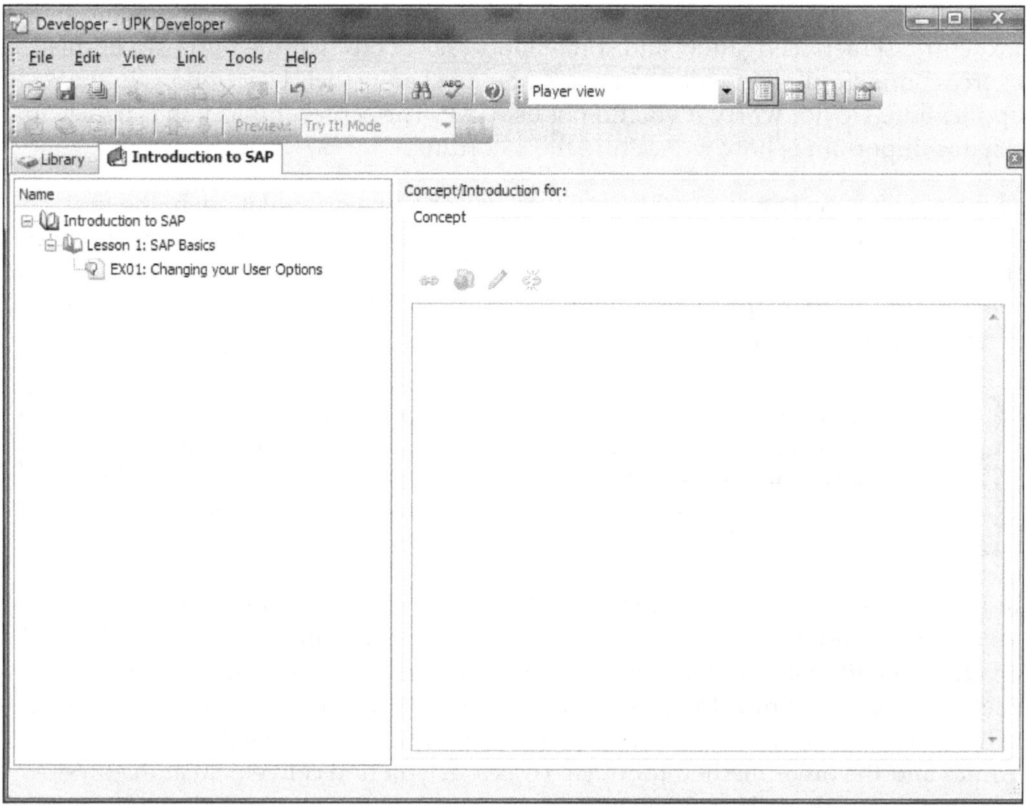

You can now either proceed immediately with recording the Topic, or can exit from the Outline (or after creating additional empty Topics) and come back to recording it either from the Outline or from the Library at any point in the future. Note that you do not need to save the Outline—the assignment of objects (Topics or other Outline Elements) to Outline Elements is automatically committed.

Recording an empty Topic

To record the content for an empty Topic that you previously created, carry out the steps described below:

1. Click on the empty Topic in either the Library or the Outline (it does not matter which), to select it.
2. Click the Record button (icon) on the *Standard* toolbar. Alternatively, you can double-click on the Topic. The UPK window (which was showing the Library or Outline) is hidden, revealing the last application that you had open on your screen. The UPK *Recorder* window appears in the upper-right corner of the screen (see *The Recorder window* section, below).
3. Make sure that you are at the correct start point in the application that you want to record.
4. Press *Prt Scr* to start the capture of the screenprints and actions.
5. Perform a *single* action.
6. Press *Prt Scr* again, to capture the action and the resulting screenprint.
7. Repeat Steps 5 and 6 for all actions throughout the transaction.
8. Once you have finished, click the **Finish** button in the *Recorder*.

Once you finish the recording, you will be passed directly into the Topic Editor, from where you can make any necessary adjustments (and there *will* be adjustments) to the recording. Note that if, in your Options, you select the option **Open the Topic Editor | After each screenshot**, then you will be passed into the *Topic Editor* every time that you press *Prt Scr*. This option is discussed later in the section *Setting your Recorder options*.

Recording a Topic immediately

To record the content for a brand new Topic (that is, not an **empty topic**), carry out the steps described below:

1. In the Library, navigate to and select the folder in which you want the Topic to be created. Note that, as explained in Chapter 5, *Building an Outline*, this does not necessarily need to relate to the Outline in which the Topic will be included for publishing.

2. Select menu option **File | New | Topic**. The UPK window (which was showing the Library) is hidden, revealing the last application that you had open on your screen. The UPK *Recorder* window appears in the upper-right corner of the screen, as shown in the screenshot in the *The Recorder window* section of this chapter.
3. Make sure that you are at the correct start point in the application that you want to record.
4. Press *Prt Scr* to start the capture of the screen prints and actions.
5. Perform a *single* action.
6. Press *Prt Scr* again, to capture the action and the resulting screen print.
7. Repeat Steps 6 and 7 for all actions throughout the transaction.
8. Once you have finished, click the **Finish** button in the *Recorder*.

Once you finish the recording, you will be passed directly into the Topic Editor, from where you can make any necessary adjustments (and there *will* be adjustments) to the recording. Note that if, in your Options you select the option **Open the Topic Editor | After each screenshot**, then you will be passed into the *Topic Editor* every time that you press *Prt Scr*. This option is discussed further in the section *Setting your Recorder options*, below.

The Recorder window

Regardless of the method that you use to record your Topics, ultimately, you will be passed into the Recorder, and the Recorder window will be displayed in the upper-right corner of the screen. Note that this is not a fixed position—you can move this window by clicking on the title bar and dragging it to a new position on the screen. You will need to do this if you need to capture an action on a screen element that is located underneath the Recorder window. The following screenshot shows the standard "manual" *Recorder window:*

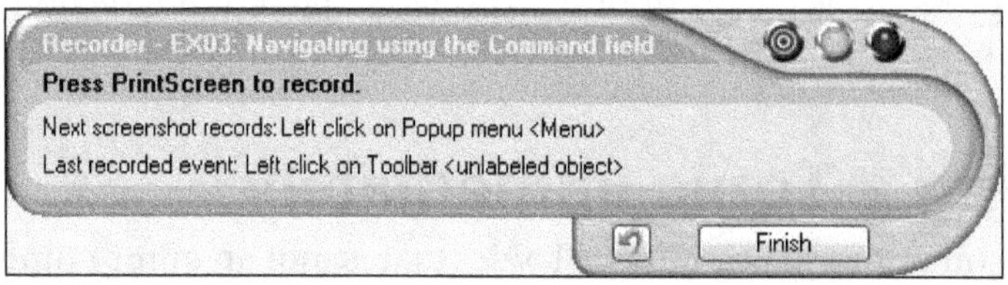

There are a couple of interesting things to note in this Recorder window. Firstly, the name of the Topic that you are recording is shown in the "title bar" of the window (unless you are recording the Topic immediately, in which case the name is shown simply as "New Topic"). The line immediately below this (**Press PrintScreen to record.**) reminds you of the key (or key combination) that has been defined as the "capture key" (see the section *Setting your Recorder options*). The line below this (**Next screenshot records:...**) specifies the action that will be captured if you press *Prt Scr* at this point. You will note that this changes as you move the cursor over different screen elements or perform other actions. The bottom line (**Last recorded event:...**) identifies the last action that was captured by the Recorder.

> When you start recording, always check the "Next screenshot records" text, to see if it is necessary to press *Prt Scr* to start recording, before performing your first action.

In the upper-right corner of the window, there may be one or more indicators (the previous screenshot shows all possible indicators, for completeness). The green one (second from the right) is "lit" when UPK is ready to capture a screenshot—that is, you are free to press *Prt Scr* whenever this indicator is on. The red indicator (on the right) is "lit" if UPK is busy, which it normally is when saving (or preparing to save) a screenshot. The final indicator, on the left, may not always be present. If it is present, then this means that UPK "knows" the application that you are recording, and will capture the context of the action as you record it. Capturing the context is one of the key capabilities of UPK, and is explained more fully in Chapter 6, *Publishing Your Content*.

> **Version Difference**
>
> The green and red "traffic light" indicators exist in OnDemand 9.1, but were discontinued in UPK 3.5.

At the bottom, on the left, is the **Undo** button. This can be used to cancel the last screenshot (and action) that was captured. Effectively, it undoes the last use of the *Prt Scr* key. Finally, at the bottom, on the right, is the **Finish** button. You need to click on this button when you have finished recording the Topic, in order to close the Recorder window.

Note that UPK will automatically hide the Recorder window whenever you press *Prt Scr*. It will also hide the UPK Developer application button from the Windows Taskbar.

> When recording, if you are unsure whether an action has been captured (for example, if you were interrupted by a telephone call) then re-perform the action and/or press *Prt Scr* again. As a general guideline, when in doubt, *over-record*. It is much easier to remove extraneous screen prints than it is to go back and insert missing actions.

The Recorder window for automatic recording

If you are using the automatic recording option, then the *Recorder* appears slightly differently, as shown in the following screenshot:

Here, there are very few options—only a single button for canceling the recording, and a couple of lines of instruction telling us how to start and stop recording.

Once you press *Prt Scr* to start recording, the *Recorder* window will be hidden and you will not see it again during the recording. When you press *Prt Scr* to stop the recording, you are passed directly to the *Topic Editor*, as before.

Our sample exercise

For the record, these are the exact steps that I carried out in order to record the sample exercise that we will use throughout the rest of this book:

1. Logged on to SAP to reach the *SAP Easy Access* screen.
2. Switched to UPK, selected the new exercise, and then clicked on the *Record Topic* button. UPK flipped me back to the *SAP Easy Access* screen, with the *Recorder* panel now displayed in the upper-right corner of the screen.
3. Pressed *Prt Scr* to start the recording.
4. Clicked on the **System** menu to expand it. Pressed *Prt Scr*.
5. Pointed to **User Profile** on the drop-down menu. Pressed *Prt Scr*.
6. Clicked on **Own Data**. Pressed *Prt Scr*. The *Maintain User Profile* screen is displayed.

7. Clicked in the **First Name** field. Pressed *Prt Scr*.
8. Selected the existing text in the *First Name* field ("Dick") and typed "Dirk" on the keyboard. Pressed *Prt Scr*.
9. Clicked in the **Function** field. Pressed *Prt Scr*.
10. Typed "Training Analyst". Pressed *Prt Scr*.
11. Clicked on the **Defaults** tab. Pressed *Prt Scr*.
12. Clicked the drop-down list button for the **Decimal Notation** field. Pressed *Prt Scr*.
13. Clicked on the entry **for X 1,234,567.89**. Pressed *Prt Scr*.
14. Clicked the drop-down list button for the **Date Format** field. Scrolled up to the top of the list. Pressed *Prt Scr*.
15. Clicked on the entry for **1 DD.MMYYYY**. Pressed *Prt Scr*.
16. Clicked on the **Save** button. Pressed *Prt Scr*.
17. Clicked on the **Finish** button in the recorder.

If you have access to SAP, go ahead and recreate this Topic by following the steps described above. If you don't have access to SAP, but still want to follow along with the exercises, then you can download all of the samples used in this book from the Packt web site. All exercises are contained in a single `.odarc` file, which you can load into your Library using the **import** function described in Chapter 7, *Version Management*. The sample exercise for this chapter is in the Topic EX01-03 Changing your User Options (Chapter 3).

If you've been skipping ahead (to Chapter 5, *Publishing Your Content)*, and already know how to preview your exercise, preview it now. Are you happy with the result? If you are, then you can stop reading this book here. If you're not happy with the result (and I hope that you're not!) then there is a lot that we can do to improve the exercise. So keep reading!

Setting your Recorder options

There are a couple of options relevant to recording that are worth knowing about. These are defined via menu option **Options | Recorder**, as shown in the following screenshot:

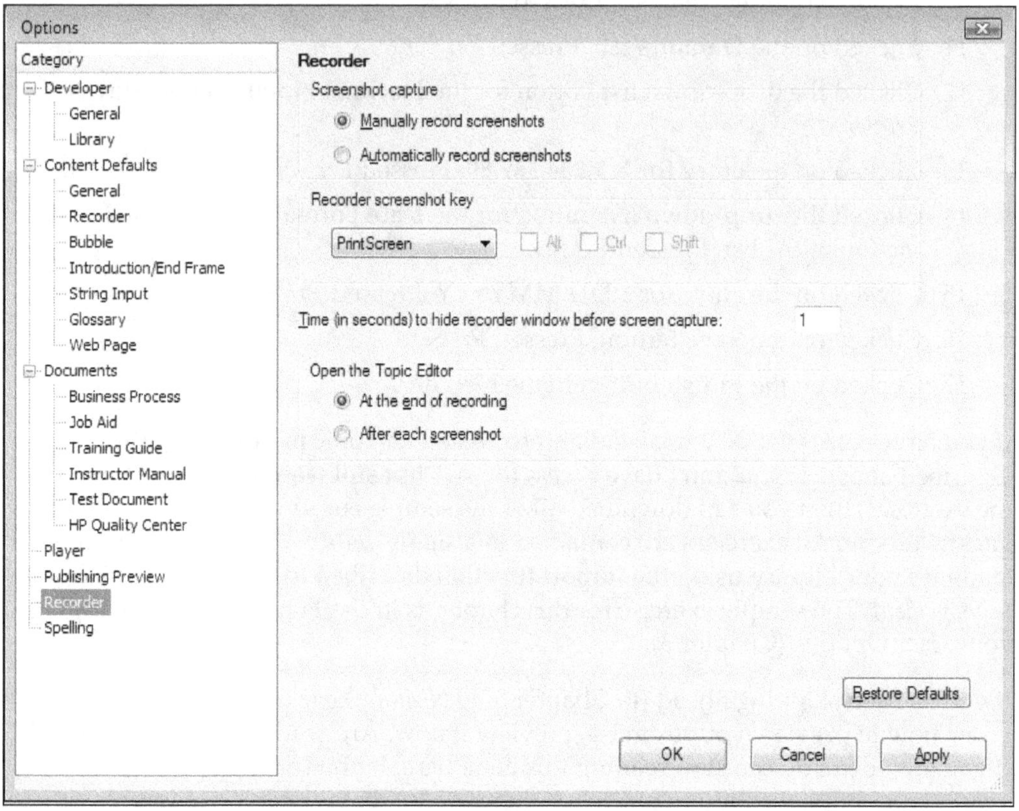

Let's take a quick look at each of these options.

Option	Description
Screenshot capture	This option is new for UPK version 3.5 (it is not available in OnDemand), and has two options. If you select **Manually record screenshots**, then you need to explicitly press the *Prt Scr* button (or other designated button) whenever you want UPK to capture a screenshot (and action). If you select **Automatically record screenshots**, then UPK will automatically capture a screenshot every time that the screen changes, which is, in theory, every time that you perform an action.

Option	Description
	Which option should you choose? Well, manual recording is the traditional way of working, and is the method that gives you the most control over what screenshots your Topic will include. Automatically recording screenshots is useful if you are forgetful in nature and tend to miss capturing screens because you forgot to press *Prt Scr*, or if (as discussed) you are trying to capture everything that an SME does in the most unintrusive way possible. However, it does result in *everything* being captured, and this may not necessarily be what you want. The author's recommendation is to use manual recording, for the control it affords.
Recorder screenshot key	This option specifies which key should be used to indicate to UPK that it should capture a screenshot (and the preceding action). By default, this is the *Prt Scr* key, but you can use the drop-down list and the checkboxes provided to select any other key combination. Whichever key combination you choose, you should make sure that this key combination is not used by the application that you are recording (specifically, make sure that you do not want to capture this key or key combination as an action). This book uses *Prt Scr*, throughout. If you use the **Automatically record screenshots** option then you still need to select a key, but this key is only used to start the recording and stop the recording. You cannot use a key combination for this (you can only use a single key).
Time (in seconds) to hide recorder window before screen capture	This option defines the number of seconds that UPK will wait after you (the developer) press *Prt Scr*, before capturing the screenshot. Generally, you should set this to be at least **1**. Anything less, and there is a danger that the screen capture will include the recorder panel itself. This used to be a problem in earlier versions of OnDemand, but UPK may have resolved this issue. This option only applies to manual recording.
Open the Topic Editor	If this option is set to **At the end of recording** (which is the default option), then you will be passed into the Topic Editor when you press **Finish** in the Recorder window. If this option is set to **After each screenshot**, then you will be passed into the Topic Editor every time that you press *Prt Scr*. This latter option is more disruptive to the overall recording process, but it does have the advantage that you can enter any Custom Text, or adjust the action, as you go along, rather than having to go through the whole recording from the beginning, trying to remember what you were trying to teach. This option only applies to manual recording.

Recording drag-and-drop activities

Most actions that you will record fall into one of the following categories:

- Clicking on a particular area of the screen
- Pressing a specific key or key combination on the keyboard
- Entering a text string

These types of activities are relatively straightforward for UPK, with its philosophy of capturing screenshots and the actions between them, to record and play back. For mouse-clicks, UPK simply takes a screenshot before the mouse-click (as part of the *previous action)*, and a screenshot after the mouse-click. During playback, UPK simply displays the *before* screenshot, and then displays the *after* screenshot once the user has clicked on the correct area of the screen. Key-presses work in a similar way.

For text entry, UPK is slightly cleverer. In addition to taking the *before* and *after* screenshots, during playback it overlays a text box on the screen, to allow the trainee to enter the required text. It is still relatively straightforward, and (largely) based on static screenprints.

However, with drag-and-drop activities, things are not so simple. As the object is dragged across the screen, the screen image is changing constantly. Ideally, UPK would capture this as a video, but unfortunately UPK doesn't work like this. In fact, UPK sticks to its guns, and tries to capture this motion using static screenshots. To pull this off effectively, UPK would need to capture a new screenshot every time the object that is being dragged moves a single pixel. However, this would be difficult to accomplish during playback (at best it would appear jerky, even on a fast network/processor, as the entire screen is being replaced each time. It would also be burdensome to work with in the *Topic Editor*.

Instead, UPK allows the object to be moved a predefined number of pixels before capturing a new screenshot. (Actually, UPK tracks the movement of the tip of the cursor, as this is easier to track.)

> Drag-and-drop does not work particularly well when dragging and dropping an object on the screen, and in these cases it may be more effective to just record the mouse-down action when selecting the object in its original location, and then record the mouse-up action when the object is dropped onto the target (that is, using *standard* action recording, and not true drag-and-drop.
>
> Where it does work well (or at least *better*) is when resizing objects by dragging their *bounding handles*. If there is a sufficiently-low distance between screenshots, this can appear *almost* true-to-life).

The number of pixels that the object moves before a new screenshot is captured is defined in your **Options**, under **Content Defaults | Recorder** (and not the **Recorder** category, for some reason), as shown in the following screenshot:

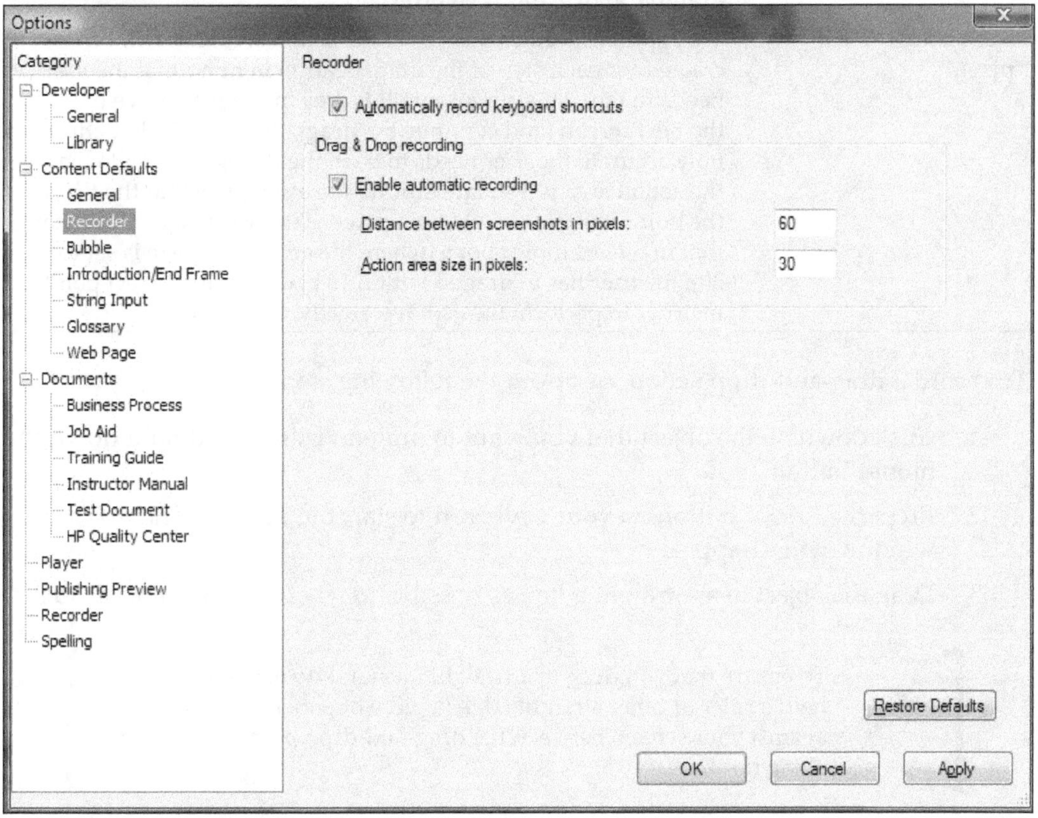

The drag-and-drop options work as follows:

Option	Description
Enable automatic recording	If this option is selected then UPK will automatically capture screenshots for the drag activity, according to the next two settings. If this option is not selected, then you (the Developer) will need to press *Prt Scr* every time a screenshot should be captured for the drag activity. In the latter case it can be difficult to achieve a smooth movement, especially as you need to move the mouse with one hand and press *Prt Scr* with the other (and things are worse if you need to *Shift*-drag, for example, to take a copy of an object!).

Option	Description
Distance between screenshots in pixels	This option specifies the number of pixels that the object needs to be moved before UPK captures another screenshot. In the example above, this is 60 pixels.
Action area size in pixels	This option specifies the size of the action area that will be created for each step of the drag. Bearing in mind that the user needs to move the cursor into this area in order to move onto the next screen (and continue the drag), this effectively defines how accurate the user needs to be in their dragging. Note that the action area is a square around the exact pixel that the tip of the pointer was over when the screenshot was taken. This means that in the example above (where the action area size is set to 30), the user has to drag to within 15 pixels of the correct point in order to perform the action correctly.

To record a drag-and-drop action, carry out the following steps:

1. Click down on the object that you want to drag-and-drop, and hold down the mouse button.
2. Press the *Prt Scr* button on your keyboard to start the capture. The *Recorder* window will disappear.
3. Drag the object in as straight a line as possible to where you want to drop it.

> To ensure that you drag in a straight line (and do not "veer off"), hold a ruler or other straight edge (a piece of paper works well) against your screen, between the drag-and-drop points, and drag along this line.

4. Drop the object at the destination, by releasing the mouse button. The *Recorder* window reappears.

Let's look at how this manifests itself in the actual recording. The screenshots ahead show the successive screenshots for a drag-and-drop action, as seen during playback:

In the first Frame, the trainee is told to click on the object that is to be dragged. This is indicated by a (by default) red marquee, which is the standard way that UPK indicates Action Areas.

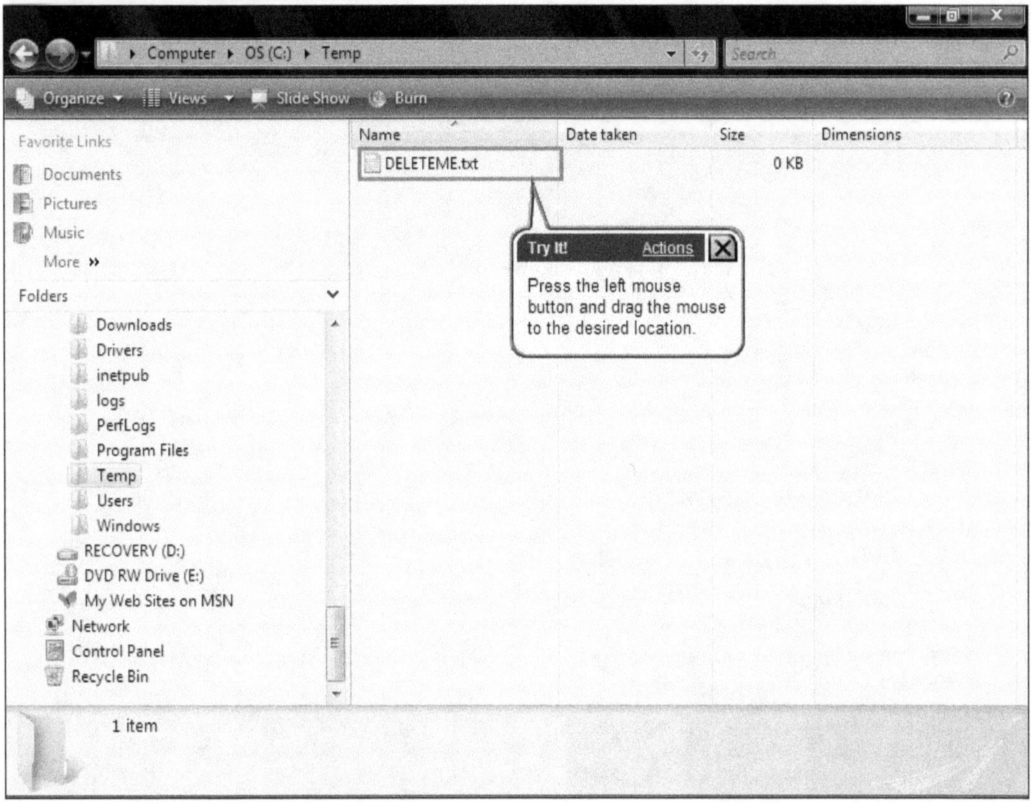

As soon as the trainee clicks on this object, the location (Action Area) to which the trainee needs to drag the object is highlighted. Note that there is no bubble on this Frame:

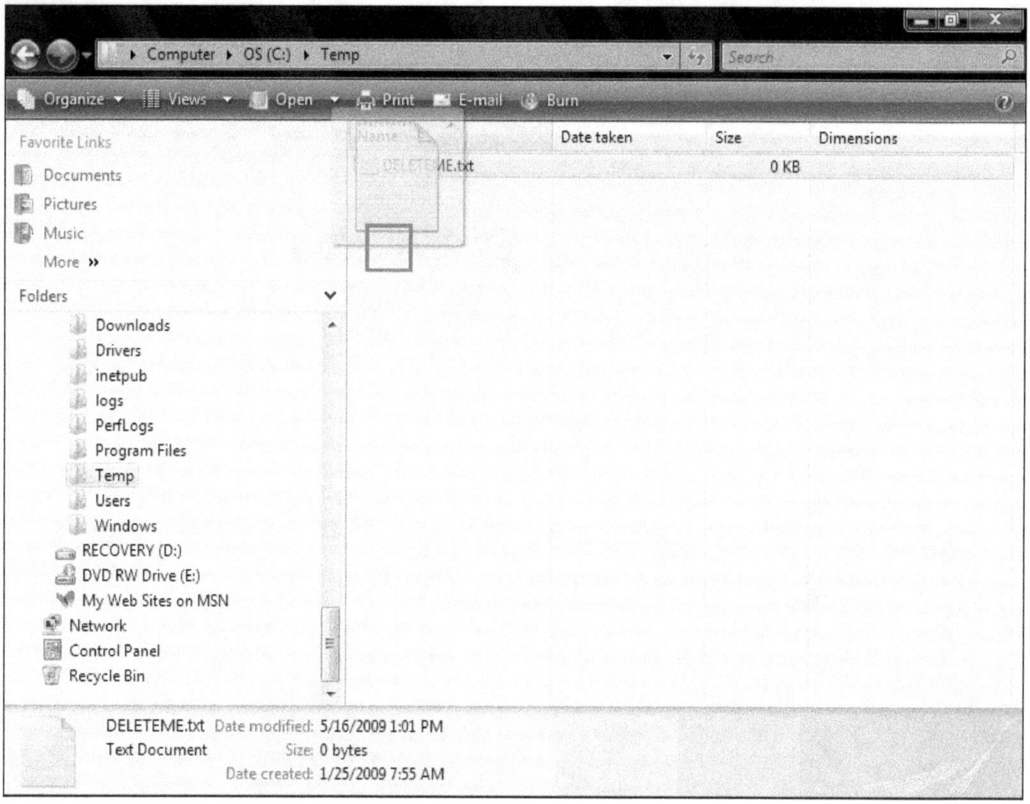

The trainee drags the mouse pointer towards the indicated area. Note that the object that they clicked on will not move, only the cursor will (which kind of ruins the illusion of reality, but it's the best that UPK can do). Once the trainee moves the mouse pointer into the indicated area, the next screenshot is displayed, showing the next Action Area.

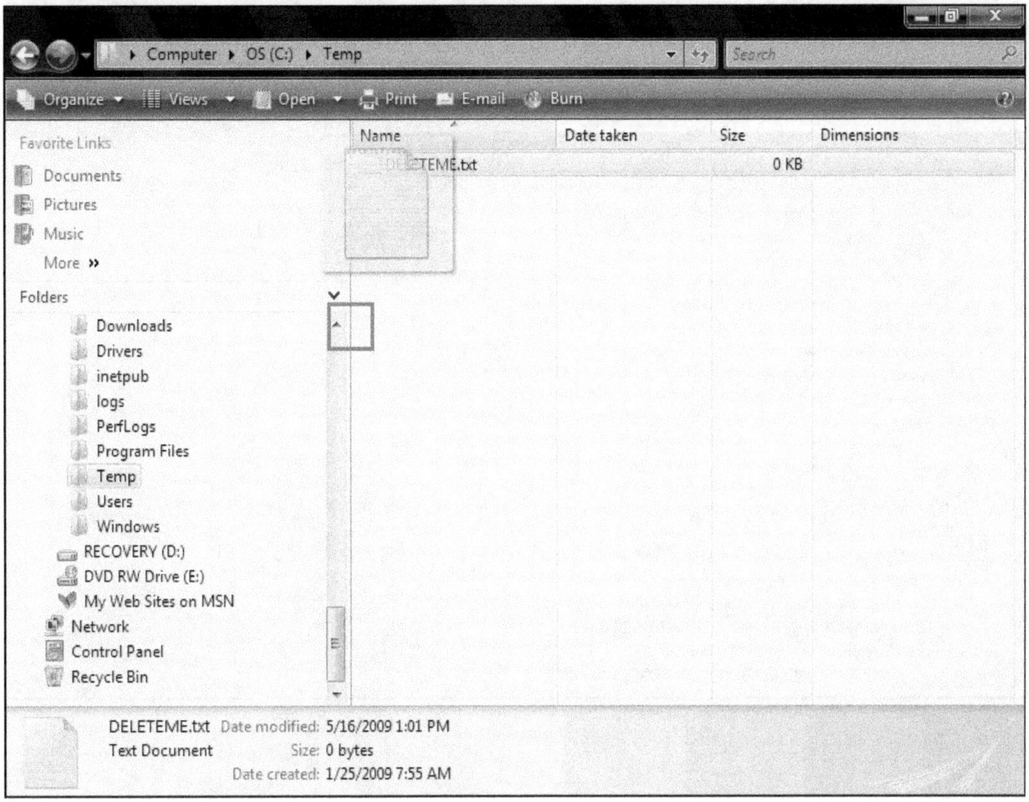

Again, the trainee moves the pointer into the indicated area on the screen (with the mouse button still depressed), and is presented with the next target area:

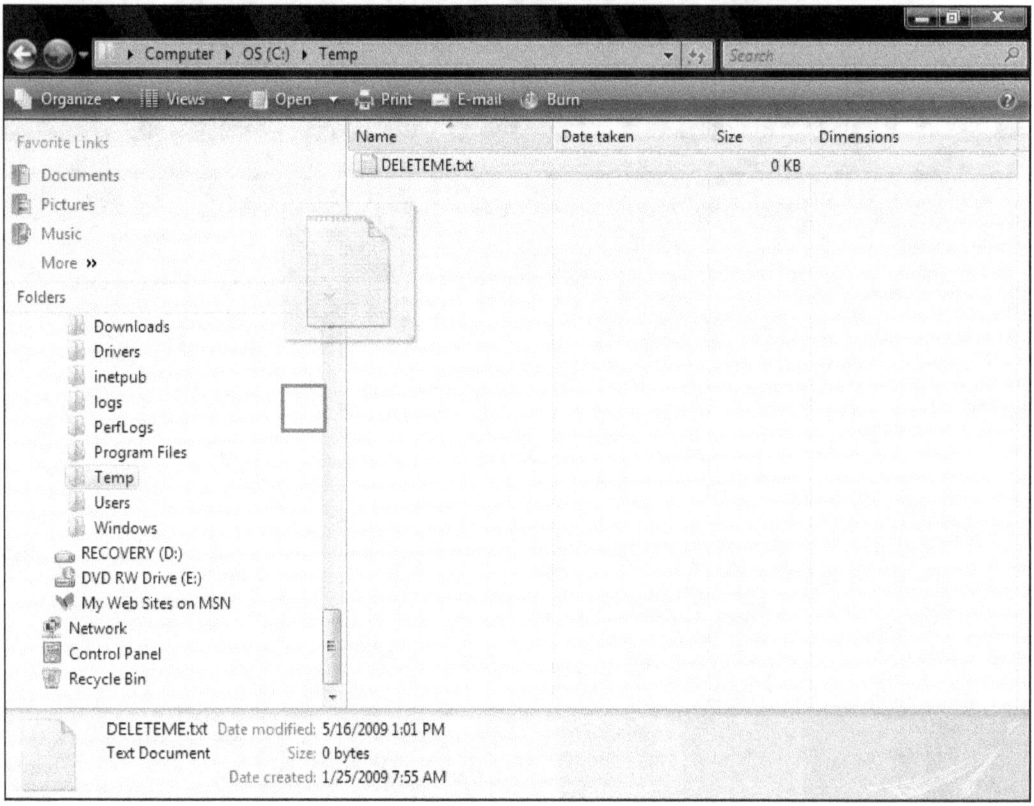

This continues into the next Frame, with the action area getting successively closer to the target area (although the trainee does not know where the final destination is).

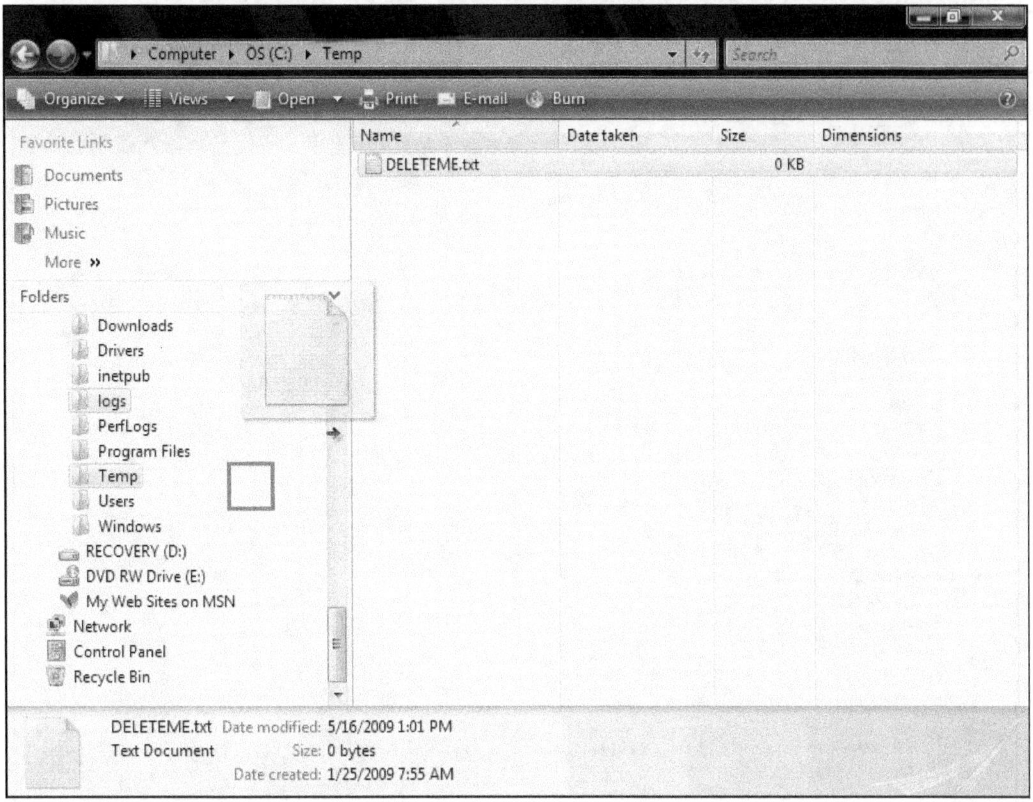

The trainee continues to drag the object into successive action areas. Note that the position of each successive area is an equal distance from the last one (in our example, the default 60 pixels). This at least keeps the playback relatively smooth.

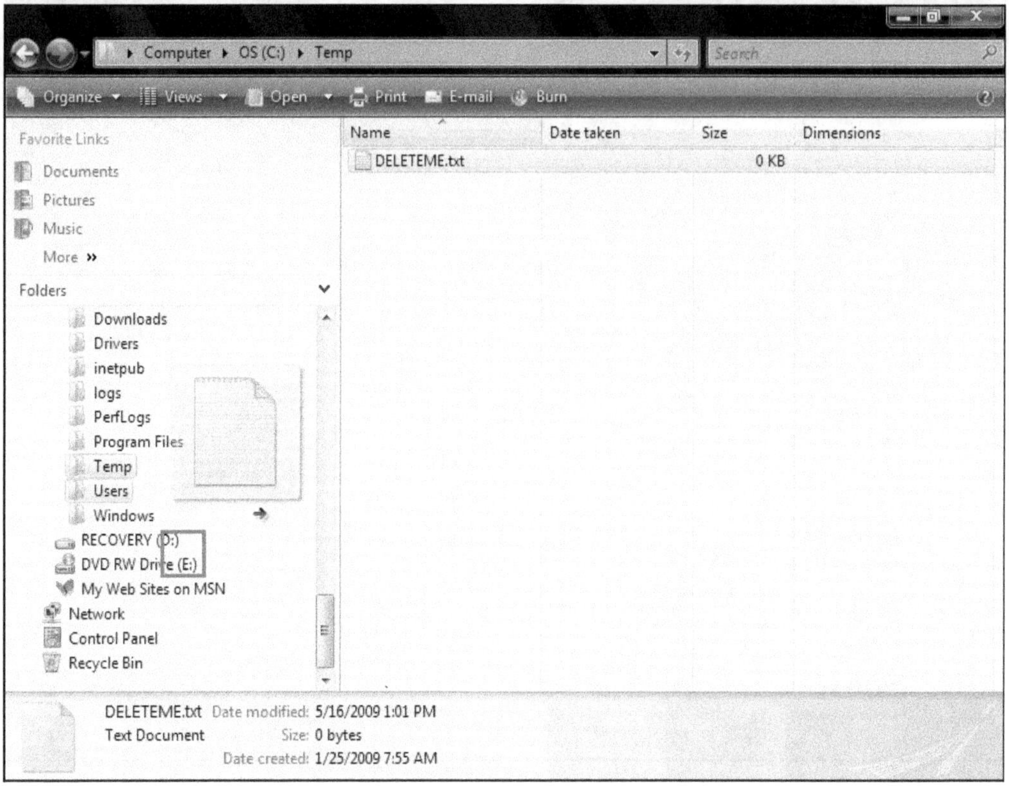

Assuming that the trainee continues to move the cursor into the designated target area, playback will continue onto the next Frame. Note that as long as the trainee keeps the mouse button held down, they can actually move the cursor all around the screen, but nothing will happen (they will not progress to the next Frame) until they move the cursor into the designated target area.

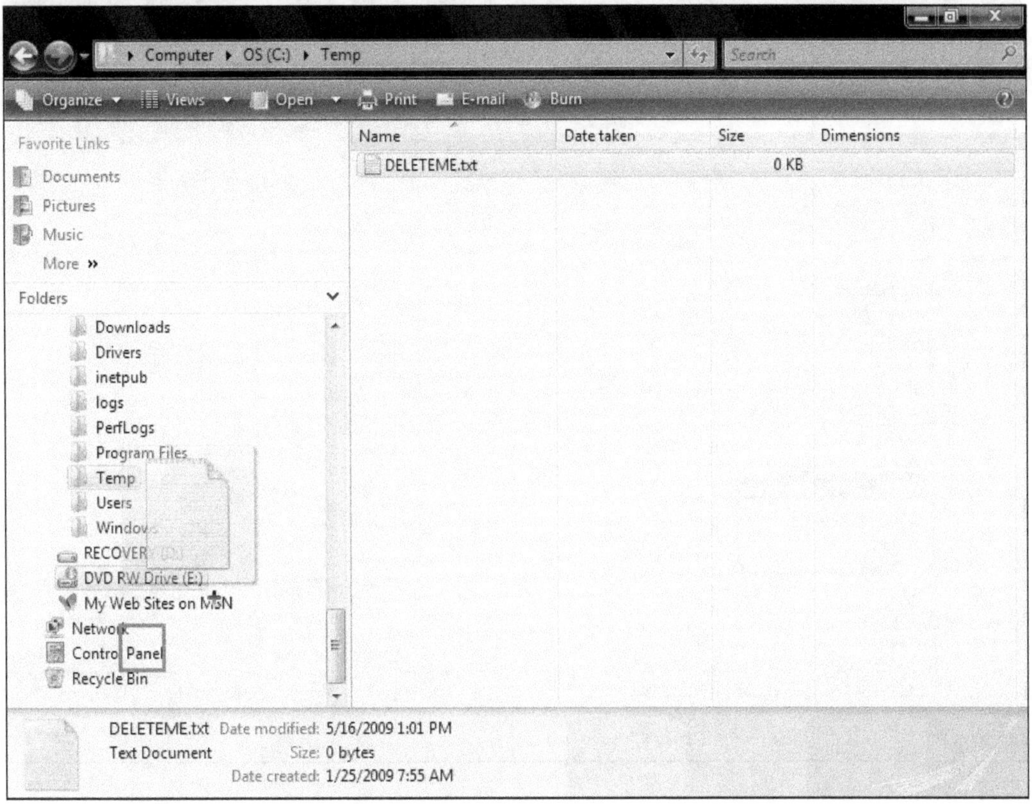

Finally, when the trainee moves the cursor over the position onto which the object was dropped during the recording, a bubble is displayed, telling the user to release the mouse button (the "drop"). Note that this is the first bubble that the trainee has seen since the initial click on the object.

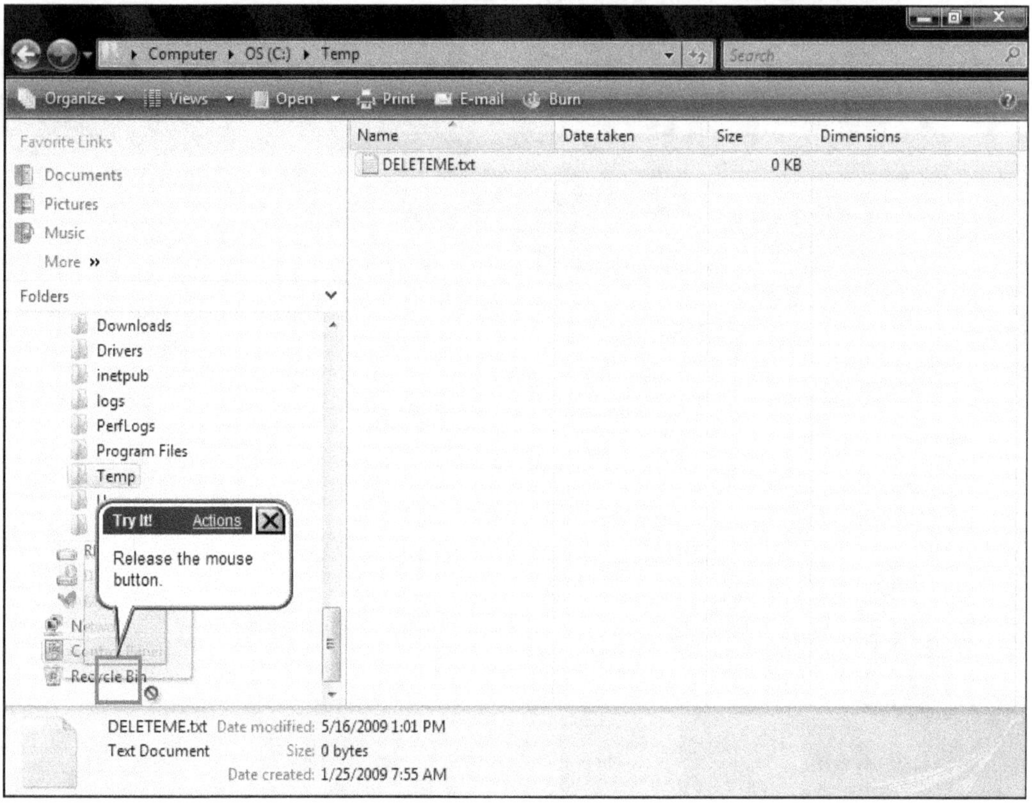

Note that we only pressed *Prt Scr* once, and all eight of these screenshots were captured for us. This is because UPK treats the drag-and-drop as a single action (if you complete the drag-and-drop action in the Player and then select **Action | Previous step** from the bubble menu, UPK will return you to the first frame in the sequence). However, this single action consists of at least three frames in the recorder, as follows:

1. A single Frame with an Action Type of **Left begin drag**. This is the first screen print in the sequence above.
2. One or more Frames with an Action Type of **Drag**. In the example above, six Frames were created. These are the six Frames that do not have Bubble Text in them.
3. A single Frame with an Action Type of **Left button up**.

[Action Types are discussed in Chapter 4 *Editing a Topic.*]

You must have these three frames, with these three specific actions (and not simply **Left button down** in Step 1) for the drag-and-drop to work correctly in the Player.

Play this exercise back (it is available on the Packt web site, in the same `.odarc` file as before, as EX99-03 Deleting a file (Chapter 3) or if you want to do it the low-tech way, cut the images out of this book, staple them together along one edge, and use them as a flip-book!). You will note that the playback is a bit jerky, as the screens flip from one to the next. You could reduce the effects of this by using a smaller capture interval in the **Distance between screenshots in pixels** option setting, but after a certain point this will become self-defeating as it will take the Player longer to load the screenshots than it takes to move from one to the next, resulting in more jerkiness.

Note also the size of the action area. The user has to move the cursor into this area in order to move onto the next frame in the sequence. You can cut the user a little slack by increasing the size of the action area (either in the **Action Area size in pixels** option before you start recording, or by manually adjusting the action area in the Topic Editor after you have captured the recording; how to do this is explained in Chapter 3, *Editing a Topic*) but be careful that your action areas do not become too close, or overlap, as this will cause problems with the playback.

One last comment on drag-and-drop activities. In *Know It?* mode, there is no square around the action area to provide the user with a visual clue as to where to drag. It is unrealistic to expect the user to correctly follow an invisible path that is (by default) only 30 pixels wide. Therefore, during playback in *Know It?* mode, the user is not required to perform the drag-and-drop activity. Instead, the Player performs this activity for them. They are not marked for this action. You should therefore be wary of providing simulations in *Know It?* mode where the majority of the simulation consists of drag-and-drop activities.

Summary

UPK *records* simulations by capturing sets of action/screen print pairs. Each pair consists of a screen print of a screen, and the action used to get to that screen. An *action* typically consists of a mouse-click, a key-press, or the entry of a text string, but it is also possible to capture drag-and-drop actions.

UPK can capture simulations automatically, or manually. If you choose the manual option, then you need to tell UPK when to capture each action/screenshot pair. With the automatic option, it will capture the action/screenshot pair every time that the screen changes.

It is possible to record simulations immediately, or create "placeholders" for them, so that they can be recorded later.

Having now recorded (the R in PREP) a basic simulation, we need to edit this (the E in PREP) to bring it up to our required standards. And that is the subject of the next chapter.

4
Editing a Topic

As exciting as the Library is, the core of your work (and certainly if you want to create *quality* exercises) will be in the **Topic Editor**. In this chapter, we will look at the information that is shown on the **Topic Editor** screen. We will then proceed to edit the Topic that we recorded in Chapter 3, *Recording a Simulation*, looking at all of the tools and options that are available in the **Topic Editor**, as we go. This is a long chapter; you may not want to read it all in one sitting (you are probably desperate to just get started with your work), but you will undoubtedly find it useful as an ongoing reference.

In this chapter, you will learn:

- What the Topic Editor is
- What the main components of the Topic Editor screen are, and how to interact with them
- How to change Bubble Text
- How to insert missing Frames
- How to delete Frames
- How to recapture screenshots

Throughout this chapter, we will build on the sample exercise that we recorded in the last chapter. If you want to follow along, we will start with *EX01-03 Changing your User Options (Chapter 3)*. If you just want to skip straight the finished result, refer to *EX01-04 Changing your User Options (Chapter 4)*. Both of these exercises are available in an `.odarc` archives, from the Packt web site.

Understanding the Topic Editor screen

The **Topic Editor** is where you edit your recorded Topics. You will automatically be passed into the **Topic Editor** either when you finish recording the Topic, or after each screen capture, depending on your options (see Chapter 3, *Recording a Simulation)*. You are also passed into the **Topic Editor** whenever you double-click on a Topic in the Library (or in an Outline). The following screenshot shows an example of a typical **Topic Editor** screen:

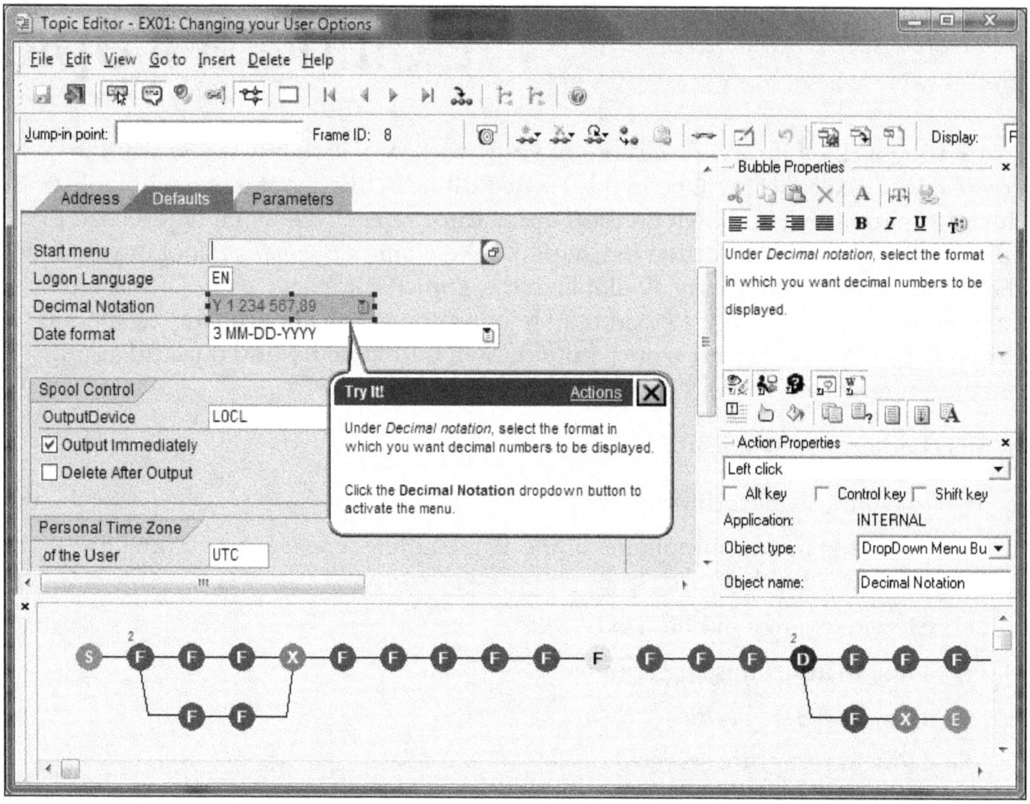

As you can see, the **Topic Editor** screen is split into several distinct areas. Let's look at each of these. Don't worry about the menus and toolbars—we'll get to them in good time.

The Screenshot pane

The largest portion of the screen (the upper-left pane) is taken up by the Screenshot pane.

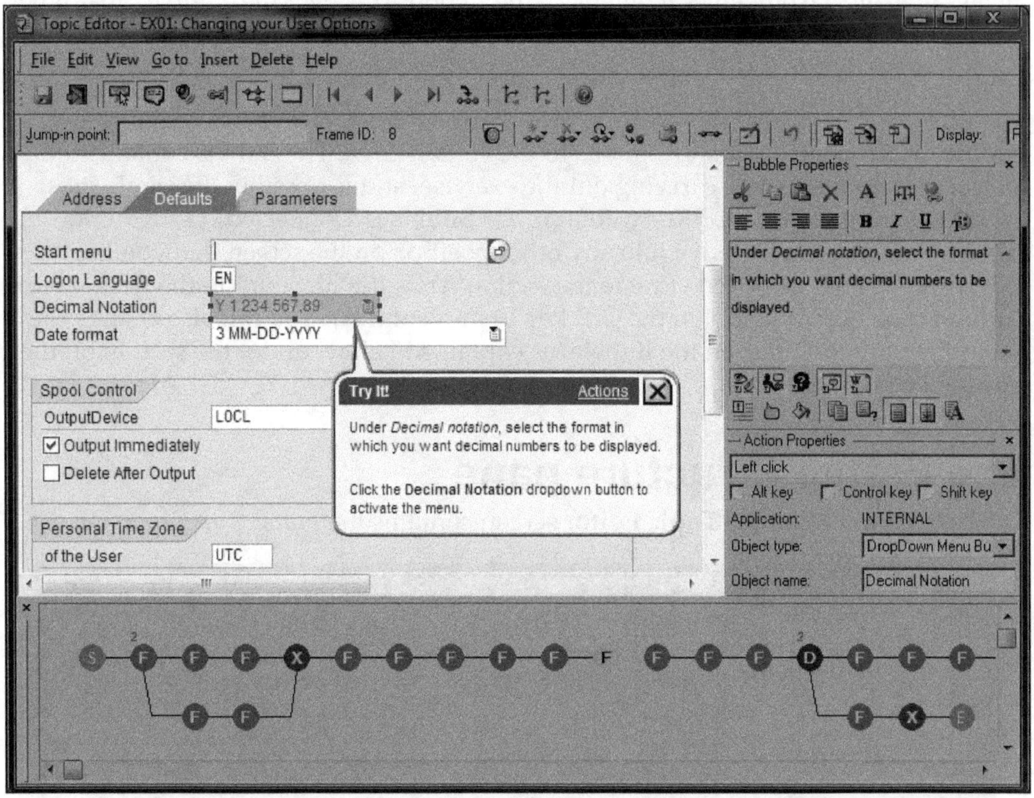

The Screenshot pane contains the screenshot that you captured during the recording. This is shown full-size, UPK does not provide an option to scale this so that you can (for example) fit the entire screenshot into this area. This means that you will need to scroll around using the vertical and horizontal scroll bars to see the different areas of the screenshot. (Or edit the Topic on a screen set to a higher resolution than the resolution at which the Topic was captured.) Never mind; you typically only want to see the area of the screenshot containing the **Action Area** (and therefore the Bubble) so you don't really need to scroll around that often.

> You can navigate around the screenshot by right-clicking on it and dragging it around the *Screenshot* pane.

The Action Area is represented by an opaque red box, as can clearly be seen in the center of the *Screenshot* pane in the previous example. The Action Area is the area of the screen that was clicked on, or into which text was entered, during recording. UPK generally does a pretty good job of correctly sizing this around the object, but it doesn't always manage it (sometimes it will place the Action Area over the entire toolbar when you click a button on the toolbar). In these cases, you can move or re-size the Action Area, as described in the section *Adjusting Action Areas* later in this chapter.

The *Screenshot* pane also shows the Bubble for the Frame. This is the "speech bubble" that (again, by default) points to the Action Area. The Bubble contains the instructions to the trainee carrying out the exercise, and is possibly the single most important component of UPK. By default, the Bubble is "connected" to the Action Area, although you can move it to any other position on the screen that you like. However, when it is moved close to the Action Area, it will "snap" to the Action Area (although you can hold down the Ctrl key to prevent this). You can also change the position of the "pointer" on the Bubble, as explained below, under the section on the **Bubble Properties** pane.

The Frame Structure pane

The bottom section of the **Topic Editor** screen contains the *Frame Structure* pane.

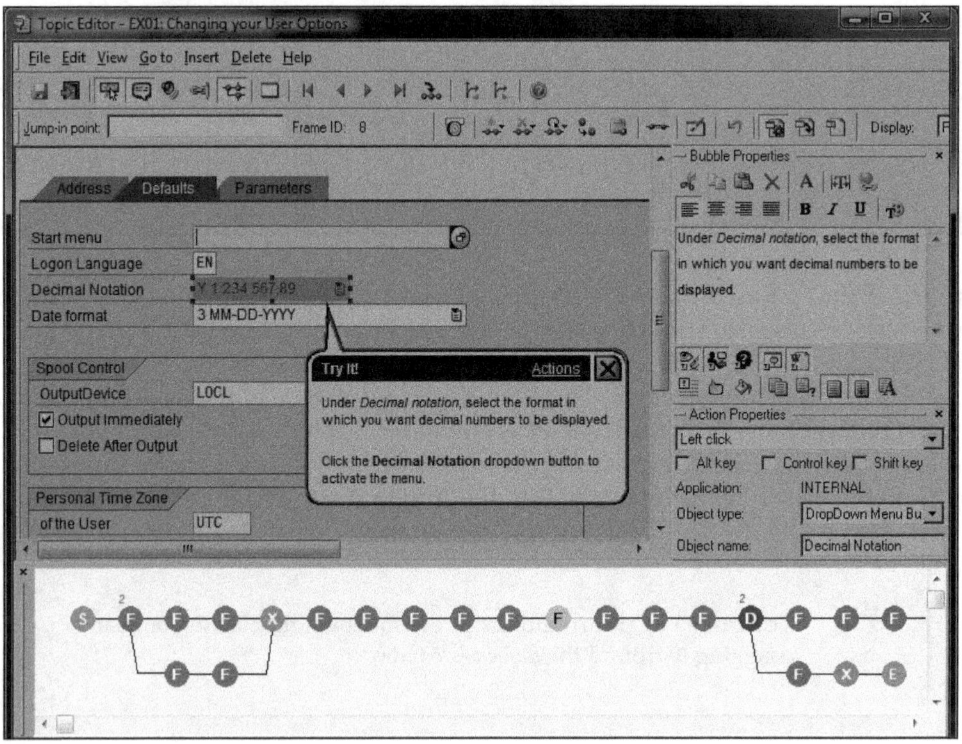

The Frame Structure pane is displayed by default whenever you open the **Topic Editor**, but you can hide (or re-display) it by clicking on the show/hide Frame Structure button ( ) on the Standard Toolbar. The *Frame Structure* provides a graphical representation of all of the Frames (almost exclusively screenshots) in the Topic, and the path(s) through them (that is, the order in which the Frames are replayed). As you can see from the example above, there may be more than one path through the Topic. Don't worry about this for now; it is all explained in Chapter 8, *Allowing Alternatives*.

> By default, the Frame Structure pane is docked at the bottom of the screen. If you prefer, you can dock it at the top of the screen, by dragging its leftmost sidebar and dropping the pane at the top of the screen.

UPK uses the following types of Frames:

Frame Icon	Description
	**Start Frame**: This is the first Frame in the Topic; each Topic can have only one Start Frame. The Start Frame is created automatically by UPK when you start recording, and uses the same screenshot as the one used in the Frame immediately following it (that is, the first Action Frame in the Topic). The Start Frame should contain the introductory text for the Topic—this is the same text that is displayed (by default) in the *Introduction* pane in the Outline. (Outlines are discussed in Chapter 5, *Building an Outline*). This Frame is sometimes referred to in UPK as the **Introduction Frame**. In this book we use the term Start Frame.
	**End Frame**: This is the last Frame in the Topic. Unlike the Start Frame, a Topic can have more than one End Frame—if the Topic includes a *Branch*. (Branches are discussed in Chapter 8, *Allowing Alternatives*.) Similar to the Start Frame, the End Frame is created automatically by UPK when you finish recording. In Know It? mode, the user's score is overlaid on top of the End Frame, so this Frame may be seen more than once.
	**Action Frame**: Most Frames in a Topic are Action Frames. Action Frames are the ones that contain the recorded actions for your Topic, and are created each time you press *Prt Scr* (or whichever other key combination you have selected) during recording.
	**Decision Frame**: A Decision Frame asks the user to make a choice from a number of options, and will direct playback down a specific path based on the choice made by the user. Decisions are discussed in more detail in Chapter 8 *Allowing Alternatives*. A Decision Frame can only be inserted from within the Topic Editor (it cannot be captured during recording), and takes its screenshot from the Frame immediately following it.

Frame Icon	Description
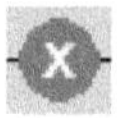	**Explanation Frame**: An Explanation Frame is a special kind of Frame on which the trainee is not required to perform any specific action (such as a mouse-click or key-press). Explanation Frames are typically used to provide additional information to the trainee, or to draw the trainee's attention to specific elements on the screen. An Explanation Frame can only be inserted from within the Topic Editor (it cannot be captured during recording), and takes its screenshot from the Frame immediately following it. Explanation Frames are discussed in more detail in Chapter 9, Adding Value to Your Topics.

When you hover the mouse pointer over a Frame in the *Frame Structure* pane, a thumbnail image of the screenshot is shown next to the pointer. This thumbnail also shows the unique identifier of this Frame within the Topic, in a yellow box. An example of this is shown in the following screenshot:

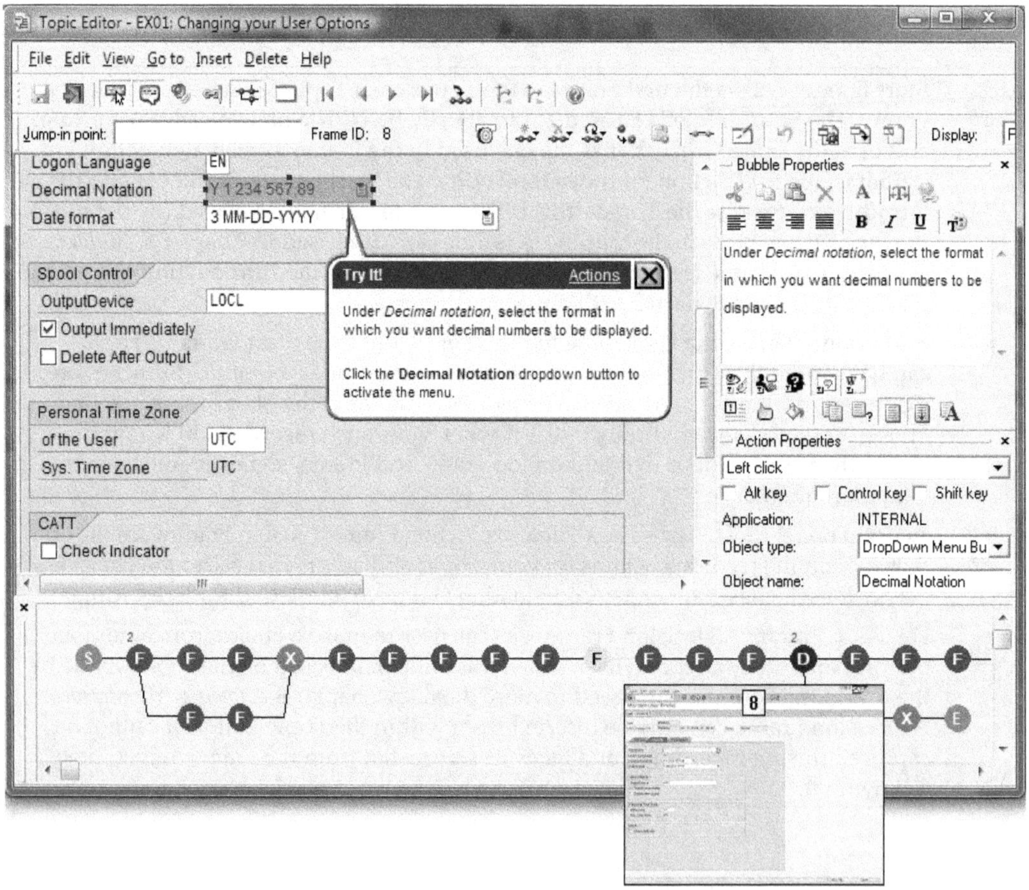

In this example, the mouse pointer is hovering over the currently active Frame (which is highlighted). Although in practice you wouldn't normally want to see the thumbnail of the currently active Frame as you can see it in the Screenshot pane. The identifier of this Frame is **A**, which is shown in the top center of the thumbnail. You can also see that the Frame identifier of the currently active Frame is shown to the left of the text **Frame ID:** in the *Editing Toolbar*. Note that the Start Frame and End Frame do not have identifiers.

> Frames are numbered, starting at **1** for the first Action Frame, in hexadecimal—which is why the 10th Frame in the example above is **A** and not **10**. UPK will number Frames in the order in which they are recorded, which is not necessarily the order in which they appear in the *Frame Structure* pane.

Knowing the identifier of a Frame can be useful for jumping directly to a specific Frame, as we will see when we look at the *Standard Toolbar*, below.

The currently-active Frame (that is, the Frame whose screenshot is currently displayed in the Screenshot pane) is highlighted in green, as shown in the previous example. You can click on the icon for any Frame in the Frame Structure pane to make that Frame the current Frame. You can also navigate between Frames by using the following buttons on the *Standard Toolbar*:

Button	Name	Purpose
	**First Frame**	Click on this button to go to the first Frame in the Topic. This is the Start Frame.
	**Previous Frame**	Click on this button to go to the previous Frame (that is, the Frame immediately preceding the currently active Frame). If the current Frame is at the convergence point of multiple paths, then focus will move to the previous Frame on the default path. (Alternative Paths are described in Chapter 8, *Allowing Alternatives*.)
	**Next Frame**	Click on this button to go to the next Frame (that is, the Frame immediately following the currently active Frame). If the current Frame has multiple paths coming from it, then focus will move to the next Frame on the default path. (Alternative Paths are described in Chapter 8, *Allowing Alternatives*.)
	**Last Frame**	Click on this button to go to the last Frame in the Topic. This is the End Frame on the default (or only) path.
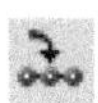	**Go To Frame**	If you want to go to a specific Frame, then you can click on this button, and then enter the identifier of the Frame in the **Go To Specific Frame** dialog box that is displayed. This assumes that you know the identifier of the Frame; you can locate this as explained above, under the explanation of Frame thumbnails.

> You can hold down the *Alt* key and press the left arrow or right arrow key to move backwards or forward through the Frames. This is very useful when you are editing a newly-created Topic for the first time, and are adding to or adjusting the Bubble Text (as explained later in this chapter); you can keep the focus in the **Bubble Properties** text field, and use the left arrow and right arrow keys to move through the presentation, without having to move your hands from the keyboard to the mouse.

The Property Editor panes

On the rightmost side of the **Topic Editor** screen, a number of **Properties** panes may be displayed. The screenshot at the start of this section shows the default screen layout, with the **Bubble Properties** pane and the **Action Properties** pane displayed on the rightmost side of the screen. You can choose to hide or display each of these individually, but you can also hide all of them (regardless of their individual setting) by clicking on the *Show/Hide Property Editors* button (). Clicking on this button again will re-display the property editors that are currently selected for display. The three *Properties* panes, and the buttons to show or hide them, are shown in the table below:

Button	Name	Purpose
	**Show/Hide Action Properties**	Show or hide the **Action Properties** pane. This pane is displayed by default. The **Action Properties** pane is explained in the section *Adjusting Action Areas*, below.
	**Show/Hide Bubble Properties**	Show or hide the **Bubble Properties** pane. This property editor is displayed by default. The **Bubble Properties** pane is explained in the section *Changing the Bubble Text*, below.
	**Show/Hide Sound Properties**	Show or hide the **Sound Properties** pane. The **Sound Properties** pane is explained in Chapter 11, *Incorporating Sound into Your Topics*.

You can undock any of the properties panes, and position them anywhere on the screen, by clicking on the pane title bar and dragging the pane to a new location. If you drag a property pane to the left or right sides of the **Topic Editor** window, then it will snap back to a docked position.

We will examine each of these panes—both their content and their purpose—in the following section (*Adjusting actions*), as we use them to edit the example exercise that we recorded in Chapter 3, *Recording a Simulation*.

Adjusting actions

In this section, we will look at how to work with Actions and Action Areas.

The Action Properties pane

The **Action Properties** pane contains all of the information related to the Action that was captured during the recording. As explained earlier, there are effectively three types of Actions that UPK can capture: mouse-actions, key-presses, and string input.

The table below lists the types of Action that UPK can capture, in alphabetic order. In this table, the *Action* column shows the value of the **Action Type** field, which is the first field in the **Action Properties** pane (regardless of the type of Action). The *Description* column describes what is captured for this Action Type. Finally, the *Category* column identifies the broad category of action that this Action Type falls into. Unsurprisingly, the **Action Properties** pane is slightly different for each of these categories—although there are several common elements, as we shall see. The description of the **Action Properties** property editor is provided separately for each of these categories, later in this chapter.

Action	Description	Category
Drag	Dragging an object across the screen. A drag-and-drop action will typically consist of a **Left begin drag** action, followed by one or more **Drag** actions, ending in a **Left button up** action. Refer to the section *Recording drag-and-drop activities* in Chapter 3, *Recording a Simulation* for more information.	Mouse
Keyboard	Pressing a single key or key combination on the keyboard.	Keyboard
Left begin drag	Clicking down with the left mouse button on an object on the screen, and beginning to drag it, while continuing to hold down the left mouse button.	Mouse
Left button down	Pressing down on the left mouse button, without releasing it. Normally, this would be followed by a **Left button up** action, where the trainee is required to click and hold an object for a period.	Mouse
Left button up	Releasing the left mouse button after it has previously been held down (see also **Left button down**).	Mouse
Left click	A single click on an object with the left mouse button.	Mouse
Left double-click	Double-clicking on a screen object with the left mouse button.	Mouse
Left triple-click	Triple-clicking on an object with the left mouse button.	Mouse

Action	Description	Category
Middle begin drag	Clicking down with the middle mouse button on an object on the screen, and beginning to drag it, whilst continuing to hold down the middle mouse button.	Mouse
Middle button down	Clicking down on the middle mouse button.	Mouse
Middle button up	Releasing the right mouse button, after it has previously been held down.	Mouse
Middle click	A single click on an object, with the middle mouse button.	Mouse
Middle double-click	Double-clicking on a screen object, with the middle mouse button.	Mouse
Middle triple-click	Triple-clicking on an object, with the middle mouse button.	Mouse
Point	Pointing to an object on the screen (effectively, hovering the cursor over it).	Mouse
Right begin drag	Clicking down with the right mouse button on an object on the screen, and beginning to drag it, whilst continuing to hold down the right mouse button.	Mouse
Right button down	Clicking down on the right mouse button.	Mouse
Right button up	Releasing the right mouse button, after it has previously been held down.	Mouse
Right click	A single click on an object with the right mouse button.	Mouse
Right double-click	Double-clicking on a screen object with the right mouse button.	Mouse
Right triple-click	Triple-clicking on an object with the right mouse button.	Mouse
String input	Entering a text string.	String input
Wheel	Scrolling the mouse wheel. Note that UPK does not distinguish between scrolling the mouse wheel up and scrolling it down.	Mouse

Let's look at the three varieties of the **Action Properties** pane, by way of a few examples.

Working with mouse Actions

When you record a mouse Action in a simulation, UPK identifies the screen element on which you clicked—most of the time. Sometimes it does not manage to identify the exact object, and even if it does identify the correct object, it sometimes (generally when an unsupported level of SAPGui is used, or when a terminal application is being recorded) allows an unfeasibly large area around where you actually clicked. Sometimes it identifies entirely the wrong object, or even thinks that you performed a different type of action. Let's look at an example of this.

Open up the sample Topic that we recorded in Chapter 3, *Recording a Simulation*, and navigate to Frame 1 (this is the first **Action Frame**). For your reference, this Frame, as it appears in the **Topic Editor**, is shown in the following screenshot:

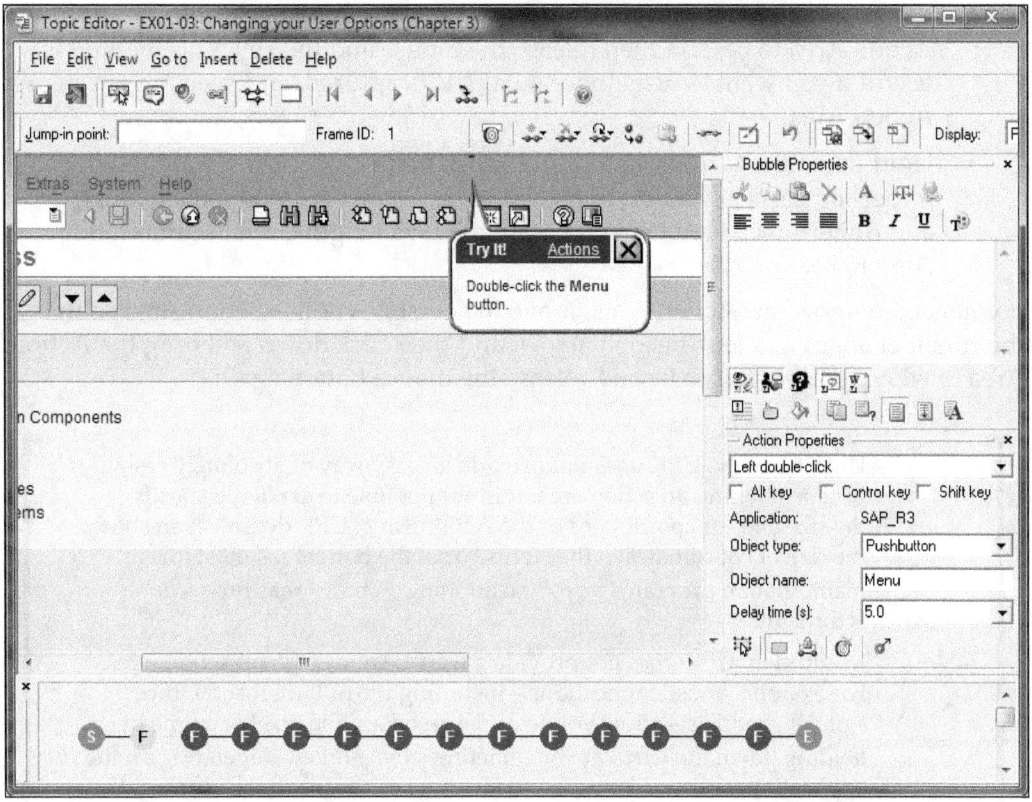

In this example, the action that we actually performed was a single-click on the **System** menu. Instead, the recording has captured a double-click somewhere on the menu bar, but identified it as a button and not a menu option. (To be fair, although UPK does occasionally make these mistakes, it typically doesn't make all of them at the same time—the example above has been "doctored" for the sake of illustration.)

Let's look at how to correct these mistakes.

Adjusting Action Areas

The first thing that we need to do is adjust the Action Area. There are three ways of adjusting the Action Area. These are:

- Drag the "handles" on the boundary of the Action Area to re-size it. This method is useful for making slight adjustments to the Action Area—for example, to set the edges of the Action Area closer to the object on which the user needs to click.
- Hold down the *Ctrl* key and click on where you want the upper-left corner of the Action Area to be. Then, with the mouse button and the *Ctrl* key held down, drag the marquee to where you want the bottom-right corner of the Action Area to be, and then release the mouse and the key. This method is useful if you want to just ignore what UPK captured, and specify your own Action Area.
- Hold down the *Ctrl* key and double-click on the where you want the upper-left corner of the Action Area to be. Then, hold down the *Shift* key, and double-click on where you want the lower-right corner of the Action Area to be.

If you need to move the Action Area, move the cursor over the Action Area so that the cursor changes to a four-headed arrow, and then click down and drag the Action Area to where you want it to be and release the mouse button again.

> Unfortunately, UPK does not provide an easy way of absolutely resizing or repositioning an action area. It is not possible to explicitly specify the size and/or coordinates of the Action Area. UPK doesn't even show the size or coordinates in the status bar at the bottom (as most image manipulation programs do) so positioning Action Areas *precisely* is difficult.
>
> In addition, UPK does not provide a way of "nudging" an Action Area. For example, most applications—including the full Microsoft Office suite of products—allow you to move an object one pixel at a time by holding down the *Ctrl* key (or sometimes the *Alt* key, depending on the application) and using the cursor (arrow) keys to move the object in the required direction. UPK does not.
>
> These limitations mean that the only way to change the size or position of an Action Area is by using the mouse, and a mouse is not a great tool for pixel-perfect positioning (and a trackball or track pad is even worse!).

There are a few other buttons in the **Action Properties** pane that are relevant to Action Areas. These are described in the table below:

Button	Name	Purpose
	**Action Area on/off**	Selecting this button will prevent the border around the Action Area from being displayed in the output format. This may be a useful option if you don't want to give the trainee too much in the way of visual clues. It is also useful if you want to give the appearance of automatically responding to a user's Action, and have several Alternative Paths (and therefore several Action Areas) defined for the same Frame. We look at this latter possibility in Chapter 8, *Allowing Alternatives*.
	**Modify Action Areas**	If you click on this button, then a drop-down menu is displayed, with a further three buttons. These buttons are shown in the next three rows of this table.
	**Create new Action Area**	Select this option if you want to create another Action Area on the same screen. If you do this, then the user will be allowed to click on either of the Action Areas in order to progress to the next screen. Note that is not something that you would normally want to do, as the Bubble can only point to a single Action Area, regardless of how many Action Areas you define. However, you may find it useful if (for example) you have a hyperlink over two (uneven-length) lines.
	**Delete Action Area**	Select this option if you want to delete an Action Area. Note that you must have at least one Action Area (for mouse or string input actions), so you would only want to do this if you had previously created an additional Action Area and then decided that you didn't want it after all. You need to make sure that you select the Action Area that you want to delete before you click on this option.
	**Copy Action Area**	Select this option if you want to delete the current Action Area on a Frame (or all Action Areas, if you have defined more than one) and replace them with a copy of the Action Area from the previous Frame. This would conceivably be useful if the user has to click in exactly the same spot on successive steps, but realistically, this is not likely to happen a lot. One practical use is where you want the Action Areas on successive Frames to be exactly the same size (because UPK does not provide a feature to specify an explicit size, and adjusting the Action Area by mouse is sometimes hit-and-miss, especially for small Action Areas).

Adjusting Bubble Text

The next thing that needs to be fixed in our sample exercise is the Bubble Text. In the preceding example, the captured text is **Double-click the menu button**, which is clearly incorrect. So where does this text come from? The text comes from the Template attached to the Topic (see the section *Setting your content defaults* in Chapter 3 *Recording a Simulation*. The text generated by the template is determined by what UPK determines to be the *context* of the action. During recording, UPK captures three things specific to the action:

- The **Application** in which the action was performed
- The type of object against which the action was performed (**Object type**)
- The name of the specific object that the action was performed against (**Object name**)

These three things are shown in the **Action Properties** pane. The diagram below shows an example of the **Action Properties** pane, along with the associated Bubble text from the Player, and identifies the relationship between the two.

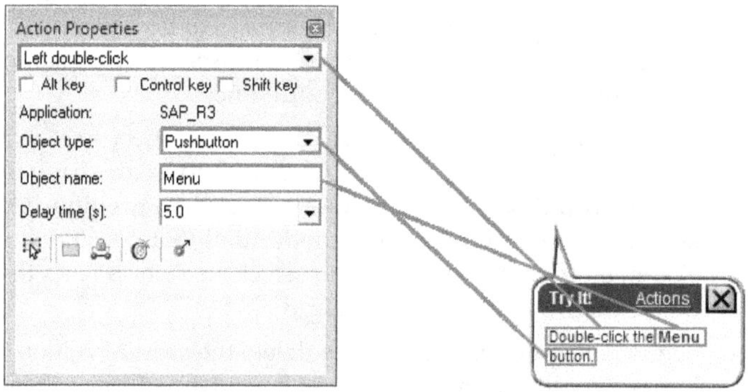

So if we want to change the Bubble Text, we can simply adjust the values of the context-related information in the **Action Properties** pane. Of these three, the **Application** cannot be changed, and the **Object name** is simply a text field that can be over-typed with any value that you like—regardless of whether this is actually a valid object name or not.

The **Object type** is a little more restrictive. UPK only recognizes a certain set of object types, and it is only possible to select one of these predefined object types in the **Object type** field. Appendix B, *Object Types* lists all of the possible Object Types, and specifies the Bubble Text generated by the Template for each of these types.

> Actually, with a little work, you can define your own object types, which we will do in Chapter 12, Configuring UPK.

Many of the Template Texts are unimaginative. Some don't even make sense (such as "**Click the <ObjectName> sound**"). There is also little point in having separate Object Types that give exactly the same result (as all of the `Pager` ones do, and all of the `Scrollbar Button` ones do). However, bear in mind that UPK is doing its best to capture the context of what you do (that is, the actions that you perform during the recording), and uses the captured Action, Object Type, and Object Name to provide the most meaningful Template Text that it can. No, it's not always right, but it is acceptable more often than not. Additionally, providing multiple Object Types (even if it does not manage to correctly identify all of these all of the time) does allow for a certain amount of flexibility. Firstly, you can change the Bubble Text simply by selecting a different Object Type in the Action Properties pane. Secondly, you can change the Bubble Text for a specific Object Type by customizing the templates themselves. (Customizing templates is covered in Chapter 12, *Configuring UPK*.)

Now that we understand the context a little better, let's look at how we can use this new-found knowledge to fix our example. You will recall that the Bubble Text generated from the Template was "**Double-click the Menu button.**". Our fixes involve doing the following:

1. The "**Double-click**" text can be replaced by "**Click**" simply by changing the Action (in the first field of the **Action Properties** pane) to **Left Click**.
2. The "**Menu**" text can be replaced simply by over-typing the **Object name** field with the correct menu name, which in our example is "**System**".
3. The "**button**" designation can be changed by selecting a new object type in the Object type field. Based on the table in Appendix B, *Object Types*, we will choose an Object Type of "**Menu entry**".

After making these changes, our **Action Properties** pane and the resultant Bubble Text are as shown in the following diagram:

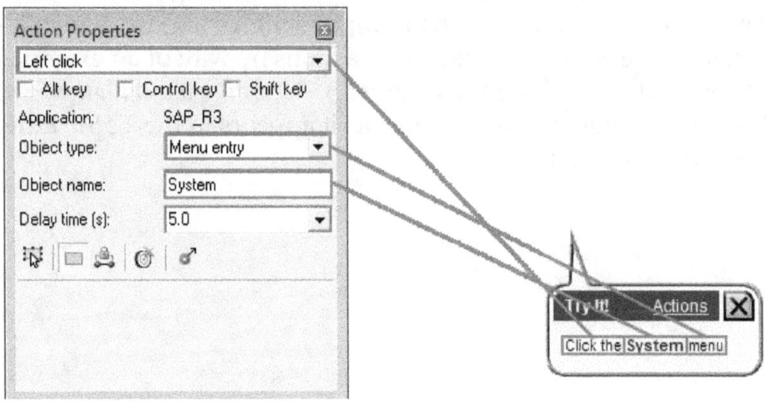

So there we have it. The Bubble Text now says just what we wanted it to and we didn't even touch the **Bubble Properties** pane (which we'll look at, next).

In some circumstances, you may not to want to use UPK's context capture at all. To do this, click on the Ignore context button ( ). This has two effects:

1. Template Text will not be used, because UPK has no context information on which to base it. However, there are other ways of removing the template text from a Bubble, as we will see in the section *Working with string input actions*, below.
2. If you are using context-sensitive help links from your application, then the current Frame (for which you disabled the context) will not be considered as a target for help. For example, normally, if the Frame is describing an action on the Change Purchase Order screen, then if the user selects your help option from this screen, then they will be taken directly to the first Frame of the recording that includes a screenshot of the Change Purchase Order screen. If you choose to ignore the context for a Frame then this will not happen. More information on application help links can be found in Chapter 6, *Publishing Content*.

For the sake of completeness, there is one final button in the **Action Properties** pane that we have not yet looked at. This is the **Change end point button** ( ). This is not strictly related to Action Areas, so we will not cover it here. Instead, we will describe it in Chapter 8, *Allowing Alternatives*.

Working with keyboard Actions

The second category of action that we will look at is the **keyboard** category. This category includes all actions that consist of a single key-press or key combination. It excludes the use of the keyboard to enter one or more characters into an input field on the screen; that is covered by the **string input** action category, which is explained later in this chapter. Let's examine keyboard actions by way of an example. Open up the sample Topic that we recorded in Chapter 3, *Recording a Simulation*, and navigate to Frame **D**. For your reference, this Frame, as it appears in the **Topic Editor**, is shown in the next screenshot:

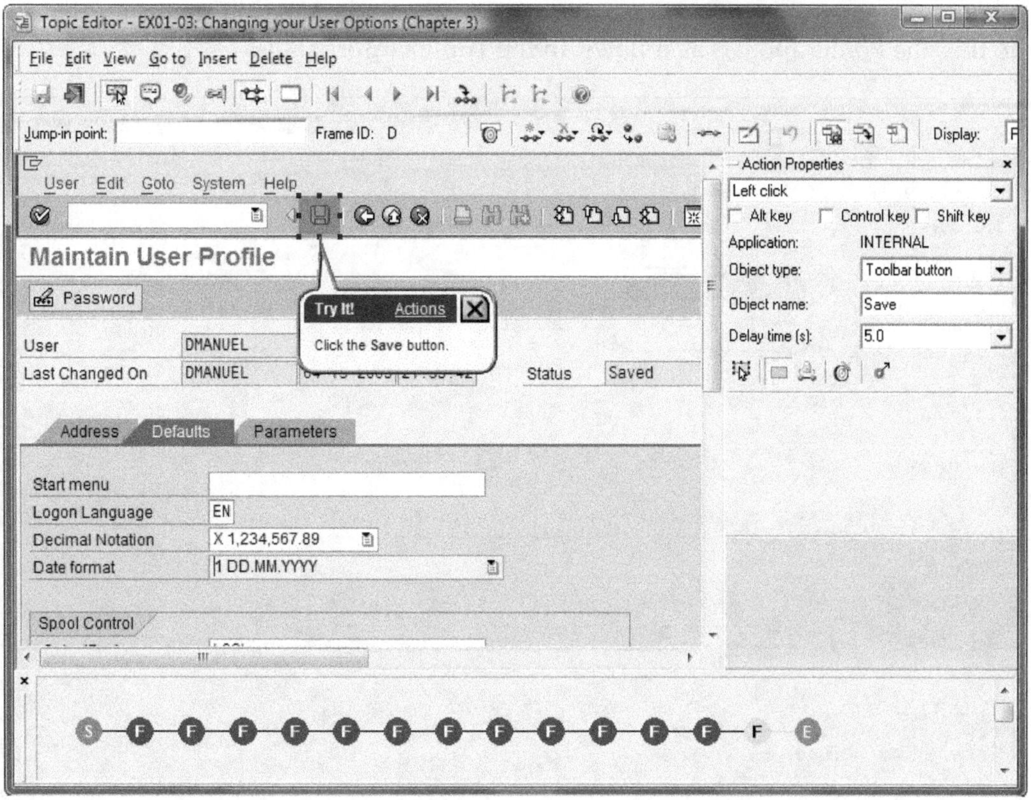

In this Frame, we are asking the trainee to save their changes by clicking on the **Save** button on the toolbar. This is a mouse-click action. However, for the sake of variety, we want the trainee to use the keyboard shortcut *Ctrl+S* instead. We could do this by recapturing the action (via the **Recapture action** button (), or menu option **Edit | Recapture action**), but handily, UPK lets you change the type of action for a Frame directly from within the **Topic Editor**. You can change a mouse-click action into a key-press action (as we will do here); you can change a single-left-click into a double-right-click; you can even change a mouse-click action into a string input action. All you need to do is select the required action in the **Action Type** field of the **Action Properties** pane.

> Changing the action type in the **Topic Editor** also has the advantage that you do not need to go back into the application and *record* anything new. This can be useful if recreating the scenario that you originally captured is problematic.

In our example, we will change the **Left click** action to a **Keyboard** action. Once we do this, the Frame appears as follows, in the **Topic Editor**:

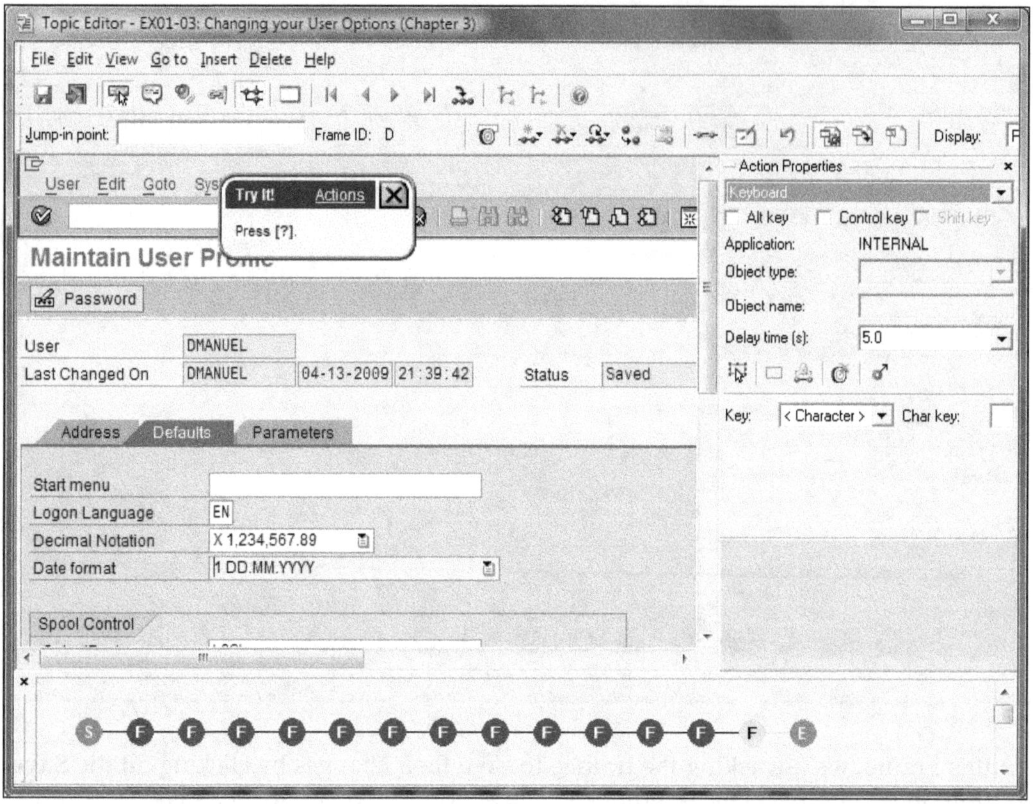

The first thing to notice here is that the Action Area (which was on top of the **Save** button) has disappeared. This makes sense, as keyboard Actions do not have Action Areas (they are the only category of Action that do not). The next thing to notice is that the template text has changed (from **Click the Save button**) to **Press [?]**. The **[?]** does not mean that the user should press the "question mark" key; it means that UPK does not know what key the user should press, because we haven't told UPK this, yet. In fact, UPK will not let you exit or navigate away from this Frame without specifying a key. You specify the key (or key combination) in the **Action Properties** pane, which is shown docked on the right in the previous screenshot.

Now that we have an **Action Type** of **Keyboard** selected in the **Action Properties** pane, the **Object Type** and **Object Name** fields are grayed out. This is because they (like the Action Area itself) are not relevant for keyboard actions. To compensate for this, two additional fields are now available in the **Action Properties** pane. These are the **Key** field, and the **Char key** field, and they are mutually exclusive (that is, you can specify one or the other, but not both). If they keyboard action is to press a single *character* key (*a-z, 0-9, !@#$%^&*()_+*, and so on), then you would simply enter this in the **Char key** field. If the keyboard action is to press a *special* key (*Enter, Escape, Delete, F1-F12*, and so on), then you would select this key from the **Key** field's drop-down list.

There are three additional options that are available in the **Action Properties** field, that relate to **Keyboard** actions. These are the **Alt key**, **Control key**, and **Shift** key checkboxes. These are used for specifying key combinations. So if the action that you want the trainee to perform is to press *Ctrl+Alt+Delete*, then you would select **Delete** in the Key field, and select both the **Alt key** and **Ctrl key** checkboxes. Note that although these three options are most commonly used with keyboard Actions, they can also be used with mouse-click Actions so you can (for example) record a "shift-click" Action.

For our exercise, we want the action to be pressing *Ctrl+S*. We therefore need to enter **S** in the **Char key** field, and select the **Control key** checkbox. Our Frame then looks like the example shown in the following screenshot:

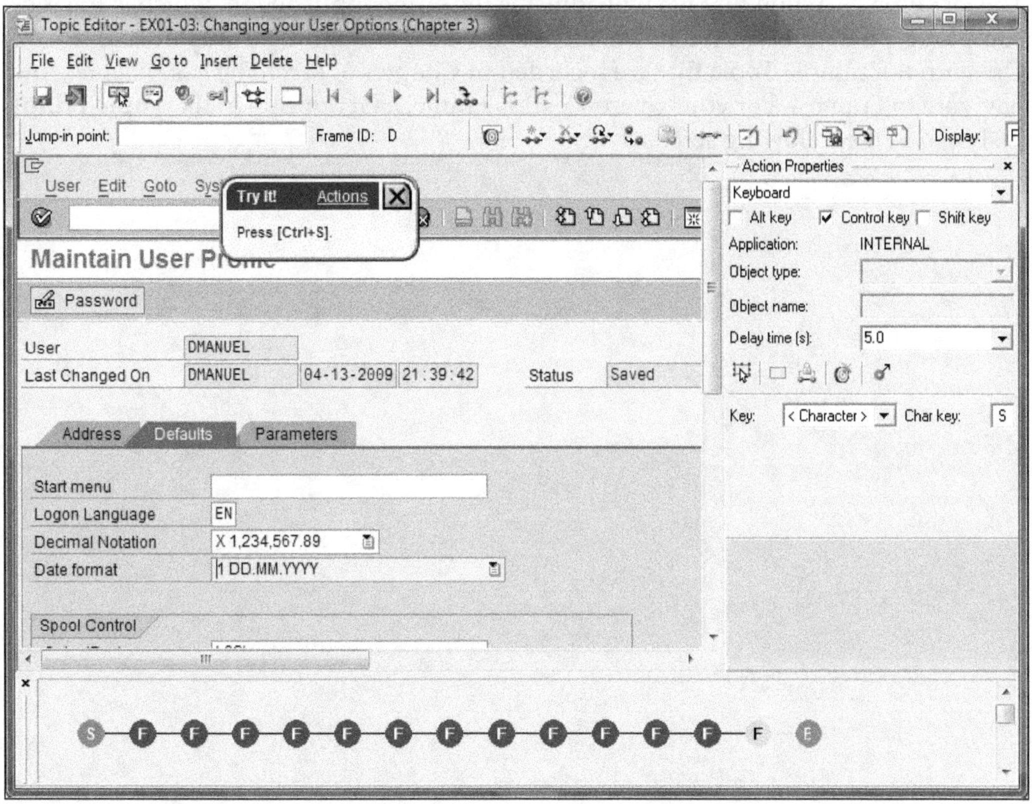

As you can see, our Bubble Text now correctly specifies "**Press [Ctrl+S]**". We have now completely changed the Action Type for the Frame. If we wanted to, we could change it back, but UPK will have forgotten our **Object type** and **Object name**, so we would have to enter these again. It would, however, have remembered the size and position of our Action Area, so at least we wouldn't have to recreate that.

> What we have done here is fairly unrealistic and done purely for the purposes of demonstration. In this particular case, what we are more likely to do is leave the mouse-click action as it is, and add the key-press an **Alternative Action**. Alternative Actions are covered in Chapter 8, *Allowing Alternatives*.

That's really all there is to know about keyboard Actions. There are no further settings, and nothing else that we can do with them. So let's proceed on to the most interesting (and most complex) category of Action—string input.

Working with string input Actions

The last type of Action that we will adjust is the string input action, which is the most complex type of Action. Again, we will examine these Actions by way of an example. Open up the sample Topic that we recorded in Chapter 3, *Recording a Simulation*, and navigate to Frame 4. For your reference, this Frame, as it appears in the **Topic Editor**, is shown in the following screenshot:

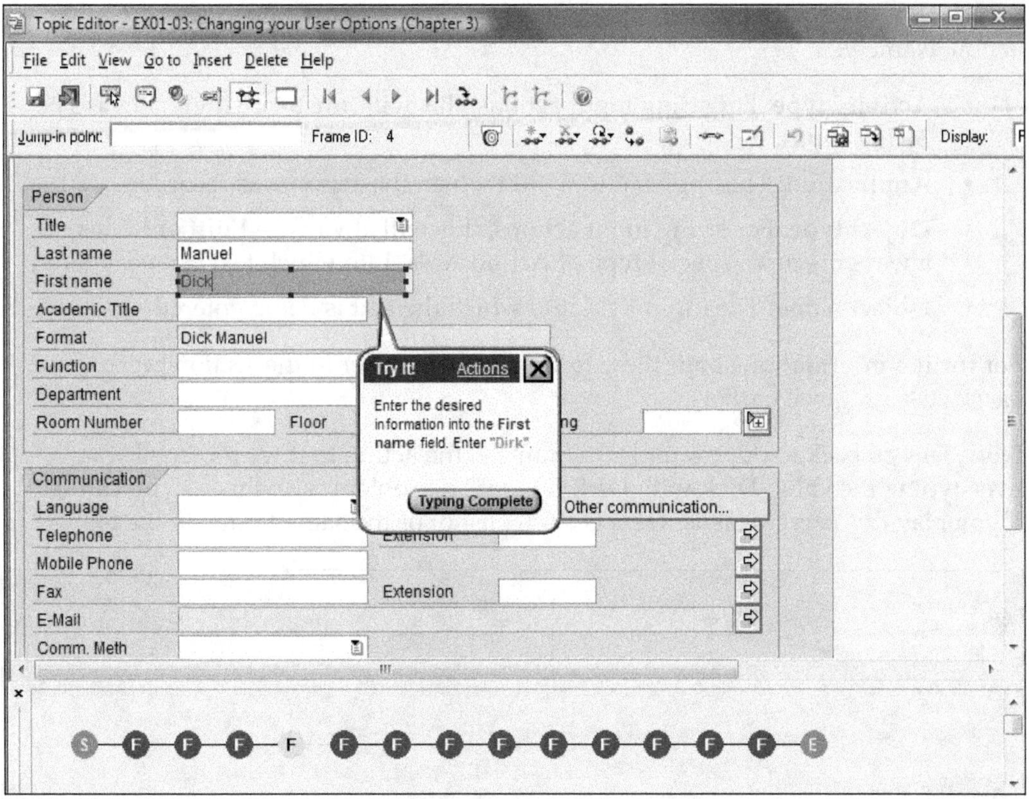

The **Action Properties** pane for this Frame is shown below:

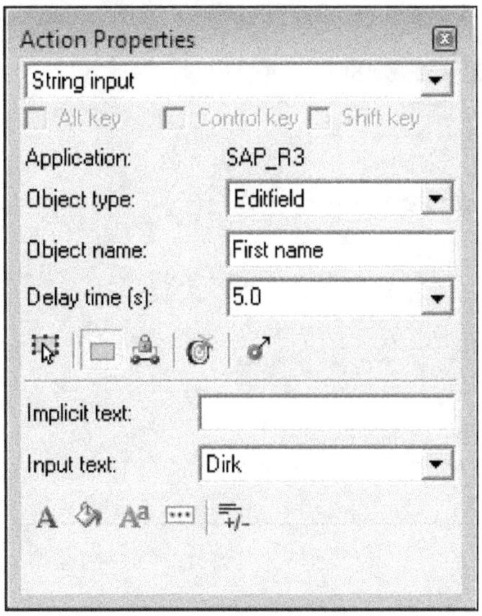

Some of the information in this pane is the same as for other categories of action. Namely:

- **Activity type**: For string input actions, this will (unsurprisingly) always be **String input**.
- **Application**: The application within which the action was recorded.
- **Object type**: For string input actions, this will always be **Editfield**. This always creates a special type of Action Area, into which text can be entered.
- **Object name**: The input field into which the text is being entered.

For further information about these four properties, refer to the section *Working with mouse Actions*, given earlier.

Now, let's go back to our example. In Frame 4, the action that we recorded was over-typing the value **Dick** with **Dirk**. There is a problem with this, as you can see if you play this exercise as-is. Here is a screenshot of the same Frame in the Player:

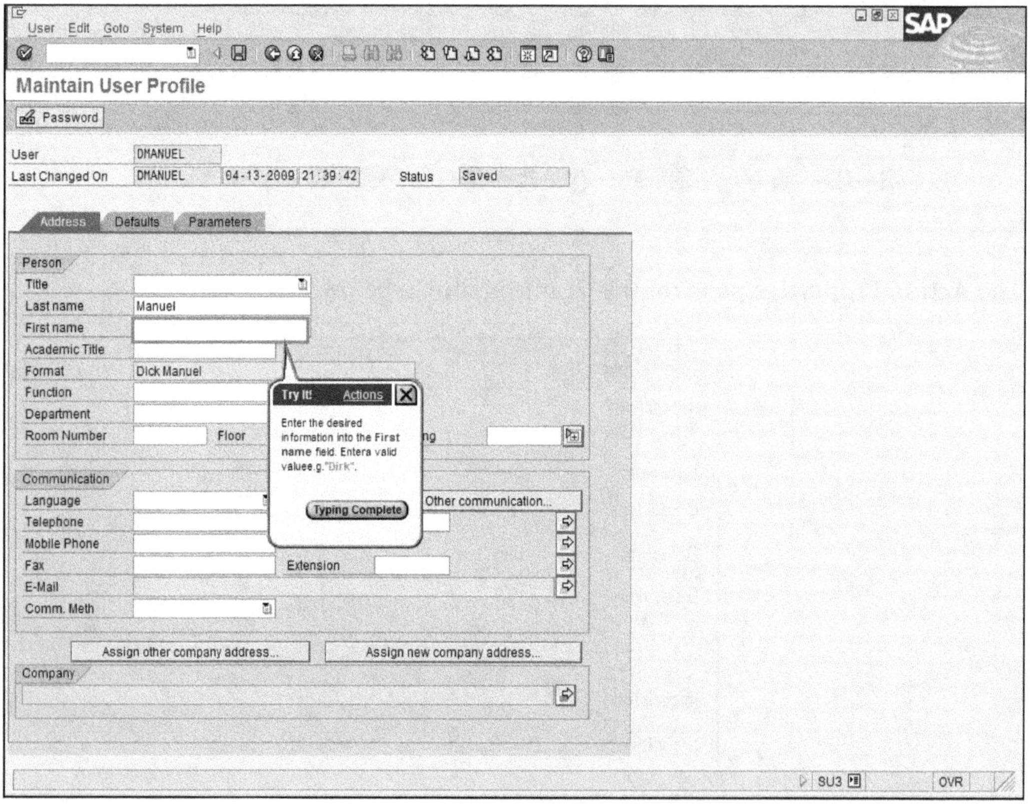

Notice anything missing? If you need a hint, compare this screenshot from the Player with the screenshot from the **Topic Editor** earlier. The original text of Dick that we want to over-type is missing. As mentioned above, the **Object type Editfield** is a special type of Action Area. In fact, it is a text box, with a solid background, that is overlaid onto the screenshot (unlike mouse-click Action Areas, which are rectangles with a transparent background). What you can see in the screenshot above is a white rectangle (with a red border) overlaid on top of the screen input field. This is hiding the actual field, and making it appear empty. If we want the field to look correct (with the initial value in the field) then we need to explicitly specify this text (UPK is not clever enough to "scrape" the screen and retrieve this value for us). You can do this via the **Implicit text** field in the **Application Properties** pane. For our example, we need to enter an **Implicit text** of **Dick**. This is shown in the following screenshot example:

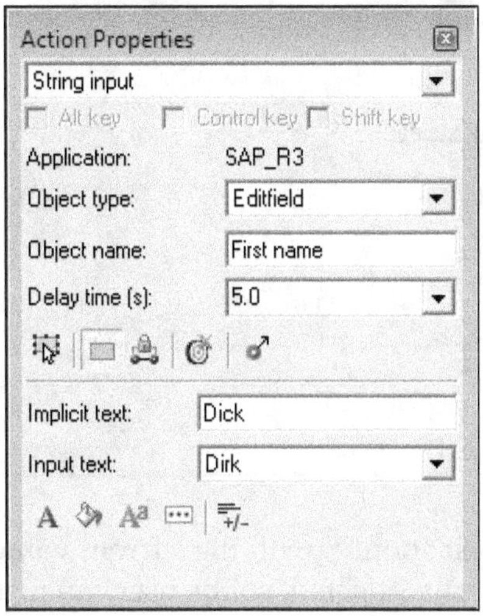

Now, the screen appears correctly in the Player, as shown in the next screenshot:

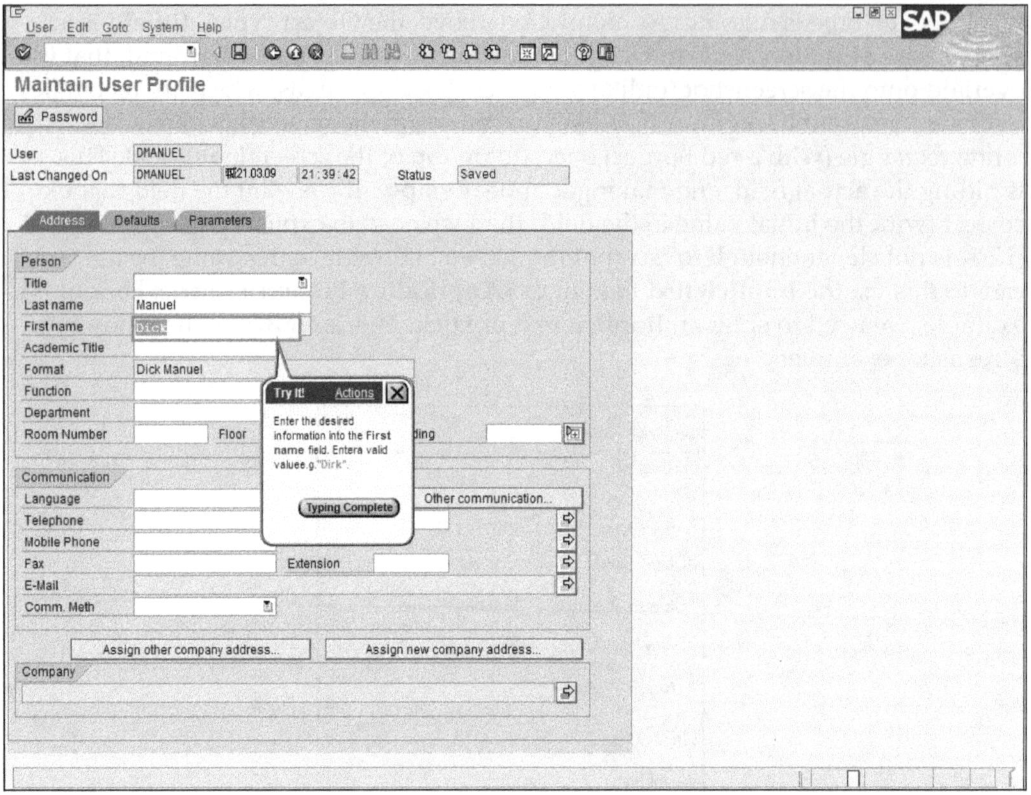

The screen now appears as it should, with the current value of the field appearing correctly. This is automatically selected, so the user can just start typing to replace it. Note also that this is a fully-functional text field. The trainee can click anywhere in the text string, use the cursor to move through the text, character by character, and use the *Delete* or *Backspace* keys to delete some or all of the text. This is very useful as it means that the trainee will not be marked incorrect in Try It? mode if they happen to use a different way of editing the text, as long as the final text is correct.

There are still a couple of other problems with this field that we need to fix. Firstly, the Action Area is larger than the actual field. This is not so easy to see in *See It!*, *Try It!*, and *Do It!* mode, where the border of the Action Area masks the problem, but if you play the exercise in *Know It?* mode, where the border of the Action Area is not shown (or you can simply hide the border by clicking on the **Action area on/off** button ( )), then the problem is more obvious.

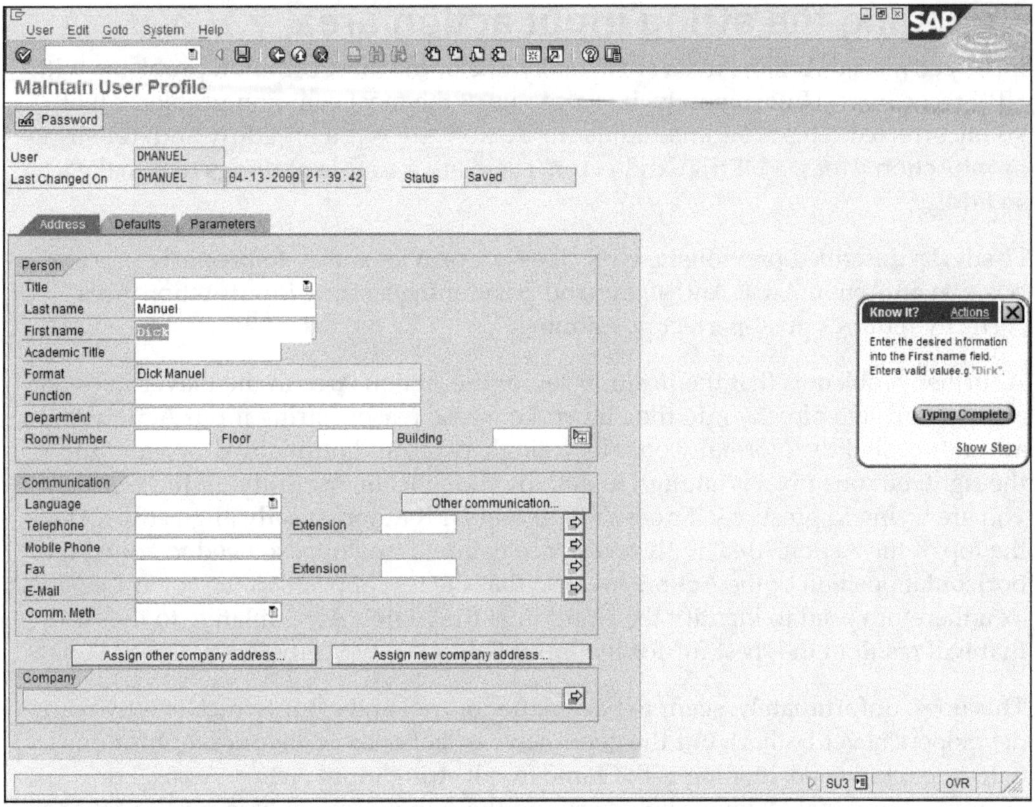

There are three specific problems with this:

- The Action Area is a different size (narrower and deeper) than the actual input field on the screen.
- The background color of the Action Area is different to the color of the input field.
- The text in the Action Area is using a different font than the application itself.

> I have accentuated these problems for the sake of illustration. UPK isn't usually as "wrong" as this!

Let's look at how to correct each of these problems.

Adjusting the string input action area

Incorrectly sized Action Areas are actually one of the most common problems with UPK recordings. Unfortunately, it is also one of the most common problems that go uncorrected. This is because adjusting Action Areas is a bit fiddly and, for string input Action Areas, a bit trial-and-error. There are a couple of things that make it so fiddly.

Firstly, as described previously, UPK does not provide a way to precisely size and position an Action Area. And sizing and positioning a string input Action Area correctly requires pixel-perfect positioning.

A further problem is that the position set for the Action Area in the Player does not always translate directly into the Player. For some reason, string input Action Areas are shifted slightly. Normally only by a single pixel, and normally down and to the right, but one pixel is enough to destroy the "illusion of reality", which is what you are trying to preserve. It doesn't help that UPK automatically aligns the text at the top of the Action Area, with zero space before it, so you also need to adjust the horizontal position of the Action Area, so that the text appears in the correct position. You therefore need to identify the position of the Action Area, relative to the field, that will result in the "best fit" for the input field.

This does, unfortunately, seem to be a matter of trial and error (which is why many developers never bother), but the good news is that once you work it out for one field, the relative positioning is the same for all string input Action Areas. For example, I find that leaving a space around the Action Area of zero pixels at the top, one pixel on the left and right, and two pixels at the bottom, results in a good fit in the Player. This is shown in the following screenshot, which has been scaled up to emphasize the spacing:

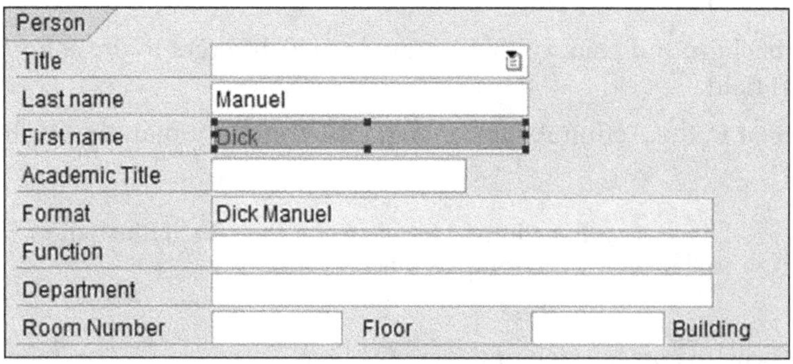

Yes, it is fiddly, but it does create a good fit in the Player (as you can see in the "final version" screenshot at the end of this section). Besides, this book is all about creating *quality* training, right?

How to adjust the size and position of the Action Area is explained earlier, in the section *Working with mouse Actions*. Refer to that section, and adjust the Action Area for our string input Action as described above.

Note that in order to make the exercise as realistic as possible, we also need to make sure that the background color of the Action Area is *exactly* the same color as the actual input field in the application. This is what we will look at adjusting next.

Adjusting the background color

As explained above, string input Action Areas are the only types of Action Areas that are not "transparent". They have a background color because the field may contain **implicit text** (explained previously) which would "show through" if the action area was transparent. By default, the background color of a string input Action Area is white, but you can change this to any color you like, by clicking on the **String input background color** button (). Clicking on this button displays the standard color selection panel, where you can choose one of the predefined standard colors or, by clicking on the **Define custom colors** button, specify or select the exact color that you want to use from the Color dialog box (shown below).

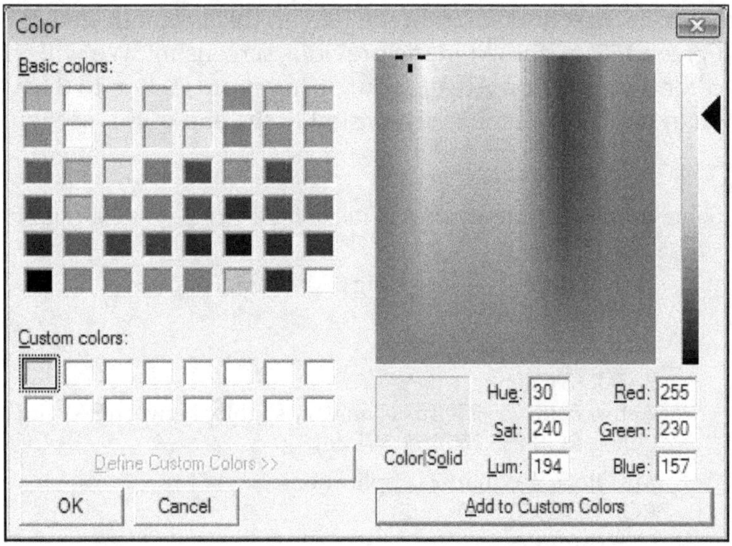

Bear in mind, when choosing a background color for the string input Action Area, that the background color must *exactly* match the color of the text field in the application **as it appears in the Player**. This last caveat is very important. UPK will (by default, although you can remove this option) down-sample screen prints to use only 256 colors. UPK does this because it makes the screenshots smaller, and therefore faster to load. This is not necessarily an issue in most Windows applications, although you may want to disable this option when recording color-sensitive applications such as photo editors. However, it does mean that there may well be slight differences between the colors in the actual application and the colors in the Player. You should therefore aim to match the color in the Player (as this is what your trainees will see) and not the color in the application. This means that you will need to publish (or preview) your first exercise, so that you can see the correct color, before you can truly finalize the exercise.

Unfortunately, UPK does not include a *dropper*, which would allow you to select the required color by clicking on it. Happily, many applications do, so you can use the dropper in another application to identify the correct hue/saturation/luminescence or red/green/blue values, and then simply type these values into the input fields in the lower-right corner of the **Color** dialog box, as shown previously.

For our exercise, we are recording in the SAP application, and the active field in SAP has a deep yellow background color. In the Player, this is manifested as red **255**, blue **230**, and green **157**, as shown in the previous screenshot. We will change the background color of the Action Area for our string input Action to this value. The result is shown in the "final version" screenshot at the end of this section.

Some common applications and the default string input background colors are as follows:

- Web applications, including SAP CRM, PeopleSoft, JDE (in Internet Explorer):
  RGB 255, 255, 255 (White)
- SAP R/3 Client:
  Active field: 255,230,157 (Can vary slightly between SAPGui releases)
  Other: RGB 255,255,255 (White)
- MS Office / Windows applications:
  RGB 255,255,255 (White)
- Oracle E-Business Suite:
  Mandatory fields: RGB 255 250 156
  Non-mandatory fields: RGB 255,255,255 (White)
  Search fields: RGB 223 234 247 (Blue)

Adjusting the font

The last thing that we need to adjust in this example is the font used for the text string. This change will apply to both the *Input text* and any *Implicit text*. To change the font used for the text, click on the **String input font button** (A). This will display the **Font** dialog box, shown below, which lists all of the fonts available on your computer.

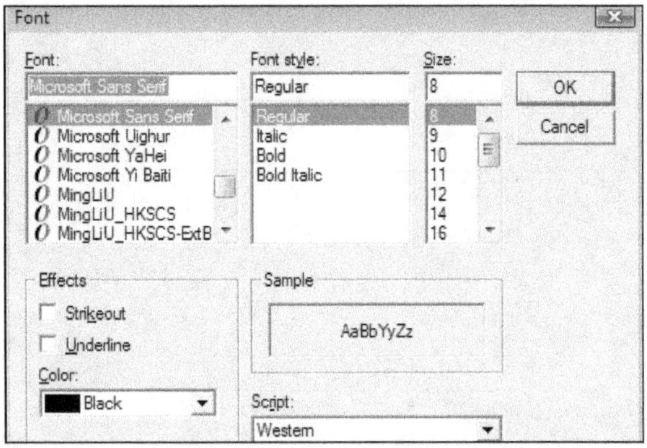

Select the required font from the **Font** list. You can also choose the font size, style and color, and set the font to be underlined or struck-through (you'd never do this for a string input field, but this same dialog box is re-used in other areas of UPK, where such options make more sense).

As with the background color, it is important that the font that you choose *exactly* matches the font used in the application. This might take a little trial and error, but once you find the correct font, it is normally the same for all input fields within the application.

> Some common applications and the default fonts are as follows:
>
> - **Web applications, including SAP CRM, PeopleSoft, JDE (in Internet Explorer)**:
>   Arial 10 pt
> - **SAP R/3 Client**:
>   Most fields: Arial Monospaced for SAP 9 pt
>   Some fields: Arial 9pt
> - **MS Office / Windows applications**:
>   Microsoft Sans Serif 9 pt
> - **Oracle E-Business Suite**:
>   Most fields: Arial 10 pt bold
>   Search field: Arial 10 pt normal

We've now fixed the Action Area size, the background color, and the font. Our Frame will now look like the example shown in the following screenshot (taken from *Know It?* mode, so that you can better appreciate the sizing and positioning of the input field):

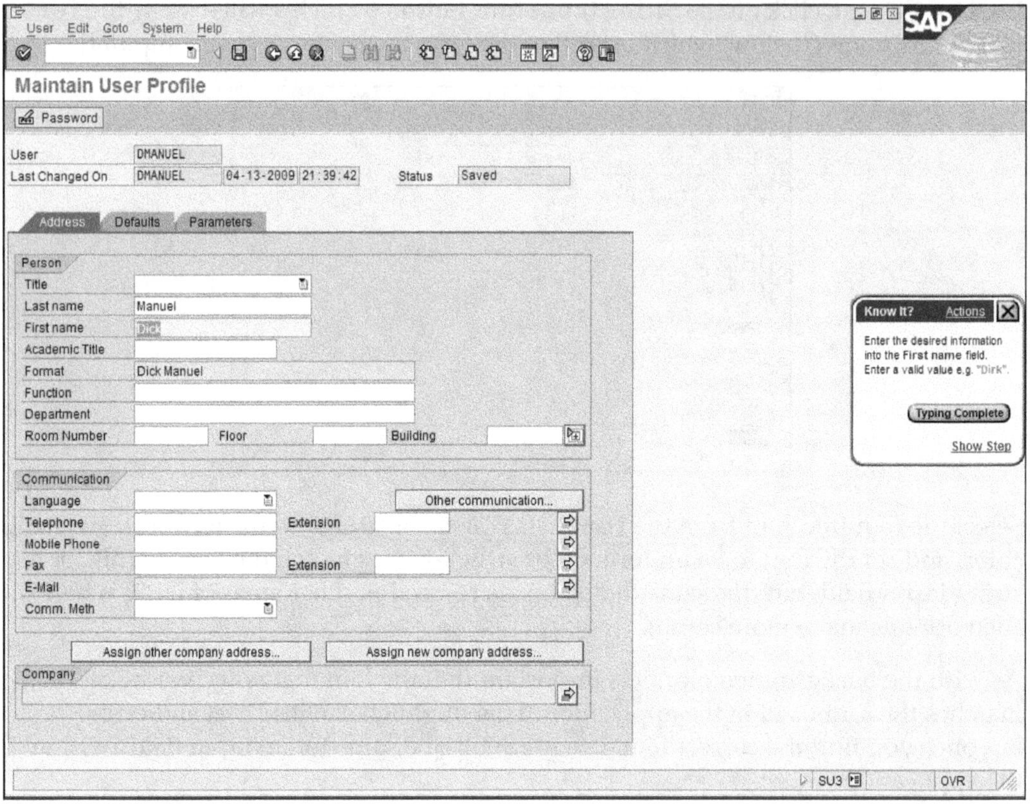

This is now perfect. You would be hard pushed to tell the difference between this Frame with an Action Area, and the actual screen in the application. This is exactly the level of quality that we are aiming for.

Controlling what the user can enter

The *appearance* of the text field is now perfect. However, there are still things that we can improve (or at least that we could change—whether it is an improvement, in this particular case, is possibly debatable). If you look at the Bubble Text in the example above you will see that the trainee is instructed to **Enter a valid value, e.g. "Dirk"**. As it turns out, "**a valid value**" is actually anything at all. The trainee could enter "**Dirk**", "**Dork**", "**asdfgh**", or anything else that they felt like. These would all be considered equally valid, and if the trainee was carrying out the simulation in *Know It?* mode, they would "pass" the test. In some cases, this may be perfectly valid. After all, what you are testing is the user's ability to enter information in the correct fields; it is not necessarily a typing test. However, in other cases, it may be important that the user enters exactly the value specified and nothing else. You can control what the user can enter via the **String input options** button (). Clicking on this button displays a pop-up menu containing further options. These options are explained below. Note that several of these options can be combined.

The first two options directly relate to the actual text string that the user can enter.

Button	Name	Purpose
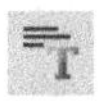	**Add new text**	By default, the user can enter only the value captured during the recording. By using this option, you can specify alternative strings that the user can enter. A good example of when you would want to do this is where the user is required to enter a monetary value of zero. Here, you may want the user to be able to enter **0** or **0.00** and still be considered "correct'. You can specify as many alternative texts as you like. All of them will be listed in the Bubble, as shown in the following example: 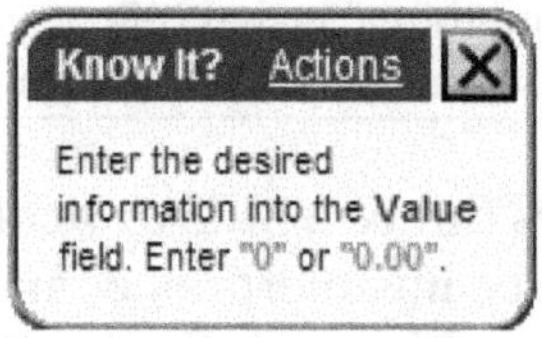
	**Replace text**	This option allows you to change the **Input text** field from the value captured during the recording (for some reason, the Input text field is not directly editable itself—although the **Implicit text** field, which is directly below it, is). Note that if you want to change an *alternative* string (added via the **Add new text** option), then you must first select the alternative string (by using the **Input text** field's drop-down list button) so that it is displayed in the **Input text** field, and then select the **Replace text** option.

The next three options are mutually exclusive. If you add one of these options to the "allowed" list, then you will not be able to add either of the other two options.

Button	Name	Purpose
	Add 'something'	Selecting this option will add **<something>** to the "allowed" list. This will allow users to enter *any* text (regardless of whether this is the recorded text), but they must enter something (that is, they cannot leave the field blank). Note that you cannot select this option if you have specified more than one text value (via the **Add new text** button).
	Add 'anything'	Selecting this option will add **<anything>** to the "allowed" list. This will allow users to either enter *any* text (regardless of whether this is the recorded text), or just leave the field blank. Note that you cannot select this option if you have specified more than one text value (via the **Add new text** button).
	Add 'blank'	Selecting this option will add **<blank>** to the "allowed" list. This will allow users to leave the input field blank and still progress to the next step. The difference between this option and simply adding "anything" is that it is possible to specify multiple alternative texts in conjunction with this option.

These last three options can be a little difficult to understand. The names of the possible selections can be misinterpreted, and it is also possible (indeed, necessary, in some cases) to specify multiple values. It is therefore worth examining these options in more detail, by way of some examples.

The main "option" for the **Input text** field is the actual value entered during simulation capture. In our sample exercise, we recorded the entry of a text string of **Dirk** in the **First name** field. The **Action Properties** pane for this initially appears as follows (with the **Input text** drop-down displayed, for easy reference):

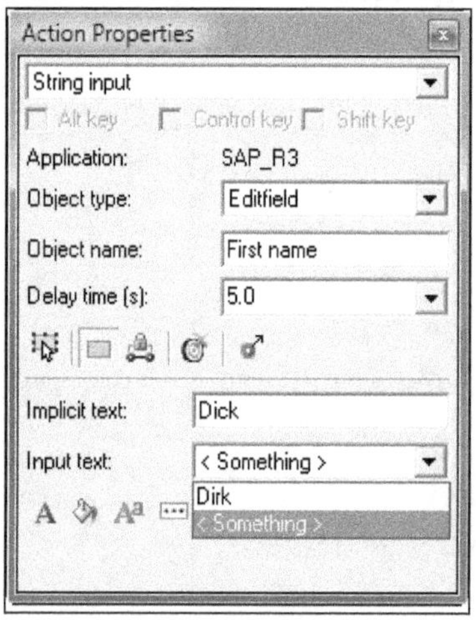

Note that the **<Something>** option is added automatically, along with the text that we explicitly entered. The option **<Something>** can be read as "The user must enter *something*" (that is, they cannot leave the field blank). Therefore, our Bubble Text (assuming that we are using the default Standard Template) will be as follows:

See It! **and** *Try It!* **modes**	*Know It?* **mode**	*Do It!* **mode**
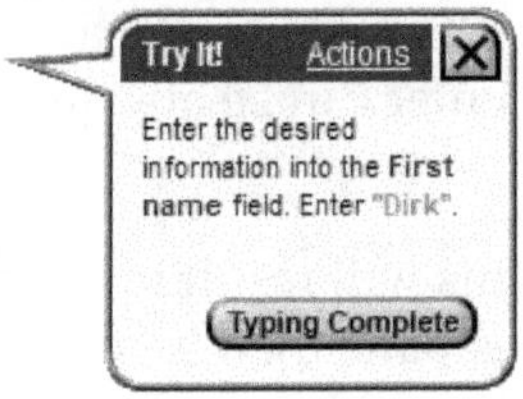	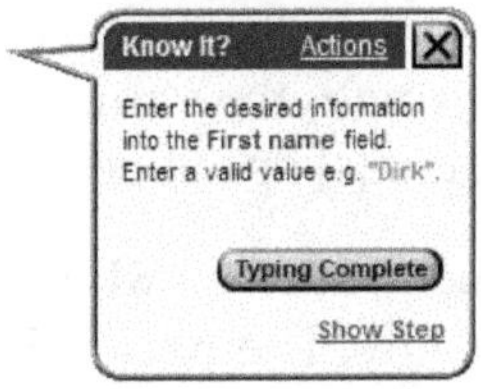	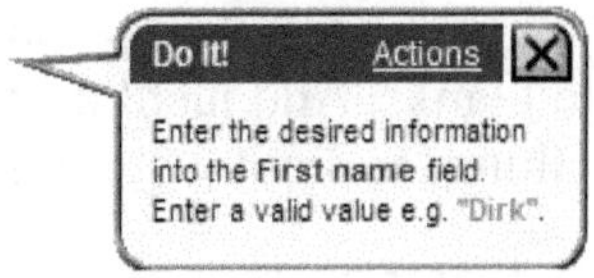

Now let's remove the **<Something>** option, and replace it with **<Anything>**. The **Action Properties** pane then shows:

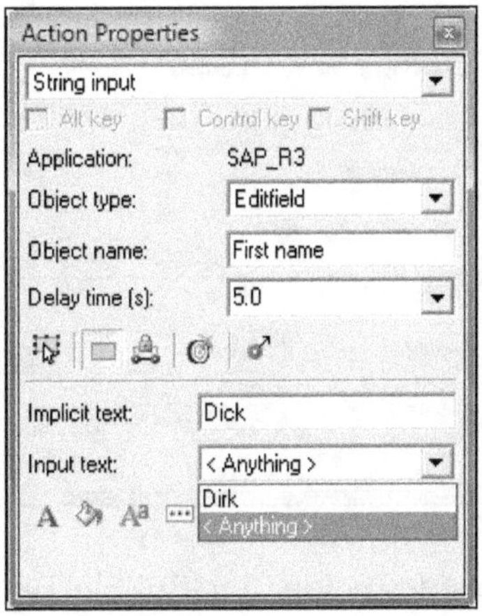

This will give us the following Bubble Text (again, assuming that we are using the default Standard Template):

See It! **and** *Try It!* **modes**	*Know It?* **mode**	*Do It!* **mode**
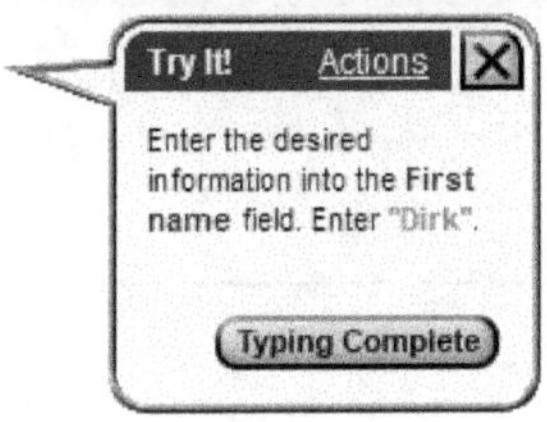	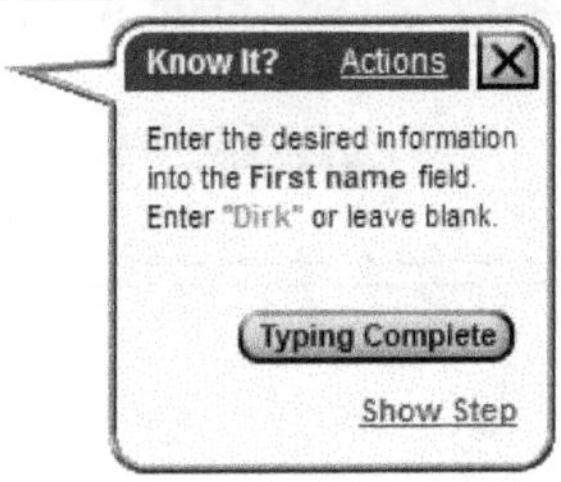	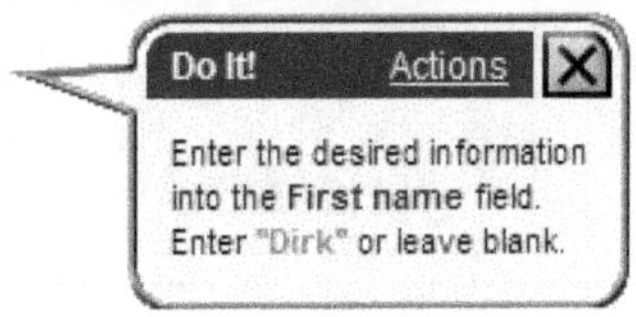

The only difference with these texts and the previous ones (from **<Something>**) is that the text **or leave blank** has been added for the *Know It?* and *Do It?* modes. Interestingly, you can see that in *See It!* and *Try It!* modes, the user is not given the option to leave the field blank, but they are in *Know It?* and *Do It!* modes. Maybe this is the way it is supposed to work; maybe it is just a bug. Either way, it is something to be aware of when choosing text input options.

In general, **<Anything>** can be read as "The user can either enter a value or leave the field blank". And just like **<Something>**, the value that they enter can be absolutely anything, and not just the explicit text(s) specified.

Note that if we remove **<Anything>** but add **<Blank>** then this will result in exactly the same Bubble Text, as shown below. The **Action Properties** pane then becomes:

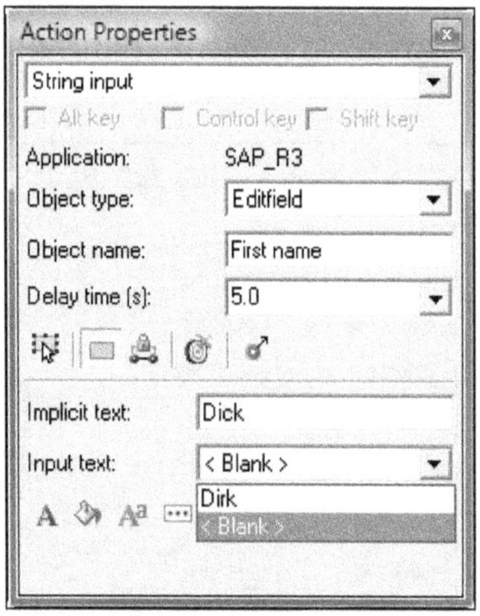

As you can see from the examples below, the Bubble Text is exactly the same as the previous example:

See It! **and** *Try It!* **modes**	*Know It?* **mode**	*Do It!* **mode**
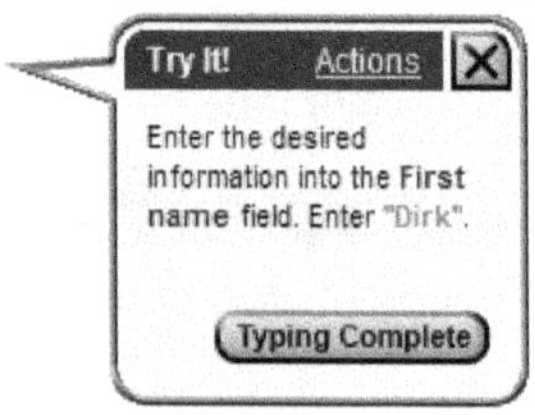	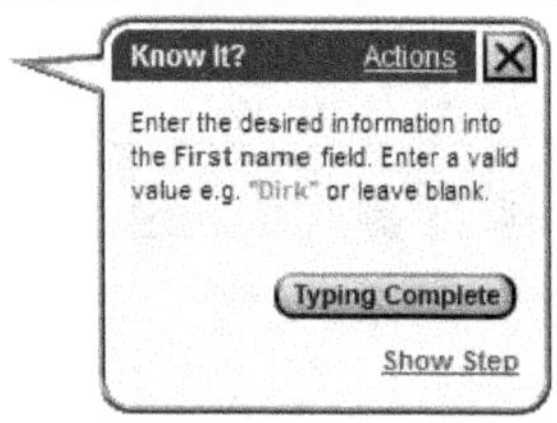	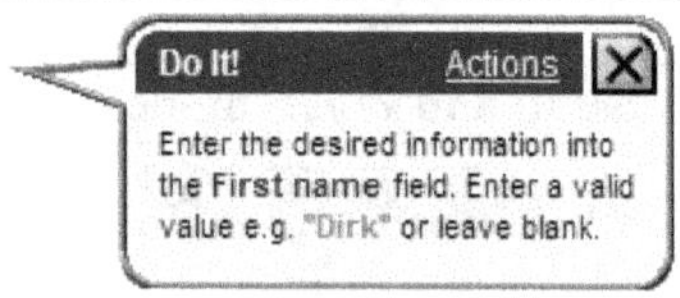

Finally, for the fun of it, we'll remove all of the text input options apart from the original explicit text (captured during the recording). The easiest way of doing this is to select the **Clear List** option () from the **String input** options context menu. The **Action Properties** pane is then as shown in the next screenshot:

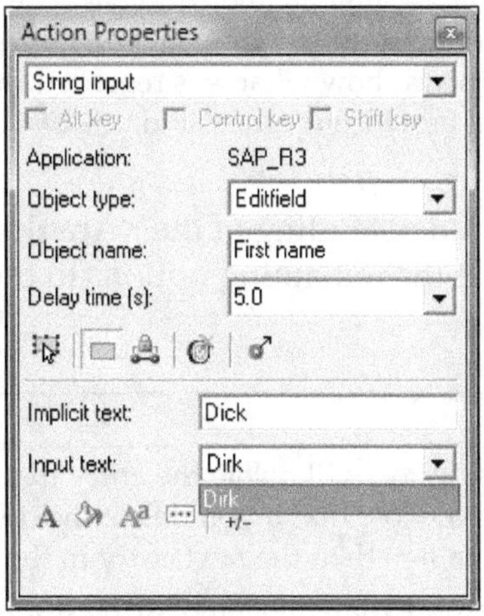

The Bubble Text for this is then as follows:

See It! **and** *Try It!* **modes**	*Know It?* **mode**	*Do It!* **mode**
		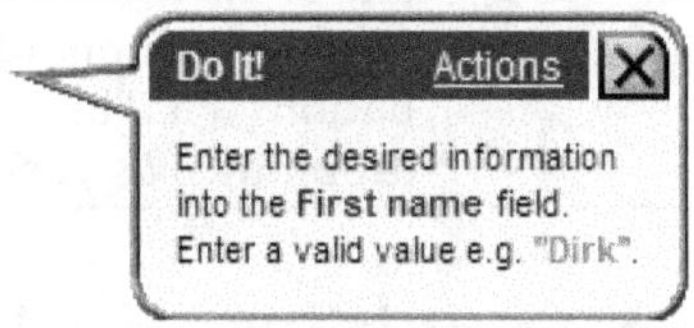

Hmm, well that's interesting! In *Know It?* mode you get nothing? Well, by default, yes. If you look at the **Bubble properties** pane (which is described later), you'll see that the **Display template text in Know It? mode** button () has been deselected. This option is automatically selected when you include the **<Something>** option in the **Input text** options, but as soon as you take this option off, UPK (for some reason only known to its developers) deselects this option. Fortunately, all you need to do is manually re-select it, and the template text will appear in *Know It?* mode again (the text will be exactly the same as the text for *Do It!* mode, as shown previously).

> I recommend that you *always* remove the **<Anything>**, **<Something>**, and **<Blank>** options. There are two very good reasons for doing this. Firstly, although it can be argued that the exercises are not typing tests, it is not unrealistic to test that your trainees are capable of entering specified information correctly—after all, they quite likely need to do this a lot in their actual jobs. Secondly, regardless of what you let the trainees enter, the next screenshot will always show what was recorded, and not what they entered. This can appear at best incongruous, and at worst confusing.

Now that we have a better understanding of the **<Anything>**, **<Something>**, and **<Blank>** options, let's look at the remaining options in the **String input options** context menu:

Button	Name	Purpose
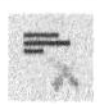	**Delete entry**	Selecting this option will delete the entry that is currently shown in the **Input text** field. Note that if you delete the default entry (the first entry in the drop-down list) then the next entry in the list will become the default.
	**Set to default**	If you define more than one valid string (for example, 0.00 and 0) then these will appear in the **Input text** field drop-down in the order in which you define them (starting with the string that was captured during recording). The option at the top is the **default option**. This is the string that will appear in the Bubble Text, although the user will be able to enter any of the texts in the list. To make another string the default option, select it from the **Input text** drop-down list, and then click the **Set to default** button (). The selected option will then be moved to the top if the drop-down list, and will be used as the default.

Case sensitivity and password fields

There are two last options related to input fields that we have not yet looked at. We do not need to use them in our example exercise, but for the sake of completeness, they are explained here.

Button	Name	Purpose
	**String input case sensitivity**	By default, string input actions are case insensitive. So for our example, the trainee could enter Dirk, dirk, dIRK, and so on, and still be considered correct. If you want the trainee to enter the text string exactly as given (but bearing in mind that in some cases they may not be given anything in *Know It!* mode), then you can click on this button to force this.
	**Set as password field**	For applications that require the user to enter a password, their entry is usually masked so that their input cannot be seen. If your string input action is for such a password field, then you can select this option. The trainee's input will then be masked when they type it. However, note that UPK chooses to mask the input using small circles ('bullets'), so if your application uses asterisks for masking (as is often the case - or at least more often than circles are used) then you will not be able to ensure a perfect match.

Changing the Bubble

In the previous section, *Adjusting actions*, we looked at how to change Actions, and in the process, influence the Bubble. However, this is only half of what we can do to change the Bubble Text. In this section, we will look at how to change the format of this Bubble and the text that it contains, and how to influence what text is displayed in which modes. All of this is controlled via the **Bubble Properties** pane.

The Bubble Properties pane

The **Bubble Properties** pane contains information relating to the yellow "speech Bubble" that is overlaid on the screenshot. You can control the appearance and content of the Bubble in this pane. An example of the **Bubble Properties** pane (undocked from its usual position) is shown in the following screenshot:

Changing the Bubble format

Although the Bubble is generated automatically, there are a number of things that you can change about it. These are described below.

Changing the Bubble pointer

The Bubble pointer is the "arm" that comes out of one corner of the Bubble, and points to a particular area on the screen. For Bubbles on Action Frames for mouse-click actions and string-input actions, UPK will create a Bubble with a pointer, and have this point to the Action Area. For keyboard actions, and Explanation Frames (discussed in Chapter 9, *Adding Value to Your Topics*), the Bubble will not have a pointer.

You can change the position of this pointer on the Bubble (that is, determine the position from which it extends from the Bubble), or remove the pointer altogether. This can be done for all Action Frames, and for Explanation Frames. You cannot add a pointer to a Decision Frame (discussed in Chapter 8, *Allowing Alternatives*). Additionally, note that Bubbles in *Know It*? Mode do not have pointers in the published version (although they are visible in the Topic Editor).

To change the position of a pointer on a Bubble, carry out the steps described below:

1. Go to the Frame that contains the Bubble for which you want to change the pointer.
2. In the **Bubble Properties** pane, click on the **Bubble Pointer** button ( ). The following drop-down list appears below the button:

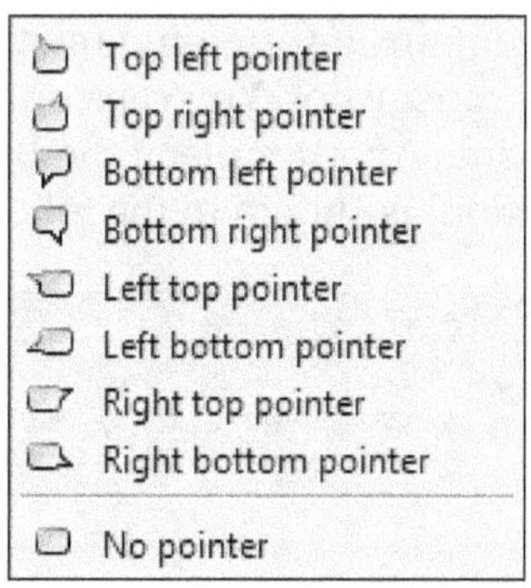

3. Select the appropriate entry for the position at which you want the pointer to appear (or select the **No pointer** entry to remove the pointer altogether).

Note that UPK will automatically "snap" and "glue" the Bubble to the Action Area, and will therefore reposition the Bubble on the most appropriate edge of the Action Area, depending on the position of the pointer. If there is not enough space on the screen to attach the Bubble to the required side, then UPK will automatically change the pointer position and reposition the Bubble on another side. If you want to manually change the position of the Bubble, refer to *Repositioning the Bubble*, next.

Repositioning the Bubble

By default, UPK will "attach" Bubbles for Frames that include an Action Area to the Action Area. If you move the Action Area, then the Bubble moves with it. For Frames without Action Areas (typically, Action Frames for keyboard actions), and Explanation Frames, the Bubble is placed in the middle of the screen by default, although you can move it.

In either case, you can move the Bubble as explained below. You would typically want to do this if the default position is obscuring a section of the screen that you want to be visible, or if you are moving the Bubble for an Explanation Frame, and want to point to specific information on the screen,

To move a Bubble on a Frame, carry out the steps described below:

1. Go to the Frame that contains the Bubble that you want to move.
2. Click on the Bubble header (which is blue, and contains the name of the mode for which it is being displayed), and drag it to the new location. Release the mouse button when the Bubble is in the required position.
3. If you are moving a Bubble for a Frame with an Action Area, then if you move the Bubble pointer into the proximity of the Action Area a light-blue marquee is shown around the Action Area. If you release the mouse button at this time, the Bubble will be snapped to the Action Area. You can stop the Bubble from snapping to the Action Area by holding down the *Ctrl* key when moving the Bubble.

Note that you cannot move the Bubble for a Decision Frame.

Note also that in *Know It?* mode, the Bubble will always be displayed in the horizontal middle of the rightmost edge of the Player screen, regardless of where you position it in the *Topic Editor*. The trainee has the ability to move the Bubble if it is obscuring key data, although if you know that the Bubble will obscure key data, you may want to include a text in the Bubble (and tag it for *Know It?* mode only, as explained later in this chapter) to inform the trainee that they should move the Bubble, as it is not immediately obvious that you *can* (let alone *should*) move it.

Changing the size of the Bubble

The Bubble is automatically resized to accommodate the amount of text (both Template Text and Custom Text) that is to be displayed in it. This is extremely useful because (as we shall see later) the amount of text in the Bubble may vary depending on the Player mode used.

The downside to this automatic resizing is that it is not possible to set a specific size or dimension for the Bubble. Although UPK generally uses Bubbles of the same proportion (horizontal to vertical ratio), sometimes it will generate a short, wide Bubble, or a long, tall one. In other cases, the default shape may be obscuring key information on the screen that you could make visible if only you could resize the Bubble. Unfortunately, you can't.

What you *can* do is manually "force" the shape of the Bubble by judicious use of non-breaking text (via the *Non-breaking Text* button ( )) and/or line breaks. However, bearing in mind that UPK may resize the Bubble depending on the mode in which it is displayed, this is extremely hit-and-miss. It is difficult to manually force a dimension that works well in every mode, so it is recommended that you do not even *try* to do this.

Adding an icon to a Bubble

You can add one of 35 built-in icons to a Bubble. You may want to do this to draw attention to a particular Bubble, or to identify specific types of information. In Chapter 9, *Adding Value to Your Topics* we use an icon to identify Explanation Frames. An example of a Bubble containing an icon is shown in the next screenshot:

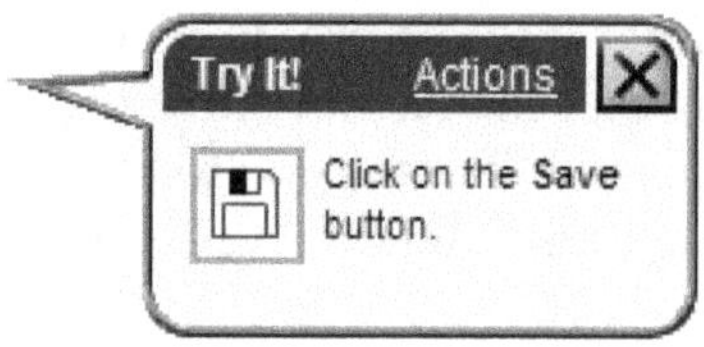

To insert an icon into a Bubble, follow these steps:

1. In the **Bubble Properties** pane, click on the Bubble icon button ( ), to display a drop-down list of available icons, as shown in the following figure:

2. Click on the icon that you want to add to the Bubble.

You can add an icon to any Bubble, on any kind of Frame (except Decision Frames), by using this option. However, you should use icons sparingly and consistently (that is, always use the same icon to identify the same kind of information and across all Topics in your Library).

> If you add an icon to a Bubble and then subsequently decide that you do not want to use an icon in the Bubble, then you can select the blank square in the upper-left corner of the icon drop-down list.

Changing the Bubble Text

The most important aspect of the Bubble is the text inside it. This is what tells the user what they should be doing, or looking at. Fortunately, UPK provides a great deal of flexibility in determining what text is displayed, and how this text appears.

Template Text versus Custom Text

Most of the **Bubble Properties** pane is taken up by the **Custom Text** field; this is the yellow area in the center of the pane. This is where UPK gets interesting. In the images below, compare the text in the **Bubble Properties** pane on the left, with the resulting Bubble, which is shown on the right.

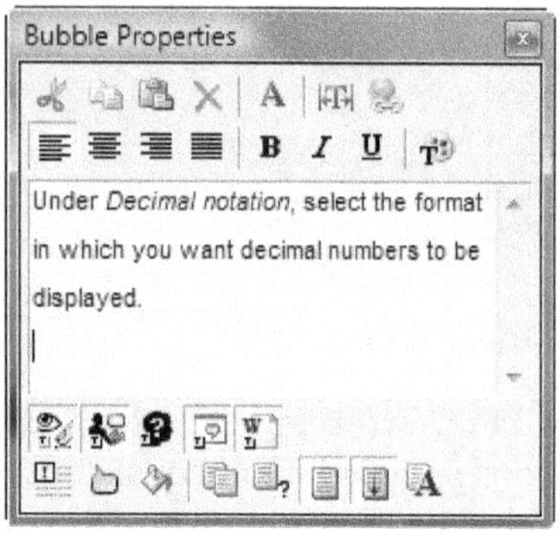

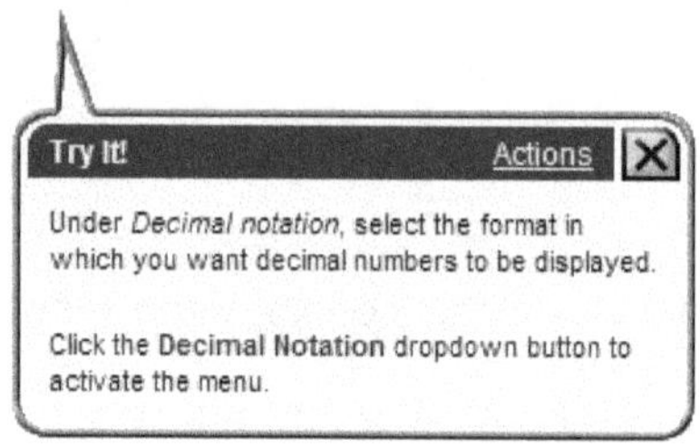

You will notice that the Bubble contains more text than is in the **Bubble Properties** pane. Why? Well, the text that is displayed in a Bubble is (potentially) composed of two distinct elements: Template Text and Custom Text. In the example above, **Click the Decimal Notation dropdown button to activate the menu** is the Template Text. This is inserted automatically by UPK when you capture the recording, based on the context of the action that you are recording (which we looked in the section on the **Action Properties** pane, above), and the Templates (which we will look at more closely in Chapter 12, *Configuring UPK*).

> In the example above, the **Use Template Text** button ( ) is selected. This indicates that the Template Text will be displayed in the Bubble, regardless of whether or not any Custom Text is specified.

The text **Under Decimal notation, select the format in which you want decimal numbers to be displayed** is Custom Text. This is text that we, as the developer, have entered ourselves.

When we first record the Topic, the Bubble will contain only the Template Text, and the Custom Text field (in the **Bubble Properties** pane) is empty. Adding Custom Text is all part of adding value to a recording, and covered extensively in Chapter 9, *Adding Value to Your Topics*. The recording itself only captures key-strokes and mouse-clicks—nothing more. If we want to explain why the user needs to carry out the action, or what will happen as a result of this, or put any kind of business context around what they are doing, then we need to include Custom Text.

Using Custom Text

To add Custom Text to your Bubble, carry out the steps described below:

1. Go to the Frame for which you want to add Custom Text.
2. Enter the required text in the **Custom Text** field (the big, yellow area) of the **Bubble Properties** pane.
3. If you will also include the Template Text in your Bubble, then include an additional line break either before your custom text (if the Template Text is to be displayed first) or after your custom text (if the Custom Text is to be displayed first). This is necessary because by default UPK will show one text immediately after the other, on separate lines, but with no inter-paragraph spacing. Determining which texts will be displayed, and in what order, is explained under *Choosing which texts are displayed*, ahead.

For our example, we want to provide some additional guidance on the **Decimal Notation** field in SAP. The screenshot below shows our **Bubble Properties** once we have entered this custom text into it:

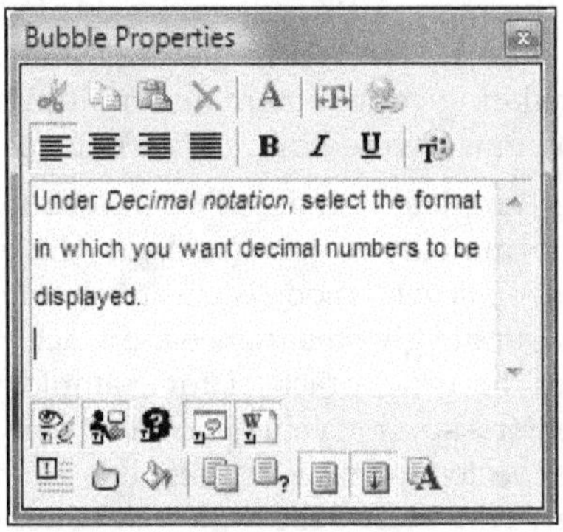

The effective use of Custom Text is covered extensively in the section *Providing context in Bubble Texts* of Chapter 9, *Adding Value to Your Topics.*

Choosing which texts are displayed

There are a number of possibilities for using the Template Text and/or Custom Text. These are controlled by a number of buttons that are available in the **Bubble Properties** pane. The following table describes these buttons and their use:

Button	Name	Use
	**Insert template text as user text**	By default, the Template Text exists in the template files, and not directly in the Topic. Effectively, this text is "built dynamically" from the Template. If you change the template (as discussed in Chapter 12, *Configuring UPK*), then the Template Text that is displayed in the Bubble will automatically be updated to use the new text from the Template. If you find that the Template Text is inadequate for your purposes (as is often the case) then you can click the **Insert template text as user text** button () to copy the Template Text into the Custom Text field, where you can change it to your heart's content. Note that this severs the link between the Template and this text, which means that any subsequent changes made to the Template will not be reflected in the Bubble Text. Furthermore, UPK will not be able to "automatically" translate the Bubble Text, which may be a concern if you are planning on translating your content into multiple languages. (Translating content is covered in Chapter 13 *Localizing Your Content*.)
	**Template text visible in Know It? mode**	The Template Text describes the action that the trainee needs to perform in the exercise (such as, where to click, or what keys to press). *Know It?* mode is effectively a *test*, and so you would typically not want to give the trainee the exact instructions. However, in some cases this is not practical, for example, when the trainee is required to enter a specific value into a text field, and they cannot reasonably be expected to know or guess this. In this case, you probably want to give the trainee the same instructions in *Know It?* mode as you give them in *Try It!* mode (or any other mode). To do this, select the **Template text visible in Know It? mode** button.
	**Use templates**	As mentioned above, the default option is for the Template Text to be used in the Bubble. The **Use templates** option is therefore selected by default. If you enter Custom Text and want to use only this Custom Text, then you can deselect the **Use templates** option, and the Template Text will be suppressed. Another handy use of this button is if you have copied the Template Text into the Custom Text field (via the option *Insert template text as user text*) at which point the **Use templates** option is automatically deselected but then decide if you want to use the template text or not. In this case, you can delete all of the text in the **Custom Text** field and then reselect the **Use templates** option to go back to using the Template Text.

Button	Name	Use
	Show custom text first	If you choose to use Custom Text as well as the Template Text, then both of these text elements will be displayed in the Bubble. By default, the Template Text is displayed first, followed by the Custom Text. If you want the Custom Text to be displayed before the Template Text, then select the **Show custom text first** option. For some reason best known to the UPK developers (actually, the OnDemand developers, before them) UPK places a single carriage return after the first text element (either Custom Text or Template Text, depending on whether the **Show custom text first** option is selected or not) and the second text element (the other one), and not a paragraph return. To make the Bubble Text more appealing, it is usually a good idea to insert an additional carriage return at the end of the first text element, as has been done in the previous example.

Formatting Bubble Text

In addition to controlling what text is displayed, the **Bubble Properties** pane allows you to control the appearance of the text itself. This includes the usual formatting options, plus a couple of options that are unique to UPK. All of these are explained in the following table:

Button	Name	Use
	Bold	Click this button to render the selected Custom Text in bold.
	Italics	Click this button to render the selected Custom Text in italics.
	Underline	Click this button to underline the selected Custom Text.
	Font Color	Select some text and then click this button to open up the **Color** dialog box, from which you can change the color of the selected Custom Text. You can either choose a standard color, or can specify a specific color by entering the RGB or hexadecimal value of the color.
	Custom Text Font	Select some text and then click this button to display the **Font** dialog box, from which you can choose the font-family and size of the Custom Text. You can also select whether the text should be rendered in bold, italics, or underlined, but these options effectively duplicate the Bold, Italics, and Underline buttons also available in the **Bubble Properties** pane. You can also set the default font for custom texts in your **Options** (see Chapter 3, *Recording a Simulation*).

Button	Name	Use
	Template Text Font	Click this button to display the **Font** panel, from which you can choose the font family and size of the Template Text. Unlike the Custom Text, you cannot choose whether the text is displayed in bold, italics, or underlined. This is controlled in the templates themselves. You can also set the default font for template texts in your **Options** (see Chapter 3, *Recording a Simulation*).
	Non-breaking Text	Select some text and then click on this button to make the selected text non-breaking. This means that all of the selected text will be displayed on a single line in the Player.
	Hyperlink	Select some text and then click on this button to turn the selected text into a hyperlink. Hyperlinks are covered in more detail in Chapter 9, *Adding Value to Your Topics*.

Tagging Custom Text for different modes

The previous sections explain how to control which texts are displayed in the Bubble, and the format of these texts. But UPK offers a further level of customization by allowing you to specify exactly what text will be displayed in the various modes in which the Topic can be played. In fact, UPK automatically does this (as best it can) for Bubble Text for string input actions. Consider the following examples:

These two texts are both generated from the same Template Text. This is shown in the illustration below. Note that in this screenshot the Template Text was copied into the **Custom Text** field so that we can see exactly how it is structured. Note also that this particular screenshot was taken with the **Display** property set to **Player-See It!/Try It!**.

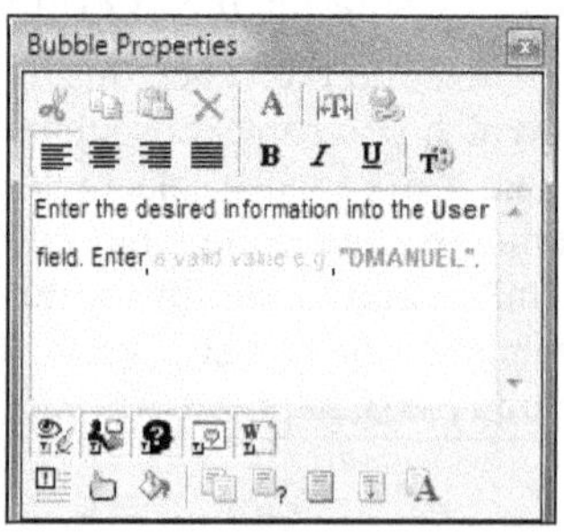

The first thing that you will notice is that one section of the text is "low-lighted" in gray. Coincidentally, this is the same section of text that appears in *Know It*? mode but not *Try It!* mode. If you look closely at the previous example of the **Bubble Properties** pane, you will see that there is a small "tick" just underneath the baseline of the text, exactly at the point where the text changes from appearing in both modes to appearing in only the *Know It*? mode. What is all of this doing, and how is it working?

In short, UPK allows you to tag different sections of a text for display in specific modes. The text **a valid value e.g.** in the **Bubble Properties** pane above has been tagged to appear only in *Know It?* mode. As the **Bubble Properties** pane is being displayed in **Player-See It!/Try It!** mode, the text is low-lighted – this can be interpreted as "this text appears in another mode, but not this one". The tick marks identify the points at which the tagging changes from one mode to another. Tagging text for a particular more is done by selecting the text in the **Custom Text** pane, and then clicking on the appropriate mode button, as shown ahead:

Button	Name	Use
	**Visible in See It!/ Try It!**	Select the text and then click this button if you want the text to appear in *See It!* mode and *Try It!* mode. Note that these two modes use the same formatting. The only difference is that one is an automatic demonstration and the other is a hands-on exercise.
	**Visible in Do It!**	Select the text and then click this button if you want the text to appear in *Do It!* mode.
	**Visible in Know It?**	Select the text and then click this button if you want the text to appear in *Know It?* mode.
	**Visible in Player**	By default, all text will appear in the on-line deployment formats, in the relevant mode for which it has been tagged via the first three buttons. If you do not want the text to appear in the on-line deployment formats, then you should click on this button to deselect it (but then the text must be tagged to appear in the printed output (see the last button).
	**Visible in Print**	By default, all text will appear in the printed deployment formats, in the relevant mode for which it has been tagged via the first three buttons. (Printed output is discussed in Chapter 6, *Publishing Your Content*.) If you do not want the text to appear in the printed output (for example, because it refers to a "simulation"), then click on this button to deselect it.

A standardized approach to string input Bubble Text

In general, I advocate using the Template Texts as much as possible. This cuts down on development time, and also simplifies translation and the provision of sound. However, the Template Text for string input actions leaves a lot to be desired. Although it is possible to customize this (as we do in Chapter 12 *Configuring UPK*) it is difficult to find a truly satisfactory solution.

Given that I also advocate judicious use of Custom Text to provide business context, I usually end up completely replacing the Template Text for string input actions, and using all Custom Text. I lose some of the flexibility and convenience of using Template Texts, but this is an acceptable trade-off for being able to provide meaningful instructions to the trainee.

Although providing Custom Text takes time, especially if it has to be tagged for various playback modes, if you use the same words, and the same sentence structure, you will find that you can actually do this fairly quickly. I always use the structure shown in the example below for string input Bubble Text:

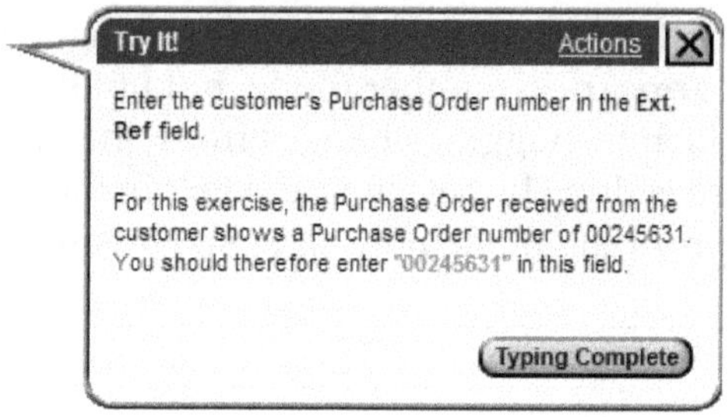

This includes business context, as well as the actual data required. Using this format also makes tagging the text for the various modes very simple, as explained below:

1. Select *all* of the text in the Bubble, and tag it for *See It!/Try It!* mode (![]) and *Do It!* mode (![]). Make sure it is not tagged for *Know It?* mode.
2. Select everything from the end of the first paragraph until the end of the second paragraph, and **deselect** *Do It!* mode. (It is important that you start your selection from the end of the first paragraph, so that you capture the two carriage returns.)
3. Select the first sentence in the second paragraph, and tag it for *Know It?* mode (![]).

This then leaves the *Try It!* mode text as shown in the example above, and provides text in *Do It!* mode and *See It?* mode as shown in the following two examples:

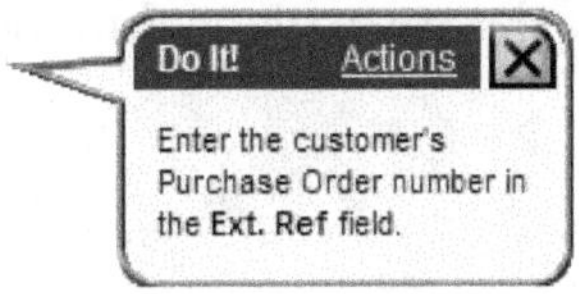

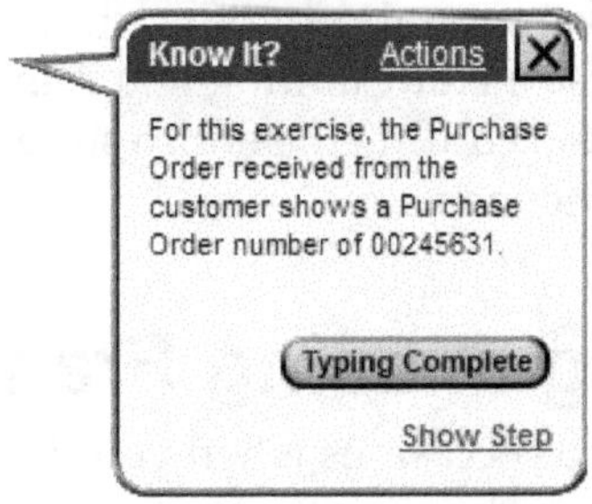

This then provides three separate texts for the three selectable modes, and without having to tag individual words, mid-sentence (as the Template Text does). It also conforms to the following golden rules:

- In *See It!* and *Try It!* modes, the trainee is given the **instructions** and the **data**
- In *Know It?* mode, the trainee is given the **data** only
- In *Do It!* mode, the trainee is given the **instructions** only

So we have now provided Custom Text for our string input action, and tagged it perfectly for the three selectable modes. And all in little more time than it takes to type the text into the **Custom Text** field.

Undo

At this point it is worth noting that the Topic Editor includes an **Undo** function (and a **Redo** function). Unfortunately this is, at best, very limited, and at worst it is hugely unreliable. In a throwback to the days of OnDemand 8.7, where changes were saved as soon as you navigated away from the Frame, the **Undo** button ( ) will only undo changes on the current Frame. Once you leave a Frame your changes are *committed* (although you can always exit without saving if you haven't done too much).

Sometimes the **Undo** button does not undo anything at all, and other times it seems to roll back the past several changes. It is therefore better not to not rely on this feature, and manually reverse your changes if you need to.

Adjusting your recording

Beyond changing the actions that were captured during the initial recording, there are also a number of other things that you can do to adjust the simulation as a whole. These include adding and removing Frames, replacing or editing screenshots, and even re-recording the entire simulation. These tasks are explained in the following sections.

Adding missing Frames

There may be occasions when you finish capturing a recording, and then realize that you missed out a couple of screens (or, as is more often the case, the developers forgot to tell you about some requirement). Never fear; there is no need to recapture the entire recording—UPK allows you to insert new Frames (screenshots) into an existing Topic.

Let's look at an example. In our sample exercise, we have explained how to use the **Address** tabbed page and the **Defaults** tabbed page. Now we look at it, we think that it would be useful to explain the last tabbed page, **Parameters**, as well. So we would like to insert some new Frames to explain this page.

To add new Frames to an existing Topic, carry out the steps described below:

1. Start up the application that you want to capture, and navigate to the exact point (screen) at which you want to start recording. In our exercise, this would be positioned on the **Defaults** tabbed page.
2. Open the Topic into which you want to insert the additional Frames, in the **Topic Editor**.
3. Select the Frame after which you want to insert the new Frames. For our exercise, this will be Frame **C** (immediately prior to the "save" Frame—Frame **D**).
4. Select menu option **Insert | Missing Frame(s)** ( ). You are passed into the application, and the **Recorder** pane is displayed.
5. Record the missing actions and Frames, as explained in Chapter 3, *Recording a Simulation*. Once you have captured the last new screenshot, click the **Finish** button in the **Recorder** pane. Be careful about the Frame on which you stop recording. In our example, this would be immediately prior to clicking the **Save** button (because we already have this recorded, and this will be the next Frame after our newly inserted Frames).
6. Once you have finished recording, you will be passed back into the **Topic Editor**, and can edit the newly inserted Frames as normal.

You now have a newly-expanded recording, as you can see from the following screenshot. Note that the additional Frames that have been recorded are identified by a border around them:

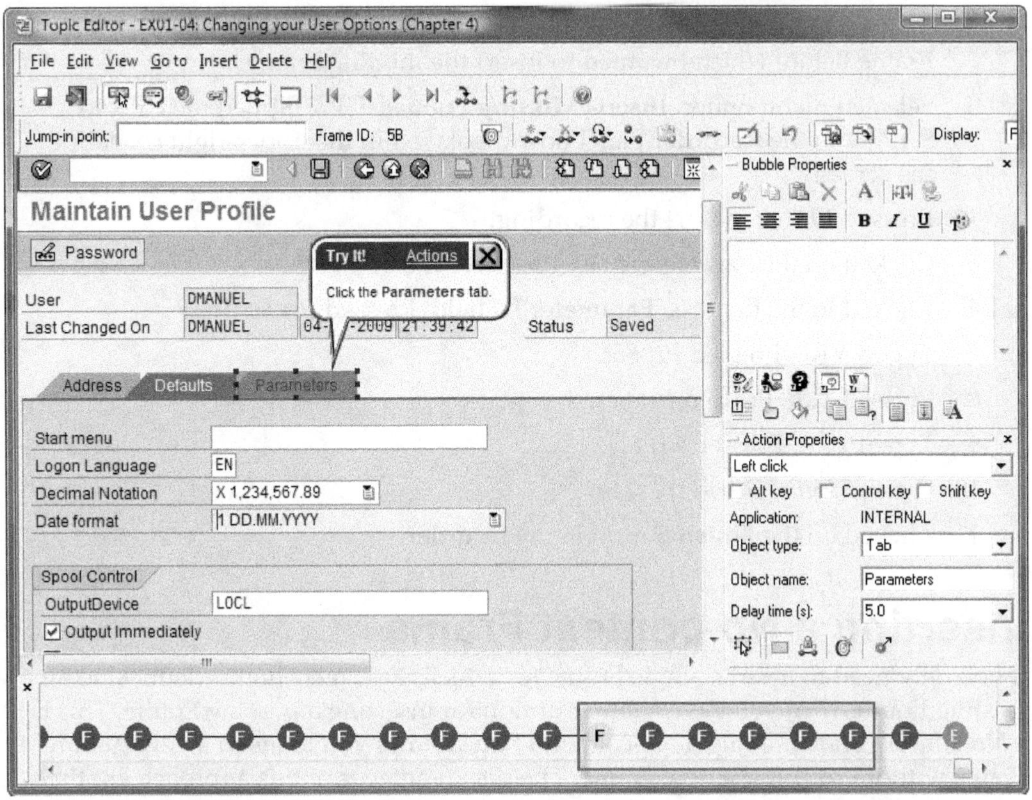

Note that the **Frame ID** for the first of these new Frames is `5B` (the new Frames run from `5B` to `60`) even though they have been inserted between Frames C and D (which are still called **C** and **D**). This is because Frame numbers *never* change. Any new Frames will be given a new number after the last Frame number previously used (or some way after this, in this example), regardless of whereabouts they appear. Remember that *Frame IDs* are simple references—they are not position-significant.

For the record, I carried out the following steps to insert these missing Frames:

1. Logged on to SAP, and navigated to the **Defaults** tab in the **Maintain User Profile** transaction.
2. Switched to UPK, opened up the Topic in the **Topic Editor**, and selected the Frame before which I wanted to insert the missing Frames.
3. Selected menu option **Insert | Missing Frames**. UPK flipped me back to SAP, with the **Recorder** panel now displayed in the upper-right corner of the screen.
4. Pressed *Prt Scr* to start the recording.
5. Clicked on the **Parameters** tab. Pressed *Prt Scr*.
6. Clicked in the first free **Parameter** ID field. Pressed *Prt Scr*.
7. Typed **VK0**. Pressed *Prt Scr*.
8. Pressed **Tab**. Pressed *Prt Scr*.
9. Typed **1001**. Pressed *Prt Scr*.
10. Pressed *Enter*. Pressed *Prt Scr*.
11. Clicked on the **Finish** button in the recorder.

Inserting a No-context Frame

If you only need to insert a single Frame for which the screenshot is identical to an existing Frame, then you have another option for inserting a missing Frame. This is a **No-context Frame**. Using a No-context Frame allows you to insert a new Action Frame without *recording* a new Frame. The disadvantages of this approach are that (1) no context information is available (that's why they call it a "No-context" Frame), and (2) you can only use a screenshot that already exists in your Topic. That said, the No-context Frame is often a useful option if you do not have the ability to go and re-capture the correct screen (for example, because you were recording a difficult-to-recreate scenario, or because you have "consumed" your data).

A No-context Frame will take its screenshot from the Frame immediately following it. This is a one-time copy, which means that you can insert a No-context Frame and then edit the screenshot that it uses (as described below), without affecting the Frame from which the No-context Frame originally took its screenshot. Note that this does not necessarily mean that you are limited to inserting a No-context Frame to immediately before the Frame that contains the screenshot that you want to use (although most of the time this will be the case). You can insert a No-context Frame before the Frame whose screenshot you want to copy, and then cut-and-paste (actually, copy-and-paste and then delete the original) the No-context Frame into the position where you really want it to appear. (How to copy-and-paste screenshots is explained in Chapter 9, *Adding Value to Your Topics*.)

A No-context Frame will take its Action Area from the same Frame as that from which the screenshot is taken. Any Custom Text will also be copied over, but the Template Text will not (because there is no context, and UPK needs the context information to determine which template texts to use).

To insert a No-context Frame, carry out the steps described below:

1. Open the Topic into which you want to insert the No-context Frame, in the **Topic Editor**.
2. In the **Frame Navigation** pane, select the Frame **before** the Frame from which you want the screenshot to be taken.
3. Select menu option **Insert | No-context Frame** ( ). (You could also click on the **Insert** button ( ) on the *Standard Toolbar*, and then select **No-context Frame** ( ) from the drop-down menu.) The No-context Frame is inserted into your Topic.
4. Adjust the Action Area as required.
5. Change the Custom Text as required (there will be no Template Text).

Replacing screenshots

Sometimes, you may find that you need to recapture a single screenshot in a recording. Maybe some extraneous information got captured by mistake, or you realize that not all of the required data was set up correctly. Given what you learned in the previous section, you could be forgiven for thinking that all you need to do is delete the Frame containing the incorrect screenshot, and then insert a missing Frame to capture the new screenshot. Sure, that would work; but UPK provides a much easier way of doing this: **replacing** a screenshot.

If we look back at our sample exercise, you will recall that we added several new Frames, to explain an additional tabbed page. The problem with this is that when we recorded the initial exercise, we saved our changes when the **Defaults** tabbed page was displayed. Once we have added in our missing Frames, the user should now be saving their changes from the **Parameters** tabbed page. However, because we inserted our new Frames *before* the "save" action, the screen print for the "save" action still shows the **Defaults** page, as shown in the following screenshot:

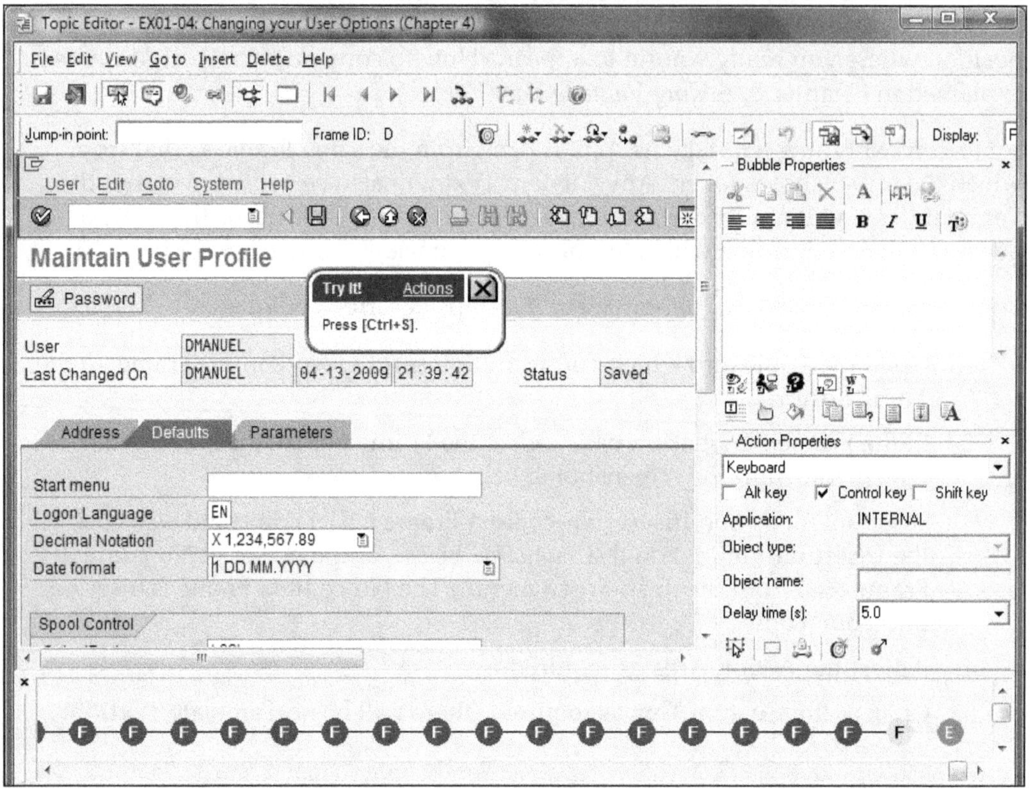

What we need to do here is replace this screenshot with a screenshot showing the **Parameters** page. Because the action is still exactly the same (and in exactly the same position), it is easier to just swap out the screenshot rather than re-record Frames.

To recapture a screenshot, carry out the following steps:

1. Go to the application that you are creating the simulation for, and position yourself on the replacement screen (that is, the screen that you want to use in your Topic).
2. Open the Topic in the **Topic Editor**.

3. Select the Frame containing the screenshot that you want to replace (Frame **D**, in our example).
4. Select menu option **Edit | Recapture screenshot** (). You are passed into the application.
5. Press the *Prt Scr* button. The screenshot is recaptured, and you are returned to UPK.

Our Frame (Frame D) now appears as shown in the following screenshot. Note that the Action is still the same, and the Bubble is still in exactly the same place. These things do not change when we replace a screenshot.

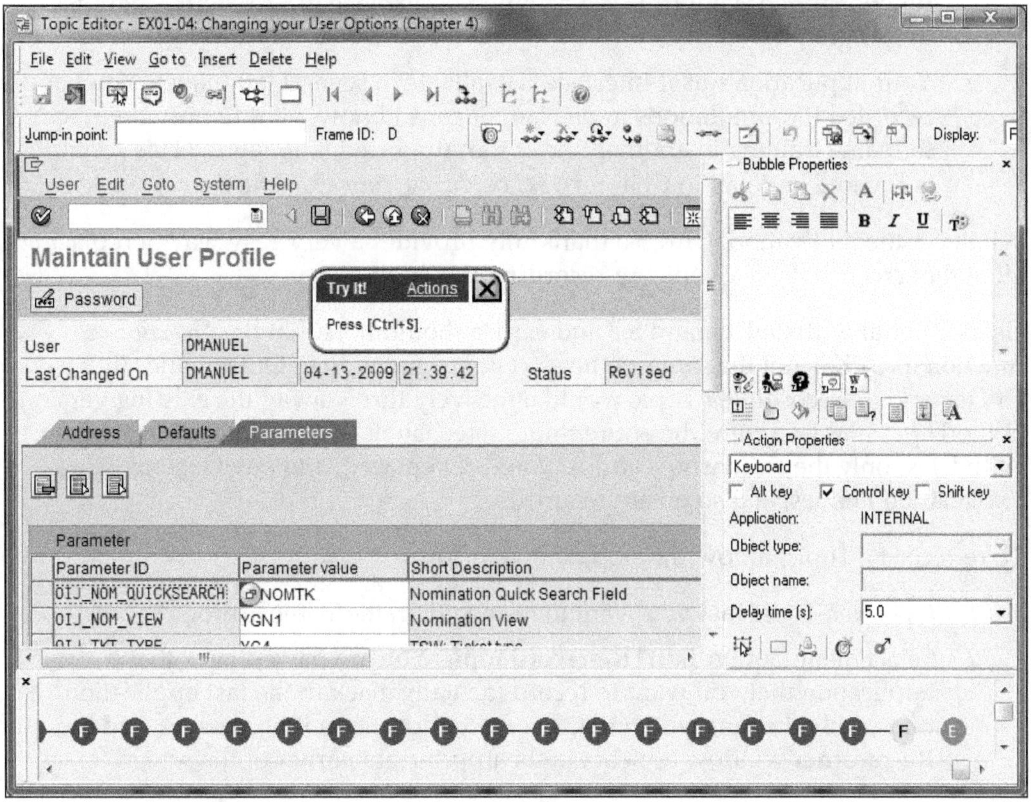

Re-recording a Topic

In some cases, you may find that you need to replace all of the screenshots in a Topic. A few example scenarios for this are as follows:

- You have captured an entire simulation, but then noticed that you left the Windows Taskbar displayed when you do not want to include it in your exercise (or there was some other element that you did not want to be included in your training material).
- The software application that you have developed your training for is being upgraded, and the user interface has changed even though the basic functionality has not (this is a common occurrence in SAP, with upgrades to SAPgui).
- Your application's user interface is available in several languages. You have recorded the simulations in one language, and now want to provide exactly the same training in another one of the supported languages. (This scenario is covered in detail in Chapter 13, *Localizing Your Content.*)

Whatever the motivation, UPK 3.5 thankfully provides a very easy way of replacing all of the screenshots in a Topic: **re-recording** the Topic.

Users familiar with OnDemand 8.7 and earlier should note that the `Re-record` function in UPK is not the same as the `Re-record` function in OnDemand. In OnDemand, re-recording a Topic would effectively throw away the existing version of the Topic, and recapture the entire thing, screenshots and Actions all over again. With UPK, only the screenshots and Actions are replaced, and any Custom Text, Explanation Frames, and so on are retained.

To re-record a Topic, follow the steps shown below:

1. Open the Topic that you want to re-record, in the Topic Editor.
2. Select menu option **Edit | Re-record topic**. You are passed back to the application that you want to record (actually, back to the last application that you had open; switch to the correct application if necessary), and the **Re-recorder** window appears in the upper-right corner of the screen.

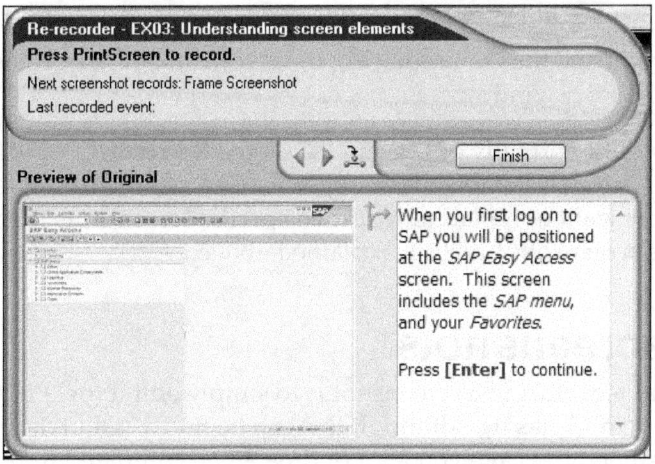

A thumbnail (actually, a sufficiently large image) of the screenshot for the current Frame is shown in the lower-left portion of the **Re-recorder** window, and the Bubble Text (Template and/or Custom) is shown in the lower-right portion of the window. This makes it very easy to recall exactly what you originally recorded in the exercise.

3. If you do not want to replace the screenshot for this Frame, then you can use the **Next Frame** and **Previous Frame** buttons to move through the recording, to locate the next screenshot that you do want to replace.
4. When you are positioned in the **Re-recorder** window on the screenshot that you want to replace, and are positioned in the application on the screen that you want to replace it with, **carry out the action specified** and then press the *Prt Scr* button, as usual. The screenshot is replaced, and you automatically advance to the next screenshot in the Topic. Note that if there are multiple paths in the Topic then the **Re-recorder** will record one path before looping back to re-record the screenshots in the Alternative Path. The *Alternative* icon will be highlighted if you are in an Alternative Path.

5. Repeat Steps 3 and 4 for all additional screenshots that you want to replace.
6. When you have finished replacing the screenshots, click on the **Finish** button in the Recorder window.

Note that you would normally only want to use the **Re-record Topic** function if you have a non-trivial exercise, and want to replace all or most of the screenshots in the Topic. If you only want to replace one or two specific screenshots then it is easier to use the **Replace screenshot** function explained above.

Editing screenshots

An alternative to recapturing a screenshot is to simply edit it (or "Photoshop" it, as common parlance now has it). Although this can be fiddly (and requires pixel-perfect editing), it can sometimes save you a lot of time when compared to recapturing the screenshot—especially if you would need to set up data all over again to get the application in a state where you can capture the screenshot that you need. Another case would be where you need to remove sensitive data.

> I would advise against editing screenshots to "pixilate" or "blur" sections of the screen to obscure sensitive information. I would also advise against drawing borders around sections of the screen to which you want to draw the trainee's attention. Remember that you are trying to match reality as closely as possible. More judicious selection of data can eliminate the need to edit screenprints to remove unwanted or unwelcome data, and Explanation Frames can be used to draw the trainee's attention to specific information on the screen.

Choosing an image editing application

Before you can edit a screenshot you need to tell UPK which image editing application you are going to use. Although you can use almost any image editor, you should make sure that it can handle Bitmaps correctly, as UPK saves the `.png` format screenshot as a `.bmp` file, and passes this to the image editor, and then converts the edited `.bmp` file back to a `.png` image before inserting it back into the Topic.

In the absence of anything else, UPK will find **Microsoft Paint** on a Windows PC, but Paint is not particularly good for image editing. **Microsoft PhotoEditor** works well if you have a copy of that (it used to be bundled free with Windows, but was dropped in later versions). I have tried using **Macromedia Fireworks**, but could not get it to copy my changes back into UPK. I tend to use **TechSmith SnagIt Editor** Version 9, which is relatively inexpensive, and very easy to use.

To specify your default image editor, carry out the steps described below:

1. From the main **Developer** screen, select menu option **Tools | Options**.
2. Select the **Developer | General** category of options. The **General Developer Settings** screen is displayed, as shown in the screenshot below:

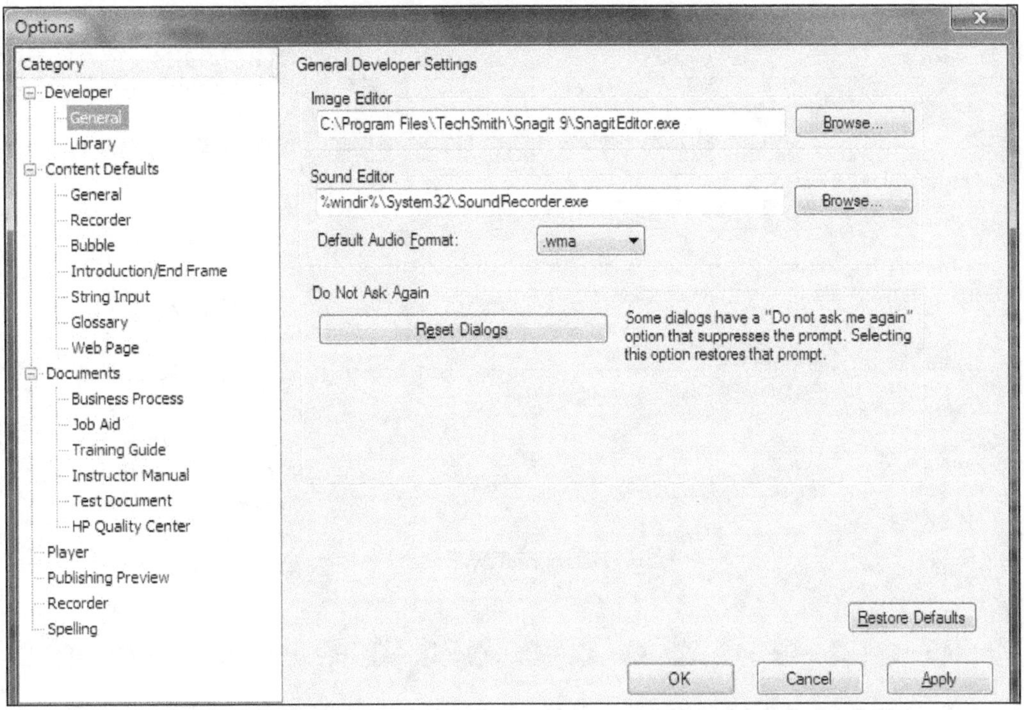

3. Click on the **Browse** button to the right of the **Image Editor** field to navigate to and select the program file for the image editor that you want to use.
4. Click on the **OK** button to save your setting.

Editing a screenshot

Editing a screenshot is fortunately very easy, and can be done directly from the **Topic Editor**.

One of the problems with our sample exercise is that the screenshots taken by UPK include the bar cursor (which indicates the insertion point) in the input fields. This can be distracting, especially for string input actions, where the cursor may not be completely masked by the Action Area. If you look at Frame **4** in our original recording, you will see that the screenshot includes the cursor (immediately after the text "Dick" in the **First name** field), and that it protrudes out slightly below our Action Area, as shown in the screenshot below. We should remove this.

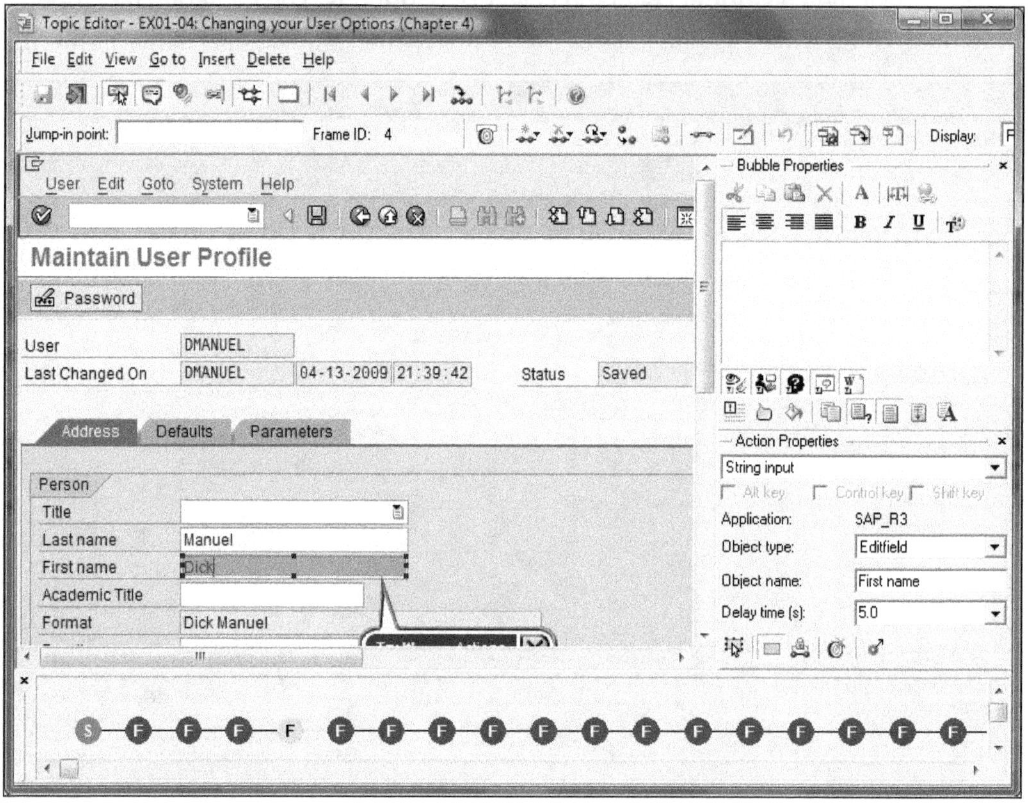

> This may seem overly fiddly, but bear in mind that we are trying to create a quality exercise that matches reality as closely as possible. You may not think this level of attention to detail is entirely necessary, but don't say you weren't advised.

To edit a screenshot, carry out the steps described below.

1. Open up the Topic in the **Topic Editor**.
2. Select the Frame that contains the screenshot that you want to edit.
3. On the *Editing Toolbar*, click on the **Edit screenshot** button ( ). Your image editing application is started (it is best that it is not open already), and you are passed into it, as shown in the following screenshot:

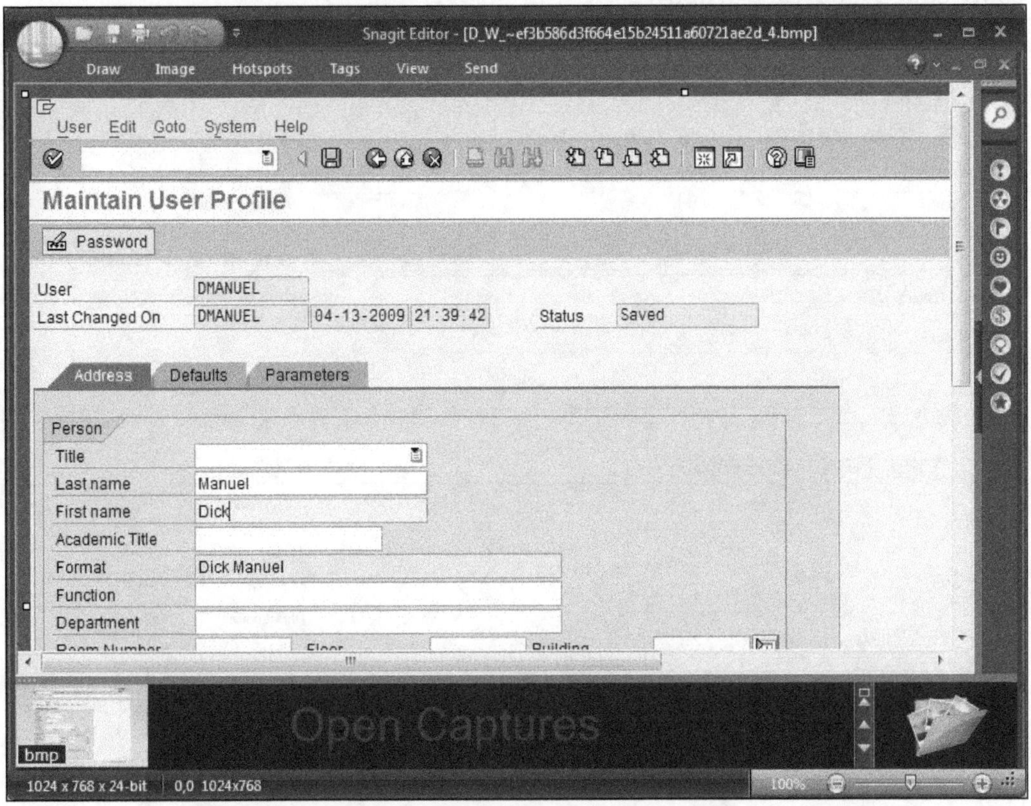

(Note that the file name in the window title bar shows a `.bmp` file.)

4. Edit the screenshot as required. How you do this will depend on your image editing software.

5. Once you have finished editing the screenshot, **close** your image editing application.
6. In response to the message asking you if you want to save your changes to the `.bmp` file, click on **Yes**. You are passed back into UPK.

> It is recommended that your image editing application is not open before you click on the **Edit screenshot** button, and that you **close** it again once you have editing the screenshot. If you do not close the image editing application then the updated image will not be saved back to UPK.

You will now see that the screenshot has been changed in the **Topic Editor**. The example below shows our edited Frame **4**. The cursor is now no longer visible, as we edited it out Step 3, above.

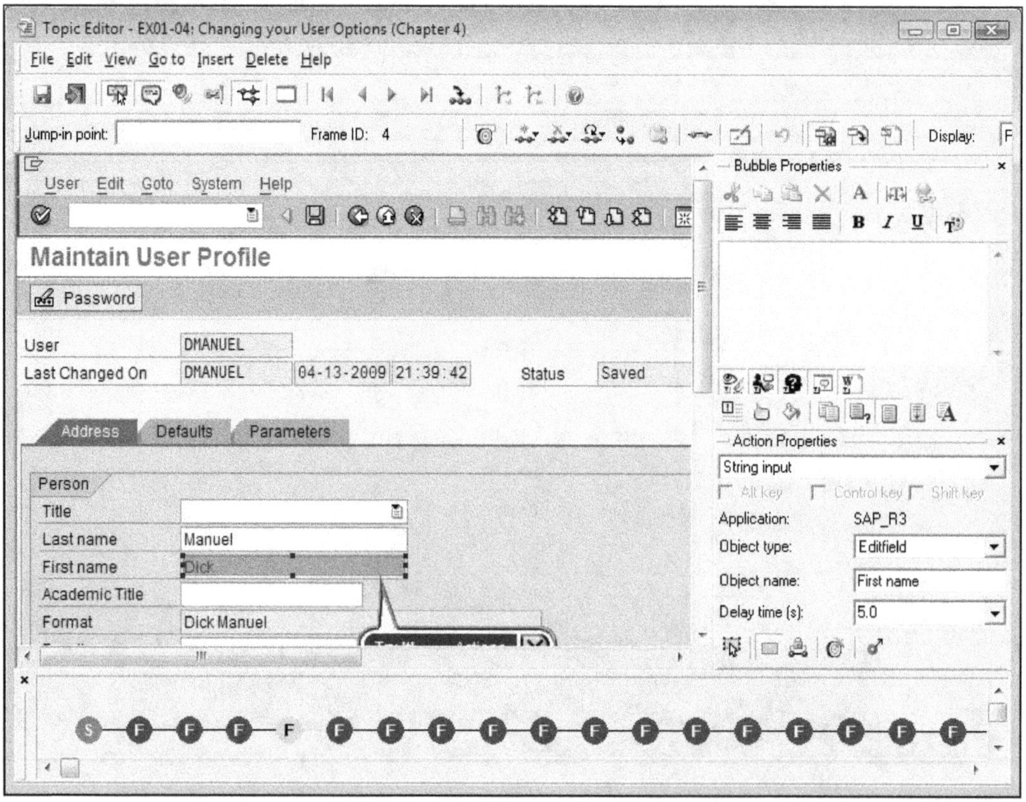

Deleting Frames

It is a good practice to "over-capture" when recording. Capture every single thing that you do, regardless of whether you think that you will need it in the final recording. This is a useful tactic, especially if you are recording a difficult-to-reproduce scenario, or consuming data that is time-consuming to set up. Alternatively, you may adjust some element on the screen (such as resizing or repositioning a dialog box) to create a more effective screenshot, but do not want this adjustment to be included in the final recording.

In these cases (and no doubt in countless other cases), you may need to delete a Frame from your recording.

In our sample exercise, we have a further example of where it is desirable to delete a Frame. When we recorded the Action to select a date format, the date format that we want the trainee to select is at the top of the drop-down list, and is initially not visible. We therefore had to scroll up in this list, and then select the required entry, as shown in the following screenshot:

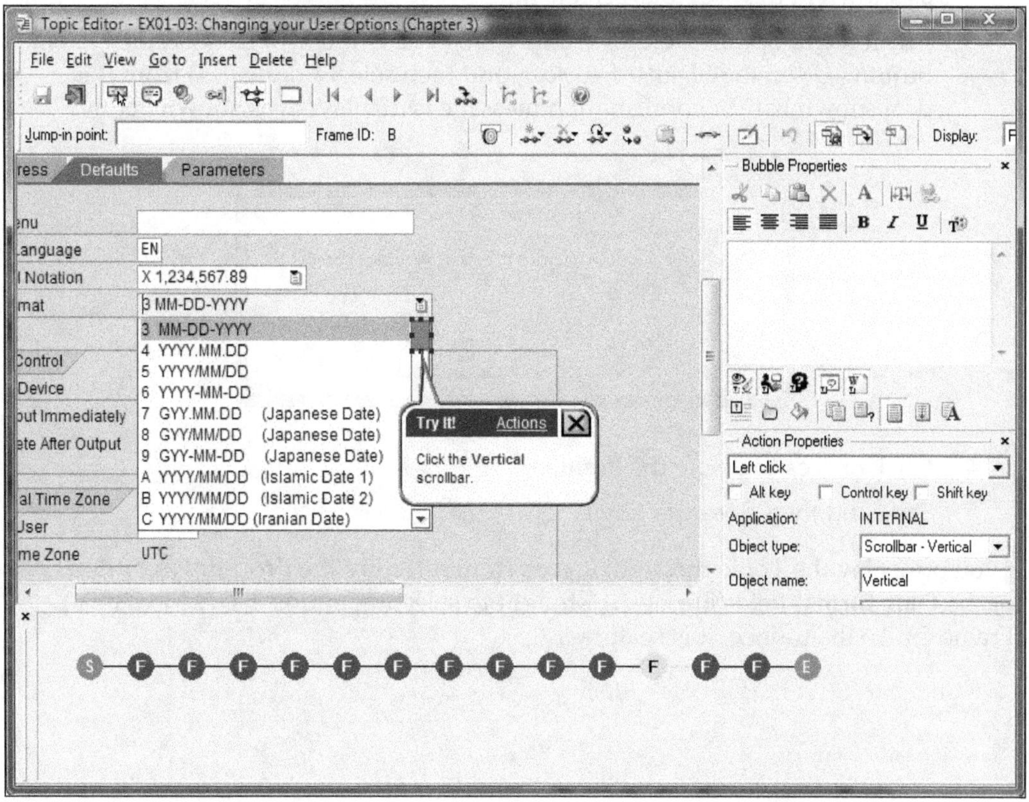

Our exercise would be more effective if the drop-down list showed the required entry when we first opened it, so the trainee can just click on the required entry.

Although this is not strictly "as we did it', or "true to life", this will not be evident in our final recording. It is important, when building exercises, to think about exactly what you need to teach your trainees. The chances are (in this example) that our trainees are already familiar with scrollbars, so having them scroll up is not really a "value-add" learning activity. In addition, consider *Know It!* mode—do you really want to test your trainee's ability to correctly use the scrollbar? Probably not.

So, for our sample exercise, we will remove this Frame (on which the trainee is required to scroll up) from our recording.

To delete a Frame from a recording, carry out the steps described below:

1. Open the Topic from which you want to delete the Frame, in the **Topic Editor**.
2. Click on the Frame that you want to delete. In our example, this is Frame **B**, as shown in the previous screenshot.
3. Select menu option **Delete** | **Frame** (). (You could also click on the **Delete** button () on the *Standard Toolbar*, and then select **Frame** () from the drop-down list.) A confirmation message is displayed, as shown below:

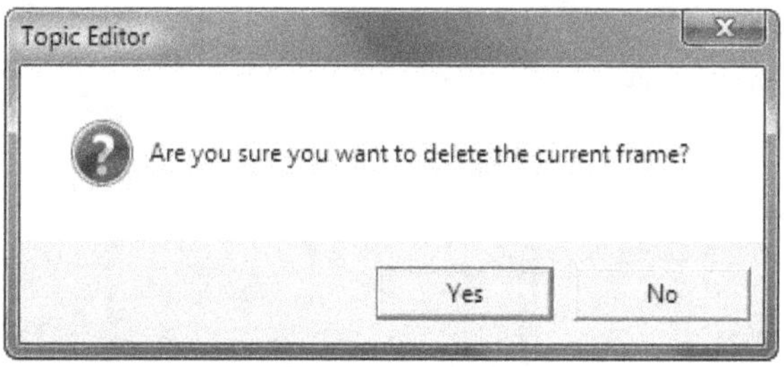

4. Click on **Yes** to delete the Frame.
5. Save and then close the Topic.

If you now play the Topic through, it goes from selecting the drop-down button for the **Date format** field (Frame A), straight to selecting option **1 DD.MM.YYYY** (Frame C). To the trainee, it is seamless.

Note that you cannot delete a Frame that has Alternative Actions recorded for it. In this case, you need to first delete the Alternative Action and then delete the Frame, once it only has only one Action associated with it. The same applies to Frames with Alternative Paths (including Decision Frames); you must first delete the Alternative Path. Alternative Actions and Alternative Paths are described in Chapter 8, *Allowing Alternatives*.

At this point, it is worth mentioning another opportunity for *streamlining* recordings that include string input actions. Typically, in an application, you need to position the cursor in a field (either by clicking in it or by pressing the *Tab* key—possibly several times to get to the correct field), and then enter a value. If you provide a true-to-life recording, then you also record the action of navigating into the field, as well as the action of entering the text. This can slow down the *flow* of the simulation, and (again) provide unnecessary opportunities to slip up in *Know It!* mode. You therefore might want to remove these "navigation" steps, so that the recording simply progresses from string input to string input. **Yes**, it is less "realistic", but again, you need to consider what you need to teach the trainees. Clearly, if identifying the correct field to enter the value into is also a skill then you should include this step, but in most cases, it simply adds "clutter" to the exercise.

However, there is one word of caution with this approach. Some applications (such as SAP and Oracle) identify the "active" field (that is, the field that has focus, and into which the text will be entered) by shading it, or otherwise highlighting it. If you remove the action to click in the correct field, then you must be careful to ensure that the field into which the text is being entered (as the string input action) is indeed the active field. This creates a further problem, in that in *Know It?* mode, the field into which the trainee needs to enter the value is highlighted for them, which may be a bit more of a "clue" than you want to give them on what is effectively a test. Again, think carefully about exactly what you need to teach your trainees.

Summary

Although it is relatively quick to *record* a simulation, a simulation can hardly be called "finished" once it is recorded (despite what the Oracle salesperson may tell you). If you are extremely lucky, the simulation will actually *work* as recorded, but even if it does work, you will want to edit it to improve the overall quality of the simulation.

Fortunately, UPK makes it easy to change just about every aspect of a recording. Screenshots can be changed, Action Areas adjusted, Action Types changed, and just about every conceivable change can be made to the Bubble Text.

Much of this editing work is painstakingly detailed, but if we are to create *quality* training exercises, then this work is absolutely essential.

Editing takes place in the **Topic Editor**, which provides the following key components:

- The **Screenshot** pane that shows the captured screenshot for the Frame that is currently being edited, and the content and position of the Bubble.
- The **Frame Navigation** pane, which shows the path(s) through the recorded Frames.
- The **Bubble Properties** pane, which can be used to select Template Text, enter Custom Text, format these texts (and the Bubble containing them) and tag text for different modes.
- The **Action Properties** pane, which specifies the Action Type and Object Type captured during the recording. You can change these to influence the Template Text used.
- The **Sound Properties** pane (covered in Chapter 11, *Incorporating Sound into Your Topics*), which can be used to assign sound files to Frames.

In the next chapter, we will look at how to insert our newly edited simulation into an Outline, so that we can play it, which we'll look at how to do in the chapter after that.

5

Building an Outline

In Chapter 2, *Organizing your Library*, we looked at the environment in which the developer works. In that chapter, we also saw the split between the Library that the developer sees, and the Outline that the trainee sees. In this chapter, we will examine how to build Outlines.

In this chapter you will learn:

- The differences (and similarities) between Modules and Sections
- How UPK 3.5 differs from OnDemand 8.7 with regard to Outlines
- How to build an Outline by using Modules, Sections, and Topics

Outlines versus the Library

One of the key changes introduced in OnDemand Version 9.1 is the distinction between the Library, seen by the developer, and the Outline, seen by the trainees. This is a significant conceptual change from how OnDemand 8.7 and earlier worked. Before looking at how OnDemand 9.1/UPK 3.5 works, it is worth looking back at how OnDemand 8.7 worked. This will serve two purposes—First, it will provide a useful reference point for developers familiar with OnDemand 8.7. Second, it will provide some context for our examination of UPK and help to explain why UPK does some of the things that it does.

In OnDemand 8.7, the concept of a "Library" was fulfilled by the Title. It was technically possible to have multiple Titles, although OnDemand did expect all simulations for a given targeted application to be contained within the same Title. Therefore, developers would often work within a single Title. The Title did not contain folders in the way that the UPK Library does. Instead, the developer was required to use organizational elements called **Modules** and **Lessons** to group their **Topics** (simulations) into the structure in which they wanted them to be displayed to the trainee. The use of Modules, Lessons, and Topics was rigidly controlled. A Title consisted of a collection of Modules. Modules could only contain Lessons, and Lessons could only contain Topics.

When publishing one or more exercises, although it was possible to select content at the Topic, Lesson, Module, or Title level, the resulting player would always contain exactly (and only) these three (Module, Section, and Topic) key levels. Even if you only selected a single Topic for publishing, the resulting player would include the selected Topic, as well as the Lesson and Module in which it was contained.

OnDemand Version 9.x relaxed this arrangement somewhat. The Title disappeared, effectively being replaced by the Library, and the Lesson element was renamed to Section. Most significantly, Sections could now contain Modules (that's right—they can include what was once a "higher-level" element—hence the renaming), and Modules could also contain Topics. This change was significant, as it meant that it was finally possible to move beyond the limitation of a strict three-level (Module, Section, and Topic), hierarchy by nesting Modules to any level necessary. This meant that there was no longer any distinction between the way a Module works and the way that a Section works. The only difference between the two is the color of the icon in the Library: Modules are purple and Sections are blue (although even this small distinction disappears in the Player, where they are both purple).

UPK 3.x uses the same Library concept as OnDemand 9.x. There have been no significant changes to its structure or use.

As we saw in Chapter 2, *Organizing your Library*, the developer can organize their content objects into folders in any way that they see fit. It is no longer necessary for Topics that are to appear within the same Section in the Player to be stored in the same folder within the Library. Instead, an **Outline** is used to organize Modules, Sections, and Topics into a structure for presentation to the trainee, regardless of the folder within the Library in which these Outline Elements are located. You could have the Modules in one folder, the Sections in another, and the Topics spread all over the place (although this would probably be a little confusing).

In UPK 3.5, you publish a specific Outline Element - regardless of whether this is a Module or a Section, or the level within the Outline hierarchy at which it appears. UPK will then create a Player (or other deployment format) that contains as many hierarchical levels as the Outline Element that was selected for publishing.

Organizing your Topics

Now that you understand the limitations (or *lack* of limitations if you are coming from a background of OnDemand 8.7 or earlier) of Outline Elements, you need to decide how you want to structure your Outline (just as in Chapter 3, *Organizing Your Library* you decided how to organize your Library).

There are a few key points to bear in mind while choosing an Outline, which are as follows:

- An Outline is for the benefit of the trainee. You should structure your Outline in a way that makes sense to your trainees.
- You can have as many Outlines as you like. An Outline is really just a "publishable unit", and if different trainees would benefit from different Outlines, then you should create different Outlines. There are some limits on the use of multiple Players if you choose to link your Player to an application (as described in Chapter 6, *Publishing Your Content*), but it is perfectly acceptable to publish distinct Players for different groups of trainees.
- Any given Topic can appear in multiple Outline Elements. If you want to publish separate Players for each user group, and want to include some common Topics in all every Player, then you can do this and without having to duplicate the Topics.
- Related to this last point, you can include Outlines in other Outlines (strictly speaking, Outlines are just Outline Elements themselves). This means that if you create a separate Outline for each user group, you can also combine all of these individual Outlines into a single, "master" Outline for integrating into your application help.

How you organize your Outline(s) is entirely up to you and your individual requirements. Just be sure that you use a structure that makes sense to your trainees. Some options are:

- Creating a single Outline for each application and including everything to do with that application within it. You may want to use one Outline element per application *area* if your application is a particularly large one.
- Creating separate Outline for each of the application's functional areas. Note that if you want to provide context-sensitive help in Oracle or SAP, then you can only link to a single Outline. In this case, all of the content for the application needs to be in this single Outline.
- Creating an Outline for each user group, which contains only the content that those users need. (Note that you also have the possibility to publish by role, as explained in Chapter 6, *Publishing your Content*, or filter your Topics based on the user's role, as explained in Chapter 10, *Adding Value in the Player*.)
- Creating a separate Outline for each training course. Given that role-based training is now almost taken for granted, this option and the preceding one (creating an outline for each user group) may well be the same.

It is worth consulting your user base to see which option they find most intuitive. Perhaps dummying up a few options for them to try would help.

Although the Outline Elements can be nested to as many levels as you like, in any combination of Modules and Sections, and Topics can appear at any level in the hierarchy, some degree of restraint is advised. When the trainee first displays the Outline (for example, in the Player), all levels of the hierarchy will be collapsed. The trainee will be required to expand their way down the hierarchy to reach the required content. Having too many levels, or having Topics at inconsistent levels, will simply annoy trainees.

In general, I advocate a three-level hierarchy for training content, where the first level of the hierarchy (a Module) represents the course, the second level (a Section) represents the lessons (or sections, or units, depending on your terminology) within the course, and the lowest level represents the actual exercises (Topics) themselves. This works very well for relatively small, self-contained courses, although you may need to expand this model if you want to build out an entire training curriculum. We will be using this three-level, course-based structure when building our example Outline.

Building an Outline

Let's build an Outline to house the Topic that we recorded in Chapter 3, *Recording a Simulation*. We will create an Outline for a single course that contains two lessons, with three simulations in each lesson.

Step 1: Creating an Outline

An Outline is simply an Outline Element (either a Module or a Section) that contains Topics and (optionally) other Outline Elements. Creating an Outline, therefore, effectively consists of creating a Module or Section, and then inserting the Topics and additional Modules or Sections within it. For our sample exercise, we will use a Module for the highest level of the Outline.

To create an Outline, carry out the following steps:

1. In the Library, select the folder in which you want to create the Outline. As explained earlier, it is advisable to keep the outline elements in the same folder as the Topics that they contain, unless you have a good reason for not doing so (for example, if you have a habit of sharing Topics across Outlines, or because you want to provide different levels of security for Outline Elements and Topics in UPK 3.5). For our example, we have a folder named `GSAP-002 Introduction to SAP`, into which we placed our initial Topic. We'll store our Outline Elements in this same folder.

2. Select menu option **File | New | Module** (icon). The **New Module** dialog box is displayed, as shown in the following screenshot:

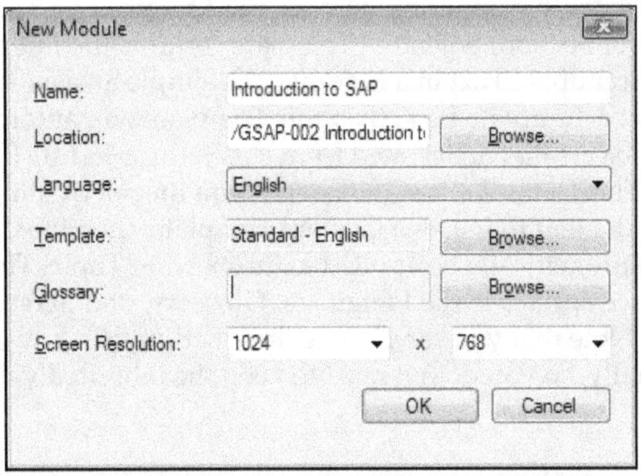

3. In the **Name** field, enter the name of the Module. For our example, because this is an Outline for a course we will give it the name of our course, which is **Introduction to SAP**.
4. The **Location** field will default to the current folder. This is the one that you selected in Step 1, if you've been following along correctly. You can select any other folder by clicking on **Browse** and navigating to and selecting the required location, if necessary.
5. In the **Language** field, you can change the language of the spell-checker that will be used when spell-checking the Module—but not the content objects within the Module; they have their own language definition, as we shall see.
6. The **Template** field defines the Template that should be used with the Module. If you have a Custom Template, then you can select it here. Custom Templates are described in exhaustive detail in Chapter 12, *Configuring UPK*. For now, we'll just accept the default of **Standard - English**.

> **Why do we need Templates for Modules? There's no Bubble!**
>
> You're probably wondering why we need to specify a Template for a Module (or Section) when the Template controls the Bubble Text and there is no Bubble Text in a Module. The simple answer is: *inheritance*. If you select a Template here, then this Template will automatically be used for any objects that are created from *within* this Module (in the Outline Editor). This last point is significant. If you link an existing Topic into an Outline Element that uses a Custom Template, then the Custom Template will *not* automatically be applied to the existing Topic. The same inheritance applies to the **Language**, **Glossary**, and **Screen Resolution** settings. Note that you can change these settings for any element individually, so you do not need to keep the inherited value.

7. If you have an existing Glossary defined, then you can use the **Browse** button for the **Glossary** field to navigate to and select it. Glossaries are covered in Chapter 9, *Adding Value to your Topics*, so we will leave this field blank for now.
8. The **Screen Resolution** should be set to be the same as the Topics that will be contained within the Module. Note that this only serves as a reminder. A different resolution can be specified for the Topics recorded from within this Outline Element.
9. Once you have specified all required information (Steps 3 to 9), click on **OK**. The Module is created and opened for editing in the *Outline Editor*.

The *Outline Editor* appears as another tab within the main *UPK Developer* screen, as shown in the example below. Note that a new toolbar is available. We'll look at the various buttons on this toolbar as we need them.

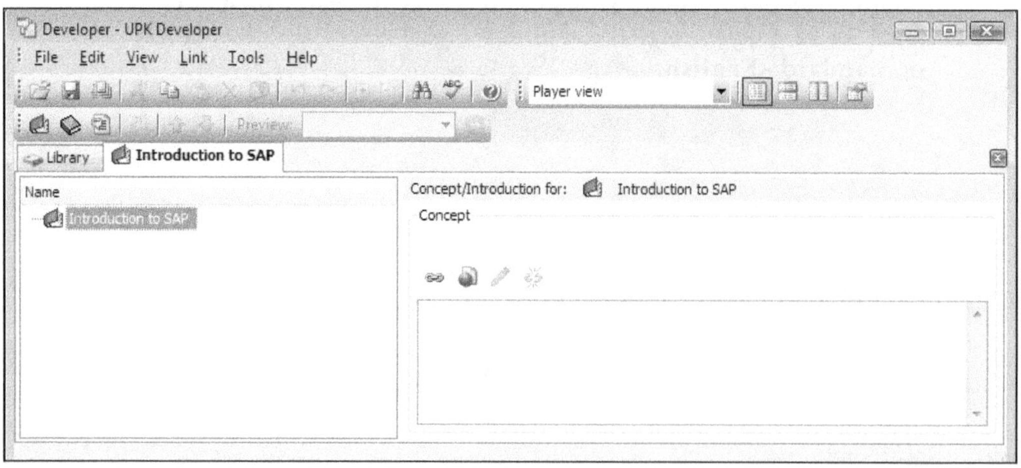

Step 2: Inserting Outline Elements into an Outline

Next, let's insert the two Sections into our Module.

To insert Outline Elements into an existing Outline, carry out the steps described below:

1. Select the Outline Element below which you want to insert the new Outline Element. In our example, we only have one Outline Element, our Module.
2. Click on either the **Link New Module** button ( ) or the **Link New Section** button ( ) depending on what type of Outline Element you want to insert. For our exercise, we will insert a Section.

> Do not use menu option **File | New | Module** (or **File | New | Section**) here as this will create a new Module or Section, but will not automatically insert it into the Outline Element that you are currently editing.

3. A new Outline Element is added below the selected element. This is given an initial name of **New Section** (or **New Module**, as appropriate). However, the name is open for editing. Change this to the required name for the Section. For our example, we will use **Lesson 1: SAP Basics** for the name of our first Section.
4. Press *Enter* to confirm your new name.
5. Repeat Steps 1 to 4 for all additional Outline Elements that you want to add to the Outline. For our example, we will insert another Section, and name this **Lesson 2: Working in SAP**.

Our example Outline now looks as follows:

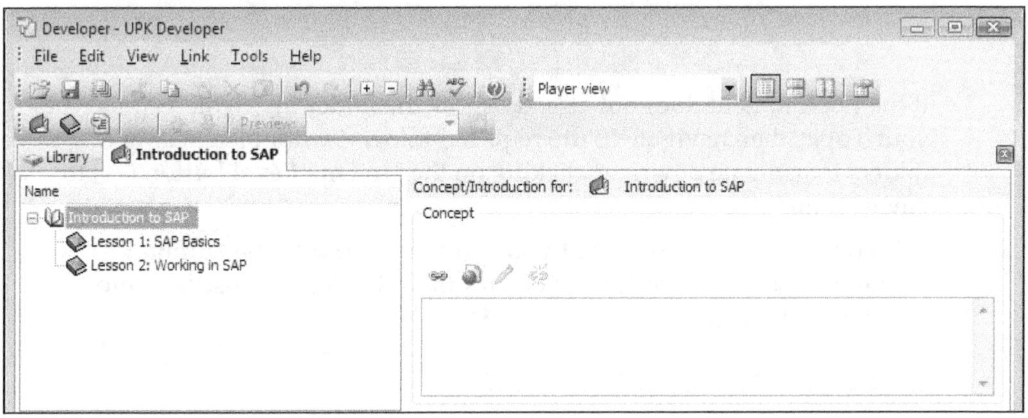

Note that the Sections have exactly the same attributes as Modules: **Language**, **Template**, **Glossary**, and **Screen Resolution**. You can change these by displaying the Properties for the Section and specifying the required values as explained for Modules.

Step 3: Inserting a Topic

Now that we have our Sections in place, we're ready to insert the Topic that we recorded in Chapter 3, *Recording a Simulation*.

To insert Topics into an Outline Element, carry out the steps described below:

1. Click on the Section (or Module, depending on the structure that you have chosen) within which you want the Topic to appear. In our example, this is **Lesson 1: SAP Basics**.
2. Select menu option **Link | Existing Document**. The **Link Existing Document** window is displayed, as shown in the following screenshot:

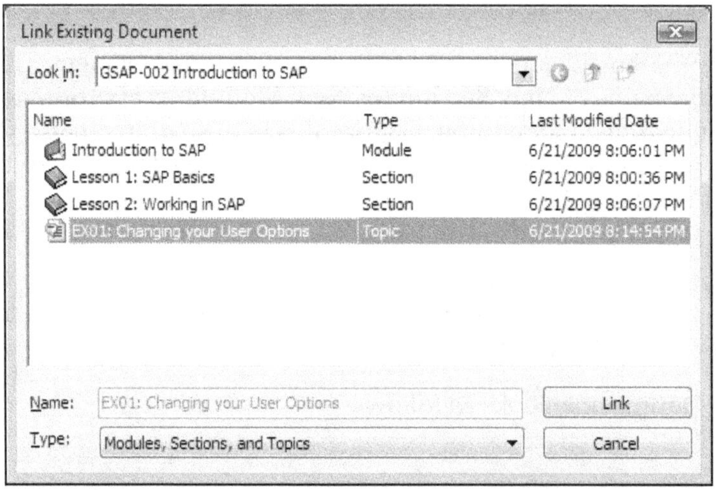

3. If the **Look in** field does not already show the folder into which you saved your Topic, then navigate to the required folder, by double-clicking on folders to navigate down, or clicking on the **Up One Level** button ( ) to navigate up.
4. Click on the existing Topic that you want to insert into the Outline Element, to select it, and then click on **Link**. The Topic is inserted into the Outline Element.

Our Outline now looks as shown in the following screenshot:

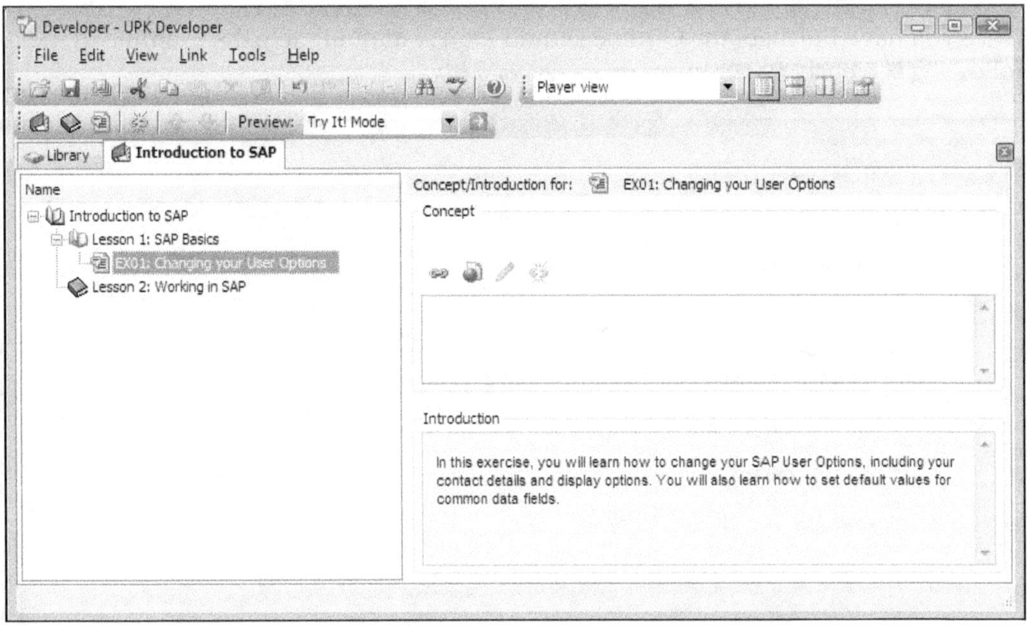

Step 4: Inserting Topic placeholders

Although we have technically done as much as we need to with our Outline, we'll finish things up by inserting placeholders for the remaining Topics that we will create for this course. Building the full Outline even before you have recorded the Topics is a good way of making sure that you don't miss anything. It also allows you to gauge the full content of the Outline before you start work. If you are coordinating the work of several developers, this is useful for identifying where everyone's work will go. You can also assign the empty Topics to specific individuals for recording , via the **Assigned to** property.

To insert Topic placeholders, carry out the steps described below:

1. Click on the Module or Section within which you want the empty Topic to appear.
2. Click on the **Link New Topic** button ().
3. A new Topic is inserted, and given an initial name of **New Topic**. Change this name to the correct name of the Topic. For the Topic names for our example, refer to the screenshot of the completed Outline, below. Press *Enter* to confirm the new name.

4. Repeat Steps 1 to 3 for all additional Topics that you want to add to the Outline.

Once you have finished, the Outline should look something like the example in the following screenshot:

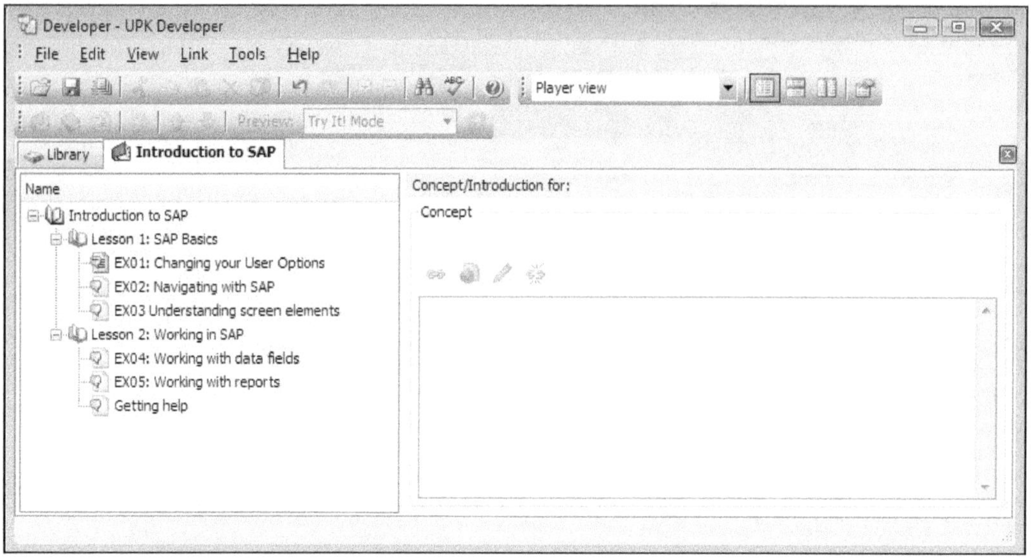

Note that the icons for empty Topics ( ) are different from the icon used for recorded Topics ( ). This allows you to easily identify what is left to be done.

When you are ready to record the simulation for one of these empty Topics, simply select it and then click the Record button ( ) on the *Standard* toolbar (you can also double-click on the topic). You'll then be taken directly to the Recorder. Refer to Chapter 3, *Recording a Simulation* for additional instructions on recording Topics.

For now, we are finished so we can click on the **Save** button ( ) to save the Outline, and then close the Outline Editor tabbed page.

Adjusting the Outline

So, we now have a working Outline. Or do we? There is actually a problem with this outline. However, this will not become apparent until we publish it. So for the sake of illustration, we will fast-forward several chapters and assume that we now have a fully-populated Outline. The following screenshot shows our finished Outline (so you're also getting a sneak peek of where we're going!):

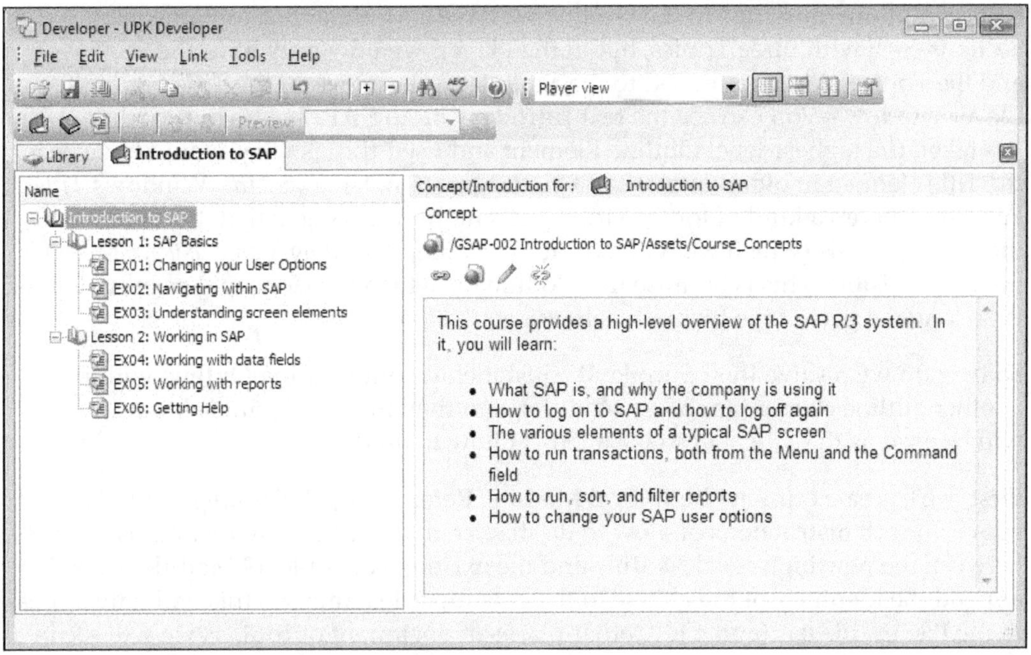

Now let's look at how this appears in the Player:

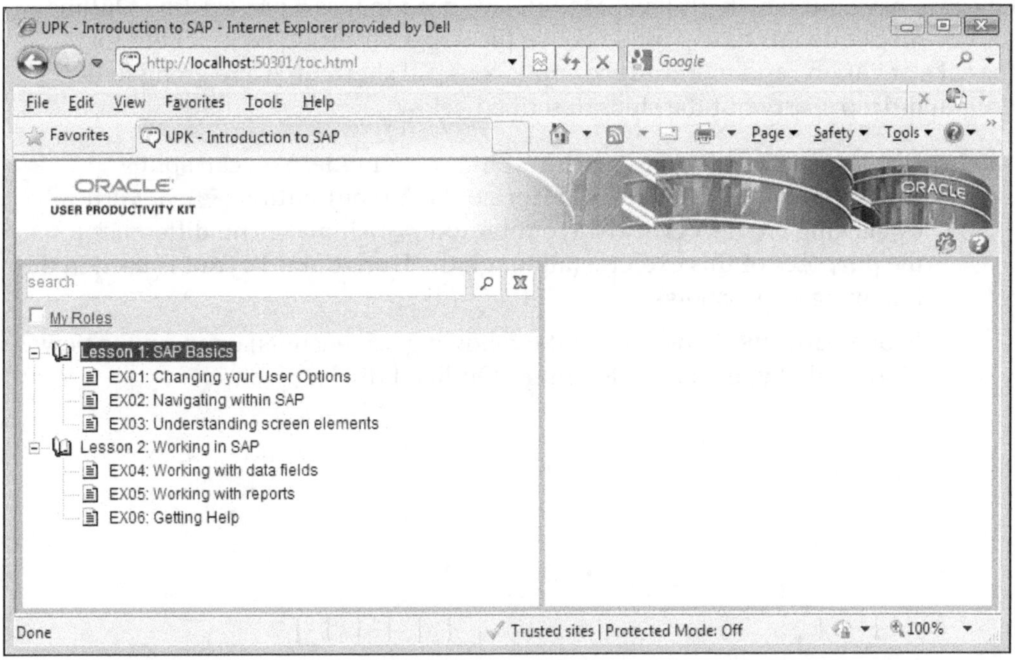

Notice anything missing? In the Outline we have a Module that contains two Sections each with three Topics, but in the Player, we now only have the Sections and the Topics. What happened to the Module? Take a look at the Title bar of the Player window—you can see the text **Introduction to SAP**. This is our Module. UPK has taken the highest-level Outline Element and used this as what would have been the Title element in older versions of OnDemand (OnDemand *Title*: Windows *Title* Bar—see, there's a kind of logic to it). What's more worrying is that, the content of the Concept pane (which we will look at in Chapter 9, *Adding Value to your Topics*) is no longer visible. This is because the Module for which the Concept has been defined is no longer a part of the hierarchy shown on the left.

So how do we resolve this? Simple. We just include our existing Outline within another outline element (another Module), and then that new (outer) Module will be used as the Title. Let's take a look at how to do this.

First, we'll create our new high-level Module. Refer to *Step 1: Creating an Outline* above, for full instructions on how to do this. To make it easier to distinguish between the new high-level Module and the existing course-level Module, we will append the identifier of the course to the new module name. As this will only appear in the Player title bar (and a few other places in document output, as we will see in Chapter 6, *Publishing your Content*), this is not too intrusive. We will therefore use a Module name of **GSAP-002 Introduction to SAP**.

Once we have our new high-level Module, we need to insert our existing Outline into it. We can do this as explained above (in Step 3: Inserting a Topic) but for the sake of variety, and to introduce you to a useful shortcut, we're going to use drag-and-drop. Carry out the steps described below:

1. Display the **Developer** screen, in split-screen mode. You can split horizontally by clicking on the **Horizontal Layout** button (), or vertically by clicking on the **Vertical Layout** button () - it makes no difference for the purposes of this exercise (although the **Horizontal Layout** is used in the following screenshots).
2. In one pane (the upper one in the following screenshots) open up the new Module that you just created in the Outline Editor.

3. In the other pane (the lower one in the following screenshot) open the Library and navigate to the folder containing all of the content objects that we have created so far. Your screen should now look similar to the example shown next:

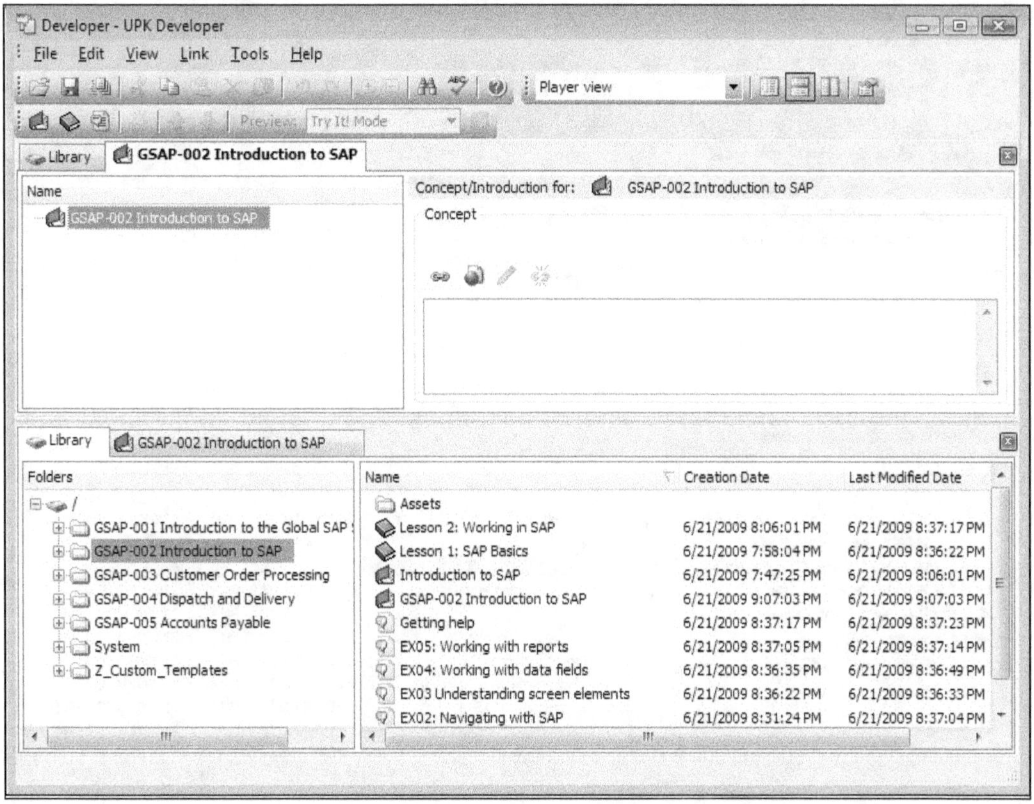

4. In the Library pane, click on the original course Module (**Introduction to SAP**) and drag this onto the *Outline* pane. As you hover the Module over its new location, UPK will indicate where it will be inserted, by the text **<documents will be inserted here>**, as shown in the following example. This allows you to make sure that you get your indentation correct.

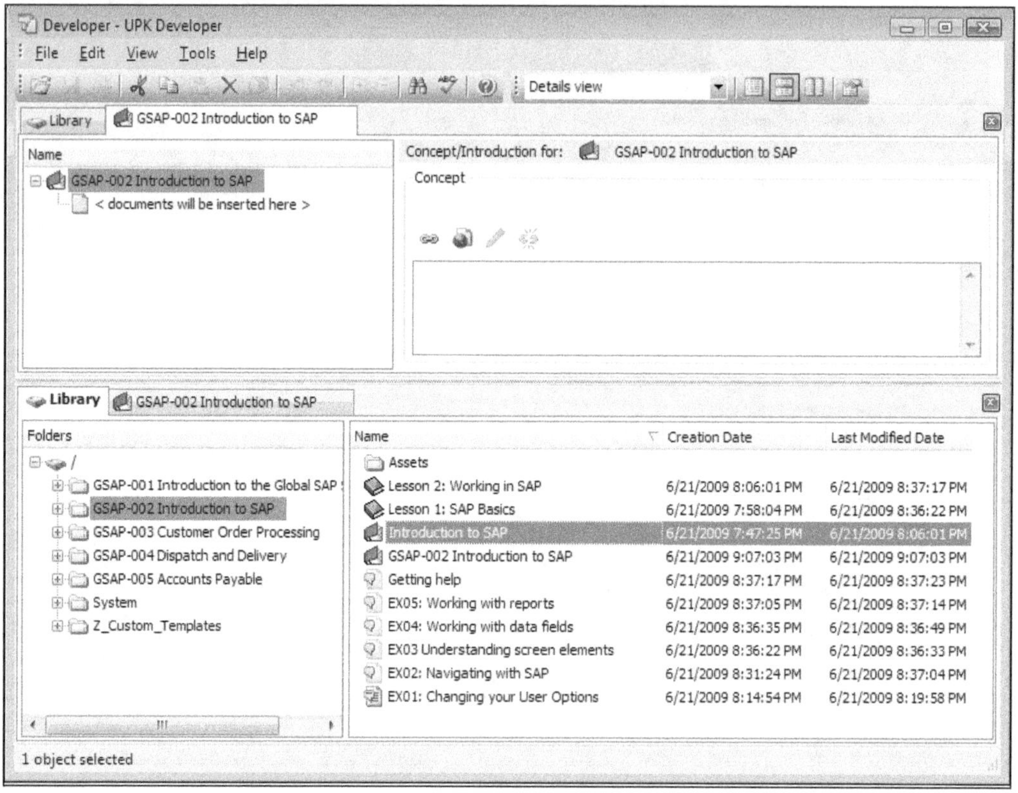

> You can use this same drag-and-drop approach to insert any kind of element in an Outline. You can even drag from one Outline to another.

5. Click on the **Save** button to save your changes to the new Module, close the Outline Editor tabbed page, and then click on the **Single Layout** button ( ) to exit from split-screen view. Open up the new Module (**GSAP-002 Introduction to SAP**), and the Outline should now appear as shown in the following screenshot:

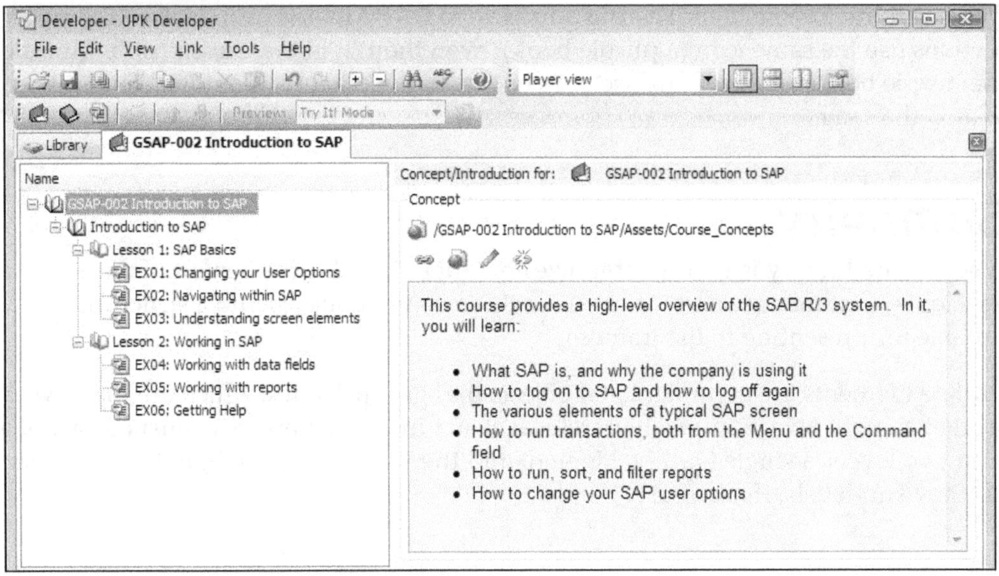

We have now created an additional Module that contains nothing apart from the original course Module. We have given this new Module the same name as the course Module, but you could also use a more generic name (say, of "End User Training")—just use whatever you want to appear in the Player window title bar. In the example, the title bar now contains what we want it to, and the course concepts are correctly displayed, as shown in the following screenshot:

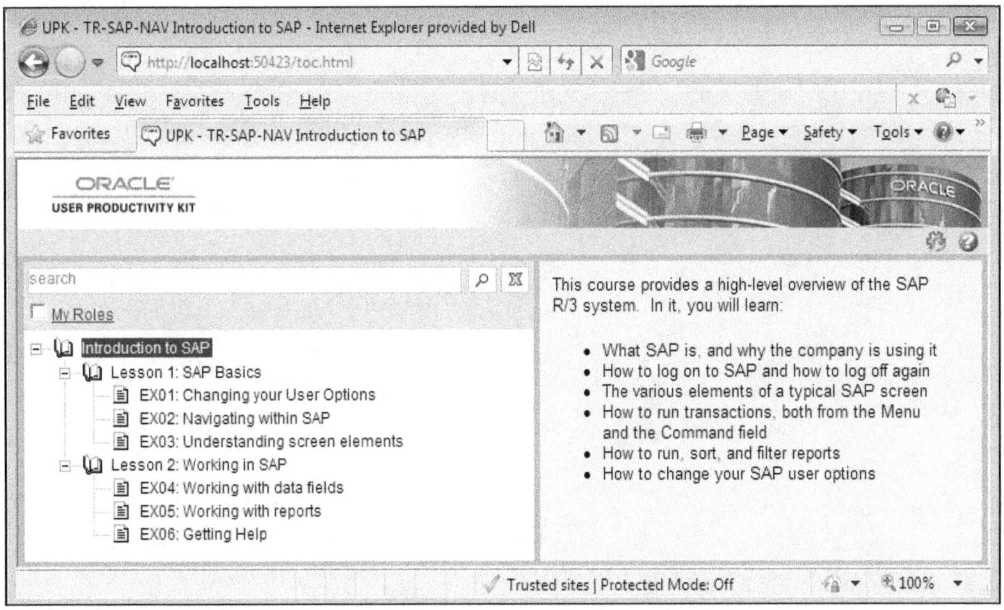

One last thing to note here: The **Introduction to SAP** Module and the two *Lesson* Sections use the same icon (a purple book), even though in the Outline only Modules use purple books and Sections use blue books. In the Player, all outline elements are treated the same.

Summary

Whereas the Library is used to organize content objects for the benefit of the developer, Outlines are used to organize these content objects into a structure suitable for presenting to the trainees.

Outline Elements are organizational objects that group Topics, which are the lowest level of content objects, into a hierarchical structure. This hierarchy must consist of at least two levels: a single Outline Element and the Topic(s) within it, but can consist of many sub-levels, if necessary.

6

Publishing Your Content

In this chapter, we will look at how to publish the Topics and Outlines that you have created. We will also look at some of the things that you should always do before publishing your content, in order to check that your deliverables are of the best quality possible.

This chapter also takes a close look at the available output formats, and provides examples for each of them. If you are not sure which format best suits your needs, or you just want to see what else is available to you, then you may find this chapter to be a useful reference.

Bear in mind that although publishing will always be the last thing that you do, you will also publish your content at regular periods throughout the development process, to check your work, or to provide review copies to reviewers, and so on. Hence, it helps to have a solid understanding of the options available when publishing your content, before you get as far as your final delivery.

Note that you can only publish (or preview) content from an Outline. If you want to publish a Topic, you will first need to add it to an Outline Element. Refer to Chapter 5, *Building an Outline* for more information on Outlines and Outline Elements.

In this chapter, you will learn:

- How to spell-check your content
- How to test your simulations
- How to publish to online formats
- How to publish your content as documents
- How to integrate your simulations into presentations
- How to integrate your UPK environment into the application for which you have created the simulations

Pre-publication checks

Before publishing your content, there are a few things that you should always do. These are summarized in the following list, and then explained in further detail in the sections following this list.

- Perform a full spell-check on the content that you will be publishing.
- If you have defined a glossary (see Chapter 9, *Adding Value to Your Topics* for details) then re-generate the glossary links.
- Test your content in *all* of the modes in which it will be published.

You will typically do all of these things many times throughout the development process (especially the testing), but it is important to perform all of these tasks again, immediately prior to publication. This is particularly important if you are working in a multi-developer environment and will be publishing content that was created or changed by other authors, whose checks may not be as thorough as yours.

Checking your spelling

To check the spelling of a content object, select the content object in either the Library or the Outline, and then click on the **Check Spelling** button ( ). Note that you can also select a folder, an Outline Element, and/or multiple content objects, depending on what you want to spell-check. Before publishing an Outline, it is recommended that you select the highest-level element in the Outline. The spell-checker will then include all sub-elements within this, as explained below.

Once you click on the **Check Spelling** button, UPK will determine if there are any other documents related to the object(s) that you selected, and, if it finds any, will display the following dialog box:

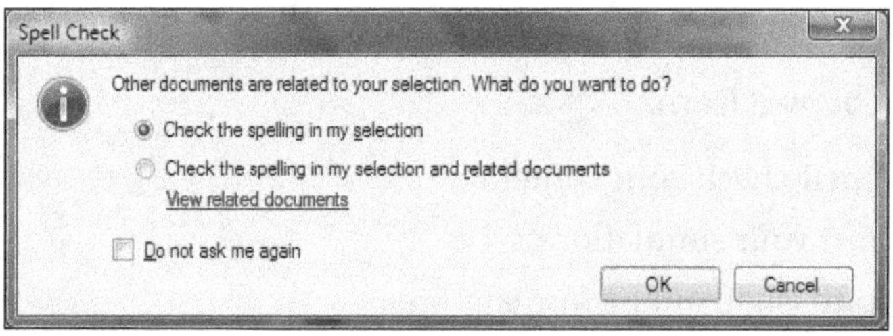

What are these related documents? If you selected an Outline Element to spell-check, then this will include all of the sub-elements within the selected element whether these are Modules, Sections, or Topics. If you want to see exactly which content objects UPK has identified, you can click on the **View related documents** link. This will display a dialog box similar to the following one:

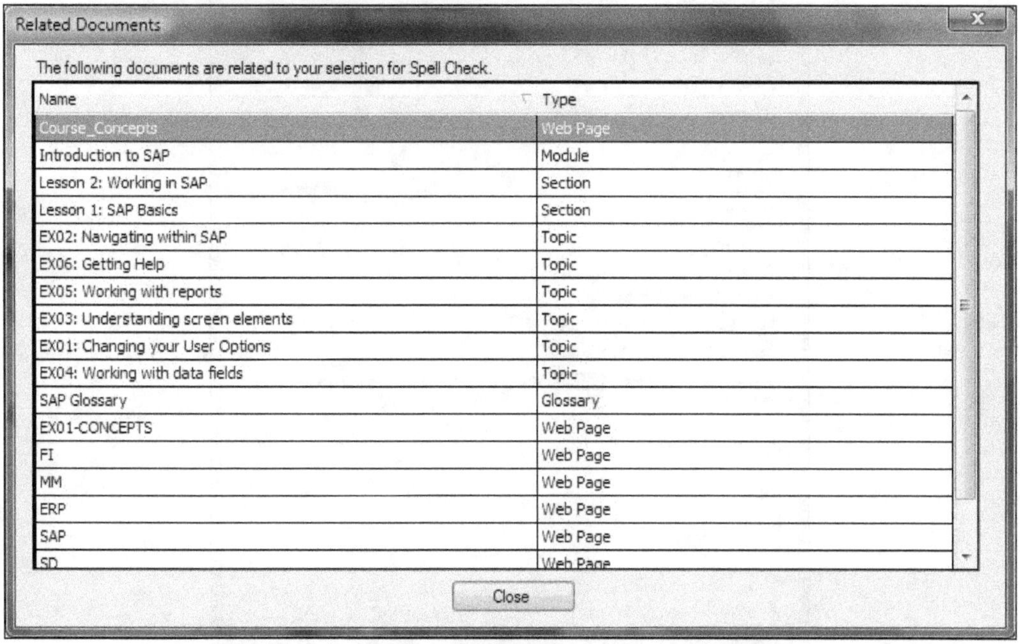

In the screenshot above, we selected a course-level element. UPK has identified several Modules, Sections, and Topics as related documents. These are the other content objects in the selected Outline. However, UPK has also identified a number of Web Pages. Where did these come from? Typically, they are Web Pages that have been attached to one of the Topics (or other elements) already identified—for example, Web Pages used in the *Concepts* pane. (Web Pages are discussed in detail in Chapter 9, *Adding Value to Your Topics*.)

UPK will also include any Glossaries that have been attached to any of the content object(s) that you are spell-checking. As the check for related documents is recursive, it will also include *all* of the Glossary entries (Web Pages) included in the Glossary (and not just the Glossary entries actually *linked* to the content object). This means that if you spell-check three Topics separately that all use the same Glossary then you will end up spell-checking the Glossary, in its entirety, three times. You can mitigate this to some degree by adding the Glossary terms to the custom dictionary the first time that you spell-check them, but UPK will still check them every time.

Choose whether or not you want your spell check to include these related documents by selecting the relevant option in the dialog box (shown earlier), and then click on **OK**. The following dialog box is displayed:

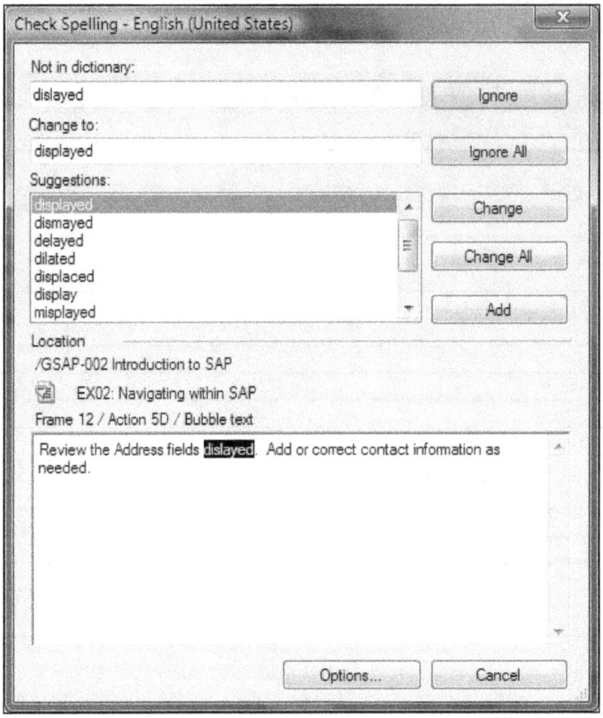

This is similar to the spell-checker in many other applications. The first input field in the dialog box is the text that the spell-checker objects to. Below this, the spell-checker provides a suggested alternative (in the **Change to** field), followed by a list of other possible alternatives, in the **Suggestions** box. You can accept the proposal (click on **Change**), select any other suggestion (by double-clicking on it in the **Suggestions** list), or simply overtype the **Change to** field with your own value. Of course, you also have the usual options of **Ignore**, **Ignore All**, **Change**, **Change All**, and **Add** (to custom dictionary).

The **Location** section of the **Check Spelling** dialog box contains much more useful information. The first line of this specifies the location (folder) in the Library in which the content object being spell-checked can be found, and the line immediately following this specifies the name of the object itself. If you are spell-checking a Topic, then the third line specifies the exact point within the Topic that is being inspected at which the spelling "mistake" was found. This consists of up to three identifiers, separated by slashes ('/'). These are:

- **Frame identifier**: This is useful if you do not want to accept the spell-checker's suggestion as it is, but do want to go to this frame in the **Topic Editor** to manually adjust the text.
- **Action identifier** (for action frames): This is the sequential number of the Action within the Topic. This is almost useless as it is impossible to identify an action within the **Topic Editor** based on this number.
- **Text type**: This specifies the type of text element in which the potential spelling mistake was found. This is normally **Bubble text**, but could just as easily be the **Object Name**, **String input text**, and so on.

Finally, the **Check Spelling** dialog box contains a text area (at the bottom of the dialog box), that provides the full text of the element being spell-checked. This is extremely useful for seeing the text that the spell-checker objected to in its full context, so that you can determine if it really is invalid, or is acceptable.

Once the spell check is complete, a confirmation message is displayed. As you can see from the following example, this shows the number of changes made (across all selected documents).

If you are working in a client/server environment and corrected the spelling in any documents that were not currently checked out to you, then UPK will automatically check these out to you, and will inform you of the number of content objects that were checked out, as shown in the example below.

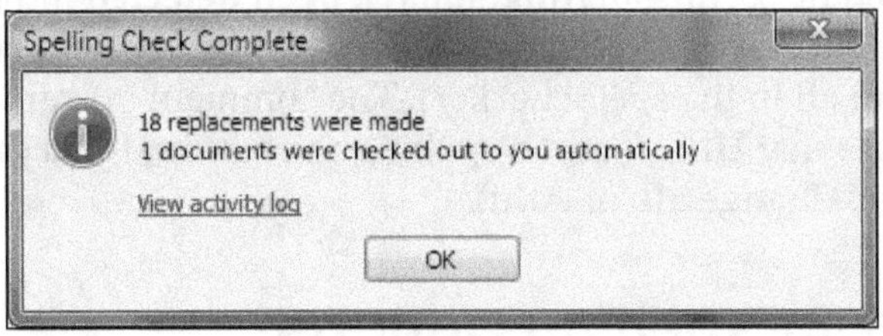

If you click on the **View activity log** link, UPK will display a list of what was changed. This is not as useful as it sounds, as the activity log contains one entry for each content object changed, and not one entry for each replacement. However, it is useful if you are working in a sever environment, as you will be able to see exactly which documents were checked out. You will need to know this in order to check them back in again. (Although, of course, if you choose the **Check in related documents** when you check in the main content object that you selected for spell-checking, then once again UPK will identify these checked-out documents as related documents, and include them in the list of content objects to check in. Refer to Chapter 7 *Version Management* for more information on checking in content objects.) An example of the activity log is shown below:

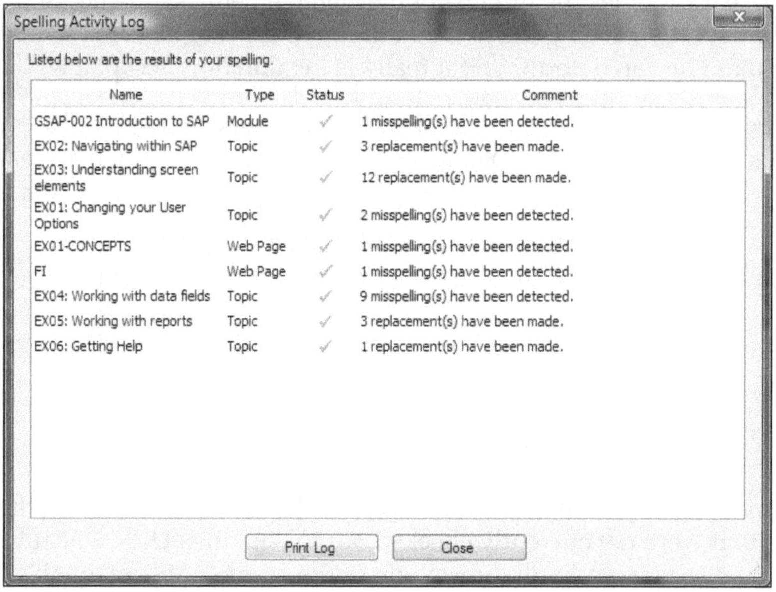

Note that the comment **"x" misspelling(s) have been detected** indicates that UPK found what it thought was a spelling mistake, but you chose to ignore it (by clicking on **Ignore** or **Ignore all** in the spell-checker). The comment "**x**" **replacement(s) have been made** indicates that UPK found a spelling mistake and you corrected this (by clicking on **Change**, **Change all**, or **Add**).

Changing your spelling options

At the bottom of the **Check Spelling** dialog box is the **Options** button. Clicking on this button displays the **Options** dialog box, with which you are no doubt familiar by now, but with only the **Spelling** category available. An example of this is shown in the following screenshot:

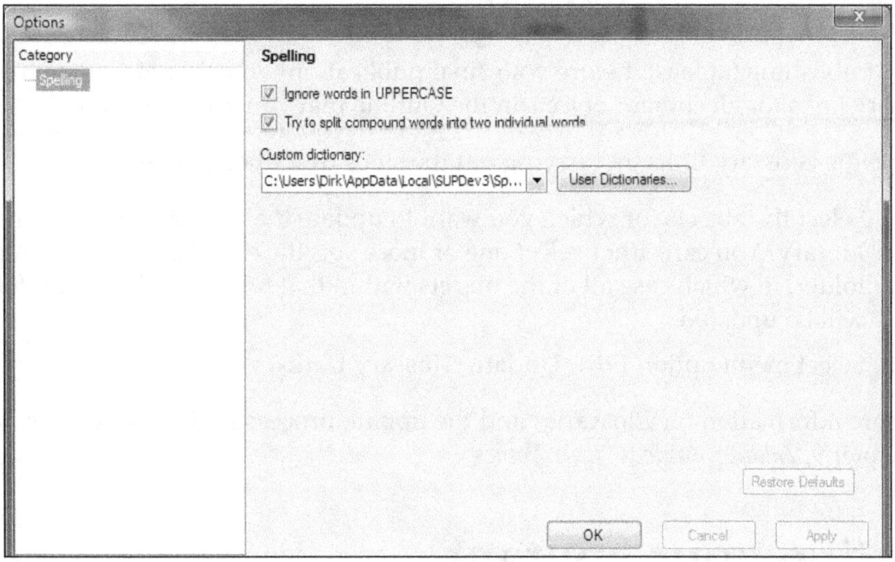

> You can access this same set of options at any time by selecting menu option **Tools | Options** and then selecting the **Spelling** category.

The following table describes the options that are available:

Option	Use
Ignore words in UPPERCASE	This is a fairly standard option in many spell-checkers, and simply tells the spell-checker to ignore all words that entirely in UPPERCASE (working on the assumption that these are acronyms or technical words).
Try to split compound words into two individual words	If you select this option then the spell-checker will suggest splitting compound words (words made up of two other words) into their component words. For example, it will suggest changing "spell-checker" to "spell checker". Some style guides recommend splitting compound words for clarity, although this may not always be what you want to do. This is a useful option as long as you review each suggestion rather than simply accepting them all.
Custom dictionary	This option can be used to specify the location of the user dictionary – that is, the dictionary to which non-standard words are added by the user when they click on the **Add** button in the **Check Spelling** dialog box (see earlier). By clicking on the **User Dictionaries** button, you can even specify multiple user dictionaries (for example, for multiple languages. You can also attach an existing dictionary (`.tlx` file), which is very useful if you have an in-house user dictionary that all developers should use.

Updating the Glossary links

Before publishing (at least, before your final publication) you should update the Glossary links for all content objects in the Outline that you are publishing.

Update the Glossary links by carrying out the steps described below:

1. Select the objects for which you want to update the Glossary links, in the Library. You can either select one or more specific objects, or you can select a folder, in which case all of the objects within that folder (and any sub-folders) will be updated.
2. Select menu option **Edit | Update Glossary Links**.

For more information on Glossaries and the update process for Glossary links, refer to Chapter 9, *Adding Value to Your Topics*.

Testing your content

Before you publish your content, you should *always* test your simulations. This may seem to be such a truism that it does not even need to be said. However, I have seen several "final" simulations that simply don't work in one or more of the published modes, so apparently it *does* need to be said. Again: Before you publish your content, you should *always* test your simulations.

Note that testing does not mean simply running through the simulation once, in *Try It!* mode, with "skip" enabled, and checking that it doesn't "break". It means making sure that every Frame in every path in every mode has the correct Bubble Text and the correct Action.

Here is a good set of steps for testing a single scenario:

1. Open the Topic in the **Topic Editor**.
2. In the **Display** field, select **Player - See It / Try It**.
3. Visit *every* Frame and check that the Bubble Text is correct and that the action area is in the correct place. Make sure that you go to every Frame, every Alternative Path, and every Alternative Action.
4. Repeat Steps 2 and 3 for all of the other modes (that you are using). A few things to watch out for in each of the modes, are:

   See It! mode:

   - Check the speed of the transition from one Frame to the next.
   - Check that Explanation Frames (discussed in Chapter 9, *Adding Value to Your Topics*) are displayed where necessary.

- Check that Decision Frames (discussed in Chapter 8, *Allowing Alternatives*) are not displayed (unless required).

Try It! mode:

- Check that the trainee is provided with both the instructions and the data required to complete each Action (see also Chapter 4, *Editing a Topic* for a discussion on Bubble Text in different modes).
- Check that the Action Area is a realistic size, and that string input Action Areas look good (that is, it is correctly sized, and using the correct font and background color).
- Check that Bubbles are correctly positioned, and do not obscure information on the screen to which the trainee needs to refer.

Know It? mode:

- Check that the trainee is provided with the data but not the instructions required to complete each Action.
- Check that the 'pass score' is realistic.
- Check that adequate Alternative Actions (discussed in Chapter 8, *Allowing Alternatives*) are provided, in order to give the trainee a sporting chance.

Do It! mode:

- Check that the trainee is provided with the instructions but not the data required to complete each Action.
- Check that *linked* Frames (where the **Keep with next** option has been used – see Chapter 4, *Editing a Topic*) are used appropriately.

5. Close the **Topic Editor**, and go to an Outline containing the Topic.
6. **Preview** (see instructions ahead) the Topic in *See It!* mode. Although *See It!* and *Try It!* mode use the same bubble text it is worth running through them separately so that you can check the timing of the auto-advance in *See It!* mode. Check that every Action works correctly, and that the Bubble Text correctly describes these Actions. If you have Alternative Paths and/or Alternative Actions, make sure that you test each of these, even if it means running through the Topic several times in each mode.
7. Repeat Step 6 for all of the other modes (that you are using).

It is a good idea, when testing your content, to have both the Player and the **Topic Editor** open at the same time. That way, as soon as you notice something wrong in the Player, you can flip to the **Topic Editor**, make the change, then flip back to the Player and continue testing. This is much easier than going through the entire Topic in the Player, and remembering or making a note of everything that needs to be fixed before going back and making any changes. This method of working is even more effective if you have two screens attached to your computer (as is an increasingly common practice, especially with laptop users) as you can display the Player and the **Topic Editor** side-by-side, while you are working. Note that you can play the Topic either by publishing it and then opening the Player, or simply by using the **Preview** option from the Outline (as explained in the next section of this chapter). Both methods will allow you to flip between the Player and the **Topic Editor**.

Previewing a Topic

UPK provides the ability to play or display a Topic without first publishing the Outline Element in which it is contained. This is normally quicker than publishing (and more convenient, as the content is launched immediately), which makes it a good option for testing your content during development. Unfortunately, you can still only do this from within the **Outline Editor** (which makes it a marginally less useful option), but it is still useful.

You can preview a Topic in *See It!*, *Try It!*, *Know It?*, or *Do It!* mode, or in any of the six document formats. (See later in this chapter for a description of each document type.) If you have defined your own deployment formats (as described in Chapter 12, *Configuring UPK*) then you can also preview in these custom formats.

To preview a content object, carry out the following steps:

1. Open the Outline Element (Module or Topic) that contains the Topic you want to preview in the **Outline Editor** (refer to Chapter 5, *Building an Outline* for further details of the **Outline Editor**, if necessary).
2. In the **Outline Editor**, click on the Topic that you want to preview.
3. In the **Preview** field in the **Outline Editor** toolbar, use the drop-down to select the mode in which you want to preview the Topic.
4. Click on the green **Go to** button ( ) to the right of the **Preview** field.

The Topic is displayed on the screen in the selected mode or document format. Once you close the Topic (or document), you are returned to the **Outline Editor**. Note that the preview version of your Topic is not saved (as published versions are).

Publishing your content

UPK allows you to publish your content in a number of formats, as shown in the **Formats** pane of the **Publish Content** dialog box (see the following screenshot). This includes four formats for online (interactive) use, and six documentation formats. The overall approach for publishing in any of these formats is the same, and so is described only once, under *Publishing content – a generic approach*, next. The options available, and the format of this output, obviously vary depending on the chosen format, and these are described separately, in subsequent sections.

> **Version Difference**
> OnDemand (up to Version 9.1.5) provided two further "publishing formats", the *Context ID Report*, and the *Missing Sound Report*. These have been discontinued in UPK 3.5.

Publishing content—a generic approach

1. Open the Outline Element (Module or Topic) that you want to publish, in the **Outline Editor** (refer to Chapter 5, *Building an Outline* for further details of the **Outline Editor**, if necessary).
2. In the **Outline Editor**, click on the Outline Element that you want to publish. Note that this does not have to be the same Outline Element as you opened in Step 1 - you can publish at any level within the Outline. You can even select an individual Topic to publish only this Topic (although UPK will also include the Modules and/or Subjects within which it is contained – but not other content objects within them).

3. Click on the **Publish** button (). You can also select menu option **File | Publish**. The **Publish Content** dialog box is displayed, as shown in the following screenshot:

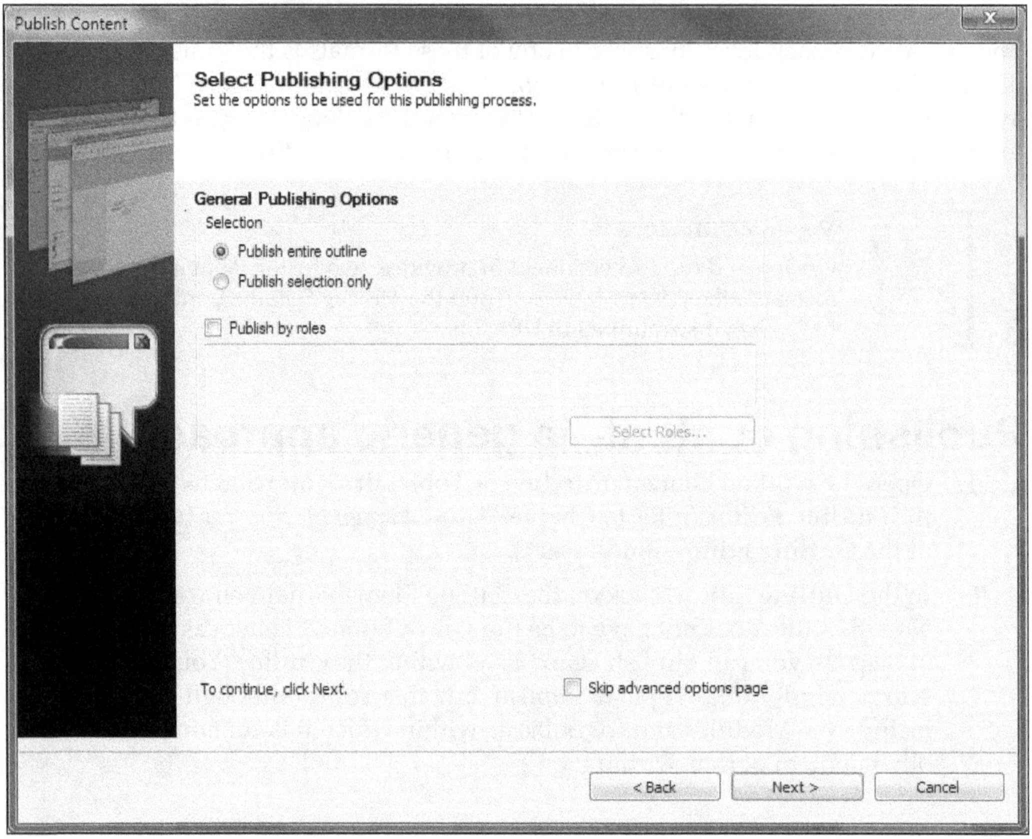

4. Specify (or navigate to and select, via the **Browse** button) the folder to which you want to publish your content.

5. Click on **Next**. The following screen is displayed:

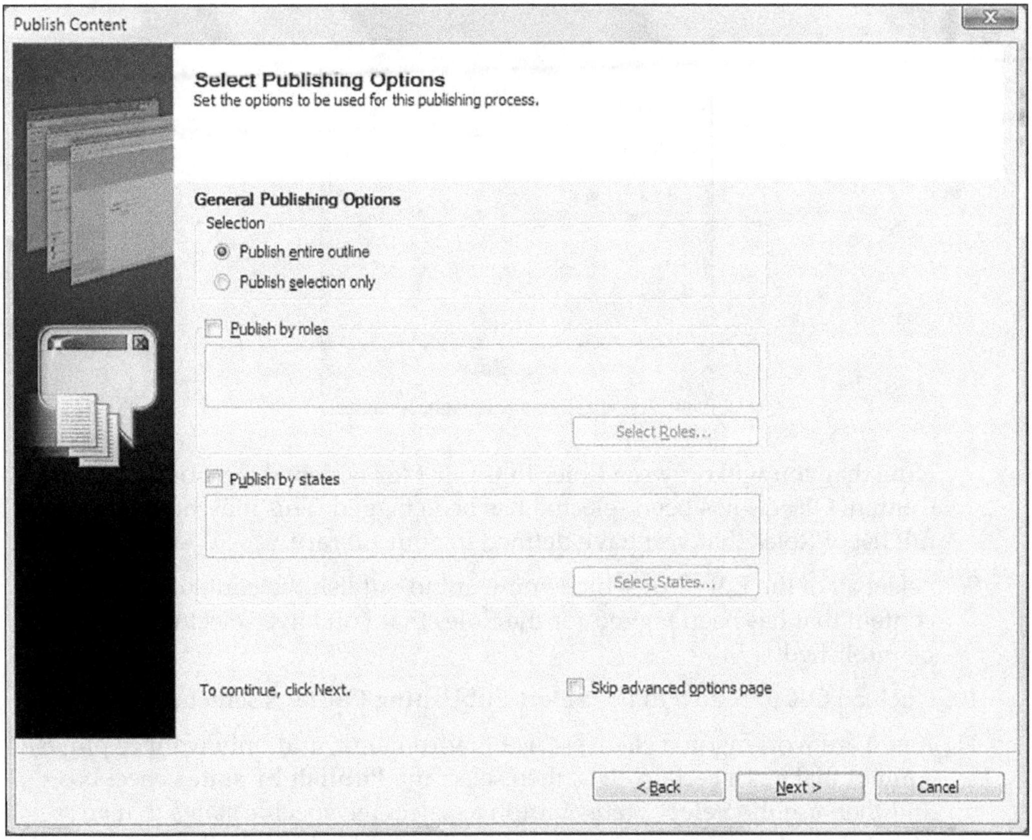

6. Under **General Publishing Options**, **Selection**, specify whether you want to publish the entire Outline (option **Publish entire outline**), or only the selected content object and everything under it (option **Publish selection only**).
7. If you have Roles defined and only want content tagged for specific Roles to be published, then select the **Publish by roles** checkbox and continue with Step 8. Otherwise, go directly to Step 11.

> Roles are described in Chapter 10, *Adding Value in the Player.*

8. Click on **Select Roles**. The **Select Roles** dialog box is displayed, as shown in the following screenshot:

   Note that you will only see Roles in this list for which at least one of the Content Objects has been selected has been tagged. This may not be the full list of Roles that you have defined in your Library.

9. Select all of the Roles for which you want to publish the content. Only content that has been tagged for the Roles that you have selected will be published.
10. Click on **OK** to return to the **Select Publishing Options** screen.
11. If you are working in a client/server environment, and only want to publish content that has a certain *state*, then select the **Publish by states** checkbox, and then use the **Select States** button to select the specific states that an object should have in order to be selected for publishing, in the same way that you selected roles. You can use this option to (for example) publish only **Final** content, or only content that is **In Review** (for example, for sending to a reviewer), and so on. (Refer to the section on *Workflow* in Chapter 7, *Version Management* for more information on content objects' *State* property.)

> The option to publish by state is only available in a client/server environment. This option is not available in the standalone (single user) environment, because the *State* Property is simply not available in a standalone environment.

> **Version Difference**
>
> The option to publish by state was introduced in UPK 3.5.0, and is not available in earlier versions.

12. Make sure that the **Skip advanced options page** checkbox at the bottom of the **Select Publishing Options** screen is *not* selected.
13. Click on **Next**. The **Advanced Publishing Options** screen is displayed, as shown in following screenshot:

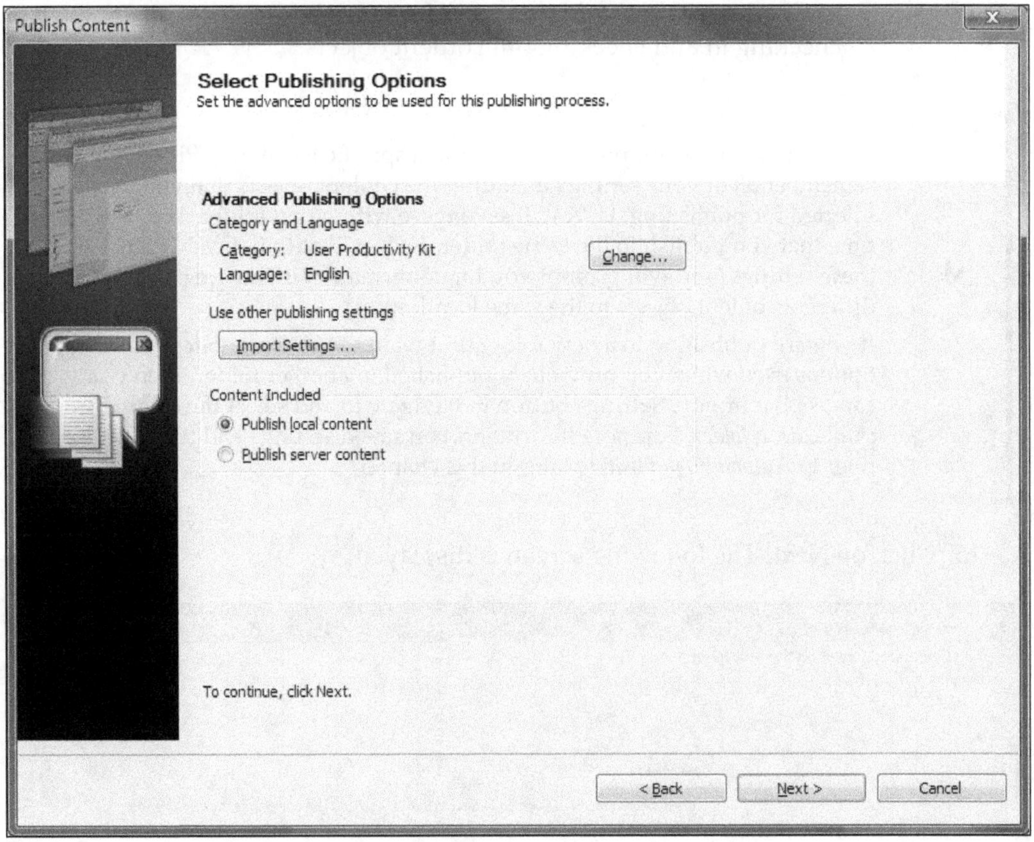

14. In the **Advanced Publishing Options** dialog box, select the appropriate settings as follows:
    - To change the Publishing Category or language, click on the **Change** button, and then select the required category and/or language.

For more information on Publishing Categories, refer to Chapter 12, *Configuring UPK*. For more information on local language support, refer to Chapter 13, *Localizing Your Content*.

- If you are working in a client/server environment, then select whether you want to include only content that has been checked in to the server (select the **Publish server content** option) or want to include content that you currently have checked out (select the **Publish local content** option). Refer to Chapter 7, *Version Management* for more information on checking in and checking out content objects.

> The first time that you publish content to a specific location, UPK will remember all of your settings including the content objects that you selected for publishing. UPK will save these within that folder. The next time that you publish to the same folder, UPK will automatically load these settings (and will prompt you for confirmation if you are publishing different content objects to the same location).
>
> If you are publishing to a new folder, but want to use the publication options used when you previously published to another folder, then you can use the **Import Settings** button to navigate to and select the original publication *folder*. For more information on saved settings and their use, refer to *Automatic publishing* later in this chapter.

15. Click on **Next**. The following screen is displayed:

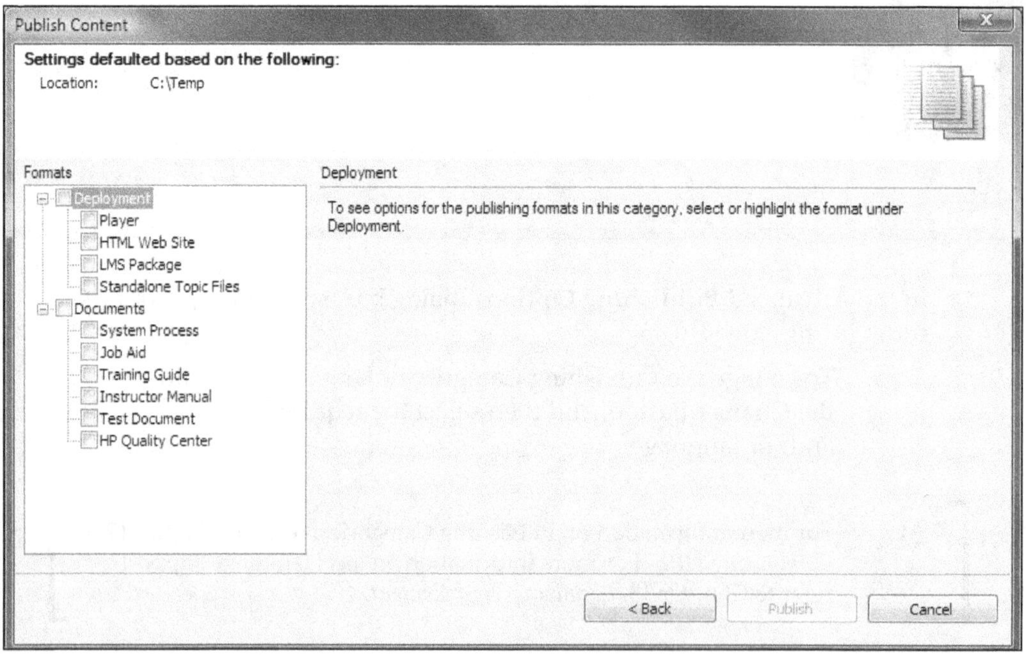

16. In the **Formats** pane on the leftmost side of the dialog box, select the checkbox for the format in which you want to publish the content. Note that you can select multiple formats at the same time. You can also select the checkbox for a *category* (**Deployment** or **Documents**) to publish to all formats in that category.

> **Version Difference**
>
> The ability to publish to multiple formats at the same time was introduced in OnDemand 9.1—in previous versions, you could only publish to one format at a time)

17. Depending on the format that you select, the pane on the rightmost side of the screen will be populated with the options available for the format. (Note that even if you click on the format name, the options will be grayed out until you select the checkbox for that format.) The options for each format are explained separately below. Refer to the relevant section and make any necessary adjustments to the options, before continuing with the next step.
18. Click on **Publish**. Your content is published in the selected format(s). While this is happening, a **Publishing Progress** dialog box will be displayed, as shown in the following screenshot:

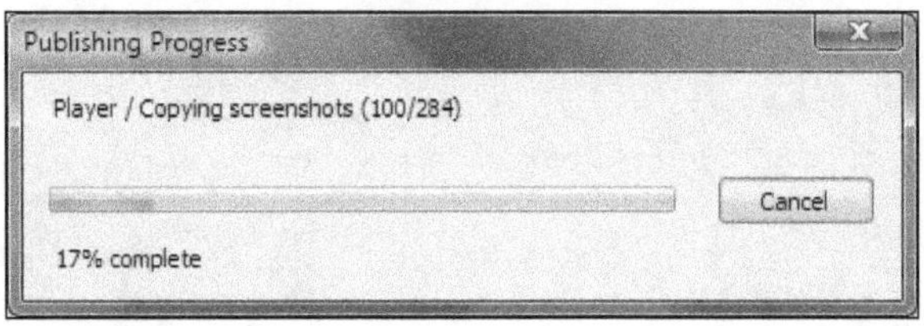

19. Depending on the volume of content that you are publishing, and the number of formats in which you are publishing it, this may take some time. Once the content has been published, the **Publishing Complete** dialog box will be displayed. An example of this dialog box, in this example for the publication of a Player, is shown in the following screenshot:

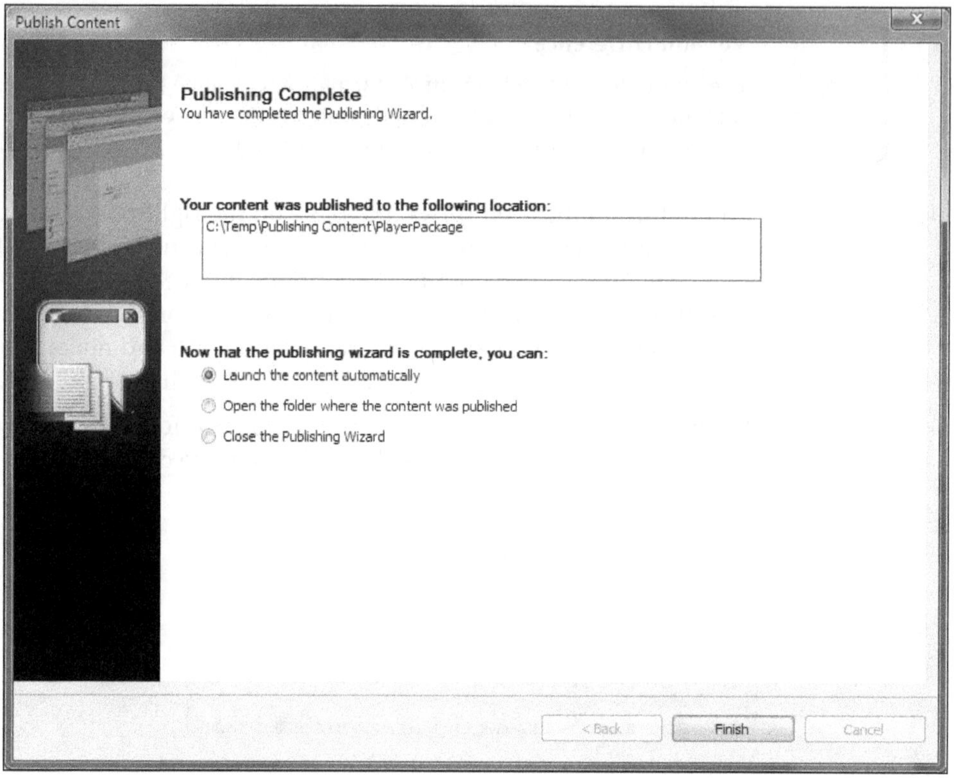

20. Depending on the format into which you have published your content, and whether there are any errors during the publication process, you will be given the options to:
    - Launch the content immediately (which is useful for testing)
    - Open the folder into which the content has been published (which is useful if you need to rename or move the published content)
    - Display the publication log, which will list any errors found (such as missing sound files, broken links, and so on)
    - Exit from the Publishing Wizard

Generally, you should select **Launch the content automatically** (for Player packages) or **Open the folder where the content was published** (for other formats) so that you can check your work. Even if you have only made a very minor change, it is worth checking that the changes have been correctly implemented.

Published folder structure

If you choose to display the folder into which the content was published, you will see a structure similar to the one shown in the following screenshot:

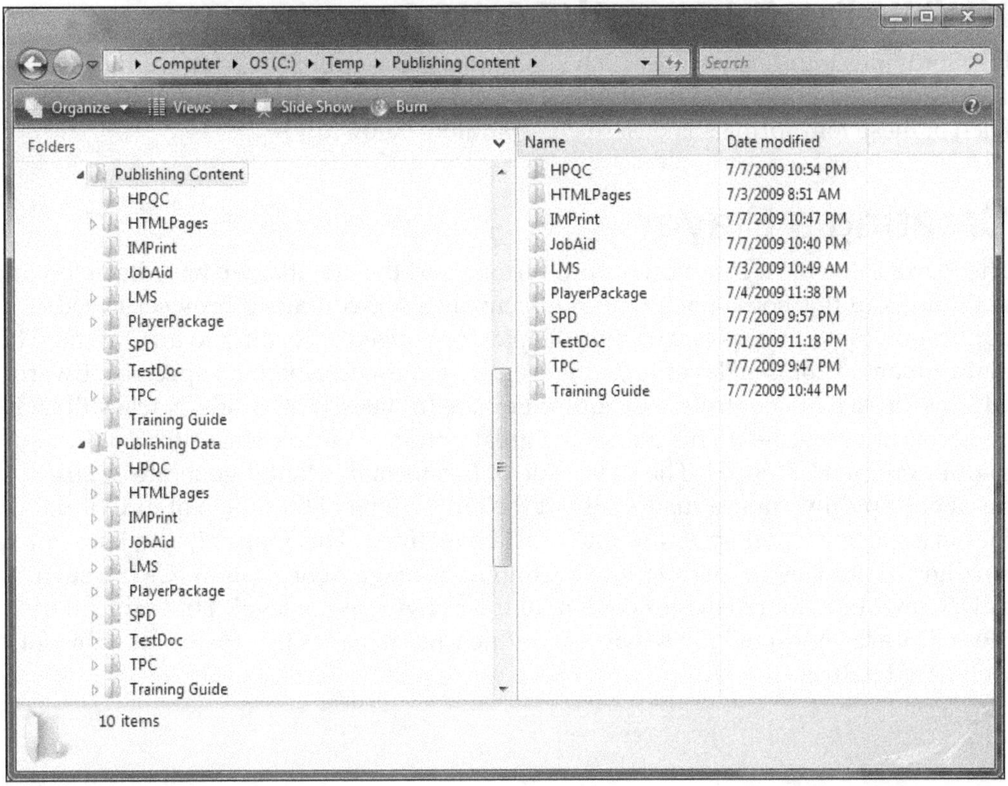

Note that there are two sub-folders in the destination folder (`C:\Temp` in this example): `Publishing Content` and `Publishing Data`. You can ignore the `Publishing Data` folder. This contains work files that UPK generated during the publication process. You do not need to refer to these files, although they will be used by UPK for incremental publishing (for example, when republishing an existing Outline within which only one Topic has changed).

Within each of these main folders there is one folder per publication format. The previous example shows all of the possible folders. The exact content of these folders will depend on the publishing format to which it applies. Refer to the relevant section below for additional information.

> The folder names that are used are defined in the Deployment Package for the output type. Refer to Chapter 12, *Configuring UPK* for more information on Deployment Packages.

Publishing for online use

UPK provides four formats in which an Outline can be published for online use. These are listed under the **Deployment** category in the **Publish Content** dialog box. Each of these four formats is described separately below.

Creating a Player

The *Player* is the most common output format, and the one that we have been looking at throughout this book. The *Player* is effectively a self-contained browser-based application that contains one or more Topics, organized according to an Outline. The main advantage of the Player is that it is entirely self-contained; no special software, add-ins, or ActiveX controls are required by the trainees. (Although Oracle still levies an end-user license fee.) This makes it a great option for web sites, or for publication to (for example) CD-ROM. The downside of this format is that it generates a large number (typically, thousands for all but the most trivial of Outlines) of individual files in a specific folder structure that must be retained. This makes it unwieldy for emailing to trainees, or loading into a **Content Management System** (**CMS**), such as Documentum, that manages content at the individual file level. That said, all of these files are very small (30 KB or less), which again makes this format suitable for web-based delivery.

Publishing options

The following screenshot shows the options that are available when publishing content to a Player.

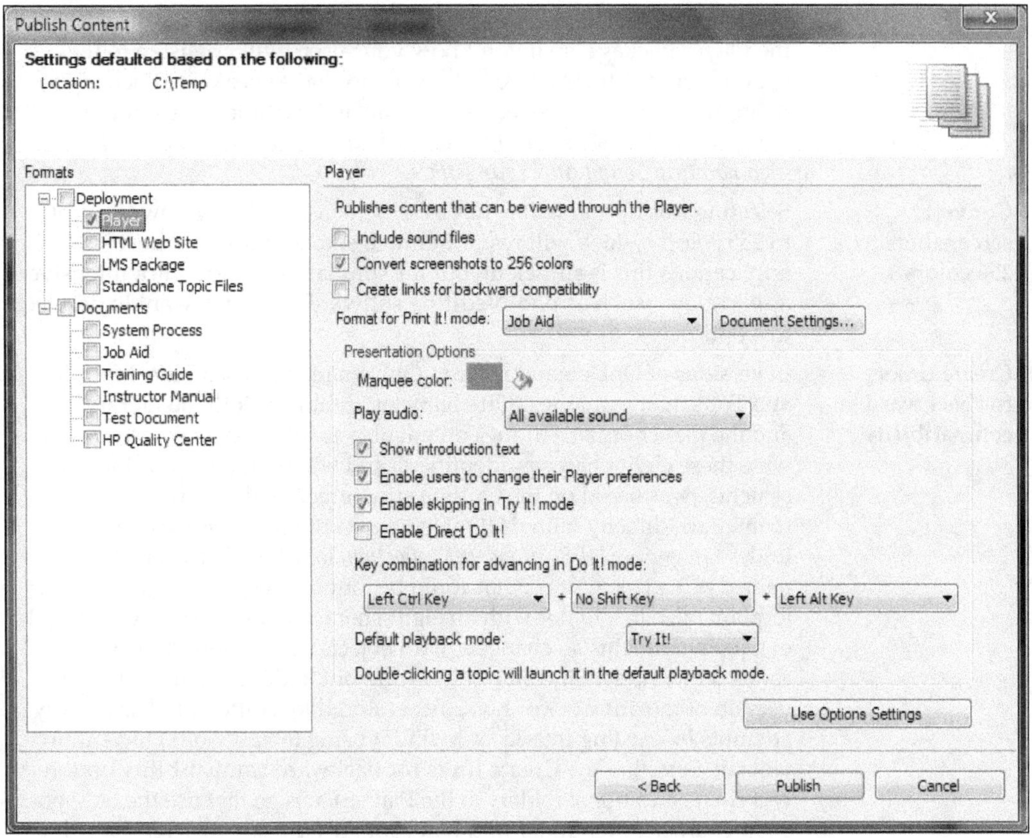

The table below lists the options that are available, and explains their use.

Option	Use
Include sound files	If this option is selected, then sound files will be included in the Player. The use of sound tends to significantly increase the overall size of the Player package, so if you know your users will not listen to the sound (perhaps their workstations do not have speakers attached to them) then you can deselect this option and exclude the sound files altogether. The use of sound is described in detail in Chapter 11, *Incorporating Sound into Your Topics*.
Convert screenshots to 256 colors	Selecting this option will result in all screenshots being down-sampled to 256 colors, which will result in much smaller files. For most applications this is sufficient, but for simulations of graphics-intensive applications (such as photo-editing software) you may want to deselect this option.
Create links for backward compatibility	In versions of OnDemand prior to OnDemand 9.1, each Title, Module, and Topic had a unique eight-character identifier. Both the Library and the Player organized the content objects into folders whose names were these eight-character identifiers, and whose (folder/sub-folder) structure was based on the Outline structure. Applications wanting to interface directly with the OnDemand content objects (as explained under *Integrating UPK into your application*, later) made use of a file named `dhtml_kp.html` that could be found at a specific known location (also in a folder with an eight-character name). With version 9.1 of OnDemand, this all changed, with objects being referred to by a 32-character identifier, and stored in a different folder structure. The new version of the `dhtml_kp.html` file is stored in a different place, so any attempts by existing interfaces to find it using the previous convention will fail. Selecting the **Create links for backward compatibility** option will create additional folders in the Player Package that use the old-style eight-character identifiers, and that contain a `dhtml_kp.html` file that can be used with existing interfaces.
Format for Print It! mode	This option allows you to select the document format that will be displayed if the trainee selects the *Print It!* mode in the Player. You can choose any of the document formats, and can also choose, via the **Document Settings** button, the specific settings for the chosen document type. (These document settings are identical to the settings available when publishing to that document format, and so are explained under the relevant document format, below.)
Marquee color *	This option defines the color of the rectangle that is shown around the action area during playback of the simulation. By default this is red, but if you need to (for example, if the application you are recording uses red prominently in its screens) then you can change this color by clicking on the **Fill** icon to the right of this option, and selecting the required color.

Option	Use
Play audio *	This option allows you to specify which sounds should be played during playback. The choices are: • **No sound**: No sound will be played. • **All available sound**: All sound files used in the simulation will be played, including bubble text sound files. • **Keyboard and mouse-clicks**: Only the sounds for keyboard presses and mouse-clicks will be played. Sounds for bubble text will not be played. Note that these options are (obviously) only relevant if the **Include sound files** option is selected. You may wonder why there is a **No sound** option here, when you could just deselect the **Include sound files** option. The simple answer is that the **Play audio** settings are only defaults. The trainee (who is playing the simulation) can (by default, but see **Enable users to change their Player preferences**) change this setting themselves, and/or switch on or off the sound on their computer.
Show introduction text	By default, the Bubble Text specified on the Start screen of the simulation will be displayed on the first screen of the Topic playback. If this option is deselected, then the introduction text will not be displayed during playback—in fact, the entire Start Frame will be omitted from playback. For more information on this option and the Start Frame, see Chapter 9, *Adding Value to Your Topics*.
Enable users to change their Player preferences	If this option is selected, then users will be able to change a number of Player options within the Player window itself. The options that they can change are: **Marquee color**, **Play audio**, **Show introduction text**, **Enable skipping in Try It! mode**, and **Key combination for advancing in Do It! mode**. I usually deselect this option, as I do not want users skipping in *Try It!* mode (see below). This option is covered in more detail in Chapter 10, *Adding value in the Player*.
Enable skipping in Try It! mode *	If this option is selected, then users can progress through the screens in *Try It!* mode simply by pressing the *Enter* key on their keyboard. As the whole point of *Try It!* mode is that the users are trying it (!) allowing them to skip through the simulation is counter-productive. However, it can be useful when testing to be able to do this. I therefore always leave this option selected during development, and then deselect this option for the final publication. Note that this is just a default setting. If you deselect this option, but select **Enable users to change their Player preferences**, then although users will not initially be able to skip through a simulation, they will be able to go into their Preferences (assuming they know how to do so) and re-enable it. Therefore, if you deselect this option, you should also consider deselecting **Enable users to change their Player preferences**. Either that, or consider removing this option altogether, as described in Chapter 12, *Configuring UPK*.

Option	Use
Enable Direct Do It!	The **Direct Do It!** feature was introduced in UPK 3.5. If this option is selected, then if a user invokes context-sensitive help from within the application and only one Topic matches this context, then that Topic will automatically be launched in *Do It!* mode (versus being listed in the Player, for the user to select). This option applies only to *targeted* applications for which in-application performance support has been enabled (see the section *Integrating UPK into your application* below).
Key combination for advancing in Do It! mode *	In *Do It!* mode, the UPK window is displayed on top of the application with which the user is interacting. If the key combination specified by this option is pressed, then the instructions in the UPK window will advance to the next step (screen) in the UPK window, even though the application (and not UPK) is still the active window. (See the *Introduction* to this book for a more detailed explanation of Do It! mode.) You can use any (one-, two-, or three-)key combination, but should choose one that is not used in the application to which the simulation applies. Note that you will have to educate your users on this key combination, especially if you deselect the **Enable users to change their Player preferences** option as the users will not even know that it exists.
Default playback mode	As of UPK 3.5, trainees can double-click on a Topic in the Player to launch it (as opposed to single-clicking on the Topic to select it and then clicking on the appropriate mode button). This option allows you to choose the mode in which the Topic will be launched when the user double-clicks on it. This defaults to *Try It!* mode.

Options marked with an asterisk (*) are *default* options that can be overridden in the Player by the trainee (assuming that the **Enable users to change their Player preferences** option is selected).

Generated files

In the `PlayerPackage` folder, you will find several files and folders. If you will be making your Player available on a Web Server (or other file server) then you will need to copy the complete contents of this `PlayerPackage` folder to your server.

In order to provide access to this Player package, you should provide a link to either the `index.html` file (for Apache servers), or the `default.html` file (for IIS servers).

> For Apache servers, it is also possible to simply provide a link to the folder containing the `index.html` file.

If you try accessing the Player locally (for example, from the Publishing Content folder on your local workstation) then you need to run the `Play.exe` file instead, to avoid any browser security warnings.

Example output

Although you are no doubt completely familiar with the Player by this stage in the book, for the sake of completeness (or in case you are flicking through this book as a reference), an example of the Player output format for our sample exercise is shown in the following screenshot:

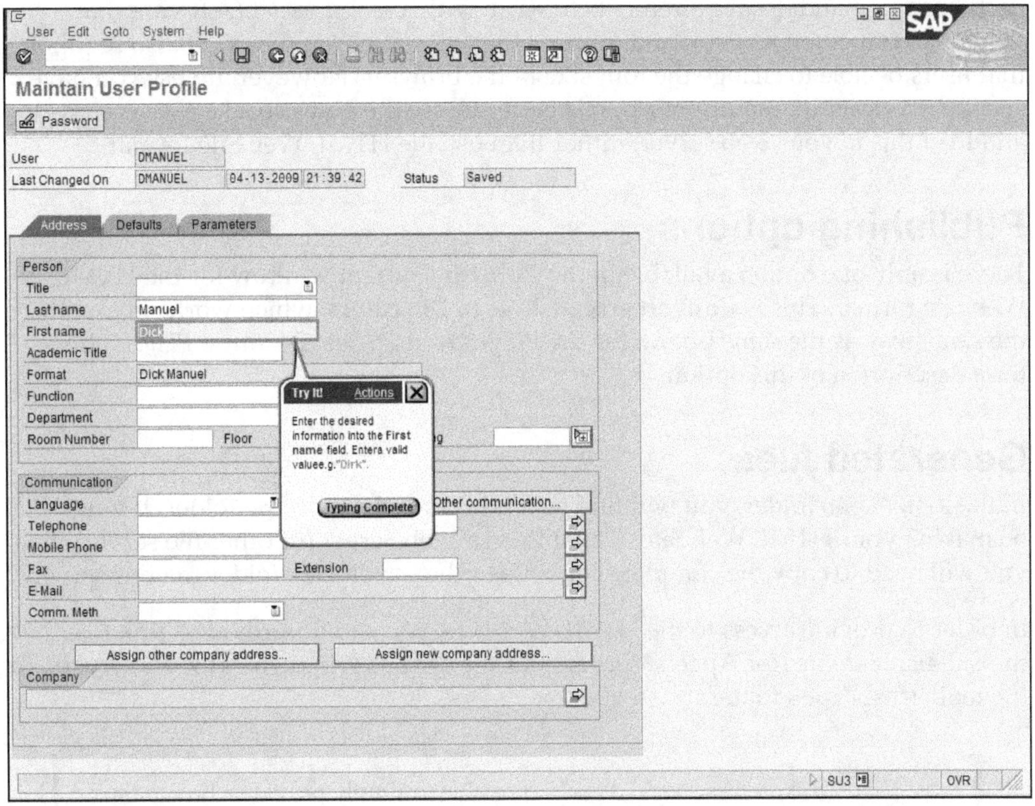

This example is taken from *Try It!* mode. For an explanation of the different play modes and the differences between them, refer to Chapter 1, *Oracle User Productivity Kit*.

Creating an HTML Web Site

The **HTML Web Site** format generates a version of the Player that is, in theory, better-suited for use as a web site. This is because UPK generates only HTML, CSS, and PNG files. There is no JavaScript, as there is in the Player. However, in doing so, UPK sacrifices a good deal of its functionality. The HTML Web Site only allows the Topics to be executed in *Try It!* mode, Bubble Text is actually displayed below the Frames, string input is not possible, and Alternative Actions are not supported at all.

Given that almost all Web Browsers support JavaScript, the only real advantage to the HTML Web Site format is that it confirms to Section `508c` accessibility standards. Section `508c` mandates requirements to work with a *screen reader* (software that reads the content on a screen and outputs this via speech synthesis). It also requires that users be able to change the font size in the browser. However, unless you have specific accessibility requirements, it is better to use the Player package (see above), and load this to your web server, rather than use the HTML Web Site format.

Publishing options

There is only one option available in the **Publish Content** window for the HTML Web Site format. This is **Convert screenshots to 256 colors**, which works in exactly the same way as the same option for the Player format. See *Creating a Player*, above, for a description of this option.

Generated files

In the `HTMLPages` folder, you will find several files and single `tpc` folder. If you will be making your HTML Web Site available on a Web Server (or other file server) then you will need to copy the complete contents of the `HTMLPages` folder to your server.

In order to provide access to the HTML Web Site, you should provide a link to either the `index.html` file (for Apache servers), or the `default.html` file (for IIS servers) in the main `HTMLPages` folder.

> For Apache servers, it is also possible to simply provide a link to the folder containing the `index.html` file.

Example output

An example of the output for the HTML Web Site format is shown in the following screenshots. The first screenshot shows the main `index.html` file, which is the first screen that the trainees will see (this is the *HTML Web Site* equivalent of the *Player* Outline, which incidentally, is also called `index.html`):

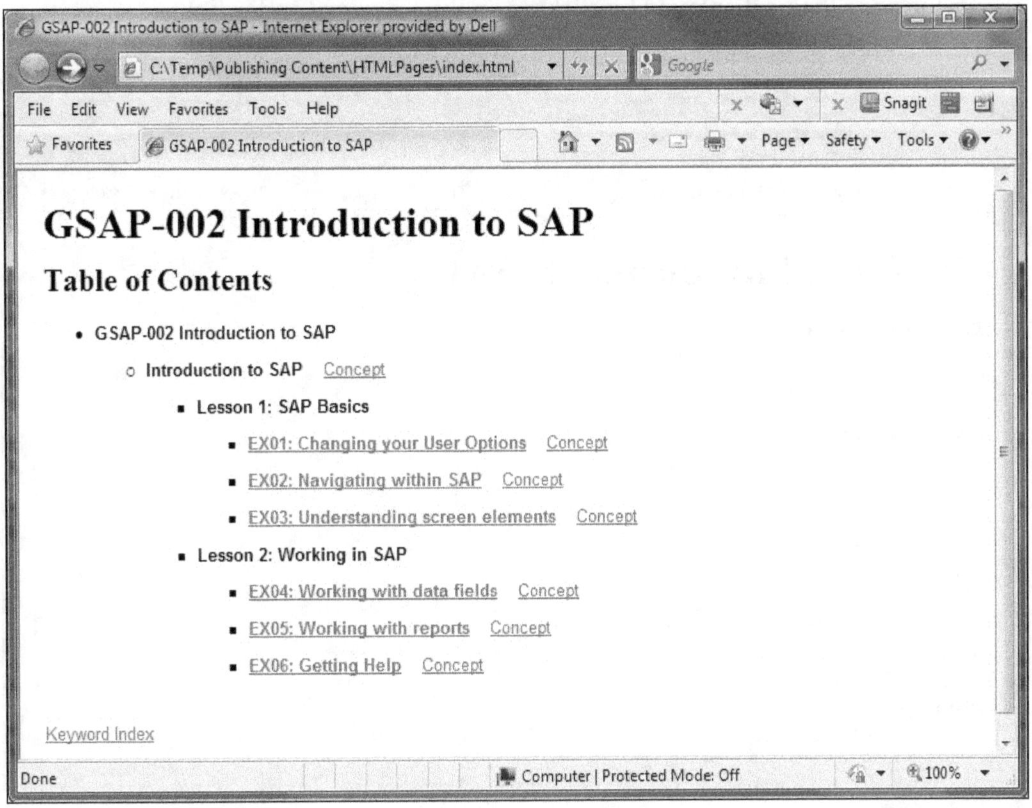

As you can see from the above example, the Outline structure is maintained, but there is only a single link available for each Topic, which leads to a limited version of the *Try It!* mode. Trainees can also see any information attached to the **Concepts** pane for a content element by clicking on the **Concept** link. Note that there is no ability to filter by Role, and there is no *Search* function. To compensate for this latter limitation, a new link, **Keyword Index**, is provided at the bottom of the page. The following screenshot shows the page that is displayed by clicking on the **Keyword Index** link:

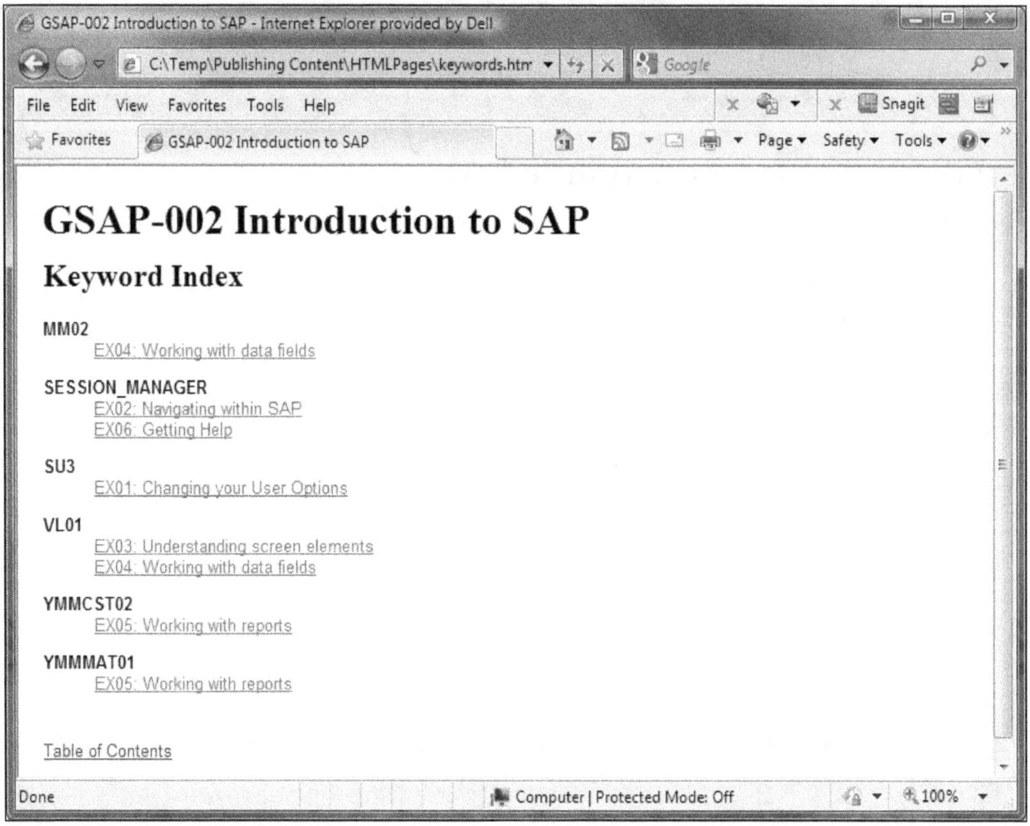

This **Keyword Index** page (above) provides an index to the Topics in the HTML Web Site organized according to the Keywords assigned to each Topic (if any). This could prove to be quite a useful page depending on the purpose that you have assigned to your keywords (it would actually be useful to have this feature in the Player). Given that the HTML Web Site format does not provide us with a Roles index, if you do organize your Topics according to Roles, you might want to consider using your Role names as Keywords. Your **Keyword Index** would then give access to your Topics organized by Role. Of course, the page would still be called "Keyword Index", but you could always change this, as explained in Chapter 12, *Configuring UPK*.

Keywords are explained in detail in Chapter 10, *Adding Value in the Player*.

The **Table of Contents** link at the bottom of the **Keyword Index** page links back to the main index page, discussed earlier.

Clicking on the link for a Topic displays a page similar to the one shown in the following screenshot:

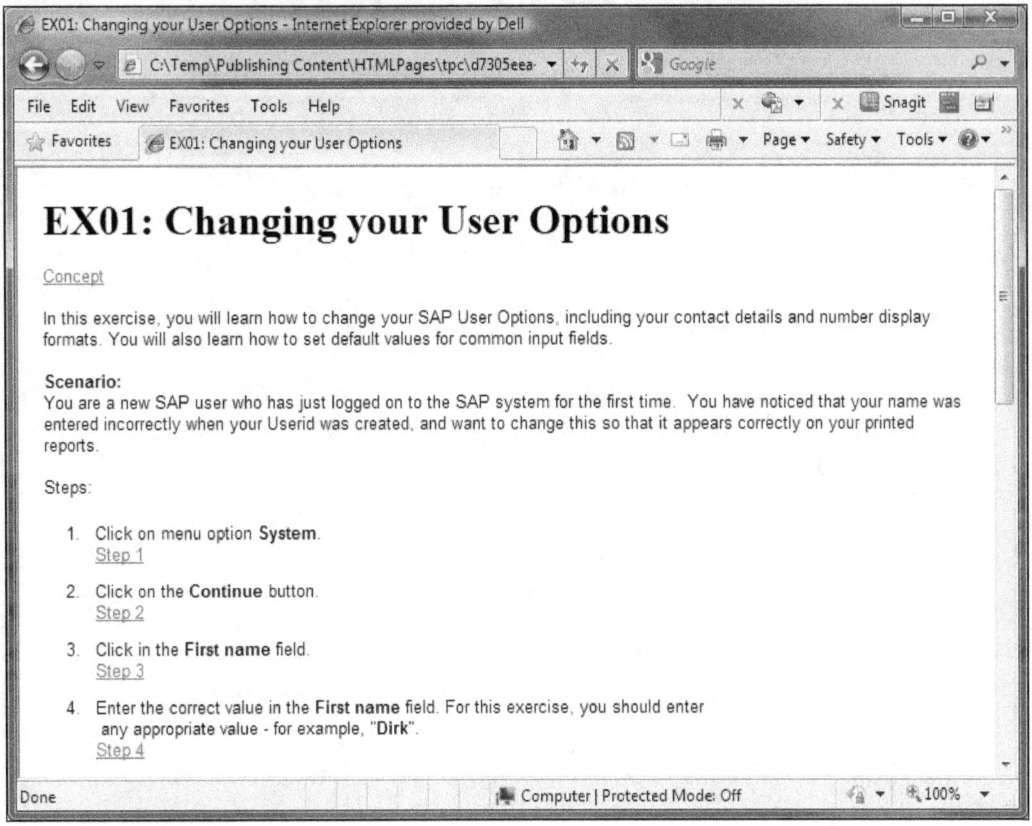

This initial page is very similar to the *Job Aid* output described below, in that it is a text-only version of the instructions, with the addition that for each step, a hyperlink to the screenshot is provided. Clicking on a hyperlink displays a page similar to the one shown in the following example. Note that this screenshot was taken from the middle of our sample exercise, for the purposes of illustration.

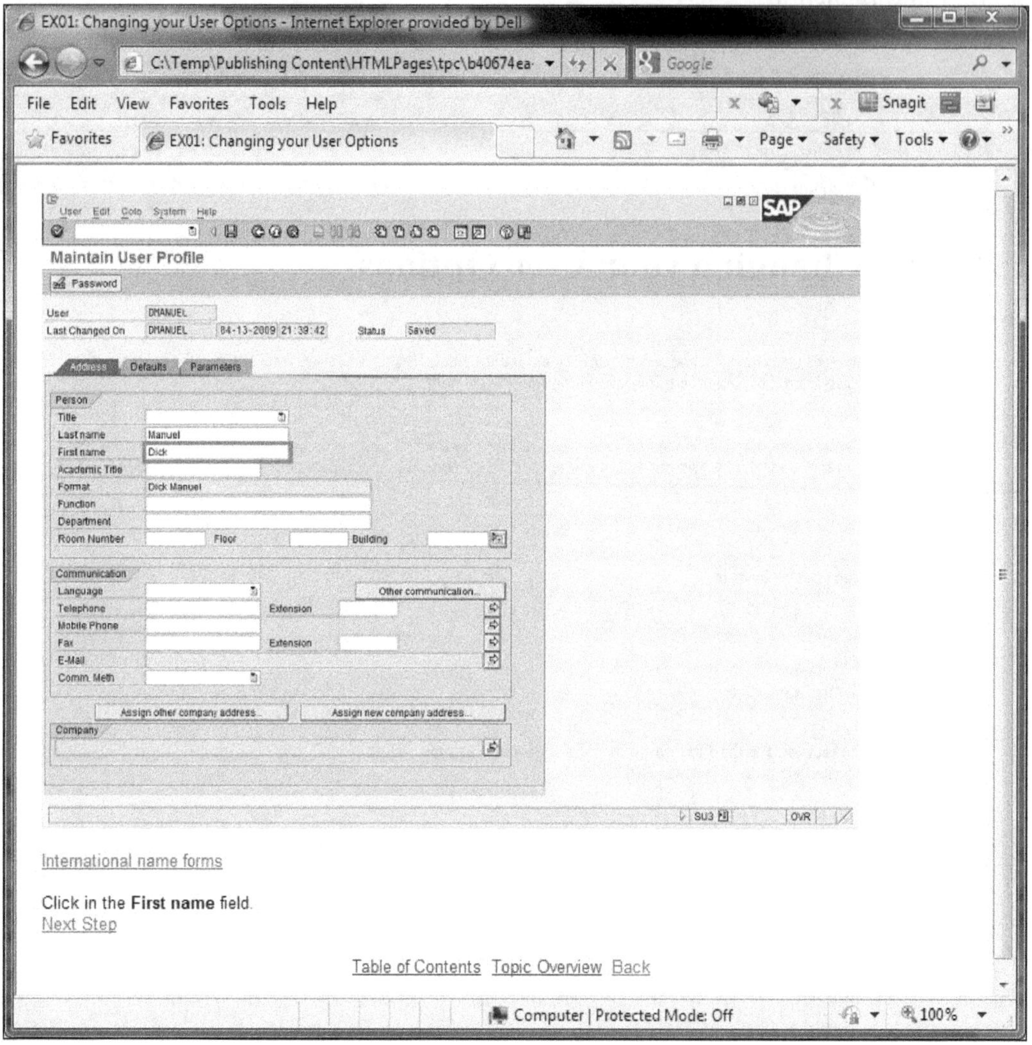

In this example, you can see that the Action Area is highlighted (and works; if you click on it, UPK uses image-maps, and you will move to the next step), but the Bubble Text is shown below the screenshot (which has been scaled down to fit on the screen). You can also see that links are provided to any (UPK) Web Pages attached to the Frame, such as the link **International name forms**, in this example. (Web Pages are described in Chapter 9, *Adding Value to Your Topics.*) Finally, links are provided to the next step (**Next Step**), to the Web Site index page (**Table of Contents**), the initial page of this Topic (**Topic Overview**), and the previous step (**Back**).

Creating an LMS Package

The **LMS Package** publishing option will create a package that is suitable for loading into a **Learning Management System** (**LMS**). This package is both AICC and SCORM compliant. The way in which this package is integrated into your LMS will vary depending on the specific LMS used, but the exercises will appear similarly to how they appear in the Player. Note that *Do It!* mode is not available in an LMS Package.

AICC is the acronym for the **Aviation Industry Computer-Based Training Committee**, an international association of technology-based training professionals that develops guidelines for aviation industry in the development, delivery, and evaluation of CBT, WBT and related training technologies.

SCORM is the acronym for **Shareable Content Object Reference Model**, which is a collection of standards and specifications for developing and delivering online (web-based) training.

Most LMSes are AICC and/or SCORM compliant. UPK is both AICC and SCORM compliant, which makes it compatible with most LMSes.

Publishing options

The publishing options for the LMS Package format are as shown in the following screenshot:

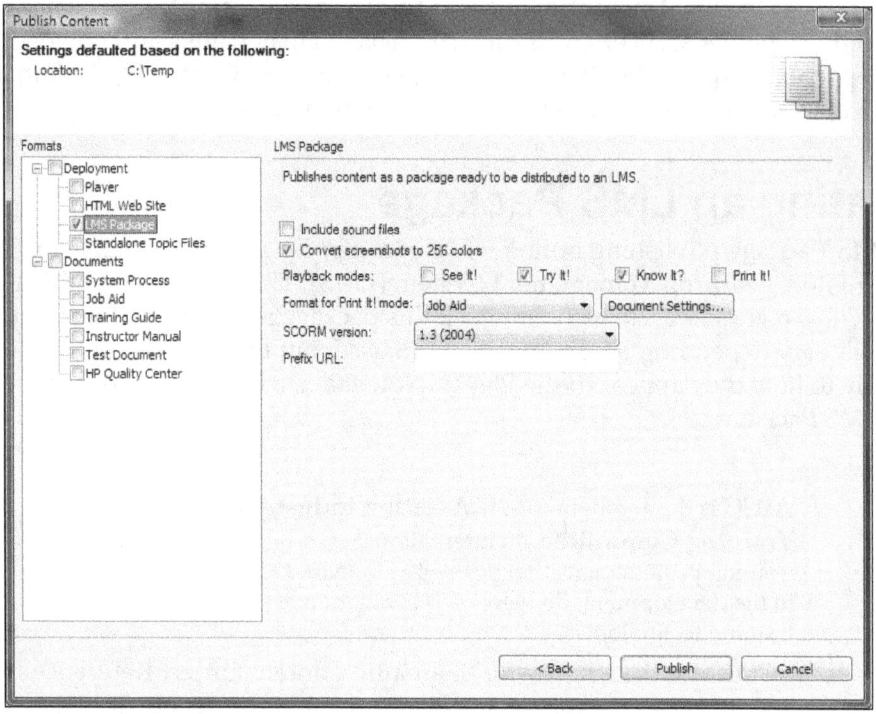

The following table lists the options that are available, and explains their use.

Option	Use
Include sound files	If this option is selected, then sound files will be included in the LMS Package. The use of sound tends to significantly increase the overall size of the LMS Package, so if you know your users will not listen to the sound (perhaps their workstations do not have speakers attached to them) then you can deselect this option and exclude the sound files altogether. That said, sound is an important consideration in self-paced learning so it may be wise to include sound in the LMS package (assuming that you have recorded the sound in the first place—see Chapter 11, *Incorporating Sound into Your Topics*).

Option	Use
Convert screenshots to 256 colors	Selecting this option will result in all screenshots being down-sampled to 256 colors, which will result in much smaller files. For most applications this is sufficient, but for simulations of graphics-intensive applications (such as photo-editing software) you may want to deselect this option.
Playback Modes	This option allows you to select the playback modes in which you want the Topics to be available in the LMS. Note that *Do It!* mode is not available. If you have selected a specific mode in the **Properties** for the Topic, but do not select that mode here, then the Topic will *not* be available in this mode in the LMS Package. Similarly, if you select a mode here that is not selected in the **Topic Properties**, then again the mode will not be available in the LMS Package.
Format for Print It! mode	This option allows you to select the type of document that will be made available in *Print It!* mode in the LMS Package. The various document types are discussed under *Publishing Documents*, later in this chapter. You can click on **Document Settings** to change the individual settings that should be used when generating this document. Again, these are described under the relevant document in the section *Publishing Documents*, later in this chapter.
SCORM Version	This option allows you to select the version of SCORM with which the generated package should be compliant. This will depend upon the version supported by your LMS. The options available are 1.2 and 1.3. 1.3 (which is also known as SCORM 2004 4th Edition) is the latest version, and so is selected by default. Note that there are no AICC-specific options. All versions of SCORM are also AICC compliant.
Prefix URL	If your content will be published to an external content server (and not the LMS) then you need to specify the URL of the location at which the package will be placed on the content server. This URL is prefixed to all of the assets in the LMS Package, to ensure that all links work correctly. If the content is imported into the LMS directly, then relative links are used, in which case this option should not be used.

Generated files

In the `LMS` folder, you will find several files and sub-folders. The files to be loaded will depend on the specific LMS that you are using.

Example output

The output generated cannot be seen until the content is loaded into a Learning Management System. The format of this output will then depend on the LMS being used, but will generally be similar to the example below:

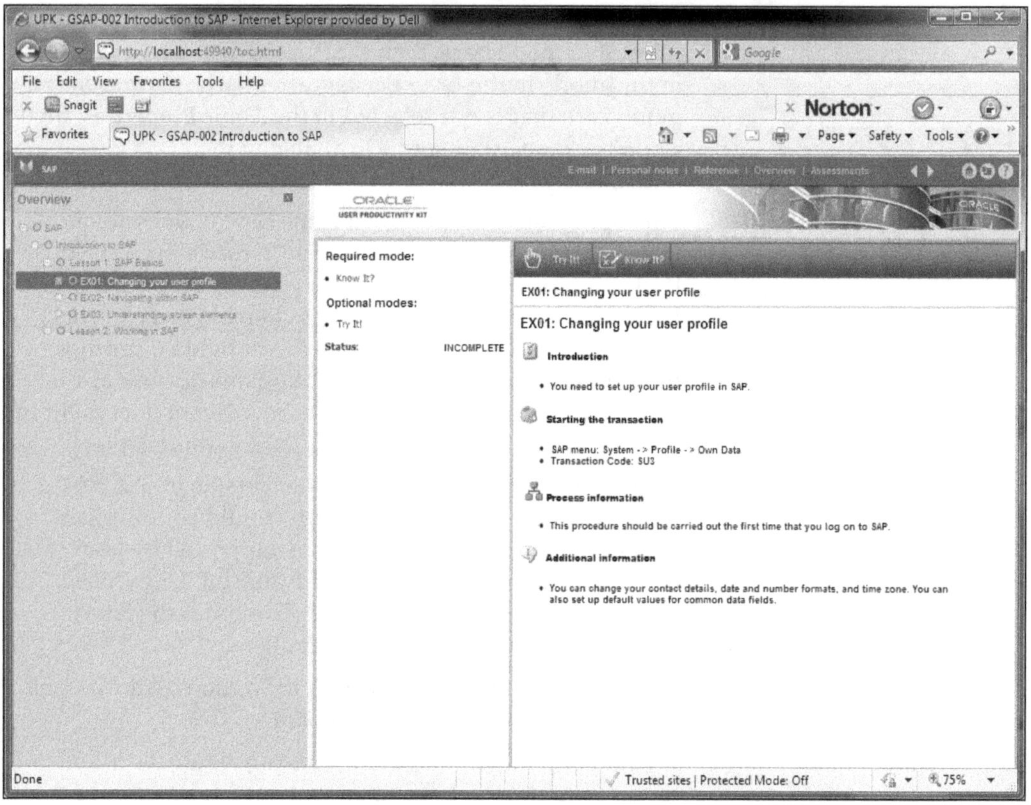

Creating Standalone Topic Files

Standalone Topic Files are complete, self-contained versions of Topics. A separate, single file is generated for each Topic, and this contains everything necessary to play the Topic as if it was opened in the Player. This includes all modes, Web Pages, Packages, and so on, all bundled up into a single "executable" file, of file type `.odtpc`. The advantage of this format is that there is only a single file, which makes it suitable for emailing, or storing in a Content Management System that manages content at the individual file level. However, the disadvantage is that `.odtpc` is a proprietary format, and trainees will need a Topic Player to be able to open it (see *Appendix A* for instructions on how to install the Topic Player). Another disadvantage is that `.odtpc` files tend to be large, so transmission across a network may be slow.

Publishing options

The publishing options for the Standalone Topic File format are as shown in the screenshot below.

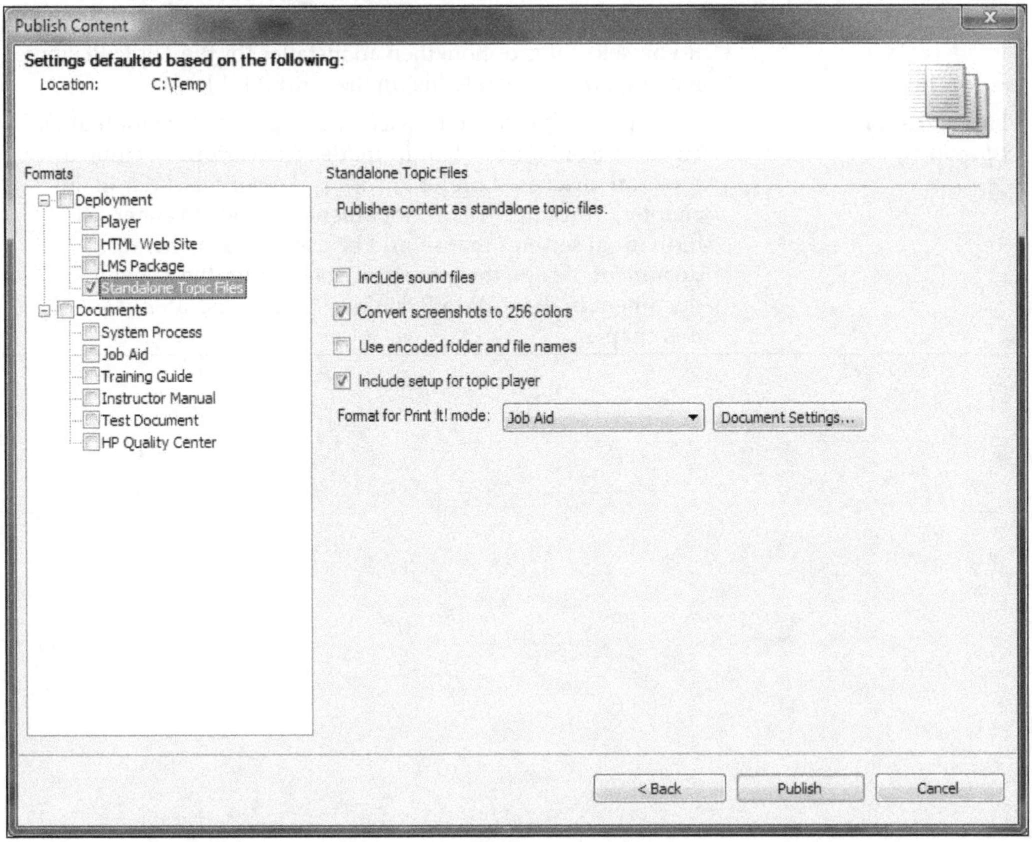

The following table lists the options that are available, and explains their use:

Option	Use
Include sound files	If this option is selected, then sound files will be included in the Standalone Topic File. The use of sound tends to significantly increase the overall size of the file, so if you know your users will not listen to the sound (perhaps their workstations do not have speakers attached to them) then you can deselect this option and exclude the sound files altogether.
Convert screenshots to 256 colors	Selecting this option will result in all screenshots being down-sampled to 256 colors, which will result in much smaller files. For most applications this is sufficient, but for simulations of graphics-intensive applications (such as photo-editing software) you may want to deselect this option.
Use encoded folder and file names	If you select this option, then the file name for each `.tpc` file will be UPK's internal 32-character object identifier for the Topic. Otherwise, the file name will be the Topic name.
Include setup for topic player	As stated earlier, trainees must have the UPK Topic Player installed in order to be able to open the Standalone Topic File. If you select this option, then an installer for the Topic Player is included (as a separate file) in the output folder.
Format for Print It! mode	This option allows you to select the type of document that will be made available in *Print It!* mode. The various document types are discussed under *Publishing Documents*, later in this chapter. You can click on **Document Settings** to change the individual settings that should be used when generating this document. Again, these are described under the relevant document in the section *Publishing Documents*, later in this chapter.

Generated files

In the `TPC` folder, you will find a single `.tpc` file for each Topic within the published Outline. Each of these is a Standalone Topic File. You can distribute these files as required.

If you selected the **Include setup for topic player** option, then the `TPC` folder will also contain a sub-folder, called `installer`. This contains a copy of the installation file for the UPK Topic Player. If your trainees (the recipients of your Standalone Topic Files) do not already have the Player installed, then you should also send them this installer (which is actually a single executable file, `odweb.exe`).

> You can find instructions on installing the Standalone Topic Player in Appendix A, *Installing UPK 3.5*.

Example output

When a trainee launches a Standalone Topic File, they are presented with the following dialog box:

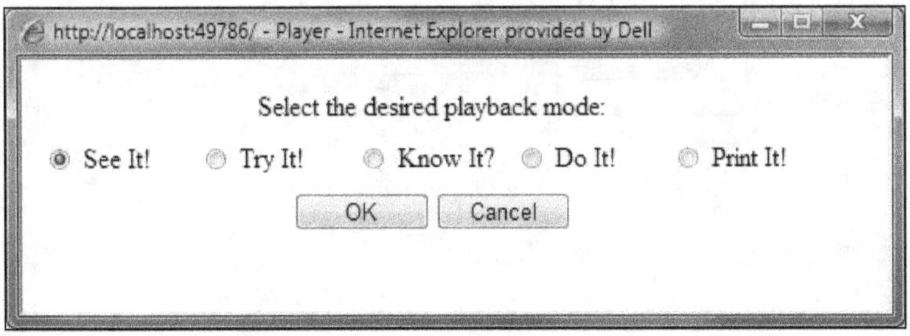

The trainee is required to select the mode in which they want to see the Topic, and then click on **OK**. The Topic is then launched. This provides *exactly* the same functionality as the Player package—including all Bubble Text, Action Areas, hyperlinks, and so on. The following screenshot shows a sample Frame from the *Try It!* mode. Note that the format of the *Print It!* mode document will be exactly as described under the section *Publishing Documents*, next in this chapter.

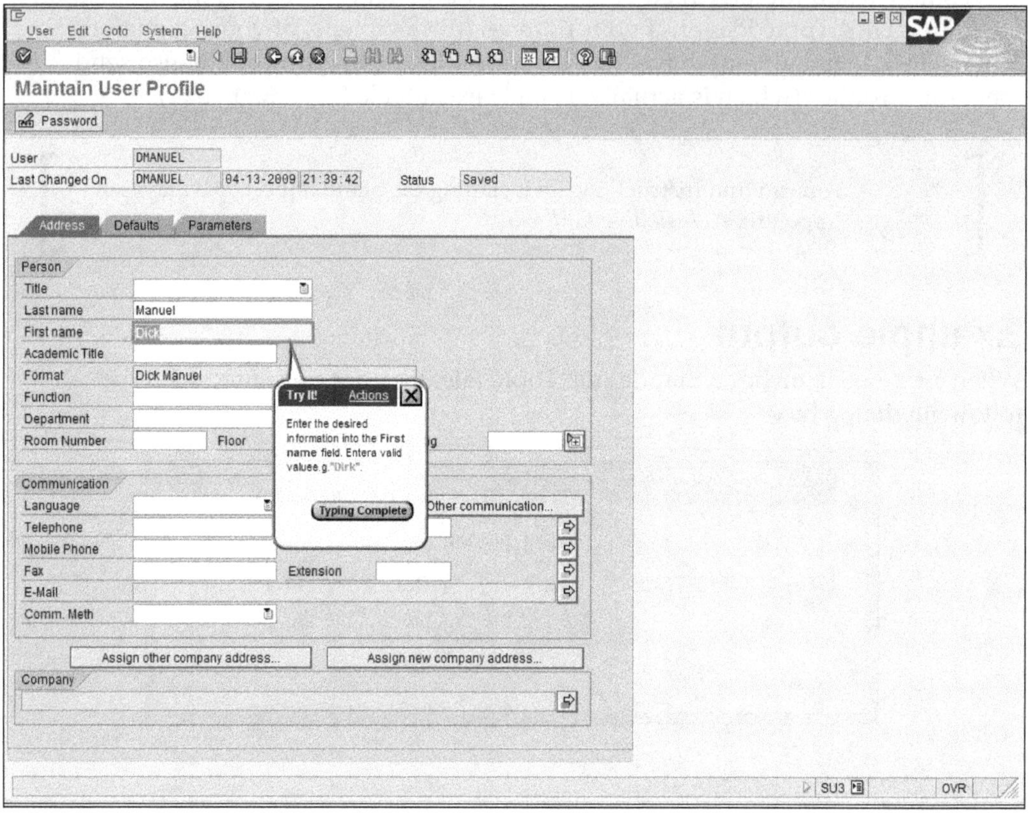

Publishing Documents

UPK provides the capability to publish to a number of different document formats. Obviously, this information is almost entirely the same as the on-line output, with the addition of one or two specialized pieces of information that are defined via the Topic's Properties. The publishing process is exactly the same as above, but the output is different.

All of the additional information is pure text (that is, there is no *contextual* information associated with it), so in theory you could put whatever information you wanted into these Properties. However, the labels will still say what UPK wants them to say. You can customize the output documents (as explained in Chapter 12, *Configuring UPK*), but the labels in the **Properties** pane in the Library will still be the same.

You can choose to have any of the document output types output to Adobe PDF, Microsoft Word, or both, although if you choose PDF, UPK simply outputs the content to Word anyway, and then creates a PDF from that (before deleting the Word document if you did not choose both).

> In order to publish to PDF you need either a full version of Adobe Acrobat (not just the Reader), or (for Office 2007) the **Microsoft Save as PDF or XPS** plug-in.

Publishing a System Process document

The **System Process** document is probably the most commonly used of the available UPK document formats. This document can also be thought of as a user procedure, work instruction, job step, and so on, and is designed to explain the steps required to complete a specified task in the application. The UPK-generated document contains all of the actions carried out in the Topic (screenshots and Bubble Texts), plus an additional page of *context* information. This includes the contents of any *Concept* Web Page linked to the Topic, plus other information taken directly from the Topic's Properties.

Document Properties

The **Properties** that are relevant for System Process documents are shown in the following screenshot (ignore the fact that the property category says **Business Process Document** this is just a(nother) minor inconsistency in UPK, owing to the fact that the System Process document used to be called Business Process Document).

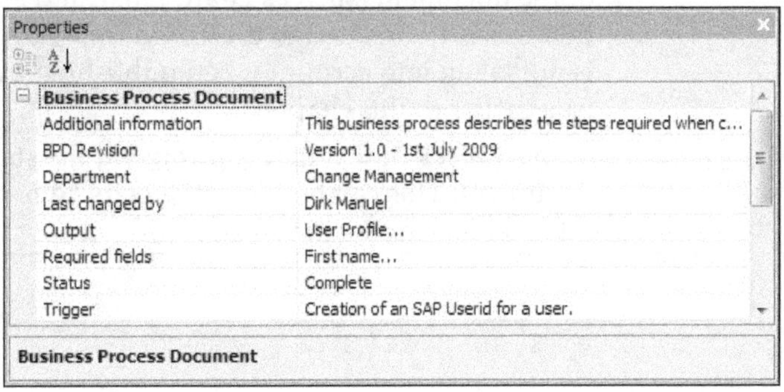

The table below describes some possible uses of these Properties, although it should be noted that they can really be used for any suitable purpose; there is no data validation against what you enter.

Property	Use
Additional information	A short block of text that is printed immediately prior to the actual instructions. Possible uses include specifying prerequisites, or providing additional information about the overall process of which this activity is a part.
BPD Revision	A single line of text. This can be used to specify the revision number of the document. This appears both within the text of the document and in the generated file name, which means that previous revisions will not be overwritten when you re-publish.
Department	A single line of text. This can be used to specify the business function responsible for carrying out this procedure, Given that any role assignments (explained in Chapter 10, *Adding Value in the Player* are not included in the System Process document, you may find it useful to specify the roles in this field.
Last changed by	A single line of text. This can be used to specify the person who either made the change (that is, the content developer), or the person who requested or authorized the change. The latter would be more useful.
Output	A two-column table, with column headings of **Result** and **Comments**. This can be useful for specifying the results of carrying out this procedure.
Required Fields	A two-column table, with column headings of **Required Fields** and **Comments**. Most usefully, this can be used to specify the information that the user needs to know in order to carry out the procedure.
Status	A single line of text. This can be used to specify the status of the document (such as Draft, Final, and so on). Note that this is not related to the Topic *State* Property, and is not taken into account when publishing by state (see earlier in this chapter).
Trigger	A short block of text that is printed at the start of the document. This can be used to specify "when to use" information for the procedure.

Publishing options

The publishing options available for System Process documents are shown in the following screenshot:

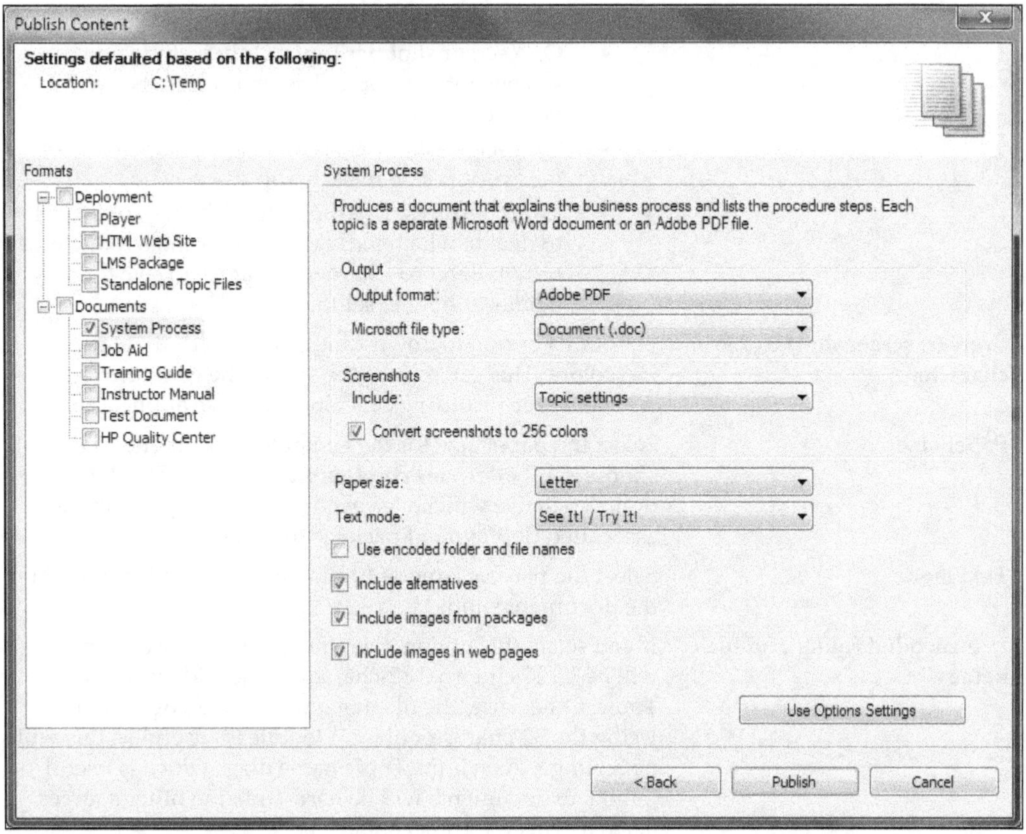

The following table lists the options that are available, and explains their use:

Option	Use
Output format type	Select the file type to be generated. This can be Microsoft Word, Adobe PDF, or both. Printing to Adobe PDF requires Adobe Acrobat 7.0 or greater.
Microsoft file type	Select the type of Word document to be generated. This can be either `.doc` (Microsoft Word format) or `.docx` (Word 2007 format).

Option	Use
Screenshots	Select whether or not screenshots should be included in the document, and how many should be included if they should. The available options are: • **None**: Do not include any screenshots. • **One screenshot per topic**: Only include one screenshot per Topic. The first screenshot will be used. • **One screenshot per frame**: Include a screenshot for every Frame in each Topic. • **Topic settings**: Use the settings in the Topic itself to decide which individual screenshots to include or not. Refer to Chapter 4, *Editing a Topic* for details of how to set this.
Convert screenshots to 256 characters	Select this option to down-sample the screenshots to 256 colors. This can reduce the size of the generated file, especially for recordings of color-intensive applications.
Paper size	Select the paper size for the generated documents. You can choose **A4**, **Letter**, or **Print template setting**. This latter option will use whichever page size is configured in the associated deployment package template.
Text mode	Select the playback mode from which the text included in the document should be taken.
Use encoded folder and file names	If you select this option, then the file name for each file will be UPK's internal 32-character object identifier for the Topic. Otherwise, the file name will be the Topic name. Using the 32-character object identifier is useful as this will not change, even if the Topic name does, which is useful if links to documents will be hard-coded in other sources (such as via an intranet site).
Include alternatives	By default, the document will include any alternative paths recorded in the Topic. If you want to exclude these, then deselect this option.
Include images from packages	If any image files have been attached to the Topic via Packages, then by default the document will include these. If you do not want to include attached images, then deselect this option.
Include images in web pages	If any (UPK) Web Pages attached to the Topic include images, then (by default) the document will include these. If you do not want to include these images, then deselect this option.

Generated files

In the `SPD` folder, you will find a separate (Word or PDF) document for each Topic within the published Outline. Each file contains a single System Process document.

Example output

Sample pages from the System Process document for our sample exercise, using the information shown in the **Properties** pane above, are shown next. The first example shows the additional information that is pulled from the Properties settings:

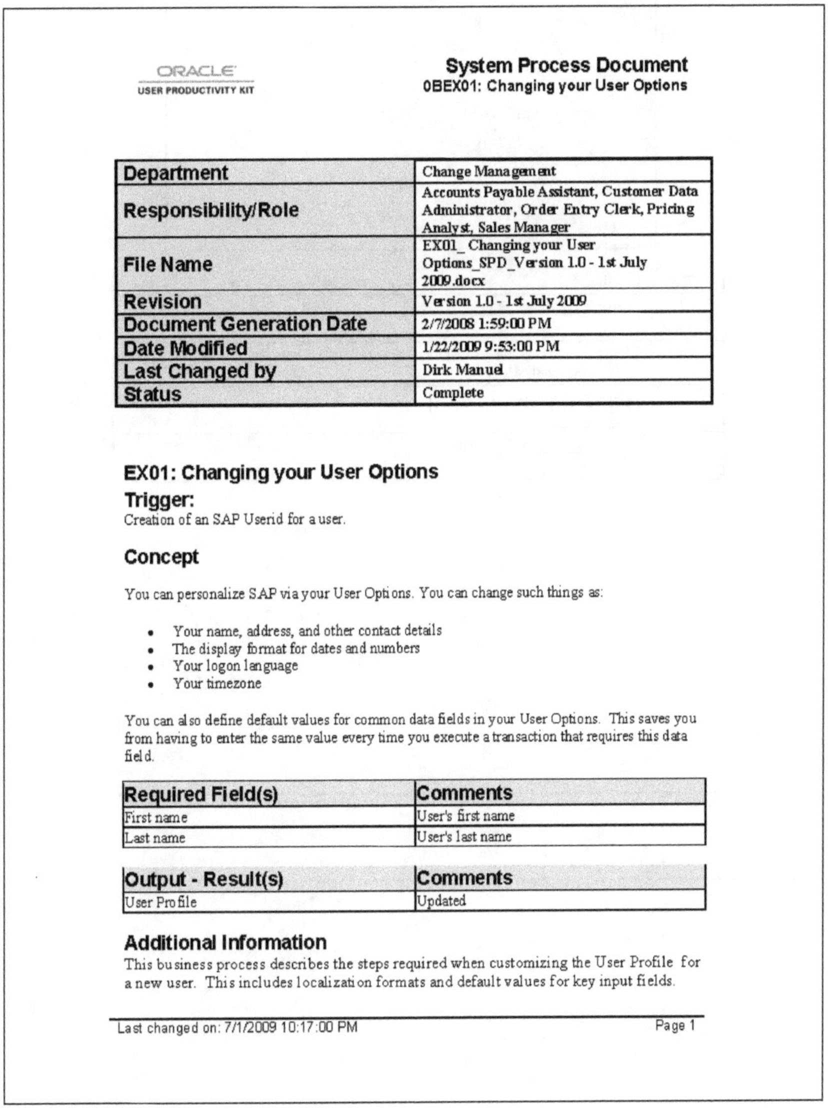

ORACLE
USER PRODUCTIVITY KIT

System Process Document
0BEX01: Changing your User Options

Department	Change Management
Responsibility/Role	Accounts Payable Assistant, Customer Data Administrator, Order Entry Clerk, Pricing Analyst, Sales Manager
File Name	EX01_ Changing your User Options_SPD_Version 1.0 - 1st July 2009.docx
Revision	Version 1.0 - 1st July 2009
Document Generation Date	2/7/2008 1:59:00 PM
Date Modified	1/22/2009 9:53:00 PM
Last Changed by	Dirk Manuel
Status	Complete

EX01: Changing your User Options

Trigger:

Creation of an SAP Userid for a user.

Concept

You can personalize SAP via your User Options. You can change such things as:

- Your name, address, and other contact details
- The display format for dates and numbers
- Your logon language
- Your timezone

You can also define default values for common data fields in your User Options. This saves you from having to enter the same value every time you execute a transaction that requires this data field.

Required Field(s)	Comments
First name	User's first name
Last name	User's last name

Output - Result(s)	Comments
User Profile	Updated

Additional Information

This business process describes the steps required when customizing the User Profile for a new user. This includes localization formats and default values for key input fields.

Last changed on: 7/1/2009 10:17:00 PM Page 1

The second example shows a page taken from the middle of the System Process Document, which illustrates how screenshots and actions are presented:

System Process Document
0BEX01: Changing your User Options

ORACLE
USER PRODUCTIVITY KIT

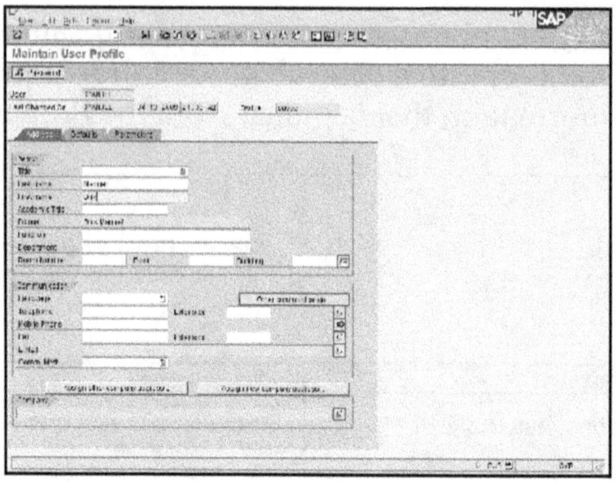

Step	Action
7.	Click in the **Function** field.
8.	Enter the correct value in the **Function** field. For this exercise, you should enter "**Training Analyst**".
9.	Click the **Defaults** tab. Defaults
10.	Click the **Decimal Notation** list. Y 1 234 567,89

Page 6 Last changed on: 7/1/2009 10:17:00 PM

Publishing an Instructor Manual

The **Instructor Manual** provides a simple run through the screens and actions in whichever mode you select for publication. The only unique information provided in the Instructor Manual comes in the form of a block of *Instructor Notes*. These are defined in the Topic **Properties**, and then included in the document immediately before the "procedure" itself.

Document Properties

The Properties that are relevant for Instructor Manual documents are shown in the following screenshot:

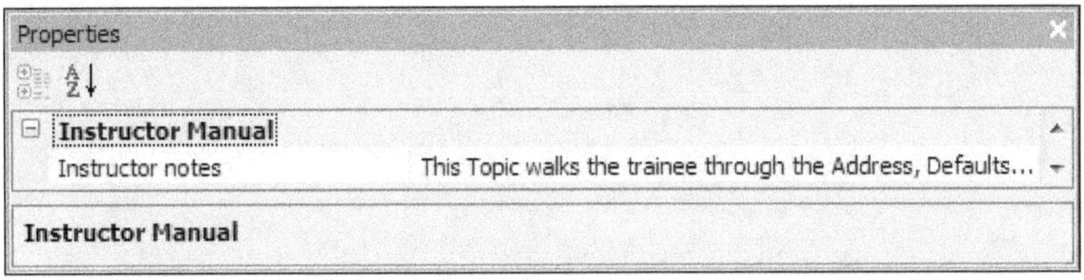

The table below describes possible uses of this Property:

Property	Use
Instructor note	A short block of text that is printed immediately prior to the Topic details. This can be used to provide the instructor with information about how the Topic should be used in the classroom. This could include a description of the alternative paths, or mentioning if this exercise builds on previous ones, and so on.

Publishing options

The publishing options available for Instructor Manual documents are exactly the same as those for System Process documents. Refer to *Publishing a System Process document*, for details.

Generated files

In the `IMPrint` folder, you will find a single (Word or PDF) document for the entire Outline. This contains the Instructor Manual.

Example output

A sample page from the Instructor Manual document for our sample exercise, using the information shown in the **Properties** pane above, is shown in the following screenshot:

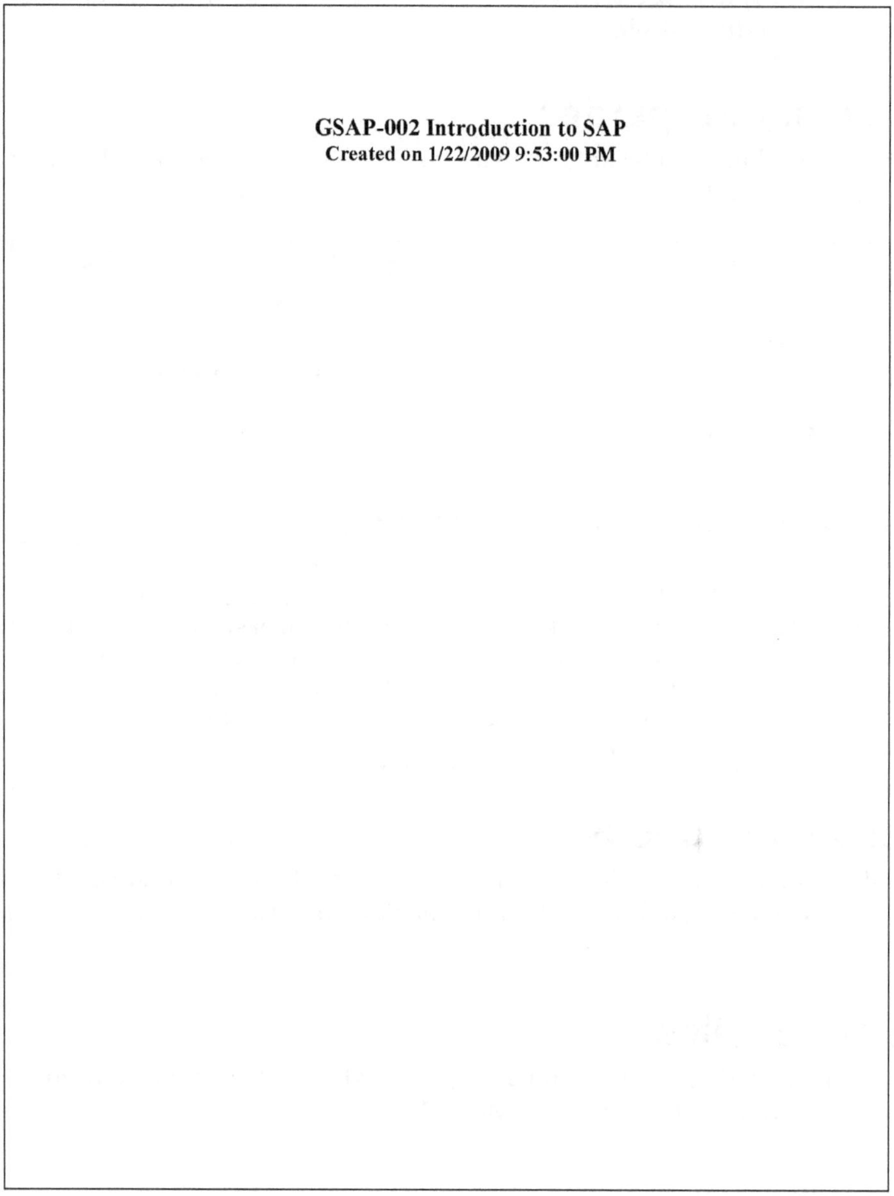
GSAP-002 Introduction to SAP
Created on 1/22/2009 9:53:00 PM

Publishing a Job Aid

The **Job Aid** is a very scaled-down extract of a Topic and simply lists all of the actions as a single numbered list, formatted in a table. By default, screenshots are not included, but you have the option to include a single screen-print per Job Aid, one per Frame, or to use the settings in the Topic itself.

The Job Aid format is commonly used as the default document format for the *Print It!* mode (which is available in UPK 3.5 and above).

Document Properties

The Properties that are relevant for Job Aid documents are shown in the following screenshot:

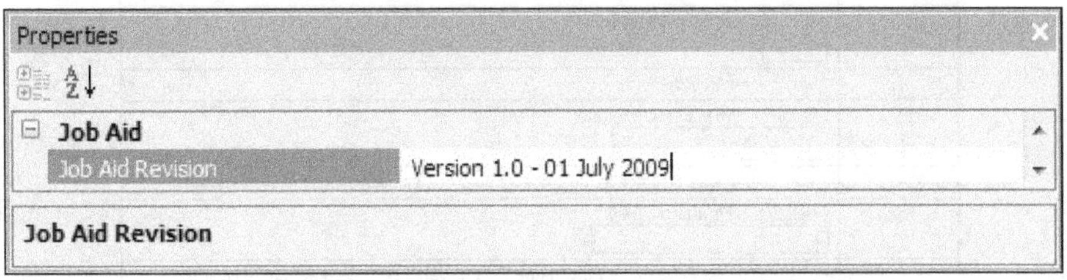

The table below describes possible uses of this Property:

Property	Use
Job Aid Revision	A single line of text. This can be used to specify the revision number of the document. Note that this is not used within the printed document, but does appear in the generated file name, which means that previous revisions will not be overwritten when you republish.

Publishing options

The publishing options available for Job Aid documents are broadly the same as those for System Process documents, with the exception that the two image-related options (**Include images from Packages** and **Include images in Web Pages**) are not available. Refer to *Publishing a System Process document* for details of the available options.

Generated files

In the `JobAid` folder, you will find a separate (Word or PDF) document for each Topic within the published Outline.

Example output

A sample page from the Job Aid document for our sample exercise, using the information shown in the **Properties** pane above, is shown below. Note that the **Job Aid Revision** property is only used in the file name and not within the body of the document itself (which is why you do not see it here).

ORACLE
USER PRODUCTIVITY KIT

Job Aid

EX01: Changing your User Options

Step	Action
1.	Click on menu option **System**. System
2.	Point to **User Profile**.
3.	Click on menu option **Own Data**. Own Data
4.	Your family name is shown in the *Last name* field. You can change this if necessary.
5.	Click in the **First name** field. Dick
6.	Enter the correct value in the **First name** field. For this exercise, you should enter any appropriate value - for example, "**Dirk**".
7.	Click in the **Function** field.
8.	Enter the correct value in the **Function** field. For this exercise, you should enter any appropriate value - for example, "**Training Analyst**".
9.	Click the **Defaults** tab. Defaults
10.	Click the **Decimal Notation** list. Y 1 234 567,89
11.	Click the **X 1,234,567.89** list item. X 1,234,567.89
12.	Click the **Date format** list. 3 MM-DD-YYYY
13.	Click the **1 DD.MM.YYYY** list item. 1 DD.MM.YYYY
14.	Click the **Parameters** tab. Parameters
15.	Click in the first free field in the **Parameter** column.
16.	Enter the correct value in the **Parameter value** field. For this exercise, you should enter any appropriate value - for example, "**VKO**".
17.	Press **[TAB]**.
18.	Enter the correct value in the **Parameter value** field. For this exercise, you should enter any appropriate value - for example, "**1001**".

Date Created: 7/1/2009 11:02:00 PM Page 1

Publishing a Test Document

The **Test Document** contains several additional pieces of information related to testing, such as the purpose of the test, the set-up instructions, the expected time to complete, the additional validation instructions, and so on. For each step in the "procedure", the Test Document includes space to record the input (data entered or action taken), expected result, and whether the test (or step) was passed or failed.

Document Properties

The Properties that are relevant for Test Document documents are shown in the following screenshot:

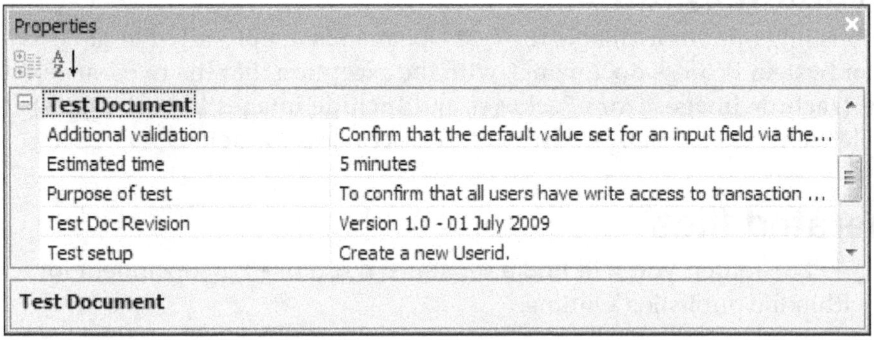

The following table describes possible uses of these **Properties**:

Property	Use
Additional validation	A short block of text that is printed at the very end of the Test Document. This can be used to specify any additional validation steps that should be performed and that are not directly tied to the test steps. For example, you could provide details of what additional actions the tester should perform to validate that the test has indeed done what it was supposed to.
Estimated time	A single line of text. This can be used to provide the tester with the amount of time that they will require to complete the test. In the printed document this is formatted as a table, with space for the tester to enter the actual time taken to complete the test.
Purpose of test	A short block of text that is printed prior to the test steps. This can be used to specify what the test is proving.

Property	Use
Test Doc Revision	A single line of text. This can be used to specify the revision number of the document. Note that this is not used within the printed document, but does appear in the generated file name, which means that previous revisions will not be overwritten when you re-publish.
Test setup	A short block of text that is printed prior to the test steps. This can be used to specify any prerequisite activities, or to describe the data that is required (or other environment information) in order to execute the test.

Publishing options

The publishing options available for Test Documents are broadly the same as those for System Process documents, with the exception that the two image-related options (**Include images from Packages** and **Include images in Web Pages**) are not available. Refer to *Publishing a System Process document* for details.

Generated files

In the `TestDoc` folder, you will find a separate (Word or PDF) document for each Topic within the published Outline.

Example output

A sample page from the Test Document document for our sample exercise, using the information shown in the **Properties** pane above, is shown opposite. Note that the **Job Aid Revision** property is only used in the filename and not within the body of the document itself.

ORACLE
USER PRODUCTIVITY KIT

Test Document

Purpose of Test

To confirm that all users have write access to transaction SU3.

Test History

Date	Tester	Pass/Fail	Notes

Time to Test

Estimated Time	5 minutes
Actual Time	

Test Setup

Create a new Userid.

Test Procedure

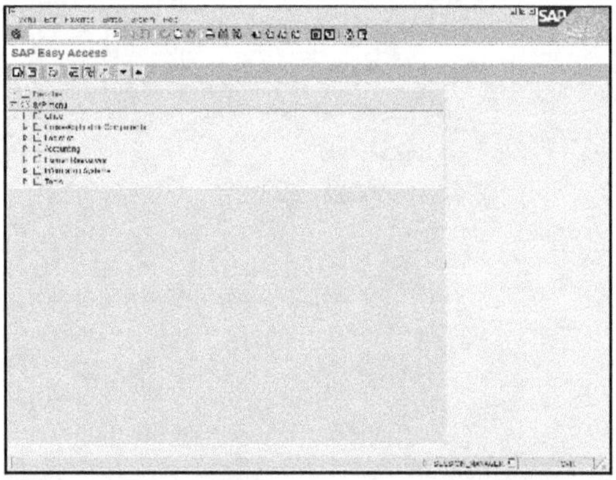

Step	Action	Input	Expected Results	Pass	Fail
1.	Click on menu option **System**. System				

Last changed on:7/1/2009 11:16:00 PM Page 1

Publishing an HP Quality Center test script

The **HP Quality Center** format generates a Microsoft Excel file that is identical in format and content to those produced by HP Quality Center (previously known as Mercury TestDirector).

Document Properties

There are no Topic Properties unique to HP Quality Center, but the `Estimated Time` property from the Test Document Properties is included in the output.

Publishing options

The publishing options available for the HP Quality Center format are shown in the following screenshot.

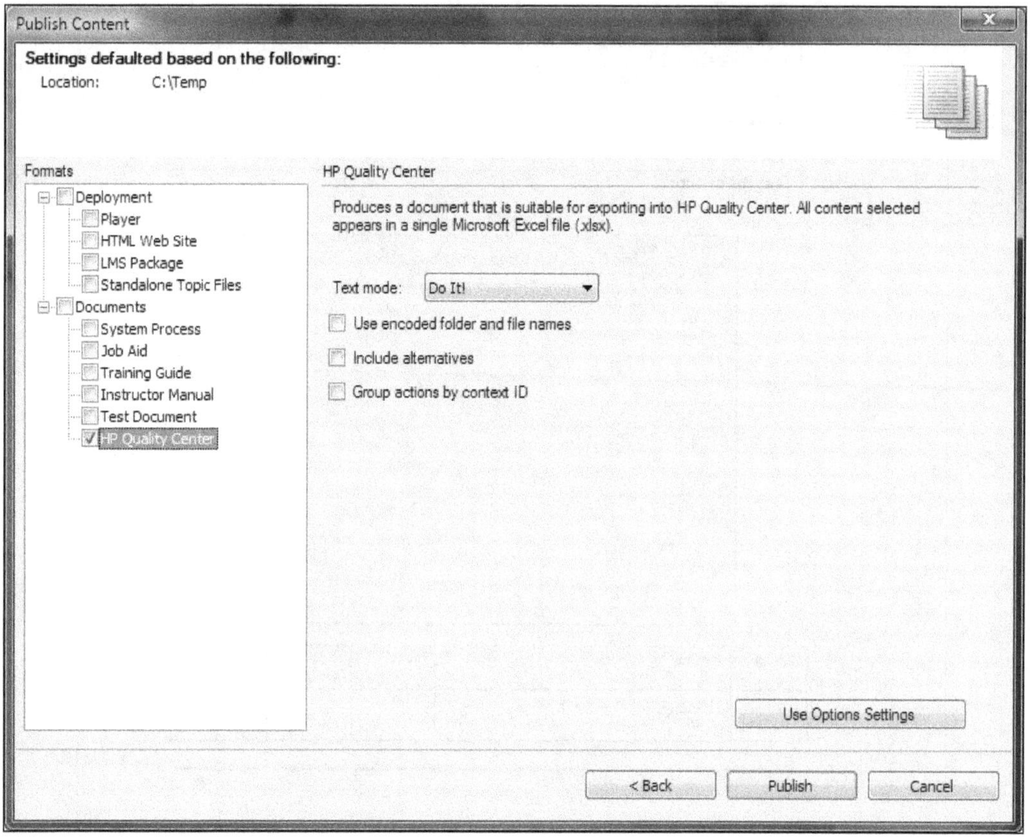

The next table lists the options that are available, and explains their use.

Option	Use
Text mode	Select the playback mode from which the text included in the document should be taken.
Use encoded folder and file names	If you select this option, then the file name for each file will be UPK's internal 32-character object identifier for the Outline Element. Otherwise, the file name will be the Topic name.

Option	Use
Include alternatives	By default, the document will include any alternative paths recorded in the Topic. If you want to exclude these, then deselect this option.
Group actions by Context ID	By default, the generated file will include each step (action) on a separate row. If this option is selected, then all actions for the same Context ID will be grouped into a single row (per Topic).

Generated files

In the `HPQC` folder, you will find a single Microsoft Excel Workbook for the entire published Outline.

Example output

A sample page from the HP Quality Center worksheet for our sample exercise is shown next:

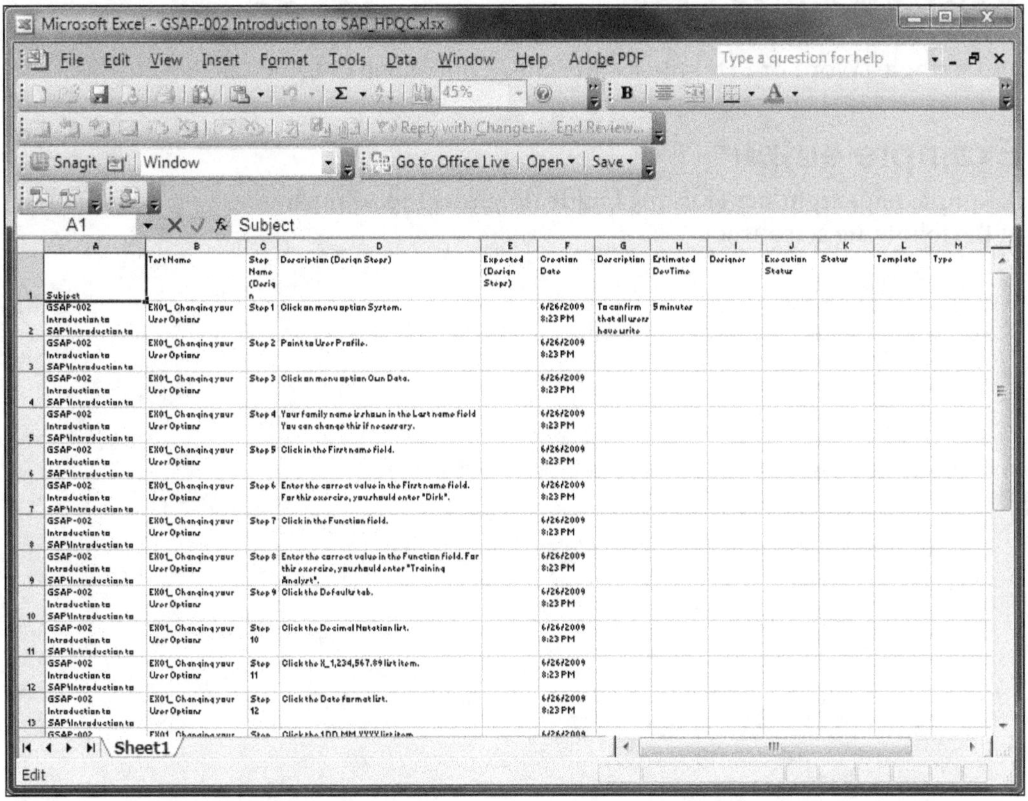

Publishing a Training Guide

The **Training Guide** is effectively a complete print-out of all of the Topics in the published Outline. This includes all screenshots and instructions, along with the content of any Web Pages used in the **Concept** panes or otherwise attached, and so on.

Document Properties

There are no Topic Properties for the Training Guide document.

Publishing options

The publishing options available for Training Guide documents are exactly the same as those available for System Process documents. Refer to *Publishing a System Process document* for details.

Generated files

Training Guides are published to the `TrainingGuide` folder. In this folder, you will find a single (Word or PDF) file for the entire published Outline.

Example output

A sample page from the Training Guide document for our sample exercise is shown in the following screenshot:

Training Guide
GSAP-002 Introduction to SAP

ORACLE
USER PRODUCTIVITY KIT

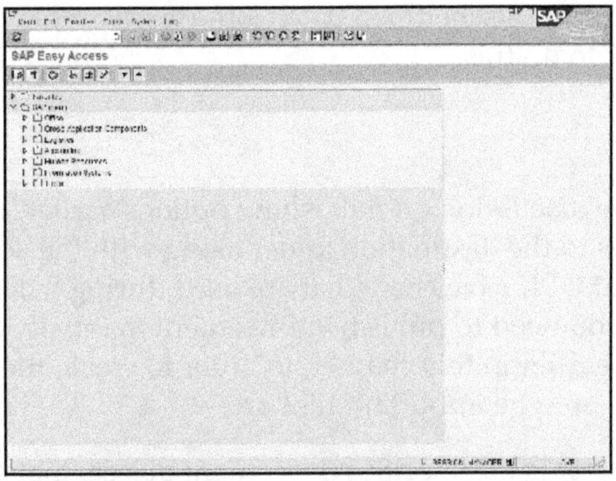

Step	Action
1.	Click on menu option **System**. System

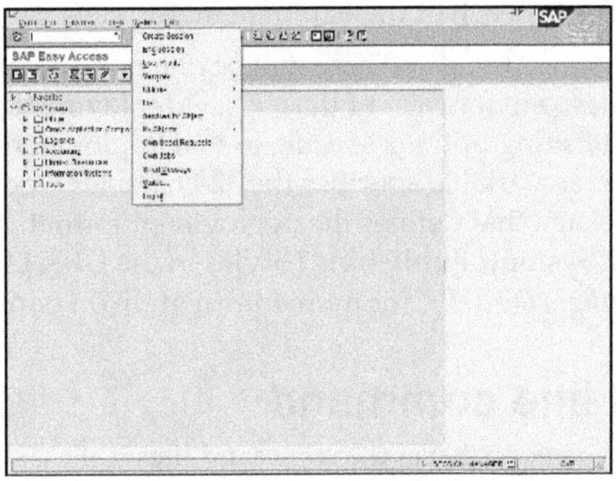

Page 2

Note that the previous example is of **Page 2** of the Training Guide. Page 1 is the same as the example shown for Instructor Guide, but without the **Instructor Notes**.

Automatic publishing

UPK provides the ability to execute publishing tasks via the Windows command line. This is a useful feature, as it allows you to put the publishing commands in a batch file and submit this via a scheduled batch job—for example, during off-peak times. Let's look at how to do this.

Settings files

You may recall from the discussion on publishing options earlier, that UPK saves your publishing options to the destination folder along with the actual published output. It is the files that UPK saves here that are used during batch publishing. This means, of course, that you need to publish your content manually at least once, using the methods described earlier in this chapter, in order to create these files, before you can publish via a batch job. The important files are:

- `Selection.xml`: This file specifies the content objects that are to be published. It is this file to which the publication command must refer.
- `Publishing.project.xml`: This file defines the "global" publishing options that apply to all output formats. It also contains a list of the individual configuration files for each of the deployment formats.
- `<format_guid>.config.xml`: There will be one or more of these configuration files, one for each of the chosen deployment formats. Each file contains the publishing options specific to that deployment format. Note that the `<format_guid>` variable specifies the 32-character Document ID of the deployment package that defines the deployment format. You can find these packages under **System** | **Publishing** | **Styles** in the UPK Library. (Refer to Chapter 12, *Configuring UPK* for more information on deployment packages.)

The command line command

The executable file that you execute via the command line is `CommandLinePublish.exe`. You can find this command in the program folder for your UPK installation (that is, the same folder that contains the `OdDev.exe` executable).

The format of the command is:

```
CommandLinePublish.exe <settings> /profilename:<profile> /
password:<password>
```

or:

```
CommandLinePublish.exe <settings> /profile:<profile> /
password:<password>
```

or (for a standalone implementation):

```
CommandLinePublish.exe <settings>
```

The following table explains the command-line parameters:

Parameter	Description
`<settings>`	This is the path to the `Selection.xml` file in the destination folder. This can be a relative path, as long as it is relative to the folder containing the `CommandLinePublish.exe` file.
`/profilename:<profile>` *	Use this parameter to specify the name of the user profile within the `UserProfiles` folder that should be used for the publication process. If the user's password is not stored within the profile, then the `/password` parameter must also be used.
`/profile: <profile>` *	If you want to use a user profile that is not stored within the `UserProfiles` folder, then use this parameter to specify the full path and file name of the user profile that should be used for the publication process. If the user's password is not stored within the profile, then the `/password` parameter must also be used.
`/password:<password>` *	If the password for the user profile that you are using does not contain the password, then use this parameter to specify the password.

Note that parameters marked with an asterisk (*) apply only to a client/server (multi-user) environment. In a standalone implementation, only the `<settings>` parameter is used.

To execute the command, simply open a Windows command prompt, and enter the command. You should either do this from the same folder in which the `CommandLinePublish.exe` file is located, or prefix the command with the path to this file.

During the publishing process, a succession of status messages will be displayed, indicating the progress of the publishing activities, as shown in the following example:

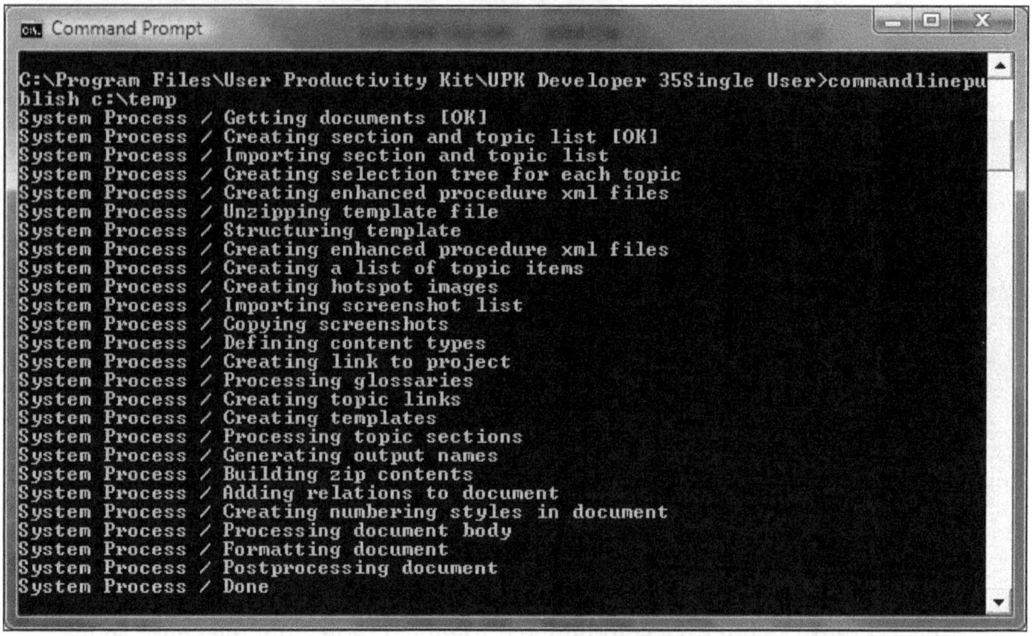

Once you see the message **Done**, publishing is complete.

Publishing via a batch job

Publishing via a batch job is very simple, given the command-line functionality explained above. Simply place the command in a batch file (file type `.bat`), as shown below:

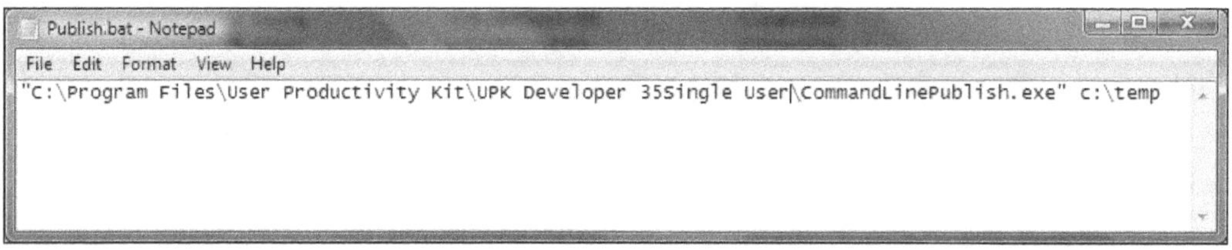

You can then publish your content simply by double-clicking on this file in Windows Explorer. Note that you can include multiple commands within the same batch file, as long as each command is on a separate line. Note also that if you include the path to the command executable, and this path includes spaces, then you need to enclose the full path/file specification in quotes, as shown in the preceding example.

You can now set this batch job to run at a specific time, or at regular intervals. How to do this will vary depending on your Operating System, but is likely to be some variation on the Windows Task Scheduler. Use your operating system's Help function to search for "Schedule a task" for details of how to set up batch jobs.

> The Task Scheduler for Windows Vista allows you to specify the program, parameters, and the folder from which this will be executed for a task. This allows you to call `CommandLinePublish.exe` directly, saving you the need to create a batch file.

Integrating published content into other environments

In most cases, you will probably publish your Topics to a content server or LMS, and then have your trainees carry out the simulations from there, via the published Outline. However, in some cases you may want to provide access to Topics in other ways. This section explains some of these ways. Note that this is certainly not an exhaustive list of possibilities, but it will hopefully provide you with some food for thought.

Integrating a Topic into a presentation

When you publish to a Player, UPK also creates an additional, "hidden" HTML page that can prove extremely useful to you as a developer. This page is `kp.html`, and can be found in the `Publishing Content/PlayerPackage` folder (that is, exactly the same folder as the `index.html` and `default.html` pages). This file was initially developed as part of Global Knowledge's Knowledge Pathways application (which is now included in Oracle UPK Professional) as a way of providing easy access to individual Topics from within an e-learning environment, but it has its uses for "regular" (and not just "professional") UPK developers.

If you open this `kp.html` file, you will see something like the example shown in the following screenshot:

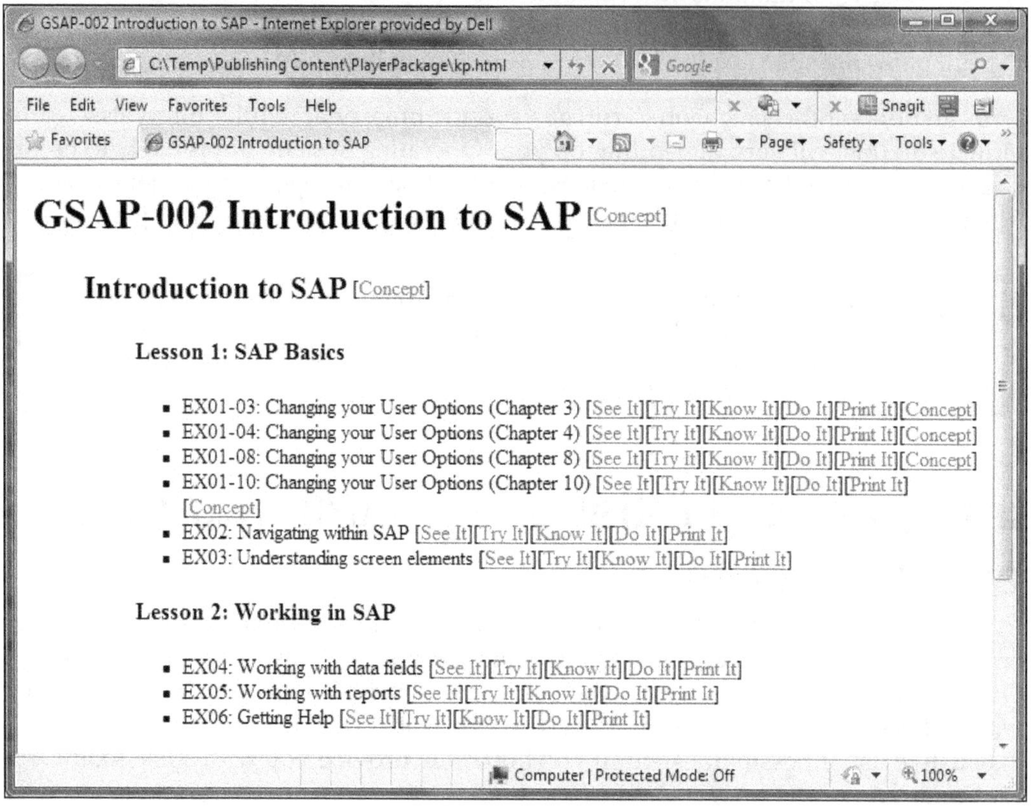

As you can see, this page provides a very basic way of accessing each of the Topics in the published outline in any of the five (four, prior to UPK 3.5) standard modes (assuming that the Topic is available in all modes), along with all of the Web Pages linked in as Concepts. Just click on the relevant link, and the Topic will be launched exactly the same as if you had selected it in the Outline and clicked on the Player button for that mode. Obviously, this is not really an interface that you'd want to give to your trainees, but for the developer, it is indispensable, because what this page is really doing is providing you with direct URLs to the Topics.

Why is this useful? Well, consider the case where you are building a standalone course designed to be used for self-paced learning (as opposed to instructor-led classroom conduct). You have built a presentation in Microsoft PowerPoint, and want to integrate your UPK simulations into this. You *could* simply provide instructions telling your trainees to go and access the UPK server, select their course, navigate to the correct exercise, and then run it in the required mode. All of which they *may* bother to do, and all of which they *may* actually do correctly. However, wouldn't it be better if they could just click on a link within the presentation and immediately be taken to the correct exercise, in the required mode? To do this, all you need to do is get the URL of the specific Topic/mode combination, and use this as a link in the presentation. And the `kp.html` file will give you this link.

To copy the link for a specific Topic/mode combination, carry out the steps described below:

1. Open the `kp.html` file in your web browser.
2. Locate the Topic to which you want to provide a link.
3. Right-click on the link for the relevant mode, and then select **Copy shortcut** from the context menu. (The option name may be different in browsers other than Internet Explorer.)
4. You can now use this URL in any link you like. You can use it in a presentation, as discussed, or email it to a reviewer, or even use it to build your own frontend for your UPK training exercises. Note that depending on where you displayed the `kp.html` file from (for example, the final content server, or your local machine), you may need to change the server specification in the URL (basically, everything between `http:/` and `Publishing Content`).

Let's take a closer look at this URL. Starting from the `PlayerPackage` folder, it is:
`PlayerPackage/dhtml_kp.html?Guid=d7305eea-5139-408f-b4f6-f126b662440a&Mode=S&Back`

You can see that this is effectively calling a specific web page (`dhtml_kp.html`) within the `PlayerPackage` sub-folder, and passing this web page three parameters separated by ampersands (`&`). These parameters are the crucial part, and are:

```
Guid=d7305eea-5139-408f-b4f6-f126b662440a
```

This specifies the **Document Id** of the specific Topic. You may recall that UPK uses its own 32 character identifier to refer to all content objects; this is that identifier. For reference, a snippet of the Library, showing the same identifier, is shown below:

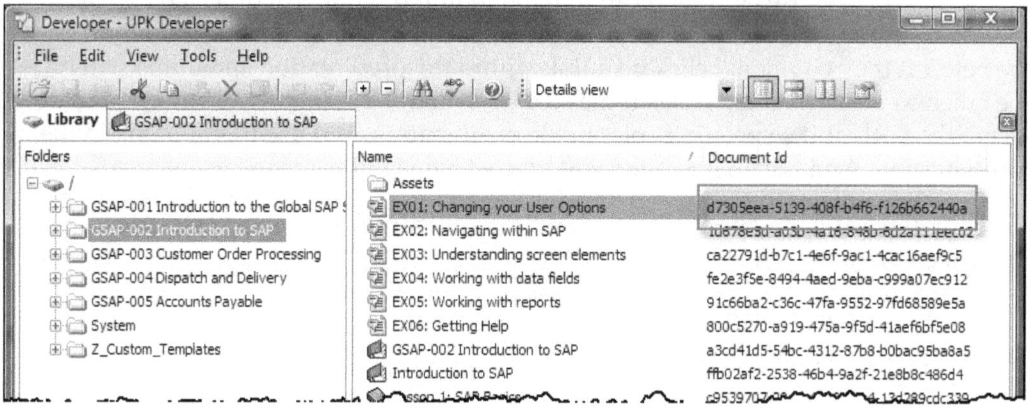

`Mode=S:` This parameter specifies the mode in which the Topic will be played. The following values are possible:

- **S**: See It! mode
- **T**: Try It! mode
- **K**: Know It? mode
- **D**: Do It! mode
- **P**: Print It! mode

`Back:` This parameter does not take a value, and simply means that once the simulation has completed, the window should be closed and control returned to the calling application. This is normally what you would want to happen.

> The question mark (?) in the URL means that what follows it is one or more parameters. This is standard web functionality. However, some applications may not support the use of a question mark in a URL, and interpret it differently. If you find that you cannot successfully call this URL from within your application, then try replacing the question mark with a hash mark (#), sometimes referred to as a *pound* or *hex* sign. This is also standard web functionality. Both are supported by all standard web browsers.

By using all of this information, you can manually build your own hyperlinks to Topics (without displaying the `kp.html` file), as long as you know the **Document Id**. This can be useful if you need to provide hyperlinks (for example, for use in an external access mechanism) before you have even published your content to its final location.

Integrating UPK into your application

UPK can be used to provide an online help library for just about any application. However it really comes into its own when integrated with an application for which UPK can capture context information (referred to as *targeted applications*). As of UPK 3.5.1, these applications are:

- Agile
- JD Edwards Enterprise One
- JD Edwards World
- Microsoft Dynamics CRM
- Oracle E-Business Suite
- PeopleSoft
- SAP
- Siebel

What is context capturing, and what does it do?

You may recall from Chapter 4, *Editing a Topic* that the **Action Properties** pane contains a couple of fields that are specific to the application being recorded. For reference, an example of the **Action Properties** pane for a Frame in our sample exercise is shown in the following screenshot:

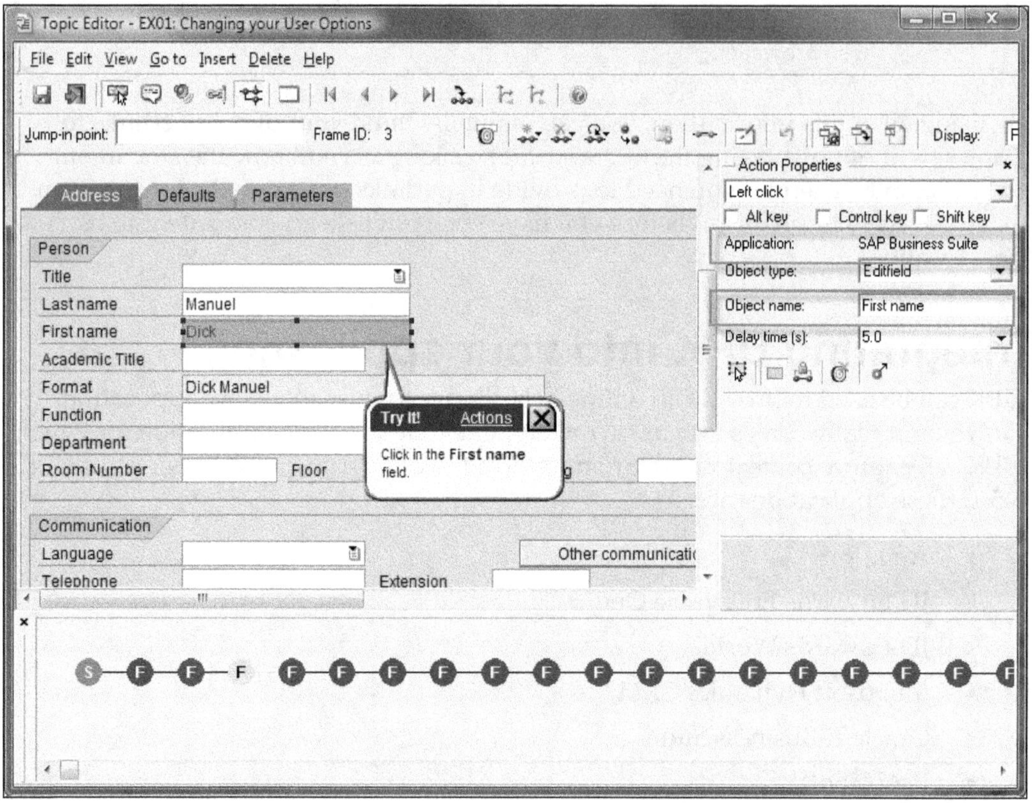

This information (highlighted in the previous screenshot) is part of the *context* that UPK captures—the actual object within the application that has been acted upon. In the example above, UPK has captured the following information:

- Application: SAP Business Suite.
- Object Name: The name of the object that was clicked or the field into which text was entered.

In addition to this information, UPK is also capturing some other, "under the hood" context information. You can see this additional information if you select menu option **Edit | Context ID**. The screenshot below shows the context information for the same screen to which the **Action Properties** pane shown above applies:

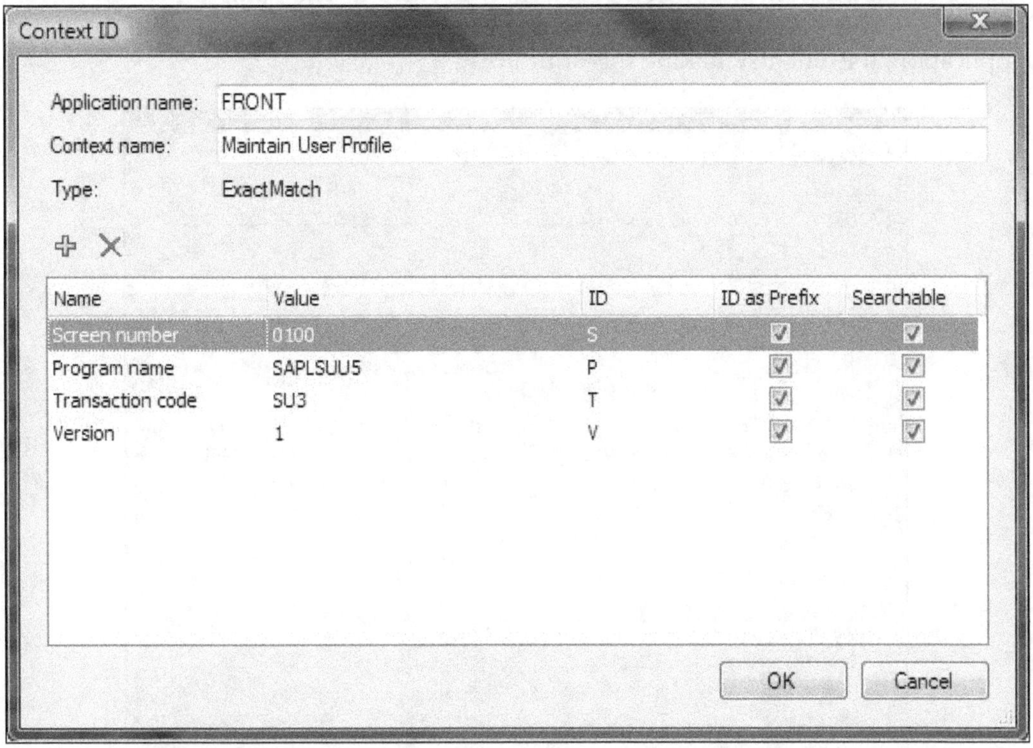

This information is the true context of the action. It identifies the exact screen within the application that was recorded. Note that the information shown in the example above is for the SAP application. Other information may be captured for other applications.

> In addition to being able to change any of the information in the Context ID dialog box, you can also recapture the context for any Frame within the Topic Editor. To do this, select menu option **Edit | Recapture Context ID**, then re-perform the action in the correct context within the application, and press *PrtScr* to recapture the context.

If we display the technical information for our application, we will find this same information. In the following screenshot, we see the technical information for the same screen as the context information shown previously. This information will obviously vary depending on the specific application that you are recording. This example is taken from SAP, but that is largely irrelevant. The point of this screenshot is simply to show that UPK is *capturing* this key information: the context from the application; it is not just making this stuff up!

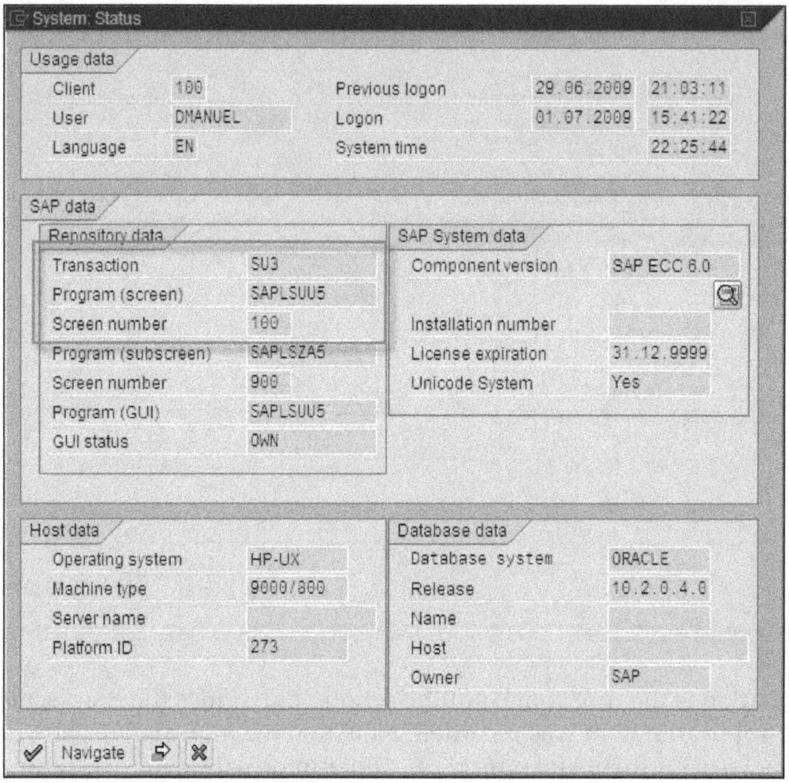

So far so good, but what does this context information do for us? Put simply, the context information provides the ability to support *context-sensitive help* in our application. With context-sensitive help, if a user in the application selects the on-line help option, the application will pass details of the *context* within which the help option was selected (typically, the program, screen, and/or field) to the help system. The help system can then see if it has help for this particular context, and display that context-specific help topic. In this way, users get help on exactly what they need, rather than being presented with the main index page of the help system and having to find what they are looking for themselves.

How to integrate UPK into your application is beyond the scope of this book, but it is useful to understand how it works once it is in place. We will therefore just look at a simple example of integrated application help. For details of your own application, and how to set up this help integration, you will need to refer to your local application support team. The Oracle-provided documentation in the folder `/User Productivity Kit/{version}/Documentation/{language}/Reference` also provides a brief implementation guide for each supported system.

Our sample exercise was recorded for SAP. In the SAP application screens, custom help is provided by way of another option on the **Help** menu, as shown in the next screenshot:

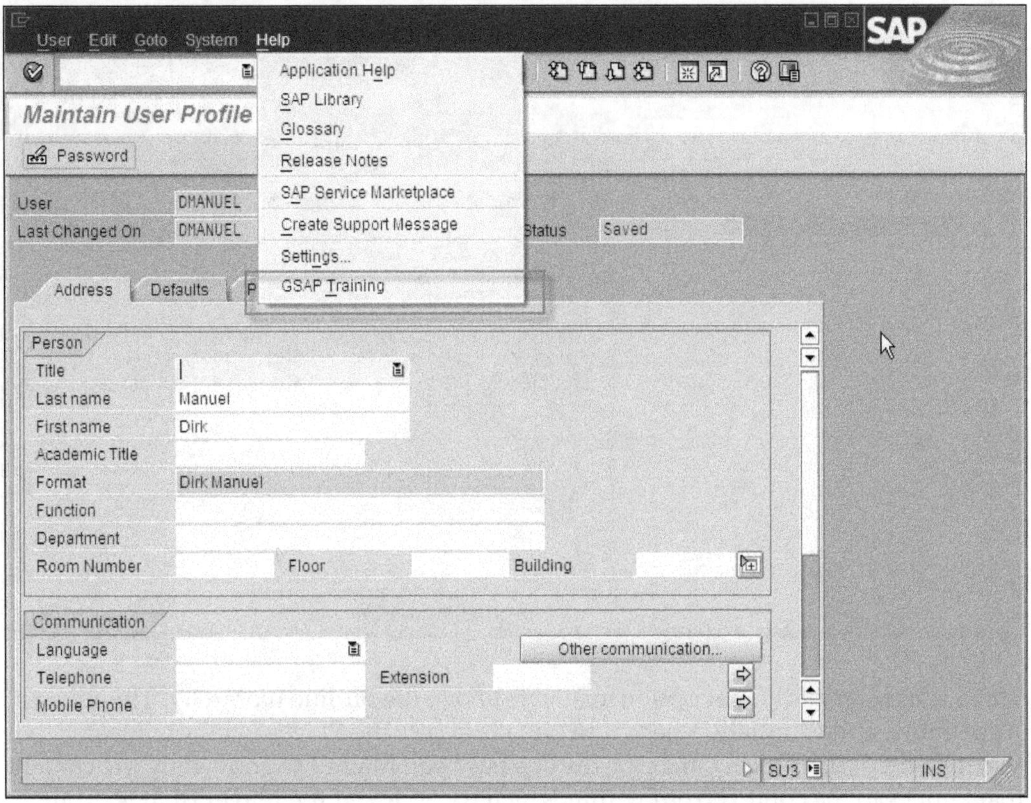

This menu option, **GSAP Training**, is configured within SAP to point to a UPK Player on a server. If a user selects this help option, then the specified UPK Player is opened in the browser. The clever part is that the content of the Player is automatically filtered to show only Topics that apply to the exact context that was passed by the application. In our example, we selected **Help** from the initial screen of transaction **SU3**. The context-sensitive Player then appears as follows:

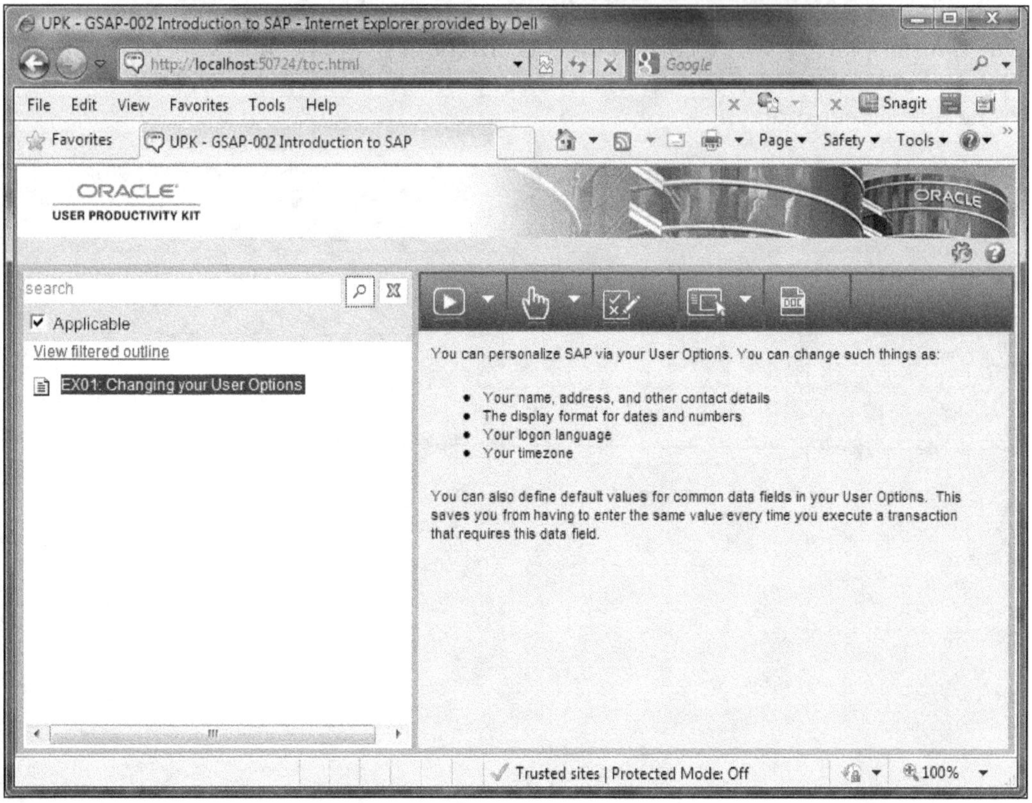

There is now an additional option available above the outline hierarchy. This is **Applicable**, and is initially selected (when we access the Player via the context sensitive help). This means that the outline has been filtered to show only the content that applies to the context from within which we accessed the Player (that is, from within which the help option was invoked in the application). The trainee can always deselect the **Applicable** checkbox to return to the full view of the Player.

Note that the list of topics is displayed as a simple list, as opposed to in the actual Outline hierarchy. This is to simplify access where multiple applicable Topics are found in several Outlines. (This is new in UPK 3.5; in OnDemand 9.1, the hierarchy was still used, and the same Topic could appear under several branches). The trainee can click on the **View filtered outline** link to display the *applicable* Topics within their respective Outline Elements. This is useful if additional information is provided in the **Concept** panes of the Outline Elements.

> It is only possible to point your application to a single Player. You therefore need to ensure that when you publish this Player it includes all of the Topics that you want to be available via the context-sensitive help in your application. If your basic approach is to publish separate Players for each course, or for loading into your LMS, then you will need to create a separate Outline that contains all of the Outlines for all of your other Players, and then publish this to the location in which your application's help option is configured to look.

So now you know how it all works. Most of this is just "for your information", as the set up and configuration is beyond the scope of this book. But it does highlight the need to correctly capture the context in your Topics (and avoid the use of No-context Frames). The reverse side of this is that you should provide Topics for all of the screens for which you want to be able to provide context-sensitive help.

SmartMatch and SmartHelp

The context sensitivity described above applies only to the "targeted applications" listed at the start of this section. This functionality is sometimes referred to as **ExactMatch**, because it provides *exact* context matching. UPK provides similar functionality for the increasing number of browser-based applications (that are not targeted applications). This functionality is called **SmartMatch**, and works in a similar way to context-sensitivity in targeted applications, but using analytics similar to those used by search functions to identify the context.

SmartHelp is a way of providing help menu integration for web-based applications. SmartHelp adds a new button to the browser toolbar that can be used to call up UPK simulations relevant to the user's (browser) screen, in a similar way to how the help menu integration for targeted applications works, by using the SmartMatch capabilities of UPK.

The implementation of SmartMatch and SmartHelp is something that is best left to the system administrators, and is therefore beyond the scope of this book. For more information, refer to the UPK *Content Deployment Guide*.

Summary

In addition to generating the commonly-used Player package format, UPK provides the ability to deploy content in a number of formats. UPK provides four online formats (including the Player), plus six printed document formats. These formats are:

- **Player package:** A suite of interactive simulations.
- **HTML Web Site:** A limited-interaction version of the simulations, suitable for use with low-bandwidth/low-functionality browsers (such as those on mobile phones).
- **LMS Package:** A package suitable for loading into a Learning Management System.
- **Standalone Topic Files:** A single, self-contained file per simulation. This format requires a separate Topic Player in order to be played.
- **Business Process:** A document that contains (by default) screenshots and action steps. This is suitable for use as a User Procedure.
- **Job Aid:** A "slimmed-down" version of the Business Process, which (by default) does not contain screenshots. This is suitable for use as a quick reference.
- **Training Guide:** A printout of the full content of all Topics for a published Outline. This is suitable for use as a handout for trainees.
- **Instructor Manual:** A printout of the full content of all Topics for a published Outline, including brief instructor notes. This is suitable for use as a "teacher's edition" of a Training Guide, for use by an instructor during classroom training.
- **Test Document:** A test script that guides testers through the steps that they need to perform in order to complete a test.
- **HP Quality Center test script:** A test script in a format that is compatible with HP Quality Center. This file can be fed into HP Quality Center to facilitate the tracking of test execution.

Each of these formats has specific options that can be used to tailor the layout and content of the output. The overall publication process is largely the same for each format.

Which of the deployment formats you use will depend upon your individual requirements. Many corporations do not look beyond the Player package, but even though the document formats are not always "pretty", and take significant work to match in-house style guides, they do have their uses, as described in Chapter 1, *Oracle User Productivity Kit*.

You can incorporate the output from UPK into other applications—for example, linking to Topics from a presentation. You can also link UPK to the Help system for the application for which the simulations were recorded, in order to provide in-application performance support.

In this chapter, we have covered a lot of information. You will likely not need all of this information to start with, depending on the formats that you choose to use. However, this is information that you need in order to see the results of your work (even in Preview mode). In the next chapter, we will get back to some more practical topics, by looking at version management, backups, and importing and exporting content.

7 Version Management

This chapter applies primarily to a client/server environment (sometimes referred to as a multi-user environment, although a client/server setup could still be used with only one user). If you are a lone developer working in a *stand-alone* environment (sometimes referred to as a single-user environment), you may want to just skip straight to the section *Exporting and importing content*, at the end of this chapter. Sorry, but version management in a stand-alone environment is almost nonexistent, so you're largely on your own.

In a client/server environment, all content objects are stored on a central server. Developers create and edit content on their own workstation (typically, a PC), and then send this content to a database on the central server for storage when they have finished with it. This is referred to as **checking in** a content object. If they subsequently want to change a content object that is on the server, they need to **check out** the content object, change it, and then check it back in.

In this chapter, you will learn how to:

- Check in a content object
- Check out a content object
- Display the version history for an object
- Revert to an earlier version of an object
- Restore a deleted content object
- Export content to a backup file
- Import content from a backup file
- Import content from a previous version of UPK or OnDemand

Checking in a content object

When you create a content object in a client/server environment, the content object is stored in your **local repository** (that is, on the client side of the client/server set-up). It is important to understand that your local repository is located on your *local* workstation. This means that if you have a content object in your local repository, and then move to another workstation, you will not see your local version of this content object on the new workstation. This is because they are located on the workstation on which you created them or checked them out. You should, therefore, always use the same workstation, or check in all of your content objects before moving to a new workstation.

> **Version Difference**
>
> In UPK 3.5.1 client/server edition, it is possible to choose a specific location for your local repository.

Documents that are checked out to your local repository are identified by a green check-mark ( ) to the left of the object details in the Library. You will need to check these objects in if you want them to be stored in the central library so they will be accessible to other developers. Generally, you should do this whenever you have finished working on a content object. However, there are good reasons for checking in objects more frequently. Your local repository is (typically) in the `C:` drive of your computer, whereas the central library is on a central server. Unless you are very fastidious about backing up your PC, the chances are that the server is backed up more often than your PC, and is usually backed up automatically. Placing your files in the central library will, therefore, provide greater security in terms of having a backup that you can revert to in the event of a disaster.

In addition to this, whenever you check in a content object, a back-up of the previous version is taken. Should you need to back out your changes, you can simply revert to a back-up version of the content object. Related to this, content objects are never really deleted from the server library. Actually, they can be deleted, but only by an Administrator, and typically as part of a cleanup. However, if you delete an object (that has never been checked in to the central server) from your local repository, it is gone. Forever!

Finally, it is not unheard of that for a local repository to simply disappear when UPK crashes (which thankfully doesn't happen that often, but it has been known to happen). If this does happen to you, then you may again lose all of the content that you currently have checked out even though the *Lost documents* view, introduced in UPK 3.5, may save you.

For all of these reasons, and more, it is recommended that you check in all of the content that is stored in your local repository to the server at least at the end of each work day. Fortunately, UPK provides a quick way of doing this. If you click the **Check In All** button ( ), then all of the content objects that you currently have checked out will be checked in again. The downside of this is that if you do check in all of the documents that you are currently working on at the end of the day, you need to remember which objects these are so that you can check them out again the next day.

> Before checking the documents in, you can use the **All Checked Out** view to identify all of the documents that you currently have checked out. You can then print this list, and will know which files you need to check out again the next day.

There is one further thing to bear in mind when deciding how often you are going to check in your content objects. As mentioned above, UPK retains every version of a content that has been checked in. These are accessible via the Document History, as we will see later. This means that if you check in a content object ten times, then UPK will retain ten versions of it. This can also make it difficult to identify the "released" versions of the content object in the Document History, should you subsequently need to roll back to the last-released version. The Administrator can clean up the database periodically, but the only way of differentiating between versioned drafts and versioned released content objects is by using the check-in comments. These are explained in the section *Step 2: Confirming the scope of the check-in*, ahead.

UPK Workflow

The down-side to checking in content objects that you may not have finished working on is that these objects could be mis-perceived as being final, and actually used or published. In some cases, you may have checked some of them out not because you want to change them, but specifically to stop anyone else from changing them.

UPK does not provide you with a simple, automatic solution to these shortcomings, but there is a manual workaround that you can use. This is to use the Workflow properties of the objects.

> UPK does not have a "real" workflow, it does not have "routing" of content objects based on their status, or automatic email notification of content objects that are due for review, or any of the things that you'd expect from workflow functionality. Of course users can use a Custom View (as explained in Chapter 2, *Organizing Your Library)* to display content objects according to their *Workflow* properties, but this is still not really "workflow".

If you display the *Properties* for a content object, by clicking on the **Properties** button ( ), the last category of properties (at the end of the *Properties* list) is the **Workflow** category. Within this, there are two properties:

- **Assigned To**: This property allows you to select (from a drop-down list) the user ID of any developer who is authorized to access the content object. If you select your own user ID in this field, then this is an indication to the other developers that they should not work on this content object themselves.
- **State**: This property can be used to specify the current status of a content object. The default values are (`blank`), `Not Started`, `Draft`, `In Review`, and `Final`. If you select a status of **Draft**, then this is an indication that you have not finished with the object.

An example of the **Properties** pane, showing the **Workflow** category, is in the following screenshot:

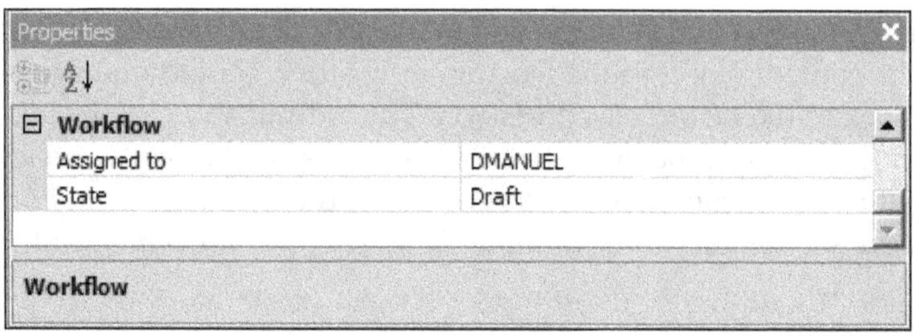

Of course, these **Properties** do not provide "hard checks". You still rely on people seeing, and then paying attention to, these **Properties** but it is a start. Some strong guidance from your Project Manager or Team Leader would help, here. For information on making specific properties visible in the Library, refer to Chapter 2, *Organizing your Library*.

> Administrators can add, remove, or rename statuses. It is recommended that a suitable set of statuses are established and defined prior to any development work starting, and that these statuses and their meaning are communicated to all developers.

Step 1: Selecting the content objects

To select content objects for checking in, carry out the steps described below:

1. In the Library, select the content objects that you want to check in. Normally, you will want to check in specific content objects, so you would only select these. As always, you click on a content object to select it. You can *Ctrl*-click to select multiple objects, or *Shift*-click to select a series of objects. You can also select a folder in the Library to check in all of the content objects in that folder. Do not worry if some of the objects that are included in your selection are not checked out; UPK will simply ignore these objects during check-in (it will not "error-out").

   > You can also check in content objects by selecting them in an Outline Element.

2. Once you have selected all of the content objects that you want to check in, click the **Check In** button ( ).

Step 2: Confirming the scope of the check-in

When you check in one or more specific content objects and have not selected a folder in the Library to check in, UPK will automatically check for any content objects that are related to the object that you are checking in. You will be prompted to check these in, as well. An example of this prompt is shown in the following screenshot:

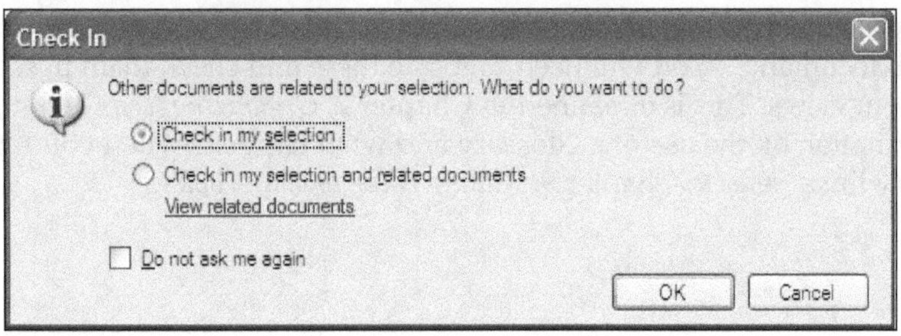

What are **related documents**? In general, they are Web Pages and Packages used by the content object that you are checking in. For example:

- If you have created, or changed, an Outline Element (Module or Section) then UPK will automatically select all of the content objects (Modules, Lessons, and Topics) included in this Outline Element, along with any Web Pages used by any of these content objects will be selected as well.
- If you are checking in a Topic for which you have also created a Web Page that is linked to the Concepts pane, then UPK will automatically select this Web Page as a related document during check-in.
- If you have created a Glossary and are checking this in, the related documents will be all of the Web Pages for the content definitions used by the Glossary.

An example of the **Related Documents** dialog box is shown in the following screenshot:

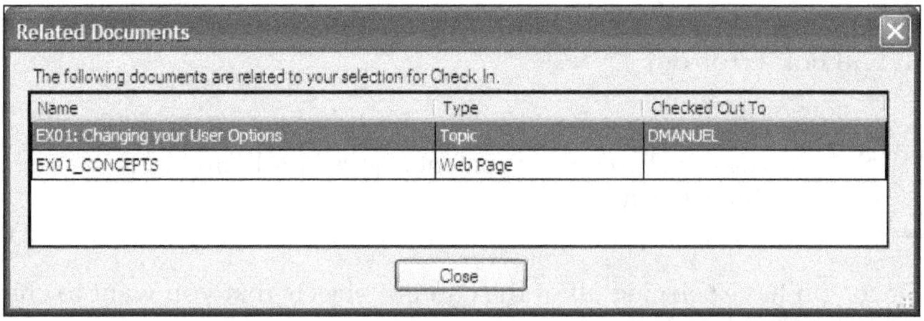

This list of related documents can be confusing, as it does not match the list that you see in the **Related Documents** pane for the content object that you are checking in. The list will include Web Pages that have been explicitly linked to from the content object that you are checking, but will not include Glossaries, Templates, Packages, or icons, all of which are listed in the **Related Documents** pane.

This limitation is important to understand. If you checked out, and updated, a Glossary and as a result UPK checked out several content objects during the glossary link regeneration, UPK will *not* identify all of the Glossary elements (Web Pages) as "related documents". You will need to locate these and check them in separately using custom views. This is explained in Chapter 2, *Organizing Your Library*. For more information on the use of a Glossary and what happens when you regenerate the glossary links, refer to Chapter 9, *Adding value to your Topics*.

Adding to the confusion, the list of related documents will include **all** of the explicitly-linked content objects, and not only those objects that are currently checked out to you. Do not worry about this - UPK will only physically check in the content objects that you do have checked out (these are the ones that have your User ID in the Checked Out To column of the **Related Documents** dialog box). In the example above, we are checking in an Outline Element that contains one Topic, which in turn contains a Web Page. The Topic is checked out, but the Web Page is not.

Step 3: Specifying a reason for the change

When you check in one or more content objects, you will be prompted to enter a short description of the change, as shown in the following screenshot:

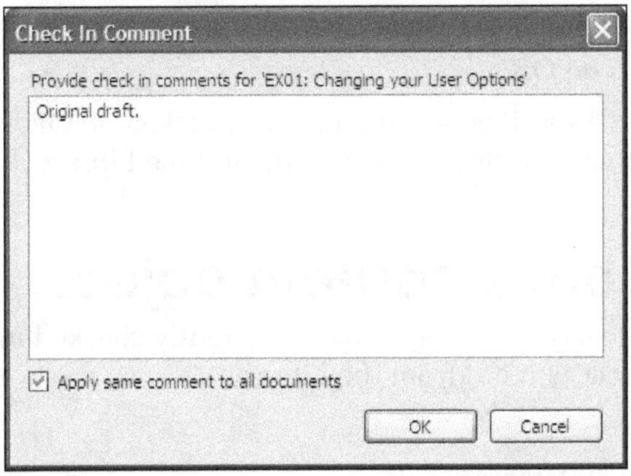

The title of the content object that you are checking in is shown above the comment text box. If you are checking in multiple content objects, then this will initially specify the first object and (assuming that you deselect the **Apply same comments to all documents** option) will specify the next object when you click **OK**. It then moves on to the next object. In this way, you can provide separate comments for each content object, even though you are checking them all in at the same time.

> Although it is entirely optional, it is a very good practice to always enter a comment. This comment will appear in the object *History*, and therefore serves as a useful audit log.

Specify a reason for the change by carrying out the steps described below:

1. Enter a suitable comment in the space provided. Note that you do not need to specify the date and time of the change, or your user ID. These are captured automatically by UPK.
2. If you are checking in multiple objects, then UPK will initially suggest applying the same comments to all of the objects. You will see that the **Apply same comments to all documents** checkbox toward the bottom of the dialog box is selected. If you do not want to use the same comment for all objects that you are checking in, then deselect this checkbox. Now, when you click on **OK**, the **Check In Comment** dialog box for the next content object in the check-in selection will be displayed. You can repeat the above processing from Step 3.
3. Once you have entered your description of the change (or reason for the change), click on **OK**.
4. Once you have specified a comment, and clicked on **OK** for the last time, then the content objects are checked in, and the Library screen is redisplayed.

Checking out a content object

If you want to change a content object that is currently checked in to the server library, you need to check it out from the Library.

> **Version Difference**
>
> As from UPK 3.5.1, if you try to open a content object for editing that you currently do not have checked it, UPK will ask you if you want to check it out first. Prior to version 3.5.1, UPK did not warn you (other than a small text of "Read only" in the title bar - which was easily overlooked), and would simply prompt you to save the read-only content object as a new content object when you tried to save it. This is a significant improvement.

To check out a content object from the server, carry out the following steps:

1. In the Library, click on the content object that you want to check out.

2. Click on the **Check Out** button () on the Versioning toolbar. If there are other content objects related to the content object that you are checking out, then UPK will ask you if you want to check out these objects as well, as shown in the following screenshot:

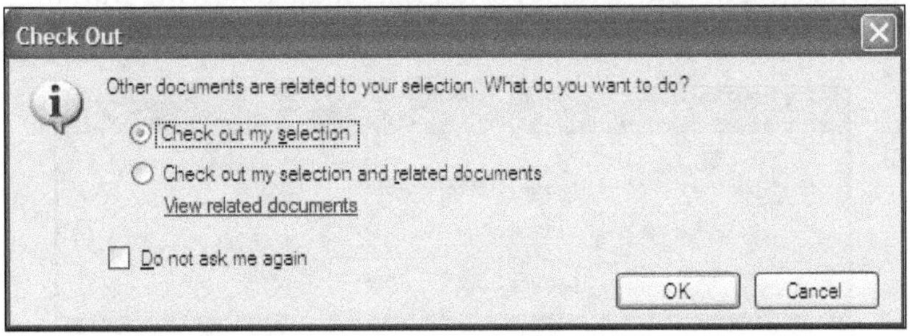

3. Select whether you want to check out only the selected document, or the selected document and all related documents. Then click on **OK**. Refer to *Checking in a content object*, for additional guidance, if necessary.

The document is checked out into your local repository. A green check-mark () is shown to the left of the content object's name to indicate that the content object has been checked out. All other developers will see a lock symbol (), indicating (to them) that another user has the content object checked out. If you have a content object checked out, then other developers can still display the currently checked in version of the content object. However, they will not be able to make any changes to it as this would necessitate them checking it out themselves, which they will not be able to do. They will also, obviously, not see any changes that you have made to the content object since you checked it out (as these changes exist only in your local repository).

You can now edit this content object as required. Once you have finished editing the content object, you should check it back into the server.

Cancelling the check-out of a content object

If, after checking out a content object, you realize that you do not want to change it after all, you can cancel the check-out. If you do this, then any changes that you have made to the content object will be discarded.

To cancel the check-out of a content object, carry out the steps described below:

1. In the Library, select the object for which you want to cancel the check-out.
2. Click on the **Cancel Check Out** button ( ). If you have changed the content object in your local repository, then the following warning message is displayed:

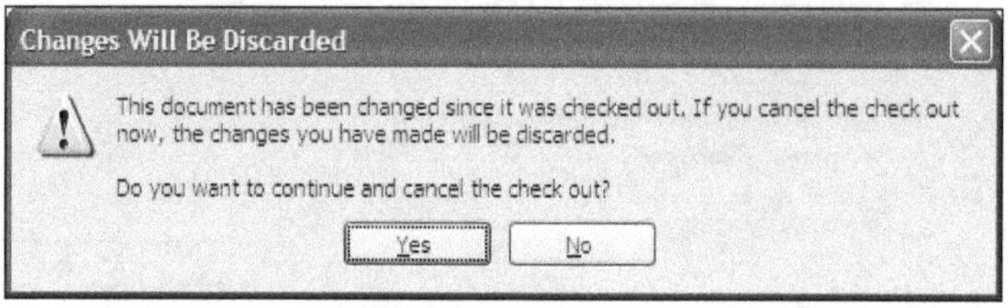

3. Click on **Yes** to confirm the cancellation of the check-out.

The document is removed from your local repository and will be available to other users for check-out. This will not create any entries in the version history.

If you did not actually make any changes to the content object, then it is simply "unlocked"—nothing is *moved* to the server, and no new version is created.

Working with document versions

Every time that you check in a content object (and not every time that you save it in your local storage), UPK takes an archive copy of the previous version. You can list all of the previous versions of any content object by clicking on the object to select it, and then selecting menu option **Document | History**. An example of the resulting **History** dialog box is displayed in the following screenshot:

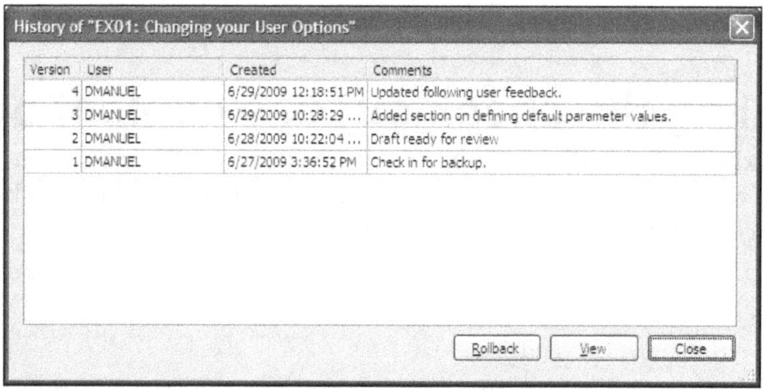

The **History** dialog box lists every version of the content object since it was first created, along with the **User ID** of the person who created the version (that is, the person who checked in the content object) and the date and time at which this was done. The **Comments** field shows the comments that were entered when the document was checked in.

Displaying an earlier version

You can display any version of a content object from the History. To do this, follow the steps shown below:

1. Select the content object in the Library.
2. Select menu option **Document | History**.
3. In the **History** dialog box, select on the version that you want to.
4. Click on **View**.

The content object is opened in the relevant editor: *Outline Editor*, *Topic Editor*, *Web Page Editor*, and so on. The title bar shows the version number that you are displaying, as shown in the screenshot below:

In this example, we are displaying version 3 of the content object.

Reverting to an earlier version

If you have checked in a content object, and then realize that you do not want to keep your latest changes (or you are an Editor and want to back out someone else's work because they made a rubbish job of it) then you can revert to an(y) earlier version of the content object. To do this, follow the steps shown below:

1. Select the content object in the Library. Note that the document must be checked in; you cannot roll back a document that is currently checked out (by you or any other user).
2. Select menu option **Document | History**.

3. In the **History** dialog box, click on the version to which you want to revert back to. This is shown in the following screenshot:

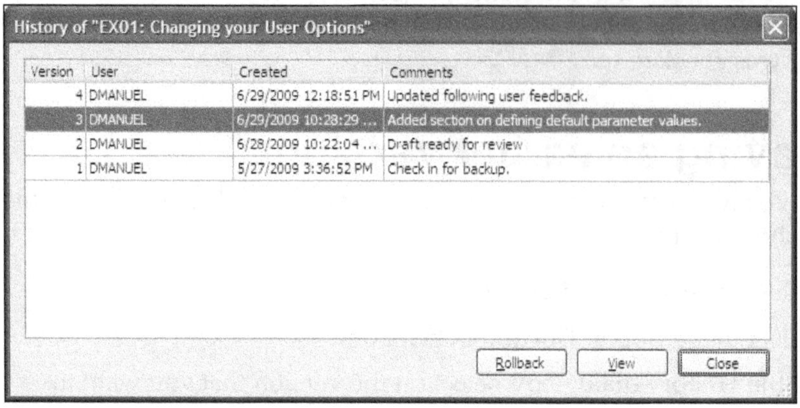

4. Click on **Rollback**.

The version that you selected becomes the latest version again, with the *Comments* set to **Rolled back to version** "X", as shown in the screenshot below:

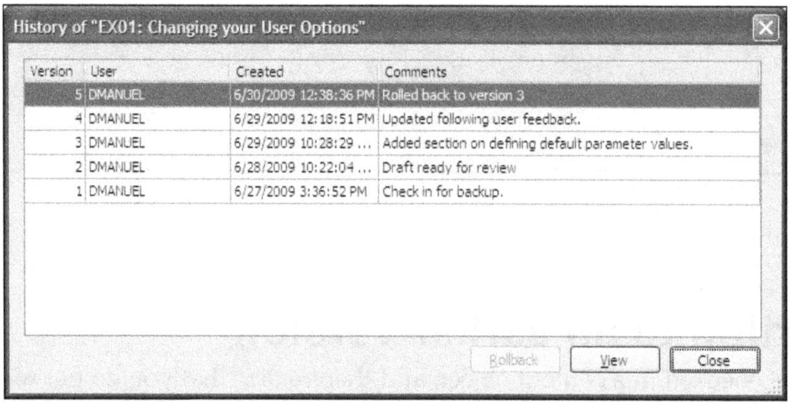

What has happened is that a new version has been created, by taking a full copy of the selected version. The version that you wanted to back out has not been deleted, it is still available, but it has just been superseded by the new (copied) version. This means that if you subsequently realize that you shouldn't have reverted to the earlier version, and really do want to keep your latest changes, then you can simply select the last version before the rolled back version (in the example above, this would be version 4), and roll back to that. In the example above, this would be version 4.

Also note that the content object is not checked out when you revert to an earlier version.

Restoring a deleted document

In a client/server environment, content objects are never really deleted; they still exist on the server. Instead, they are removed from the Library folders so that they are not visible within the Library itself. However, they will appear in the **Deleted documents** view, from where developers can display and restore them. The only way they can be truly deleted is by the Administrator purging them. The advantage of this is that you can always (up until the point that the Administrator has purged it) "un-delete" a content object, if you realize that you deleted it by mistake.

To restore (un-delete) a content object, carry out the following steps:

1. From the **Library** screen, click on the drop-down button for the **View** field (which will normally indicate *Details view*) on the **View** toolbar, and select **Deleted documents**. A list of all of the content objects that have been deleted (but not purged) is displayed, as shown in the following screenshot:

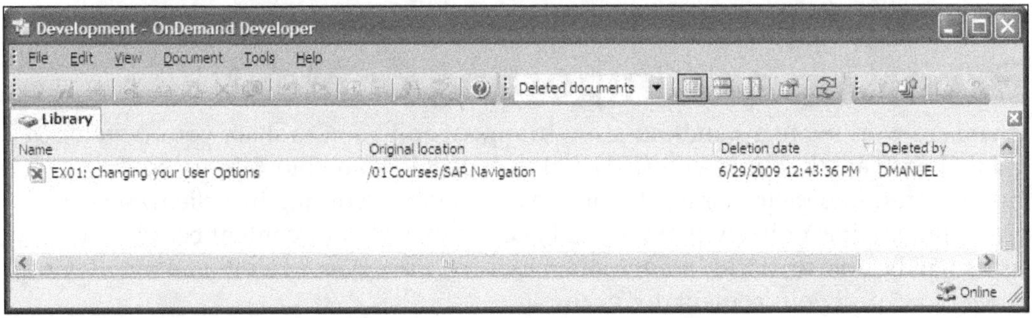

2. Right-click on the document that you want to restore, and select **Restore** from the context menu. This is the only option available on this context menu.

The document is restored to the Library, and placed back in the folder it was originally deleted from. This location is also shown in the **Original location** column in the **Deleted documents** view. This will create another version in the version history for the content object—just as deleting it did. This is shown in the screenshot below:

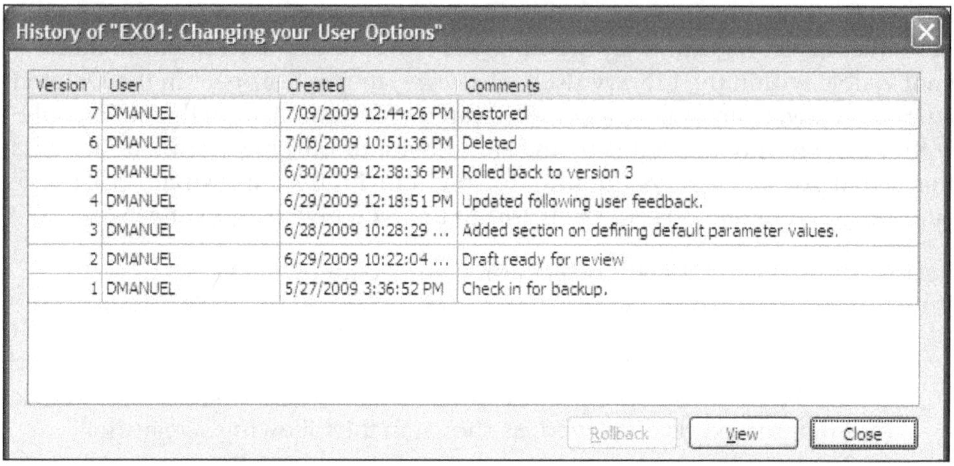

Exporting and importing content

If you are working in a stand-alone environment and want to share your developed content with another user, you will need to export it from your Library so they can import it into their Library. If you are a developer working in a client/server environment, it is unlikely that you will need to export your content because all users will be able to access it in the same Library. However, even then there may be a need to export your content, for example:

- Your company may use a "staged" approach to implementation, whereby all content is developed in a Development library before being migrated to a more secure production environment

> If you are working with multiple libraries, then it is recommended that you always export/ import *folders*, and not simply Outline Elements and their contents. This will reduce the possibility of elements that appear in multiple outlines being overwritten on successive imports.

- You have developed content in one environment (for example, your personal stand-alone environment) and now want to bring it into your company's client/server environment

- You want to take a copy of everything you have done, as a personal back-up
- You want to export all of your content before upgrading to a new version of UPK and importing your content into the new version's Library

Whatever the reason, UPK makes it easy to export content. In this section we'll look at just how to do this.

> You would not normally use this approach to export content for *translation*. If you want to extract content from UPK so that you can pass it to a translator, you should instead use the approach described in Chapter 12, *Localizing your content*.

Exporting content objects

You can use the **Export** function to export content objects as an archive, publishing options, sound files, and content objects for localization. This section covers exporting content objects as an archive.

You can export any type of content object to an archive: Modules, Sections, and Topics, as well as Web Pages and Packages. You can also export any of the objects in the System folder, such as Templates and Publishing Packages.

To export a content object, carry out the following steps:

1. In the Library, select on the content objects that you want to export. You can select a single object, or multiple objects of various types. You also have the option of selecting a folder and exporting all of the content within the folder.
2. Select menu option **Tools | Export | Documents**. The **Export** dialog box is displayed, as shown in the following screenshot:

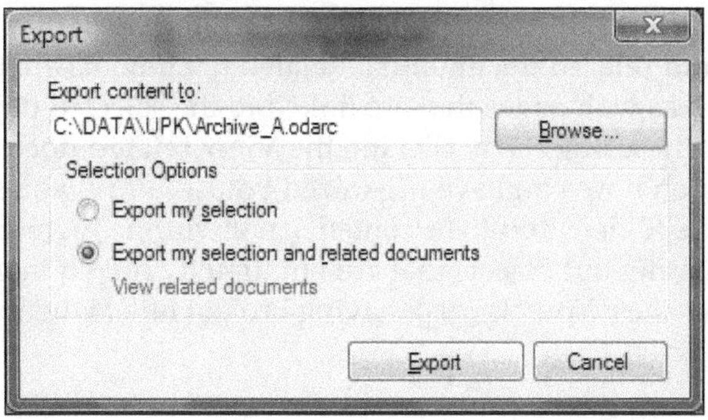

3. Click on the **Browse** button next to the *Export content to:* field. The **Save As** dialog box is displayed, as shown below:

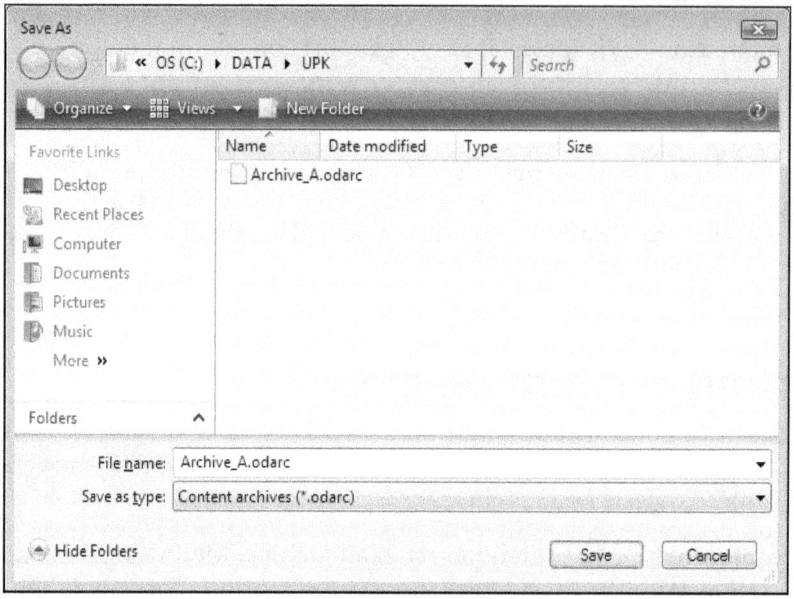

4. Enter a suitable file name for your export file in the **File name** field.
5. Note that UPK will automatically select a file type of **Content archives (*.odarc)** and add the file prefix `.odarc` (for **On**Demand **Arc**hive. Note the reference to OnDemand even though the product is no longer called OnDemand!).
6. Click on **Save** to confirm the destination folder and file.
7. Back in the **Export** dialog box, under **Selection Options**, select whether you want to export only the specific content that you have selected (**Export my selection**), or the selected content and all related documents (**Export my selection and related documents**). Related documents are typically content objects such as web pages that are linked to the selected object(s). You can see a list of these objects by clicking the **View related documents** link. Depending on how you have organized your Library, you should normally export entire folders and their contents, not Outline Elements. Otherwise, you risk missing out objects that are not directly linked into the Outline, such as Packages. You also risk having broken links when you (re)import the content object(s).

8. Click on **Export**. The selected content objects (and all related documents, if you chose that option) are exported to the specified file. While this is being done, a progress indicator is displayed for the object currently being exported, and the overall percentage complete. The export may be very quick, especially if you are only exporting one or two Topics so don't blink or you'll miss it. An example of the progress indicator is shown below:

9. Once the export is complete, you are returned to the Library.

As the content is exported to a single file, you can easily send the file to another Developer for importing into their UPK Library, save it to CD as a back-up, and so on. How to import content objects is described next.

Importing content objects

You can import UPK content that has previously been exported from another implementation of UPK. You can also import content from your own implementation as a back-up.

> **Version Difference**
>
> Do not use the **import** function to import content from version 8.x or earlier of OnDemand into UPK because the format in which content objects are stored changed significantly between version 8.x/2.x and version 9.x/3.x. In this case, you should use the **convert** function described in the section *Converting content from a previous version of UPK or OnDemand* that appears later in this chapter.

To import previously exported content objects, carry out the steps described below:

1. Select menu option **Tools | Import | Documents**. The **Import** dialog box is displayed, as shown in the following screenshot:

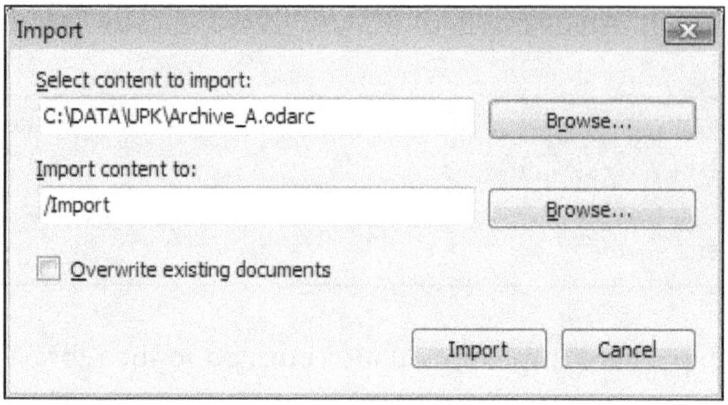

2. Click on the **Browse** button to the right of the **Select content to import** field. Navigate to, and select the archive file that contains the content that you want to import. This must be a file with a file type of `.odarc`.
3. The **Import content to** field specifies the folder within your Library into which the imported content will be placed. This defaults to `/Import`, and UPK will create this folder if it does not exist already. If necessary, you can use the **Browse...** button to navigate to, and select any other folder within your Library. If you don't know exactly what content is contained within the archive, it is probably a good idea to not import it directly into your "production" libraries. In this case, consider accepting the default folder as you can always move the imported content into the correct folders, once the import is complete.
4. If UPK finds that your Library contains versions of any of the objects contained in the archive, then the archive version will not, by default, be imported. If you *do* want to import this content, and are happy to overwrite any existing versions that you have in your Library, then you can select the **Overwrite existing documents** option in the **Import** dialog box.

> If you are importing content from one Library to another, for example, if you have separate Development and Production Libraries, then you should always select **Overwrite existing documents**. Otherwise, any changed Content Objects will not be re-imported.

Note that UPK does not use the file name, or the folder into which it is being imported, to determine whether a file already exists. It uses its own internal 32-character identifier that is retained when the object is exported.

5. Click on **Import** to begin the import.
6. If the folder that you specified in the **Import content to** field does not already exist, then the following message will be displayed:

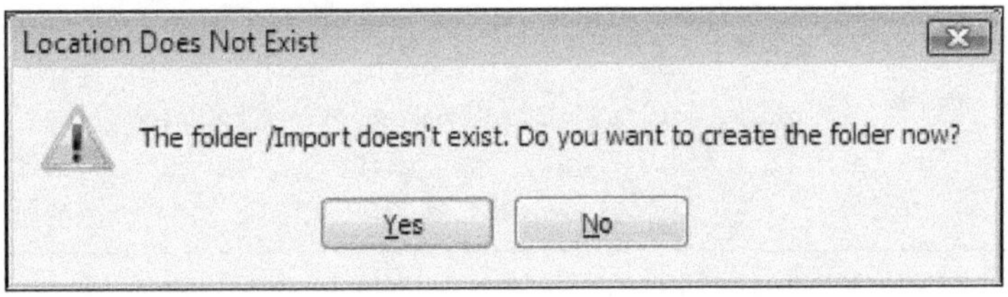

Click on **Yes** to create the folder.

7. The content is imported. During the import, a progress indicator is displayed showing the object currently being imported, and the overall percentage complete. The import may be very quick, especially if you are only importing one or two Titles. Again, don't blink or you'll miss it. An example of the progress indicator is shown in the following screenshot:

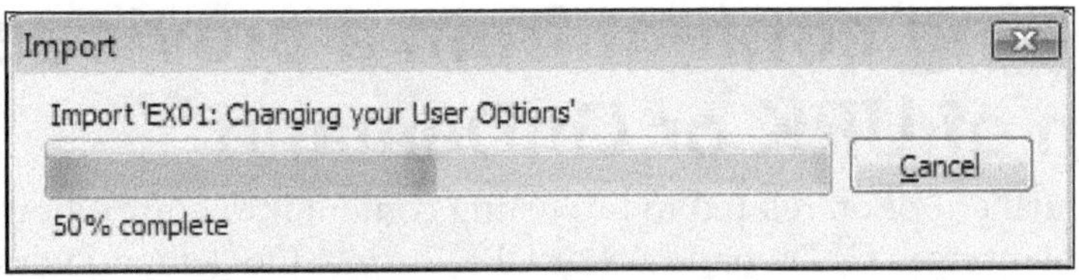

8. If some content already exists in the target folder, and you did not select the **Overwrite existing documents** option, a warning message is displayed, as shown in the next screenshot:

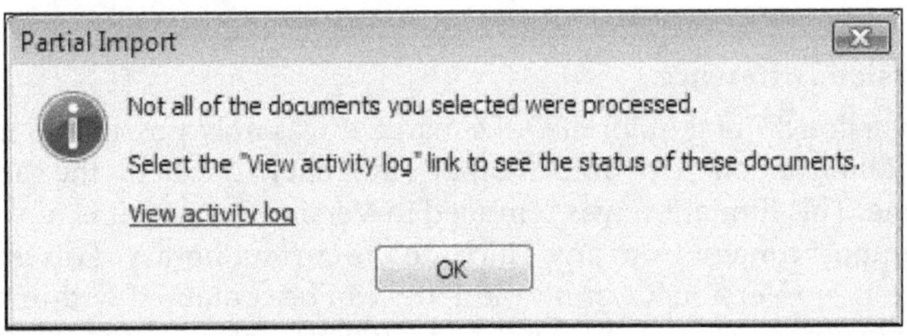

Always click on the **View activity log** link to display the list of files that were and were not imported. An example of the **Activity Log** is shown in the next screenshot:

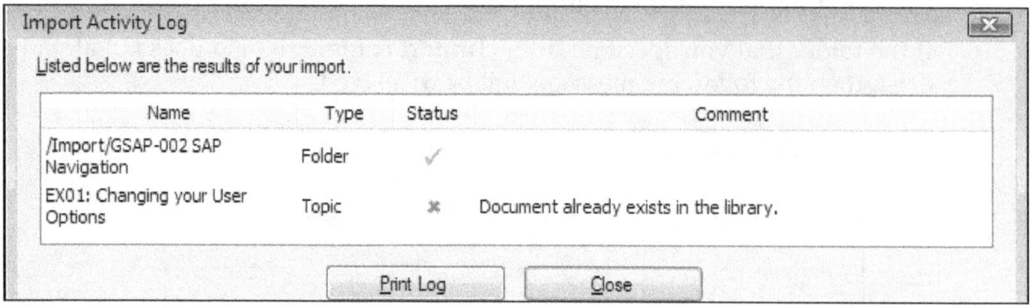

In this example, one Folder was imported and one Topic was not imported because it already exists in our Library. Click on **Close** button to close this dialog box. Back at the *Partial Import* dialog box, click on **OK** to close the dialog box.

Once the content has been imported, you are returned to the Library. You can now navigate to the **/import** folder and work with the imported objects the same way as you work with objects that you created yourself.

Converting content from a previous version of UPK or OnDemand

There is one further option related to importing content into your Library. This is importing content from OnDemand 8.x or UPK 2.x into OnDemand version 9.x or UPK version 3.x. The format in which Content Objects are stored changed from flat files in 8.x/2.x to a database in 9.x/3.x. This means that if you want to import content created in one of these older versions into a more recent UPK library, you will need to convert it to the new format. Luckily, UPK provides functionality for doing just this.

> **Version Difference**
>
> In version 8.7 and older of OnDemand, it was only possible to import content from one Title into another Title that had exactly the same folder name. This limitation was removed in Version 9.x, and it is now possible to import content from any Title into the current library. This is largely because in Version 9.x, multiple Titles can be contained within the same single library, so such a limitation no longer makes sense.

To import content from a prior version of UPK or OnDemand, carry out the steps described below:

1. Create a new folder into which you want to import the content.
2. Select menu option **Tools | Convert From 2.x | Content**. Note that the "2.x" refers to "UPK prior to version 3.0", which also includes OnDemand version 8.x.

> If you have content developed using OnDemand version 6.x or 7.x, then you should first convert this content to version 8.x, and then convert it from 8.x to 9.x/3.x. If you do not have access to an 8.x environment, then contact UPK Support for assistance.

The **Content Conversion Wizard** is displayed in the following screenshot:

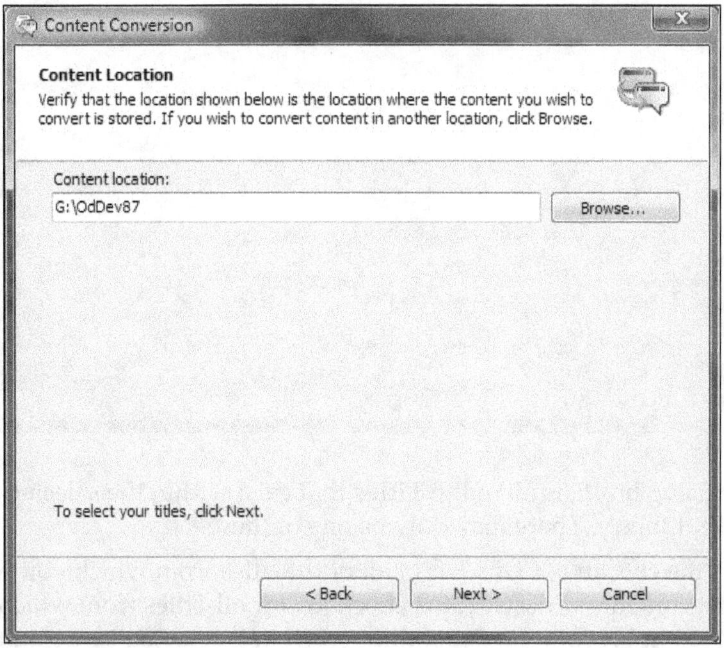

3. Click on the **Browse** button to the right of the **Content location** field. Navigate to and select, the location in which the `OnDemand.ini` file for the library from which you want to import content is located. Note that it is extremely important that you locate the `OnDemand.ini` file. This is the file that tells OnDemand what simulations exist within the Library. For UPK, the file is *still* called `OnDemand.ini`.

> If you do not have access to the `OnDemand.ini` file (for example, if you only have a set of publisher files) then you will not be able to import the content as described here, and should contact UPK Support for assistance. They may be able to manually create the UPK file for you, and help you import your content.

4. Once you have specified the source location, click **Next**. The **Title Selection** dialog box is displayed, as shown ahead:

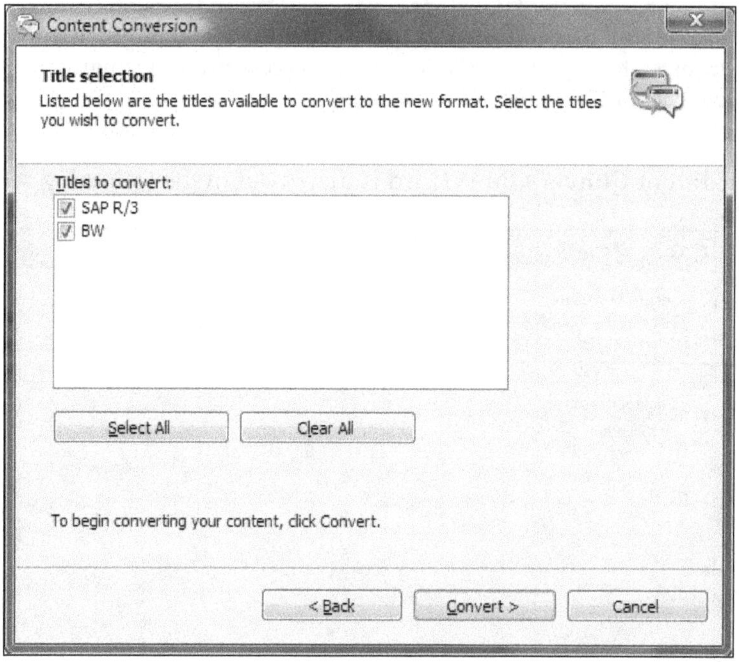

This dialog box lists all of the **Titles** that exist within the selected OnDemand or UPK Library. There may only be one of these.

5. Select the checkbox to the left of all of the titles from which you want to import content (or deselect the checkbox for all Titles from which you do not want to import content, depending on what is selected by default). Note that you cannot select specific Modules within a Title - you need to import the entire Title, and then delete what you don't want.
6. Click on **Convert**. A progress tracker will be displayed. Note that depending on the amount of content being imported, this may take 30 minutes (or more) to complete.

Once the content been imported, a confirmation dialog box is displayed, listing the Titles that have been imported. This can be seen in the following screenshot:

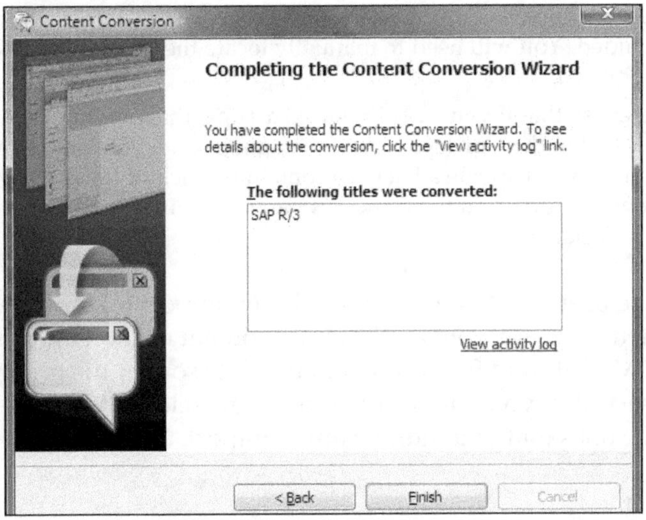

7. If there have been any problems during the conversion, then these will be listed in the **Activity Log**. To display the **Activity Log** (which you should *always* do), click on the **View activity log** link. An example of the **Activity Log** is shown below:

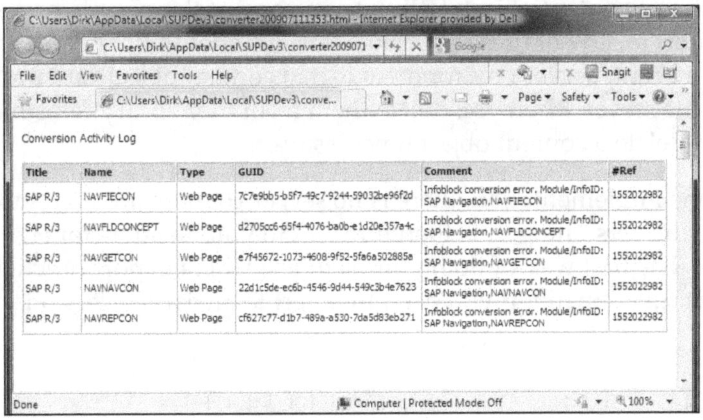

8. Check any errors listed. Most of this will mean nothing, but you can locate the objects in the Library via either the **Name**, or the **GUID** (which is the 32-character identifier assigned to the object by UPK when it imported the object). Close the **Activity Log** to return to the **Conversion Wizard** dialog box.
9. Click on **Finish**. You are returned to the Library screen.

> If you are importing several Modules that each includes the same Infoblock (Web Page or Package in UPK 3.5), then UPK will create multiple copies of this Infoblock, one for each Module in which it is included. You will need to manually locate these and consolidate them, if required.
>
> Note also that if you have imported a Topic that had multiple Infoblocks attached to the **Concept** pane (for example, a text file and an image file), then UPK will create a Package containing each of these Infoblocks, and provide a link from the **Concepts** pane of the imported Topic to this new Package.

A folder will have been created below the selected import folder for each Title that has been imported. This will contain the entire content of the Title with a sub-folder created for each Module and Section within the Title so that the original Library structure is preserved. If you only wanted to import selected exercises, then you need to delete the ones that you didn't want to import.

Summary

The need to make regular back-ups of your work is extremely important. In a client/server environment, this is simplified by the fact that the server is backed up on a reasonably-regular basis. So, as long as you check in your content, it will be backed up as well. The other advantage of checking in your content is that each time that you check in a content object, UPK takes a copy of the previous version. You can display, or revert to, any of these previous versions should the need arise. A further advantage of a client/server environment is that content objects are not immediately deleted from the server when you delete them from the Library. This means that it is possible to un-delete a content object if necessary.

In a stand-alone implementation, there is no server so there are no regular backups, and no automatic versioning. It is therefore, left to you, the developer, to take your own back ups. The best way of doing this is to use UPK's export functionality and then its import functionality if you need to revert to an earlier version.

8

Allowing Alternatives

As we have seen in the previous chapters, UPK is good at recording the execution of a task. The developer simply executes the task, one action at a time, from beginning to end, recording as they go. What this gives you is a linear recording. But this is not all that UPK can do. With a little more effort, it is possible to add alternative routes through the exercise. In this way, an exercise could cover multiple scenarios. Adding alternative ways of doing something also makes an exercise more realistic, especially in *Know It?* mode, as we will see.

In this chapter you will learn how to:

- Add Alternative Actions
- Add Alternative Paths
- Add Decision Frames
- Add Branches
- Respond automatically to user actions

Adding Alternative Actions

An Alternative Action (in UPK terms) is another way of doing the same thing on a single Frame. If you remember the initial description of what UPK captures during recording, you'll recall that what it captures is a set of action/screenshot pairs—effectively, a screenshot and the action carried out to get there. With this in mind, an **Alternative Action** is another action that will also get you to the same screenshot. This is probably best clarified by way of an example.

In the exercise that we have been working on throughout this book, we have a Frame where the user was required to refresh the screen by clicking on the **Enter** button on the toolbar. In the **Topic Editor**, the Frame appears as follows:

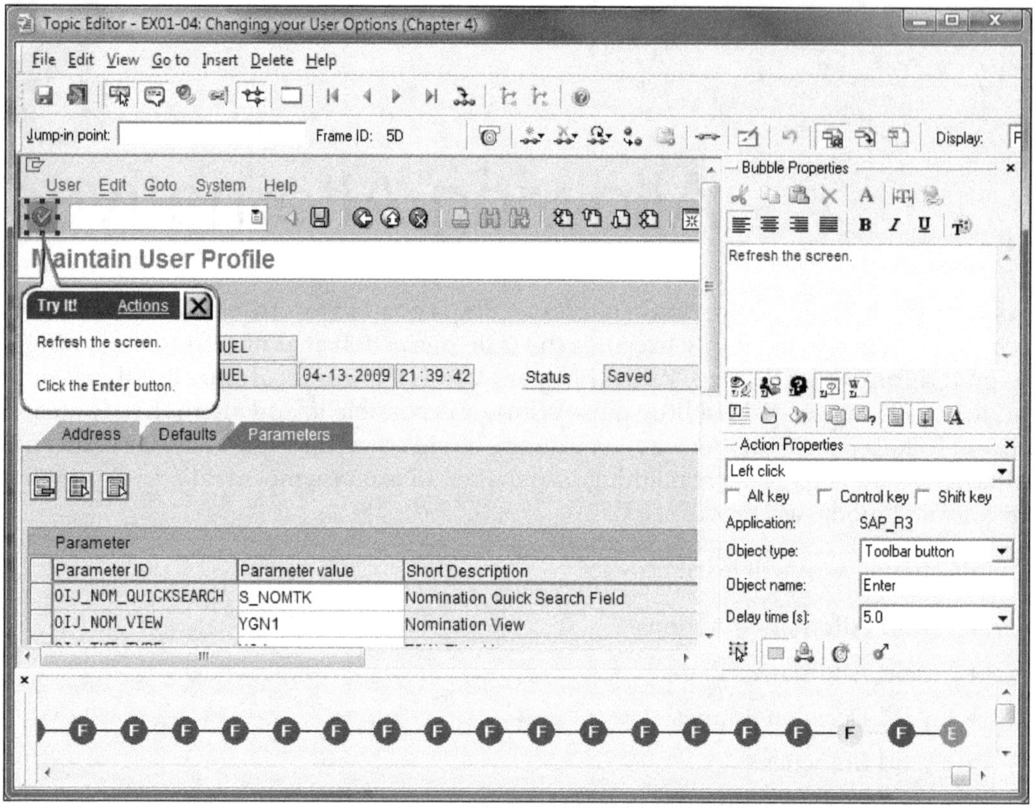

In reality, the user can either click the **Enter** button on the toolbar (as currently recorded), or press the *Enter* key on the keyboard. Which option they use is largely a matter of choice. One could argue that it is best to stick to teaching people only one method so as not to confuse them. However, there is often strong feeling about mouse actions versus keyboard actions, and users seem to appreciate being given the choice of suffering from either repetitive strain injury or carpal tunnel syndrome.

There is also another strong driver for providing Alternative Actions in exercises: *Know It?* mode. Consider the example above. In *Know It?* mode, the user is asked to refresh the screen, but is not told how to do this (the **Template text visible in Know It? mode** button ( ) is not selected, which is the default). You can see from the **Action Properties** pane that the Action is **Left click** on the **Push button** object named **Enter**. If the user carries out this exercise and they press the *Enter* key, which is a perfectly valid way of refreshing the screen, then they will be marked incorrect, and (depending on the required pass percentage, and their performance on the rest of the exercise) could fail. This is a bit harsh given that they did something that would have worked in the actual system.

One solution to this problem would simply be to display the template text in *Know It?* mode, but then it hardly seems like a test at all. A better solution would be to allow pressing the *Enter* key as a valid Action as well. We can do this by recording the pressing of the *Enter* key as an Alternative Action.

To record an Alternative Action for a frame, carry out the following steps:

1. Make sure that you are positioned on the correct screen in the application.
2. In the Topic Editor, select the frame for which you want to record the Alternative Action.
3. Select menu option **Insert | Alternative Action** ( ). (You can also click on the **Insert** button ( ) on the editing toolbar, and then select Insert **Alternative Action** ( ) from the context menu.) You are passed back to the application, with the **Recorder** panel displayed in the upper-right corner of the screen, as usual.
4. In the application (from Step 1), perform the Alternative Action and then press *Prt Scr* to capture the Action. Note that you do not need to press *Prt Scr* an initial time to start recording (UPK will always display a message stating when you need to press *Prt Scr* to start recording). As soon as the Action has been captured, you are passed back into the *Topic Editor*.

> When you capture an additional Action, no screenshot is captured. The Alternative Action is applied to the same screenshot as the initial Action. In addition, for keyboard actions, the context is still captured, even though there is no **Object type** or **Object name** captured. You should, therefore, capture alternative actions on the correct screen in the correct application. Otherwise, the context-sensitive help will not identify this alternative action as applicable help.

Now, the Frame appears as follows, in the **Topic Editor**.

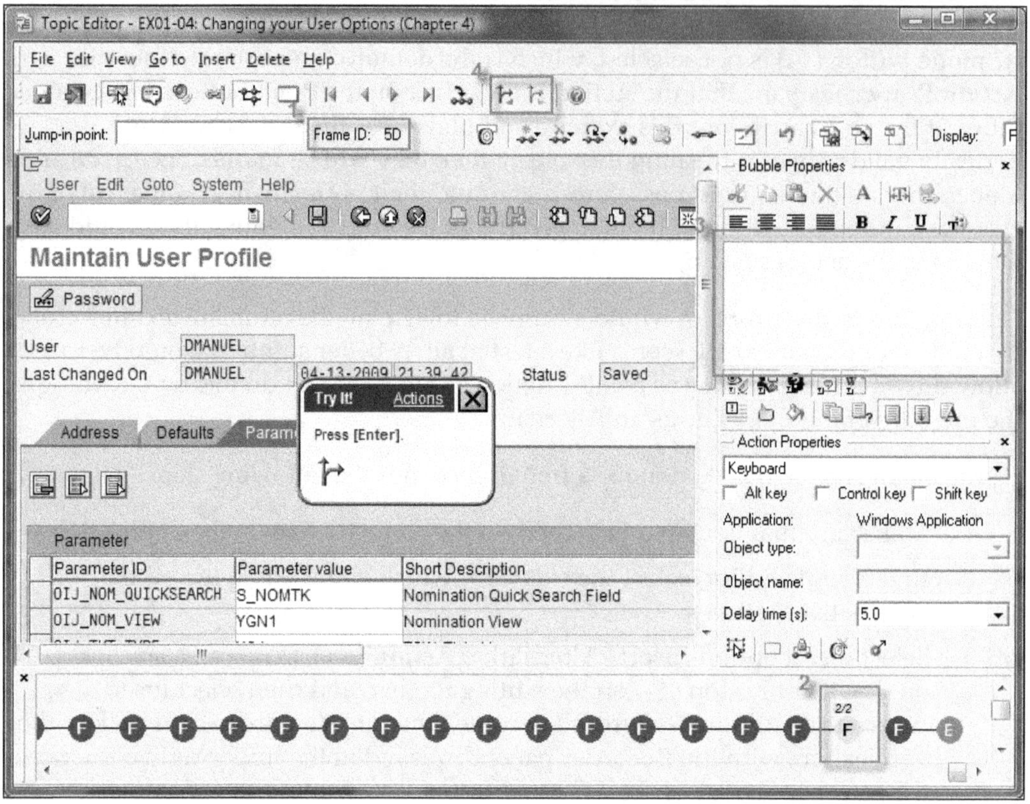

There are a few things worth noting here. These have been highlighted in the above screenshot, and are explained below:

1. The new Action (which is specified in the **Action Properties** pane) has been performed against Frame 5D. This is the same Frame as the one against which the original Action was recorded (see the previous screenshot). This confirms that no new screenprint has been captured.
2. In the **Frame Structure** pane, the indicator for this frame now has the text **2/2** displayed above it. This text indicates that there are two actions for the Frame, and the details of the second Action are currently being displayed. (For reference, the first digit is the number of this Action, and the second digit is the total number of Alternative Actions, like "x of y".)

> You can add as many alternative actions as you like. Although more than two or three might be overwhelming for the trainees. Providing a single mouse-click action and a single key-press action is usually sufficient.

3. The *Custom Text* field is empty (compare this with the previous screenshot). This is because we are now looking at the Bubble for the Alternative Action. You *could* enter the same Custom Text here as for the primary Action, but this will never be displayed in *Know It?* mode.
4. The **Previous action** button (⊢) is now "active" (look at the previous screenshot, where it is not active because there was no previous Action). If you click on this button then the details of the previous Action are displayed, the Previous action button is deactivated (⊢), the Next action button (⊢) is activated, and the numbers above the frame indicator in the **Frame Structure** pane changes to **1/2**. The following screenshot shows these situations:

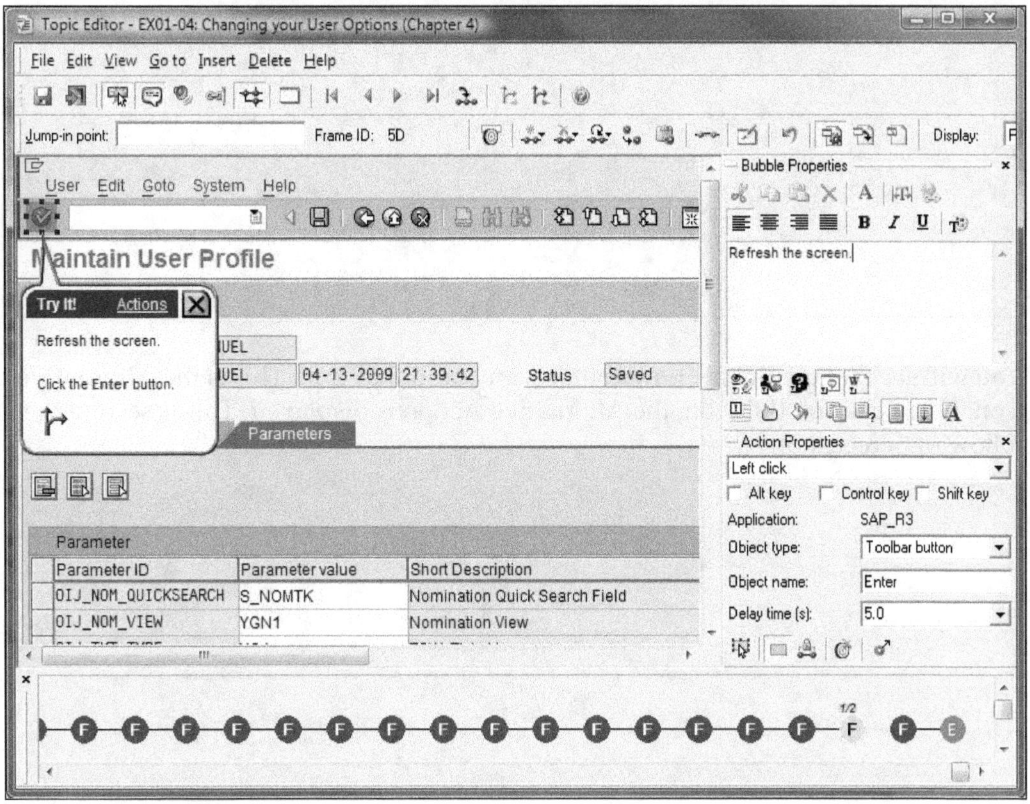

Let's take a quick look at how this manifests itself in the Player. The following screenshot shows the previous Frame in *Try It!* mode:

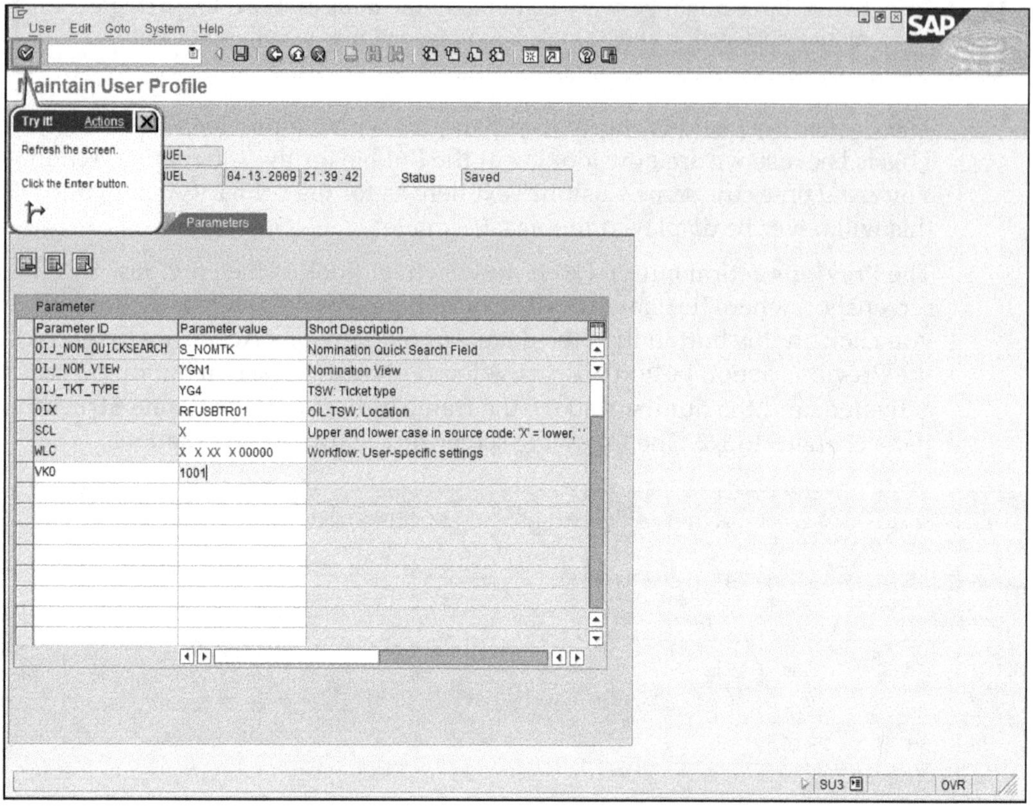

You will see that the Bubble now contains an additional icon. This is the **Alternative** icon. If you click on this icon, the Alternative Action is displayed. This is seen in the following screenshot:

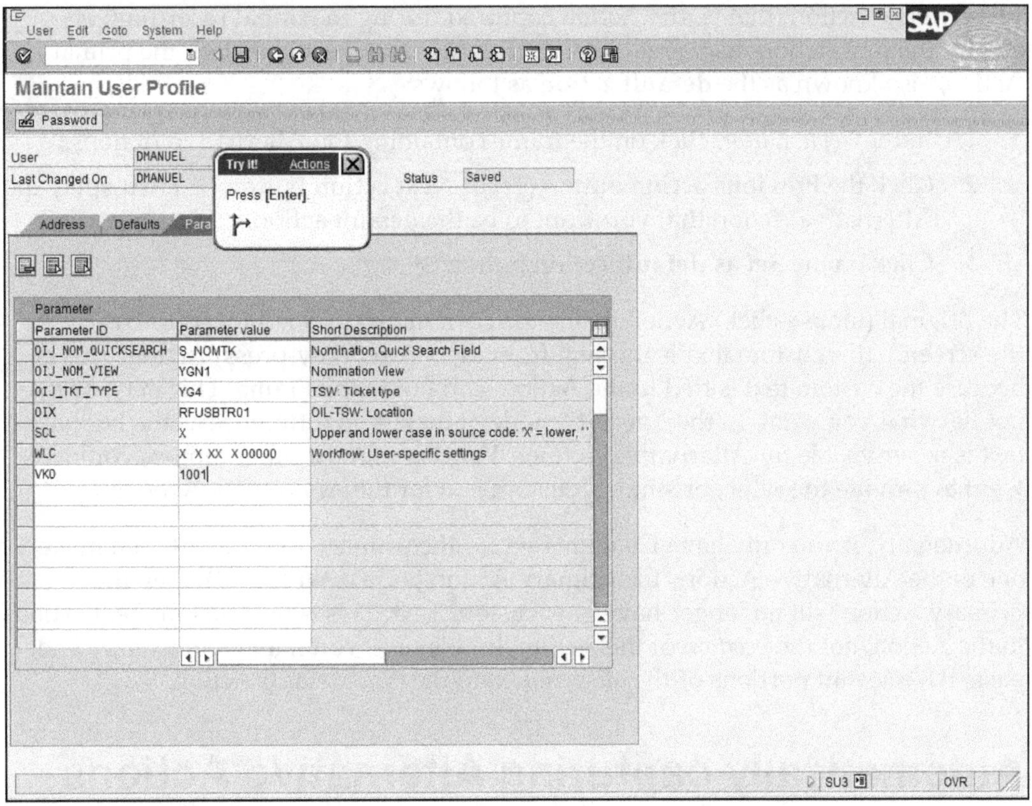

Note that the user can perform either Action, regardless of the actual instructions that are displayed on the screen. Although these screenshots are taken from the *Try It!* mode, the same holds true for the *Know It?* mode. The only difference is that in the *Know It?* mode, the alternative icon is not displayed.

You can actually record as many Alternative Actions as you like (or at least, as many as make sense in the application that you are recording). If there are more than two Alternative Actions, then these will be "daisy-chained" together in the Player. Clicking on the **Alternative** icon from the first Action will display the second Alternative Action. clicking on the **Alternative** icon from the second Action will display the third Alternative Action; and so on. Once the last Action is reached, clicking on the **Alternative** icon (for the last Alternative Action) will take you back to the first (primary) Action.

The primary Action (that is, the Action captured during the initial recording) is always the first Action displayed. However, you can make any Action the primary Action, also known as the **default action** as follows:

1. In the *Topic Editor*, click on the frame containing the Alternative Actions.
2. Click the **Previous action** button () or **Next action** button () to display the Alternative Action that you want to be the default action.
3. Click on the **Set as default action** button ().

The original (mouse-click) Action had some custom text defined for it (**Refresh the screen.**), this custom text is missing from the second (key-press) Action. This is because the custom text is tied to the Action, and not to the Frame. This may, or may not be, what you want. In the *Know It?* mode, it makes no difference as the bubble text is never visible for Alternative Actions. However, in the other modes, you may want to provide the same, or similar, custom text for the Alternative Actions.

Additionally, if you only have Custom Text for the primary Action, but then make one of the Alternative Actions the primary Action (as just explained), then the primary Action will no longer have any Custom Text. This is the Custom Text is tied to the Action, not the *position* of the Action. In this case, you may want to copy and paste the relevant portions of the custom text to the new default Action.

Automatically capturing Alternative Actions

Many applications include keyboard shortcuts for mouse actions. If UPK *knows* the application (that is, it can capture the context information), then it can usually also identify the keyboard shortcuts. You can ask UPK to automatically capture the Alternative Actions for you, by setting your user options as follows:

1. From the Library, select menu option **Tools | Options**.
2. In the **Options** dialog box, expand **Content defaults** and then click on the **Recorder** category.
3. In the **Recorder** options on the right, make sure that the **Automatically record keyboard shortcuts** option is selected.
4. Click **OK** to save your settings.

This setting is shown in the following screenshot:

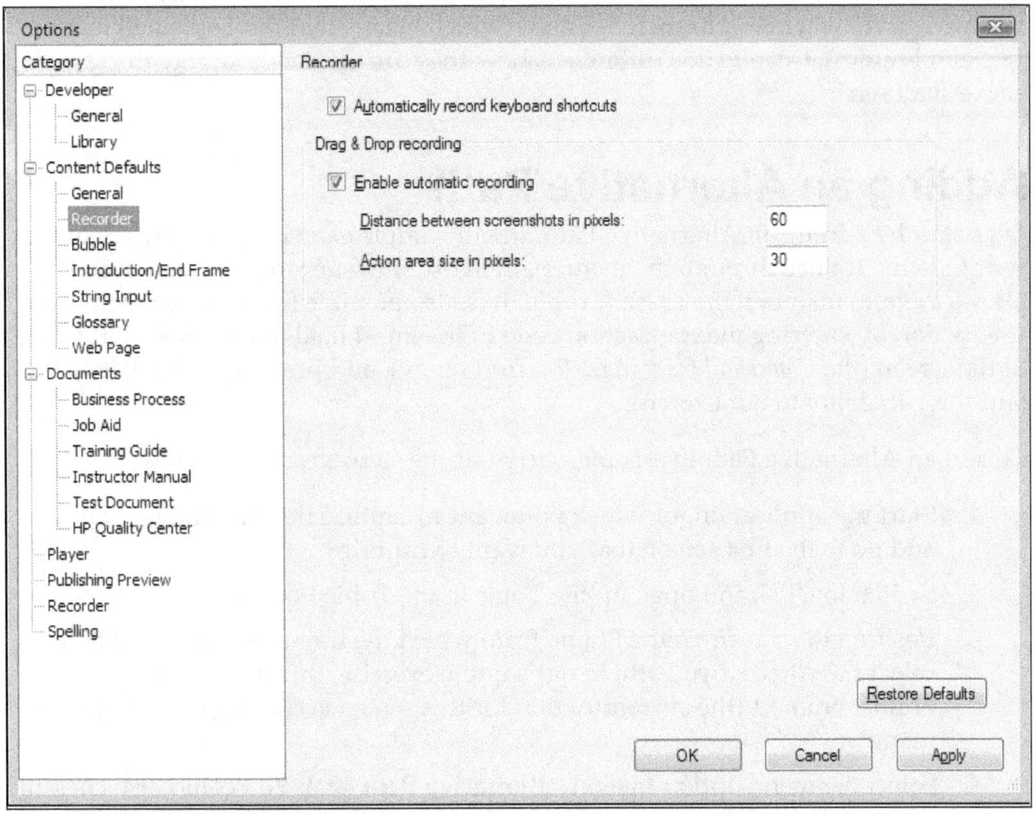

Alternative Paths and Branches

An **Alternative Action** takes place on a single Frame (the Frame against which the original Action was recorded), and is another Action that has exactly the same effect as the original Action. Meaning, it takes you to the same screen (the *next* Frame in the recording). But what if the Alternative Action should take you to an entirely different screen? What if the Alternative Action has an entirely different outcome from the primary Action? Or, what if you just want to be able to describe two possible scenarios in the same single exercise? UPK can support these requirements through the use of Alternative Paths and Branches.

Alternative Paths and Branches are similar with one exception: an **Alternative Path** will always rejoin the main path (that is, both paths eventually share common Frames again), whereas a **Branch** does not (which means that the Topic will have two end Frames). Despite this difference, how they are created is largely the same, as we shall see.

Adding an Alternative Path

Let's start by adding an Alternative Path. In our sample exercise, you may recall that we guide the trainee through the menu path in order to start the transaction that allows them to maintain their User Profile. It is also possible for users to reach this transaction by entering the transaction code in the input field in the upper-left corner of the screen (the *Command field*, in SAP terminology), and pressing *Enter*. We will add this capability to our exercise.

To add an Alternative Path to a Topic, carry out the steps described below:

1. Start the application for which you want to capture the Alternative Path, and go to the first screen that you want to capture.
2. Switch to UPK, and open up the Topic in the Topic Editor.
3. Position the screen on the Frame from which the trainee should be able to select the Alternative Path. In our sample exercise, this is on the very first Frame, Frame **1** (the current Action for this screen is clicking on the **System** menu).
4. Select the menu option **Insert | Alternative Path** (). You could also click the Insert button () on the Editing toolbar, and then select Insert Alternative Path () from the drop-down menu.
5. The pointer changes into an arrow, with a black "E" (for End) at the bottom. In the **Frame Structure** pane at the bottom of the screen, navigate to the Frame at which you want this Alternative Path to re-join the Main Path, and click on it. Note that as you hover over a frame, its thumbnail is displayed. Also, you will see the **Frame ID** (as shown in the example below), to help you in selecting the correct frame. For our exercise, we will choose to rejoin the main path at Frame **3**.

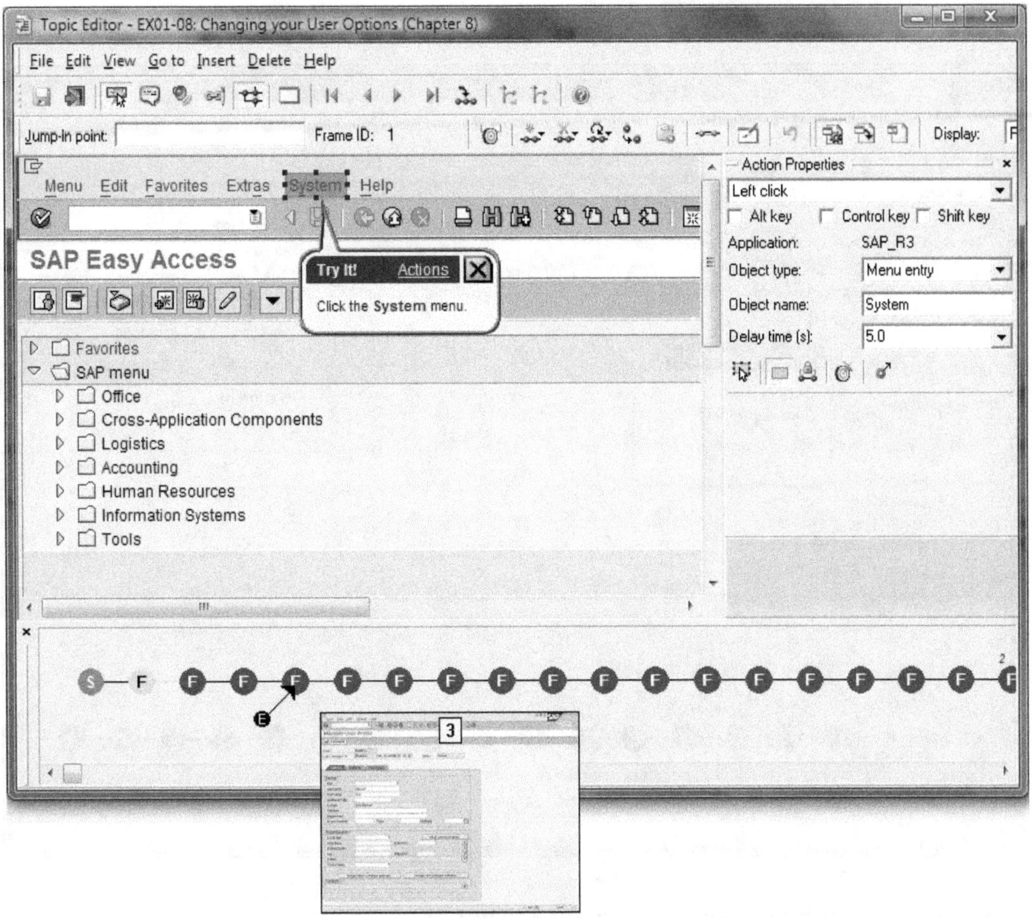

6. You are passed into the application for which you want to record the Alternative Path. Press *Prt Scr* to start recording. Record the actions for the Alternative Path as usual. (Refer to Chapter 3, *Recording a Topic* for additional guidance, if required). For our sample exercise, we recorded the following actions:
    - Clicked in the Command field, to make this the active field
    - Entered the transaction code SU3
    - Clicked the Enter button on the toolbar
7. When you have finished (when you are positioned on the screen at which you are rejoining the main path), click on the **Finish** button in the **Recorder**. You are passed back to UPK.

The Alternative Path has been inserted, as shown in the following example:

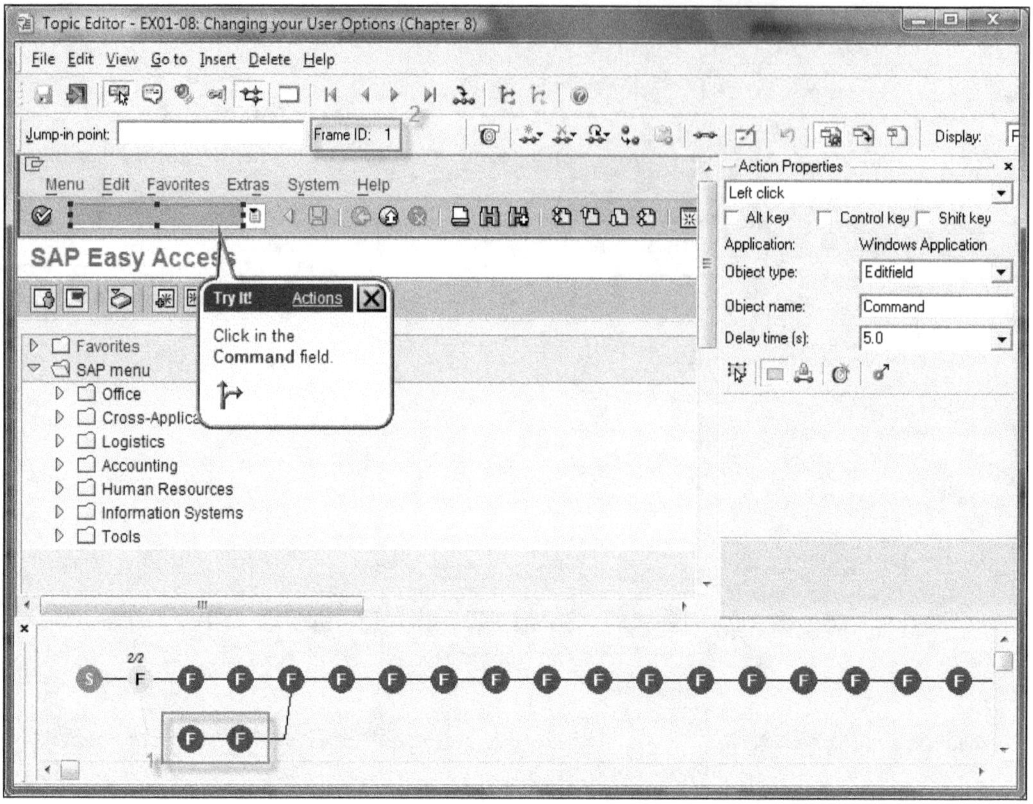

There are a few things to note in this screenshot.

First, although we recorded three actions there are only two additional Frames in the recording (1). This is because the first Action that we recorded (clicking in the **Command** field) was recorded against the Frame from which we started our Alternative Path (2). Second, the path that the Action is currently being shown for is highlighted in green in the **Frame Navigation** pane. This may not show up too well in black and white print (you'll just have to take my word for it). This is useful for understanding what you are looking at on the screen (and which frame will be navigated to next if you click on the Next Frame button ( ), or press *Alt+Right Arrow* on the keyboard).

Changing the end point of an Alternative Path

If you mistakenly select the wrong Frame at which you want to rejoin the main path, then you can change it.

> The ability to change the re-join point for an Alternative Path is a welcome feature that was introduced in OnDemand 9.1. Prior to this there was no way to change the re-join point without a lot of manual work-around.

To change the re-join *point* for an Alternative Path, carry out the following steps:

1. Select the last Frame in the Alternative Path (that is, the Frame immediately before the Alternative Path rejoins the main path).
2. Click on the **Change end point** button ( ) in the **Action Properties** pane. The pointer changes to the End arrow we saw earlier when we were selecting the original end point for the Alternative Path.
3. Click on the Frame where the Alternative Path should now rejoin the main path.

Note that if you have defined Alternative Actions for the last Frame in the Alternative Path (that is, the Frame from which you are changing the re-join point) then you will need to change the re-join point separately for each Alternative Action.

Deleting an Alternative Path

If you need to delete an Alternative Path, then you can do so as follows:

1. Select the frame on which the Alternative Path starts.
2. Click the Next alternative button ( ) or the Previous alternative button ( ) so that the Action shown on the screen is the first Action of the Alternative Path.
3. Check which path is highlighted (in green) in the **Frame Navigation** panel, and make sure that this is the Alternative Path that you want to delete. This is extremely important as it is very easy to mistakenly select the main path and delete that. Once it is deleted, you can't undo the deletion.
4. Select menu option Delete | Path ( ). (You can also click on the Delete button ( ) on the Editing toolbar, and then select Delete Path ( ) from the drop-down menu.)
5. In response to the message **Are you sure you want to delete the selected path?**, click on **Yes**.

Inserting a Decision Frame

The Alternative Action and Alternative Path that we have seen so far are benign choices. They are there and the trainee can choose to use any of the alternatives by clicking on the Alternative button in the Player, and then carry out the associated Action. What if we want to *force* the user to make a choice? What if we want to explain each of the Alternative Paths before the trainee makes their choice? This is where Decision Frames come into play.

A **Decision Frame** is a special kind of Frame where the user is presented with two or more choices (technically, you could have only one choice, but what would be the point in that?), each of which directs them down a different Alternative Path. In addition to the name of each path being shown, a short introductory text can also be provided. Let's look at this by way of an example.

In our sample exercise, we describe the use of three tabbed pages: the **Address** page, the **Defaults** page, and the **Parameters** page. After consulting with our subject matter experts, we learn that most casual users won't ever define any default parameter values and therefore, don't need to be taught about the **Parameters** page. Instead, we'll provide an Alternative Path that bypasses the **Parameters** page, and use a Decision Frame to ask the trainee whether or not they want to learn how to maintain their parameters.

To insert a Decision Frame, carry out the steps described below:

1. In the **Topic Editor**, position yourself on the Frame *after* which you want the Decision Frame to appear. (This is the frame *before* the first frame in one of the paths resulting from making a decision.) In our sample exercise, we will select Frame C, because the following Frame, **5B** is the Frame containing the Action to click on the **Parameters** tab.
2. Select menu option **Insert | Decision Frame** (). (You can also click on the Insert button () on the Editing toolbar, and then select Insert Decision Frame () from the drop-down menu.) The **Create New Decision Path** dialog box is displayed, as shown in the following screenshot:

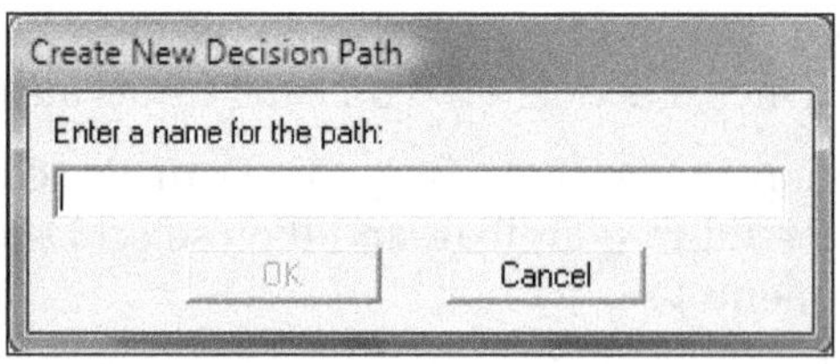

3. In the **Enter a name for the path** field, enter a short text description of the current path. This is the path that has already been recorded. In our sample exercise, this is the path that teaches the trainee how to maintain their parameters, so we will enter a description of "I am a frequent user; I want to see how to define parameters."

> If you subsequently need to change the text description for a path, select the path in the **Path** list, and then click on the **Rename** button (). In the **Rename Decision Path** dialog box that is displayed, change the name as required, and then click on **OK**.

4. Click on **OK** to save your description and create the Decision Frame.

The Decision Frame has now been inserted in the Topic, and is identified by a "D" icon in the **Frame Structure** pane, as shown in the following screenshot:

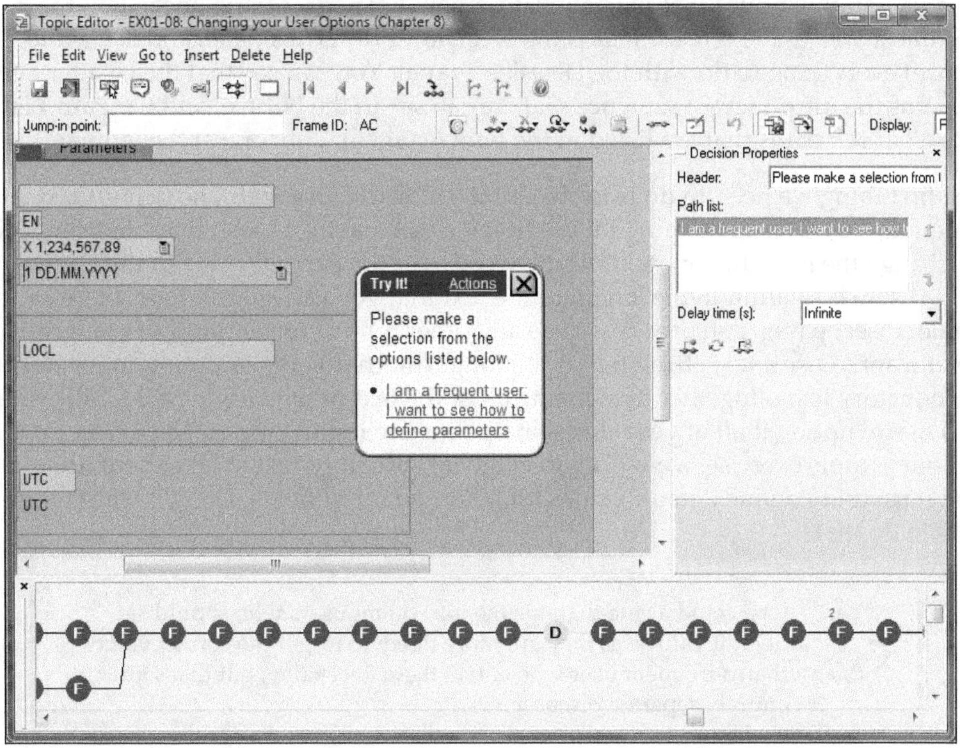

There are several things to note about this new Frame.

First, the screenshot used for this Frame is a grayed-out version of the screenshot from the Frame immediately following it. This is actually the first Frame in our main path, but the same screenshot will also (out of necessity) be the first Frame of all other paths, so this is logical. However, this is a one-time copy (the Frames are not linked), so if you wanted to use a more neutral screen as the background for your decision, then you could either recapture or edit the screenshot for the Decision Frame. The screenshot of the next Frame, from which the Decision Frame screenshot was taken, will not be affected.

Next, we have a new type of Bubble overlaid on the screenshot. This has an introductory sentence (the **Header**) about the decision, followed by a bulleted list of the options that are available (although at the moment there is only one option because we have not yet recorded any Alternative Actions for this decision).

Finally, you will notice that we now have a new **Properties** pane docked on the rightmost side of the screen. This is the **Decision Properties** pane, and is used to control everything to do with the Decision Frame. You can see that the Header field contains the introductory sentence that we can see in the bubble, and the **Path List** lists all of the paths that are listed in the bubble (again, only one at the moment).

The first thing we need to do is to change the introductory text. The default text is adequate, but if we are aiming for quality, we can make this a bit more meaningful. To change the introductory text, simply type over the current value in the Header field. There is no limit to the length of the text that you can specify here, but you cannot insert paragraph breaks (or use any other type of formatting) so you probably don't want to use a text string that is too long. Alternatively, you can remove the introductory text altogether by deleting all of the text in the Header field. This would be a useful option if all of your decision options are in the format "Click here to..." For our sample exercise, we will change the introductory text to "Frequent users may find it useful to define default values for common input fields. Do you want to see how to do that?"

> One could argue that it is the infrequent users who should set default values, as they are more likely to forget the correct values than a frequent user who enters them every day, but that's an entirely separate discussion.

Inserting a Branch

We are now ready to insert another path for this decision. Inserting an Alternative Path from a Decision Frame is slightly different from the method described above (in Adding an Alternative Path), in that it needs to be done from the **Decision Properties** tab.

For our sample exercise, we are providing the trainees with an alternative to bypassing the description of the **Parameters** page entirely. Because the **Parameters** tab is the last thing described in the simulation, we will use a Branch that just exits from the transaction.

> This is actually the *wrong* choice in this case. The two choices (seeing and bypassing the **Parameters** page) do actually share a subsequent Frame. This is the very last Frame in the simulation where we see the confirmation message. Therefore, it would be better to use an Alternative Path. However, for the sake of variety in our sample exercise, we'll use a Branch. This will also give us the opportunity to look at some other interesting functionality later in the book, and give us the opportunity to try to work around this mistake.

To insert a Branch, carry out the following steps:

1. In the application that you are recording, make sure that you are positioned on the screen from which you want to start your path.
2. In the Topic Editor, select the Decision Frame to which you want to add the path.
3. In the **Decision Properties** pane, click on the **Insert Path** button ( ). The **Create Decision Path** dialog box is displayed, as shown in the next screenshot:

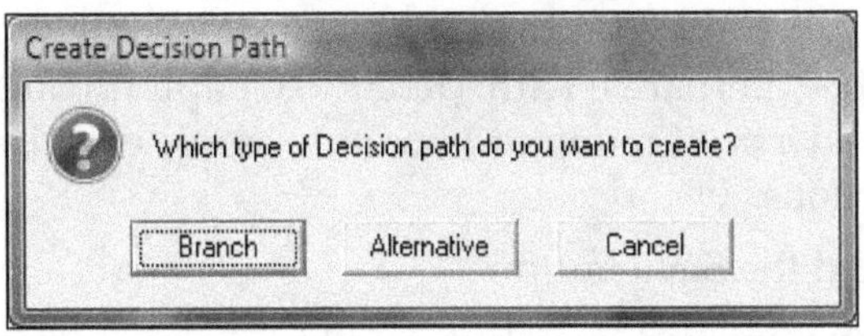

4. Note that this dialog box is only displayed if you are creating an Alternative Path from a Decision Frame. It is not displayed if you are creating an Alternative Path from an Action Frame. This dialog box is also the only place from which you can insert a Branch (although you can insert an Alternative Path via the Editing Menu, as described earlier). This means that you can only insert a Branch if you have a Decision Frame, which is a little inconsistent, but I'm sure UPK has its reasons.
5. Click on the appropriate button, depending on whether your new path will rejoin the main path (Alternative) or will not (Branch). For our example, we will select Branch. Either the **Create New Decision Path** dialog box or the **Create New Branch dialog box** is displayed (as appropriate). The content and purpose of both is the same, so they are not described separately.

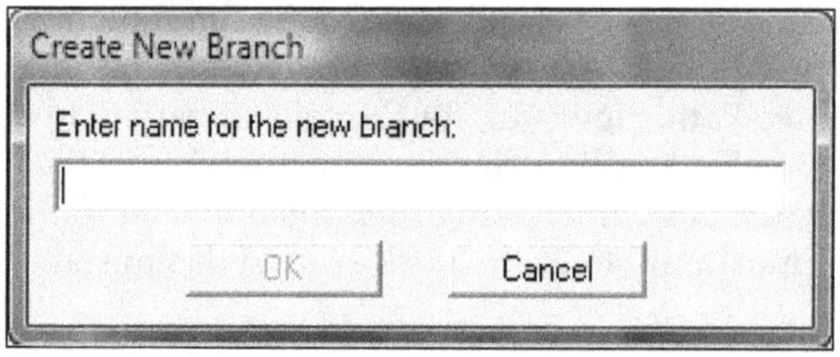

6. In the **Create New Branch/Decision Path** dialog box, enter a short text name for your new path, and then click on **OK**. For our sample exercise, we will enter a path name of "I am an occasional user; I don't need to know that."
7. If you are creating an Alternative Path (as opposed to a Branch) then you will be prompted to select the end point for the path in exactly the same way as you would for an Alternative Path without a decision frame (see Adding an Alternative Path).
8. You are passed into the application for which you want to record the Alternative Path. Press *Prt Scr* to start recording, and then record the Actions for the Alternative Path. (Refer to Chapter 3, *Recording a Topic* for additional guidance, if required.) For our sample exercise, we recorded the following Actions:
    - Clicked the **Save** button
9. When you have finished, which should be when you have completed the activity (transaction, in this example) as you are not re-joining the main path, click on the **Finish** button in the **Recorder**. You are passed back to UPK.

The Branch has now been inserted, as shown in the following screenshot:

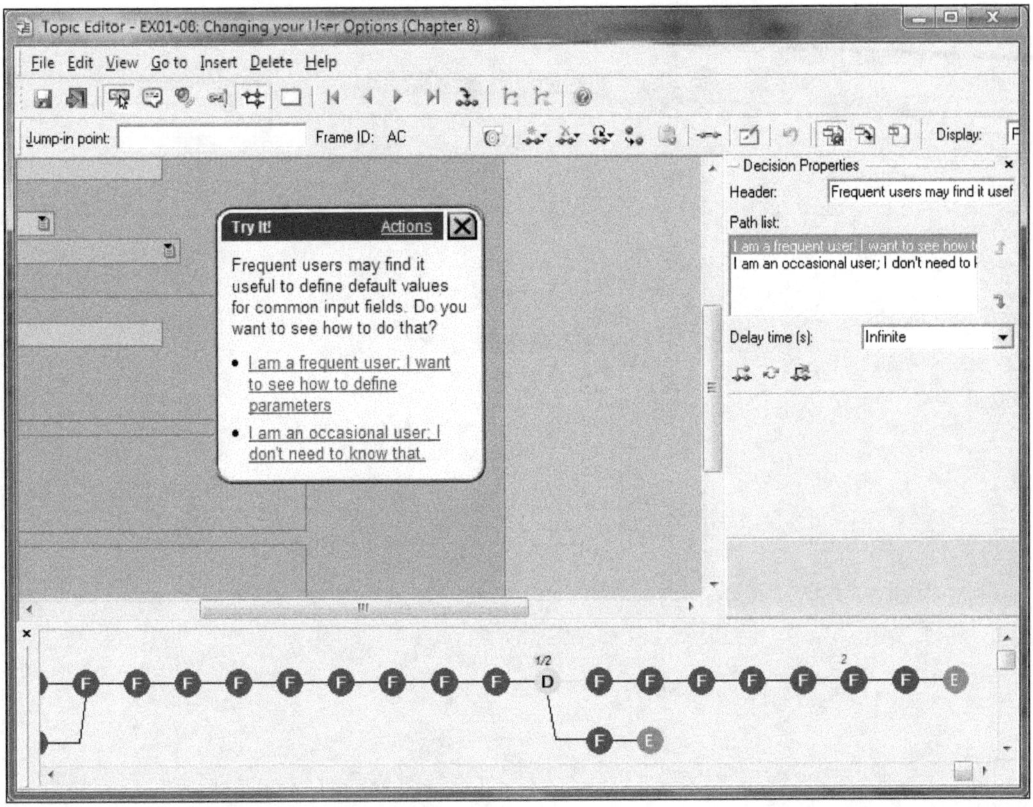

You can see that the Decision Frame now contains two options. Each one ties in with the list of paths shown in the **Path list** in the **Decision Properties** pane. You can also see from the **Frame Navigation** pane that we now have two end points for the Topic. This is because we used a Branch.

Let's look at how this manifests itself in the Player. The next screenshot shows what the trainee will see when they reach the Decision Frame:

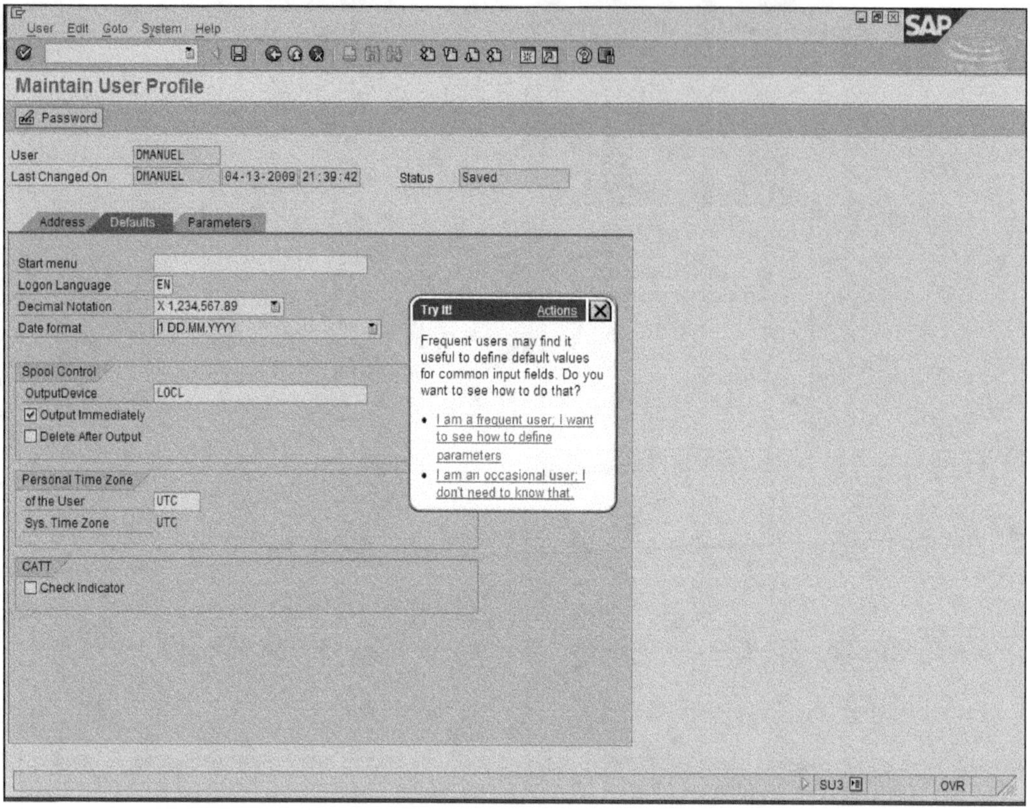

Note that you can add as many Alternative Paths or Branches as you like to a Decision Frame. You can even mix them, perhaps providing three Alternative Paths and two Branches, all from the same Decision Frame.

Changing the order of paths

Alternative Paths will be listed in the order in which they are created, but you can change this order if required. For example, you may want the most commonly-used path to be listed first. The order or the *Alternative Paths* or at least which one is listed first becomes important when considering *See It!* and *Know It?* modes (see ahead).

To change the order of the paths in a Decision Frame, carry out the steps described below:

1. In the Topic Editor, select the Decision Frame, so that the **Decision Properties** pane is displayed.
2. In the **Decision Properties** pane, click on the path that you want to reorder, in the **Path list**.
3. Click on the **Move Up** button (⇑) or the **Move Down** button (⇓) to move the path to the required position. These buttons can be found to the right of the **Path list**.

Deleting a decision path

To delete a decision path, carry out the steps described below:

1. In the Topic Editor, select the Decision Frame, so that the Decision Properties pane is displayed.
2. In the *Path list*, select that path that you want to delete.
3. Click on the **Delete Path** button ( ).

Note that you cannot delete a path if it is the only path in the Decision Frame. In this case, you would first need to delete the Decision Frame itself, and then delete the path (which would effectively delete the remainder of the recording, which you probably wouldn't want to do).

Decision Frames in See It! mode

In *See It!* mode, the Decision Frame will (by default) be displayed until one of the options is selected. This may not always be desirable, especially if the simulation is being looped in kiosk mode. Whether UPK waits for a decision or not, and how long it waits for if it does, is controlled by the **Delay time (s)** field in the **Decision Properties** pane. As you can see from the previous screenshots, this is set to Infinite by default, which is why UPK will wait forever, if necessary, for a decision to be made. If you want UPK to automatically continue down the primary path if a decision is not made within a certain period, then simply change the **Delay time (s)** field to specify how long (in seconds) UPK should wait before continuing. You can either choose one of the predefined options from the drop-down, or enter a specific number of seconds directly into the **Delay time(s)** field.

If you select a delay time of Skip, then UPK will act as though the Decision Frame does not even exist. The Decision Frame will not be displayed, and the playback will proceed immediately down the default path (this is the one listed first in the **Path list**).

Decision Frames in Know It? mode

Decision Frames effectively do not exist in *Know It?* mode. The trainee is required to carry out the actions for the default path (this is the one listed first in the Path list) only. This is in marked contrast to Alternative Actions and Alternative Paths without Decision Frames, and is an important consideration when deciding whether to have an Alternative Path with a Decision Frame, or an Alternative Path without a Decision Frame.

If you recall the first Alternative Path that we added (see Adding an Alternative Path), we gave the trainees the choice of accessing the transaction either via the menu, or by entering the transaction code. In *Know It?* mode, the trainee can perform either set of actions and will still be marked correctly. With our Decision Frame Alternative Path (see *Inserting a Decision Frame*), the trainee can only perform the Action for the default path (changing their parameters). If they try to take the Alternative Path (assuming that they somehow know about it in advance maybe because they have already carried out the exercise in *Try It!* mode) then they will be marked incorrect.

Stretching the envelope with Alternative Paths

What we have looked at so far has been fairly obvious use of Alternative Paths. However, there are a few other interesting things that you can do with Alternative Paths. Note that the key word here is "interesting". These things may not be entirely practical, but explaining them here will at least open your mind to other possibilities.

Looping back

In our examples, so far, Alternative Paths have been used to move forward through the simulation. When selecting the end point for our Alternative Path, we have always selected a Frame that is further ahead in the simulation than the Frame where the Alternative Path starts. However, there is nothing in UPK that says that you have to go forward. You could quite easily go backwards to an earlier Frame. A good use of this would be where you have several decision options, and want the user to be able to go back to the decision and choose a different path. An example of such a scenario is shown in the following screenshot:

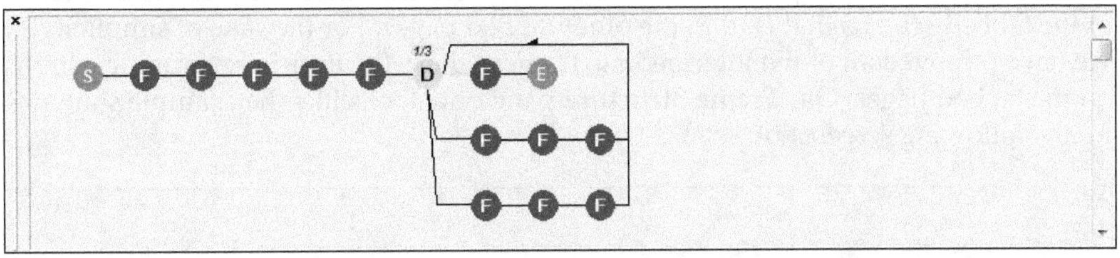

You can even have a couple of frames unique to the Alternative Path, and then rejoin the main path further back from where you originally started. This is illustrated in the following extract of the **Frame Structure** pane:

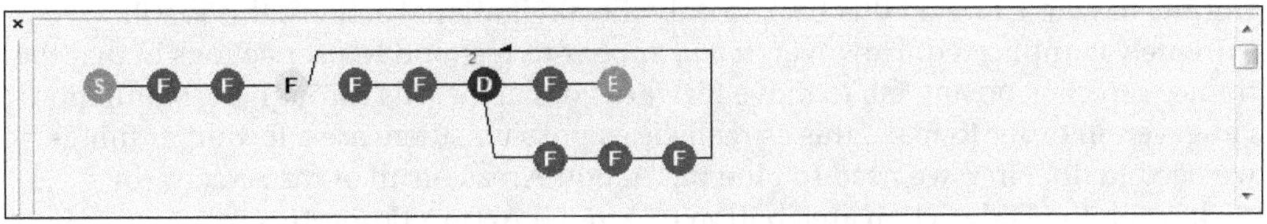

Quite under what circumstances this would be useful remains to be seen (maybe a decision of "Do you want to see that again?"), but the possibility is there.

Automatically responding to user input

As was clearly stated at the outset of this book, UPK creates recordings. Trainees carrying out UPK simulations can only perform the actions that have been recorded. They can only follow along a predefined path. As we have seen in this chapter, it is possible to extend this slightly by recording multiple paths and allowing the user to go down any one of these paths, but the recording is not automatically responding to which Action the trainee has chosen.

If Alternative Actions (and Alternative Paths leading from these Actions) have been defined for a Frame, then the trainee can carry out any of these Actions on the screen. They do not have to click on the Alternative icon (↱) to go to the specific Alternative Path to which the Action applies. You can use this capability to direct trainees down a certain path depending on where they click on the screen by defining each of these clicks as Alternative Actions on Alternative Paths.

As a simple example of this in Action, we will create a simplified version of our sample exercise. In this version, we will allow the user to click on any tab from any screen. They can also click on the **Exit** button to exit from the transaction (and therefore the simulation). We have done this by defining Alternative Paths on each of the tabbed screens that lead to the other tabbed pages. For the sake of simplicity, we have removed all of the intermediate frames where the user is performing actions on the tabbed pages. Our **Frame Structure** pane now looks like the example shown in the following screenshot:

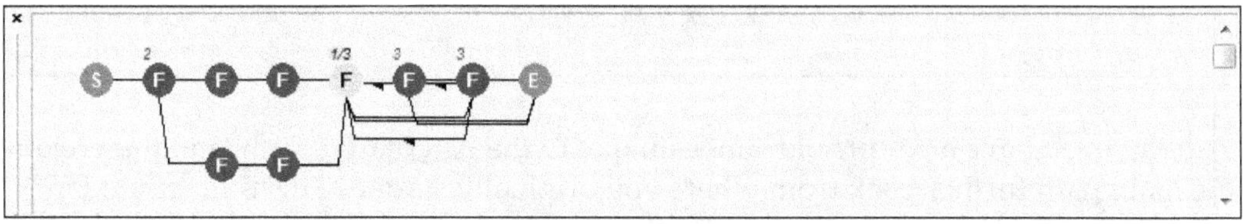

Despite having trimmed this back to only the navigational actions, this is still extremely complicated. However, it *will* appear to respond to user actions in that the trainee can click on any tab to move forwards or backwards through the simulation. However, in order to make this as realistic as possible, there are a few other things we need to do. First, we need to hide the Action Areas on all of the screens (by clicking on the Hide action area button (▭) in the **Action Properties** pane), so that the trainee has full flexibility of where to click. If you don't do this, then even though the trainee can click on any tab, the first tab will always be highlighted. Secondly, we need to remove any bubble text (custom or otherwise) that tells the trainee where to click, and replace it with some neutral text. For example, in our exercise we could say something like "Click on any tab to go to that page, or click the Exit button to quit." We need to do this for every Action on every Frame. Once we've done this, we'll have a simulation that appears to automatically respond to what the trainee does.

As this is fairly complex to set up, it is probably not worth doing for every exercise, especially once you start including "real" actions. However, there is certainly an argument to be made for using this approach for display-only activities, where trainees can roam around the various screens depending on their whim.

Summary

Providing alternatives in a Topic will make the Topic more realistic, and more flexible. There are three types of alternative:

- Alternative Actions provide another way of achieving the same result as an existing Action, on the same Frame. Alternative Actions are useful for providing such things as keyboard shortcuts for mouse-click actions.
- Alternative Paths provide different ways of progressing through the same simulation. In some cases, this may just be an extension of an Alternative Action. By providing an alternative that takes several screens—for example, navigating through more than one level of menu, versus the initial Action of clicking a button on the toolbar. They can also be used to provide alternative scenarios—for example, parking an entered invoice versus posting it. You can also use an Alternative Path to allow trainees to bypass certain parts of the simulation that may be irrelevant to them.
- An Alternative Path may use a Decision Frame, which requires the trainee to make a conscious decision about which path to take. If no Decision Frame is used, then the Alternative Path behaves in the same way as an Alternative Action.
- Branches are similar to Alternative Paths, but instead of returning to the main path (as Alternative Paths do), a Branch has its own End Frame. Branches always require a Decision Frame.

9

Adding Value to Your Topics

In Chapter 3, *Recording a Simulation,* we recorded our first simulation. Some developers would have stopped there. In Chapter 4, *Editing a Topic,* we updated our simulation so that it actually worked properly, and tidied up some of the Bubble Text so that it made a bit more sense. Most developers would have stopped there. In Chapter 8, *Allowing Alternatives,* we added some alternatives into our simulation, to make it work a bit more realistically, and to extend the *usefulness* of the Topic. Not many developers even bother to go that far. In this chapter, we will take our Topics to an entirely new level, adding a great deal of value to them, and significantly improving their quality. We will do this through the use of Custom Text, Explanation Frames, Web Pages, and Packages. We will also look at providing a Glossary, which we'll seamlessly integrate into our training.

These things are sometimes thought of as "bells and whistles", because they are added after the recording has been done, and are sometimes perceived as purely being "nice to have" (which usually translates into "don't bother", in a project plan). However, these bells and whistles can make the difference between **adequate** training and **outstanding** training, and of course you always want to aim for outstanding.

Adding the bells and whistles is even more important when the simulations are to be used as "stand-alone" learning objects. That is, objects, for self-paced learning and not within the context of a classroom conduct. In a classroom, the instructor is there to embellish on the information shown, to present additional information, and generally talk around the exercise. If the trainee sits at their own desk, all of this has to be provided in the simulation itself and this is where these bells and whistles prove to be essential. If you want your exercises to have a shelf-life beyond the first round of training, then you really need to pay attention to this chapter.

In this chapter, you will learn how to:

- Provide context through the use of Custom Text
- Use Explanation Frames
- Use Web Pages in the Concepts pane and beyond

- Use Packages and link them to content objects
- Create a Glossary

Providing context through the use of Custom Text

The easiest and simplest way to add value to your Topics is to make good use of Custom Text in the Bubbles. We looked at how to influence the Template Text, and how to add Custom Text, in Chapter 4, *Editing a Topic*, so we will not go over the same information here. Instead, we will simply look at what you can (and should) do with Custom Text. If you need additional help on Custom Text, refer to Chapter 4, *Editing a Topic*.

The Start Frame

You may recall that the very first Frame in a Topic is the Start Frame. This is sometimes referred to as the **Introduction frame**, which is largely a throwback to OnDemand, as we shall see shortly. As this Frame is the first thing that a trainee will see when they carry out a Topic, coupled with the fact that this Frame is a "non-action" Frame, in that the user does not need to actively do anything (other than pressing *Enter* to continue), it is a good place to provide some additional information to the trainee.

The first thing that you should explain in the Introduction frame is exactly what the trainee will be learning in the exercise. Certainly the title of the Topic should give them a clue, but this is not really detailed enough. A good source of information for this is the learning objectives of the course for which this exercise has been built, or the competencies, depending on your curriculum development process. For our sample exercise, we could use the bubble shown in the following screenshot:

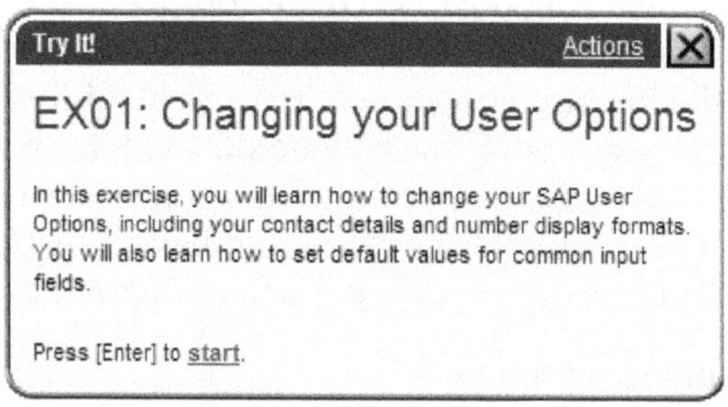

This is a good start, but we can do more.

It is always useful, with training exercises, to use realistic business scenarios to explain what the trainee is doing, to put the keystrokes and mouse-clicks into a business context. Trainees are much more likely to remember information to which they can relate. Consider telling a story and walking the trainees through that story as they carry out the exercise. Although it is a fairly spurious example, we will continue with our sample exercise. Here, we could use the bubble shown in the following screenshot:

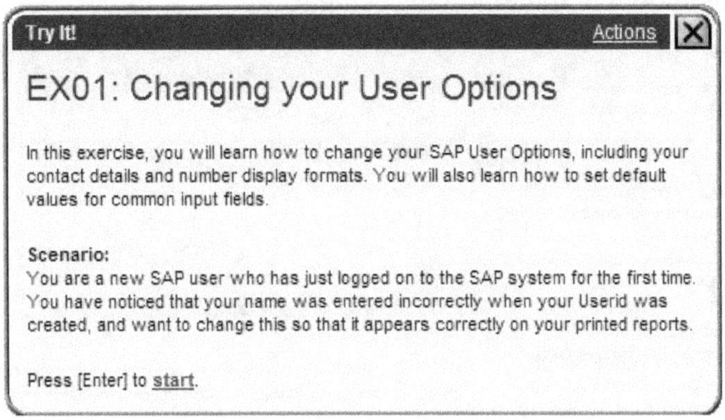

So now the trainee has a good idea of what they will learn, and they have an example that they can relate to. The text is also directed at the trainee, so the trainee will feel actively involved.

There is another strong argument for including a scenario in the form shown above. Consider the case where you are providing training for users in multiple locations (possibly countries) or departments, each of which has its own set of customers, products, and vendors. Users will always want to see exercises using *their* data: orders for their products, placed at their location, and so on. To keep everyone happy, you would need to develop a separate, customized Topic for each location or user group. If the basic process (and, most importantly for us, the Actions in the recording) is the same in each case, this is clearly inefficient. However, if you create a scenario, and say something like "You are a Customer Service Representative in the Tampa Service Center. Customer SunCo has phoned through an order for 1,000 gallons of regular gasoline. You need to record this order in the system so that it can be fulfilled by Fuel Services." then trainees who are not at the Tampa Service Center will at least understand that this is *role play*. It is *make believe*, and they shouldn't be concerned that they don't see products that they don't supply at their own location. So set the scene with a scenario in the **Introduction** pane, and then build on this throughout the exercise.

Introduction Text: Version differences

At this point, it is worth highlighting some key differences between the way the **Introduction** pane was handled prior to UPK 3.5, and the way that the **Introduction** pane is used in UPK 3.5.

If you open an Outline Element in the *Outline Editor*, and select a Topic in the navigation tree, you will see that the lower-right portion of the screen is labeled **Introduction**, as shown in the following screenshot:

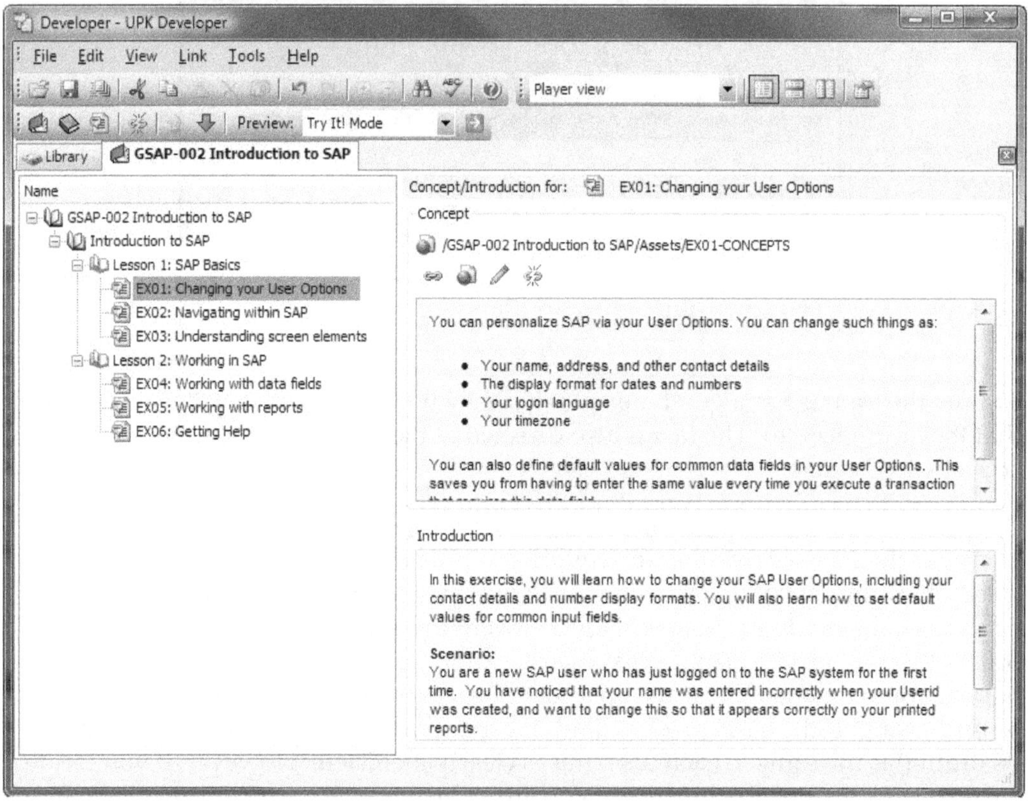

You will recall from Chapter 5, *Building and Outline*, that the *Outline Editor* is used to organize content objects into the structure that the trainee will see. However, if we look at the published version of the Outline above, we will see the following:

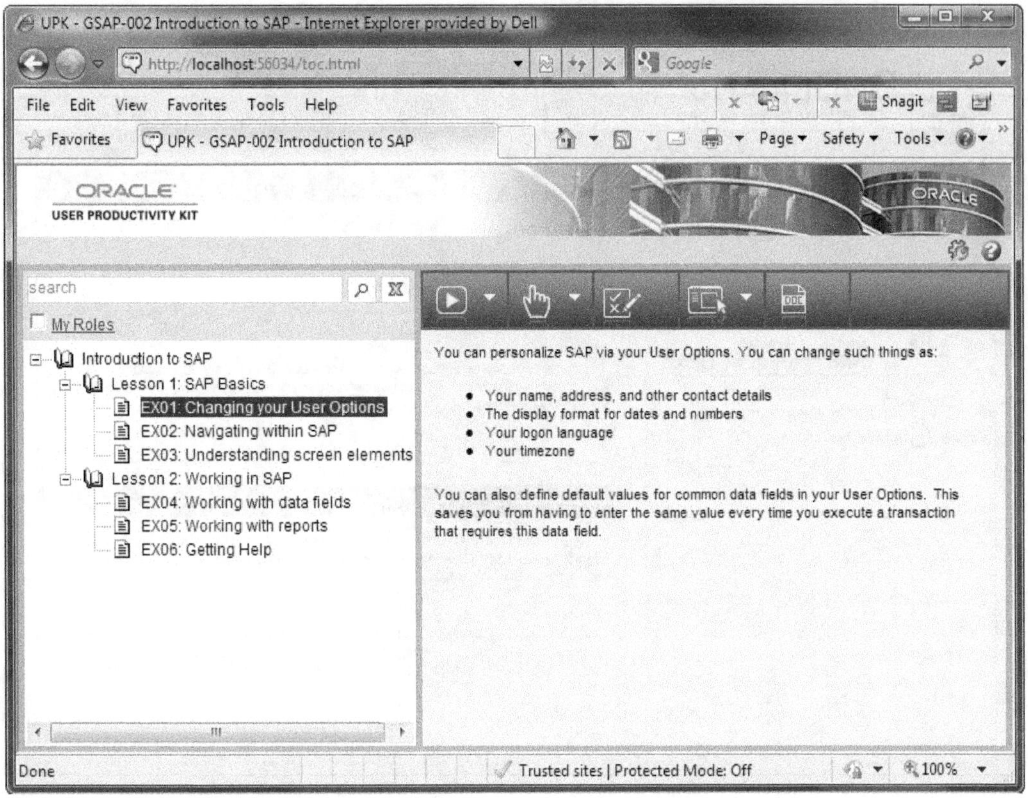

Where has the **Introduction** Frame gone? Put simply. UPK 3.5 does not display the **Introduction** Frame in the Player any more. Users of UPK 2.x or OnDemand 9.x will recall that the **Introduction** Frame certainly *used* to be displayed, as shown in the following screenshot, which is taken from OnDemand 9.1.5:

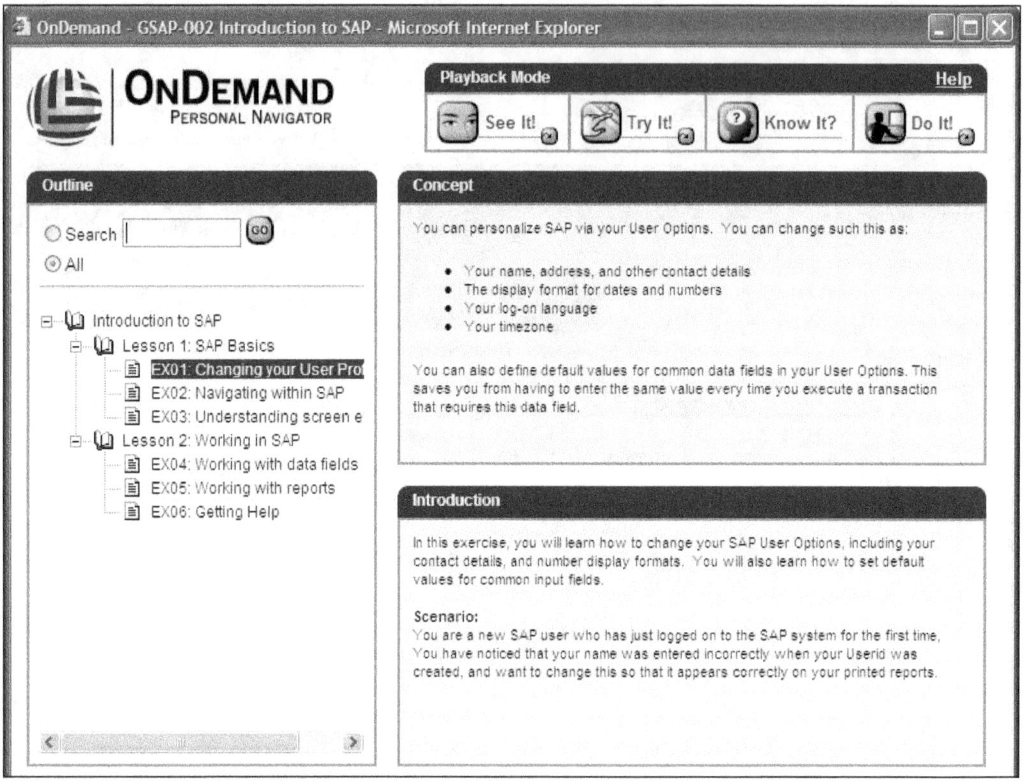

Quite why Oracle decided to change the way the **Introduction** pane is displayed (or not) in version 3.5 is a mystery (maybe they felt that with all that screen space required for the new Oracle branding, there just wasn't the space left to include the **Introduction** any more). However, it does have some important implications on the way that we are planning on using it.

This is because the effect of a publishing option associated with the **Introduction** pane has changed significantly. In the *Publishing Wizard*, the options for the *Player* package include an option to **Show introduction text**. In OnDemand version 9.1, this option determined whether the **Introduction** text appeared in the Outline *as well as* on the first Frame of the Player. However, in UPK 3.5, the **Introduction** text is *never* displayed in the Outline and the **Show introduction text** determines whether the **Introduction** text appears in the Player *at all* (effectively, it controls whether the Start Frame is included in the Player or not.

> **Version Difference**
>
> The *Content Development* manual for OnDemand 9.1.5 describes the **Show introduction text** option as working the way described for UPK 3.5. It doesn't work that way; it works the way described for OnDemand 9.1, above. This is clearly a rare case of the documentation being updated *before* the software.

For our purposes, therefore, we need to make sure that the **Show introduction text** option is *always* selected when we publish. This option can be found in the **Player** category of your **Options**, as shown in the next screenshot:

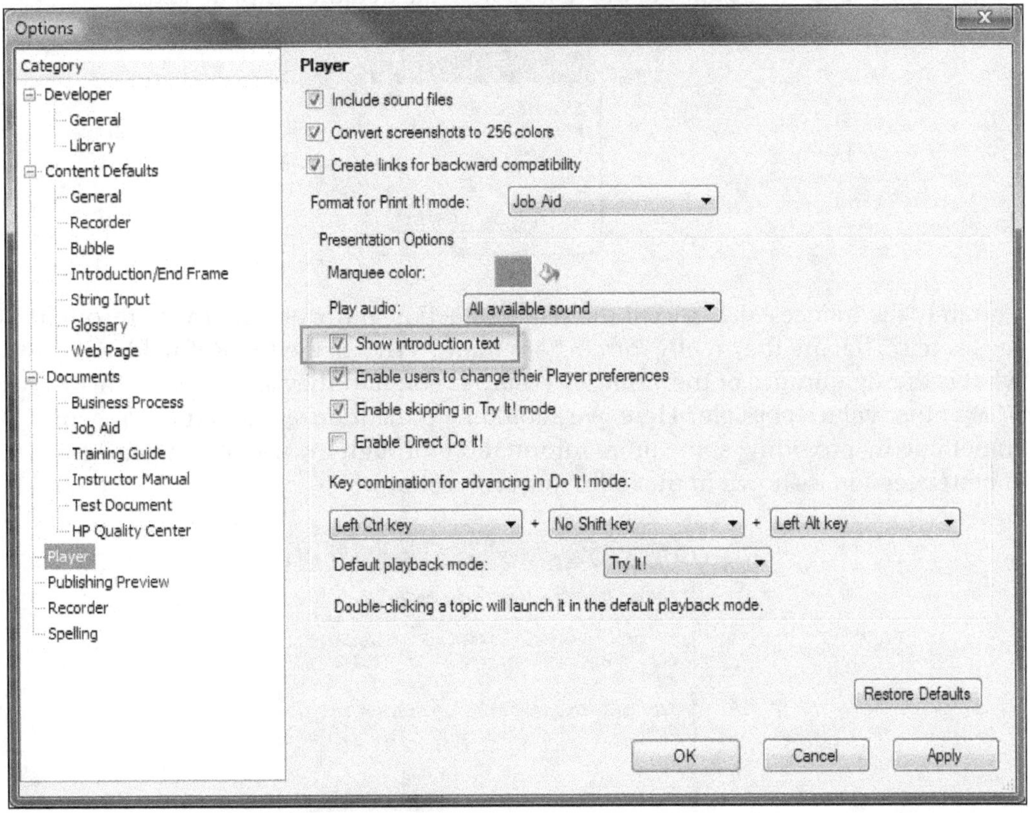

Action Frames

As we saw in Chapter 4, *Editing a Topic*, it is possible to add Custom Text to the Topic's Bubbles, either in addition to, or instead of, the Template Text. Using the Template Text has several significant advantages, especially when localizing your content (see Chapter 13, *Localizing your Content*) or providing sound (see Chapter 11, *Incorporating Sound into Your Topics*). However, the Template Text will only ever be able to describe the *mechanics* of what the user is doing, it cannot provide *business context*. You should always try to teach more than just key-strokes and mouse-clicks. Specifically, you should always take the opportunity to add business context yourself, through the liberal use of Custom Text in Action Frames.

Consider the following example that uses solely the default template texts:

Certainly the trainee can *carry out* the required action and work their way through the exercise, but are they really *learning* anything? What is the **Ext.Ref** field, and what is the significance of the value **ZBW002342**? Should they *always* enter this value, or are other values possible? Here, we should help the trainee out and *teach* them something by providing some more information through the use of Custom Text. A better version is shown in the following screenshot:

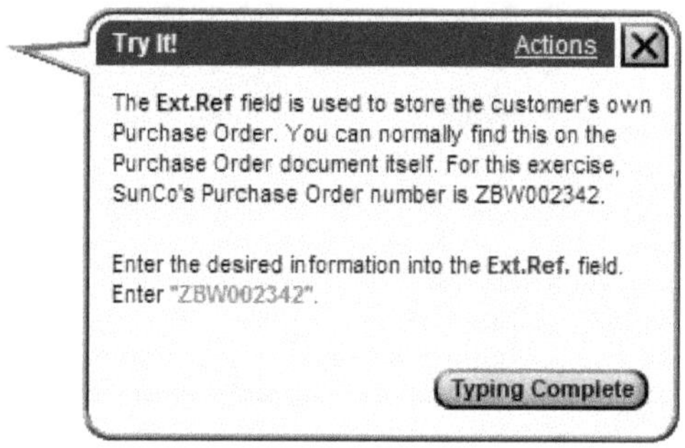

Now the trainee knows exactly what they are entering in the exercise, and understands the *business context* so they can perform the action correctly when they are doing their actual job.

Note that here, we have retained the Template Text (we did not insert the Template Text as Custom Text) which will aid in the translation (although the custom text will still need to be manually translated). We simply added the first paragraph that you see in the Bubble above as Custom Text, and positioned it before the Template Text (the **Show custom text first** button (▣) is selected by default; you can deselect this if required, to have the Template Text displayed first, but for our purposes we want the Custom Text first).

> UPK will run the Template Text in the next line immediately after the Custom Text, so you need to insert an extra line break at the end of the Custom Text if you want the two texts to appear as separate paragraphs.

In this example, note that we have continued the scenario that we described in the **Introduction** pane through into this exercise, by mentioning the customer's name. Again, it is always useful to use a scenario so that the trainee can better relate the exercise to their actual jobs. Note that the text **For this exercise...is ZBW002342** will need to be tagged to appear only in See It! and Try It! modes.

Whenever practical, you should try to provide some more information, whether this is business context, or a continuation of the scenario you are using, even if this is on every Frame. If you intend for your simulations being used outside of a classroom environment, then you should consider providing exactly the same level of information as the instructor would provide in a classroom. Think about what you would say to the trainee, what additional information or guidance you would give them if you sat next to them, talking them through the simulation, and then add *that* information into the Bubbles as Custom Text. Remember: training is the effective transfer of knowledge, and if that knowledge is incomplete, then the trainees have not been adequately trained.

The End Frame

The End Frame is always displayed as the final Frame in the simulation. There is no End Frame equivalent of the **Show introduction text** option to avoid having this Frame displayed. This is a good thing, as it means that we can use this Frame to provide some final information to the user. This should be seen as a companion to the Start Frame, and should confirm the information presented in the Start Frame.

In the Start Frame above, we told the trainee what they would learn. In the End Frame, we should confirm that they have learned this. (This much is standard training theory.) If you have described a scenario in the Start Frame, and followed this through the Action Frames, then you should make reference to this, as well. Suitable End Frame text for our ongoing exercise on SAP user options could be:

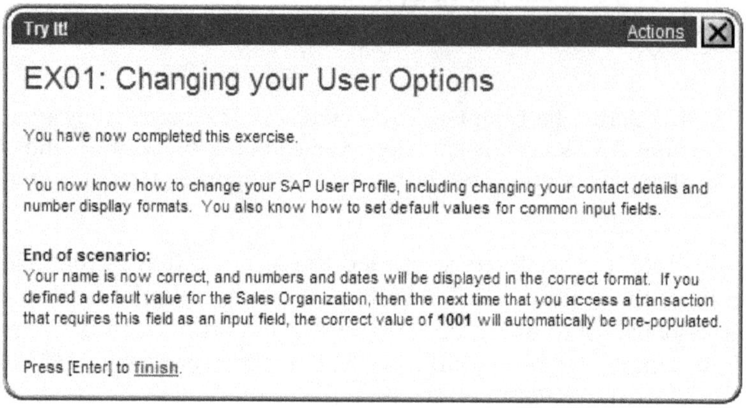

Although the scenario information is again fairly spurious in this example, it does at least give you an idea of the kind of information that can usefully be included in the End Frame. Again, this information should be tagged for *See It!* and *Try It!* modes only.

Note that in this example we have also included a message of **You have now completed this exercise**. This is a nice courtesy, and confirms to the trainee that they have reached the end of the simulation.

Explanation Frames

In the previous sections, on the Start Frame, Action Frames, and the End Frame, we have looked at ways to provide additional information into the *existing* Bubbles. In this section, we will look at how to provide information on Frames that serve no purpose other than to provide information. These are **Explanation Frames**.

An Explanation Frame is a special type of Frame that does not have an associated Action. When you insert an Explanation Frame, it takes its screenshot from the Frame immediately following it (regardless of whether this is an Action Frame, a Decision Frame, or even another Explanation Frame. This makes Explanation Frames extremely useful for drawing the trainee's attention to particular information on the screen, or explaining things that are not explicitly covered by the Action Frames. Note that, unlike Decision Frames, the screenshot used in Explanation Frames is not "grayed out".

In our sample exercise, we will add two Explanation Frames. In the first, we will add an Explanation Frame informing the user that, although the simulation does not walk them through doing so, they can still change their last name. In the second, we'll draw the user's attention to the message generated by the system when they save their user profile.

To insert an Explanation Frame, carry out the steps described below:

1. Open up the Topic to which you want to add the Explanation Frame, in the *Topic Editor*.
2. In the *Frame Navigation* pane, click on the Frame after which you want the Explanation Frame to appear. Bear in mind that the screenshot of the *next* Frame will be copied into the Explanation Frame (this is a one-time copy; you can replace or edit either screenshot without the source Frame being affected). For our exercise, we want the Explanation Frame to show the initial view of the **Address** tabbed page, so we will select Frame 2, as shown in the following screenshot:

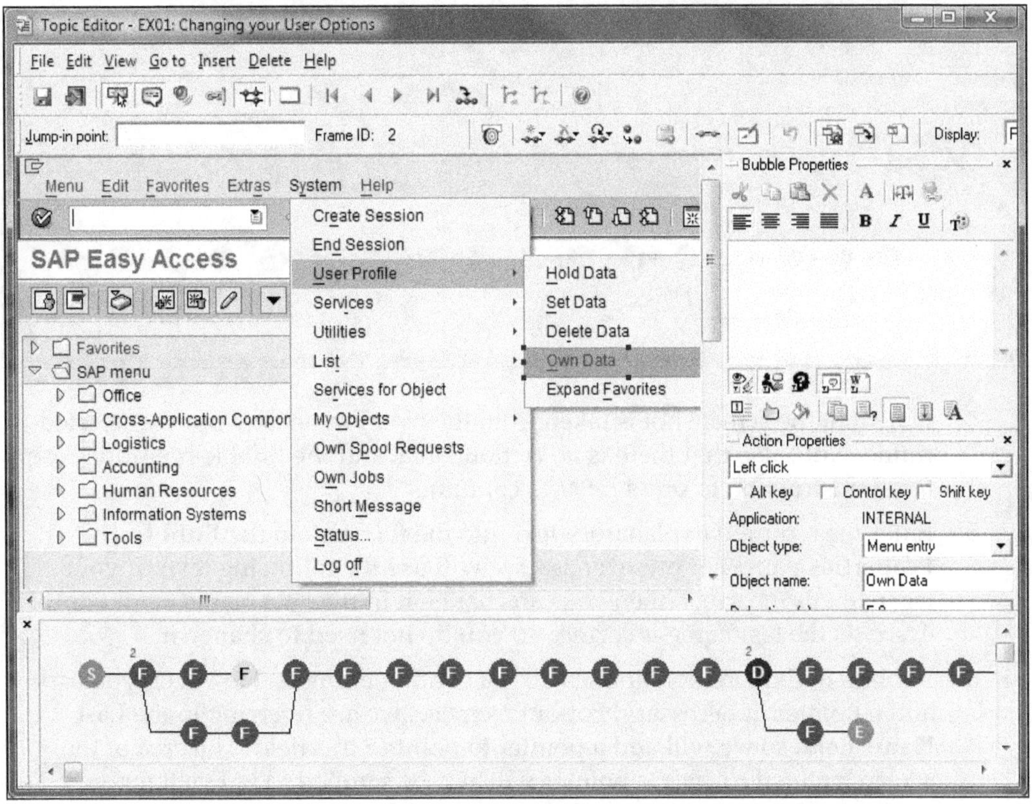

3. Select menu option **Insert | Explanation Frame** (You can also click on the **Insert** button () on the *Standard Toolbar*, and then select **Explanation Frame** () from the drop-down menu.) A new Frame is inserted, as you can see in the next screenshot:

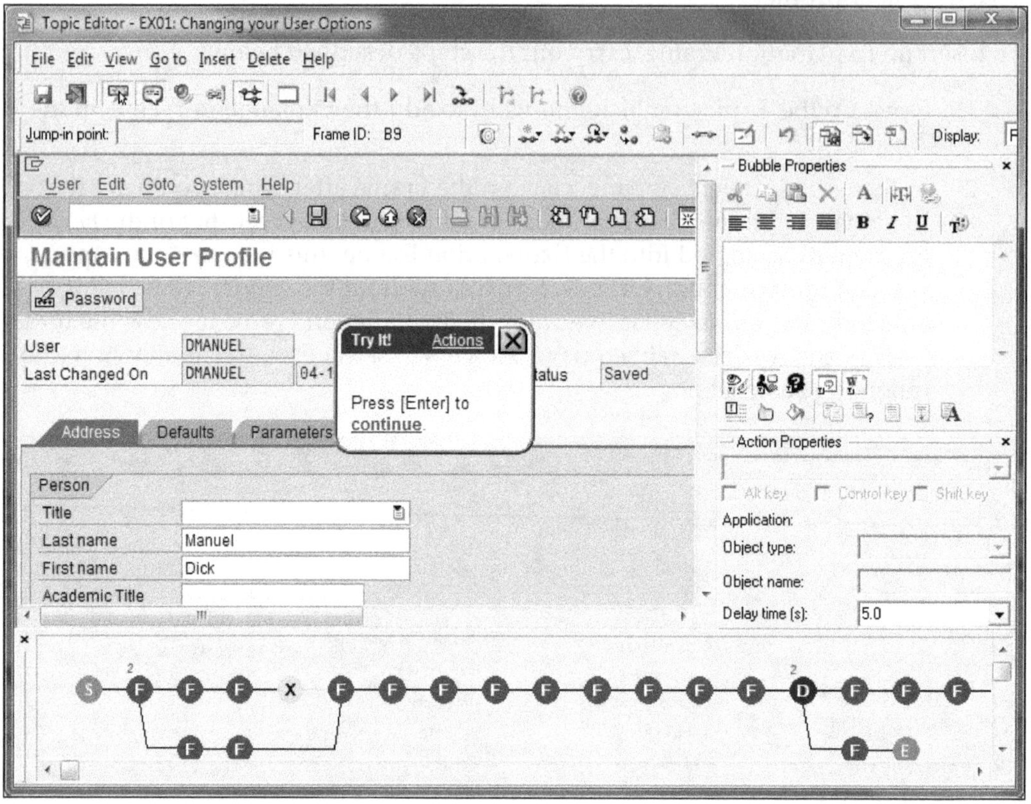

4. Note that the screenshot is taken from the next Frame, and not the selected frame. Note also that there is no Action Area, and the Bubble is empty except for an instruction to press *Enter* to continue.

5. Enter the required explanatory text into the text area in the **Bubble Properties** pane. For our exercise, we will use the following text: "If your last name is incorrect, then you can change it in the Last Name field. For this exercise, the last name is correct, so you do not need to change it."

6. Bubbles in Explanation Frames do not contain pointers. However, you can add a pointer, if necessary. For our exercise, we are referring to the **Last Name** field, so we will add a pointer to point to this field. The area of the screen 'pointed to' by the pointer will also be scrolled to in Do It! mode if the screenshot is displayed. Click on the **Pointer position** button () in the **Bubble Properties** pane to display the drop-down list of possible pointers:

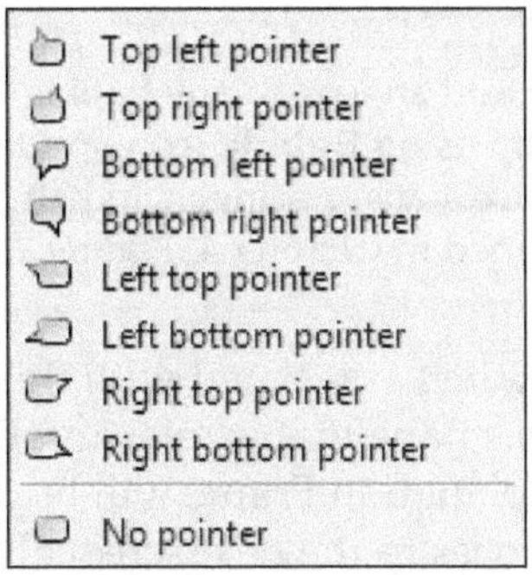

7. Click on the appropriate pointer position from the drop-down list. For our exercise, we will use the **Left top pointer**. You will also have to move the position of the Bubble so that the pointer is pointing to the required screen element. You can do this by clicking on the Bubble header, and dragging the Bubble to the required position.

> You can change the pointer position (or remove the position altogether) for any bubble, on any kind of Frame, by using Pointer position option. Refer to Chapter 4, *Editing a Topic* for more details.

8. Bubble texts do not have an associated Action; the trainee is not required to do anything other than press the *Enter* button (or click on the **[Enter]** link in the bubble) to continue. However, it is worth emphasizing this to the trainee. We can do this by inserting an icon into the bubble, which informs them that this Frame is for information only. To insert an icon, click on the Bubble icon button ( ), to display a drop-down list of available icons, as shown in the following diagram:

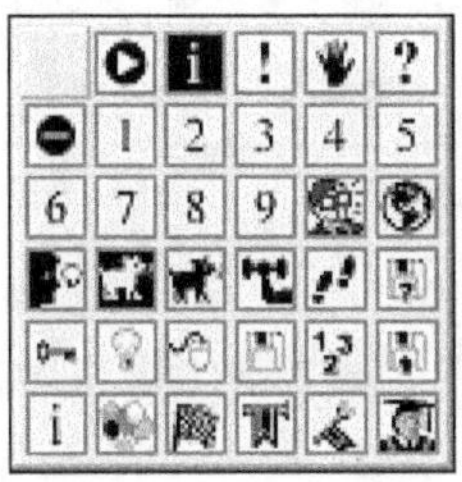

9. Click on the appropriate icon to select it. For our exercise, we will use the black "**i**" image in the top row. This icon will then appear in the upper-left corner of the Bubble (as shown in the finished Bubble for our exercise ahead).

> You can add an icon to any bubble, on any kind of Frame, by using **Bubble icon** option. However, you should use icons sparingly, and always consistently, as explained in Chapter 4, *Editing a Topic*.

10. Although there is no *Action* associated with this Frame, there is still one field in the **Action Properties** pane that is relevant: **Delay time (s)**. By default, in *See It!* mode, the Explanation Frame will be displayed for five seconds before the Player advances to the next screen. If you have a lot of text on your Explanation Frame, then this may not be enough time for the trainee to read it all. In this case, you should select or enter a longer period.

Our finished Bubble, in our Explanation Frame, now looks as shown in the next screenshot:

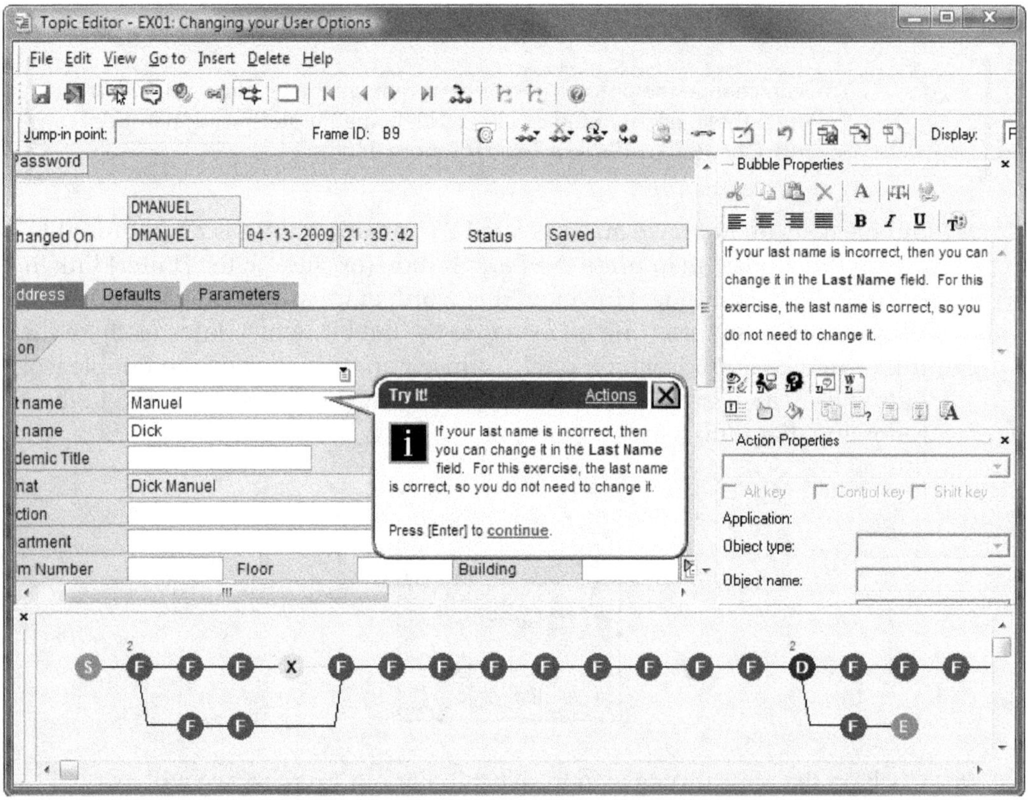

This icon isn't very eye-catching (none of the default ones are), and is only in black and white (probably as a concession to printed output). In Chapter 12, *Configuring UPK*, we will look at how to replace the default icons with our own.

So far, so good, but inserting this Explanation Frame has introduced a new problem. Our Explanation Frame has been inserted *before* the re-join in our Alternative Path. This means that if a trainee chooses the Alternative Path, (the lower of the two paths shown here) they will not see our new Explanation Frame.

We need to move the end point of this Alternative Path to re-join the main path on our new Explanation Frame. How to do this is explained in Chapter 4, *Editing a Topic*, under the section *Changing the end point of an alternative path.*

Version Difference

In early versions of OnDemand (8.7 and before) you could not move the end point of an Alternative Path. Instead, you had to either add an identical Explanation Frame to the Alternative Path, or remove the alternative path and then re-record it, joining the main path at the new Explanation Frame.

Once we have moved this end point, our *Frame Navigation* pane now looks like the example shown in the following partial screenshot:

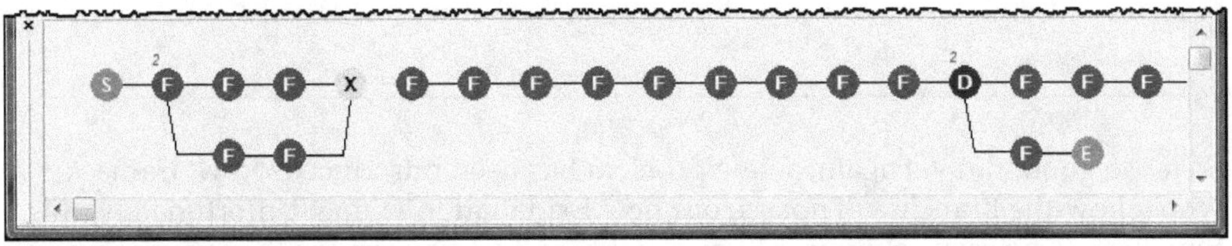

We are now ready to insert our second Explanation Frame. For this one, we are going to draw the trainee's attention to the message that is displayed when they save their changes. This message is visible only in the very last Frame, so we need to insert our Explanation Frame immediately before this.

Carry out the same steps as described above, to perform the following activities:

1. Insert an Explanation Frame as the penultimate Frame in the main path
2. Add the Custom Text "Your changes are saved, and a confirmation message is displayed at the bottom of the screen." to the Bubble.
3. Add a pointer, and point this to the message at the bottom of the screen.
4. Add the same 'i' icon as we used before to the Bubble.

Our new Explanation Frame appears as follows:

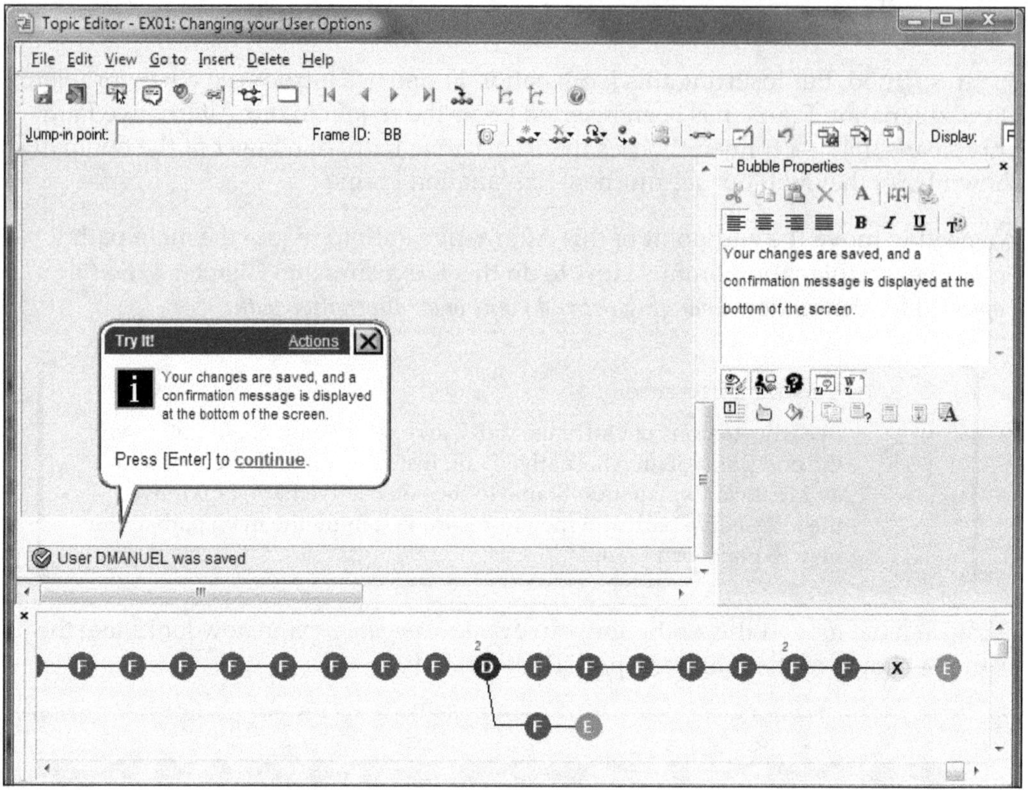

So far so good. But yet again, a new problem has been introduced. Now, trainees who follow the Branch will not see our new Explanation Frame. Unfortunately, this time there is no easy solution. Although UPK will let you change the re-join point of an *Alternative Path*, it is not possible to change the end point of a *Branch* to have it re-join the main path that is, to change a Branch into an Alternative Path. (Maybe Oracle will consider this as an enhancement for the next release of UPK.)

Copying and Pasting Frames

In the previous section, we had a problem where we had a Frame in our Main Path, which we also wanted to be available in our Branch. Fortunately, UPK 3.5 introduced some new functionality that we can use to resolve (or at least work around) this problem. This is the ability to copy and paste Frames. For our exercise, we will simply copy our new Explanation Frame from the Main Path, and paste it into the Branch. This is fairly inefficient, as it means that if we want to change the Bubble Text for this Explanation Frame we have to do it in two places (or just re-copy-and-paste). However, it will save us from having to delete and then recapture the branch, and will be faster than inserting another Explanation Frame and re-entering our Custom Text.

To copy and paste Frames, carry out the following steps:

1. Open the Topic from which you want to copy the Frames in the *Topic Editor*.
2. In the *Frame Navigation* pane, click on the Frame that you want to copy.

   Other options:

   - If you want to copy multiple Frames, then click on the first Frame in the sequence, then *Shift*+click on the last Frame in the sequence.
   - If you want to copy an entire path, then click on the first Frame that you want to copy, and then *Ctrl*+click on any other Frame in the path. Be careful when using this option, as UPK will select *all* of the Frames that will be seen by trainees who follow this path even those frames in the main path. In the following example, we (i) clicked on the first Frame in the Alternative Path, and then (ii) *Ctrl*+clicked on the second Frame in the Alternative Path. The result is that all of the Frames in the Alternative Path are selected, along with all of the Frames in the main path after the point where the Alternative Path rejoins the main path. If there are subsequent Alternative Paths, then the main path is selected. (If you want to force the use of a specific path, then simply make this the default path—seen Chapter 8, *Allowing Alternatives*, for details of how to do this—before you cut-and-paste)

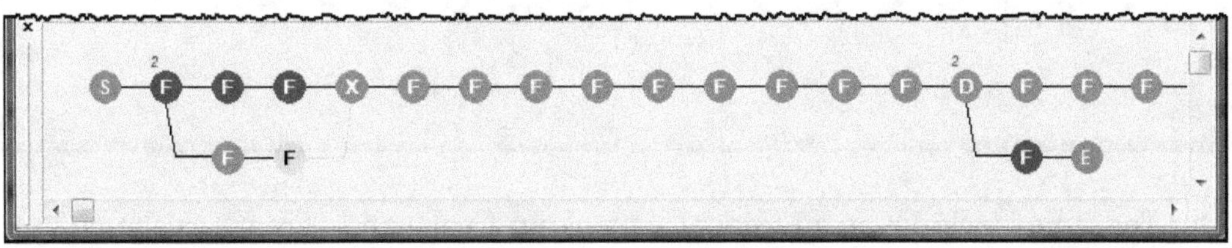

     This feature (of being able to copy an entire path) is extremely useful in cases where you have a simulation that includes multiple paths, but now want to split it out into separate Topics for each path.

- You cannot copy non-contiguous Frames (that is, you can only copy a sequence of Frames). If you need to copy multiple individual Frames, then you need to perform multiple copy-and-paste actions, or copy and paste a sequence that includes all of the required Frames and then delete the unwanted Frames from the pasted sequence.
- You can only *copy*-and-paste; you cannot *cut*-and-paste. If you need to do this, then you first need to copy-and-paste the Frames, and then come back and delete the Frames that have been copied.

3. Right-click on any of the selected Frames, and select **Copy Frames** from the context menu. This is shown in the following screenshot:

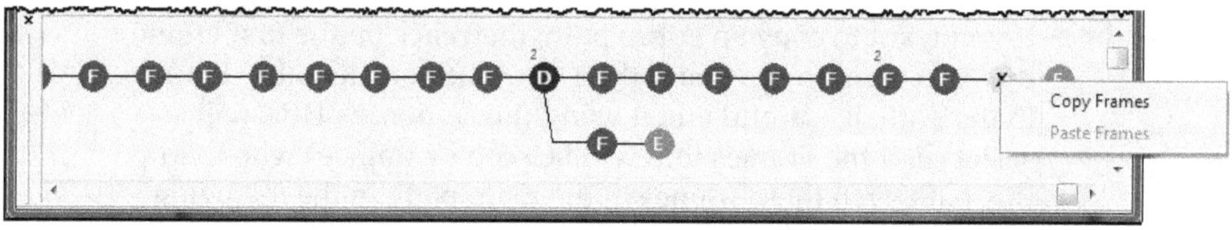

4. If you want to paste the copied Frames into a different Topic, then close the Topic Editor for the current Topic, and then open the destination Topic in the Topic Editor.
5. Right-click on the Frame after which you want the copied Frames to be inserted, and select **Paste Frames** from the context menu, as shown in the next screenshot:

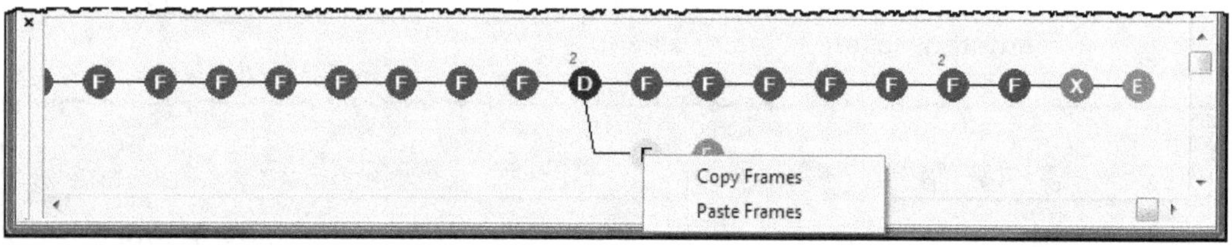

Our Topic now includes an additional copy of our Explanation Frame, as shown in the following screenshot:

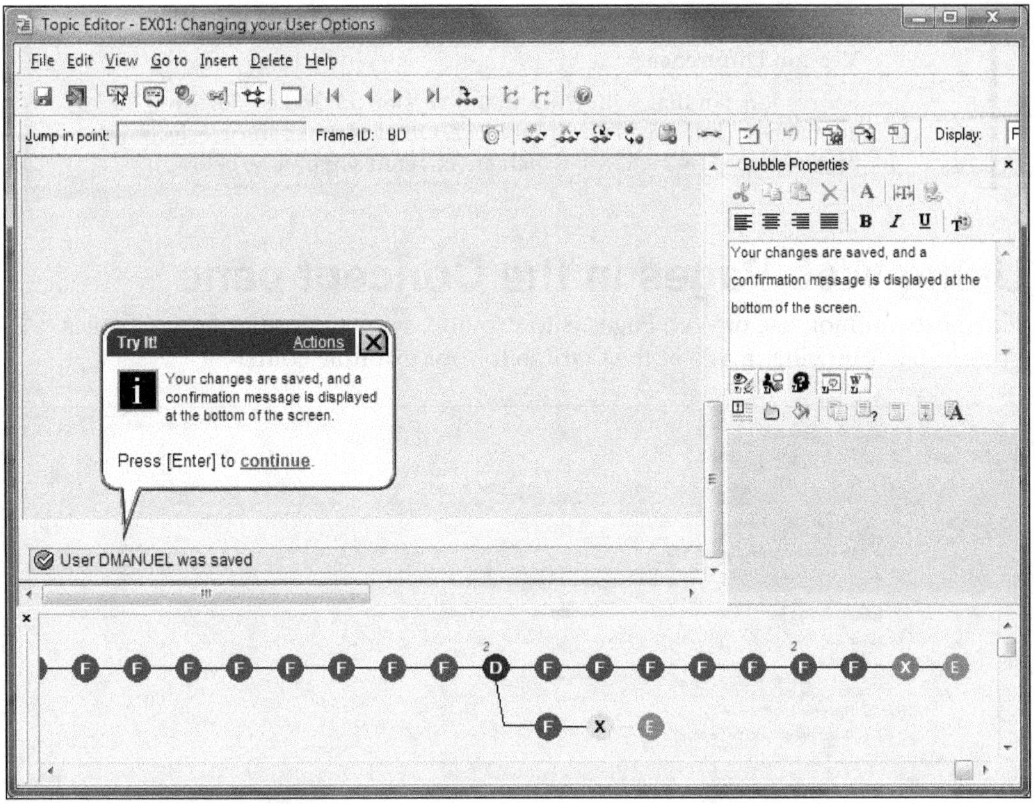

Note that the *entire* Frame and all of its contents have been copied. In our example, this is only the Bubble (including the Custom Text, icon, and pointer), but if you copy a standard Action Frame, then the Action Area (including any multiple action areas that have been defined) and Actions (including Alternative Actions, but not alternative paths) will also be copied.

Putting Web Pages to good use

A **Web Page**, in UPK terms, is a single file that can contain text or images. In this respect, Web Pages are very limited. You can perform rudimentary font formatting, provide lists, and insert images, but that's about it. You cannot insert tables, or use any HTML tags as you would be able to with real web pages (which you can only use via a **Package**). However, they are very flexible, and can be utilized in a number of ways.

Version Difference

For readers familiar with OnDemand version 8.7 and earlier, Web Pages are the new, improved *text* Infoblocks. Other types of Infoblocks have been replaced by *Packages*, which are covered separately, below.

Using Web Pages in the Concept pane

The most common use of Web Pages is to provide *context* information for Topics. Look at the following image of the Outline for our example course:

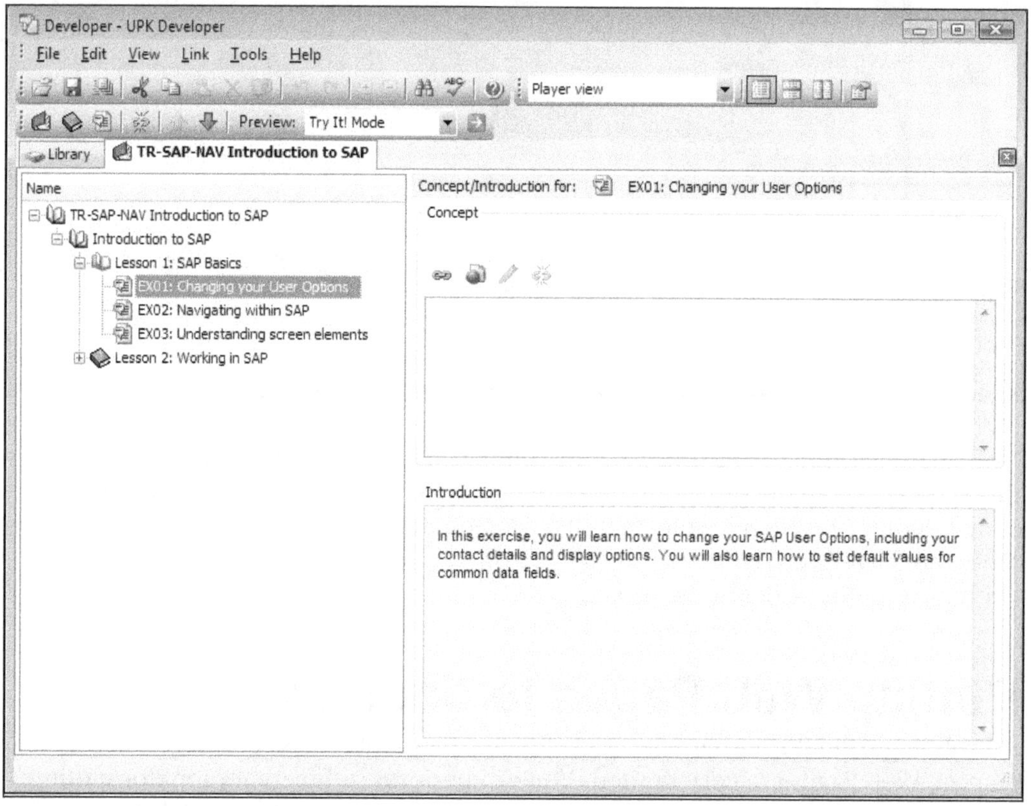

You will see that the upper-right section of the Outline window contains a pane labeled **Concept**. If you want any information to be displayed in this pane, then you need to create a Web Page and attach it to the content object in the Outline.

Version Difference

Although the **Concept** pane always appears in the Outline view, if it is empty, then it does not appear in the Player. This is, thankfully, a new feature in UPK 3.5. In previous versions, the **Concept** pane always appeared in the Player, often appearing as a blank frame, where developers couldn't be bothered to provide any concepts.

To create a new Web Page and attach it to a content object, carry out the following steps:

1. Open the Outline containing the content object to which you want to attach the Web Page, in the Outline Editor.
2. Click on the content object to select it. Although in this example we are attaching a Web Page to the concept pane for a Topic, Modules, and Sections also have concept panes, so you can also attach Web Pages to these as well.
3. Click on the **Create new web page** button () in the **Concept** pane. The **Save As** dialog box is displayed.

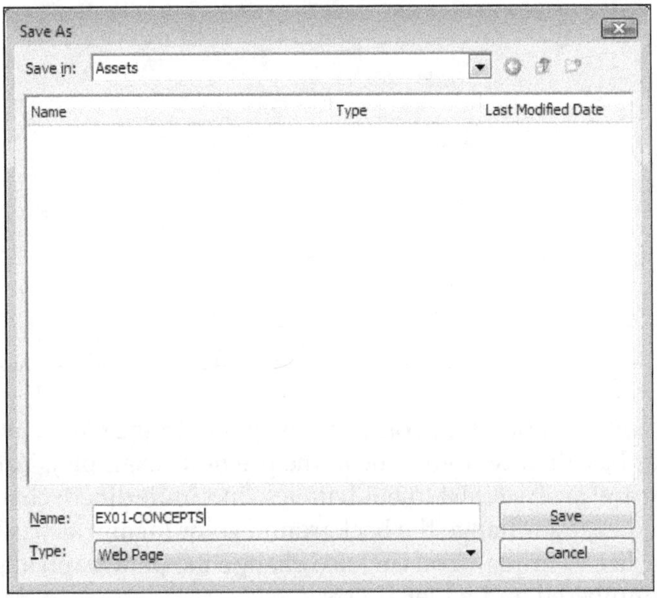

4. Navigate to the folder in which you want to save the Web Page (as explained in Chapter 2, *Organizing your Library*, we will use an `Assets` sub-folder for all of our Web Pages), enter a name for the Web Page (it makes sense to use a reference to the content object to which the Web Page relates), and then click on the **Save** button. The Web Page Editor is opened on the **Developer** screen, as shown in the next screenshot:

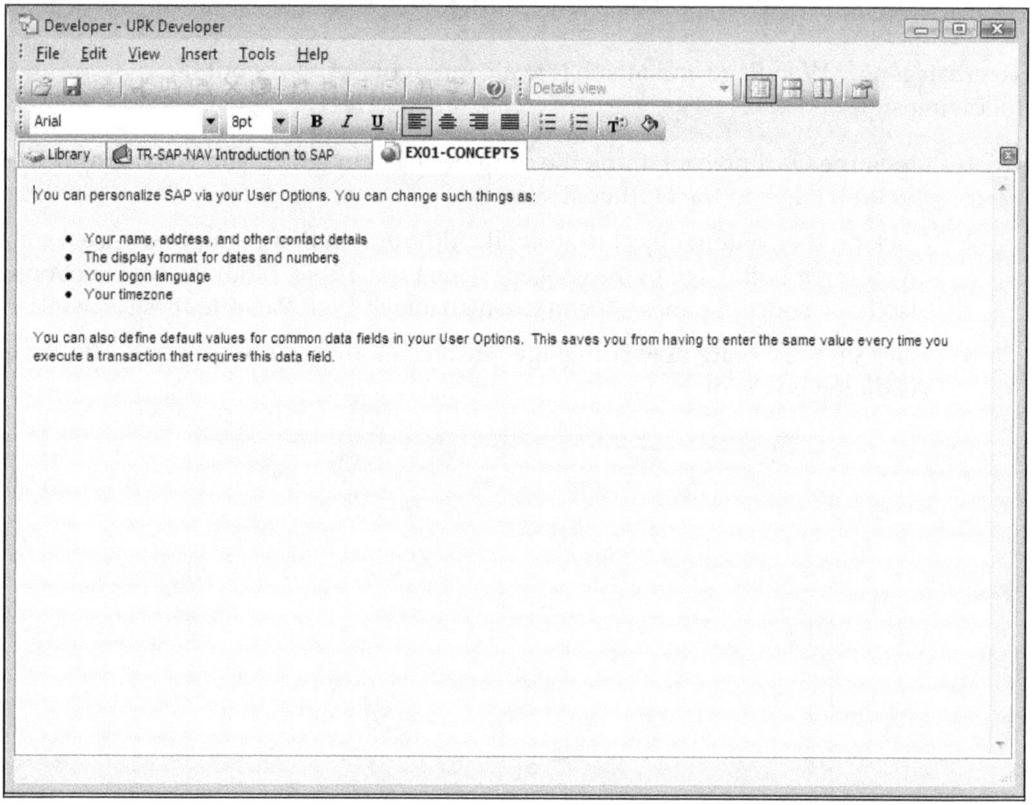

5. Enter the information that you want to appear in the **Concept** pane in the editor (as has already been done in the previous example). You can set the font face and size; set text to bold, italics, and underlined; change the text color, and change change the background color (again, as has been done in the earlier example). You can also change the paragraph alignment, and format numbered and bulleted lists.

6. Once you have entered the required text, click on the **Save** button () to save your changes, and then close the Web Page Editor tabbed page. You are returned to the Outline Editor. Now, the **Concept** pane shows the contents of the Web Page, as shown in the next screenshot:

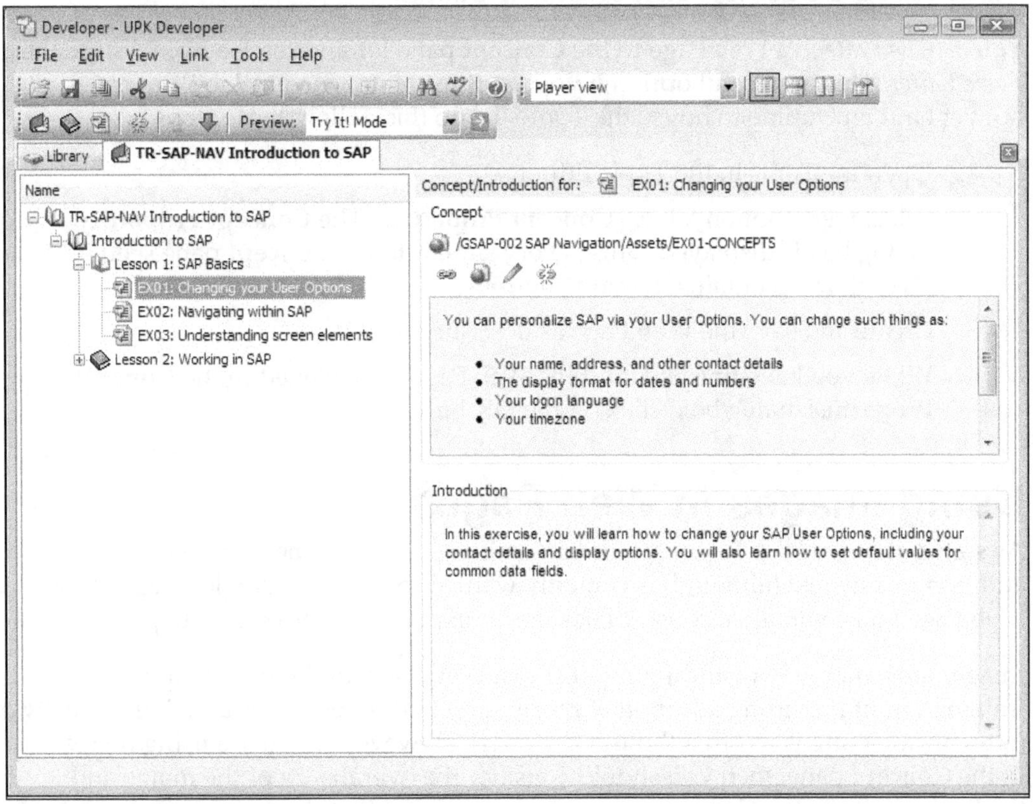

Version Difference

In UPK 3.5 (and OnDemand 9.1) you can only attach a single Web Page to the **Concept** pane. This is a change from OnDemand 8.7, where you could attach multiple Infoblocks and they would be displayed sequentially. (But note that if you convert content from OnDemand 8.7 where there are multiple Infoblocks in a single **Concept** pane, then all of the attached Infoblocks will be converted to a single Web Page in UPK 3.5.)

The above steps explain how to attach a Web Page to the **Concept** pane for an exercise from the Outline. Although this is done from the Outline, the Web Page is attached to the Topic content object and not to the outline element. If you subsequently insert the same Topic in another Outline, the same Web Page will be used in the **Concept** pane of the new Outline.

You can also attach a Web Page to the **Concept** pane for an exercise from within the *Topic Editor*. This is a useful option if you want to create *concept* Web Page but have not yet built an Outline to house the Topic. To do this, follow these steps:

1. Open the Topic in the Topic Editor.
2. Select menu option **View | Concept Properties**. The **Concept Properties** dialog box is displayed. This is very similar to the **Concept** pane seen in the Overview. It contains the same buttons.
3. Create and save the Web Page as described above.
4. When you have finished, and the Web Page is displayed in the **Concept Properties** dialog box, click on the **OK** button.

Using images in Web Pages

As stated above, a Web Page can contain an image. This can be instead of, or in addition to, any text (although if you only wanted to include a single image in the Web Page you could always use a Package, as explained later in this chapter).

Images are a nice way of adding interest to a Web Page (and therefore to your training), or of providing additional information that is better explained graphically (after all, a picture is worth a thousand words). However, if you are using images in the **Concept** pane, then you should consider the overall size of the image and the likely width of the **Concept** pane, bearing in mind that the trainee may run the Player in a smaller window than the one you design.

For our sample exercise, given that we are providing simulations for the SAP system, we will include a small SAP logo in the Web Page that appears in the **Concept** pane for our course Module. For the sake of variety, we will do this from the Library, and not from the Outline Editor.

To add an image to a Web Page, carry out the steps described below.

1. In the Library, locate the folder containing the Web Page to which you want to add the image.
2. Double-click on the Web Page, to open it in the *Web Page Editor*. As before, this is opened in a separate tab in the main *UPK Developer* window, as can be seen in the next screenshot:

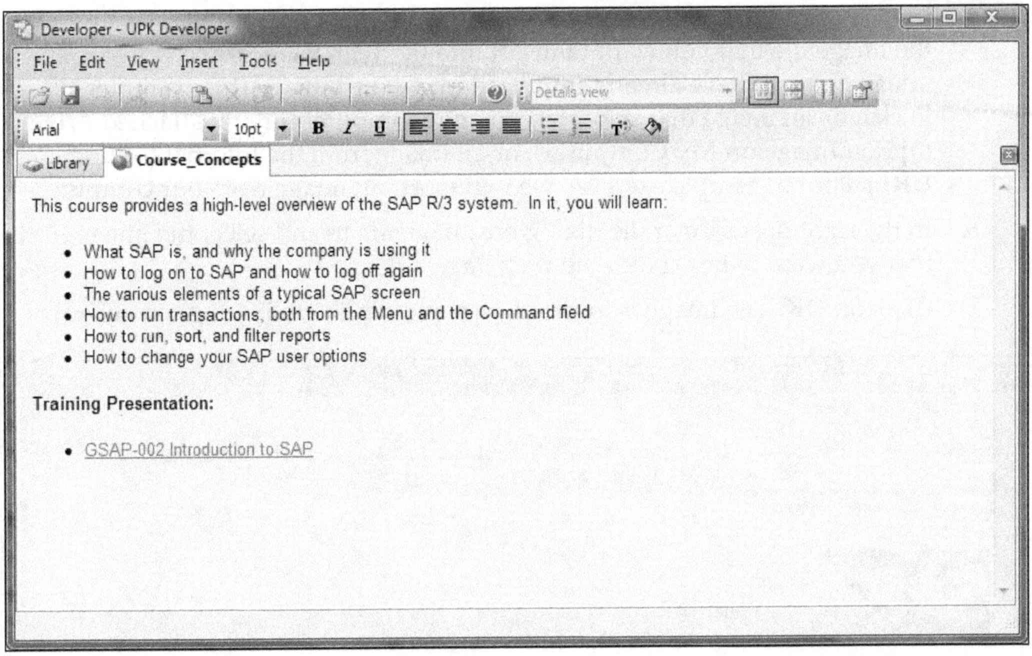

3. Within the Web Page, position the cursor at the place in the text where you want the image to appear.
4. Select menu option **Insert | Image**. The **Insert Image** dialog box is displayed, as shown in the next screenshot:

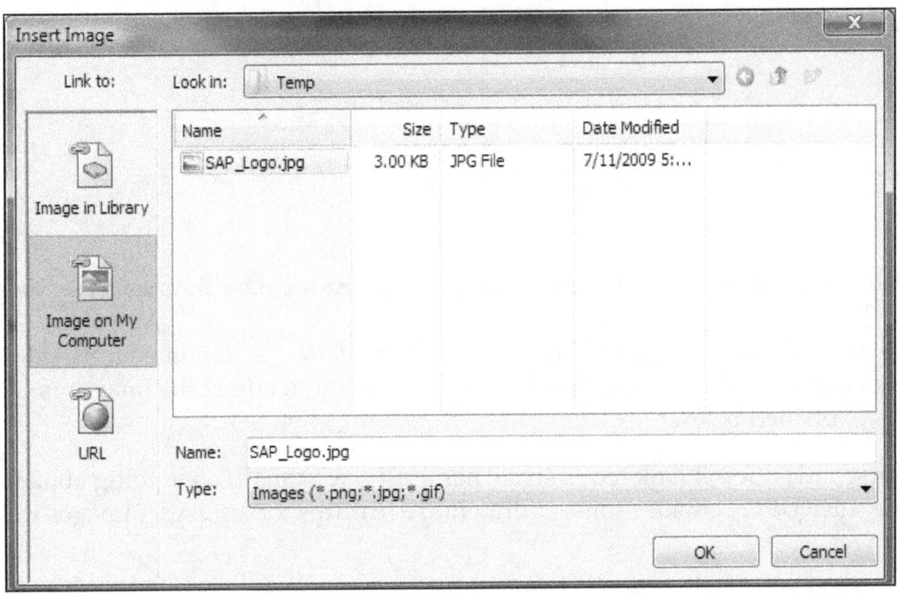

5. In the *Link to* bar on the leftmost side of the dialog box, select the location of the image file that you want to insert into the Web Page. You can insert an image that you have already imported into your Library (for example, in a Package), an image that is located on your computer (or any attached drive) (option **Image on My Computer**), or an image from the Internet (option **URL**). For our sample exercise, we will insert an image from our computer.
6. In the rightmost side of the dialog box, navigate to and select the image file that you want to insert into the Web Page.
7. Click on **OK**. The image is inserted, as shown in the following screenshot:

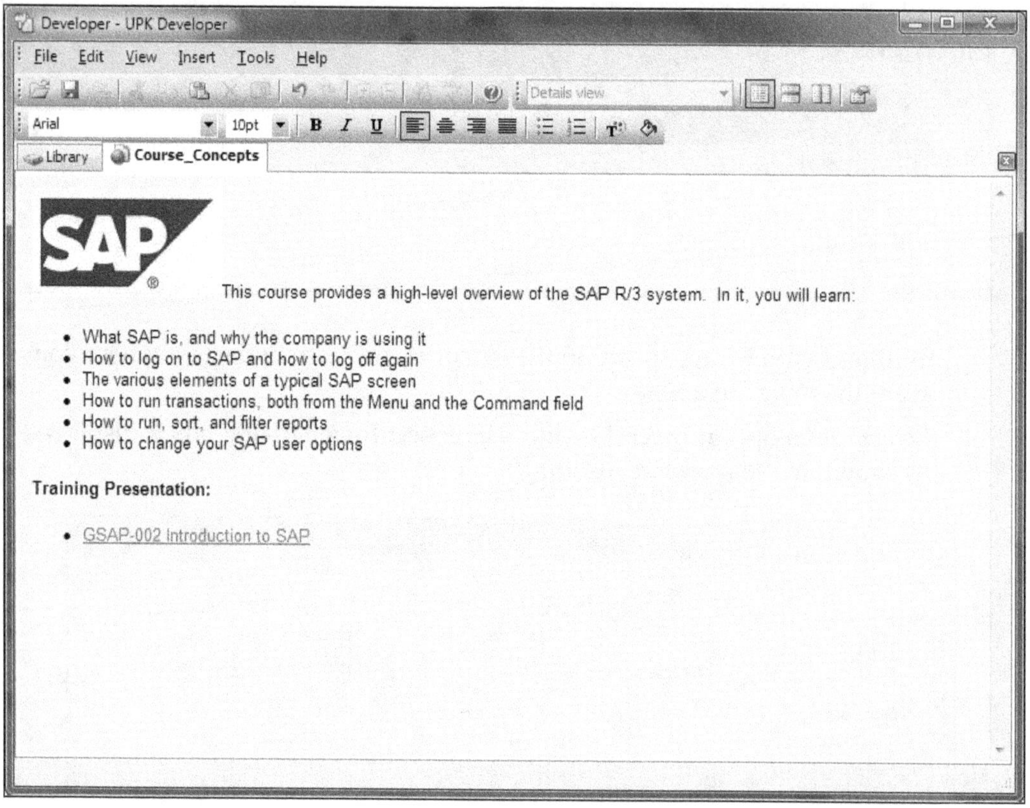

8. Save the Web Page, and close the *Web Page Editor*, if you have finished editing this Web Page. (We have not; we want to adjust the image, as explained below).

Of course, this doesn't look too pretty. Thankfully, we can do something about this, because UPK provides some rudimentary features for adjusting images in Web Pages.

To adjust the size or position of an image in a Web Page, carry out the following steps:

1. With the Web Page open in the *Web Page Editor*, right-click on the image that you want to adjust, and then select **Image Properties** from the context menu. The **Image Properties** dialog box is displayed, as shown in the next screenshot:

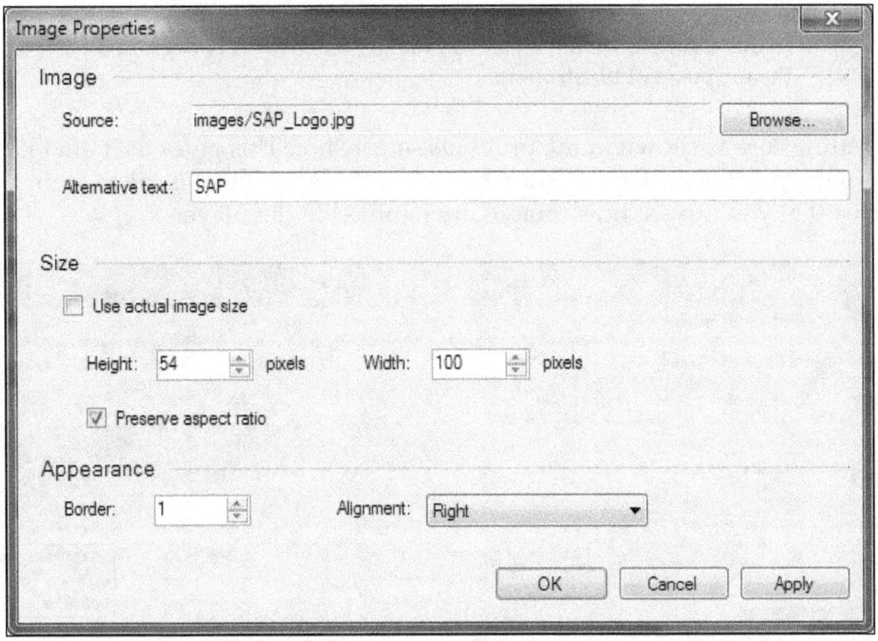

2. In the **Alternative Text** field, enter a short text description of the image. This will be used as the ToolTip in some web browsers.
3. Under **Size**, select whether you want to use the original image size or not, and specify a new height and width if you choose not.
4. Under **Appearance**, select a border width and indicate where the image should be aligned on the Web Page. Your choices are: **Top**, **Middle**, **Bottom**, **Left**, and **Right**. The first three of these (the *vertical* options) control the position of the image relative to the line of text in which it is located. The last two (the *horizontal* options) determine whether the image is left-aligned or right-aligned within the overall Web Page. Although these are two independent things (vertical and horizontal), you can only select one, so if you want the image to be right-aligned and halfway down the page, you can't do it.

5. Click on **OK** to confirm your changes.
6. Save and close the Web Page.

For our sample exercise, we resized the image, set it to be right-aligned, and added a `1pt` border around it (because it looked odd with a white background against the blue of the Web Page, without a border).

> A better option would be to use an image with a transparent background. In this example we have used an image with a solid background just for the purposes of illustration.

These settings are as shown in the previous screenshot. This gives us a final Web Page as shown in the next screenshot. Note that this screenshot is taken from the Player, so that you can see how images are handled in the Player.

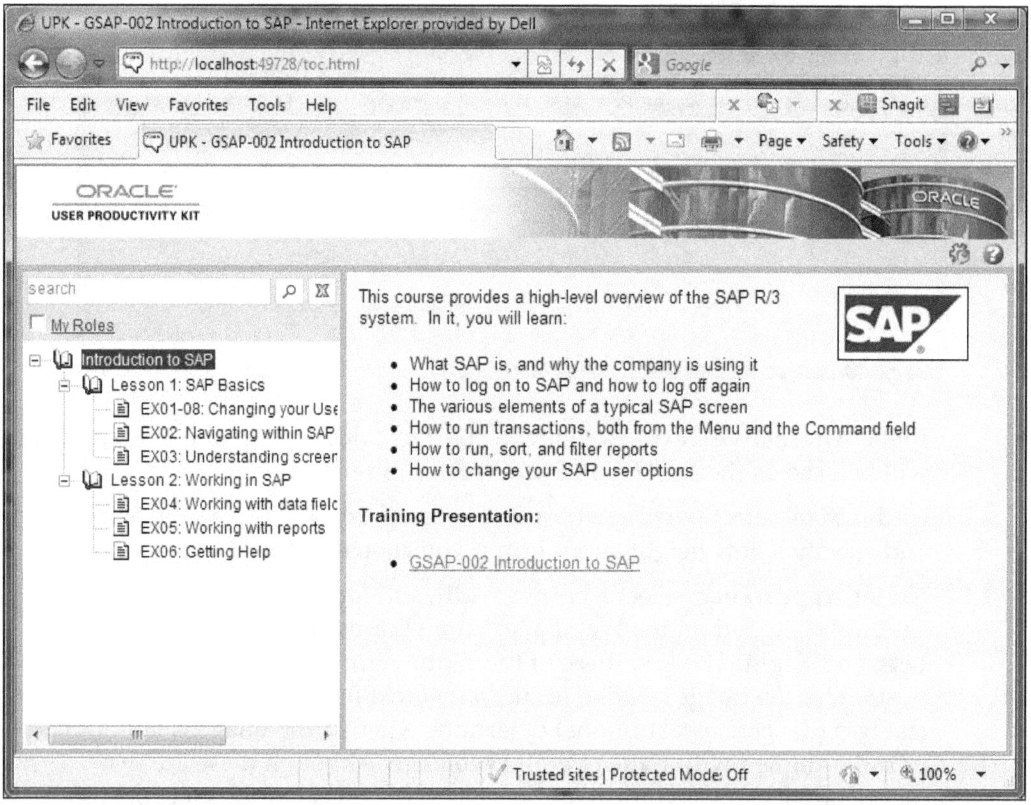

Note that the text *flows around* the image. You will see that there is a little more space to the right of the image than there is above it. This is to leave room for a scrollbar.

Creating independent Web Pages

In the previous section, we looked at how to use a Web Page to add information to the **Concept** pane of a content object. In this section, we will look at how to use Web Pages to provide information in other areas.

Observant readers will have noticed that a Web Page is in fact an independent content object itself. When you created a Web Page to attach to a **Concept** pane, you edited this Web Page in its own tabbed editor and saved it to its own folder (our `Assets` folder). Hopefully, you also noticed that in addition to the **Create new web page** button (), the **Concept** pane also has a **Create link** button () that can be used to attach an existing Web Page to the **Concept** pane. It should, therefore, come as no surprise to learn that Web Pages can be created independently of the **Concept** pane. In fact, the **Concept** pane is only one of several uses of Web Pages.

To create a Web Page that is independent of a **Concepts** pane (or anything else), carry out these steps.

1. In the Library, navigate to the folder in which you want to store the Web Page. In our example, we are saving all of the Web Pages for a module in a sub-folder called `Assets` within the course folder.
2. Select menu option **File | New | Web Page**. A *Web Page Editor* tabbed page is opened up on the **Developer** screen. The content and use of this is exactly as described above in the explanation of how to create a Web Page from within an Outline.
3. Enter the required information into the Web Page, and format it as required. We have already covered most of the available options, above.
4. Once you have made your changes, click on the **Save** button (). You will be prompted to select the destination folder (which will default to the folder selected in Step 1, although you can change this) and a file name. Refer to the description of the **Save As** dialog box above for additional help if necessary.
5. Close the Web Page Editor.

You have now created a new Web Page. Now let's look at how to use it.

Using Web Pages in Topics

If you recall our long-running exercise on maintaining your SAP user profile, you will remember that we ask the user to enter their last name and their first name. These terms may be confusing in some countries—especially in countries where the "family name" actually comes before the "given name"—so we want to provide some extra explanation of some common name formats in different countries, and how these translate into first name and last name. We'll provide this information in a Web Page, and then link to this Web Page at the relevant place(s) within our Topic.

First, we need to create the Web Page. How to do this is explained in the section *Creating independent Web Pages*, above. For our exercise, our created Web Page is as follows:

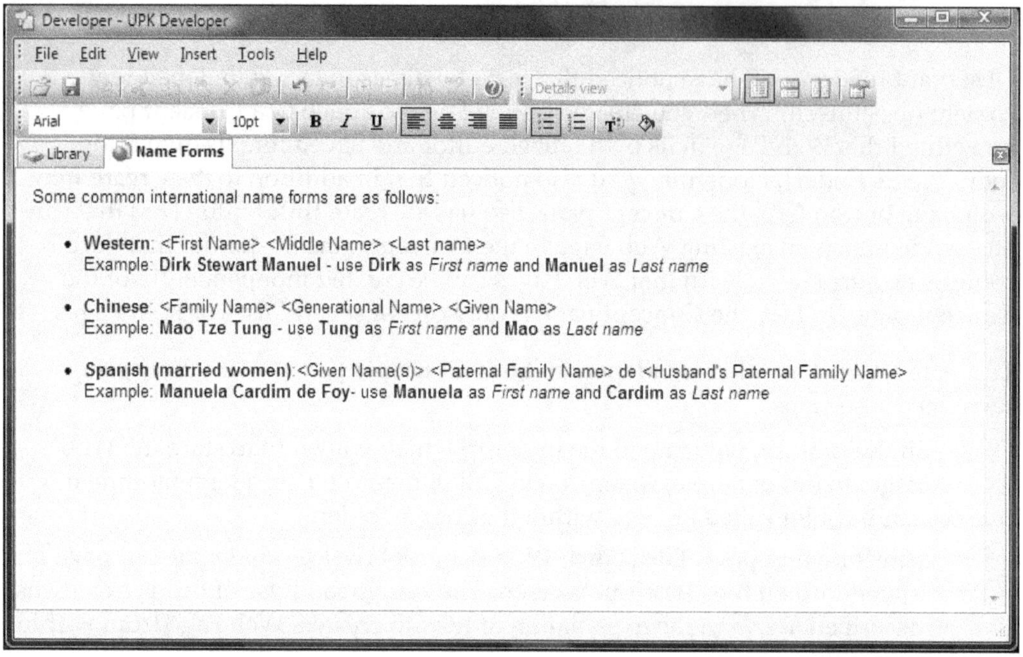

There are two ways in which you can link to a Web Page from a Topic. These are explained separately, below.

Linking via a hyperlink

With a hyperlink, the Web Page is linked from a word or phrase within the Bubble Text of a Frame. (Note that it is only possible to do this for Custom Text because you can't select the Template Text to hyperlink from.) To create a hyperlink to a Web Page from within a Frame in a Topic, carry out the steps described below:

1. Open up the Topic in the *Topic Editor*.
2. Navigate to the Frame from which you want to provide the hyperlink. In our exercise, we will link from the Explanation Frame describing the *Last name* field (this is Frame **5B**).
3. In the *Bubble Properties* pane, select the text that you want to form the hyperlink (that is, the text that the user will click on to display the Web Page).
4. Click on the **Bubble text link** button ( ) in the **Bubble Properties** pane. The **Bubble Text Link Properties** dialog box is displayed.

5. Click on the **Create link** button (🔗) to create a link to an existing Web Page (you could also click on the **Create new web page** button (●) to create a new Web Page if you have not yet created it). The **Insert Hyperlink** dialog box is displayed, as shown in the next screenshot:

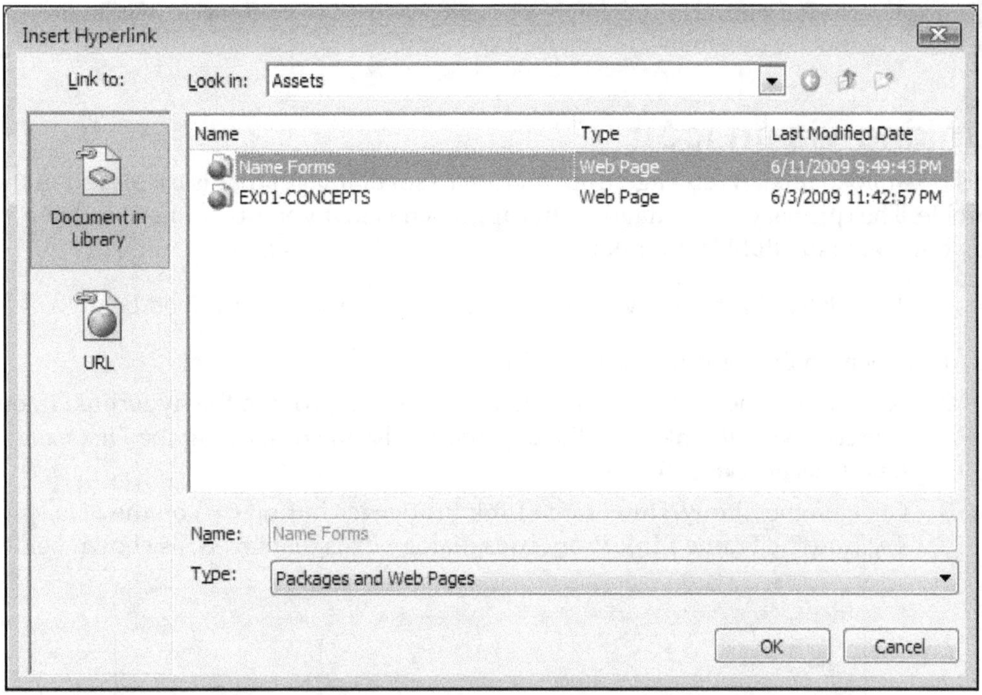

6. Make sure that the **Document in Library** option is selected in the **Link to:** bar.
7. In the **Look in:** field, navigate to the folder containing the Web Page (the `Assets` folder, in our example).
8. In the file list, click on the Web Page to which you want to create a hyperlink.
9. Click on the **Open** button.
10. Back in the **Bubble Text Link Properties dialog box**, click on **OK**.

This hyperlink will now appear as follows, in the Player:

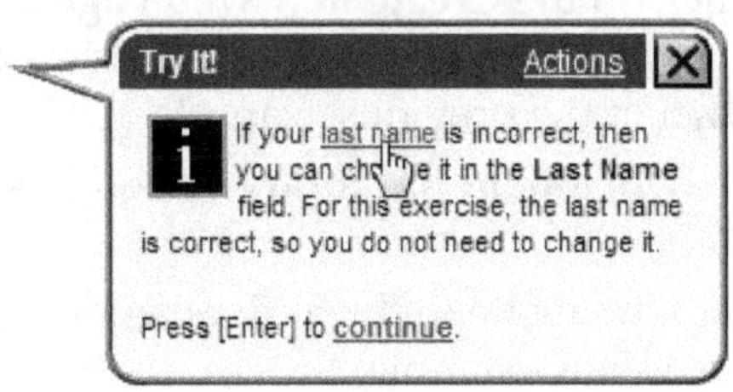

Note that there is no ToolTip for this hyperlink. There was no opportunity to enter one in the steps above, so UPK doesn't know what to use.

> **Version Difference**
>
> In OnDemand 8.7 the Infoblock name was used as the ToolTip, but this is not the case from OnDemand 9.x onwards.

Linking via an icon

It is possible to link a Web Page from an icon (a small image) that is displayed in the bubble. The (primary) advantage of this approach is that you do not need to have custom text in the Bubble, to link from.

To insert a link to a Web Page via an icon, carry out the steps described below:

1. Open up the topic in the *Topic Editor*.
2. Navigate to the Frame from which you want to provide the hyperlink. In our exercise, we will link from the explanation Frame describing the *First name* field (this is Frame **3**).
3. Click on the **Show/Hide Frame Link Properties** button ( ) on the *Standard Toolbar*. The **Frame Link Properties** dialog box is displayed, as shown below:

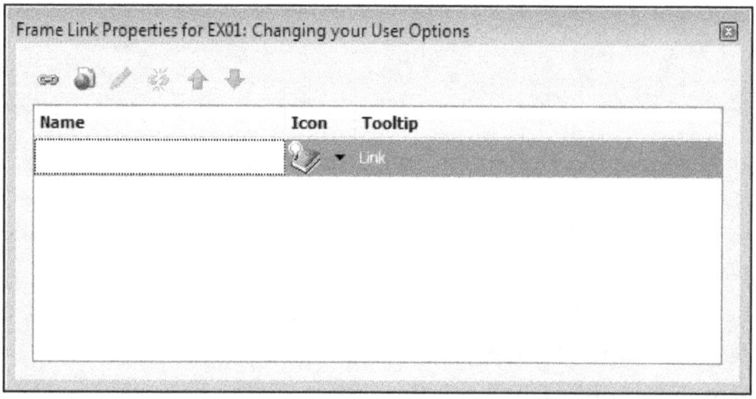

4. Click on the **Create link** button ( ) to create a link to an existing Web Page (you could also click on the **Create new web page** button ( ) to create a new Web Page if you have not yet created it). The **Insert Hyperlink** dialog box is displayed, as shown in the previous example.
5. Make sure that the **Document in Library** option is selected in the **Link to:** bar.
6. In the **Look in:** field, navigate to the folder containing the Web Page (the `Assets` folder, in our example).

7. In the file list, click on the Web Page to which you want to create a hyperlink.
8. Click on the **Open** button.
9. Back in the **Bubble Text Link Properties** dialog box, click on the drop-down button for the **Icon** field, and select the icon that you want to use. There are several to choose from.

[You can also use your own images by adding them to the Custom Package contained in the `System/Icons/Custom` folder in the Library. Custom images must be 22 x 22 pixels in size.]

10. In the *Tooltip* field, over-type the default (and unimaginative) **Link** with a suitable value (such as **International name forms**, in our example). Your **Frame Link Properties** dialog box should now look as follows:

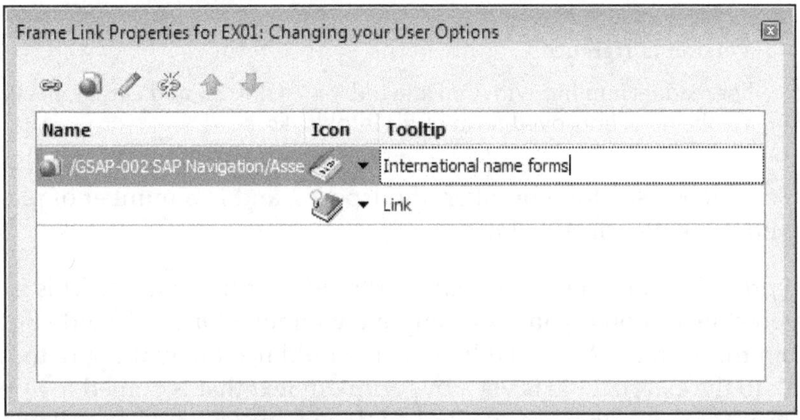

11. Close the **Frame Link Properties** dialog box (or click on the **Show/Hide Frame Link Properties** button (🔗) on the *Standard Toolbar* again) to hide this dialog box again.

This hyperlink will now appear in the player as follows:

Note the ToolTip for the hyperlink. This now shows the text that was specified in the **Bubble Text Frame Link Properties** dialog box.

Linking files through the use of Packages

UPK allows you to import external files into your Library, so that you can then link to these files from your content objects. Technically, external files are imported into *Packages* within UPK, although they are always referenced individually. That is, links to files are always to the individual file; you cannot create a link to a Package.

Packages are conceptually similar to ZIP files, in that they can contain multiple files. They can also contain only a single file. Whether you choose to store each external file in its own Package, or group all files (for example, for a course) into a single Package is your choice; it makes absolutely no difference to UPK. However, from a transparency of organization point of view, it makes sense to keep each external file in its own appropriately-named Package, except for files that are always accessed as a group (such as a complete web site, or an Articulate Presenter presentation), where it would be best to store all of the files in a single package.

> **Version Difference**
>
> For readers familiar with OnDemand 8.x / UPK 2.x and earlier, Packages are the new, improved form of *file* Infoblocks.

External files can be used for a number of purposes, and in a number of places. Some of these options are described below:

- To provide a data sheet for a *Know It!* mode verification test. This is an interesting option if you also completely remove *Know It?* mode Bubble Text from the exercise. Note that here, you would need to make sure that the link to the external file is via a hyperlink in text that is tagged to appear in *Know It?* mode, otherwise the linked document will not be available.
- To provide an image of equipment related to an exercise.
- To provide a related document, for example, a vendor's invoice for a simulation that involves entering an invoice into the application.
- To provide the presentation for the training course to which the simulations relate.

For our example, we will use the last of these examples. We will provide access to a presentation from the exercises. As you will see, there are a number of ways that we can do this. However, linking to the course presentation from the exercises is back-to-front. Logically, you should link to the exercises from the presentation (how to do this is discussed in Chapter 6, *Publishing Content*). To make things interesting and to demonstrate the concept of having multiple files within a single Package, we will import a presentation that has been published into Flash format via Articulate Presenter. This published format consists of many files (at least one per slide, plus navigational elements) all of which are launched from a single file (`player.html`), which makes it an ideal candidate for using in a Package. There are three steps that we need to carry out:

1. Create a Package in UPK
2. Add the Articulate Presenter player to the Package
3. Link the Package into our content objects

Let's look at each of these in turn.

Creating a Package

In order to be able to link to a file from within UPK, you first need to create a Package to contain the file. To create a Package, carry out the steps described below:

1. In the Library, navigate to the folder in which you want to store the Package. For our exercise, this will be the `Assets` sub-folder of our *Introduction to SAP* course folder.
2. Select menu option **File | New | Package**. The *Package Editor* is opened on the *UPK Developer* screen, as shown in the following screenshot:

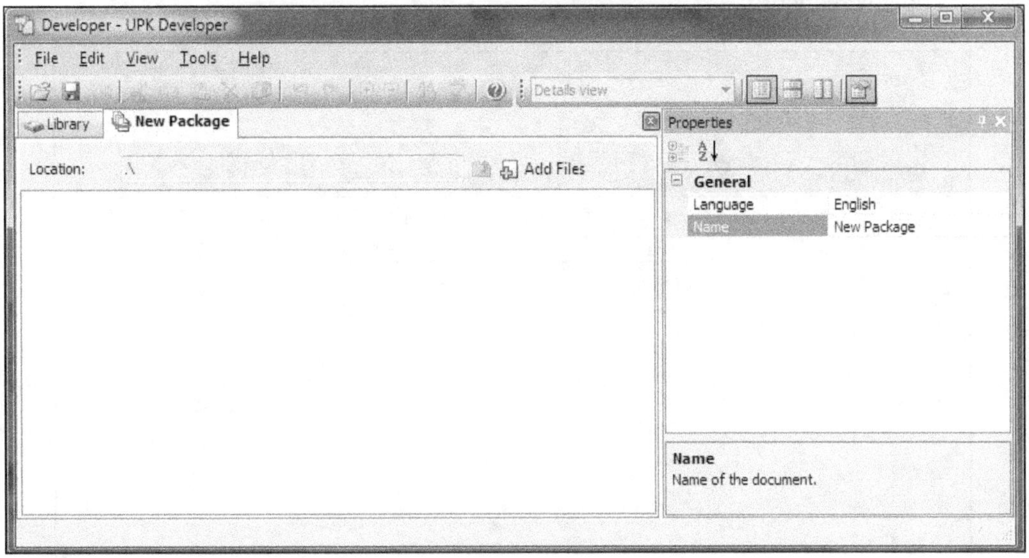

3. In the **Name** field of the **Properties** pane, over-type default name of **New Package** with a suitable name for the Package. If you do not have the **Properties** page opened, then you can click the **Properties** button ( ) now to display it, or you can just wait until the next step where you will be prompted to specify a name when you save the Package. For our exercise, we will name the Package `Presentation`, as it will contain the presentation for our course.
4. Click on the **Save** button ( ) to save your changes to the Package, and then (if you are finished with the Package for now) close the *Package Editor*.

Adding files to a Package

We now have a package. The next thing to do is to add files to the Package. To do this, carry out the steps described below:

1. Make sure that the package to which you want to add the files is open in the *Package Editor* (see above).
2. You will notice that there is an **Add Files** button, on the right of the tabbed page header (see the previous screenshot for an example of this). If you click on this then the standard (file) **Open** dialog box is displayed, as shown in the next screenshot:

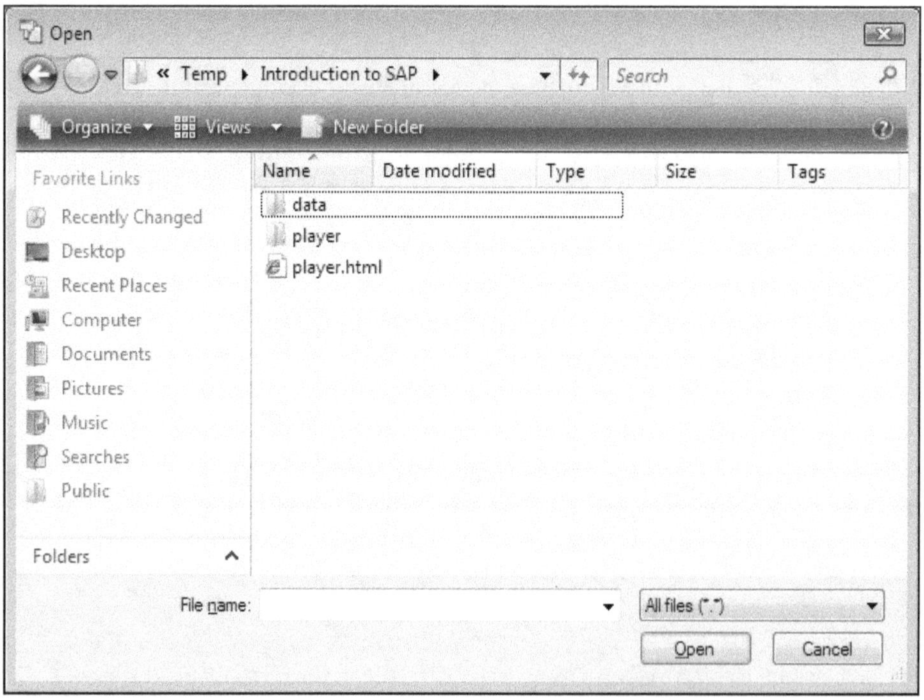

3. In this dialog box, you can navigate to, and select the file that you want to include in the Package. Unfortunately, the **Open** dialog box only allows you to select individual files (although you can include multiple files at the same time by-as usual in Windows-holding down the *Ctrl* key and clicking on multiple files, or by holding down the *Shift* key and clicking on the first and last files in a range of files). For our example, we want to include the full Articulate Presenter version of our course, which consists of a `player.html` file and two folders containing the presentation itself. The **Open** dialog box does not let us select entire folders for inserting into our Package, so we need to do something else. Close the **Open** dialog box if you have it open.
4. Open up Windows Explorer in a new window and navigate to the folder containing the files and folders that you want to add to the Package. Select all of these (again, hold down the *Ctrl* or *Shift* key to select multiple files and/or folders). Then click on the selected objects, and drag them onto the *Package Editor* in the **UPK Developer** window. Then, release the mouse button, to drop them into the package. Repeat this step to add more files to the package, as required.
5. Click the **Save** button () to save your changes to the package, and then close the *Package Editor* tabbed page.

Your package should now look similar to the one shown in the next screenshot:

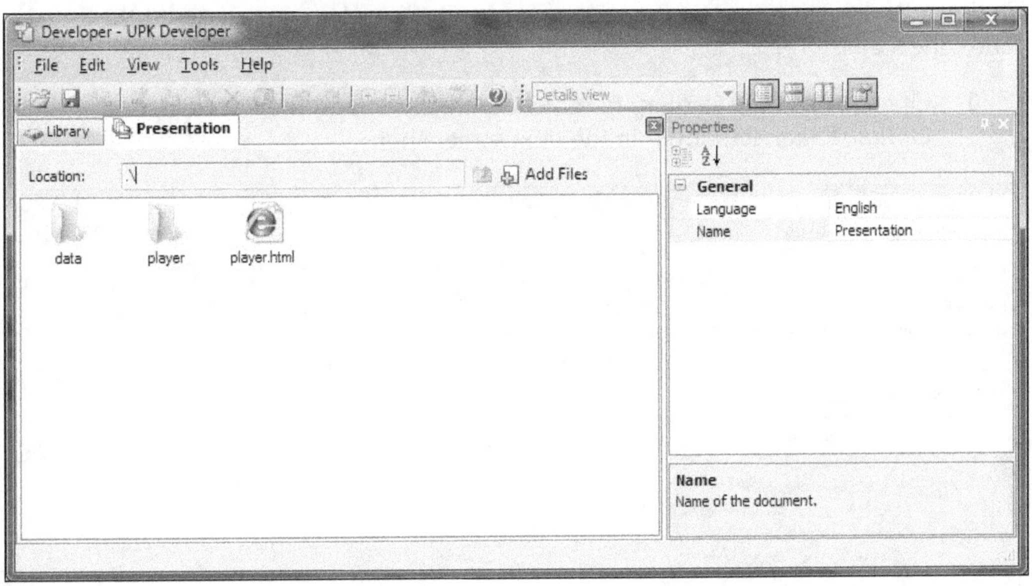

Note that the folders are imported *as*-is. That is, all files within the folders, and any sub-folders, will be imported but kept within the folder. This is important as it means that any *relative links* within these files will still work. This is extremely useful (in fact, essential) for importing entire web sites, or, as is the case in our example, a suite of interlinked files that make extensive use of relative links.

Linking a Package into a content object

The final step is to link the Package into a content object. You can link it via a hyperlink or an icon, just as we did for Web Pages above (see the section *Using Web Pages in Topics*), but there is something much more interesting that we can do. Essentially, we will link the Package (or, specifically, a *file* within the Package) into the *Contents* pane of an Outline element. Given that we have put the entire presentation for our course in the Package, it would make sense to link this into the *Contents* page of the highest-level course Outline element. Let's look at how to do this, and what it will do for us.

> Although you can link a Package via a hyperlink or an icon, icons are not displayed in *Know It?* mode. If you want a file within a package to be available in *Know It?* mode, you must link it via a text hyperlink.

To link a Package into the *Contents* pane for an Outline element, carry out the following steps:

1. Open the outline element to which you want to add the Package, in the *Outline Editor*, as shown in the next screenshot:

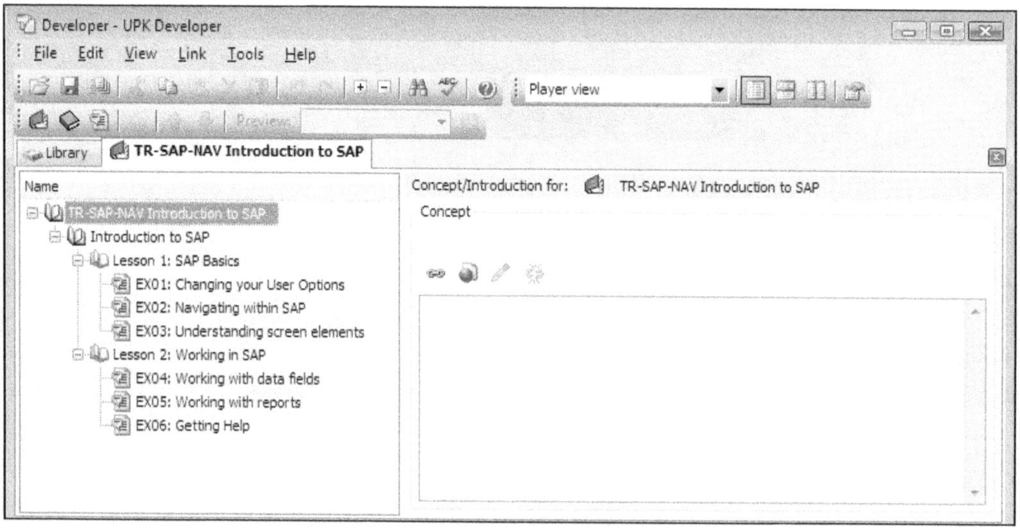

2. Click on the **Create link** button (⚭). The **Insert Hyperlink** dialog box is displayed, as shown below:

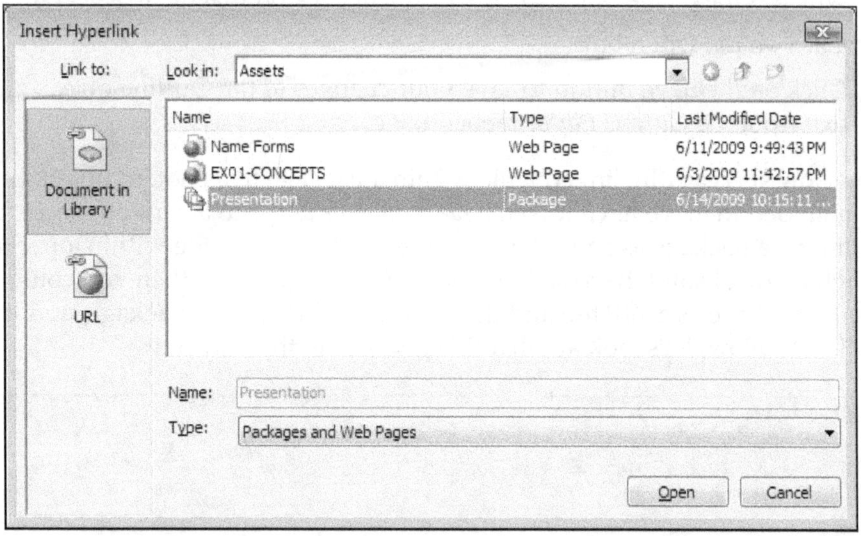

3. Make sure that the **Type** field at the bottom of the dialog box specifies either **Packages and Web Pages** or **Packages**.
4. Navigate to and select the Package that you created earlier. In our example, this is a Package named **Presentation**.
5. Double-click on the Package to open it (or click on it to select it and then click on the **Open** button). A list of all of the files and folders within the Package is displayed, as shown in the next screenshot:

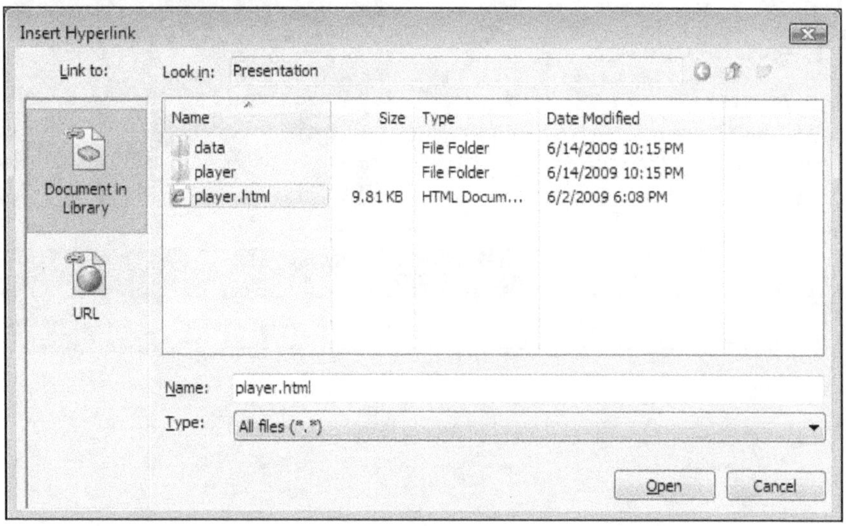

6. Click on the file within the Package to which you want to link. In our example, we want to link to the main index file of the Articulate Presentation, which is the `player.html` file, so we will click on this file to select it.
7. Click on the **Open** button.
8. Click on the **Save** button to save your changes to the Outline object, and then exit from the *Outline Editor* tabbed page.

We have now successfully linked a file within a Package to a content object. In case you missed that, we have linked *a file within a package* to a content object. You cannot link to a package as a whole; only to a specific, single file within a package. (Although if you absolutely *needed* to link to an entire package then you could bundle the package as a ZIP file and then add that ZIP file to a package, and link to the ZIP file. Now, let's look at what this gives us in the Player:

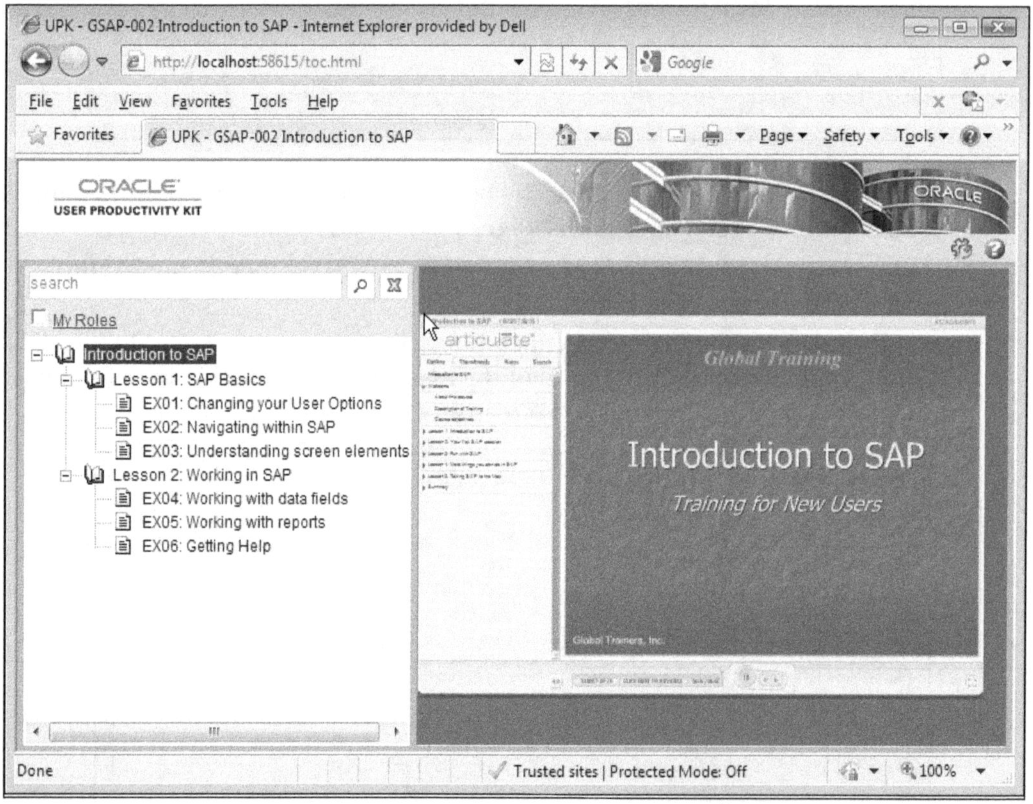

You can see that the complete Articulate Presentation has been incorporated into the overall UPK Player. This is fully-functional: you can use the navigation bar on the left to locate and select slides; you can execute any Quizmaker learning activities included in the presentation, and so on. The only problem is that some of the text is a little small.

> If you insert an Articulate Presentation (or similar package) into your Outline and this is set to auto-play, then it will start playing as soon as the user opens the outline element to which it is attached. In the example above, this is the first element in the hierarchy, so the package will start playing as soon as the trainee opens the Player. This may catch them unawares, and they may miss the start of the presentation. In this case, remove the auto-advance from the first slide in the presentation, and add a button called "Play" (or something equally obvious) that has an action of "Next Slide". Then, the presentation will not start playing until the trainee clicks on the "Play" button.

Generally, I would not advocate including a presentation in a *Concept* pane. Exercises are *components* of presentations, so presentations should link to exercises, and not the other way round. How to link from a presentation to a specific exercise is explained in Chapter 6, *Publishing content*. However, the above example does at least demonstrate the *possibilities* that UPK offers for "improving" the trainee's learning experience through the creative use of Packages.

Linking to a URL

In the previous section of this chapter, we looked at how to link to a presentation included in a Package, from the *Concept* pane of an outline element in our course. We used an example whereby we linked to a PowerPoint presentation that had been converted to Macromedia Flash via Articulate Presenter, and saw how this presentation would be launched within the *Concept* pane itself.

Although this initially seems like quite a cool thing to do, in fact the presentation is too small for effective use. In addition, we have the problem that if the presentation changes, we need to delete the old version from our Package, and then copy in the new version.

If the presentation already exists outside of our UPK Library, then a better option would simply be to provide a link to the presentation. True, the trainee will have to click on the link to display the presentation, but at least the presentation will be displayed at a sensible size, in its own window. And if the presentation changes (on whatever server it is hosted), our link will automatically point to the latest version (assuming that the new version of the presentation was published to the same location as the old version). So let's look at how to do that.

> If your presentation does *not* exist outside of UPK, and you are using UPK as your primary content repository, then it may make more sense to attach the presentations in the *Concepts* panes (possibly split by module).

In order to provide a link to an object that is located outside of the UPK server, you need to know the URL of the object. Although in this example we will be linking to the `player.html` file for an Articulate Presenter presentation, you can actually link to anything that has a URL: a file on your local LAN share, an intranet site, or even a web site on the Internet. You just need to make sure that the trainees will have access to the site to which the URL points, at the time that they access the Player. In particular, you should consider interference from corporate firewalls that may block access, and think about trainees who may not be network connected when they attend the training.

To provide a link to an external object via its URL, carry out the following steps:

1. Open the content object from which you want to provide the link. This can be a Web Page attached to a *Concepts* pane (or attached to anything else, really), or a Topic. For our sample exercise, we will provide a link from text in a Web Page.
2. Select the text that you want to form the link (that is, that the user will click on in order to display the linked object).
3. If you are linking from a Web Page, select menu option **Insert | Hyperlink**. If you are linking from Custom Text in a Bubble, click on the **Create Link** button (). The **Insert Hyperlink** dialog box is displayed.
4. Click on the **URL** button on the left-hand side of the dialog box. The dialog box is updated to show an **Address** field, as shown in the following screenshot:

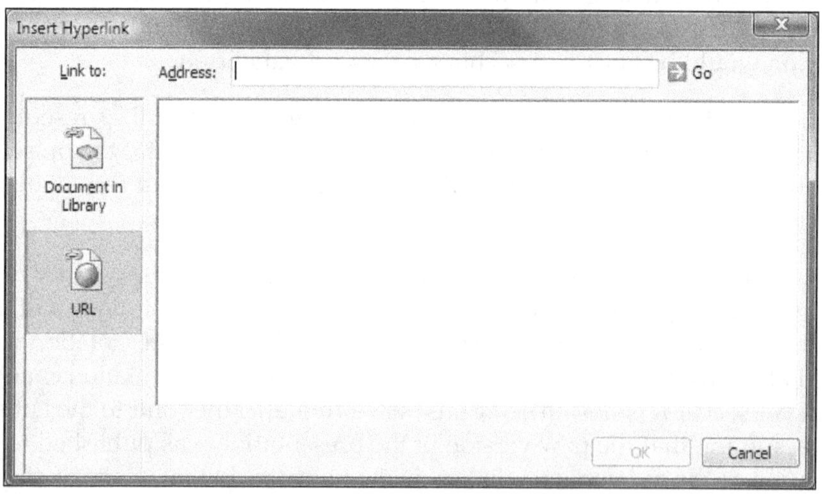

5. Enter the URL of the object to which you want to link in the **Address** field, and then click on the **Go** button to the right of the **Address** field.
6. To provide a ToolTip, right-click on the hyperlinked text and select **Hyperlink Properties** from the context menu. The following dialog box is displayed:

   Enter the required ToolTip in the **Tooltip** field (in our example, we will use the text "Presentation"), and then click on **OK**.
7. Save the Web Page, and close it.

We now have a link to an external object (in our case, the Articulate Presentation). In the Player, this will appear as shown in the next screenshot:

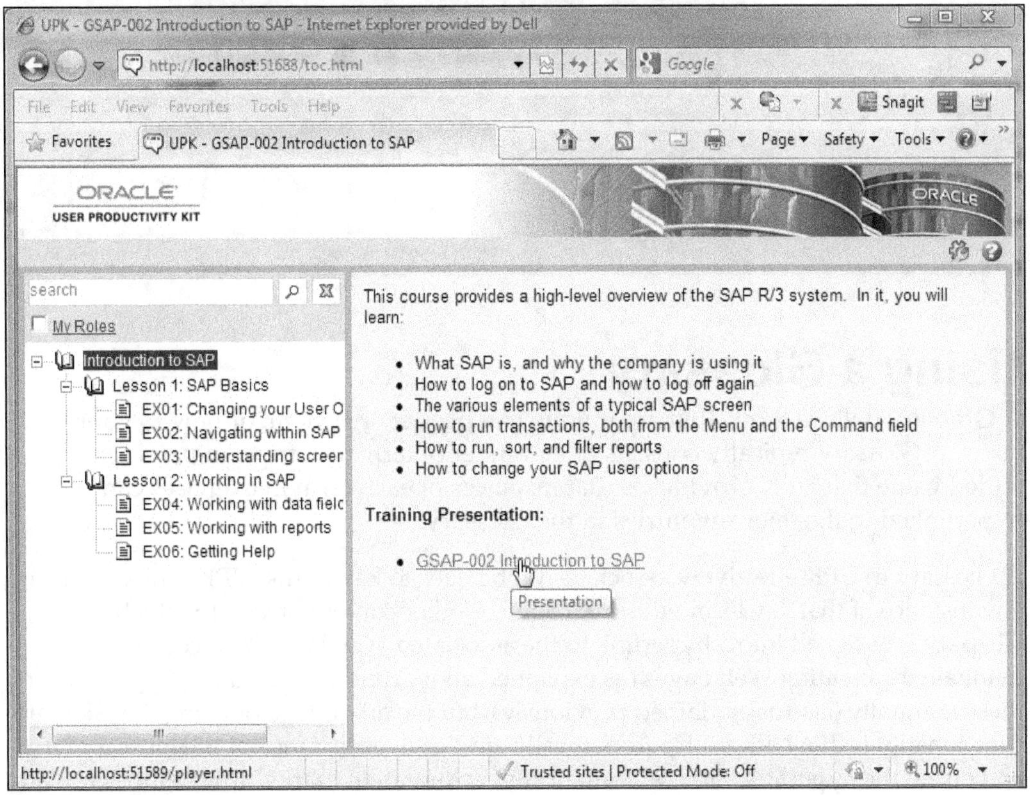

If the trainee clicks on this link, then the external object (in our case, an Articulate Presentation) will be displayed in a separate browser window, as shown in the following screenshot:

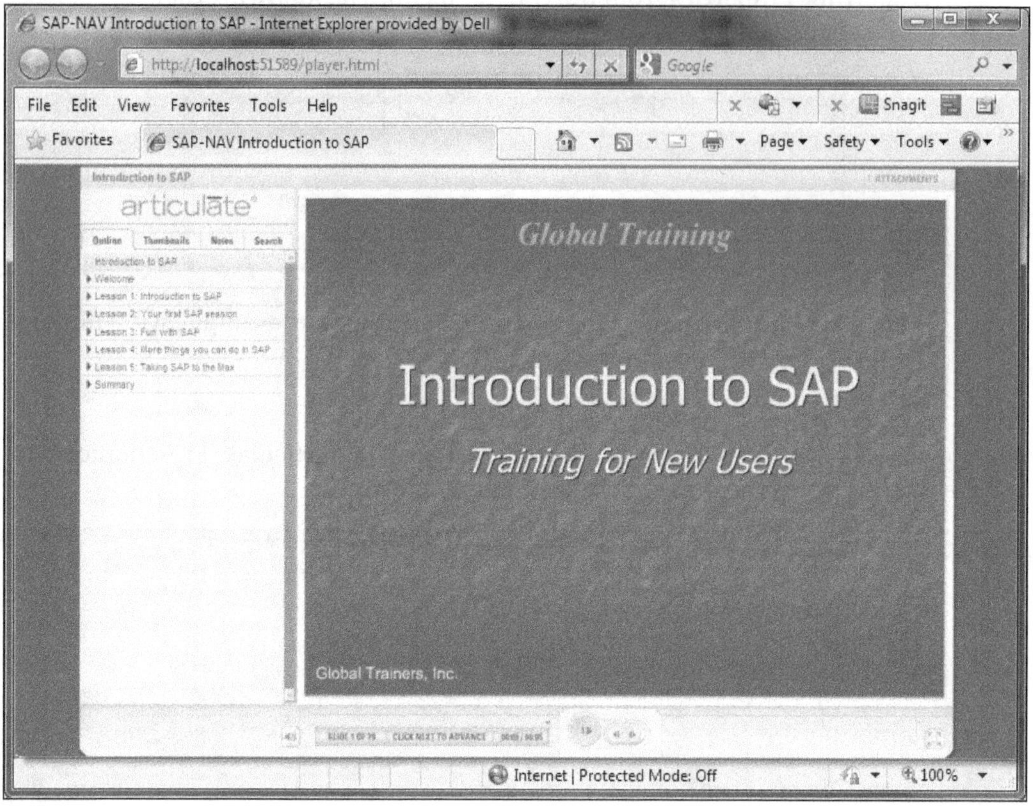

Using a Glossary

A **Glossary** defines terms that are unique to a project or system, or new to your users. A Glossary typically consists of a number of term/description pairs. The added value that UPK provides is that instances of each term in exercises can be hyperlinked to the relevant entries in the Glossary.

A Glossary in UPK effectively associates Web Pages to key terms. UPK will then turn any instance of that key term within a Topic (or other content object) to which that Glossary is assigned into a hyperlink to the associated Web Page. You could do this manually by creating Web Pages (as explained above) and then creating hyperlinks to these manually (also as explained previously), but the advantage of using the Glossary functionality is that UPK will 'automatically' find each occurrence of the glossary term and create the hyperlink. I say 'automatically' in quotation marks, as UPK does not do this *completely* automatically. You have to *tell* it to go and create the hyperlinks, but once you tell it to do so, it will dutifully go off and find 'every' occurrence of all of the terms in the glossary and create the hyperlinks to the definition.

And I say 'every' in quotation marks, because UPK won't necessarily link *every* instance of the term. UPK allows you to choose (at the Library level) whether it turns literally *every* occurrence of the term found in a location into a hyperlink, or only the first occurrence. A *location* here is effectively a single Bubble or Web Page. One could well ask why UPK doesn't provide the option to create a Glossary link only for the first occurrence of the term in a Topic. The simple answer is that it does not necessarily know *which* occurrence is the first, because the Topic could include Alternative Paths. So UPK takes an over-cautious approach, and considers each block of information separately.

This option is specified in the **Options** panel (menu option **Tools | Options**), under the **Content Defaults | Glossary** section, as shown in the following screenshot:

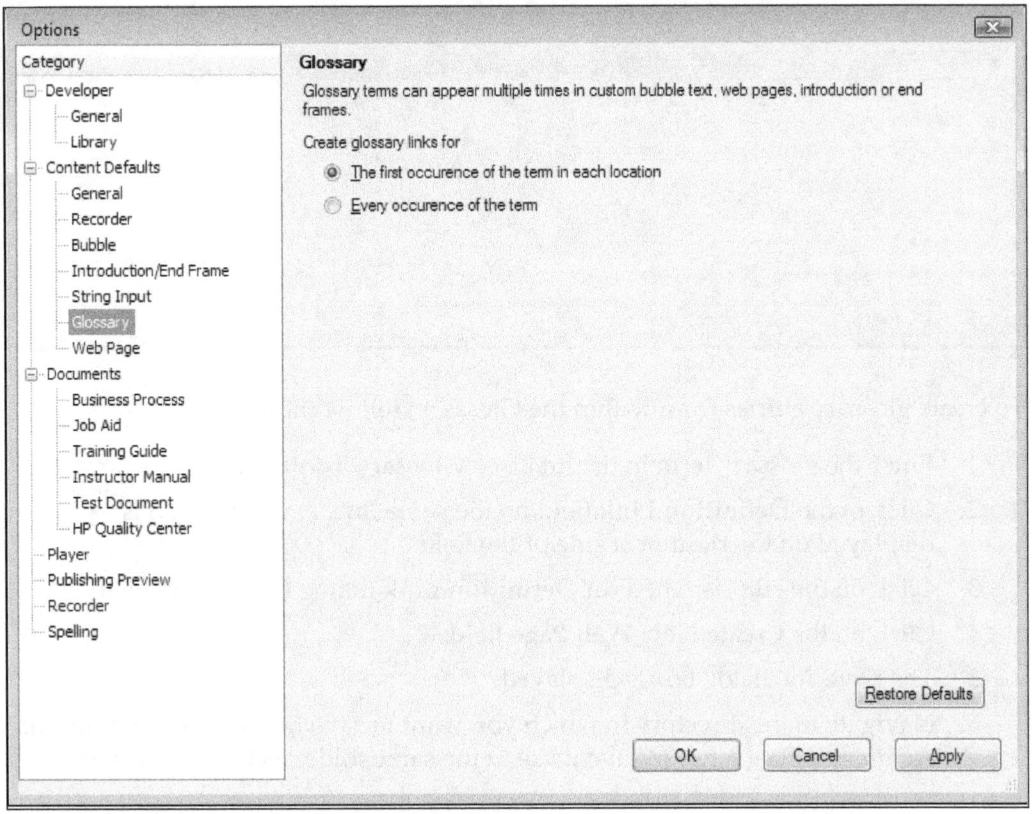

Creating a glossary

To create a Glossary in UPK, follow these steps:

1. From the main Library screen, click on the folder within which you want to create the Glossary. You can create the Glossary in any folder, but it makes sense to have a single folder that contains the Glossary file itself, and all of the Web Pages used for the terms.
2. Select menu option **File | New | Glossary**.

The *Glossary Editor* is opened in a new tab within the *UPK Developer* window, as shown in the following screenshot:

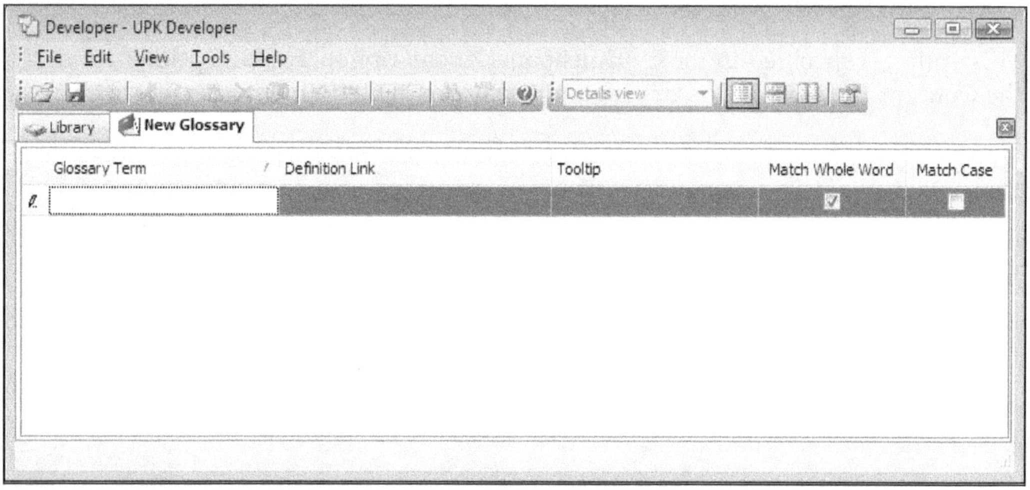

To create glossary entries from within the Glossary, follow these steps:

1. Enter the glossary term in the first free **Glossary Term** field.
2. Click in the **Definition Link** field on the same line. An ellipsis (**...**) is displayed on the rightmost side of the field.
3. Click on the ellipsis. The **Edit Definition Link** dialog box is displayed.
4. Click on the **Create New Web Page** field.
5. The **Save As** dialog box is displayed.
6. Navigate to the directory in which you want to save the Glossary definition. Again, it makes sense to save these in the same folder as the Glossary itself.

7. The **Name** field will default to the glossary term specified in the **Glossary Term** field. It is recommended that you keep this default, and use the definition term as the Web Page name. You could use any other name, if you wanted to (UPK does not use this name to locate the definition; it uses its own, internal identifier) but using the same name will allow you to easily locate the term Web Page if you need to.
8. Click on the **Save** button. A new tab is opened for the Web Page.
9. Enter the Glossary description into this page.
10. The Web Page will use the default font and colors. You can override these defaults, if required.
11. Close the Web Page by clicking on the **x** on the rightmost side of the open tab list. You are passed back to the *Glossary Editor*.
12. Enter a suitable ToolTip text for the glossary entry in the **Tooltip** field. This text will be displayed when the user hovers the mouse over the hyperlinked glossary term.
13. If only whole instances of the glossary term should be turned into hyperlinks (for example, if the term is **Order** then "Orders" and "Ordering" will not be hyperlinked), then select the **Match Whole Word** option. Otherwise, make sure that this option is not selected.
14. If only text that matches the case of the term should be turned into hyperlinks (for example, if the term is **Order** then "order" will not be hyperlinked), then select the **Match Case** field. Otherwise, make sure that this option is not selected.
15. Repeat Steps 1 to 14 for all additional terms that you want to add to the Glossary.

To create a glossary entry that uses an existing Web Page for the glossary term, follow these steps:

1. Enter the glossary term in the first free *Glossary Term* field.
2. Click in the **Definition Link** field on the same line. An ellipsis (**...**) is displayed on the rightmost side of the field.
3. Click on the ellipsis. The **Edit Definition Link** dialog box is displayed.
4. Click on the **Create Link** button. The **Insert Hyperlink** dialog box is displayed.
5. Navigate to, and select, the Web Page that contains the glossary description.
6. Click on **OK**. The **Edit Definition Link** dialog box is redisplayed.

> You can edit the Web Page directly from this dialog box, by clicking on the Edit Web Page icon. Editing Web Pages is explained in more detail earlier in this chapter.

7. Click on **OK**. You are returned to the Glossary tabbed page.

Once you have defined all required Glossary entries, save and close the Glossary, by following the steps shown below:

1. Click the **Save** button to save your changes to the Glossary. The **Save As** dialog box is displayed.
2. Navigate to the directory in which you want to save the Glossary.
3. Enter a suitable name for the Glossary in the *Name* field.
4. Close the *Glossary Editor* by clicking on the **x** on the rightmost side of the open tab list.

An example of a partially-populated Glossary is shown in the next screenshot:

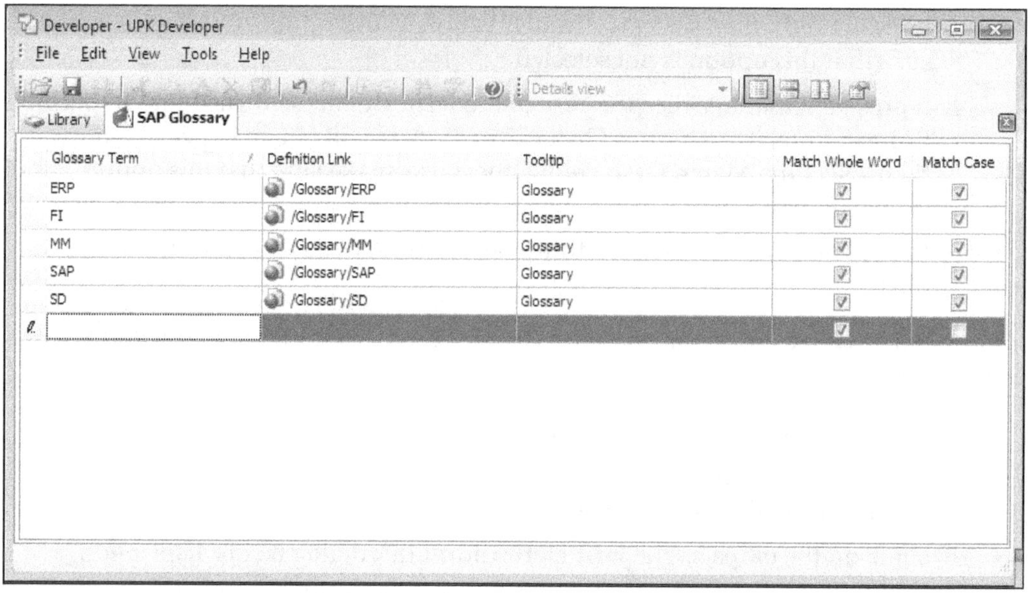

You can see from the **Definition Link** column above that all of the Glossary definition files are stored in the same, single folder, called `Glossary`. This is the same folder that the Glossary object itself is stored in. Personally, I find it useful to keep all of the content objects for the Glossary in the same single folder. This is not strictly necessary, but it does keep things organized.

You will also note that the *Tooltip* is the same in every case. I tend to always use the tooltip **Glossary** so that the user knows that the hyperlink links to the Glossary, and not to another form of Web Page.

Assigning a Glossary to content objects

Creating a Glossary is only half the story. You need to manually assign the Glossary to each object that you want to use that Glossary (that is, for which you want the terms specified in the Glossary to be hyperlinked to the Glossary definitions).

> **Version Difference**
>
> In OnDemand Version 8.7 and earlier, a single Glossary was created for a Title, and was automatically applied to all content objects within that Title. In UPK 3.5, it is possible to have multiple Glossaries within a single Library, so it is necessary to specify which content objects should use which Glossary.

This assignment is done via the content object's **Properties**, as shown in the screenshot below.

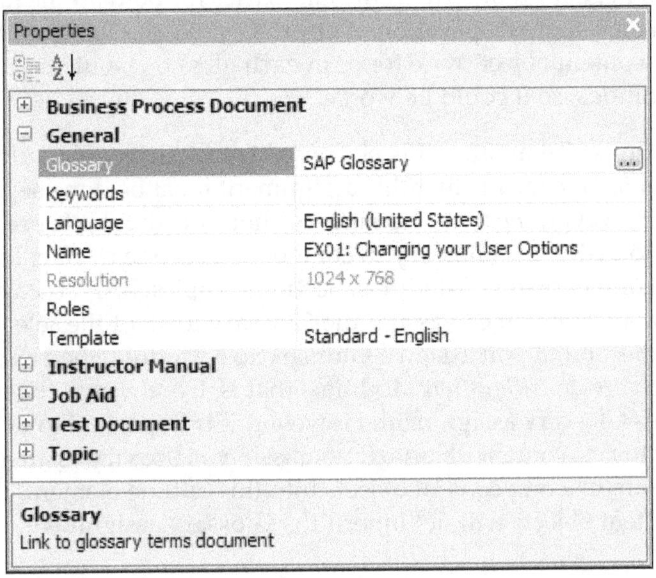

The *Glossary* property is available for Modules, Sections, Topics, and Web Pages. This means that you could potentially assign one Glossary to a Module, another Glossary to a Section within this Module, and a third Glossary to a Topic within that Section. Not that you're very likely to want to do this. But you could.

The further implication of the requirement to assign a Glossary to each content object individually is that you can define multiple Glossaries, and assign different Glossaries to different objects. I'd question the wisdom of assigning one glossary to a Module, and then an entirely different Glossary to a Topic within that Module, but I can certainly see the benefit of having multiple Glossaries available in a Library that contained (for example) simulations for multiple applications; you could create application-specific Glossaries (as you no doubt do at the moment) and then assign each Glossary to only the content objects for the relevant application.

The downside (for those of us who favor modularization and reuse) is that it is only possible to assign a single Glossary to any given object. So it is not possible to, say, create a company-wide Glossary and separate application-specific Glossaries, and then assign the company-wide Glossary and the relevant application-specific glossary to a single Topic. But more resourceful readers will have already worked out how to get around this limitation. Need a clue? Glossary entries are just Web Pages, and any given Web Page can be reused in multiple places. Need more help? A Web Page can be included in more than one Glossary. So you should first define Web Pages for all of your Glossary terms. You can then create multiple Glossaries (for example, one for each application), and include whichever terms' Web Pages you need to in each of the glossaries. If a term applies to two applications, then simply include the Web Page for that term in the Glossaries for both applications. Simple! Of course there is some slight duplication of effort as you need to create the entry in the actual Glossary content object twice (once in each glossary), but you are reusing the individual definitions, so it could be worse.

Unfortunately, unlike Templates, it is not possible to specify a default Glossary in your user defaults. This means that this assignment must be done separately for each content object. However, there are a couple of shortcuts that UPK provides which avoid the need to assign the Glossary to content objects one by one. First, if you select multiple content objects (Modules, Sections, Topics, or Web Pages) and display the *Properties* pane, then you can assign the Glossary to all of the selected objects in one fell swoop. Second, if you assign a Glossary to a Module, then any new Sections or Titles that you create *within* that Module - that is, from within the *Outline Editor* - will inherit this Glossary assignment. However, it is important to note that this will only apply to *new* content objects. If you assign a Glossary to an outline element and then insert pre-existing content objects into this outline element, then these pre-existing content objects will not inherit the Glossary assignment.

Regenerating the Glossary links

Glossary links are not created (or updated) automatically. You need to tell UPK to go and search through your content objects and turn any instances of the Glossary terms into links to the Glossary definitions. This is good in that you can at least have control over when it does this, but bad in that it is easy to forget to do so.

Updating Glossary links after updating the Glossary itself

When you close (not save) an existing Glossary, having updated it (for example, to add or remove terms), UPK will prompt you to re-generate the Glossary links by displaying the following message:

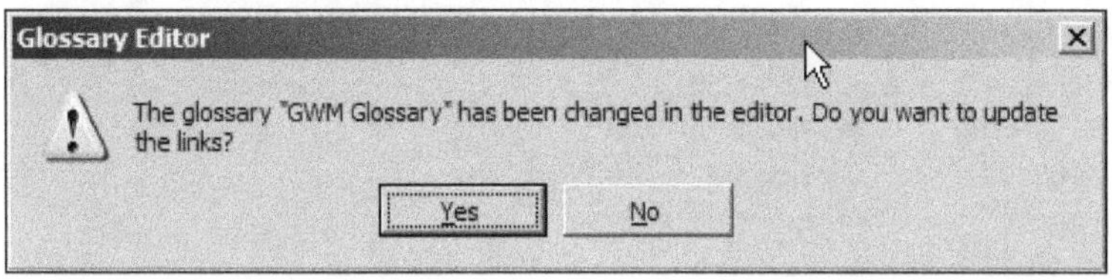

Click **Yes**. UPK will update all of the content objects that the changed Glossary has been assigned to. It will hyperlink all occurrences of the glossary terms with hyperlinks to the associated definition Web Pages. Furthermore, if you have removed any Glossary terms from the Glossary, then UPK will also remove any hyperlinks for these terms.

> **Version Difference**
>
> In OnDemand Version 8.x and earlier, if you removed terms from the Glossary then any hyperlinks to these terms would not automatically be removed when you re-generated the Glossary. This is a huge improvement in OnDemand 9.x / UPK 3.x.

Once the Glossary has been updated, the following message is displayed:

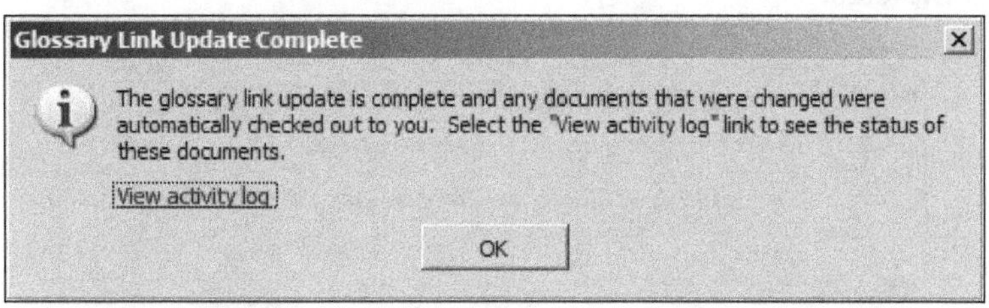

Note the text "**any documents that were changed were automatically checked out to you**". It is important to note that if you are working in a multi-developer environment then any content objects that have now been hyperlinked to your new glossary entries will have been checked out. You will need to check all of these in again (typically, when you check in the updated glossary). You should, therefore, click on the **View activity log** link and make a note of the changed documents. Alternatively, you can choose to **Check in all** when you check in the glossary, although you should be warned that this will check in all content objects that you have checked out - which may be more than just those objects changed by the Glossary link update.

An example of the *Activity Log* is shown in the following screenshot.

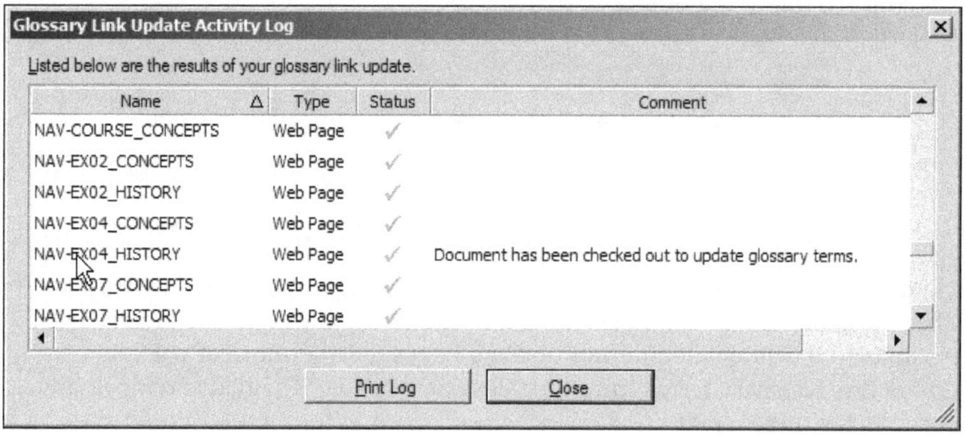

Note that the *Activity Log* lists all of the content objects that have been examined - even if they have not been updated. Also note the message "**Document has been checked out to update glossary links**". You will need to check back in all of these content objects.

It is also important to note that if UPK attempted to update the Glossary links in a content object that is currently checked out to another user, then it will not be able to. In this case, you will see a warning message similar to the one shown below when the update completes:

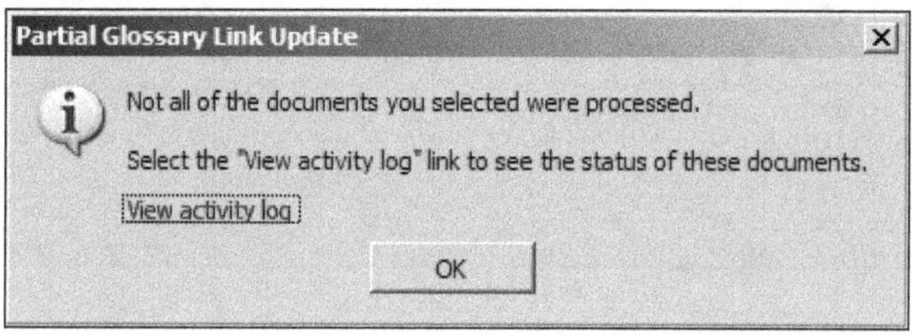

You can identify these documents in the *Activity Log*, as shown in the following screenshot:

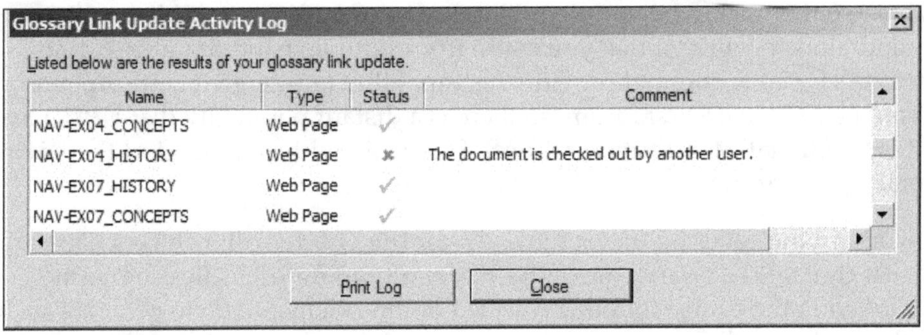

You should make a note of these unprocessed content objects. You will need to run the Glossary update again once they are checked in. Bear in mind that UPK will have identified the content object based on the most recently checked-in version of the object. The developer could well have removed the text that would have been hyperlinked to the Glossary in their edits. Conversely, it is possible that UPK did not identify a content object for Glossary updates based on the most recent version, but a developer had the object checked out and added the Glossary terms (that are eligible for *hyperlinking*) whilst they had the object checked out. For these reasons, you should run the Glossary update periodically, and definitely run it immediately before publishing your content (when all of the content objects should be checked in, anyway).

Manually regenerating the Glossary links

You can regenerate Glossary links whenever you want to, by following these steps:

1. Select the objects for which you want to update Glossary links, in the Library. You can either select one or more specific objects, or you can select a folder, in which case all of the objects within that folder (and any subfolders) will be updated.
2. Select menu option **Edit | Update Glossary Links**.

It is advisable to always regenerate the Glossary links immediately prior to publishing your content. It certainly does no harm to regenerate the Glossary links at any other time, but bear in mind that it could take a while if you have a lot of content objects and/or a lot of glossary terms. Also, bear in mind that UPK will check out every object that it updates the Glossary links in, so you will need to manually check all of these back in again which can also take time. This may also be inconvenient if you have developers working on the content objects (or are working on the content objects yourself) at the time that you want to regenerate the Glossary links.

Generating a stand-alone Glossary

After seeing the usefulness of a Glossary, you're no doubt wondering if it is possible to either include a complete Glossary in an outline, or publish a Glossary to a stand-alone document that you could (for example) hand out during training. Unfortunately, UPK does not provide this capability (although it crops up reasonably often on the *Feature Request* forum, so there is a distant possibility that UPK may add this functionality in a future release). However, with a bit of effort there is an acceptable workaround.

This workaround relies on the fact that a **Training Guide** will include a Glossary table that contains Glossary entries (term/definition) for each Glossary term hyperlinked in the course (or other selected outline element). So to generate such a table that includes *all* Glossary entries, you simply need to publish a Training Guide for an outline element that contains *all* of the Glossary terms. How to create and publish an outline element specifically for this purpose is explained below:

To create a Word-format, complete Glossary, and carry out the steps described below:

1. Open your Glossary in the Library.
2. In the *Glossary Editor*, click on the first Glossary term, to select it.
3. Scroll down to the bottom of the Glossary, and *Shift*-click on the last Glossary term, to select the full range of Glossary entries in the Glossary. Your selection should look as shown in the following screenshot:

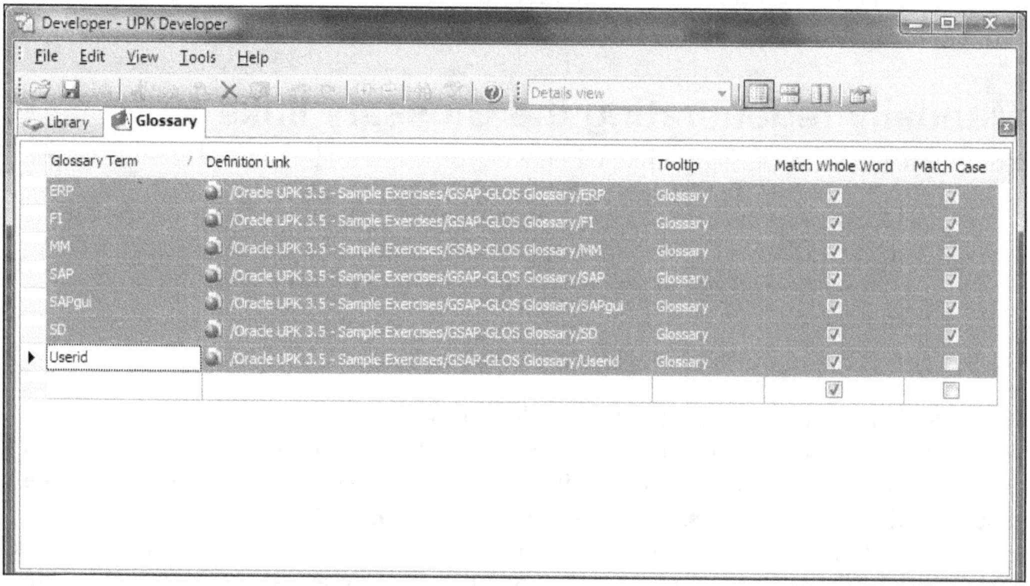

4. Copy (*Ctrl+C*) this information to the clipboard.

5. Close the *Glossary Editor*.
6. Create a new Web Page and open it for editing.
7. In the *Web Page Editor*, paste (*Ctrl+V*) the contents of the clipboard into the Web Page. This will be pasted as pure text, which will include the full file path of the Web Page, the Tooltip, and so on. But most importantly, it includes every glossary term in your Glossary. Don't worry about editing or formatting this Web Page; we will not use it in this form. Your Web Page will look similar to the example in the following screenshot:

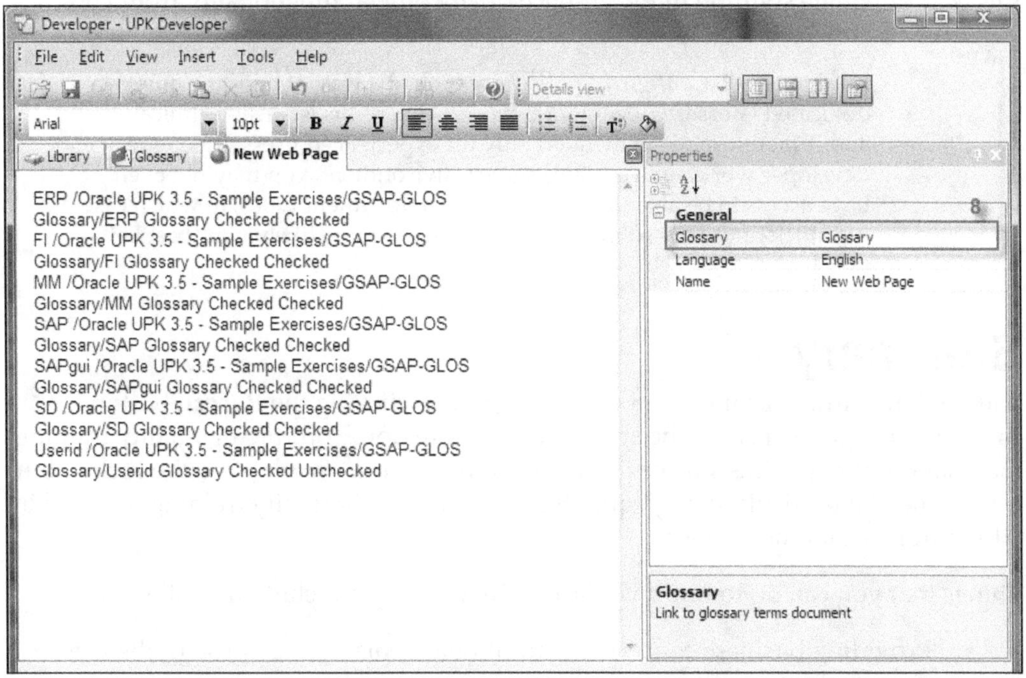

8. Use the **Properties** pane to assign your Glossary to this new Web Page (as described in a previous section of this chapter). This is very important; the glossary links will not be updated if you don't assign the Glossary to the Web Page.
9. Save and close your new Web Page.
10. Back in the Library, click on your new Web Page, and then select menu option **Edit | Update Glossary Links**. This will turn all of the Glossary terms in the Web Page into hyperlinks to the associated Glossary entries.
11. Create a new outline element (Module or Section) and attach this new Web Page to this element as the **Concept**.
12. Publish this outline element as a **Training Guide**.

Once the publishing process is complete, open the generated Training Guide. At the bottom, you will find a section labeled **Glossary** that contains a table with all of your glossary terms and definitions in it. You can then reformat this, or extract it and copy it to somewhere else, or do whatever else you want with it.

Note that this is a one-time (one-way) activity. Any new terms that you add to the Glossary will not automatically be included in your dummy Glossary outline element. However, assuming that you just want to generate a quick and simple Word-based Glossary, for example for distributing during your initial training, then this is an adequate solution in the absence of any official functionality from UPK.

> In Chapter 12, *Configuring UPK*, we look at a way of building our own dedicated Glossary document type. However, this is fairly technical and is therefore recommended only for experienced users. If you are a developer working in a client/server environment, you may not even have access to be able to define your own document types, in which case the quick-and-dirty solution offered above is quite likely your best bet.

Summary

Although recording a simulation is just a matter of clicking the **Record** button, running through the task in the system, and you're done, producing quality training material is not really this simple. Yes, the simulation may work (if you're lucky), but it won't be of a particularly high quality. Producing high-quality training material in UPK requires a lot more work.

Things that you can do to improve the quality of a Topic include the following:

- Providing business context and additional explanations through the use of Custom Text
- Providing additional information via Web Pages
- Attaching relevant documents through the use of Packages
- Providing an on-line Glossary

These things are the *bells and whistles* that improve the trainee's experience. Because they are 'add-ons' to the basic recording, some developers may choose not to use them (or find that their project management has not allocated them enough time to add them). However, taking the time to add this level of features will greatly improve the overall usability of your exercises, and you will certainly see an increase in trainee satisfaction (assuming that you take post-training feedback—which you should).

10
Adding Value in the Player

In Chapter 9, *Adding Value to Your Topics*, we looked at things that you can do to your recordings to improve their quality (regardless of the deployment format). In this chapter, we will look at a few things that you can do to improve the trainee's interaction with the Player. These are all things that the trainee has control over, although as we shall see, it is you the developer who allows them to have this control.

In this chapter, you will learn:

- How to use roles to show trainees only those Topics that are applicable to their job
- How to use jump-in points to allow trainees to start the playback of a recording from a specific point
- How to facilitate keyword searches
- How to allow (or deny) trainees the ability to change their Player options

Working with roles

It is likely that in any application there will be some features that are used by specific users, and other features that are used by a different set of users. Typically, the assignment of features—for example, transactions in SAP (and the security authorization necessary to access these features) is done on the basis of **roles**. Each user is assigned one or more roles, and based on this assignment, they have a requirement to use certain functionality. There is nothing complicated or revolutionary about this.

Your company may have a Sales department, a Finance department, and so on. Although these departments may use the same application (the application for which you are developing the training material), they are likely to use different functions, and will therefore need different training. This is the basis for *role-based training* (where each user is trained only on the functionality that they will use, rather than being trained on the whole application), which is more often than not the preferred training approach, especially with large (typically ERP) systems.

UPK *kind of* supports the concept of role-based training, in so far as it allows Topics to be *tagged* for different roles. This does not prevent trainees from accessing the content (as security roles may do in the application itself), but it does have two important uses:

- It allows users to *filter* the content that they see in the Player according to their chosen role(s) (although if you are developing true role-based training you will likely have one Player per role anyway).
- It allows developers to publish content for a specific role (which is much more useful, although for linking to in-application help you need a single player that contains all topics for all roles).

In this section, we will look at both options.

Defining your roles

Unlike OnDemand 8.7 and earlier, UPK 3.5 does not *require* you to maintain a list of roles before you can assign them to content. You can simply define the roles as you assign them to Topics. However, from a *control* (and consistency) point of view it is probably wise to pre-define all roles prior to tagging content for these roles. (You could then lock the role definitions, so that individual content developers cannot create their own ones.)

To define a list of master roles from which you can select when you are assigning roles to Topics, carry out the steps described below:

1. In the Library, open the folder `System/Roles`. Within this folder, you will see one role list per supported language, as shown in the next screenshot:

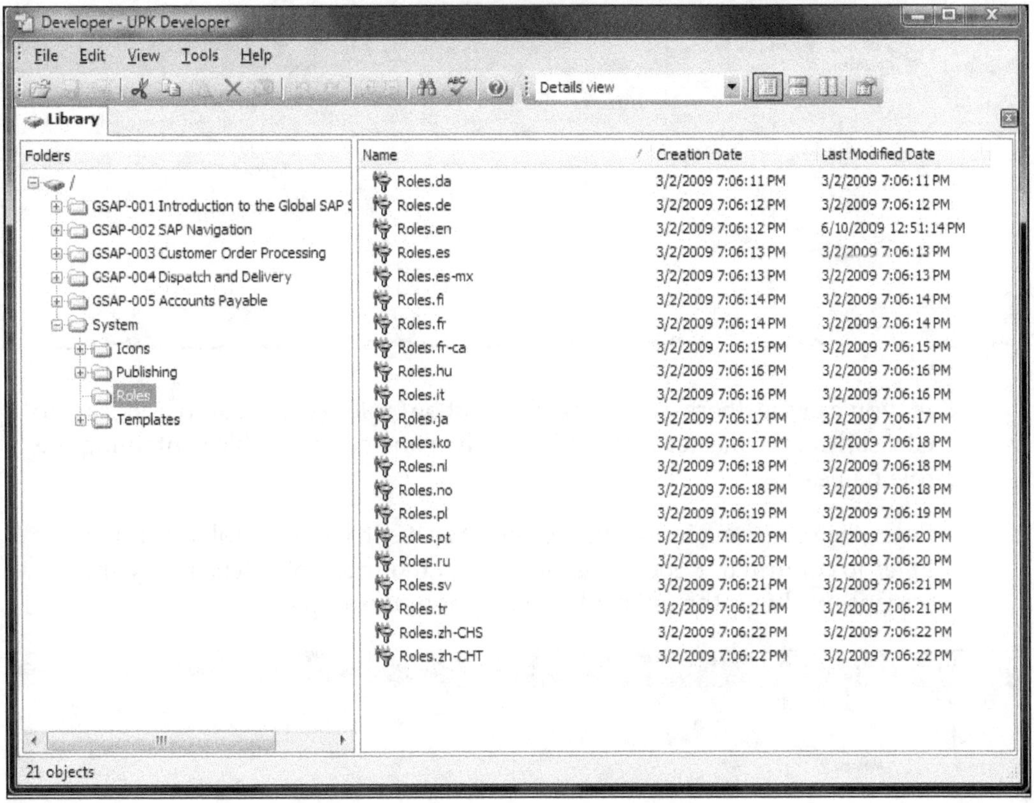

2. Double-click on the role list for your language, and the *Role Editor* will be opened up in a new tabbed page within the **UPK Developer** screen, as shown in the following screenshot:

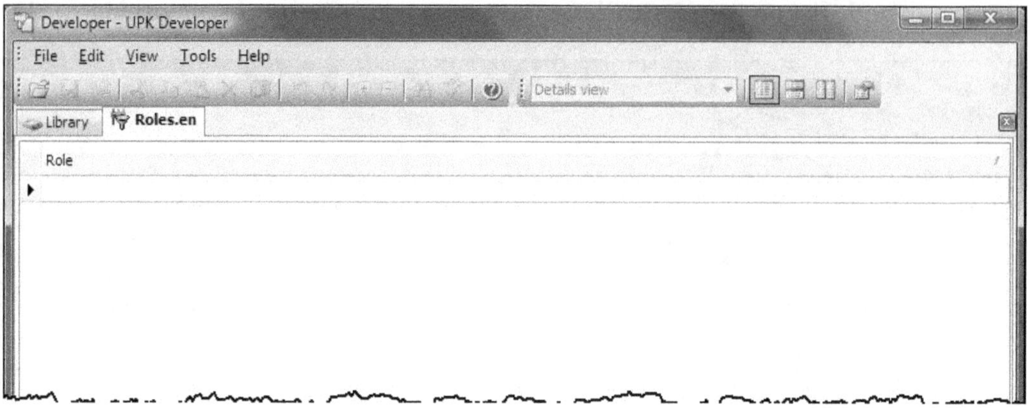

As you can see, there is nothing clever about roles (when compared, say, to Glossaries); the master role list is simply a one-column table containing the role names.

- Enter the role name in the first (or next) free entry in the table, and press *Enter* to confirm it. Repeat this step for all required roles. The following screenshot shows the finished role list for our example course:

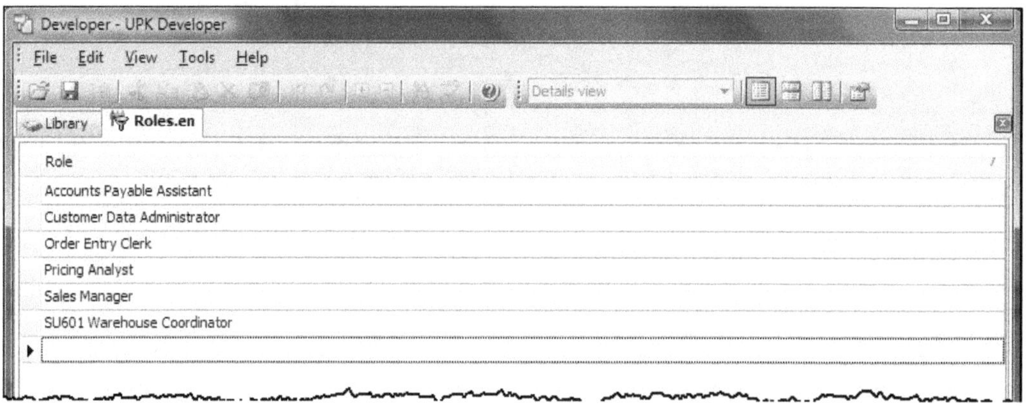

- Once you have entered all of the required role names, click on the **Save** button (), and then close the *Role Editor*.

You can now assign any of these roles to your Topics.

Assigning roles to Topics

UPK does not provide special (that is, convoluted) functionality for assigning roles to Topics; you simply use the *Properties* pane.

> **Version Difference**
>
> In OnDemand 8.x / UPK 2.x and earlier, it was necessary to define roles *before* they could be assigned to Topics. In OnDemand 9.x / UPK 3.x, roles can be defined "on the fly" as you assign them to Topics.

To assign a role to a Topic, carry out the following steps:

1. In the Library, click on the Topic that you want to tag for specific roles. Note that you can select multiple Topics if you want to assign the same role(s) to all of them at the same time.
2. Make sure that the Properties pane is displayed (click the **Properties** button () if it is not), and expand the **General** section, as shown in the following screenshot:

3. Click on the ellipsis (...) on the far right of the **Roles** field. The **Assign Roles** dialog box is displayed, as shown in the next screenshot:

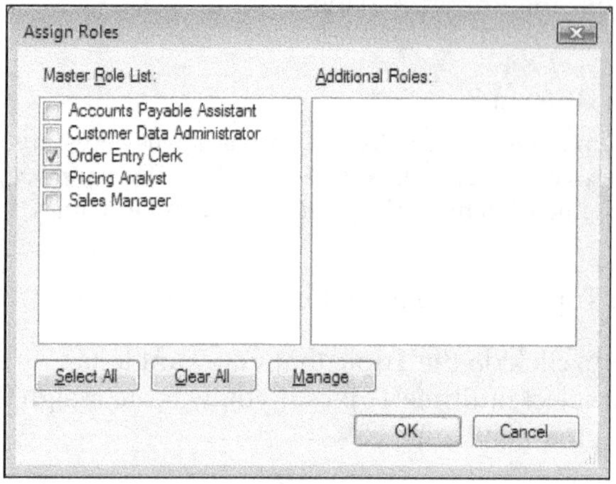

> **What are Additional Roles?**
>
> The **Additional Roles** pane on the rightmost side of the **Assign Roles** dialog box will list any roles that have been assigned to Topics in your Library but that do not exist in your master role list. How can this happen? Typically, it is because you have imported content from another Library, and the additional roles exist (and were assigned to the imported Topics) in that Library. (Refer to Chapter 7, *Version Management* for details of importing content from one Library to another.)

4. In the *Master Role List*, select the checkbox to the left of all of the roles that you want to assign to this Topic. In the previous screenshot, we have assigned the **Order Entry Clerk** role to the Topic.

> If the role that you want to assign to the Topic does not appear in the *Master Role List*, then you can click the **Manage** button and add it now.

5. Click **OK**.

That's all there is to it. Now let's look at how these roles are used in the Player, and during publication.

Selecting roles in the Player

If roles have been assigned to any of the Topics in a published Outline, then the Player for that Outline will contain an additional link, **My Roles**, in the Outline pane (below the *Search box*), as shown in the following screenshot:

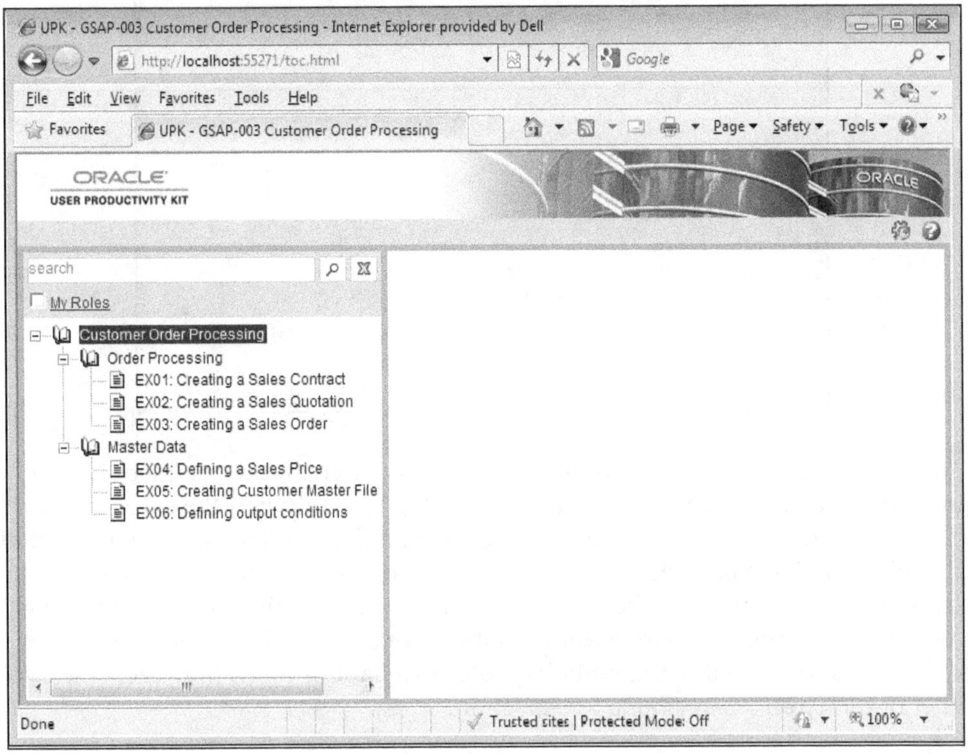

For our purposes, we will assume that the six Topics shown in the previous screenshot have been assigned to the five roles that we defined in the *Assigning your roles* section, as follows:

Exercise	Accounts Payable Assistant	Customer Data Administrator	Order Entry Clerk	Pricing Analyst	Sales Manager
EX01		X	X		
EX02			X		
EX03			X		
EX04				X	
EX05		X			
EX06					

Clicking on the **My Roles** link will display the **My Roles** dialog box. For our example, the **My Roles** dialog box appears as follows:

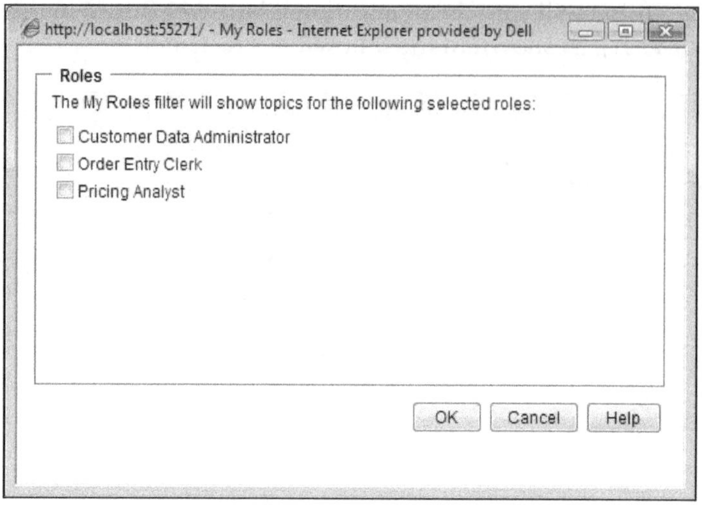

Note that there are only three roles listed, versus the five that we defined in our master role list. Why? Because the *My Roles* dialog box only lists the roles that have been assigned to the Topics included in the Outline. This may well be a subset of all of the roles that have been defined in the Library; obviously, the ability to select a role for which no content has been tagged would be both pointless and confusing. If you look at the role/exercise mapping table above, you will see that we did not assign any exercises to the **Accounts Payable Assistant** or **Sales Manager** roles, so neither of these roles is available for selection.

A trainee can select one or more roles, and then click the **OK** button to confirm their selection. The list of Topics in the Outline will then be filtered to include only content that has been specifically tagged for the selected roles. For our example, we will select the **Customer Data Administrator** role. Our Outline then appears as shown in the following screenshot:

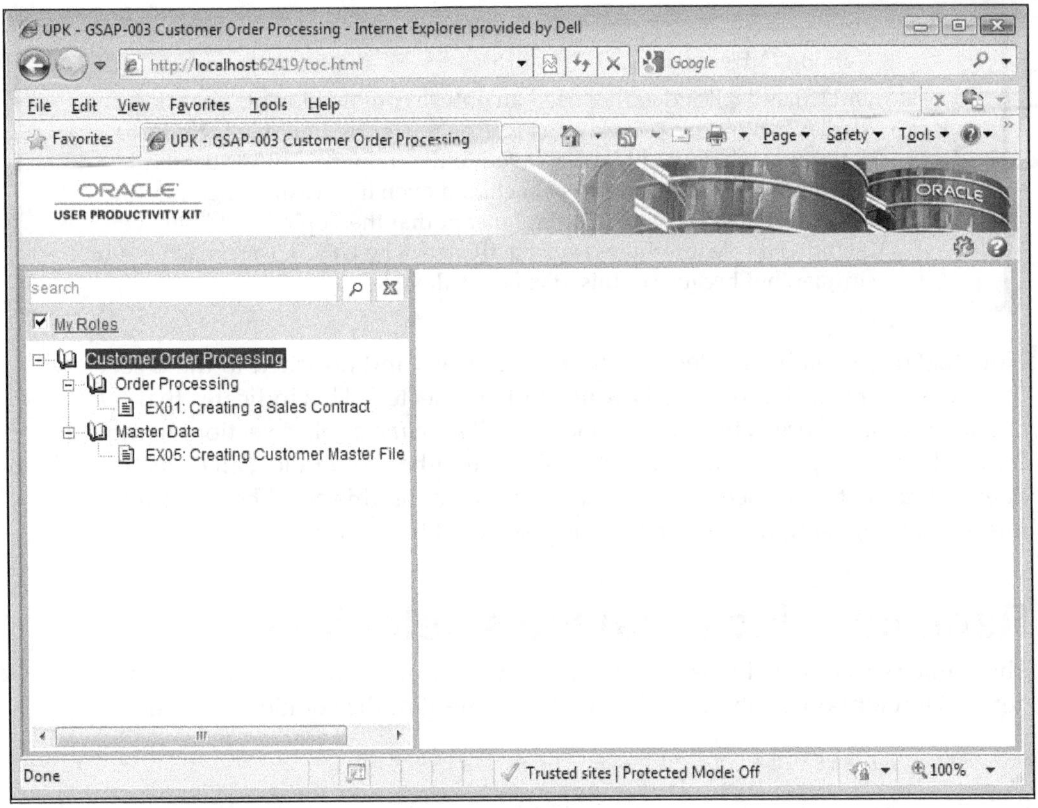

In our example, we can see only *EX01* and *EX05*. Cross-checking this against our role/exercise mapping table, we will see that these two are indeed the only Topics that have been tagged for the **Customer Data Administrator**. So, no surprises there.

It is important to understand that the Outline will include only content that has been explicitly tagged for the selected role. It will not include content that has not been tagged for *any* role (you will note that *EX06* has not been included). The implication of this is that "untagged" does not mean "applicable to all roles". If you want a Topic to be available to all roles, then you need to explicitly tag it for all roles.

Version Difference

OnDemand 8.7 and earlier used an obtuse combination of "always display" and "never display", as well as the individual role tagging, to determine what would be displayed to the trainee. "Always display" meant that the Topic would be included even if it wasn't tagged for the selected role, and "never display" meant that the Topic would only be included if role filtering was not activated. The UPK 3.5 approach is much simpler, but because of this, it is not as flexible.

Note that once you have selected one or more roles and returned to the Overview, the checkbox to the left of the **My Roles** link is selected. This indicates that *role filtering is active*. Deselecting this checkbox will *deactivate* role selection, without the trainee having to go back into the *My Roles* dialog box to deselect all of the roles. It does not *cancel* the trainee's role selection; re-selecting this checkbox will activate role filtering again, using the roles previously selected by the trainee.

Remembering a trainee's selection

The trainee's role selection is saved in a browser cookie, and this cookie has (by default) a retention period of one year. The content of the cookie is similar to:

```
OnDemandPlayerFiltering:true&Roles:Role1+Role2.
```

If a user defines their roles, and then disables role filtering, then OnDemand will still know what their roles are, because this is saved in the cookie. Should the user re-activate role filtering (by clicking the checkbox to the right of the **My Roles** link then the Outline will be filtered according to the roles that the trainee has previously selected. That is, the checkbox simply toggles filtering *off* and *on*. Using the same example as above, if the trainee has selected two roles, but has disabled role filtering, their choices are still saved in a cookie, but now the cookie will appear as:

```
OnDemandPlayerFiltering:false&Roles:Role1+Role2.
```

An implication of using browser cookies is that if multiple trainees are sharing the same workstation, and are not required to actively log on to it under a unique user ID, then any role selection made by the previous user of the workstation will apply to all subsequent users (unless they actively change it themselves). This can cause some confusion to trainees if they are not expecting this. Of course, in most corporate environments, users have unique, password-controlled logons, and so this shouldn't be an issue.

Publishing for a role

As mentioned at the start of this section, in addition to allowing users to filter the Outline according to their role(s), it is also possible to publish an Outline that includes only Topics that have been tagged for specific roles. Let's look at how to do that.

> The following explanation assumes that you are already familiar with the publishing process. If you are not, then please refer to Chapter 6, *Publishing Content* for additional details.

1. Open the Outline that you want to publish, in the *Outline Editor*.
2. Click on the outline element (Module or Section) that you want to publish, to select it.
3. Click on the **Publish** button ( ).
4. On the *Welcome to the Publishing Wizard* screen, specify the publishing destination, and then click on **Next**.
5. On the **Select Publishing Options** screen, select the **Publish by roles** checkbox (as shown in the following screenshot), and then click on the **Select Roles** button.

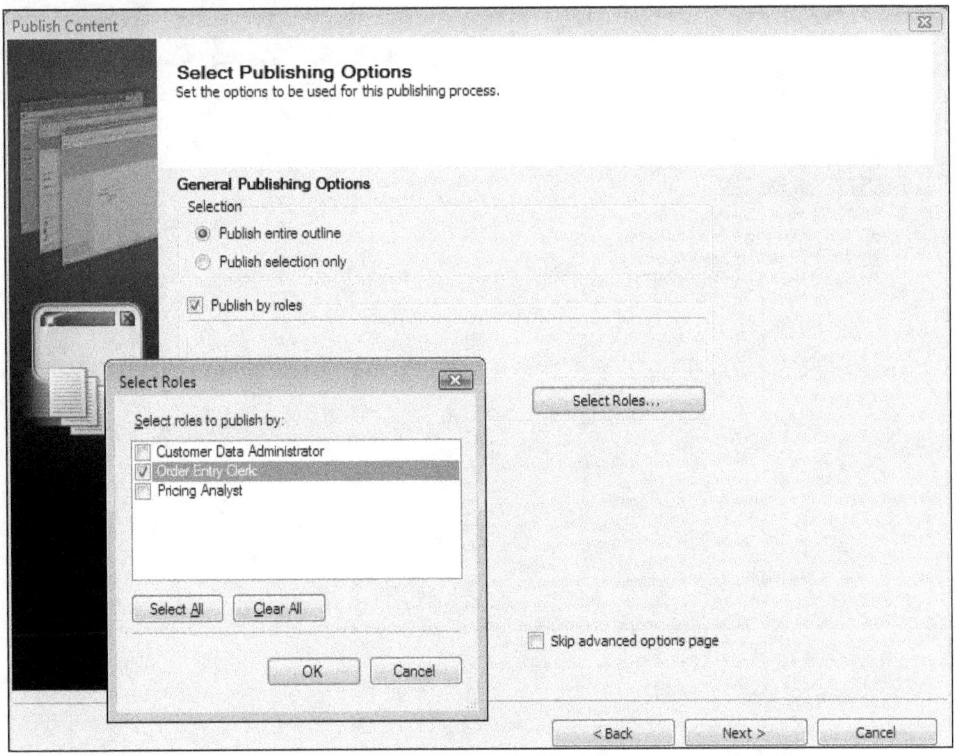

6. In the **Select Roles** dialog box, select the checkbox to the left of the role(s) for which you want to publish the content, and then click on **OK**. In our example, we are going to publish only content tagged for the **Order Entry Clerk**.
7. Back on the **Select Publishing Options screen**, click on **Next**.
8. If the **Advanced Publishing Options** screen is displayed (depending on your selection on the previous screen), make any required changes, and then click **Next**.
9. On the **Formats** screen, select the appropriate deployment format (we will select **Player**), and then click on **Publish**.

Now let's look at what this gives us in the Player. (I assume that by this far in the book you know how to launch the Player.) The following screenshot shows the Player generated for the selection that we made.

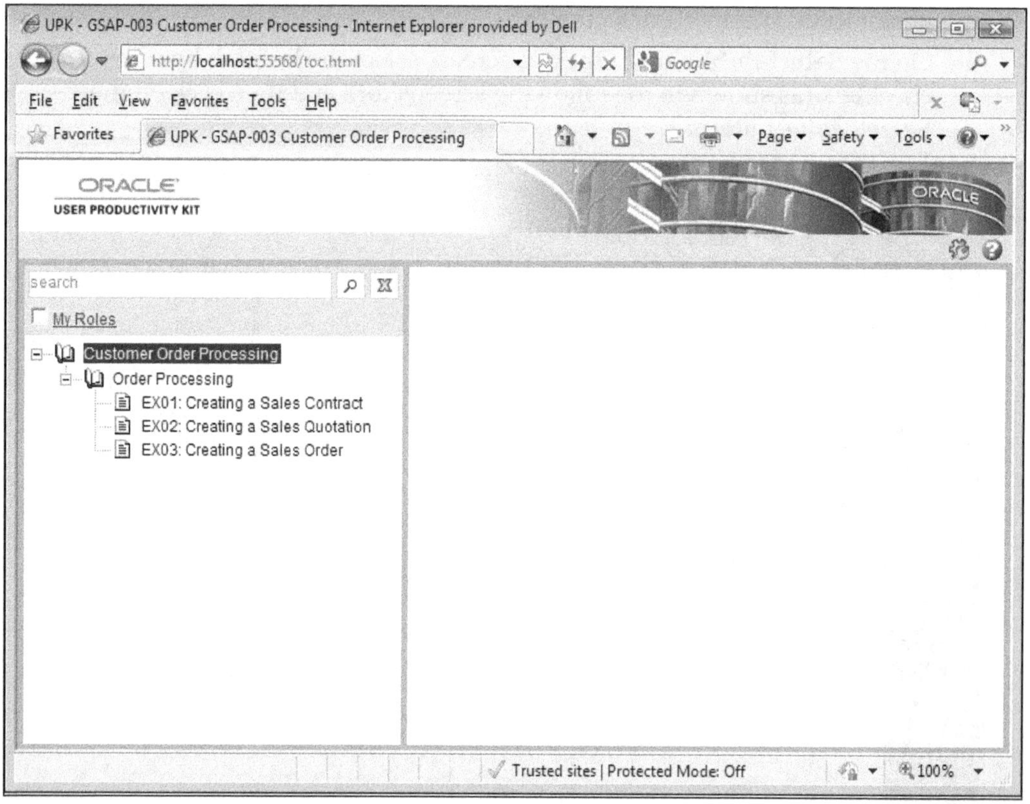

If you compare this screenshot with the earlier table that shows the roles assigned to the various exercises, you will note that (and as we would expect) the Player now only includes those Topics that were specifically tagged for the role(s) that we selected during publishing (in this example, the **Order Entry Clerk**). Success!

But wait! Why is the **My Roles** link still available? Surely if we have only published content for a specific role, then there is no need for this link (just as if we had published content that had not been tagged for any roles at all)? If you click on the **My Roles** link, you will see the following selections:

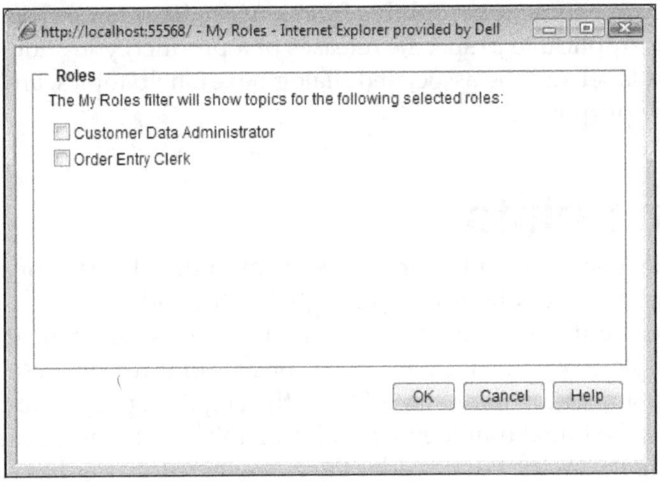

Why? The answer is simple. Some of the Topics that are tagged for the role that we selected for publishing are also tagged for other roles. Specifically, in this example, *EX01* is tagged for both the Order Entry Clerk (which we selected for publishing) and the Customer Data Administrator (which we did not). So, even though we only selected a specific role for publishing, this does not mean that no other roles will be included in the published output. This is a minor point, but one that is worth bearing in mind if you have content that is tagged for multiple roles, and something that you may need to explain to your users if they are expecting to see only content for their role (true role-based training).

Thinking beyond roles

Roles are really nothing more than *tags*. True, the tags will typically correspond to various (business) roles, but this does not necessarily have to be the case. Conceptually, this functionality is simply providing keywords on which to filter. In practice, these keywords could be the type of content, the product (or version of the product) to which the content applies, and so on. From an *information design* perspective, it is often worth looking for other opportunities to use this functionality. That said, the functionality is called *Roles*, and the option in the player is labeled "My Roles". Should you choose to co-opt this functionality for other purposes (say, to tag content as being applicable to specific releases of a product) you should also consider configuring this label and the associated dialog boxes, help topics, and so on, to match your new purpose.

Jump-in Points

Most of the time, you will want your trainees to start the playback of a simulation at the beginning, and work their way through it to the end. However, there may be cases where you want to provide the flexibility to start a simulation at some other point. For example, say you have a task that consists of three separate stages. You could allow the simulation to be started from the beginning of any of these stages. Granted, during the initial training you will probably want your trainees to go through the entire exercise, but consider the case where the user has completed training and is now performing their actual job. They remember how to carry out the first two stages of the task, but need a reminder on the last part. They would find it very frustrating if they had to run through the first two-thirds of the simulation just to get to the stage with which they need help. UPK provides a solution to this problem in the form of jump-in points.

A **jump-in point** is little more than label defined for a specific Frame in a Topic. The trainee can see defined jump-in points in the Player, and can select a jump-in point to start the playback of the Topic from the Frame to which this label has been assigned.

The advantage of jump-in points is that they take very little time or effort to set up. You just enter the label on the relevant Frame in the *Topic Editor*, and UPK does the rest. The disadvantage is that they are not immediately visible in the Player. Unless the trainee knows that they are there (or has used jump-in points before on another exercise) then they will not even know that they exist for a Topic. This is because (unfortunately) whereas the definition of roles is indicated by the presence of the **My Roles** link in the Player, the "jump-in point selection button" is present all of the time, regardless of whether jump-in points have actually been defined for the Topic or not. This means that if you use jump-in points, you will need to educate your trainees in what they are and where to find them. And if you use jump-in points for *some* exercises, then you should consider using them for *most* (if not *all*) of your exercises. If trainees check for jump-in points and find that they have not been defined in the majority of cases, then they will stop checking for them. And if that happens, you may as well not define them at all.

Defining jump-in points

By way of an example, we will add some jump-in points to the exercise that we have been working on throughout this book. You will recall that the exercise takes the trainees through three separate tabbed pages within the same transaction. We will add jump-in points to each of these pages.

To define jump-in points in a Topic, carry out the following steps:

1. Open up the Topic for which you want to define jump-in points.
2. Select the Frame to which you want to add a jump-in point (that is, the Frame to which the trainee should be able to jump).
3. Enter the text for the jump-in point in the **Jump-in point** field located on the far left of the *Editing* toolbar. This is the text that will be displayed in the jump-in list in the Player, so you should use a text that will make sense to the trainees. Note that you are limited to only 39 characters, so your text should be concise and to the point.
4. Repeat Steps 2 and 3 for all additional jump-in points that you want to create.
5. Save your Topic and exit from the *Topic Editor*.

Note that you can only specify a jump-in point for an Action Frame. You cannot provide a jump-in point for a Decision Frame or an Explanation Frame. (Or for the Start or End frames, although that wouldn't make any sense, anyway...)

The following screenshot shows a jump-in point label for our sample exercise.

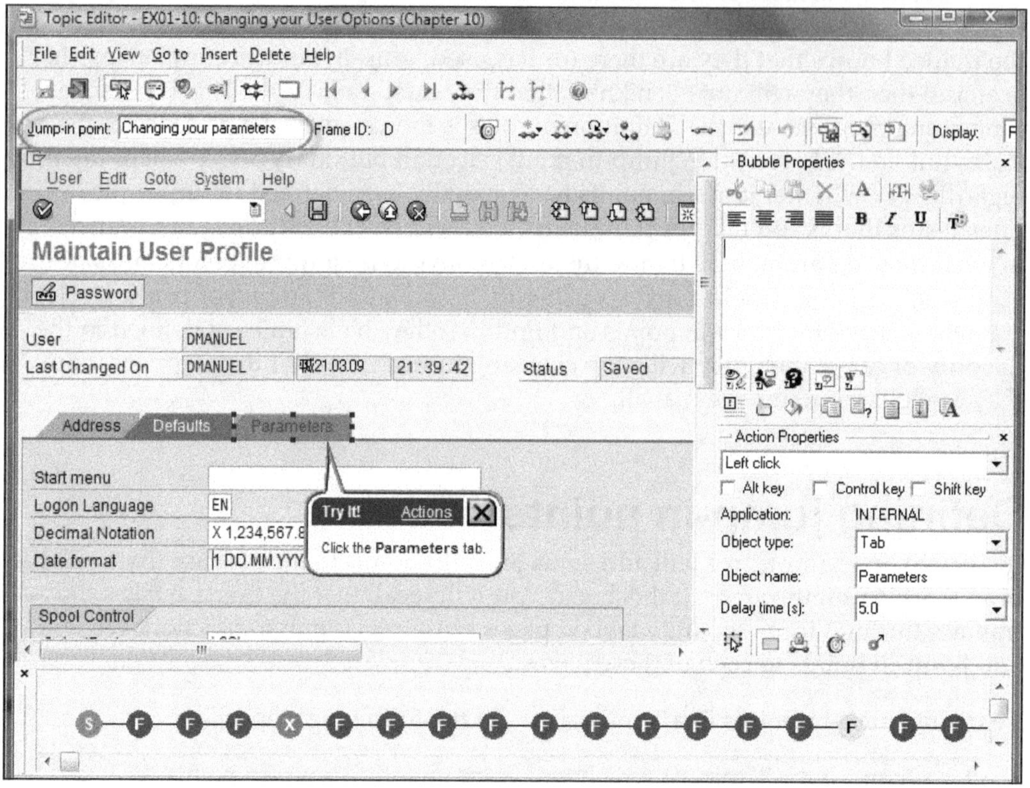

Selecting jump-in points in the Player

Let's now look at how the jump-in points appear in the Player. In the following screenshot, we have defined three jump-in points for our exercise: one for each of the tabbed pages.

Once the trainee clicks on the jump-in button (which is the small, downward-facing arrow on the right of the "mode" button), a drop-down menu is displayed, showing the available jump-in points (plus a standard "Beginning of topic" jump-in point, which is available whether you have defined any other jump-in points or not). The following screenshot shows this drop-down menu for our sample exercise:

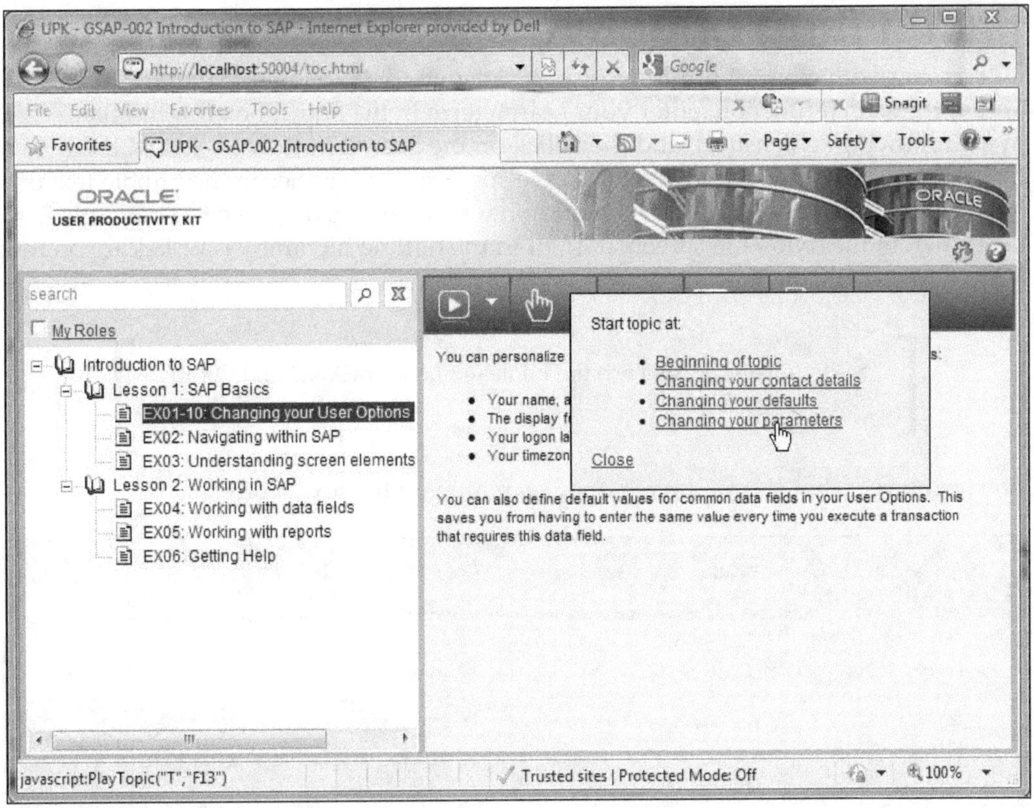

The trainee simply clicks on a jump-in point (actually, a link) and the Player immediately jumps to the Frame within the Topic to which that jump-in point relates.

How do jump-in points work?

For the technically-minded, there is one more thing of interest here. In the example above, we are pointing to the second of our jump-in points (**Changing your defaults**). If you look in the lower-left corner of the browser window, you will see the actual hyperlink for this link. This is `Javascript:PlayTopic("T","F13")`. Here, the `"T"` means **Try It!**, because this is the mode for which we selected the jump-in point. The `"F13"` is a reference to the specific Frame that the Player should jump to (Frame **13**, in this case). The Frame ID of this Frame (which you can see in the previous screenshot of the *Topic Editor*) is **D**, which is the hexadecimal value of **13**. Okay, so maybe it wasn't that interesting, but this could come in useful if you want to start creating your own hyperlinks to the middle of your exercises...

Facilitating effective searches

UPK comes with a built-in full-text search function that is available in the Player. To use the search function, enter your search term in the *Search* box (highlighted in the following screenshot), and then click on the **Search** button ( ). UPK then displays a list of all Topics that contain the specified text (either in the bubble text or an attached Web Page). You can choose to have the results displayed as a simple list (as shown in the following screenshot), or in the outline hierarchy (by clicking on the **View filtered outline** link).

> You can also use the Boolean operators AND and OR in the *Search* box.

The next screenshot shows the result of searching on the text **Profile**:

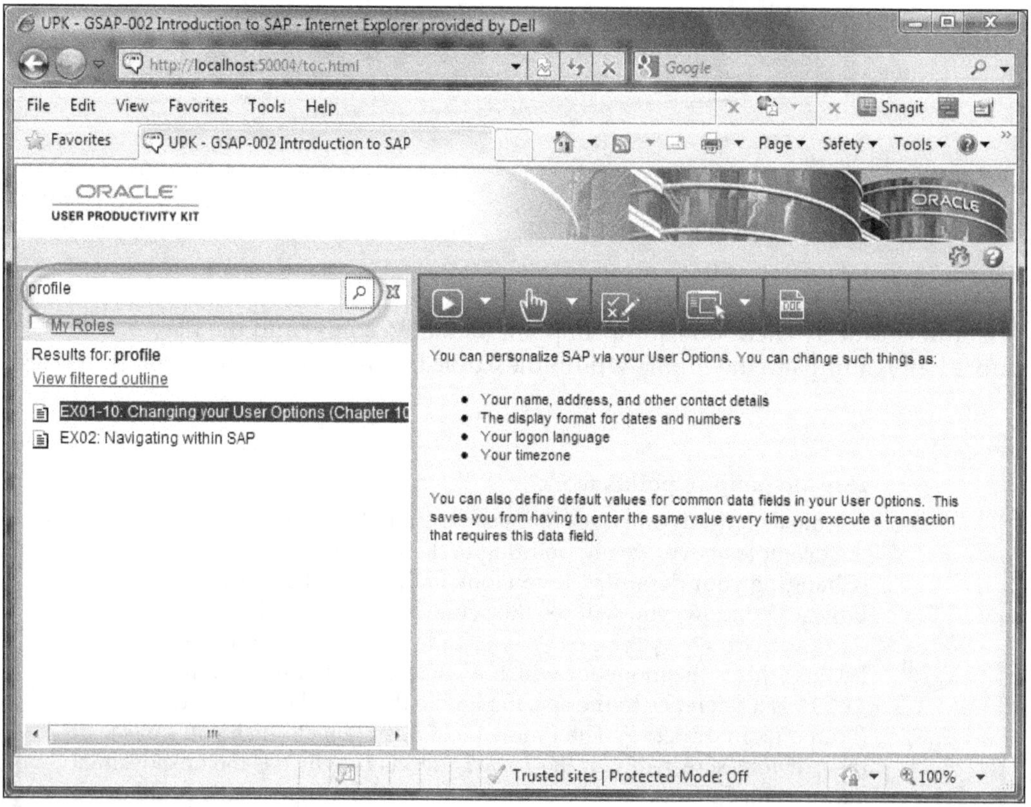

To clear the search results and return to the full Outline, simply click on the **Clear Search** button ( ).

Although the availability of a built-in search function that you (as a developer) don't need to set up, or otherwise configure, sounds like a great thing, it's not actually that useful. True, UPK will identify all of the Topics that contain the search term, but that is as far as it goes. UPK does not highlight, or otherwise identify, the search term in the Topic itself, or even identify the specific Frame(s) on which the text was found. So, the trainee could still have to hunt for the actual location of the search text.

Using Keywords

As stated above, UPK allows trainees to locate Topics that contain a specified text string within any of the Topics. It also provides the capability to locate Topics based on a text string that does not appear in the Topic. This actually makes more sense than you'd think. This functionality lets you assign *keywords* to Topics, and then these keywords are included in the list of the things that UPK will search when the trainee uses the Search function. So, if you assign a keyword of "XYZ" to a Topic that does not otherwise include the text "XYZ", then if the trainee searches for this text, that Topic will be identified and listed in the search results.

Still not convinced that this is useful? Consider the following possibilities:

- You have developed a generic Topic explaining how to run a report. You can specify the report names as keywords for this Topic so that users are directed to this Topic when they search on the report name.
- You have a Topic for a customized version of a standard transaction. You can specify the standard transaction as a keyword for this Topic so that if users search for the standard transaction they will be directed to the Topic for the customized version.
- You want to allow users to search on old terminology that is no longer used.
- And so on.

Assigning Keywords to a Topic

As an example, we will add a keyword to our sample exercise. We will add the word "localization" as a keyword, so that if a trainee is searching for details of how to localize their number display formats, they will find our exercise.

To define keywords for a Topic, carry out the following steps:

1. In the Library, select the Topic for which you want to define the keywords.
2. Make sure that the **Properties** pane is displayed, as shown in the following screenshot.
3. Expand the **General** category.
4. In the **Keywords** field, enter your keyword(s). In our example, we will enter "localization", as shown in the following screenshot:

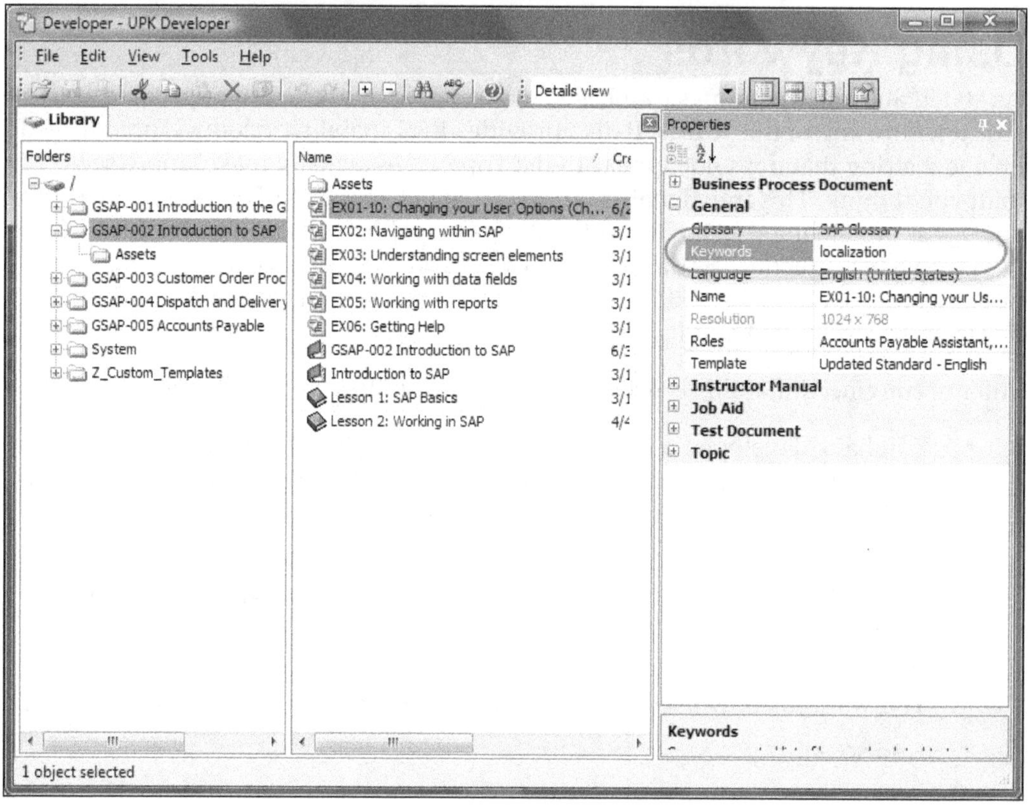

You can enter multiple keywords, separated by commas. There is a 1,024 character limit on the total length of the **Keywords** field, but this will normally be sufficient to meet most requirements.

Let's prove that this works by going to the Player and searching for the text "localization". The result is shown in the following screenshot, which proves that it is indeed working as expected.

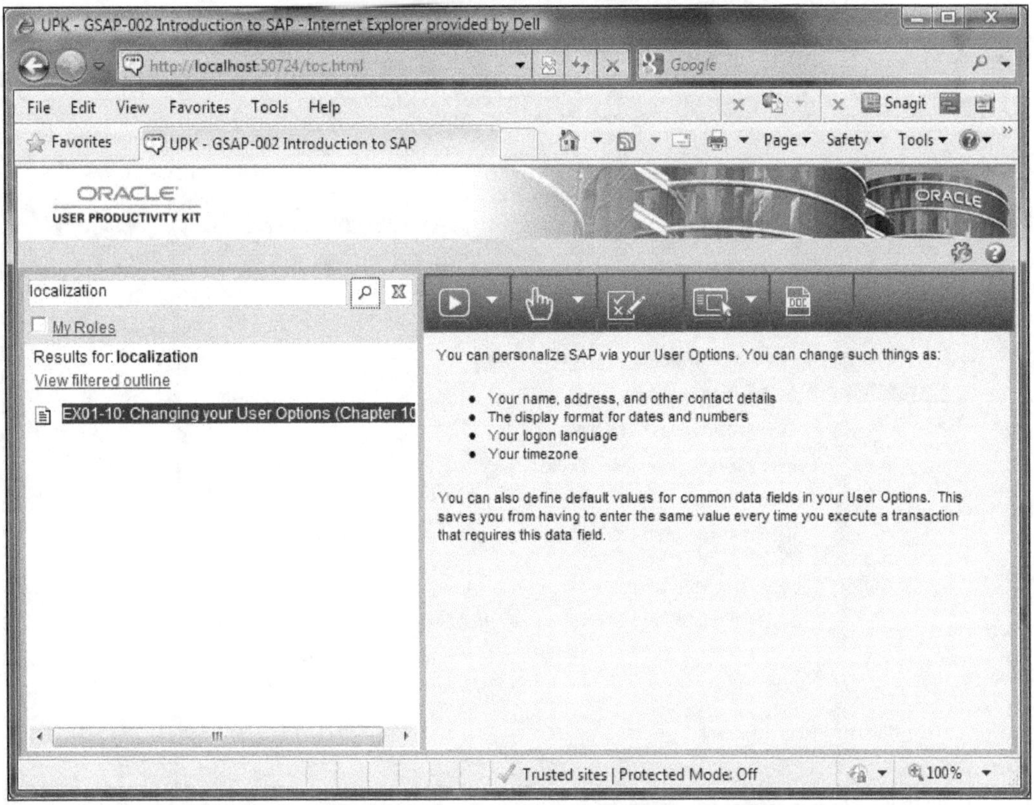

Note that you can also specify keywords for outline elements (Modules and Sections), although in this case the search results will include only the outline elements (showing any concepts defined for them), and not the Topics within these outline elements.

Allowing trainees to change their Player options

As described in Chapter 6 *Publishing Content*, when you publish to a Player package, there are several options that you can set to control the trainee's interaction with UPK. This includes such things as the color of the marquee around the action area, the key combination for advancing in *Do It!* mode, and so on.

Within the Player, there are a number of options that the trainee can configure (in addition to selecting their role(s), as explained previously). These are accessed by clicking on the **Preferences** button (⚙) in the Player. This will display the **Interface Options** dialog box, as shown below:

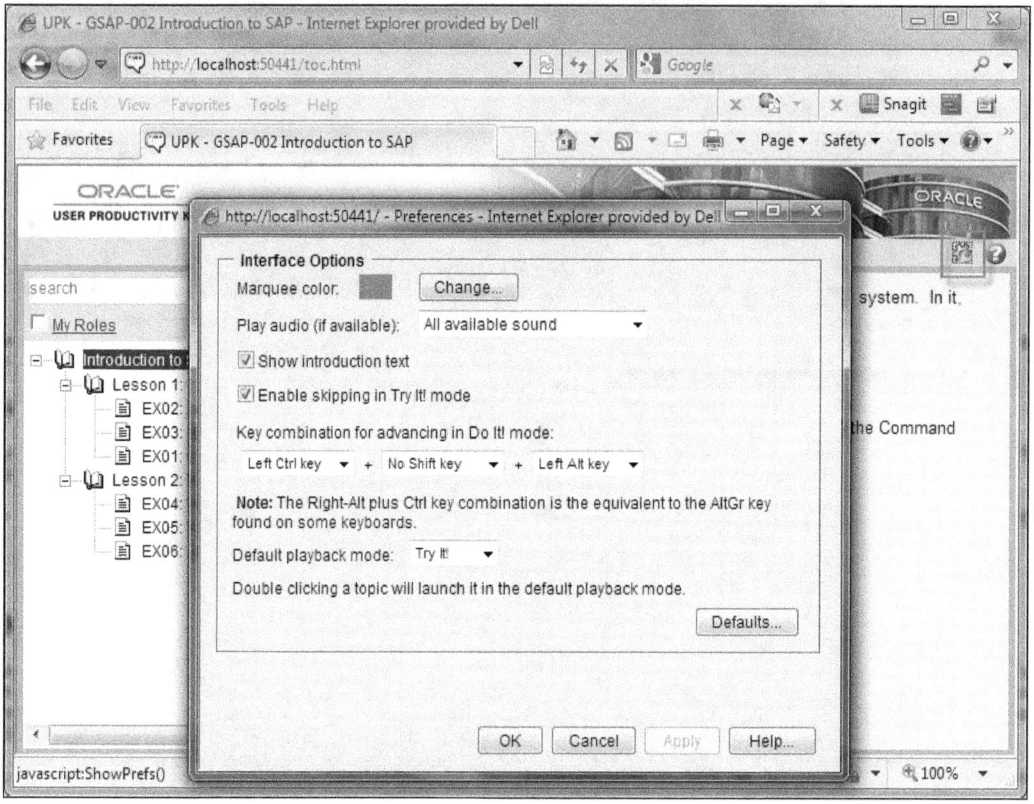

You will notice that all of these options are available to the developer, when publishing, in the **Presentation Options** for the Player output format (see Chapter 6, *Publishing Content*). When the developer sets them, they are default values; the trainee can change any of them from these default values, via the **Interface Options** dialog box above.

However, the options available to the developer include one option that is not available to the trainees. This is **Enable users to change their Player preferences**. If this option is deselected, then the **Preferences** button (⚙) will not be available to trainees in the Player, and therefore the trainees will not be able to change any of these options. Why would you want to deny the users the ability to perform this level of personalization? Because there is one very contentious option: **Enable skipping in Try It! mode**.

If the **Enable skipping in Try It! mode** option is selected, then trainees will be able to advance from one screen to the next in *Try It!* mode simply by pressing the *Enter* key on their keyboard. Specifically, they will not be required to carry out the action itself. This means that they do not need to *try* in *Try It!* mode, which reduces this mode to a kind of "manual advance" *See It!* mode. This isn't exactly teaching the trainees. I therefore always recommend disabling this option (after you, the developer, have done all of your testing—it is a useful option for being able to quickly run through a simulation).

However, it is not possible to disable only this one option; it is necessary to disable the complete ability to change a trainee's preferences in the Player. It is not even enough to deselect this option but select the **Enable users to change their Player preferences** option in the **Presentation Options** of the Publisher, because the Publisher settings are just *defaults*, and if the **Enable users to change their Player preferences** option is still selected, the trainees can simply go to their **Preferences** in the Player and select the **Enable skipping in Try It! mode** option again. So unfortunately the choice is all-or-nothing, and given that most of the other options are harmless (being able to change them adds no real *value)*, I'd recommend choosing nothing.

> It is actually possible to remove a single option from the *Preferences* in the Player, but this involves digging around under the hood of UPK. If you want to try it, refer to Chapter 11, *Configuring UPK*.

Providing training on the Player

Most of the improvements that we have made to our simulations in the preceding chapters of this book are largely intuitive to the users. The improvements that we have discussed in *this* chapter are less intuitive. If you choose to add value by using these less-intuitive features, you may want to consider providing training on the use of the Player. You may choose to do this anyway (intuitive features or not), but the use of jump-in points, keywords, and roles is a much stronger driver for the need for training on the UPK Player itself.

What to explain

Should you choose to train your trainees on the use of the Player, exactly what you need to teach the trainees will depend on the functionality that you use. A list of things that you should consider training on is given ahead:

- *See It!* mode: How to pause it and resume it
- *Try It!* mode: How to go back to the previous step, restart playback, and so on
- *Know It?* mode: Remediation levels; how to move the bubble if it is obscuring required information
- *Do It!* Mode: How to manually advance
- Role filtering: How to select roles, and activate/deactivate role filtering
- The Search function: Boolean operators; switching between search results and the full Outline
- Keywords
- Jump-in points
- In-application context-sensitive help: How to return to the full Outline

How to train on the Player

There are a number of ways that you can provide training on the Player. Some of these options are described below. There are certainly other options—this list is really just to get you thinking.

Explain the UPK Player during classroom training

UPK exercises can be used for stand-alone "computer-based training" (or "self-paced learning" as current fashion dictates), especially if they are developed to the standards suggested by this book. However, this is often not how they are used, or at least not initially. It is increasingly common for UPK exercises to be used as an alternative to providing an actual training system. In this way, they are seen as a direct replacement for the exercises that would normally be carried out in a training system during classroom-based training.

Assuming that this is the case, it is advisable to provide some brief training (perhaps in the form of a demonstration) during this classroom training—ideally, immediately prior to the trainees carrying out their first exercise in UPK. This has the distinct advantage that you can explain all of the relevant bells and whistles covered in this chapter and the last, and also affords you the opportunity to gauge the trainee's understanding of the Player, and help them through their first exercise (or two) if necessary.

Conduct a UPK "show-and-tell"

If classroom-based training will not be used, then another alternative is to conduct some kind of a "show-and-tell" session for the trainees, prior to them actually using UPK. This could be done in person (perhaps during "site visits" where you are explaining the overall training approach, or during team meetings or employee forums), or remotely by using NetMeeting, WebEx, Centra Symposium, or a similar technology. The difficulty here is making sure that all of the trainees attend this session. If you cannot enforce this, then try to at least get some key personnel (such as local trainers, "power users", or other knowledgeable "go-to" people) to attend, and then make sure that the trainees know that they can get assistance from these key people, should they need it.

Create a UPK simulation on using the UPK Player

Inevitably, some bright spark will say "Hey! Here's a crazy idea—why don't we use UPK to *train* on UPK!". That's right; it's a crazy idea. Think about it—to be able to run the simulation on using the Player, the user needs to know how to use the Player, and to know that they need to run the simulation on using the Player, but to be able to do that... etc., etc., in ever decreasing circles. That said, in some circumstances, this may be the only option. In this case, consider the carrying out the following steps:

1. Create a simulation on using the UPK Player, call it "Double-click on me second", and have this in its own Module, called "Double-click on me first".
2. Include a Web Page in the *Concepts* pane for the Module that also tells them to double-click on the Module and then double-click on the Topic. Give this a nice, bright background, and a big heading of "READ ME FIRST".
3. In the Topic itself, hide the Action Areas on all Frames. The action areas will still appear on the example that you walk them through (that is, the recording that you play back when describing the UPK Player simulation), and having two sets of Action Area would be confusing.
4. Publish the simulation in *See It!* mode only.

Do nothing

Really. Doing nothing is a valid option. The UPK Player does come with perfectly adequate built-in help. And if you find this to be inadequate, you can always provide your own specific help. If your users are in any way computer literate they should be able to work their way through the on-line help. In fact, if your users have mobile phones, then their phones are quite likely more difficult to use than the UPK Player, and if they can use their phones, they can probably use the Player.

That said, if you are expecting your users to just use the Player help, you probably want to provide some text in the *Concept* pane of the first outline element in the Player (as this is the first thing that the user will see when they start the Player) to direct them to the Player help.

Summary

There are a number of things that you can do to provide your trainees with a little control over the way that they interact with the Player, and to *personalize* their "learning experience". This includes:

- Providing the ability to filter content in the Player based on the trainee's role
- Providing jump-in points so that trainees can start the playback of a simulation from a number of different points
- Using keywords to provide a more effective search facility

Although providing these things will undoubtedly improve the usefulness of your training, and increase the trainees' satisfaction, they are not things that are immediately obvious (or intuitive) to the trainees, who may be blithely ignorant to the fact that they exist, despite the hours that you painstakingly put into providing them. You may therefore want to consider providing some form of training on the UPK Player to your trainees, if you provide these functions.

11

Incorporating Sound into Your Topics

In this chapter, we will look at a less-used feature of UPK: Sound. UPK provides the ability to incorporate sound recordings into your Topics. The purpose of this is to allow you to record speech for your texts (for both Template Texts and Custom Texts), so that trainees can hear this when they play the simulation. This may be an important consideration for Section 502, accessibility compliance.

You may recall from Chapter 4, *Editing a Topic*, that UPK builds up the Template Text for a Frame out of several smaller pieces of text (one for the Action, one for the Object Type, and so on). UPK builds the sound that is played for a Frame in exactly the same way. In fact, UPK has a sound file for each of the pieces of text, and each sound file must be recorded separately. Alternatively, you can dispense with the template structure and simply record a single sound file for the entire Frame.

Displaying sound properties for a Frame

To display the sound properties for a Frame, carry out the following steps:

1. Open the Topic for which you want to display the sound properties.
2. In the *Frame Navigation* pane, click on the Frame for which you want to display the sound properties.

3. Click on the **Sound Properties** button (🔘) on the *Standard* toolbar (see **(1)** in the following screenshot). The **Sound Properties** pane is displayed, as shown in the next screenshot:

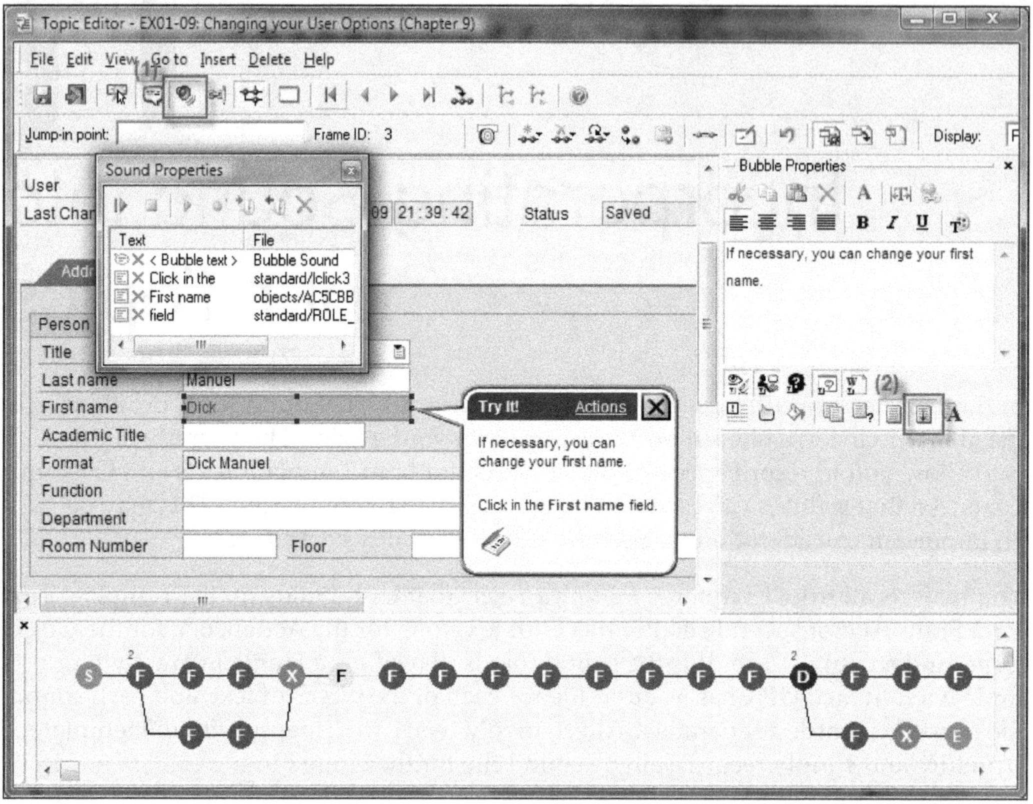

In the previous screenshot, you can also see the Frame to which the *Sound Properties* relates, and the Template Text (shown in the Bubble). Here, it is very easy to see the correlation between the sound files and the corresponding text. The **Text** column in the **Sound Properties** pane shows the template text, and the **File** column shows the expected location of the sound file. (If you want to see where UPK defines which sound file is used in each case, see the description of the `template.xml` file in Chapter 11, *Customizing UPK*.)

> **What is the <Bubble text> entry for?**
>
> The **<Bubble text>** sound file is for any Custom Text that you provide. UPK will automatically include this entry for every Frame, regardless of whether any Custom Text has actually been defined for the Frame.
>
> In the previous example, the **<Bubble text>** sound file is listed first, and will therefore be played before any of the other sound files during playback. This is because the Custom Text is displayed before the Template Text in the Bubble - the **Show custom text first** button () in the **Bubble Properties** pane is selected (see **(2)** in the previous screenshot). This is the default option. If you choose to display the Custom Text *after* the Template Text (by deselecting the **Show custom text first** button) then the **<Bubble text>** sound file will be listed *last* in the **Sound Properties** pane.

On the far left of the **Text** column in the **Sound Properties** pane is a set of two icons. The first of these identifies the type of text that the sound file is for, as follows:

- **Template text**: This sound file relates to an element of the Template Text.
- **Custom text**: This sound file can be used to provide sound for any Custom Text.

The second icon indicates whether UPK can find the sound file, as follows:

- × **Missing sound file**: UPK cannot find the file in the Library (for Template Text), or attached to the Topic (for Custom Text). This may not necessarily be a *problem*, depending on whether you want to use the sound file specified.
- ✓ **Existing sound file**: The sound file exists and can be played.

As we can see from the previous screenshot, none of the sound files can be found. This is not unusual; UPK does not ship with sound files. In addition, the *Bubble Sound* will never exist initially. Let's remedy this situation by recording some sounds for our template text.

Setting up your sound options

There are two ways to attach sound files to a Frame. You can either import existing sound files, or you can record your own from within the *Topic Editor* itself. If you want to record your own sound file, then you first need to tell UPK what software you will use to do this.

To specify a sound recorder, carry out the steps described below:

1. From the *Developer* main screen, select menu option **Tools | Options**. The **Options** dialog box is displayed.
2. Select the **Developer | General** category from the list on the left-hand side of the dialog box. The **General Developer Settings** information is displayed in the following screenshot:

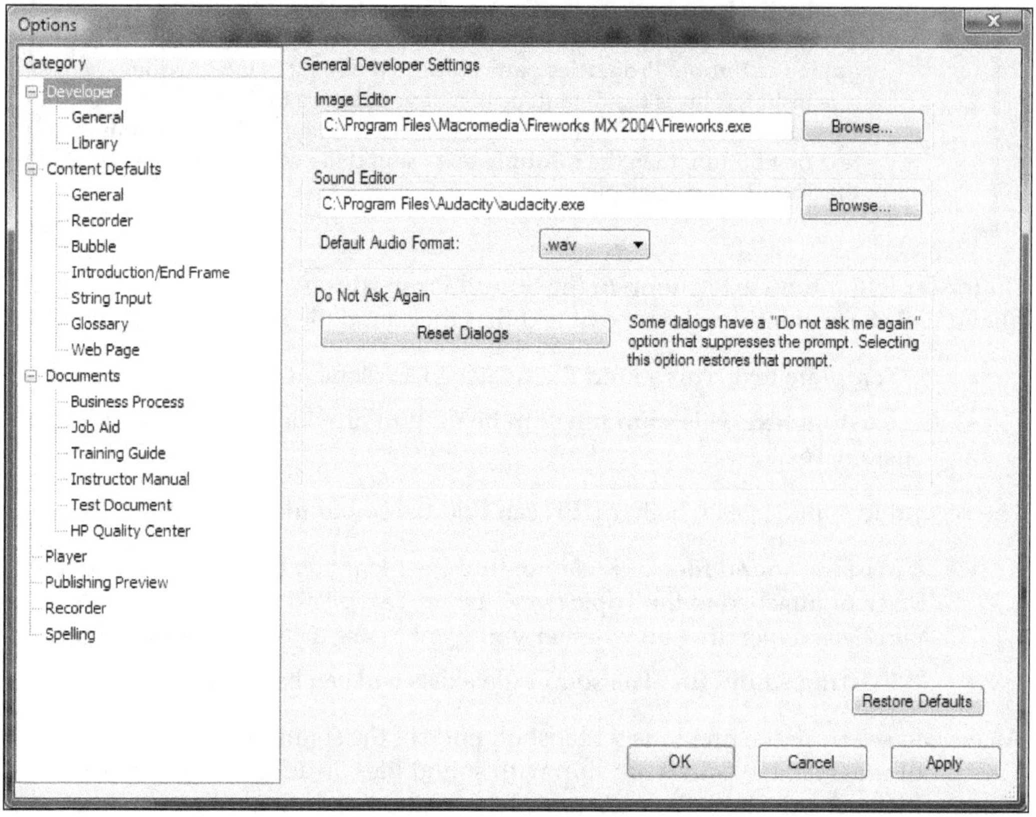

3. Use the **Browse** button to the right of the *Sound Editor* to navigate to and select the program executable for the sound recorder that you want to use. For our exercise, we are using Audacity. This is a free program available from `http://audacity.sourceforge.net`. Any application will do; I used Audacity simply because it is free, and it allows me to trim recordings, which is a useful feature that will come in handy later.

4. In the **Default Audio Format** field, select the format of the sound files that you want to record. For our exercise, we will use the `.wma` (Windows Media Audio) file format. Alternatively, you may choose to use the `.mp3` format, as the sound files are generally smaller.
5. Click on **OK** to save your options and close the dialog box.

Recording sound files for Template Text

The specific steps to be carried out when recording a sound file will vary depending on the sound recording application that you use. However, the overall process for doing this within UPK is broadly the same. This section explains how to record a new sound file within UPK using Audacity, but the steps will be broadly similar for any other application.

To record a sound file, carry out the following steps:

1. Open the Topic to which you want to add sound in the *Topic Editor*.
2. In the *Frame Navigation* pane, click on the Frame to which you want to add sound.
3. Make sure that the *Sound Properties* pane is displayed.
4. Click on the entry in the *Sound Properties* pane for which you want to record sound.
5. Click on the **Record** button (●) in the *Sound Properties* pane toolbar. The sound recording application (specified in your Options) is started.
6. If you re-record an existing Template Text sound file, then the following warning message is displayed:

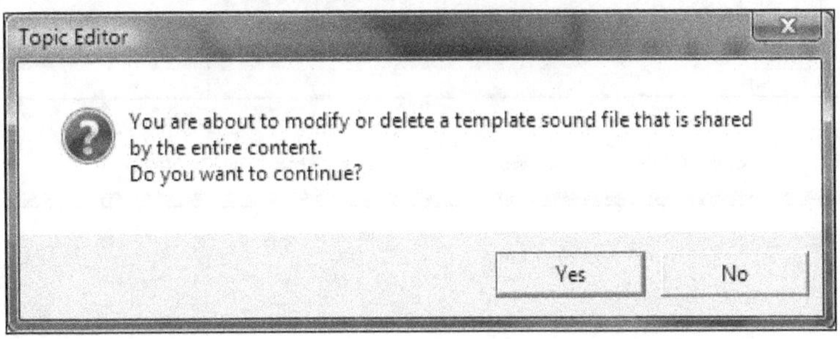

7. Click on **Yes** to confirm that this is what you want to do.

8. Within your sound recording application, record the sound file. Most sound recording applications (and Audacity is no exception) have a **Start Recording** button, and a **Stop Recording** button that you can use.
9. You should try to start and stop *immediately* before and after you start talking, to avoid too much of a lag between the different sound files when the entire bubble text is played back.

> **Ensuring a natural transition between sound files**
>
> If your sound recording software supports it, record yourself reading the entire bubble text, and then trim the recorded sound file to include only the part that relates to the specific text that you want to capture. The back-to-back playback of the files will then be seamless (although you'll need to check compatibility with other Frames, if the sound files are used in multiple places).

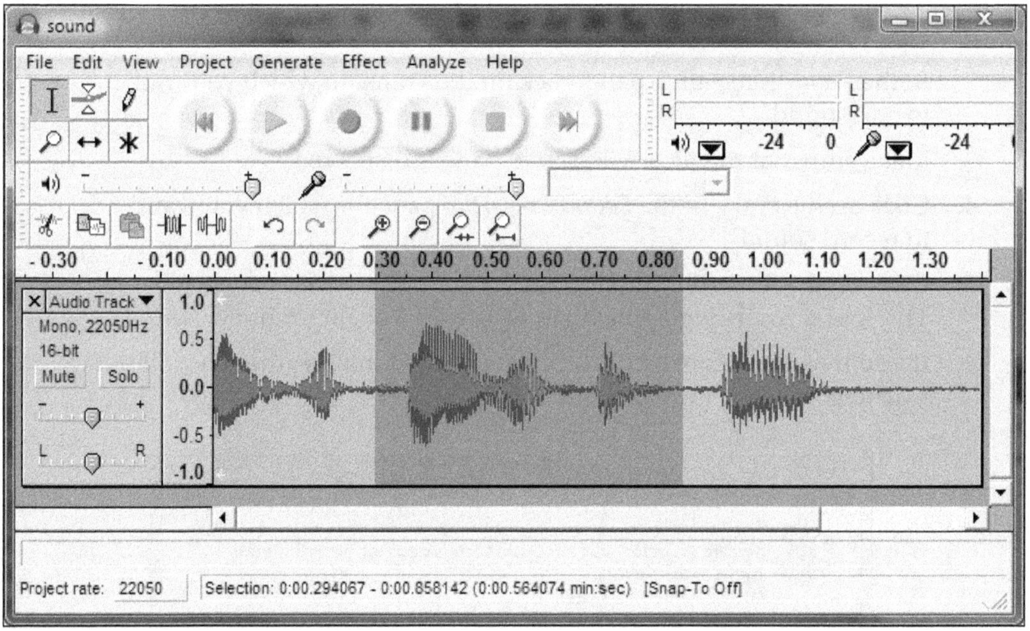

> The previous screenshot shows a recording of a complete sentence with the section for the required text being marked ready for trimming (from around 0.3 seconds in, to 0.85 seconds in):

10. When you stop recording, you will most likely be prompted to save the resulting file to your PC. Do not worry too much about this file. UPK will take its own copy of the sound file, as we shall see ahead. You therefore don't need the intermediate copy saved from within the sound recording application. You can name it anything, and save it anywhere; UPK will still find it, because UPK launched the sound recorder, and asked it to return the created file.
11. Close the sound recording application. You are returned to the *Topic Editor*. The sound file will now be marked with a green check-mark to indicate that it exists.

After recording sound files for all of the Template Text components of our Bubble, the **Sound Properties** now looks like the example shown in the next screenshot:

If you want to play back an individual sound file, click on the **Play** button () in the *Sound Properties* toolbar. If you want to play back all of the sound files in the order listed, so that you hear them as the trainee will hear them, click on the **Play all** button (). To stop the playback, click on the **Stop** button ().

Locating the sound files in the Library

As stated above, UPK will take a copy of the sound files and store them in the Library. You can find these files in the `System\Templates\{language}\Sound` folder (where `{language}` is the code for your language) as shown in the following screenshot:

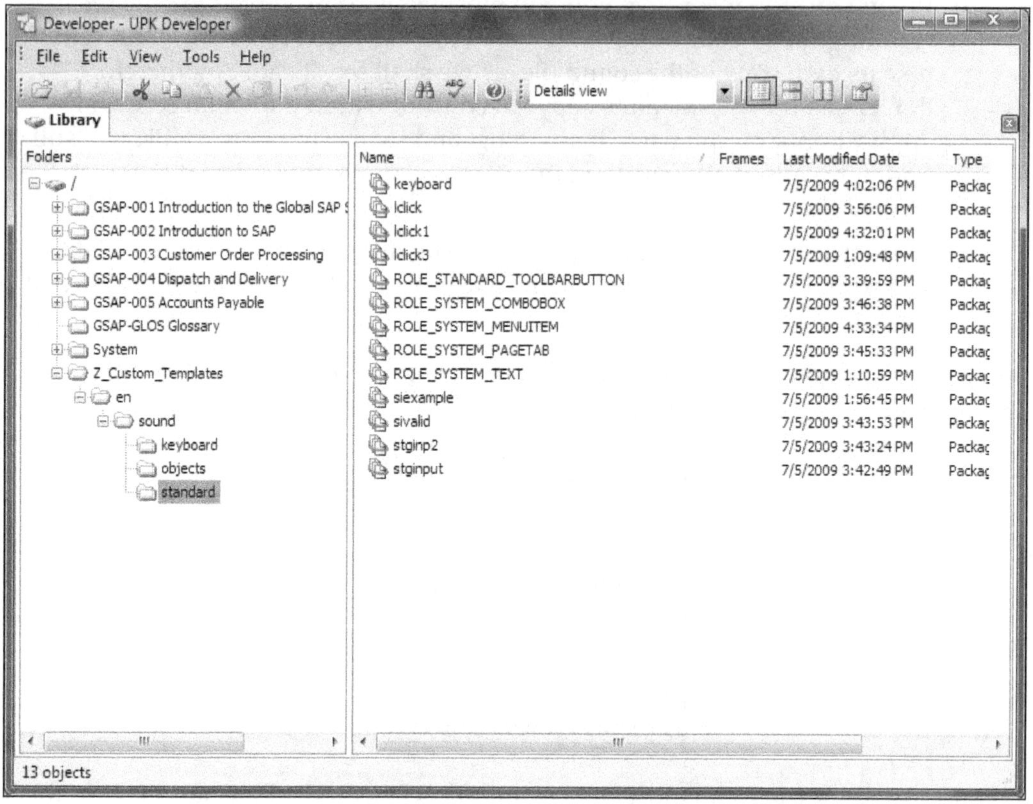

[Note that in this example we have recorded sound for our own custom template so as not to interfere with the standard templates.]

You will see that there are three folders: `keyboard`, `objects`, and `standard`. The `keyboard` folder contains the sound files for keyboard actions, the `objects` folder contains the sound files for the object names and string input (effectively, the things that UPK cannot identify by default), and the `standard` folder contains the sound files for the Template Texts. Each folder contains one or more Packages. If you open up the Package file, then you will see the sound file itself, as shown in the next screenshot:

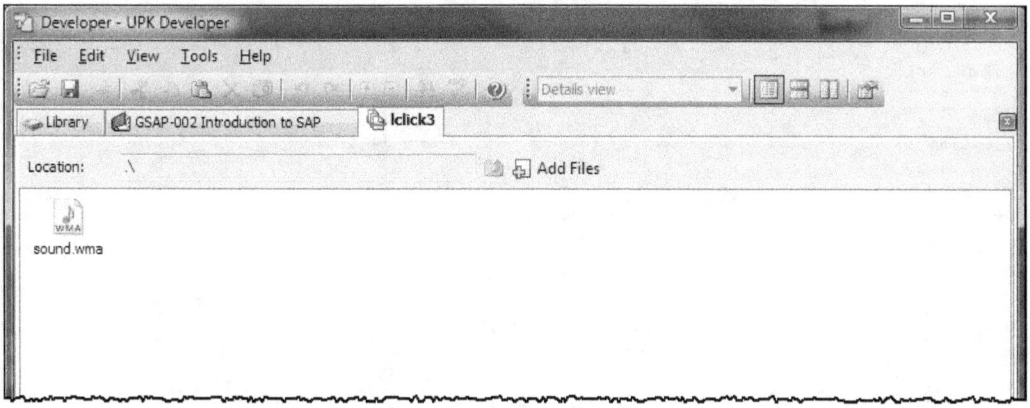

Here, we have opened the **lckick3** Package. You can see that it contains a single file, called `sound.wma` (the file type may be different depending on your settings).

> As the template text sound files are simply stored in Packages in the Library, and you (probably) have access to these, you can, in theory, create these Packages yourself and drag and drop external sound files directly into the Packages. However, you need to be extremely careful about the Package names, and must ensure that the actual sound file is always called `sound.wma` (or the appropriate file type, depending on your preferences). Unless you have a very good reason for doing otherwise, it is recommended that you always import external sound files as described ahead, instead of editing the sound Packages directly.

The fact that the sound files are stored in the Templates folder is significant. It means that the sound files are not tied to the specific Frame for which you recorded them. We can confirm this by clicking on another Frame within the same exercise (that uses at least some of the same objects). The example below shows the **Sound Properties** pane for the next Frame in our sample exercise (Frame 4, if you're following along):

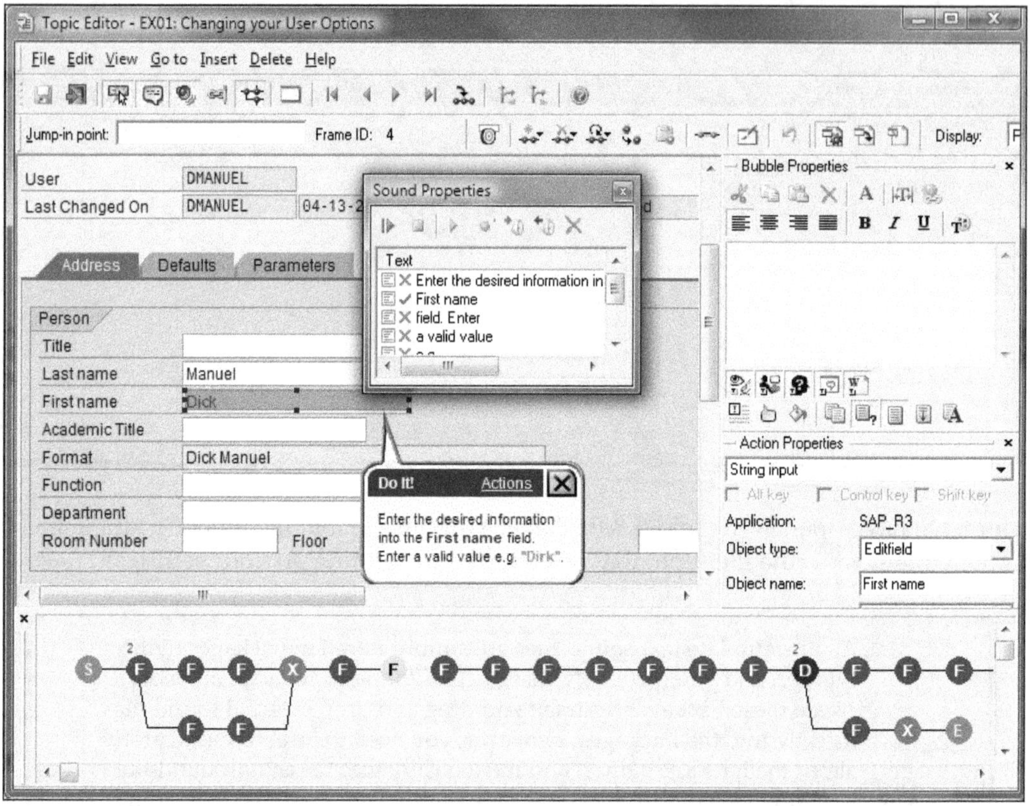

Here, you can see that one of the sound properties files has been found. This is the sound file for the **First name** object. The reason that it has been found is because we recorded it for the *previous* Frame, and it now exists in the Library. In fact, the sound files aren't only shared across Frames within the same Topic, they are common to all Topics within the Library. The advantage of this is that you only need to record the sound files once. As you progress through recording sound files for your topics, you will find that you are recording successively fewer and fewer files for each Topic. This is because you are only recording sound files for the objects that are being newly-introduced for the Topic.

Recording custom text sound files

Once you have recorded the sound files for all of the Template Texts, the Object Names and Object Types, and any string input, you will still be missing something. You will be missing the sound files for any Custom Text that you have entered into your Topic. You should also record sound files for these. How to do this is exactly the same as for Template Text sound files, but before you start recording sound for your Custom Text, consider the following.

If you play back all of the sound files for a Frame, you will probably notice that the playback is somewhat stilted. (This is impossible to demonstrate in print, but if you download and import the `.odarc` file containing the sample exercises for this book from the Packt web site, you can hear the results.) This is because what you are hearing is a succession of separate files, quite possibly recorded at separate times. It is never going to sound entirely *natural*. The problem will be further exacerbated if you have multiple developers working on content - which is almost inevitable over time. Having different people providing the speech for different elements will never sound professional (especially if you have both sexes, a handful of regional accents, or worse, different nationalities). However, recent e-learning wisdom has it that having sound *at all* is more important than having *professional* sound.

As an alternative, consider simply removing all of the template sound files and simply recording a single sound file for the entire frame. Of course, this is more work (than simply relying on sound files for Template Text, which can be re-used), but if you are in the habit of providing Custom Text anyway (which you should be, if you follow the advice in Chapter 9, *Adding Value to Your Topics*) then you will have to record a sound file for that anyway, so you may as well just record everything in one go, and at least have a consistent voice for it. The advantage to this is that you are guaranteed that you will have the same person recording the speech for both the Template Text and Custom Text. (An example of this is provided for Frame 4 in the sample exercise for this chapter, available from the Packt web site.)

An additional consideration is that there is not really any compelling reason why your recorded speech has to be an exact reading of the template text and/or custom text. You could record a more detailed explanation. You could even insert sound captured from a classroom-based demonstration of the exercise.

To record sound files for your custom text, carry out the same steps as described in *Recording sound files for template text,* above. If you want to use only the sound file for your Custom Text (and not the Template Text sound files), then carry out the steps described below:

1. In the **Bubble Properties** pane, click on the **Insert template text as custom text** button ( ) to copy any Template Text into the Custom Text field. This is necessary because if we continue to use the Template Text, then the template text sound files will still be used.

> **Caution:**
>
> Do *not* remove the existing Template Text sound files by clicking on the **Delete** button on the Sound Properties toolbar. If you do this, you will delete the sound files form your Library. For more details refer to *Deleting sound files,* ahead.

2. Navigate away from the current Frame, and then back to it, to refresh the **Sound Properties** pane (for some reason it does not automatically refresh). You will see that the **Sound Properties** now contains only the **<Bubble text>** sound file, as shown in the following screenshot:

3. Record your new sound file as described in *Recording sound files for Template Text,* above.

Note that the Custom Text sound files are not stored in the Library. They are stored within UPK's internal database, along with the Topic itself. This means that Custom Text sound files are unique to the Frame for which they were recorded. This is both good and bad. It is good in that there is no (or at least less) danger of the Custom Text sound files being accidentally deleted. However, it is bad in that it is more difficult to re-use sound files across Frames or Topics. If you do want to re-use custom text sound files, then you need to export and import them, as described in the following section *Importing and exporting sound files.*

Importing and exporting sound files

In addition to recording sound files from within the Topic Editor, you can also create sound files outside of UPK, and then import these into the Topic Editor. There are some good reasons for doing so (apart from the fact that recording from within UPK just doesn't seem to work with some software and/or hardware set-ups). The most significant of these is that you may choose to use external "talent" to record all of your sound files. Perhaps you don't personally have the most engaging voice (as you will see if you play the sample exercise for this chapter, I include myself as one of those); perhaps you have someone within your organization who sounds like Richard Burton or Don LaFontaine (now *that* would make for an interesting exercise!); or perhaps you can afford to hire a professional.

Alternatively, you may already have sound files that you want to use. Perhaps these are sound files from another Library, or a previous installation of UPK (or OnDemand, or even RWD UPerform before you "saw the light" and defected to UPK...). Or, you may have recorded a classroom demonstration of the exercise and want to use the sound files extracted from this in your recording.

Yet another possibility is that you may have already recorded sound files for one Topic (or Frame), and want to re-use these sound files in other Topics or Frames. In this case, you can export the sound files from the original Frame, and then import them into your new Frame.

For our sample exercise, suppose that we have recorded a sound file for our End Frame. Our exercise includes a Branch, so we have two End Frames. Rather than re-recording the Custom Text sound file for the End Frame on our Branch, we will just re-use our sound file for the End Frame on the main path. To do this, we will export it from the main path End Frame, and then import it into the Branch End Frame.

Exporting sound files

To export a sound file, preform the following steps:

1. Open the Topic from which you want to export the sound file, in the *Topic Editor*.
2. Select the Frame from which you want to export the sound file.
3. Make sure that the **Sound Properties** pane is displayed. (Click on the **Sound Properties** button () if it is not.)
4. In the **Sound Properties** pane, click on the sound file that you want to export to select it.

5. Click on the Export button () on the *Sound Properties* toolbar. The *Export Sound* dialog box is displayed as shown below. Note that this is effectively the standard Windows **Save As...** dialog box.

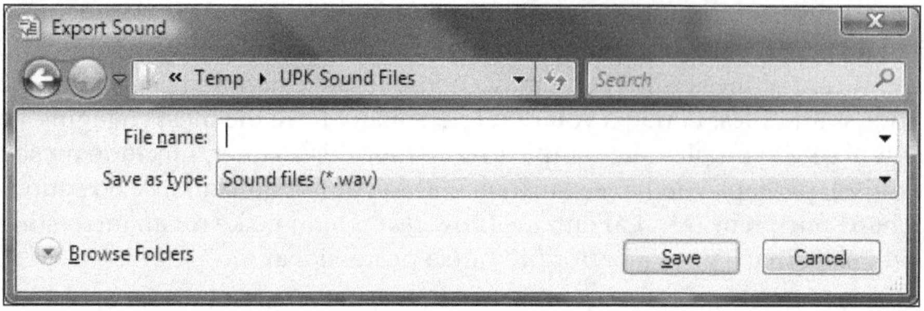

6. Navigate to the folder into which you want to save the sound file and enter a suitable name for the sound file in the **File name** field. Note that this name is not used by UPK (UPK will use its own internal identifier), but you should name it something sensible so that you can find the correct file later when you need to import it.
7. Click on **Save**.

The sound file is exported. You can now import it into another Frame, as explained in the next section, *Importing sound files*.

Importing sound files

To import an existing sound file (either one that you exported from another Frame, or a sound file that you have obtained from another source), carry out the following steps:

1. Open the Topic into which you want to import the sound file in the *Topic Editor*.
2. Select the Frame into which you want to import the sound file.
3. Make sure that the **Sound Properties** pane is displayed. (Click on the **Sound Properties** button () if it is not.)
4. In the **Sound Properties** pane, click on the entry for the sound file that you want to import to select it.
5. Click on the **Import** button () on the **Sound Properties** toolbar. The **Import Sound** dialog box is displayed, as shown below. Note that this is effectively the standard Windows **Open** dialog box.

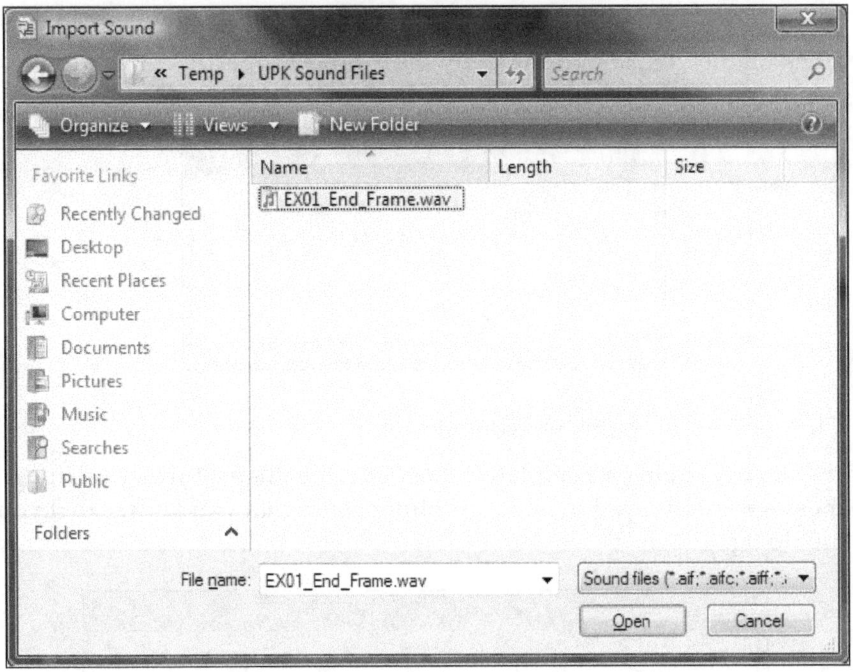

6. Navigate to and select the sound file that you want to import.
7. Click on **Open**.

The sound file is imported, and associated with the selected Frame.

Deleting sound files

If you need to delete a sound file, then you can do so as described below. In principle, however, you should never delete Template Text sound files once you have created them. This is because once you have recorded them, they become a part of the Library. Therefore, they are used by all Topics that use the template to which they are attached. Deleting Custom Text sound files is less of an issue.

To delete a sound file, carry out the steps described below:

1. Open the Topic from which you want to delete the sound file in the *Topic Editor*.
2. Select the Frame from which you want to delete the sound file.
3. Make sure that the **Sound Properties** pane is displayed (click on the **Sound Properties** button (🔘) if it is not).

4. In the *Sound Properties* pane, select the sound file that you want to delete.
5. Click on the **Delete** button (X) on the **Sound Properties** toolbar. The following confirmation message is displayed:

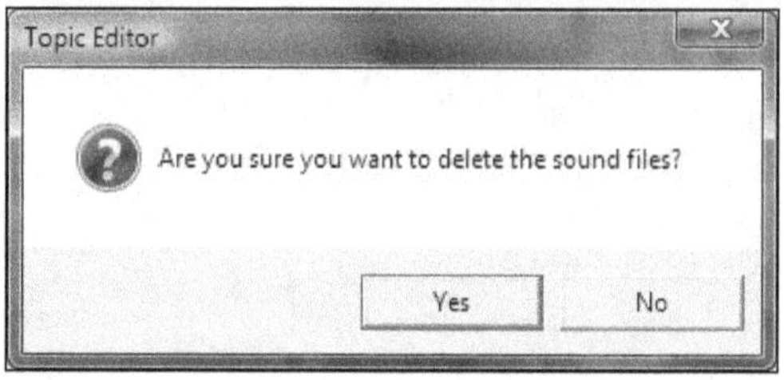

6. Click on **Yes**, to confirm the deletion.
7. If you are deleting a Template Text sound file, then a further warning message is displayed to make absolutely sure that you know what you are doing:

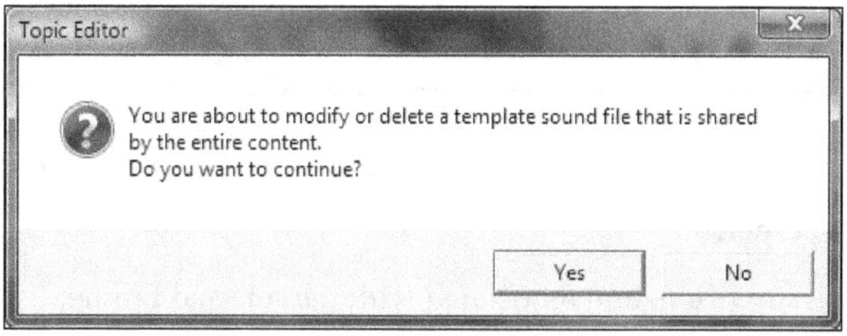

8. If you do indeed want to delete the Template Text sound file, then click on **Yes**. The sound file is deleted, and the **Sound Properties** pane will show a red cross to the left of the entry for this sound file.

Publishing sound

In order to ensure that your sound files are available to the users, there are two settings for the *Player*, *LMS Package*, and *Standalone Topic Files* deployment formats that you need to pay attention to in the *Publishing Wizard*. These are highlighted in the following screenshot:

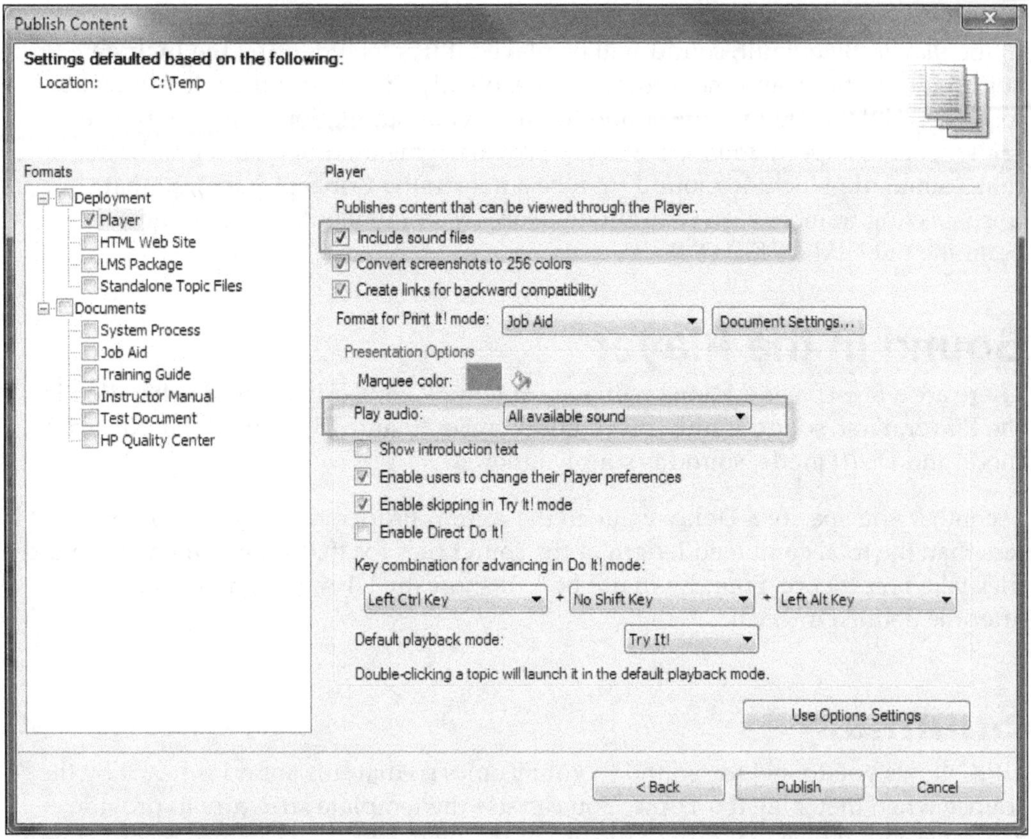

The first option is **Include sound files**. If you want the sound files to be included in the Player package, then you must select this option. This is a distinct choice, as if you have a Library of Template Text sound files recorded then these will automatically be associated with Topics that use this template, regardless of whether or not you want to use sound with the Topic. By default, this option is deselected. If you want to include sound with your Player package, then select it.

The second option is **Play audio**. Just because you have included sound doesn't mean that the trainee necessarily wants to hear it. Maybe they are in a shared office, or using a low-bandwidth network, or maybe they just don't like the sound of your voice. The trainee, therefore, has the option to turn off the sound in the player. In fact, they can choose to hear only the standard "clicks" for Actions, or hear all of your recorded sound, or hear nothing. The setting in the *Publishing Wizard* (above) sets the default value for this field in the Player.

The trainee can still override this if they want to, by changing their user preferences in the Player. By default, sound will be played if it is included (by the **Include sound files** option), and the trainee must explicitly disable it if they do not want to hear it. Unless you provide sound for all of your simulations and the trainees know what to expect, you may want to provide some kind of an alert to the fact that a simulation includes sound (maybe a note in the **Concept** pane), so that unsuspecting trainees aren't caught unaware by Don LaFontaine suddenly booming out "EXERCISE *ONE!!!*".

Sound in the Player

There are a few considerations with regard to how embedded sound is handled in the Player. First, sound is only played back in *See It!* and *Try It!* mode. In *Know It?* mode and *Do It!* mode, sound is simply ignored.

Second, if you specify a **Delay** value in the **Action Properties** pane for a Frame that is less than the total combined length of the sound files for that Frame, then the sound files take precedence. Sound will not be "cut short" by UPK going to the next Frame after the defined interval.

Summary

UPK allows you to include sound in your Topics so that this sound is heard by the trainee when they play the Topic. You can use the template structure to provide re-usable sound files that mirror the use of template text. You can also record sound files for your Custom Text. You can also use a combination of the two approaches.

Sound files can either be recorded from within the *Topic Editor*, or they can be recorded outside of UPK and then imported into UPK. Sound files for Template Texts are stored in the Library, and are therefore accessible by all Topics in your Library (and will automatically be associated with Topics based on their templates and the object used). Sound files for Custom Texts are stored in UPK's internal database.

Although providing sound may initially seem like a good idea, doing it effectively is timely, costly, and difficult to achieve. You should be absolutely sure that a genuine requirement exists for sound before including it in your Topics.

12

Configuring UPK

In this chapter, we will look at some things you can do to make UPK better meet your requirements. These things are not for the faint-hearted, as they involve digging into the bowels of UPK and tinkering with the delivered formats. However, as we will see in this chapter, a little effort can make some big improvements for your users, and that should always be the benchmark on whether or not something is worth doing.

In this chapter, you will learn how to:

- Change the existing Template Text
- Replace the default images and icons with your own ones
- Define a new object type
- Define a new output document format

Configuring Template Text

The text that appears (by default) in a Bubble is controlled by the Template Text. In many cases the Template Texts will be adequate for your purposes. However, if you want to better match your in-house styles, or simply don't like the default texts, then you can change the default texts by configuring the Template Text.

All of the Template Text is contained in a single (per language) template. Actually, the "template" consists of three separate files—a file named `template.xsl` that takes care of stylistic considerations, a file named `language.xsl` that provides some language-specific transformation functions, and a file named `template.xml` that contains the actual Template Text. It is this last file with which we are primarily concerned.

> **Version Difference**
>
> The way in which Template Text is defined changed with OnDemand version 9.x. In version 8.x and earlier, there was a separate text file for each Action Type. However, developers familiar with configuring Template Text in OnDemand 8.7 should find the transition to UPK 3.5 relatively simple, as the format of the individual Template Text elements is largely the same.

In fact, UPK ships with two templates—a "standard" one which is used by default, and an alternative one that conforms to the *Microsoft Manual of Style for Technical Publications*. In this chapter, we will be working with the Standard template, although everything that we describe is also applicable to the Microsoft template. Both templates use the same tags in the same way.

> Appendix B, *Object Types* provides a side-by-side comparison of the Template Text that is generated by each of these templates.

The template files can be found in the following folder:
`System|Templates|{language}`

In the above specification, `{language}` is the two-character ISO language code of the supported language. The following languages are supported by UPK 3.5.1, although additional languages are being added with each release.

- **da**: Danish
- **de**: German
- **en**: English
- **es**: Spanish
- **es-mx**: Mexican Spanish
- **fi**: Finnish
- **fr**: French
- **fr-ca**: French Canadian
- **hu**: Hungarian
- **it**: Italian
- **ja:** Japanese
- **ko**: Korean
- **nl**: Dutch
- **no**: Norwegian

- **pl**: Polish
- **pt**: Portuguese
- **ru**: Russian
- **sv**: Swedish
- **tr**: Turkish
- **zh-CHS**: Simplified Chinese
- **zh-CHT**: Traditional Chinese

> For more information on supporting additional languages, including using local-language templates, refer to Chapter 13, *Localizing Your Content*.

Within the appropriate language folder, you will find two Packages (see Chapter 9, *Adding Value to Your Topics* for more information on Packages)—one for each of the templates, Standard and Microsoft, as shown in the following screenshot:

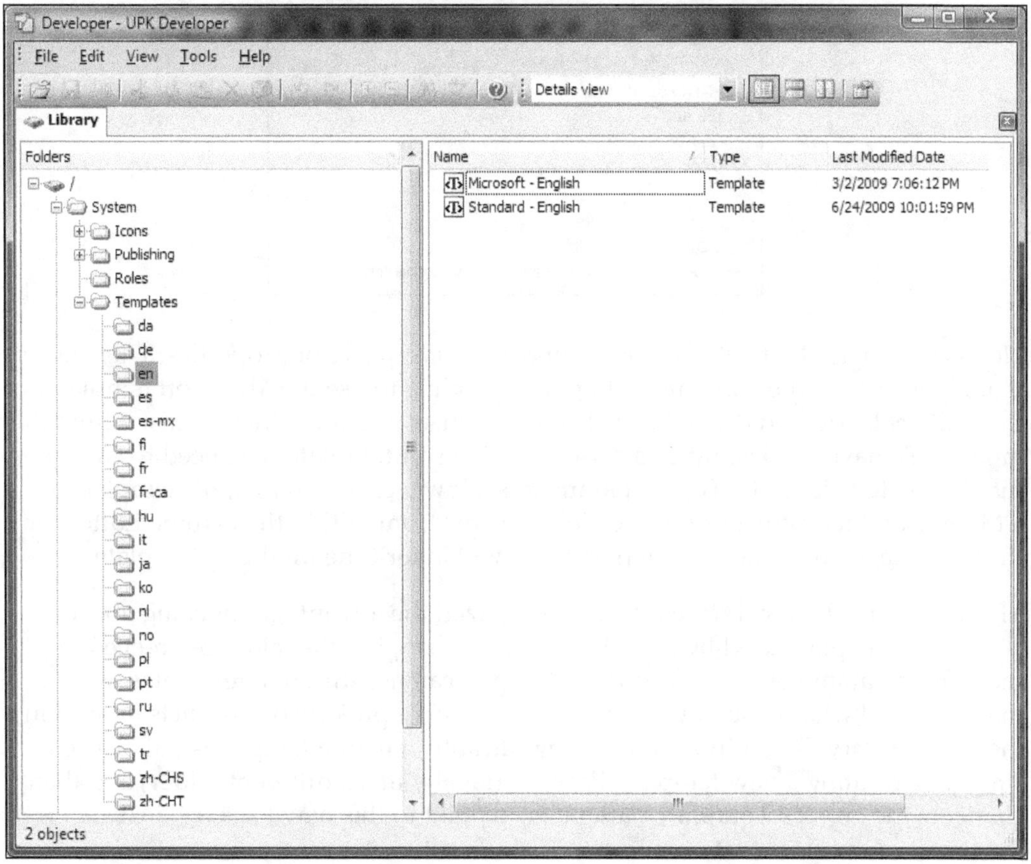

> **Version Difference**
>
> In OnDemand 9.1.5 and earlier versions, the **Standard** template was called **Default**. It was renamed to **Standard** for UPK 3.5, although the content and intent are the same.

So what tells UPK which one of these two templates to use? Each Module, Section, and Topic has a **Template** property that specifies which template file should be used for that object. By default, this is (unsurprisingly!) set to the **Standard - English** template, as shown in the following screenshot:

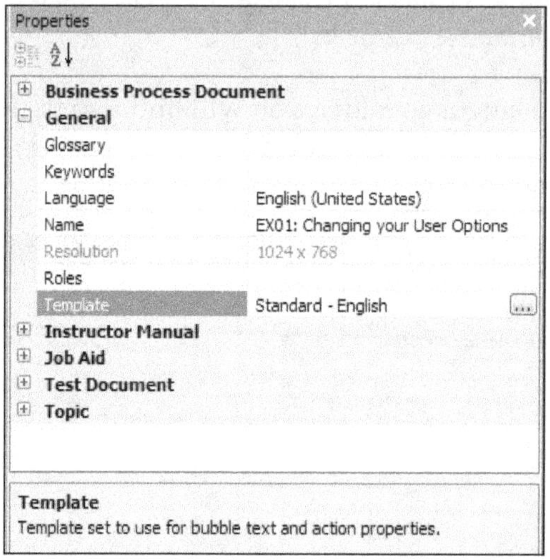

However, illogically, UPK does not support the *inheritance* of properties. This means that if you change the template setting for a Module to use the Microsoft template, this will *not* be rippled down to any Sections and Topics that already exist within this module. To have an existing Topic use the Microsoft template, you need to change the **Template** field in the Topic's parameters. However, if you assign a template to a Module and then create a new Section or Topic from within the Outline Editor for that Module, then the new Section or Topic will inherit the Module's template.

More astute readers will have already recognized the advantages of being able to change the template used by a Topic simply by changing the folder referenced in the object's parameters. Firstly, different Topics can use different templates, which may be useful where you have exercises for multiple projects or products housed in the same Library. Secondly, and more significantly, custom templates can be used simply by creating a new template Package (ideally in a a different folder) and then changing the object's **Template** parameter to point to this new Package, instead of the standard one.

So let's do that, now. We will create a new template, based on the existing default template. Of course, we will work in the English language, although these steps are equally valid for any other language.

1. Go to the folder containing the default template. In our example, this is `System/Templates/en`.
2. Copy the default, that is Standard-English, Template Package in this folder (either right-click on it and select **Copy** from the context menu, or click on it and then press *Ctrl* + *C* on your keyboard).
3. Go to any suitable folder in your library, and create a new sub-folder to house your templates. For this exercise, we will create a new folder named `Z_Custom_Templates`, immediately under our main project folder.
4. Paste the Template Package into this folder.

That's it! You've now created a custom copy of the default template. Of course, your new template contains exactly the same content as the existing template. The hard work is in changing the template to match your local requirements, and to do that, we need a thorough knowledge of the structure of the template file.

Understanding the template file

In order to gain a thorough understanding of the template file, we will look at each of its sections in detail. Don't worry, you don't need an in-depth knowledge of XML for this (although a basic appreciation of XML conventions will help); the XML file is really just a set of definitions, and these are fairly easy to understand once you know what they are defining, which is what this section will tell you.

The file header

The first few lines of code simply define the file as an XML file, and include a couple of standard XML templates. You don't need to worry too much about these lines; you will never change them. An example of these lines is shown in the following snippet:

```
<?xml version="1.0" encoding="utf-8"?>
<TemplateSet xmlns:xlink="http://www.w3.org/1999/xlink" xmlns:
xsi="http://www.w3.org/2001/XMLSchema-instance" xmlns="urn:template-
v1">
```

The <Styles> section

The `<Styles>` section defines some basic formatting for some common elements used in the template text; specifically (from top to bottom in the following example), Bubble Text, Object Names, Object Types, text that is entered, keyboard keys, and hyperlinks. For each style, the style name is given, along with the format of the text. For example, in the code below, text that is entered (`<Style Name="Content" />`) will be displayed in bold (`Bold="true"`), and in dark blue (`Color="#ff0000"`).

The default `<Styles>` section is shown below:

```
<Styles>
  <Style Name="Text" />
  <Style Name="ObjectName" Bold="true" Color="#000080" />
  <Style Name="ObjectType" />
  <Style Name="Content" Bold="true" Color="#ff0000" />
  <Style Name="Key" Bold="true" Color="#000080" />
  <Style Name="Link" Bold="true" Color="#0033cc" />
</Styles>
```

Note that these examples make use of *attributes*. The following table summarizes the attributes that are available:

Attribute	Description
`Bold`	Set to **True** if the text is to be shown in bold. If omitted, or set to **False**, the text is not shown in bold.
`Italics`	Set to **True** if the text is to be shown in italics. If omitted, or set to **False**, the text is not shown in italics.
`Color`	Set to the hexadecimal RGB value for the color in which the text is to be displayed.

Note that these are *default* values that are used in all of the class and context definitions (which are explained below). You can override any of these (should you need to, although you probably wouldn't normally want to) at the context level.

The <Events> section

The next block of code is the `<Events>` set. This defines all of the different types of Actions that can be recorded by UPK. This list corresponds to the Actions that can be selected in the **Action Properties** pane in the **Topic Editor**. A selection of these is shown, for reference, in the next screenshot:

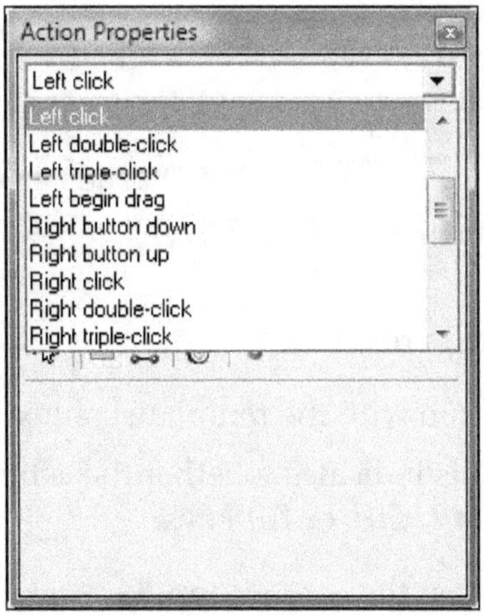

The default `<Events>` section is shown below:

```
<Events>
  <Event Type="Move" ShiftKeyPrefix="true">Point</Event>
  <Event Type="Drag">Drag</Event>
  <Event Type="Key">Keyboard</Event>
  <Event Type="LDown" ShiftKeyPrefix="true">Left button down</Event>
  <Event Type="LUp">Left button up</Event>
  <Event Type="LClick1" ShiftKeyPrefix="true">Left click</Event>
  <Event Type="LClick2" ShiftKeyPrefix="true">
    Left double-click</Event>
  <Event Type="LClick3" ShiftKeyPrefix="true">
    Left triple-click</Event>
  <Event Type="LBeginDrag" ShiftKeyPrefix="true">
    Left begin drag</Event>
  <Event Type="RDown" ShiftKeyPrefix="true">Right button down</Event>
  <Event Type="RUp">Right button down</Event>
  <Event Type="RClick1" ShiftKeyPrefix="true">Right click</Event>
  <Event Type="RClick2" ShiftKeyPrefix="true">
    Right double-click</Event>
  <Event Type="RClick3" ShiftKeyPrefix="true">
    Right triple-click</Event>
  <Event Type="RBeginDrag" ShiftKeyPrefix="true">
    Right begin drag</Event>
  <Event Type="MDown" ShiftKeyPrefix="true">
    Middle button down</Event>
  <Event Type="MUp">Middle button up</Event>
  <Event Type="MClick1" ShiftKeyPrefix="true">Middle click</Event>
  <Event Type="MClick2" ShiftKeyPrefix="true">
    Middle double-click</Event>
```

```
  <Event Type="MClick3" ShiftKeyPrefix="true">
    Middle triple-click</Event>
  <Event Type="MBeginDrag" ShiftKeyPrefix="true">
    Middle begin drag</Event>
  <Event Type="Wheel" ShiftKeyPrefix="true">Wheel</Event>
  <Event Type="StringInput">String input</Event>
</Events>
```

The important things to note here are:

- `Event Type`: This ties in with the template context, which is explained below.
- `ShiftKeyPrefix`: This indicates whether the action can be combined with holding down the *Shift*, *Ctrl*, or *Alt* keys.
- The actual text between the `<Event>` and `</Event>` tags is the text that is used in the drop-down list in the **Action Properties** pane in the **Topic Editor**.

The <Classes> section

The next sections in the template file are the `<Class>` sections. The `<Class>` sections define template formats for specific types of objects that aren't covered in the `<Defaults>` section (which is described later). In fact, if you look at some of the definitions in the `<Class>` sections, you will see that some actions only have a comment indicating that the default template is used:

```
<Class Name="ROLE_SYSTEM_ROWHEADER" ListName="Row header"
  DisplayName="row header" Gender="neutral">
  <!-- LClick1 handled by default -->
  <!-- LClick2 handled by default -->
  <!-- RClick1 handled by default -->
</Class>
```

As a more useful example, let's look at the template definitions for clicking on the Windows status bar.

```
<Class Name="ROLE_SYSTEM_STATUSBAR" ListName="Statusbar"
    DisplayName="statusbar" Gender="neutral">
  <Template Context="LClick1">
    <Text Sound="lclick14">Click the statusbar.</Text>
  </Template>
  <Template Context="LClick2">
    <Text Sound="ldblclk8">Double-click the statusbar.</Text>
  </Template>
  <Template Context="Move">
    <Text Sound="point4">Point to the statusbar.</Text>
  </Template>
```

```
    <Template Context="RClick1">
      <Text Sound="rclick11">Right-click the statusbar.</Text>
    </Template>
  </Class>
```

The <Class> element includes four attributes. These are explained in the following list:

- `Name`: This specifies the type of object for which the <Template> elements within this <Class> will be applied). In the example above, the `Name` is set to `ROLE_SYSTEM_STATUSBAR`.
- `ListName`: This is the name of the element as it will be displayed in the Object Type drop-down in the **Action Properties** pane.
- `DisplayName`: This is the name that will be used as the object type in the Bubble Text. Note that this is sometimes more of a phrase than a name. For example, for the `Titlebar` button object, the display name is "`button in the title bar`", because this gives a complete sentence of "Click on the <Name> button in the title bar.".
- `Gender`: This specifies the gender of the objects to which these <Template> definitions should apply. This may initially be confusing, but this is only because in the English language all objects are *neutral* (in terms of *masculine, feminine*, or *neutral*) so the same text can be used for all objects ("Click the XYZ button", "Press the XYZ key"). In some languages, *things* have a gender. For example, in French, a computer is male (*l' ordinateur)*, whereas a key is female (*la clé*), and hence different template texts are provided for each gender.

The <Class> element contains multiple <Template> elements. There will be one <Template> element for each type of action <Context> that can be performed against the object specified in the <Class> element's `Name` attribute. Let's look at a single <Template> element.

```
  <Template Context="LClick1">
    <Text Sound="lclick14">Click the statusbar.</Text>
  </Template>
```

At this level, the <Template> element used in a <Class> is the same as the <Template> element used in the <Definitions> section (which is described later). To save repeating ourselves, we will describe <Template> elements only once, in the *The <Template> sections*, after we have looked at the <Defaults> section.

Note that, as specified earlier, the `<Class>` sections are used to format Bubble Text relating to "objects that aren't covered in the `<Defaults>` section". So what are these objects? You may recall from Chapter 1, *Oracle User Productivity Kit* that UPK comes in multiple flavors—one for Siebel, one for SAP, and so on. The `<Class>` sections define the format of the text for objects that are application-specific. If you are using the "SAP Edition" you may see a different set of definitions in the `<Class>` sections to those that you would see if you were using the "Siebel Edition".

The <Defaults> section

Following the `<Classes>` section in the template file is the `<Defaults>` section. The `<Defaults>` section works in a very similar way to the `<Classes>` section, but whereas the `<Classes>` section is *object*-focused, containing a separate `<Class>` element for each object (which in turn contains a `<Template>` element for each action), the `<Defaults>` section is *action*-focused, containing a single `<Template>` element for each action, and having the actual object embedded within this `<Template>` element (as we shall see, below).

A small extract of the `<Defaults>` section is shown below. Note that we have only included a single (and simple) `<Template>` element, just for the purposes of illustration.

```
<Defaults Gender="neutral">
  <Template Context="LUp">
     <!-- Example: Release the mouse button. -->
     <Text Sound="lup">Release the mouse button.</Text>
  </Template>
</Defaults>
```

The `<Defaults>` element takes a single attribute, `Gender`, which specifies the gender for which the text should be used. This works in exactly the same way as the `Gender` attribute on `<Class>` elements, but here, the attribute is specified at a higher level, and applies to all `<Template>` elements within the entire `<Defaults>` element. The implication of this is that for languages in which objects can have a specific gender, separate `<Defaults>` elements need to be defined, each with the appropriate `Gender` attribute value.

The <Template> sections

The `<Template>` sections contain the true core of the template file. They define the actual text that is to be displayed in the bubble (and the sound that is to be played when this text is displayed, as we saw in Chapter 11, *Incorporating Sound into Your Topics*).

As an example, let's look at the definition for a single Template Text (effectively, the content of a single Bubble). First, let's look at an example of a <Template> definition from the <Defaults> section of the template file.

```
<Template Context="LClick1">
  <!-- Example: Click on the OK button. -->
  <Text Sound="lclick">Click on the</Text>
  <ObjectName />
  <ObjectType />
  <Text>.</Text>
</Template>
```

The <Template> element itself takes a single attribute. This is Context, which specifies the type of *action* (carried out against the object type defined in the <Class> element's Name attribute) to which this specific <Template> definition applies. In the previous example, the Context attribute is set to Lclick1. The Lclick1 action is a single-click on an object with the left mouse button. Therefore, this Template Text will be used for actions where the trainee left-clicks on a screen element.

The code within the <Template> and </Template> tags defines the actual Bubble Text, and any sound that should be played at the same time. In the example above, there are three distinct types of elements used (ignoring the comment, which is delimited by <!-- and -->, in standard HTML form). These are:

Element	Description
<Text>	This defines static text that is to be displayed in the bubble. Note that there are two <Text></Text> pairs, because there are two pieces of static text: "**Click the**" and ".". You can have as many pieces of static text as you like in a single <Template> definition. The <Text> tag takes a single argument. This is Sound, which specifies the sound file that is to be played at the time that the text is displayed. In this example, the Sound argument is set to lclick, which means that the file lclick.wav (or other sound file format) will be played. UPK will look for this in a subfolder of the Templates\en folder called Sound\Standard, and if the file is not found, no sound will be played (but no error will be generated, either). Note that UPK will automatically add the file type (such as .wav or .mp3) to the name specified on the Sound argument, depending on the default sound file type specified in your developer options. Sound files are covered in more detail in Chapter 11, *Incorporating Sound into Your Topics*.

Element	Description
`<ObjectName />`	This is a placeholder for the name of the object against which the action was recorded. The XML transformation file will automatically substitute this with the actual object name.
`<ObjectType />`	Similar to `<ObjectName>`, this statement is a placeholder for the *type* of action against which the action was recorded.

So much for the definition. Now let's look at what this does for us. Suppose we have recorded a left-click on the **Save** button. In this case, the **Action Properties** pane will look similar to the example shown below:

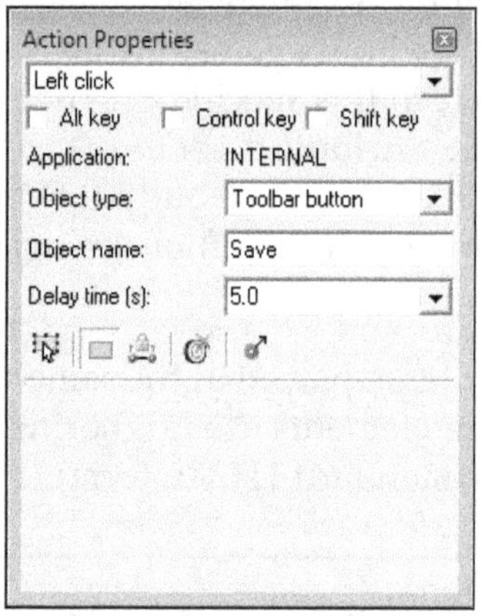

Specifically, note the **Object Type** (**Toolbar button**) and the **Object Name** (**Save**). Now let's look at what the template definition above will result in. This is shown in the following screenshot:

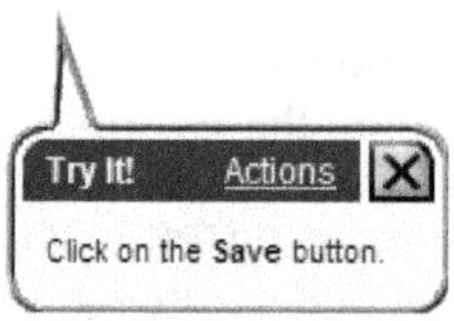

You should quite easily be able to correlate the template definition, the **Action Properties**, and the elements in the Template Text. But to make sure that we are completely clear about what is happening, the following diagram pulls it all together:

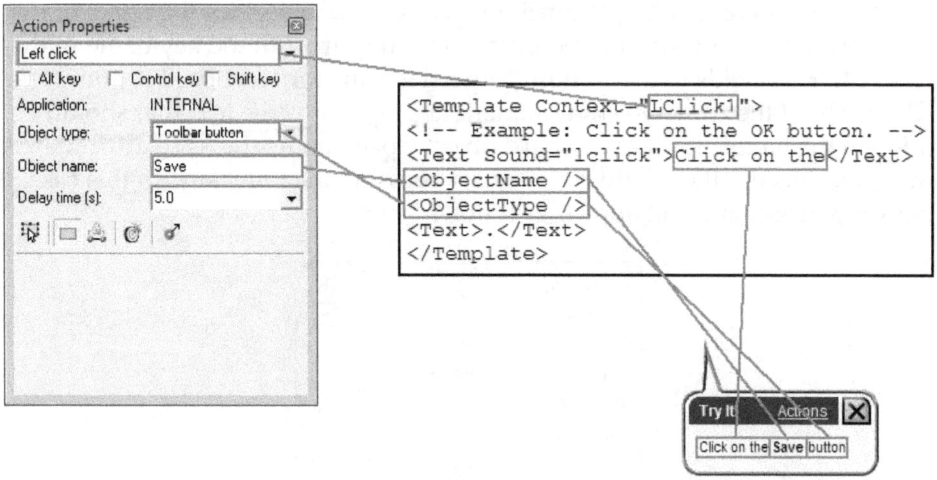

This is a simple example (String Input actions are a little more complicated), but it does clearly illustrate the relationship between the Action Properties, the template, and the resulting Bubble Text.

The <Keynames> section

The <Keynames> section of the template file defines all of the names of the keyboard objects against which an action can be performed (that is, the keys on the keyboard).

An extract of the <KeyNames> element is shown below. Note that this has been truncated in the interests of brevity as there are actually many more keys than those listed here.

```
<KeyNames>
  <Key Name="Alt">Alt</Key>
  <Key Name="Control">Ctrl</Key>
  <Key Name="Shift">Shift</Key>
  <Key Name="Space">Space</Key>
  <Key Name="Back">Backspace</Key>
  <Key Name="Tab">Tab</Key>
  <Key Name="Clear">Clear</Key>
  <Key Name="Return">Enter</Key>
</KeyNames>
```

The <KeyNames> element itself is very simple. It does not take any attributes. This is largely because they are all the same type of object (keyboard keys) and there is only one action that can be performed against these objects, which is "**Press**".

The <Key> element takes a single attribute, `Name`, which specifies the name of the key, as captured by UPK during recording. This ties up with the key name in the **Key** and **Char** *key* fields in the **Action Properties** pane for **Keyboard** actions. The actual content of the <Key> </Key> element itself contains the text that should be included in the bubble for the keyboard object (specified by the `Name` attribute). As an example, consider the recording of a user pressing the *Enter* key. In this case, the **Action Properties** pane will appear as follows:

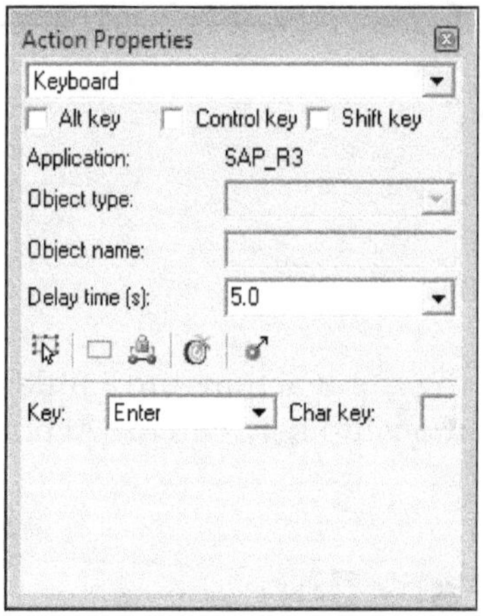

The resulting Bubble Text will be as shown in the following screenshot:

Again, let's see exactly how the template, the **Action Properties** pane and the Bubble Text all tie up.

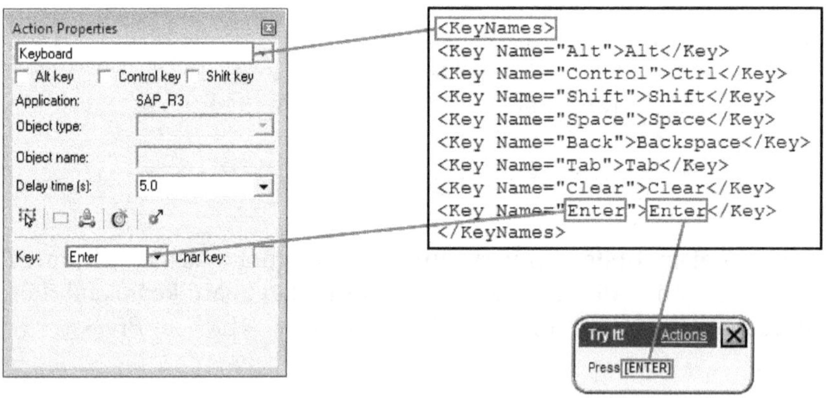

Note that the XML transformation file automatically adds square brackets when formatting the Bubble Text, even though these are not shown in the template. If you're feeling adventurous, you can find these in the `template.xsl` file.

The <ShiftKeyPrefix> section

The `<ShiftKeyPrefix>` section defines the templates for multi-key keyboard actions (for example, pressing *Ctrl* + *Alt* + *Delete*).

```
<ShiftKeyPrefix>
  <Template Context="ShiftKeyPrefixSingle">
    <Text Sound="keybrd1">Press the</Text>
    <ShiftKey ShiftKey="Alt" Braces="true" />
    <ShiftKey ShiftKey="Control" Braces="true" />
    <ShiftKey ShiftKey="Shift" Braces="true" />
    <Text Sound="sngshift">key and</Text>
  </Template>
  <Template Context="ShiftKeyPrefixMulti">
    <Text Sound="keybrd1">Press the</Text>
    <ShiftKey ShiftKey="Alt" Braces="true" />
    <ShiftKeySeparator Type="First" Style="Text" LeadingSpace="false"
      ShiftKey="C" />
    <ShiftKey ShiftKey="Control" Braces="true"/>
    <ShiftKeySeparator Type="Last" Style="Text" LeadingSpace="false"
      ShiftKey="S" />
    <ShiftKey ShiftKey="Shift" Braces="true" />
    <Text Sound="mltshift">keys and</Text>
  </Template>
  <Separator>+</Separator>
  <Separator1>,</Separator1>
  <Separator2> and</Separator2>
  <UpperCase>ABCDEFGHIJKLMNOPQRSTUVWXYZ</UpperCase>
  <LowerCase>abcdefghijklmnopqrstuvwxyz</LowerCase>
</ShiftKeyPrefix>
```

The <Instructions> section

The `<Instructions>` section contains all of the definitions for non-action-related text that is displayed, such as the static "Press Enter to continue" text that is displayed at the bottom of **Explanation** frames.

The <Instructions> element itself does not take any attributes, and simply consists of a series of <Template> elements, as shown in the following example code:

```
<Instructions>
  <Template Context="leadin">
    <Text Sound="leadin">Press [Enter] to </Text>
    <Text Style="Link" LeadingSpace="false"
      Link="javascript:HLink(0)">
    start</Text>
    <Text>.</Text>
  </Template>
</Instructions>
```

As before, note that this is a partial extract of the file. The actual <Instructions> section contains many more <Template> elements, one for each type (or use) of text. The following table lists all of the possible contexts (as specified in the `Context` attribute of the <Template> element) and describes their purpose.

Context	Purpose
`leadin`	The text that is displayed in the Start Frame, after any Custom Text, in *See It!*, *Try It!*, and *Do It!* modes.
`leadout`	The text that is displayed in the End Frame, after any Custom Text, in *See It!*, *Try It!*, and *Do It!* modes.
`continue`	The text that is displayed in an Explanation Frame, after any Custom Text. This same text is used in *See It!* mode if the trainee has paused playback.
`pauselink`	The **Pause** link that is displayed in *See It!* mode. Trainees can click on this link to pause playback.
`knowit_leadin`	The text that is displayed in the Start Frame in *Know It?* mode.
`knowit_leadout`	The text that is displayed in the End Frame in *Know It?* mode.
`knowit_nextstep`	The **Show Step** link that is displayed in *Know It?* mode if the trainee gives up.
`knowit_explanation`	The text that is displayed in an Explanation Frame.
`leadin_score`	The text that introduces the required score in *Know It?* mode.
`knowit_warningL1`	The text for the first level of remediation in *Know It?* mode.
`knowit_warningL2`	The text for the second level of remediation in *Know It?* mode.
`knowit_warningL3_0`	The text for the third level of remediation in *Know It?* mode, for non Action Area Actions.

Context	Purpose
knowit_warningL3_H	The text for the third level of remediation in *Know It?* mode, for Action Area Actions.
knowit_warningL4	The text for the fourth level of remediation in *Know It?* mode.
scoring	The table that shows the scoring information (target score, actual score, and so on) at the end of *Know It?* mode.
scoring_YES	The text that indicates that the trainee has passed the simulation in *Know It?* mode.
scoring_NO	The text that indicates that the trainee has not passed the simulation in *Know It?* mode.
knowit_continue	The text that is displayed if a step in *Know It?* mode is completed by UPK, asking the trainee to continue.
knowit_confirmdemo	The text that is displayed in *Know It?* mode if the trainee clicks the **Show Step** link, asking them to confirm that they want to see the step (and be marked down for it).
typingcomplete	The text that appears in the **Typing Complete** button for string input actions.
knowit_dragwarning	The text that tells the trainee that the action they are completing is a drag-and-drop action, and that the action will be completed for them.
knowit_finish_close	The text that is displayed when a trainee attempts to exit from a *Know It?* mode simulation before the end, asking them if they really want to exit.
strinp_suppress_example	This is not the text that is displayed, but a parameter. If it is set to `0` then examples are included in the text for *Know It?* mode. If it is set to `1` then the examples are not included.
strinp_something_text	The text that is displayed for string input actions, if the (default) option is "Something". (See the String input actions section of Chapter 4, *Editing a Topic* for more information on this.)
strinp_something_text_noexample	The text that is displayed for string input actions, if the (default) option is "Something", but the "suppress example" option has been selected (see `strinp_suppress_example`).
strinp_anything_text	The text that is displayed for string input actions, if the (default) option is "Anything". (See the String input actions section of Chapter 4, *Editing a Topic* for more information on this.)

Context	Purpose
`strinp_anything_text_noexample`	The text that is displayed for string input actions, if the (default) option is "Anything", but the *suppress example* option has been selected (see `strinp_suppress_example`).
`strinp_nothing`	The text that is displayed for string input actions, if the trainee can leave the field empty. (See the section on String input actions in Chapter 4, *Editing a Topic* for more information on this.)
`strinp_or`	The text that is used to indicate that more than one string input option is possible (for example, "Something" or "Nothing").
`strinp_formatter`	This is not the text that is displayed, but contains CSS styles that define the format of the input text.
`decision_headline`	The default text that is displayed above the decision paths on a decision frame. Note that this text can be overwritten by the developer in the Topic file, in which case the Custom Text is used and not this Template Text.

Before delving deeper into the `<Instructions>` section, let's look at the simple example provided previously. As a refresher, this is:

```
<Template Context="leadin">
  <Text Sound="leadin">Press [Enter] to </Text>
  <Text Style="Link" LeadingSpace="false"
    Link="javascript:HLink(0)">start</Text>
  <Text>.</Text>
</Template>
```

This `<Template>` element is for the text that is displayed in the **Start** frame in *See It!*, *Try It!*, and *Do It!* modes. It contains three `<Text>` elements. You should already be familiar with basic `<Text>` elements, but the second `<Text>` element in this example introduces some additional specifications.

The first of these is the `Style="Link"` specification. This indicates that the text enclosed in the `<Text>` and `</Text>` elements is to be treated as a hyperlink. If you recall, in the lead-in text "**Press [Enter] to start**", the text "**start**" is a hyperlink.

The second new specification is the `LeadingSpace` attribute. This specifies whether a space should be inserted before the hyperlink. If you look at the first `<Text>` element above, there is already a space at the end of the text, so the template does not need to include an additional one. Therefore, this attribute is set to `False` (in this example).

Finally, this example includes a `Link` attribute, which has a value of `javascript:HLink(0)`. This attribute is used to define the target of the hyperlink. Each `HLink` specification contains a unique number, and this number ties up with an index maintained internally by UPK.

Now, let's look at a much more complicated example. The following example shows the `<TEMPLATE>` definition for the 'level 4 remediation' warning that is displayed in *Know It?* mode if the user makes a mistake three times in a row (assuming that all three levels of remediation have been enabled).

```
<Template Context="knowit_warningL4">
  <XHTMLText>
    <table xmlns="http://www.w3.org/1999/xhtml">
      <tr>
        <td valign="top" id="img_icon02" name="img_icon02" />
        <td>
          <a class="InstructText">
            <b>
              <font color="#000080">
                <div xmlns="http://www.w3.org/1999/xhtml">
                The action you have performed is incorrect.</div>
                <p>When you press OK, this step will be completed for
               you.</p>
                <p>When it is complete, you may continue with the
               next step.</p>
              </font>
            </b>
          </a>
          <input type="button" width="200" value="OK"
             onClick="HLink(10)" />
        </td>
      </tr>
    </table>
  </XHTMLText>
</Template>
```

This example introduces a new pair of tags: `<XHTMLText>` and `</XHTMLText>`. These tags are used to indicate that the text between them is pure XHTML. Several of the following tags in the XHTML code have `xmlns` attributes. These specify the XML Namespaces that define what format the XHTML code can take. You do not need to worry too much about this. Everything else is standard (X)HTML, which includes a table, several paragraphs, a hyperlink, and an input button.

> The `<XHTMLText>` and `</XHTMLText>` tags are very useful indeed, as they allow you to include any kind of HTML code in your template (and therefore in your Bubbles).

Creating a custom template

OK, so far so good on the theory, but how do we actually *change* the Template Text? First, you need to decide whether your changes will apply to all simulations, or only to simulations for a specific set of exercises. For example, you may want to use separate templates for each product, project, or client (although I would hope that you strive for consistency). For our example, we will create a new template that applies only to the simulations that we will create for a specific application. We therefore want to take a copy of the existing template file, and then change this copy (and not the original). In fact, this is a very good practice, even if you intend on using your new template for *all* exercises; taking a copy will allow you to back out your changes if anything goes wrong.

Taking a copy of an existing template

To take a copy of a template, follow these steps:

1. Create a new folder for your new template. If you are creating a project-specific template, you might want to create a new template within the project's existing folder structure in the Library, and call it `Z_Custom_Templates`. It is also a good practice to follow UPK's convention of having a separate sub-folder within this for each language that you will support. Even if you only plan on supporting (for example) English, it is a good idea to still create the language sub-folder. You never know what may happen in the future, and planning for it now could save you a lot of rework in the future. Plus, mirroring UPK's set-up will make it easier for future developers and administrators to understand which custom template relates to which original template. For our example, we will create a new folder, with a name of `Z_Custom_Templates\en\`. (Using a prefix of "Z" is an old trick to ensure that the folder is listed toward the bottom of the Library folder list, out of the way of our actual content.)
2. Locate the Package for the original template that you want to copy. This will be in the `\System\Templates\en\` (in our example) folder. You have a choice of basing your new template on the `Default` template or the `Microsoft` template. For our exercise, we will use the `Default - English` template as the basis for our new custom template.
3. Click on the template that you want to copy, hold down the *Shift* key (to take a copy), and drag and drop the template onto your new folder (created in Step 1).

4. You will be asked if you want to take a copy or create a duplicate. Creating a duplicate will copy all related files, but in this case there are no related files, so you can select either option.
5. You will now have a new copy of the Template Package in your `Z_Custom_Templates` folder. You can rename this Package to be anything that you like, although you should not use *exactly* the same name as the standard template, as this will make it difficult to determine which template a Topic uses when displaying the Topic's *Properties*. Note that, as described earlier, the template Package actually consists of three separate files. All three of these files will have been copied over.

Editing a custom template

Changing a custom template is a bit fiddly, as there is no built-in editor that you can use for editing an XML file from the Library in UPK. This means that you have to save the template file to your local computer, edit it outside of UPK, and then copy the changed file back into UPK.

To change your (copy of the default) template, follow these steps:

1. Navigate to the folder containing your custom Template Package.
2. Double-click on the Template Package to open it. You will see the three files within the template.
3. Click on the file that you want to change (for example, the `template.xml` file), and drag this out of UPK and drop it into a temporary folder in Windows Explorer.
4. Locate the file in Windows Explorer, and open it using Notepad, or your preferred XML editor.
5. Make your changes as required (see the examples below).
6. Save the file.
7. Drag the file from Windows Explorer, and drop it back into the template object in UPK.
8. The **Confirm File Replace** dialog box is displayed, asking you if you want to replace the existing file. Click on **Yes**.

Customizing the Template Text

Assuming that you now know how to open up the `template.xml` file (see the *Configuring Template Text* section, given earlier in this chapter), let's now look at how to change the Template Text.

For an example, we will change the text that is displayed for string input actions. By default, this appears (in *See It!* and *Try It!* modes) as follows:

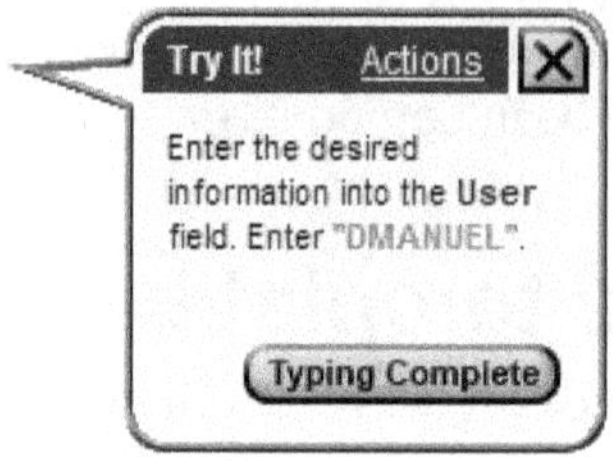

This always strikes me as a clumsy way of phrasing it. Plus, let's assume that our in-house documentation standards place field names in italics, user input in bold and black, and that we want our simulations to be consistent with this. So, we'll change the:

1. Wording
2. Formatting of field names
3. Formatting of entered text

The first thing we need to do is find the section of the `template.xml` file that generates this text. Search the `template.xml` file for `StringInput`, and you should find the following section of code:

```
<Template Context="StringInput">
  <!-- Example: Enter the desired information into the Test field.
    Enter 123.-->
  <Text Sound="stginput">Enter the desired information into
    the</Text>
  <ObjectName />
  <Text Sound="stginp2">field. Enter</Text>
  <StringInputExtension Type="anything" Sound="sivalid">
    a valid value</StringInputExtension>
  <StringInputExtension Type="example"
    Sound="siexample">e.g.</StringInputExtension>
  <Content />
  <StringInputExtension Type="blank" Sound="siblank">or
    leave blank</StringInputExtension>
  <Text>.</Text>
```

```
</Template>
```

Update this code so that it looks like the following snippet. The changed code is shown in bold.

```
<Template Context="StringInput">
  <!-- Example: Enter the desired information into the Test field.
    Enter 123.-->
  <Text Sound="stginput">Enter the appropriate value in the</Text>
  <ObjectName />
  <Text Sound="stginp2">field. For this simulation, you should
    enter</Text>
  <StringInputExtension Type="anything" Sound="sivalid">any valid
    value</StringInputExtension>
  <StringInputExtension Type="example" Sound="siexample">- for
    example,</StringInputExtension>
  <Content />
  <StringInputExtension Type="blank" Sound="siblank">. Alternatively,
    you can leave this field blank</StringInputExtension>
  <Text>.</Text>
</Template>
```

Note that in addition to changing the static text (highlighted above), we have removed one of the `<StringInputExtension>` clauses; namely the one containing the text "e.g".

> The `<StringInputExtension>` clauses relate to the <*Something*> (`Type="example"`; requires the trainee to enter some valid text), <*Anything*> (`Type="anything"`; requires the trainee to enter some valid text or leave the field blank) and <*Blank*> (`Type="blank"`; requires the trainee to enter a specific text or leave the field blank) options for input text. Refer to Chapter 4, *Editing a Topic* for more information on these.

Now let's change the formatting of the field name and the value. This is not defined in this section of the code, but you can see from this code that two placeholders are used: `<ObjectName />` and `<Content />`. So let's look for the definition of these objects in our template. Near the top of the file, you will see the following lines of code:

```
<Styles>
  <Style Name="Text" />
  <Style Name="ObjectName" Bold="true" Color="#000080" />
  <Style Name="ObjectType" />
```

```
    <Style Name="Content" Bold="true" Color="#ff0000" />
    <Style Name="Key" Bold="true" Color="#000080" />
    <Style Name="Link" Bold="true" Color="#0033cc" />
  </Styles>
```

The `<Styles>` section defines the formatting of the placeholders used in our `<Template>` definition earlier (along with some other examples not used in this example). Change these lines to be:

```
  <Styles>
    <Style Name="Text" />
    <Style Name="ObjectName" Italics="true" Color="#000000" />
    <Style Name="ObjectType" />
    <Style Name="Content" Bold="true" Color="#000000" />
    <Style Name="Key" Bold="true" Color="#000080" />
    <Style Name="Link" Bold="true" Color="#0033cc" />
  </Styles>
```

Save your changes, copy the updated template back into your Template Package in UPK, and save and close the Template Package. Then go back into the exercise (to which this template has been assigned). The Bubble Text will now appear as follows:

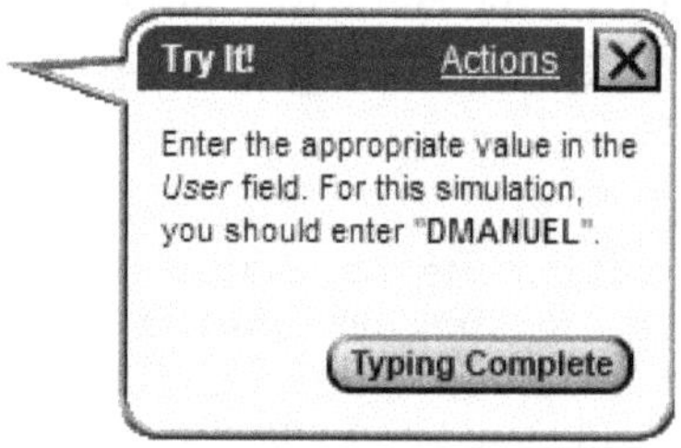

Good! Our changes have worked! Now we can use this template in our Topics.

Customizing the Template Text the "easy" way

Now that you have learned how to customize the Template Text by hand, it is time to let you into a little secret. UPK does in fact provide a *Template Editor*. However, this is not installed by default, so depending on your local implementation and your personal ability to install software, you may not even have access to this—hence my taking you through the manual approach first. Besides, the *Template Editor* is not particularly straightforward, so it is wise to understand the code behind it, before using it.

The *Template Editor* is an additional program that must be installed separately from UPK, and still only works on template files once they have been copied out of UPK and onto your local workstation (as described previously). To install the *Template Editor*, locate the file `TemplateEditorSetup.exe` in your installation directory, execute it, and follow the instructions on the screen (there are no real options, just the selection of the program folder).

To edit a template using the *Template Editor*, follow these steps:

1. If you have not done so already, copy the template that you want to edit from the Library onto your local workstation (see the previous instructions).
2. Start the Template Editor from the Windows **Start** menu.
3. From within the *Template Editor*, select menu option **File | Option**, and navigate to and select the `template.xml` file. The template will appear in the *Template Editor* as shown in the following screenshot:

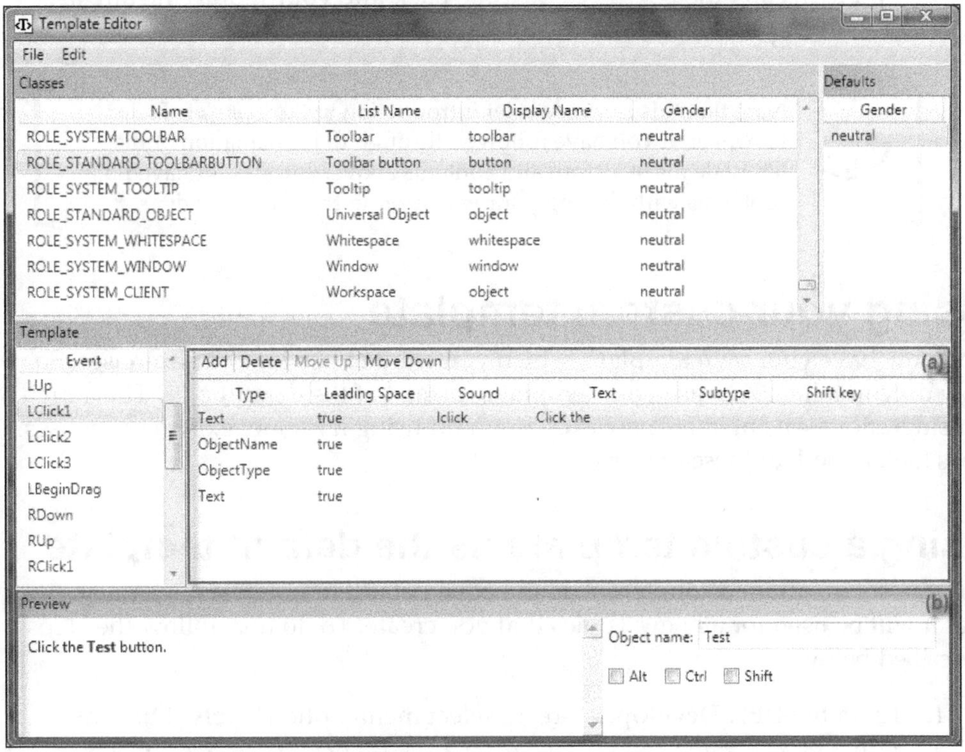

4. Select the class, gender (if required), and event, to display the template elements in the rightmost side of the Template pane **(a)**. You can see a preview of the text in the Preview area **(b)**.

5. To change the template, double-click on the element that you want to change, in the Template pane, to display the **Element Properties** dialog box, shown in the following screenshot:

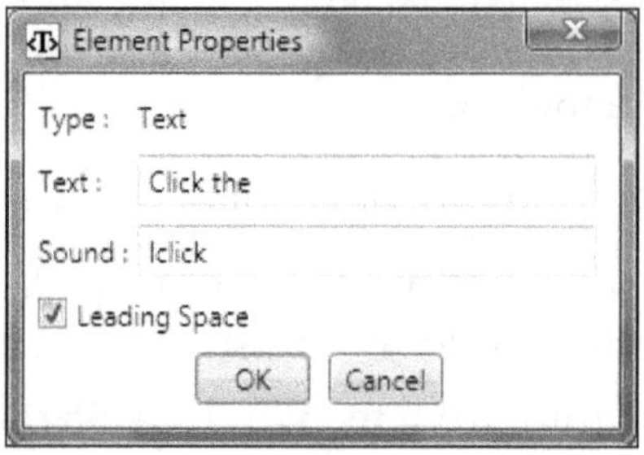

6. Change the options as required, and then click on **OK**.
7. When you have made all of your required changes, close the *Template Editor*, and then copy the `template.xml` file back into your Library (again, as described previously).

> Note that this is a very brief introduction to the *Template Editor*. However, if you have followed through the explanation of the template file structure and contents above, you should have no problems with finding your way around the *Template Editor*.

Using your custom template

You now have your own template, which you want to use for your exercises. So how do you tell UPK to use your template, instead of the default one? There are two considerations—using it for new exercises, and using it for any existing exercises. Let's look at both of these options.

Using a custom template as the default template

You can set up your custom template to be the default template, which means that it will be used for all new Topics that you create. To do this, follow the steps described below:

1. From the **UPK Developer** screen, select menu option **Tools | Options**.
2. In the **Options** dialog box, select a **Category** of **Content Defaults | General**.
3. Click the **Browse** button next to the **Template** field, and navigate to and select (click on **Open**) your custom Template Package
4. Back in the **Options** dialog box, click on **OK**

The following screenshot shows the **Options** dialog box, with a custom template selected:

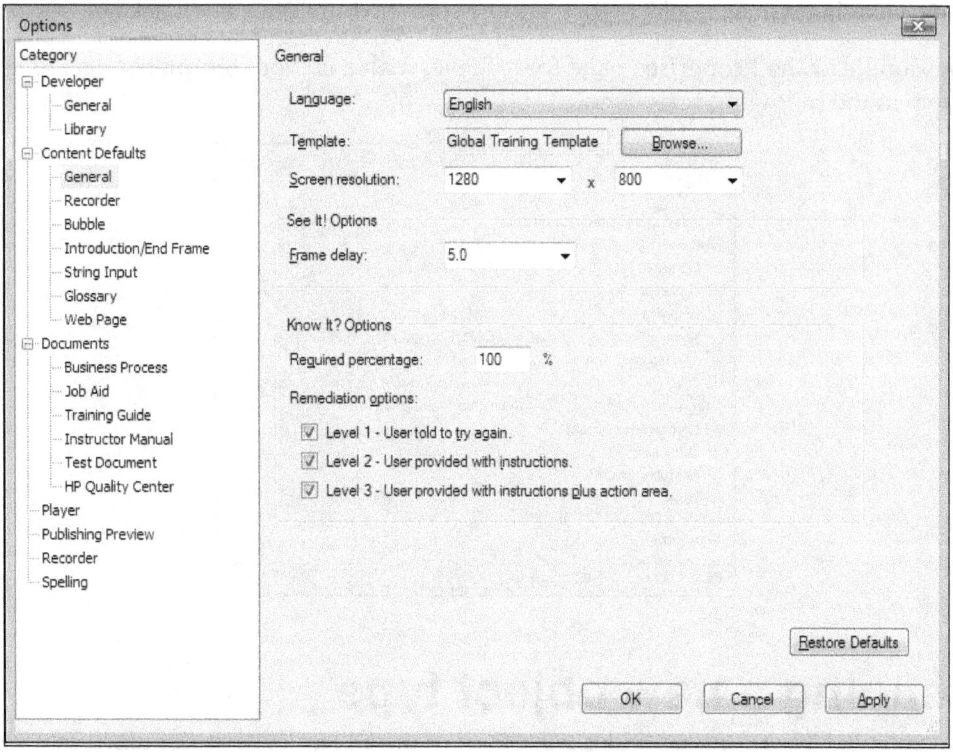

This custom template will now automatically be assigned to all new content objects that you create within your Library.

Assigning a custom template to existing Topics

Even if you have already created Topics using the standard template (or have imported Topics that do not use your custom template), you can still have these Topics use your new template. This is because the template is effectively applied at *display* time (whether this is display in the **Topic Editor**, when previewing, or during final publication). To assign a custom template to an existing Topic, carry out the following steps:

1. In the Library, select the Topic to which you want to apply the template.
2. Make sure that the **Properties** pane is displayed (click the **Properties** button ( ) if it is not).
3. Make sure that the **General** category is expanded.

4. Click in the **Template** field.
5. Click on the "ellipsis" button (...)in the **Template** field.
6. Navigate to and select (click **Open**) your custom Template Package.

An example of the **Properties** pane for a Topic, with a custom template selected, is shown in the following screenshot:

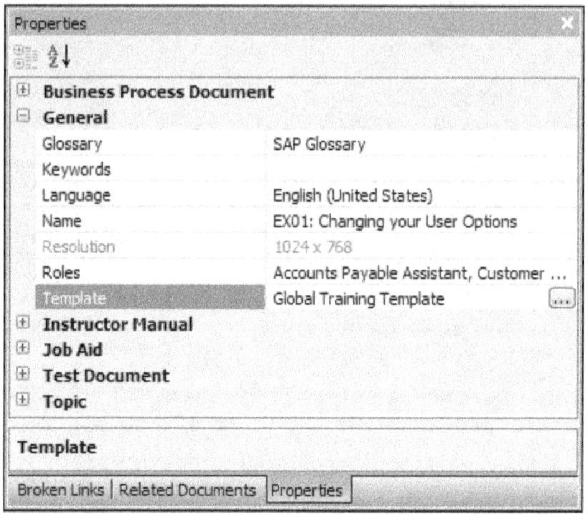

Defining a new object type

Appendix B, *Object Types* provides a list of all of the Object Types recognized by UPK, and the Template Text that is generated for each of them. Although you can customize the Template Text for any given object as described earlier in this chapter, in some cases it may be easier to just define your own Object Type. UPK will not "capture" this Object Type during the recording, but developers will be able to select it from the **Object type** field in the **Action Properties** pane (see Chapter 4, *Editing a Topic*).

We will examine how to do this by way of a real-life example. In SAP, users can select a row in a table by clicking on a button to the left of the row. This is colloquially referred to as the 'row selection button'. An example of such a table is shown in the following screenshot:

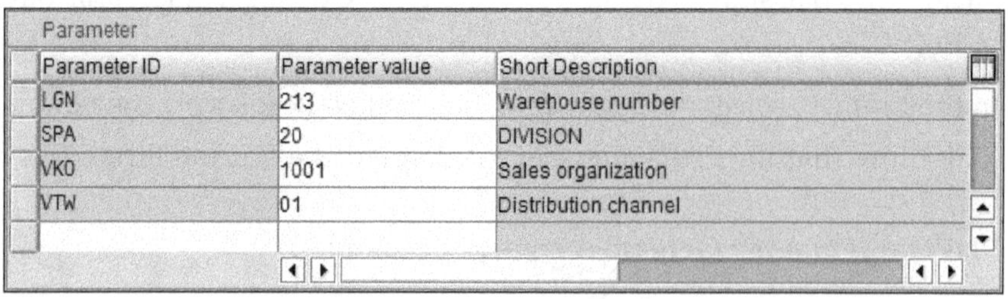

UPK identifies this action as being on the standard **Pushbutton** Object Type, and generates the following Bubble Text for this:

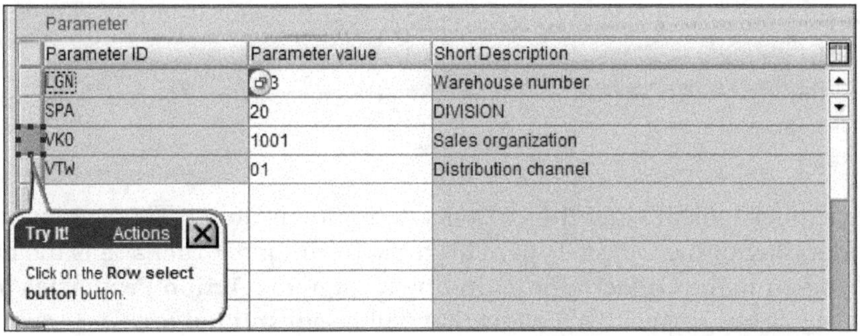

This is wrong on several levels, but rather than trying to fix it, we'll just replace it entirely with our own text. Ideally what we really want to see is the following Bubble Text.

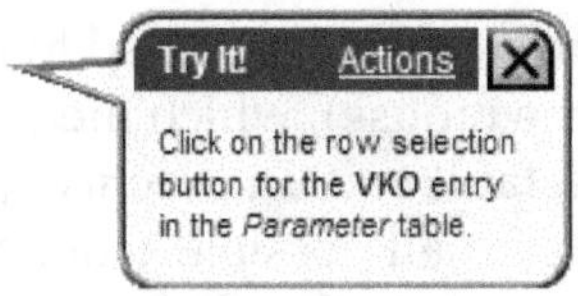

We won't be able to do this (without resorting to Custom Text, as was done to capture this example), because it requires two variables—the table name (**Parameter**) and the entry name (**VKO**), and we only have one variable to play with (the **Object name** in the **Action Properties** pane). This is a "limitation" of UPK, although, to be fair, we are "re-purposing" UPK's functionality here, so we can't really complain. We will therefore (reluctantly) compromise, and aim for the following Bubble Text:

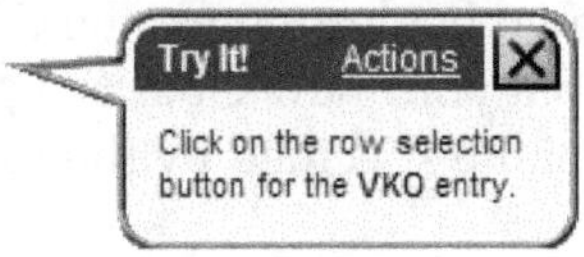

So let's look at how to do this. The first thing we need to do is to define our new Object Type. Open up your custom Template Package, and then open the file `template.xml` for editing, as described earlier in this chapter. Insert the following code into the `<class>` sections (anywhere you like - just not in the middle of another `<class>` definition):

```
<Class Name="ROW_SELECT_BUTTON"
    ListName="Row selection button"
      DisplayName="row selection button"
        Gender="neutral">
```

```
    <Template Context="LClick1">
      <Text Sound="lclick1">Click on the</Text>
      <ObjectType />
      <Text Sound="lclick1b">for the</Text>
      <ObjectName />
      <Text>entry.</Text>
    </Template>
  </Class>
```

Let's take a quick look at what the `<Class>` definition is doing. The `Name` is an internal identifier of the Object Type. This must be unique. `ListName` is the name that will appear in the **Object type** drop-down list in the **Action Properties** pane, and the `DisplayName` specifies the text that will be substituted for `<ObjectType>` in the template. Note that because we now have two `<Text>` elements, we need two `Sound` attributes. We have specified a new one (`lclick1b`), and will need to record this if we use sound in our simulations. (See Chapter 11, *Incorporating Sound into Your Topics* for more details.)

In this example, we are only providing customized template text for the `Lclick1` action (a single left-click with the mouse), which means that all other actions (like left double-click) will use the default text. In practice, you would probably want to provide customized template for all possible actions. For more information on customizing the Template Text, refer to the *Understanding the template file* section, earlier in this chapter.

Save your updated template file, and copy it back into your custom Template Package, as described earlier in this chapter. If you are currently editing a Topic in which you want to use this new Object type then close it, make sure that the updated template is assigned to it in the Topic's *Properties*, and then open the Topic in the **Topic Editor** again. Navigate to the Frame where you want to use this Object Type, and click on the drop-down list button for the **Object type** field in the **Action Properties**. You will now see that your new Object Type is available for selection (and that it is listed under the name specified by the `ListName` attribute in the template.

Select your new object type of **Row selection button**. We also need to enter the name of the entry that is to be selected in the **Object name** field. In our example, this is **VKO**. This then gives us an **Action Properties** pane as shown in the following screenshot:

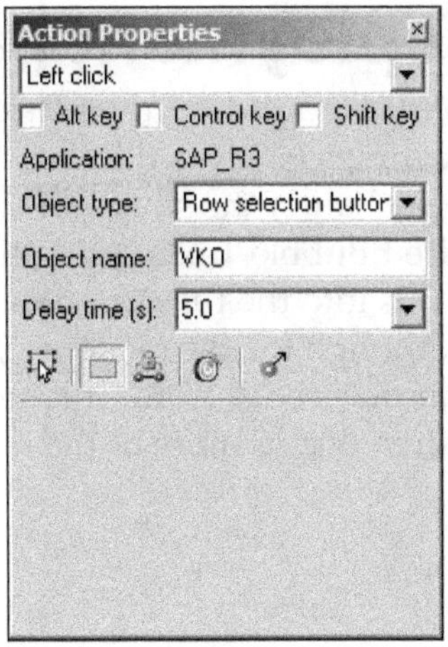

The corresponding Bubble Text (taken from our custom template) now appears as shown in the following example:

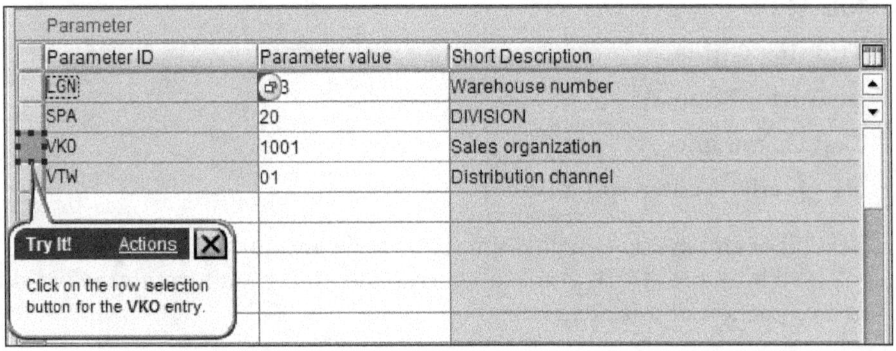

So, there you have it. A brand new Object Type, available for selection in the Topic Editor, and with its own Template Text. And all this with minimal effort.

Again, it is important to note that UPK will not automatically identify this Object Type during the recording, but at least the developers can select it in the **Topic Editor**.

Don't forget that if you are providing your training content in additional languages then you will need to add your new Object Type to all of the language-specific templates as well.

Customizing deployment packages

In the previous section, we configured the Template texts; this largely covers the Bubble Texts, plus a few other things (such as the *Know It?* mode remediation texts, and so on). However, this is only half of the story. When you publish a Topic, UPK generates all of the required Bubble Texts (using the template that we just configured), and then pushes this into the relevant deployment format, depending on your publishing choices. Although for the most part, this book has been using the Player deployment format, you may recall from Chapter 6, *Publishing Your Content* that UPK allows you to publish to one or more of the following formats:

- **Player**
- **HTML Web Site**
- **LMS Package**
- **Standalone Topic Files**
- **System Process**
- **Job Aid**
- **Training Guide**
- **Instructor Manual**
- **Test Document**
- **HP Quality Center spreadsheet**

With a little bit of effort, you can customize the style and format of any or all of these formats. With a bit more effort, you can even create your own formats, as we shall see in the next section of this chapter.

Understanding where the deployment formats are defined

So how do we create our own deployment format? Well, the first thing to do is find out where the deployment formats are defined. A clue is given in the Publishing Wizard. If you don't skip the **Advanced Options** page, you will see the **Advanced Publishing Options**, as shown in the following screenshot. Note that the **Category** field is set to **User Productivity Kit**. Click on the **Change** button to the right of this field, and you will see the **Set Category and Language** dialog box, also shown in the following screenshot.

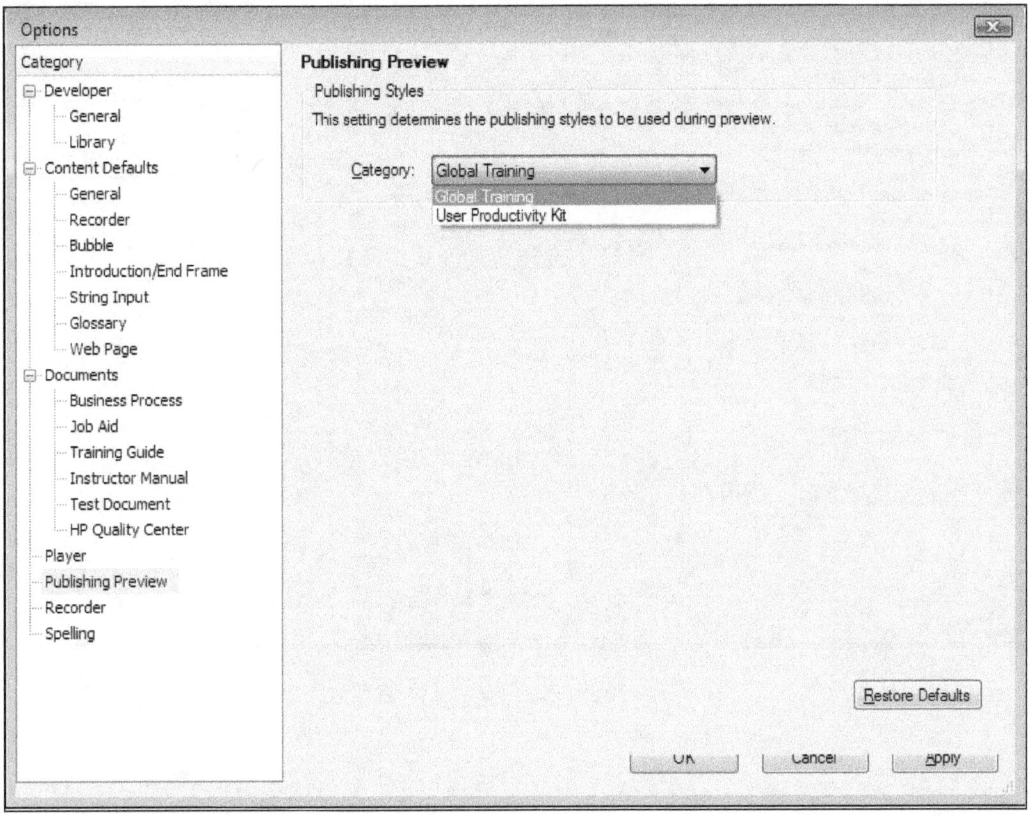

You can see, here, that it is possible to change the **Category** by selecting another value from the drop-down (shown already dropped down in the previous screenshot). However, there is only one option, **User Productivity Kit**. (This name may change in other versions of UPK, or OnDemand before it, but there will still be only one.) Cancel the wizard, and then go to the following folder in the Library: **System | Publishing | Styles**. You'll see the following:

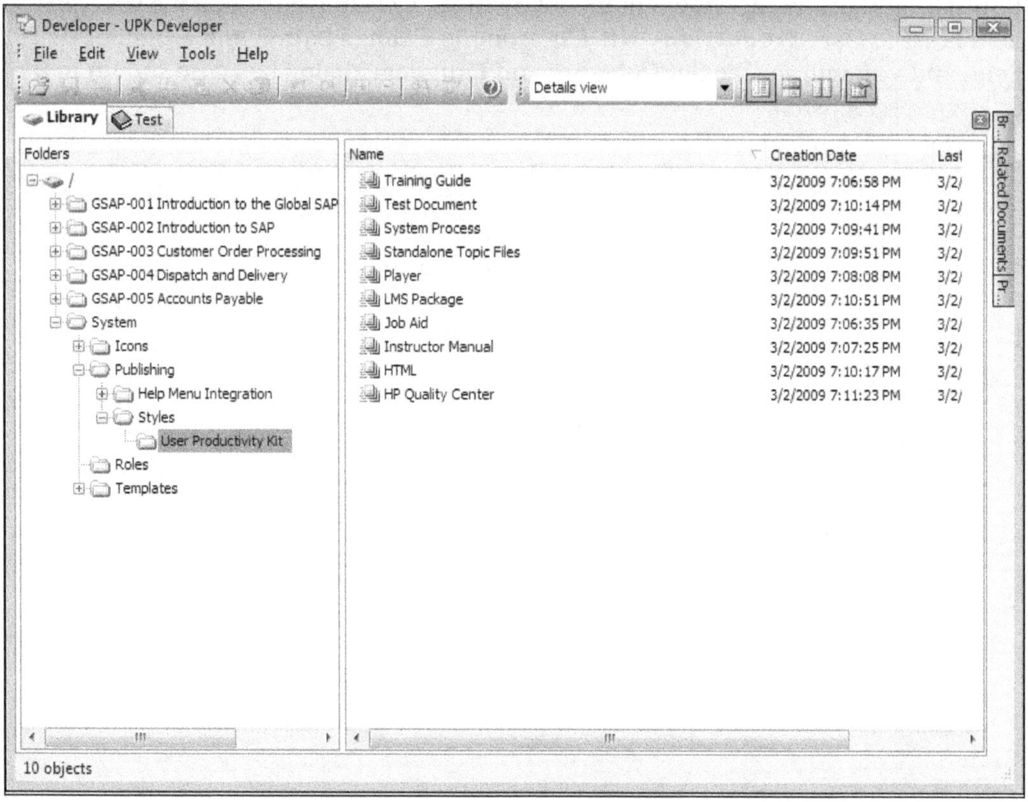

Look at the name of the folder within the `Styles` folder: `User Productivity Kit`. This is the same name as we saw in the **Category** field of the **Advanced Publishing Options**. Now look at the list of packages ( ) contained within the `User Productivity Kit` folder. Compare this with the list of possible output types at the start of this section. They're exactly the same. Is it starting to all fall into place, yet? The `Styles` folder contains the sub-folders that determine the possible publishing categories, and there is one package per deployment format within this. The Packages themselves contain the formatting for the output types; we'll look at these, shortly.

Creating your own deployment category

As you saw previously, the publishing categories that are selectable in the **Publishing Options** are controlled purely by the sub-folders in the `System/Publishing/Styles` folder. So to create a new, selectable publishing category, the first thing we need to do is to create a new sub-folder in this same folder. (It is always advisable to create your own custom copies of the standard objects, instead of directly editing them, in case you need to revert to—or just refer to—the originals.) We'll create a new sub-folder (use menu option **File | New | Folder**) for our new publishing style, and we'll call it `Global Training`.

> Note that you must create the folder for your new publication packages within the existing `System/Publishing/Styles` folder, or UPK will not find them.

Next, copy *all* of the standard packages for all of the different deployment formats into your new custom publishing category folder. You can either copy and paste them, or drag and drop them, as you prefer. It is important that you copy all of the deployment formats, even if you only want to customize one of these. Internally, UPK refers to the position of these options on the menu, and if you remove all but one Package, and UPK normally positions this Package as the seventh option, then you will get an "index error" when you try to publish your content, because there is no longer a seventh position.

We now have a copy of the standard deployment formats that we can work with, as shown in the following screenshot:

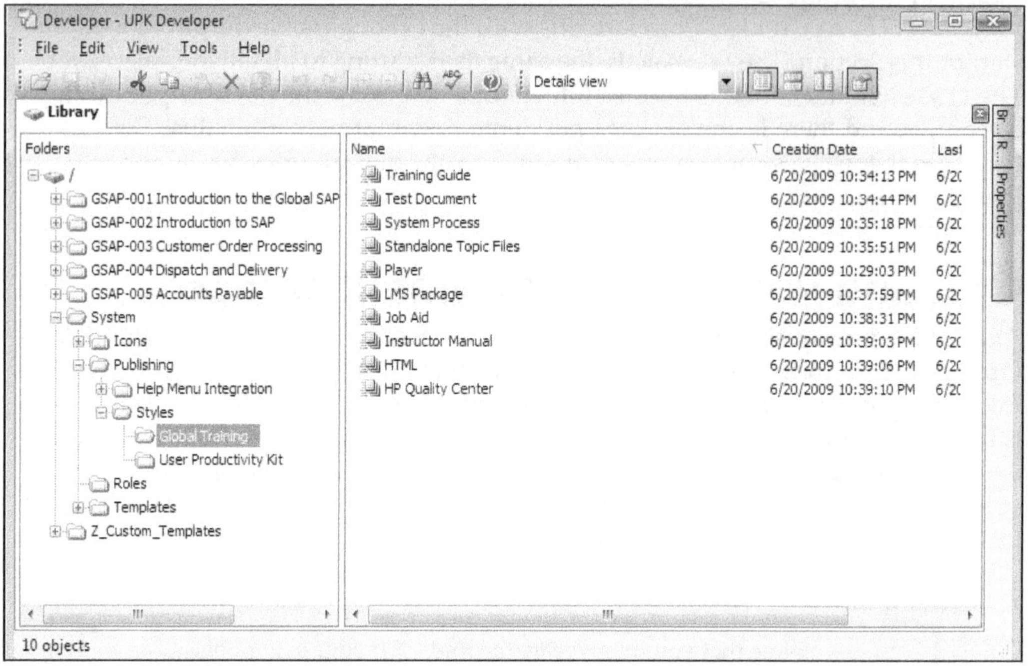

To prove that this simple copy works, select any existing content from the Outline editor, and click the Publish button ( ) to launch the Publishing Wizard. Continue through to the **Advanced Publishing Options** screen, and click on the **Change** button in the **Category and Language** area. Your custom publishing category is now selectable in the **Category** field, as shown in the next screenshot:

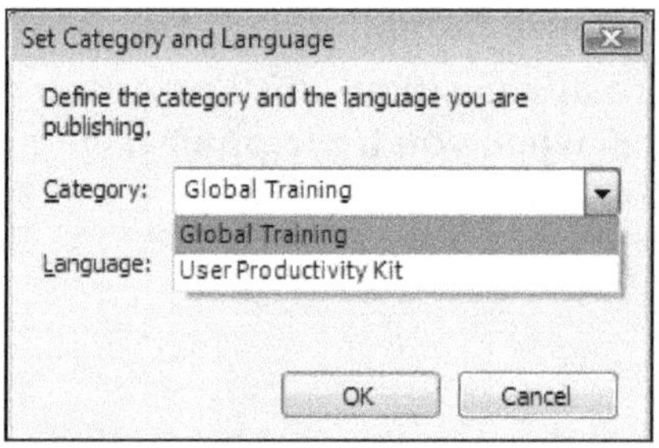

Click on **Cancel** to exit from the Publishing Wizard; we don't want to publish anything just yet as we were simply proving that UPK would find our new publishing category.

Customizing the logo

So now that we have a new custom publishing category, we can start to customize it. We will replace the Oracle logo that appears in the output formats with our own company logo. Really, this is the first thing that you should do, but many developers never bother. This is because it involved a bit of fiddling about in the previous versions of UPK/OnDemand. Thankfully, UPK 3.5 has made replacing the logo so simple that there is really no excuse for not changing it any more.

To customize the logo, carry out the following steps:

1. From the main **UPK Developer** screen, select menu option **Tools | Customize Logo**. The **Customize Logo** dialog box is displayed, as shown in the following screenshot:

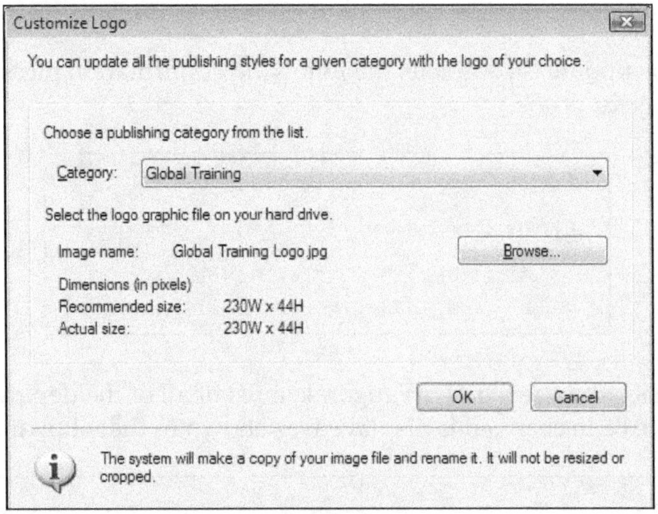

2. In the **Category** field, select the publishing category for which you want to change the logo. In our example, this will be our new custom publishing category **Global Training**, as shown in the previous screenshot. Note that UPK will replace the logo for all deployment formats in the publishing category.

> **Caution:**
>
> Make sure that you select your custom category and not the standard User Productivity Kit category, as there is no *undo* for this. (Although in a client/server environment you can simply not check in your changed files—if you notice in time...).

3. Click on **Browse**, and navigate to and select your custom logo. Note that this should be 230 x 44 pixels for the best results. This does not need to have a specific name, as UPK will rename it (to `small_logo.gif`) when UPK imports it.
4. Click on **Open** to return to the **Customize Logo** dialog box.
5. Click on the **OK** button.
6. UPK will work its way through each of the deployment formats, displaying the following status bar while the update is in progress:

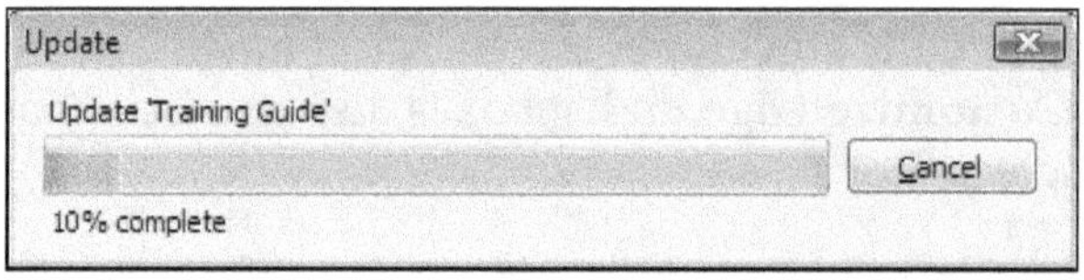

7. Once the update is complete, the following confirmation message is displayed:

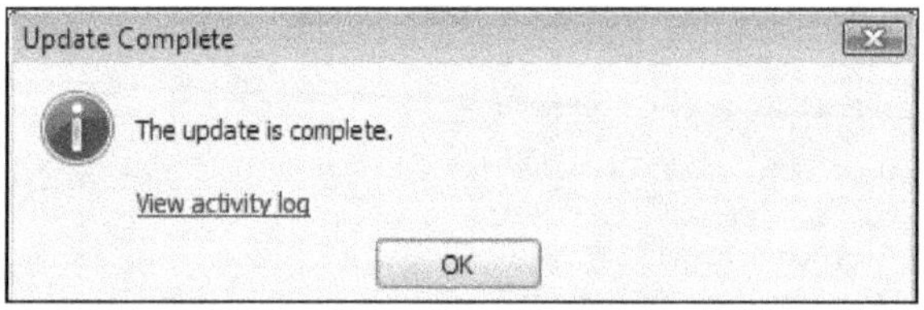

8. If you click the **View activity log** link, a list of all of the deployment formats that have been changed is displayed, as shown in the following screenshot:

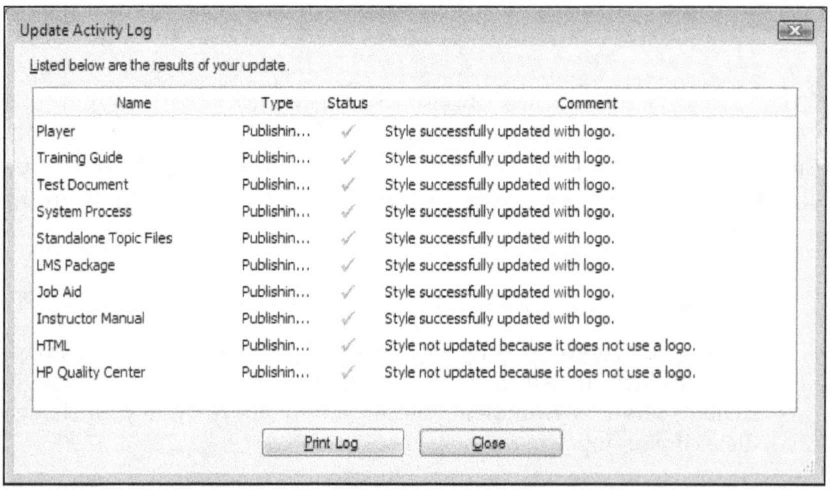

This should list all of the deployment packages (or at least all of the ones that you copied…which should be all of them).

9. Click on **Close** to close the **Update Activity Log** dialog box, and then click on **OK** to close the **Update Complete** message.

Now, let's see what this has done for us. Publish any Outline element (as explained in Chapter 6, *Publishing Your Content*) using your customized deployment format, and you should see that the logo in the Player has been changed to your company logo, as shown in the following screenshot:

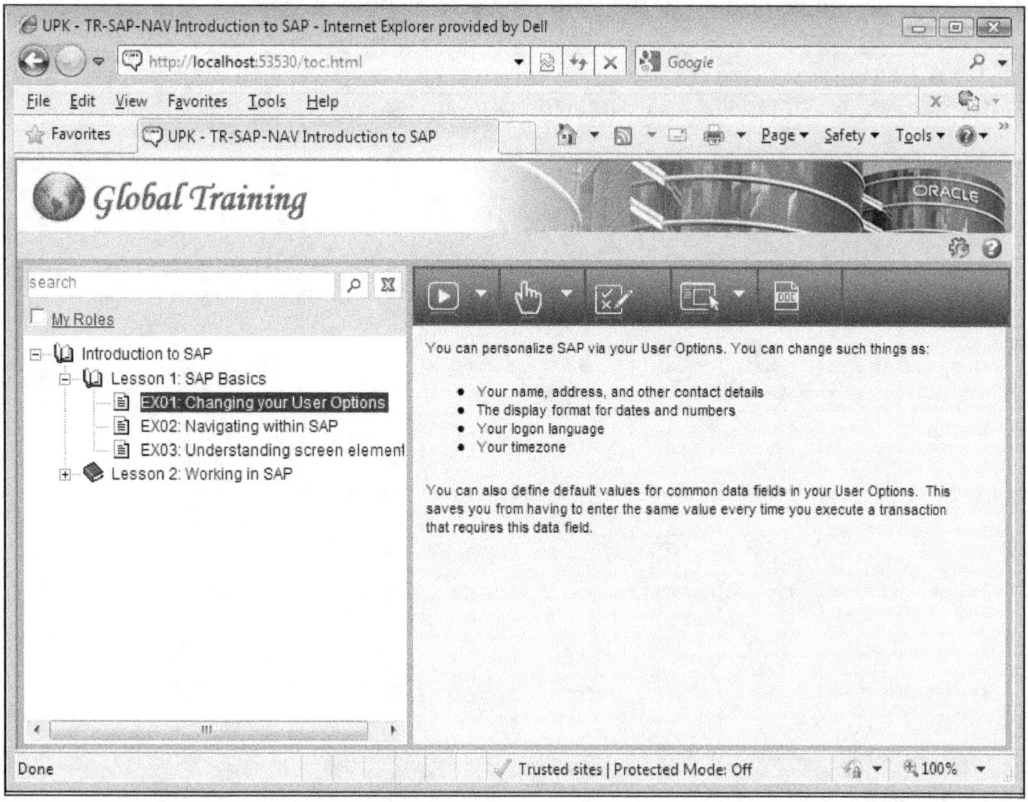

Note that UPK down-samples the image, which may appear lossy in some output formats. If you want to use a high-definition image, then you may want to replace the images one-by-one (or at least the `large_logo.gif` and `medium_logo.gif`) in the various deployment packages, as described next, in the *Customizing an output style* section.

Customizing an output style

Changing the logo in the deployment packages was an easy change. Now let's look at something a bit more challenging. The content of the deployment package, and how it can be customized, will vary depending on the deployment format, but for this example, we will customize the Player.

First, let's have a look at the content of this Package. In the Library, navigate to the custom copy of the **Player** Package, and double-click on it to open it. As with all objects in UPK (except Topics...), the editor opens in a new tab within the **UPK Developer** screen, as shown in the following screenshot:

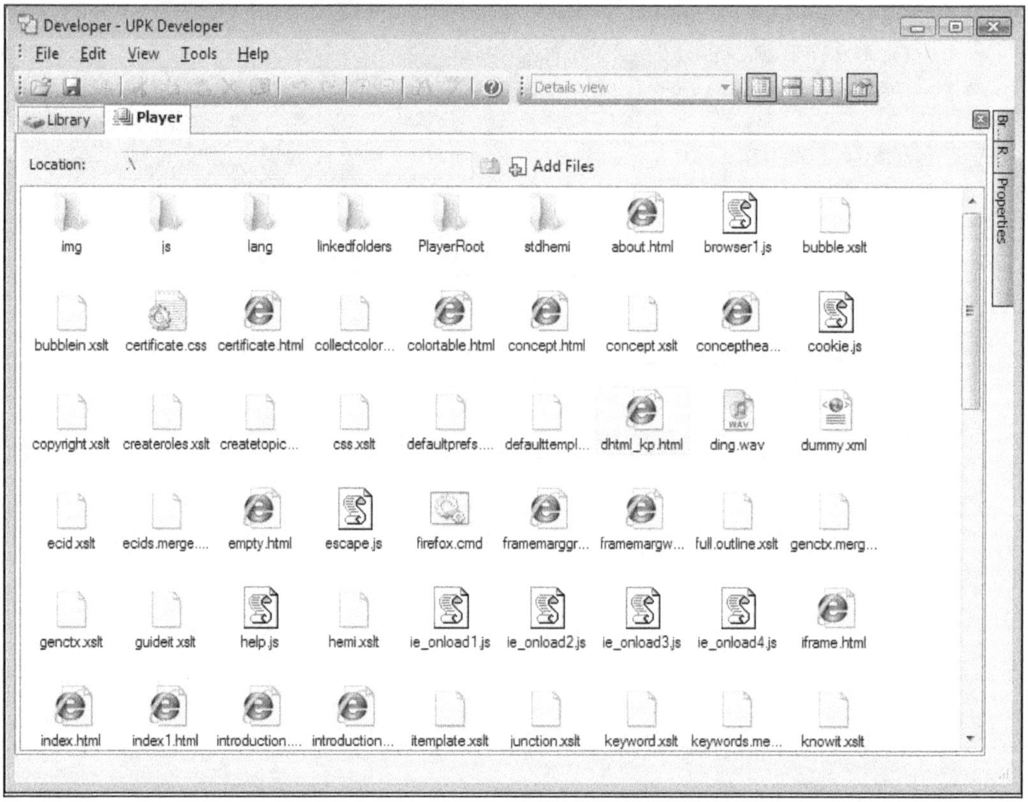

You can see that this Deployment Package, as with all packages in UPK (see Chapter 9, *Adding Value to Your Topics*) is simply a collection of files. And, as with all other packages, you can't *edit* these files from within the **Developer** screen. If you want to edit any of these files, you need to copy the file out of UPK and onto to your local PC, edit it there, and then copy it back. It is therefore recommended that you take a complete copy of the files in this Package to your PC, where you can change the view, search the files, and so on. You can then change the files locally, and copy the changed files back into the Package into UPK as you would when adding any other files to a Package.

For our example, we are going to replace the black and white "information" icon with a more interesting green one. As we saw in Chapter 4, *Editing a Topic*, it is possible to add a small icon to any bubble. We used this functionality to add an "information" icon to Explanation Frames, as shown in the following example:

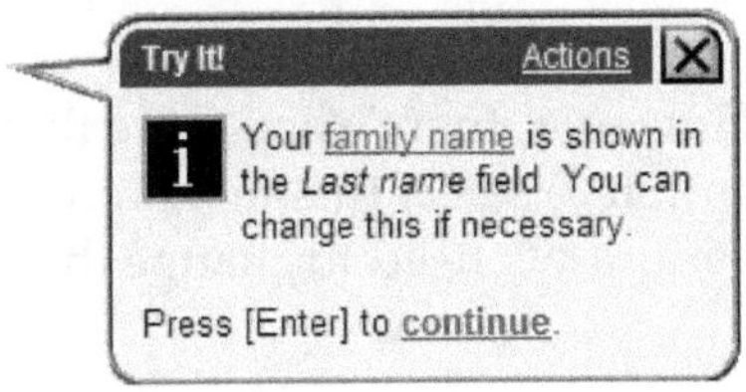

However, the icons that UPK provides are only black and white, in some cases obscure (some kind of a coughing dog??), and generally uninspiring. It would be nice to have a better-looking icon, like the one shown here:

To do this, we carry out the following steps:

1. Open the custom Package for the **Player** deployment format.
2. Double-click on the `img` folder to open it (it is opened within the same tab).
3. Click on the Add Files button ( ).
4. In the **Open** dialog box, navigate to and select the customized version of the file. For our example, this is the file `icon01.gif`. It is important that the file has *exactly* the same name as the file that you are replacing.

> As an alternative to Steps 3 and 4, you can also drag-and-drop (or cut-and-paste) the file from your local workstation, directly into the Package.

5. In response to the message that informs you that a file with the same name already exists in the package, choose to replace the existing file (remember, you still have a copy of the original file in the original package).
6. Save and then close the package.

Now, let's check that your changes have worked. Publish any Topic that uses the "information" icon (make sure you select your custom publishing category), and you should now see the following:

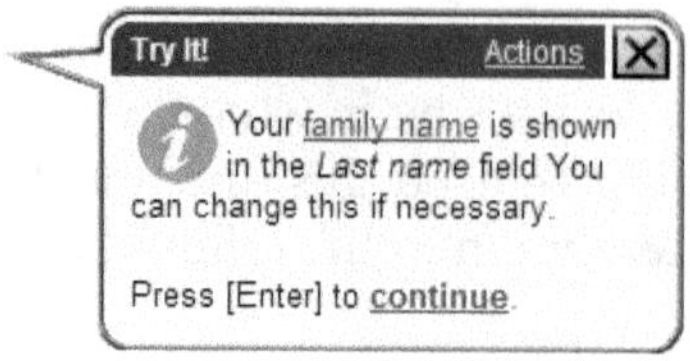

Great! Our changes work. However, there's one more thing we need to take care of—previews. There is an option to select the publishing category that should always be used for previews, and we need to change this to refer to our new publishing category.

To set the publishing category that you want to use for previews, carry out the following steps:

1. Select menu option **Tools | Options**.
2. Select the **Publishing Preview** category.
3. In the **Category** field, select your new custom publishing category.
4. Click **OK** to save your changes.

An example of the **Options** screen showing the selection of a a custom publishing category is shown in the following screenshot:

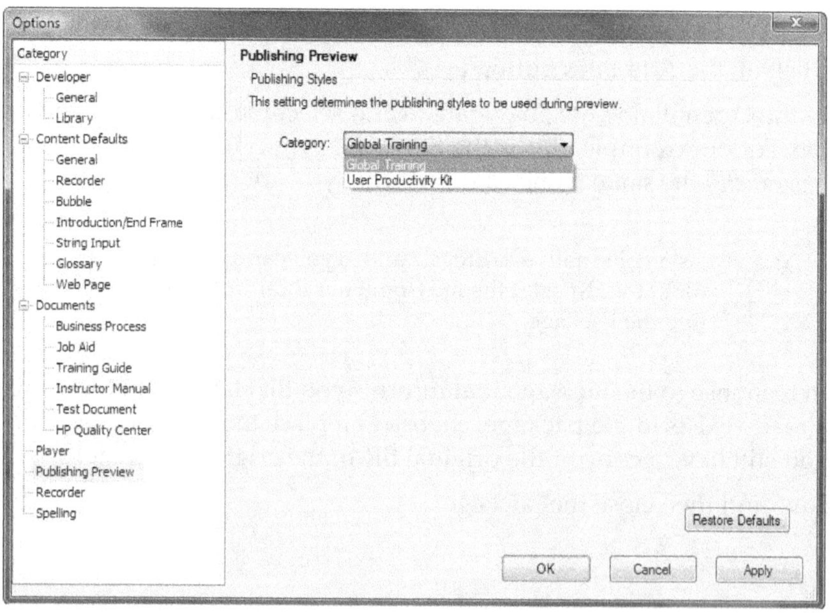

There is one more place where the old icon will appear, and this is within the Topic Editor itself:

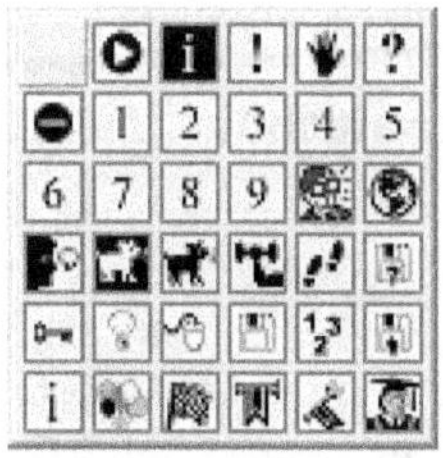

Unfortunately, there is no way to configure this.

Removing the ability to skip in Try It! mode

As discussed in Chapter 10, the UPK Player allows trainees to just press the *Enter* key to skip through the screens when playing a simulation in Try It! mode. For reasons discussed in that chapter, it is recommended that this option is disabled. Unfortunately, out of the box, it is not possible to disable this option without completely disabling the ability to change any user preferences. However, it is possible to remove this option by configuring the Player **deployment package**. In this section, we will do exactly this.

To remove the ability of users to enable skipping, carry out the following steps:

1. In the Library, open the following folder: `System/Publishing/Styles/User Productivity Kit` (or the folder that contains your own customized deployment packages).
2. Double-click on the `Player` package, to open it in the **Package Editor**.
3. Locate the file `prefmain.html`. Copy this file to your local workstation, and open it in your preferred HTML editor (or just in Notepad).
4. Within the file, locate the following statement (note that this is a single—albeit very long—statement):

```
document.write('<input type="checkbox" ID="TryItEnableSkipping"
  title="'+R_preferences_tryitenableskipping2+'"
  language ="javascript" onClick="return
  TryItEnableSkipping_onclick()" NAME="TryItEnableSkipping">
  <label for="TryItEnableSkipping" class="InstructText"
  onMouseOver="tooltip_on(\'skipping_tooltip\')"
```

```
  onMouseOut="tooltip_off(\'skipping_tooltip\')"
  onMouseDown="all_tooltips_off()">'
 +R_preferences_tryitenableskipping+'
 </label>    ');
```

5. Change this line to add the attribute `DISABLED` to the `<input>` statement, as shown below:

```
document.write('<input type="checkbox" ID="TryItEnableSkipping"
  DISABLED title="'+R_preferences_tryitenableskipping2+'"
  language ="javascript" onClick="return
  TryItEnableSkipping_onclick()" NAME="TryItEnableSkipping">
  <label for="TryItEnableSkipping" class="InstructText"
  onMouseOver="tooltip_on(\'skipping_tooltip\')"
  onMouseOut="tooltip_off(\'skipping_tooltip\')"
  onMouseDown="all_tooltips_off()">'
  +R_preferences_tryitenableskipping+'</label>
      ');
```

6. Save the file, and then copy it back into the **Player** package in the **Package Editor**.

Now, when you publish to a Player using this deployment package, trainees will still have access to the **Preferences** dialog box, but the **Enable skipping in Try It! mode** option will no longer be selectable (or de-selectable, depending on how you look at it...). The following screenshot shows our amended **Preferences** dialog box:

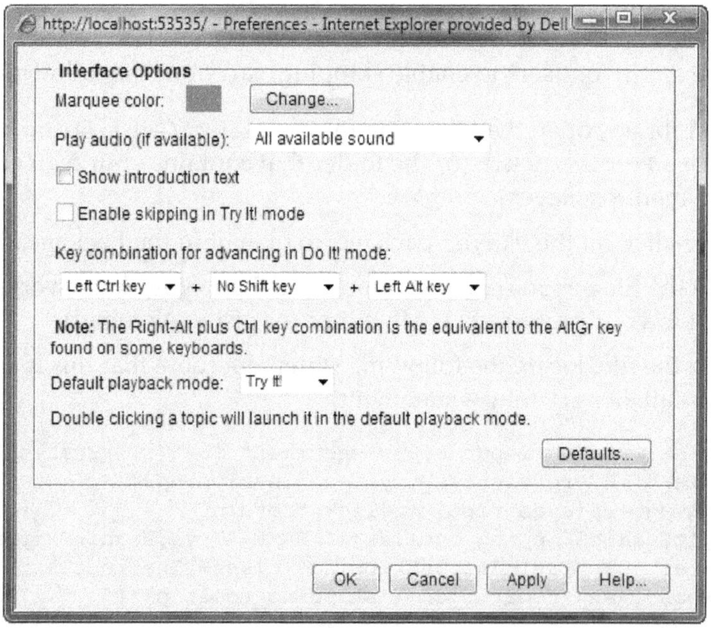

You can see that the **Enable skipping in Try It! mode** option is no longer selectable (it is shown here in a slightly lighter gray than the option above it, which is selectable). Note that it is extremely important here that the **Enable skipping in Try It! mode** option is not selected in the **Publishing** options. Otherwise it will appear as selected (but still disabled) in the Player preferences and there will be no way to deselect it.

Of course, it would be much cleaner to just remove this option altogether, so that it doesn't even appear, but that involves a lot more customization (UPK uses some clever relative references to the various form fields, which presents some problems). This, at least, is a quick-and-dirty workable solution.

Customizing document formats

Now that we have a bit of an understanding of how the deployment formats work, let's take a more adventurous step, and create our own deployment format. As explained in Chapter 9, *Adding Value to Your Topics*, UPK does not provide the ability to publish the Glossary as a stand-alone document. In this section, we will build our own Glossary output document, to address this limitation.

This is a fairly technical operation, but we'll keep the technicalities to a minimum, and explain everything as we go along. If nothing else, this section will at least take away some of the mystery, and give you the confidence to consider customizing UPK's document formats yourself, should you so desire.

Copying an existing document format

The easiest way to create a new document output format is to take one of the existing, default formats, which we know works, and then change this to meet our own requirements. You may recall from the discussion of the available document formats that the Training Guide format includes a Glossary table at the end of the document. This is exactly what we need; we just don't need all of the other content in the document type. So the first thing that we will do is to take a copy of the package for this format.

To take a copy of an existing document format package, carry out the following steps:

1. If you have not already done so, create your own, custom deployment category. How to do this is explained in the section *Creating your own deployment category*, earlier in this chapter. It is recommended that you always take a copy of the standard, delivered objects, and customize the copy. In this way, you will always have the 'vanilla' installed versions to revert to if things go wrong. For our purposes, we will use the custom deployment category **Global Training** that we created in the last section.

2. Make sure that the columns displayed for the content objects include the *Document ID* property. This will help you to distinguish between the existing package and the new package, in Step 6.
3. Open up the folder containing your custom deployment category in the Library, and click on the package for the format that you want to copy. For our exercise, we will copy the *Training Guide* package. Make a note of the *Document ID* of this content object.
4. Select menu option **Edit | Copy** (or press *Ctrl* + *C* on your keyboard).
5. Select menu option **Edit | Paste** (or press *Ctrl* + *V* on your keyboard).
6. You now have two packages, both called *Training Guide*. Locate the new copy (this is the one that does not have the *Document* ID noted in Step 3), right-click on it, and then select **Rename** from the context menu.
7. Type a new name for your new package, and then press *Enter*. You can use any name that you like. This will not be used on any screens or in any menus; the actual package name is defined within the package itself. For our exercise, we will name the package **Glossary**.

Customizing the UPK settings

If you open up the Publication Package that you have just created, you will see several dozen files, and a single folder, which contains even more folders and files. Do not worry about all of these; we will just change a few of them, so that you get an idea of what can be done. What we will do is change the name of this Package, which is important if we want to be able to select this output document formant when we publish, and customize the publishing options that you will see in UPK.

To change a document format name, carry out the following steps:

1. If you have not already done so, open the package for the document format, in the **Package Editor**.
2. Locate the file `lang\en\style.resources.xml`, and copy this to your local workstation. As explained earlier in this chapter, you cannot edit Package files directly in UPK, so you need to copy them to your workstation, change them there, and then copy them back into UPK.
3. Open up the file in your favorite XML editor (or Notepad, which we'll use here, if you have nothing else). Change the code in this file to match the following sample. The changed sections have been set in bold, for clarity.

```
<?xml version="1.0" encoding="utf-8"?>
  <Resources xmlns="urn:Publishing Resource/v1"
  xmlns:xml="http://www.w3.org/XML/1998/namespace">
    <Resource xml:id="StyleName">Glossary</Resource>
```

```
<Resource xml:id="CategoryName">Documents</Resource>
<Resource xml:id="PreviewTitle">Glossary</Resource>
<Resource xml:id="SubFolderName">Glossary</Resource>
<Resource xml:id="labelFormatDescriptionText">Produces a stand
  alone document containing all of the glossary items in the
  published Outline. The document can be generated as a
  Microsoft Word document or an Adobe PDF file.</Resource>
<Resource xml:id="groupBoxOutputText">Output</Resource>
<Resource xml:id="labelOutputFormatText">&amp;Output
  format:</Resource>
<Resource xml:id="comboBoxOutputFormatTextD">Microsoft
  Word</Resource>
<Resource xml:id="comboBoxOutputFormatTextP">Adobe
  PDF</Resource>
<Resource xml:id="comboBoxOutputFormatTextB">
  Both</Resource>
<Resource xml:id="labelMSFileTypeText">Microsoft file
  type:</Resource>
<Resource xml:id="comboBoxMSFileTypeTextD">Document
  (.doc)</Resource>
<Resource xml:id="comboBoxMSFileTypeTextX">Document
  (.docx)</Resource>
<Resource xml:id="groupBoxScreenshotsText">
   Screenshots</Resource>
<Resource xml:id="labelIncludeScreenshotsText">
  Include:</Resource>
<Resource xml:id="comboBoxIncludeScreenshotsTextS">Topic
  settings</Resource>
<Resource xml:id="comboBoxIncludeScreenshotsTextT">One
  screenshot per topic</Resource>
<Resource xml:id="comboBoxIncludeScreenshotsTextF">One
  screenshot per frame</Resource>
<Resource xml:id="comboBoxIncludeScreenshotsTextN">
  None</Resource>
<Resource xml:id="checkBoxConvertScreenshotsText">
  &amp;Convert
  screenshots to 256 colors</Resource>
<Resource xml:id="labelPaperSizeText">Paper size:</Resource>
<Resource xml:id="comboBoxPaperSizeTextA">A4</Resource>
<Resource xml:id="comboBoxPaperSizeTextL">Letter</Resource>
<Resource xml:id="comboBoxPaperSizeTextT">Print template
  setting</Resource>
<Resource xml:id="labelTextModeText">&amp;Text mode:
</Resource>
<Resource xml:id="comboBoxTextModeTextD">See It! / Try
  It!</Resource>
```

```
        <Resource xml:id="comboBoxTextModeTextC">Do It!</Resource>
        <Resource xml:id="comboBoxTextModeTextA">Know It?</Resource>
        <Resource xml:id="checkBoxIncludeAlternativesText">
          Include &amp;alternatives</Resource>
        <Resource xml:id="checkBoxIncludePackageImagesText">
          Include &amp;images from packages</Resource>
        <Resource xml:id="checkBoxIncludeWebImagesText">Include images
          in &amp;web pages</Resource>
        <Resource xml:id="checkBoxUseEncodedFolderAndFileNamesText">Use
          &amp;encoded folder and file names</Resource>
        <Resource xml:id="buttonUseOptionsSettingsText">Use
          Op&amp;tions Settings</Resource>
        <Resource xml:id="FontName">Microsoft Sans Serif</Resource>
        <Resource xml:id="FontSize">8.25pt</Resource>
        <Resource xml:id="FontType">Regular</Resource>
        <Resource xml:id="FontColor">ControlText</Resource>
    </Resources>
```

4. Do not worry about all of the other settings—we will not use most of them.
5. Save the file, and copy it back into the publications package in UPK.

We have now renamed our deployment format, so that it will appear correctly in the UPK screens. Next, we need to change the publication options for this deployment format. We based our new format on the existing *Training Guide* format, but we do not need most of the options available for the *Training Guide* format, as we will not use most of the content to which they apply.

To change the publication options for an output format, carry out the following steps:

1. If you have not already done so, open the package for the document format, in the **Package Editor**.
2. Locate the file `styles.xml`, and copy this to your local workstation.
3. Open up the file in your favorite XML editor. Change the *first section of* code in this file to match the following sample. The changed sections have been set in bold.

```
<?xml version="1.0" encoding="UTF-8"?>
  <Style xmlns:xlink="http://www.w3.org/1999/xlink"
    xmlns:xi="http://www.w3.org/2003/XInclude">
  <Name ResId="StyleName"></Name>
  <Category CategoryOrder="2" StyleOrder="7"
    ResId="CategoryName"></Category>
  <Settings>
    <Setting>
```

```
    <Name>FeatureId</Name>
    <DefaultValue>Publishing_ILT</DefaultValue>
  </Setting>
  <Setting>
    <Name>PreviewTitle</Name>
    <DefaultValue ResId="PreviewTitle">
    </DefaultValue>
  </Setting>
  <Setting>
    <Name>PreviewOrder</Name>
    <DefaultValue>10</DefaultValue>
  </Setting>
  <Setting>
    <Name>PreviewProjectFile</Name>
    <DefaultValue>preview.project.xml
    </DefaultValue>
  </Setting>
  <Setting>
    <Name>AutoLaunchPreview</Name>
    <DefaultValue>preview.txt</DefaultValue>
  </Setting>
  <Setting>
    <Name>SubFolderName</Name>
    <DefaultValue ResId="SubFolderName">
    </DefaultValue>
  </Setting>
```

4. The `StyleOrder` setting defines the position in which this output document format will appear in the **Publish Content** window. The `PreviewOrder` defines the position in which the output document format will appear in the **Preview** drop-down. We will see both of these, shortly. Note that it is important that you either position your new document format after all of the existing formats, or reposition all of the other formats, as appropriate.
5. Locate the `<Controls>` sections in the remainder of the file, and replace the `<Visible>true</Visible>` tag with `<Visible>false</Visible>` for the following controls:
    - `<Name>ScreenshotsGroupBoxSetting</Name>`
    - `<Name>IncludeScreenshots</Name>`
    - `<Name>ConvertScreenshotsSetting</Name>`
    - `<Name>TextMode</Name>`
    - `<Name>UseEncodedFolderAndFileNames</Name>`
    - `<Name>IncludeAlternativesSetting</Name>`

- `<Name>IncludePackageImagesSetting</Name>`
- `<Name>IncludeWebImagesSetting</Name>`
- `<Name>UseOptionsButtonSetting</Name>`

6. This will hide all of the publication options that are not relevant to our Glossary.
7. Save the file, and copy it back into the publications package in UPK.
8. Save your custom Publication Package.

Now, let's see what this has done for us. Close UPK and then open it again. (This is necessary to make sure that UPK picks up on your changes.) Open any outline element in the *Outline Editor*, and click on any Topic within it. Then click on the drop-down button for the **Preview** field. You should see a result similar to the one shown in the following screenshot:

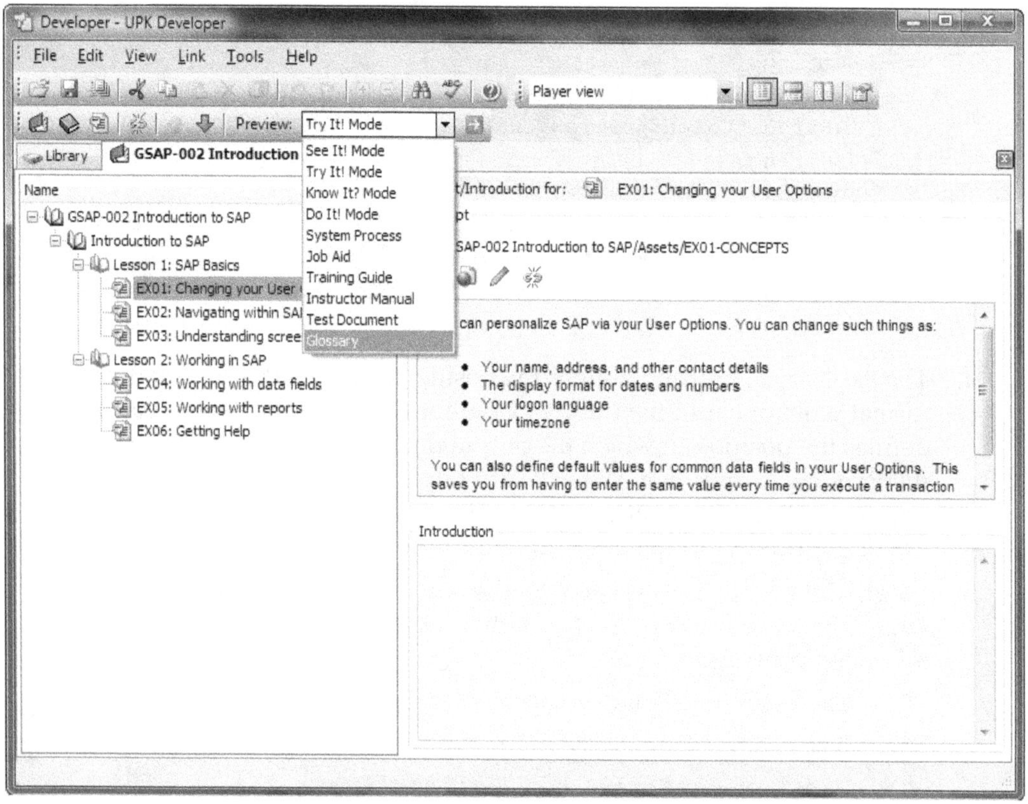

You can see that we now have a new option: **Glossary**. Note that this is the tenth entry in the drop-down. This ties in with our `PreviewOrder` value of `10`.

Next, click on the **Publish** button (), and follow the Publishing Wizard through until you reach the **Formats** window. Make sure that you select your custom deployment category in the **Advanced Publishing Options** (in our example, this is called **Global Training**), otherwise you will not see your changes. You should now see a screen similar to the one shown here:

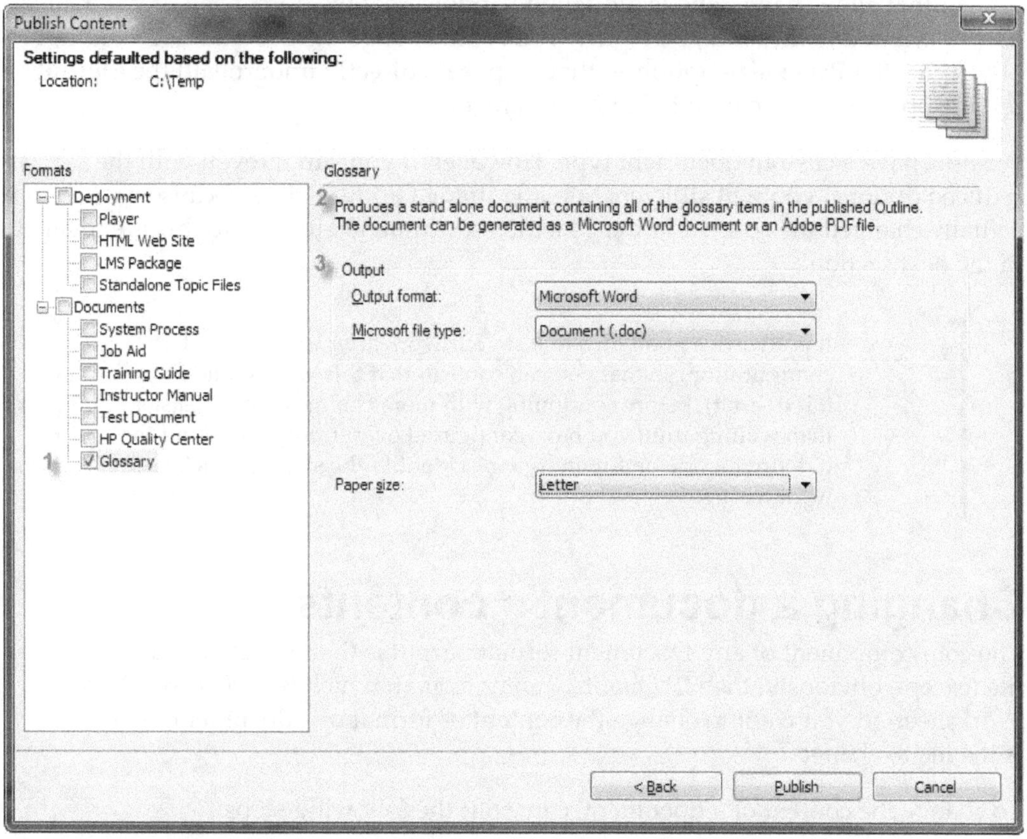

Success! Our new output format has been detected and is usable.

There are three things to note on this screen. These are numbered on the previous screenshot.

1. The **Glossary** format appears as the seventh format type on the second category (**Documents**). This ties in with our styles.xml settings of <Category CategoryOrder="2" StyleOrder="7">. The text "**Glossary**" is taken from the StyleName setting in the style.resources.xml file.

2. The description of this output format is taken from the labelFormatDescriptionText setting in the style.resources.xml file.
3. The available options are defined by the <controls> settings in the styles.xml file. Compare these options with the options available for the *Training Guide* output format (see Chapter 6, *Publishing Your Content*). You will see that all we have done is hidden the options that we don't need. If you really wanted to tidy things up, then you could change the Top and Left settings for the **Paper size** option so that it appears directly underneath the **Output** options, but we'll save that for a rainy day.

We now have a custom document type. However, if you run it (even with the reduced options) you will still generate a Training Guide. This is because we haven't actually changed the content of the generated document. How to do this is explained in the next section.

> It is always a good idea to test your work after each piece of configuration, so that you can confirm that this works (and fix it if it doesn't), before continuing with more changes. This is easier than waiting until you have configured everything to find out that it doesn't work, and then trying to identify the step at which you went wrong.

Changing a document's contents

The core component of any Document format output is the PrintTemplate.docm file (except, obviously, the HP Quality Center format, which is a Microsoft Excel Worksheet). If you want to change the content or format of a document, then this is the file to change.

To change the content of a document, carry out the following steps:

1. If you have not already done so, open the package for the document format, in the **Package Editor**.
2. Locate the file lang\en\PrintTemplate.docm, and copy this to your local workstation. (The file type .docm indicates that this is a **Microsoft Word Document with Macros**. The macros are what do all the work for us.)
3. Open up this file in Word (and enable macros, if prompted). You will see that the file contains a number of bookmarks. These are used as placeholders for the actual content, which is built separately by a series of .xslt files, and then dropped into this document. In our example, we are changing what was originally a Training Guide, which is a single file that can contain multiple Modules, Sections, and Topics, all of which can contain Web Pages

or Packages, followed by a Glossary at the end. The basic processing logic for this document (as defined by the macros) is therefore:

1. Insert the name of the outline element being published, and the creation date, followed by a page break.
2. Insert the copyright notice, followed by a page break.
3. Insert the table of contents, followed by a page break.
4. Repeat for each Module or Section in the Outline:
    i. Insert the Module or Section name.
    ii. Insert links to any websites provided via Packages.
    iii. Insert any Web Pages attached to the Module or Section.
    iv. Repeat for each Topic in the Module or Section:
        a. Insert links to any websites provided via Packages.
        b. Insert any Web Pages attached to the Topic.
        c. Repeat for each Frame in the Topic:
            I. Insert the screenshot.
            II. Insert the actions.
            III. Insert any attachments.
        d. Loop.
    v. Loop.
5. Loop.
6. Insert the Glossary.

4. Edit this file to remove all of information that you no longer want to appear in the printed output. For our example, we only want to keep the Glossary at the end, so we will remove the Module, Section, and Topic placeholders, and all of their contents. This is Steps 1 to 5 and all of their sub-steps, in the example above.
5. We will also remove the copyright notice (you'll probably always want to modify this as by default it credits Oracle, which probably isn't true for your training content). Finally, because we now have only one section (the Glossary), we don't really need the table of contents, so we'll remove that, too. We'll keep the front page with the outline element name on it—this will be useful if we publish separate glossaries for separate outlines.

6. This will give us a Word document that contains only the content shown in the next two screenshots:

   Page 1:

Page 2:

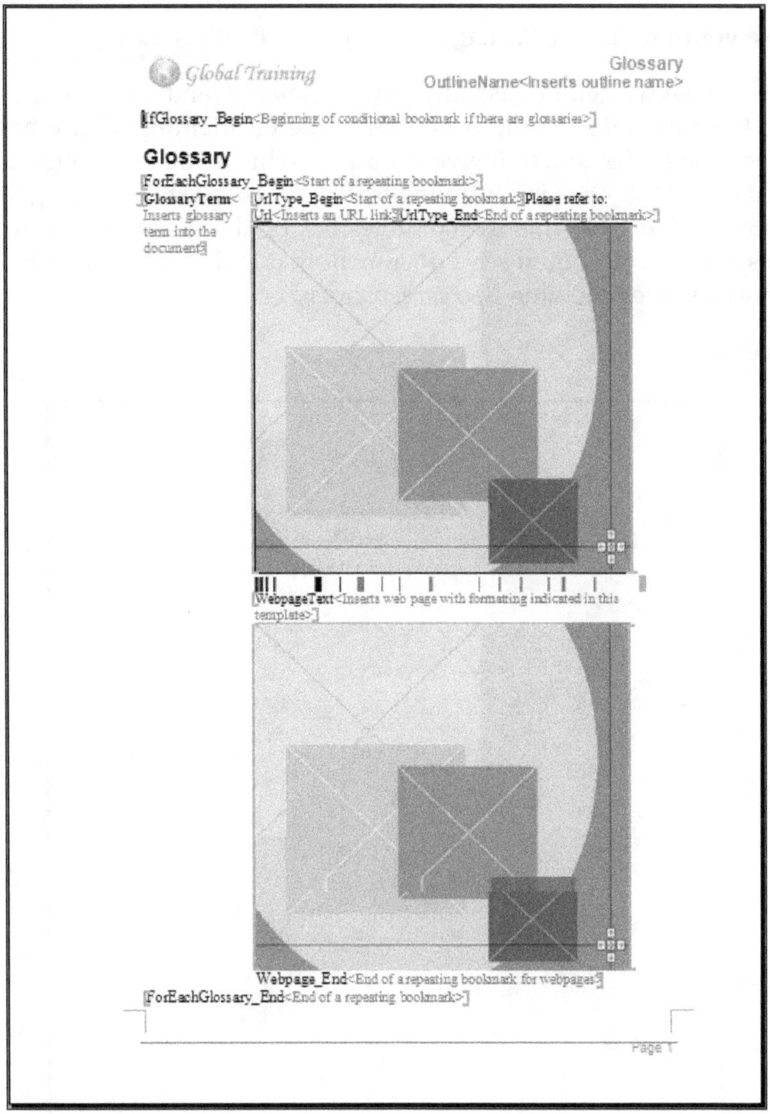

Caution:

Be very careful about editing this file; it is extremely sensitive, and it is easy to make a mistake. That said, it is safe to delete the last four lines in the original file; even though they say "DO NOT DELETE" they refer to elements that we no longer need.

7. Once your `PrintTemplate.docm` file looks like the example above, save it, and then copy it back into your Publishing Package.
8. Save your Publishing Package and close the **Package Editor**.

Now, let's see what we get. Publish any outline element, and select your new Glossary as the output document format. Once the **Publishing Wizard** has finished, open the folder containing your output (which, you will notice, is a folder called `GLOSSARY` - this is controlled by the `SubFolderName` setting in the `style.resources.xml` file, and then double-click on the Word Document that exists in this folder. You should see a document that looks very similar to the example shown in the following two screenshots:

Page 1:

Page 2:

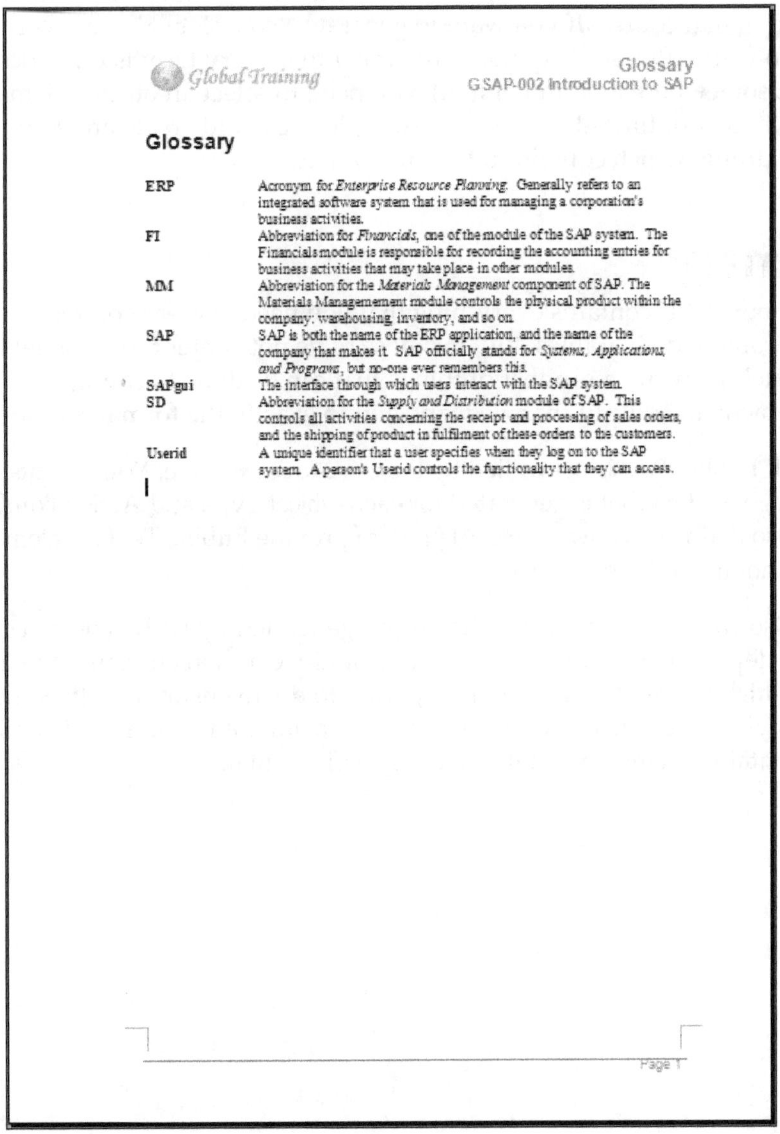

Global Training

Glossary
GSAP-002 Introduction to SAP

Glossary

ERP	Acronym for *Enterprise Resource Planning*. Generally refers to an integrated software system that is used for managing a corporation's business activities.
FI	Abbreviation for *Financials*, one of the module of the SAP system. The Financials module is responsible for recording the accounting entries for business activities that may take place in other modules.
MM	Abbreviation for the *Materials Management* component of SAP. The Materials Managemement module controls the physical product within the company: warehousing, inventory, and so on.
SAP	SAP is both the name of the ERP application, and the name of the company that makes it. SAP officially stands for *Systems, Applications, and Programs*, but no-one ever remembers this.
SAPgui	The interface through which users interact with the SAP system.
SD	Abbreviation for the *Supply and Distribution* module of SAP. This controls all activities concerning the receipt and processing of sales orders, and the shipping of product in fulfilment of these orders to the customers.
Userid	A unique identifier that a user specifies when they log on to the SAP system. A person's Userid controls the functionality that they can access.

Page 1

So there you have it. After what wasn't really that much work, we have managed to create our own document format, which generates a nice, stand-alone *Glossary* for us. Of course, you'll no doubt want to apply some additional formatting to this document, but for an hour's work, that's not bad!

Note that this solution is relatively flexible. If you select an outline element for a single course, as we did here, then you will generate a glossary that contains only terms used in that course. If you want to generate a complete glossary containing all terms in your UPK Glossary then (assuming that every term is referenced at least once, somewhere in your content), you need to select an outline element that contains all other outline elements. For example, we could create an Outline called **Global Training**, which contains all of our courses.

Summary

Out of the box, UPK contains everything that you need to create perfectly adequate training deliverables. But, for those of us not content (or unable) to stop at "adequate", there are a number of things that can be done to configure UPK to produce exactly the output that we want, and in exactly the format that we want.

The default Bubble Text is controlled by the `template.xml` file. You can customize this file to change the text that is generated for each Object Type and Action combination. You can also define your own Object Types, to provide Bubble Text for elements that UPK does not naturally recognize.

You can also change the format of the output generated by UPK. You can configure the online deployment formats, but most flexibility exists in changing the document formats, which you will more than likely want to do, to ensure that they meet your in-house styles. You can also define your own document formats, and configure these to contain specific information, in a specific format.

13
Localizing Your Content

UPK provides built-in support for several different languages, and has the ability to "automatically" translate between these languages. Actually, it is far from automatic, but in its defense, it is much faster and simpler than calling in a translator and having them manually translate all of the text in a simulation. Specifically, UPK provides a very simple automatic translation of Template Text into 21 supported languages, and provides a relatively simple mechanism for facilitating the human translation of Custom Text. In this chapter, we'll look at both of these.

In this chapter you will learn:

- How to use a foreign-language template to translate Template Text
- How to use foreign languages in the deployment formats
- How to export Custom Text for translation, via either Word or XLIFF

Foreign-language templates

In Chapter 4, *Editing a Topic*, we looked at the default templates that ship with UPK. These templates specify the text that is to be used, by default, in the screen Bubbles, during playback. In Chapter 12, *Configuring UPK*, we looked at how to define our own custom templates, and how to assign a custom template to a Module, Lesson, or Topic. Given this understanding of how templates work in general, it is not difficult to see how foreign-language templates would work. It's basically, in exactly the same way.

> In this book, we use the term foreign-language to refer to any language other than English (which is the native language in which this book was originally written). If you are reading a translated version, you should make the appropriate mental adjustments.

When we created our own custom template, we took the existing (**Standard-English**) template from the directory `system/templates/en`. Observant readers will have noticed that the `system/templates` directory also contains several other directories, as shown in the following screenshot:

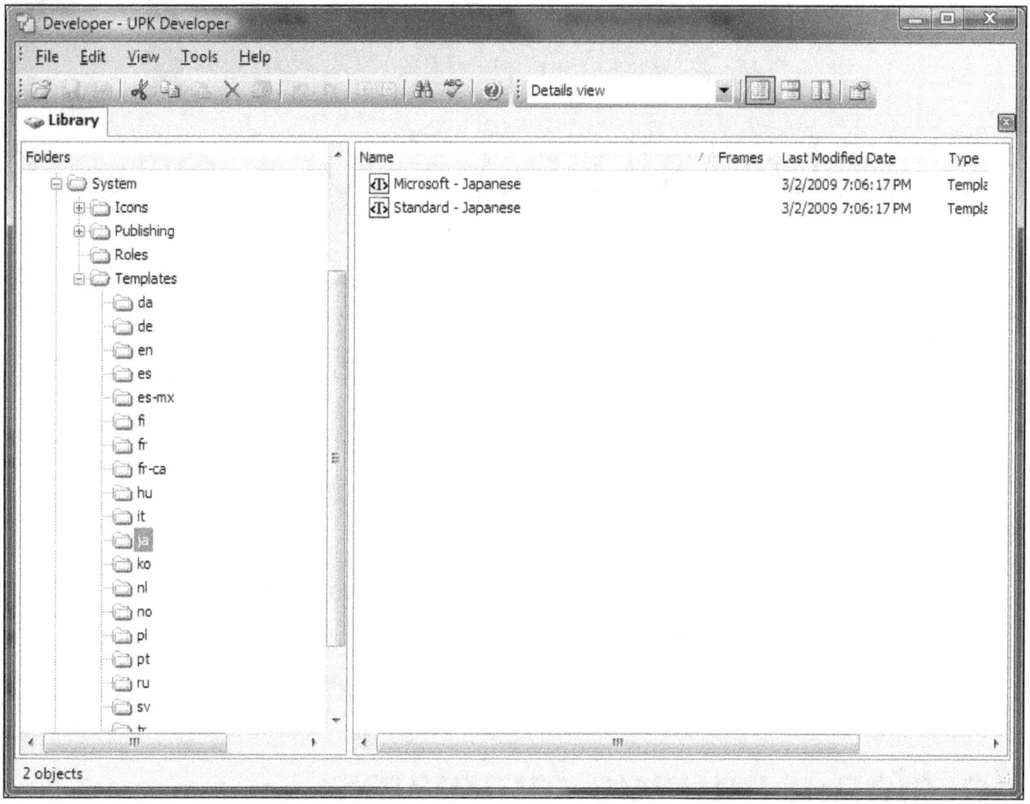

Each of these directories contains the same two Template Packages (`Microsoft` and `Standard`) as the `/en` folder, but in the language after which the folder is named. The folder names use the standard ISO two-character *language* (not country) code, plus a country/dialect suffix where necessary. So the `/fr` folder contains templates that define French-language text, and the `/fr-ca` directory contains templates for Canadian French.

Supported languages

Currently, UPK provides built-in support for the following languages:

- **da**: Danish
- **de**: German

- **en**: English
- **es**: Spanish
- **es-mx**: Mexican Spanish
- **fi**: Finnish
- **fr**: French
- **fr-ca**: French Canadian
- **hu**: Hungarian
- **it**: Italian
- **ja**: Japanese
- **ko**: Korean
- **nl**: Dutch
- **no**: Norwegian
- **pl**: Polish
- **pt**: Portuguese
- **ru**: Russian
- **sv**: Swedish
- **tr**: Turkish
- **zh-CHS**: Simplified Chinese
- **zh-CHT**: Traditional Chinese

> **Version Difference**
>
> Support for Finnish, Turkish, Polish, Russian, Hungarian, Traditional Chinese, and Korean was added in UPK Version 3.5.0.

So what do you do if you need to provide another language (other than the ones listed above)? Simple—you copy the directory for a currently supported language, (in exactly the same way as we created a custom (English) template in Chapter 12, *Configuring UPK*), rename it as appropriate, and then change all of the default text in the template(s) to the required language. (OK, so this last part might be a little time-consuming, but it is still faster than translating each individual Topic, and is reusable, too.)

Foreign-language template format

The format and content of the foreign-language templates are exactly the same as the English-language templates, which were described in detail in Chapter 12, *Configuring UPK*. The code below an extract from the default Japanese-language template (`/ja/Standard - Japanese`), showing the Template Text for string input actions. The Japanese Template Text (as opposed to tags or comments, all of which are always in English) is shown in bold, for emphasis (although I'm sure you'd be able to spot it, anyway).

```
<Template Context="StringInput">
  <!-- Example: Enter the desired information into the Test field
    Enter 123-->
  <Text>[</Text>
  <ObjectName/>
  <Text Sound="stginp2-neutral">
    ]フィールドに目的の情報を入力します。
  </Text>
  <StringInputExtension Type="anything" Sound="sivalid-
    neutral">
    有効な値
  </StringInputExtension>
  <StringInputExtension Type="example" Sound="siexample-
    neutral">(</StringInputExtension>
  <Content/>
  <StringInputExtension Type="blank" Sound="siblank-
      neutral">
    など)を入力するか、または空白のままにします
  </StringInputExtension>
  <Text>
    を入力して下さい。
  </Text>
</Template>
```

Compare this with the English-language version from Chapter 12, *Configuring UPK*, which is repeated below, for your ease of reference. Again, the actual Template Text is shown in **bold**, to simplify the comparison.

```
<Template Context="StringInput">
  <!-- Example: Enter the desired information into the Test field.
    Enter 123.-->
  <Text Sound="stginput">
    Enter the desired information into the
  </Text>
  <ObjectName />
  <Text Sound="stginp2">
```

```
      field. Enter
    </Text>
    <StringInputExtension Type="anything" Sound="sivalid">
      a valid value
    </StringInputExtension>
    <StringInputExtension Type="example" Sound="siexample">
      e.g.
    </StringInputExtension>
    <Content />
    <StringInputExtension Type="blank" Sound="siblank">
      or leave blank
    </StringInputExtension>
    <Text>.</Text>
  </Template>
```

As you can see, it's all relatively straightforward, and it's very easy to identify the foreign-language equivalent of the English text. (It also helps that the tags and the comments are still in English!) While we're here, note that whereas the `Sound` settings in the English-language version are in the form `"sivalid"`, the Japanese-language version is `"sivalid-neutral"`. As explained in Chapter 12, *Configuring UPK*, this is because in some languages (Japanese in this case) *things* can be masculine, feminine, or neutral, and the words to use can change according to this. The example shown here considers the objects to be neutral. There are similar entries for masculine and feminine objects.

Providing existing content in a foreign language

In order to provide existing content objects in a language other than the one in which they were originally developed, a number of specific steps need to be carried out. These are summarized below, and explained fully in the next several sections of this document (although not necessarily in this order, to provide a more logical explanation).

1. Take a copy of the existing content.
2. Export the Custom Text and have it translated.
3. Import the translated Custom Text.
4. Select the appropriate foreign-language template, to translate the Template Text.
5. Re-record the screenshots.
6. Re-record any sound (if used).
7. Publish the content, using the appropriate deployment language.

Taking a copy of the existing content

Before you "localize" a content object, you must make a copy of that object. This is extremely important, and bears repeating: Make a copy of that object. Later in the translation process (step 2, in the list earlier) you will need to export this *copy*. If you export the original file, then when you import it again, you will overwrite the original! In contrast, if you take a copy of the document and export the copy for translation, then when you import the translated file again, it will update this copy, leaving the original document in the original language.

> If you do not have any Custom Text, are not using sound, and will not be localizing the screenshots, then you could, in theory, simply change the template on the existing content (step 4), and publish to the appropriate foreign language (step 7), and then change the template back to the original language once you're done. However, few localization processes are this simple.

The fastest way to take a copy of a document is to select it in the Library, press *Ctrl* + *C* and then press *Ctrl* + *V*. This will take an exact copy, called exactly the same thing. You may want to rename it, or move it to another folder, to make sure that you do not select the wrong copy for export.

If you are going to translate a document and all of the documents related to it, you will need to take copies of all of these, and then link all of these copies to the copy of the original document that you made, so that the linked copies are also selected for translation, and not the originals.

Using a foreign-language template

Once you have taken a copy of a content object (a Topic, in our example), the next step is to attach a foreign-language template to it.

Before we do that, let's see how the Topic looks (in the Player) when the English-language template is used.

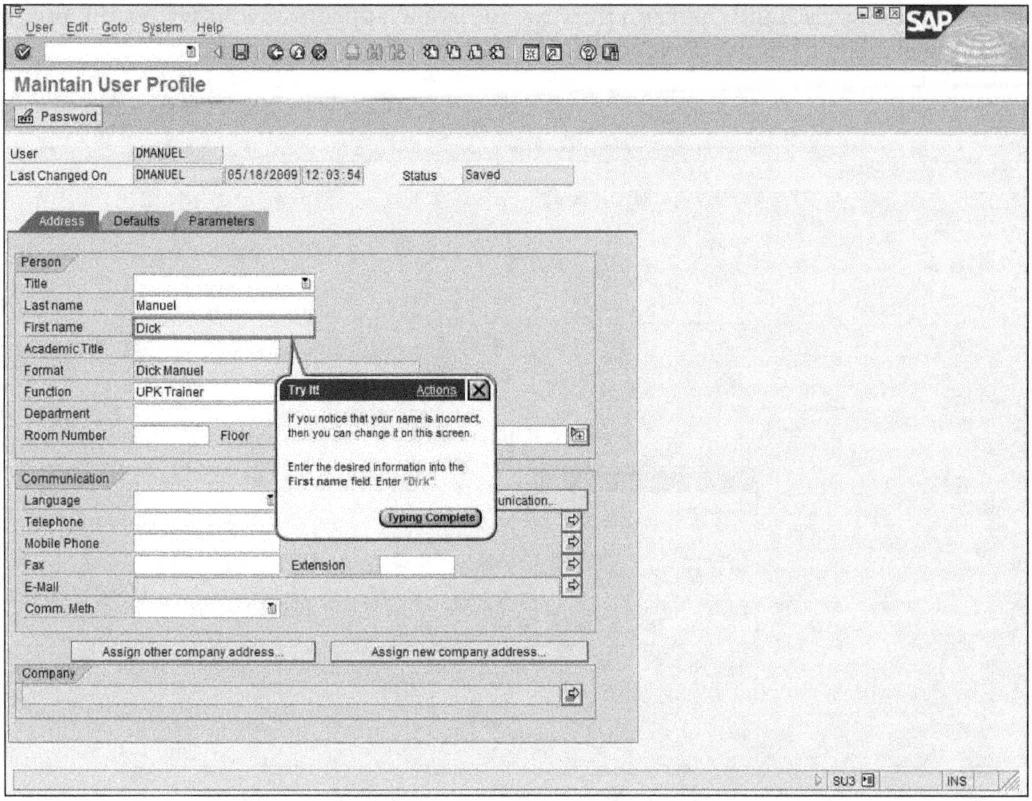

Now, let's assign a foreign-language template to this exercise. How to do this was described in Chapter 12, *Configuring UPK*, but in summary, the steps are:

1. Select the Task in the Library.
2. Display the Properties for the task by clicking on the **Properties** button ().
3. Expand the General area.
4. In the **Template** field, navigate to, and select, the `Standard - {language}` template in the relevant language directory. In our example, this will be `System/Templates/JA/Standard - Japanese`.

Publish the exercise, and then run it. Now, the Topic appears as follows (again, this example is taken from the Player):

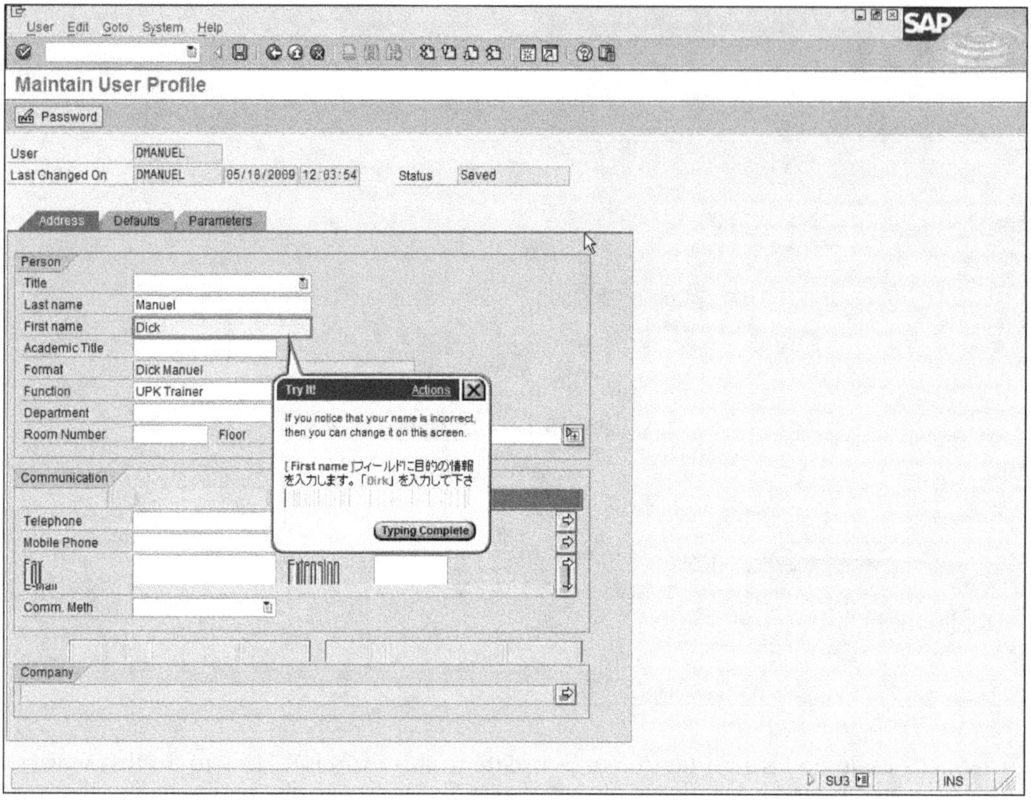

As you can see, the Template Text is now in Japanese. Success!

But wait! What about the custom text? For that matter, what about the "**Typing Complete**" bubble? And the "`Actions`" link? Fortunately, we can translate these, too, which is what we'll do in the following section.

Using a foreign-language Deployment Package

What we have done so far is translate the Template Text. The other elements that you see in English above (excluding the Custom Text, which we'll look at in the next section) are tied to the Player (actually, they are tied to the deployment format, which just happens to be a Player in this case). So, how do we translate this text? Where is it defined? To answer the first question: we don't. UPK already ships with foreign-language versions of this text.

The answer to *where* the text is defined is simple. It is defined in the same **Publishing Options** that we looked at in Chapter 12, *Configuring UPK*. All you need to do is tell UPK which language to use when generating the output, and UPK will do the rest.

To use a foreign language in your published output, carry out the following steps:

1. Follow the steps given in Chapter 6, *Publishing Your Content*, until you reach the **Select Publishing Options** screen, shown in the following screenshot:

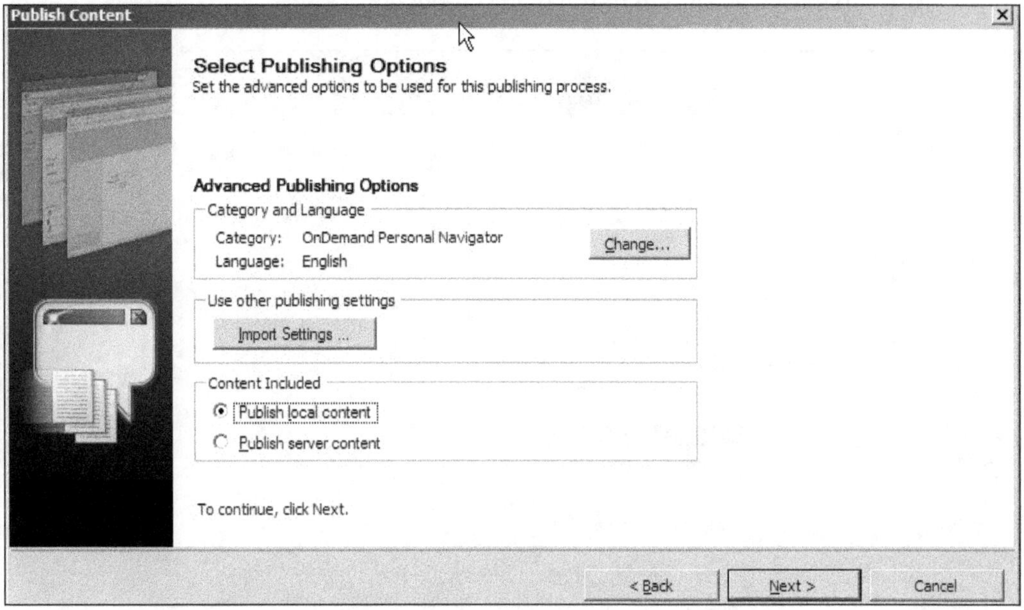

   Note the **Advanced Publishing Options** section. This includes a specification of which language to use.

2. Click on **Change**. The **Set Category and Language** dialog box is displayed, as shown in the following screenshot:

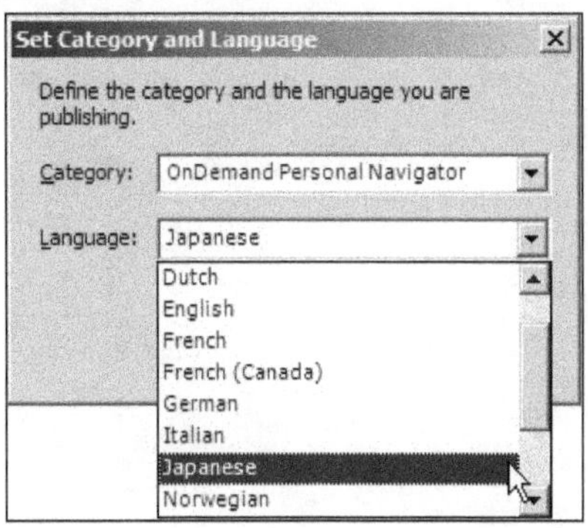

3. In the **Language** field, select the language in which you want the Player (in our case) to be generated—in our example, this is **Japanese**.
4. Click on **OK** to return to the Select Publishing Options screen, and continue with publishing the Player (again, refer to Chapter 6, *Publishing Your Content* for additional guidance if necessary).

   Once publication is complete (and the Player has been created), run it. The Topic will now (almost) be entirely in the foreign language (in our case Japanese), as shown in the next screenshot:

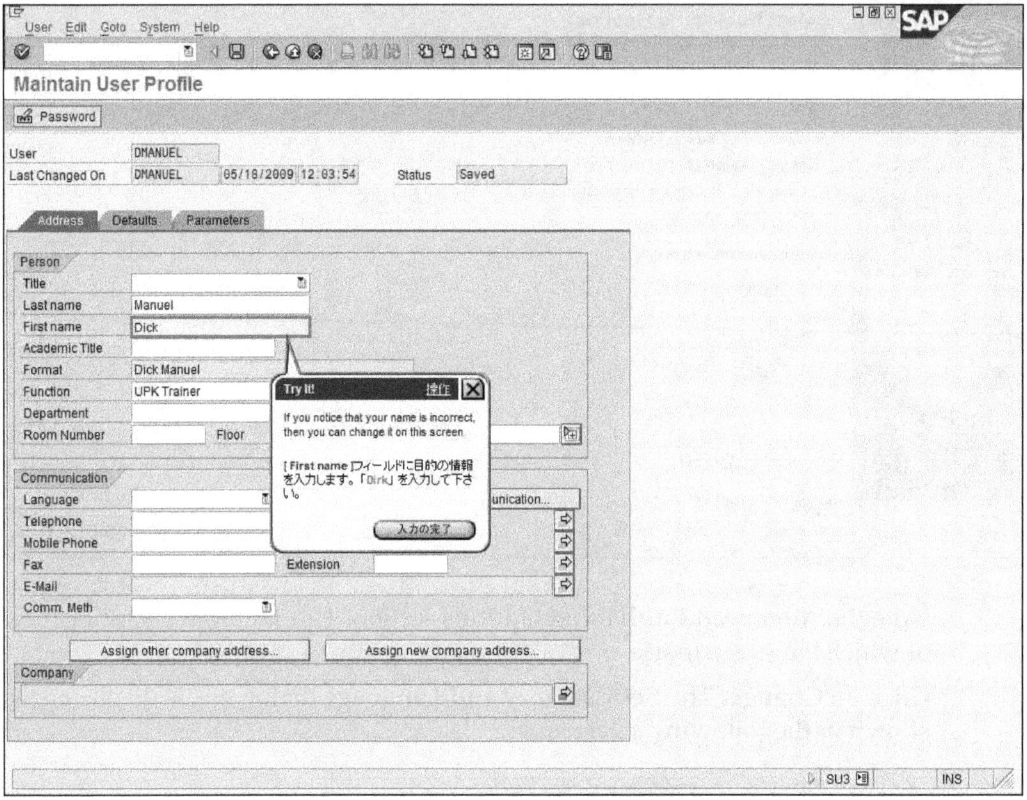

Note that the text "Try It!" in the Bubble title bar has not been translated. (Apparently UPK's four "modes" are universally recognized, and require no translation!) The only thing that hasn't been translated automatically (or if not strictly *automatically* then with relatively little effort) is the Custom Text, which you could forgive UPK for not managing to do. Next, we'll look at how to translate this.

Translating Custom Text

The steps described earlier apply to the Template texts. What if you have *Custom* Texts? These will also need translating, and no amount of fiddling around with templates or publishing options will do that for you. If you have Custom Text in your simulations—which will definitely be the case if you accept the recommendations of this book—then you will have to translate all of these yourself (or at least arrange for the translation yourself). Fortunately, UPK allows you to simply export all of the custom text to a Microsoft Word document that you can then pass to a translator for translation. Once you receive the translated file back, UPK provides an easy method for importing it again, automatically creating a translated version of the exported document(s).

> An advantage of this approach is that the translator does not need to ever see UPK—they are working purely within Microsoft Word.

Exporting content for translation

To export a content object for translation, follow the steps described below.

> **Caution**
>
> You should export the content before changing the **Language** property for the content (in the content's *Properties*) to specify the local language. This is because the language will be used in the exported files, and should therefore correctly specify the *source* language.

1. In the Library, click on the content object that you want to export for translation, to select it.

2. Select menu option **Tools | Export | Localization**. The **Export for Localization** dialog box is displayed, as shown in the following screenshot:

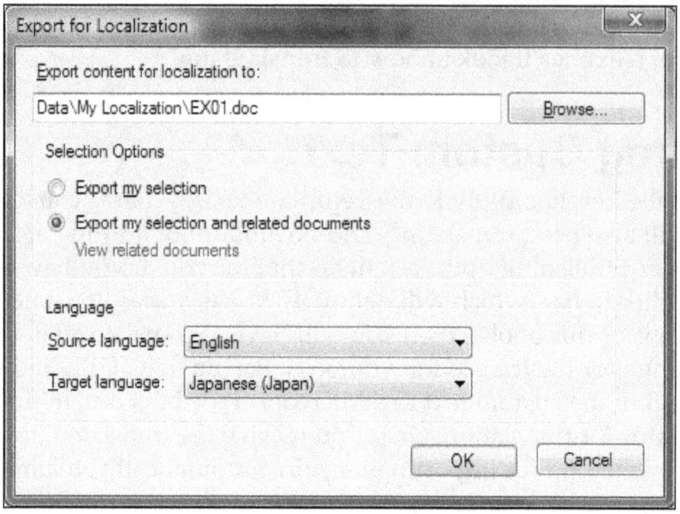

3. Click on the **Browse** button to the right of the **Export content for localization to:** field. The **Save As** dialog box is displayed.

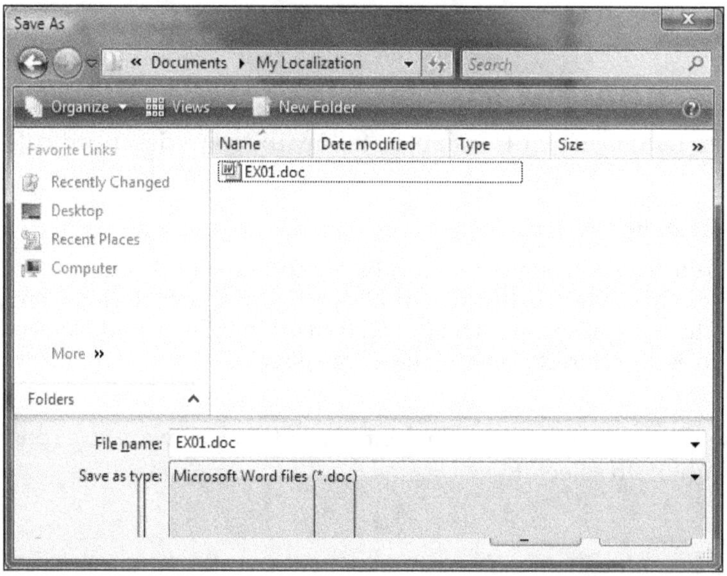

4. Navigate to and select the directory into which you want to save the exported file.

5. Enter a file name for the exported file in the **File name** field. This is largely for the benefit of the translator, so pick something sensible.
6. In the **Save as type** field, choose whether you want to save the file in XLIFF format or as a Microsoft Word document. For our exercise, we will export to **Word**; XLIFF is described separately, later in this chapter.
7. Click on **Save** to close the **Save As** dialog box and return to the **Export for localization** dialog box.
8. Back in the **Export for localization** dialog box, under **Selection Options**, select whether you want to export only the Title that you selected, or the Title and all other related content (such as included Web Pages, and so on). You would normally want to select the latter option.

   If you are not sure which documents will be selected and exported, you can click the **View related documents** link, to display a list of them. Again, make sure that you are only selecting *copies* of the original-language content, unless you want to overwrite the originals.
9. Under **Source Language**, select the current language of the content object (**English (United States)** in our case).
10. Under **Target Language**, select the language into which the content object is to be translated (for this exercise, we will select **Japanese (Japan)**).
11. If you are working in a client/server environment, then you will see an additional set of options, under **Content Includes**, as shown in the example (taken from OnDemand 9.1.5):

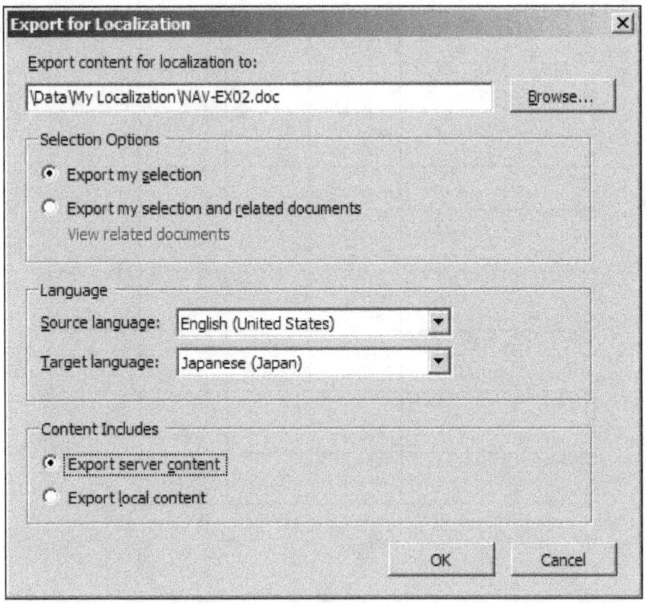

Here, you need to select whether you only want to export the version of the selected content objects that is on the server (option **Export server content**), or whether you want to include content that is in your local repository (option **Export local content**). Note that if you select **Export local content** and the content object does not exist in your local repository, then the server version will be used.

12. Click on **OK**.

The custom text is extracted from the content object (in our example, a single Title), and saved to a Word document. You can display this file in Microsoft Word (or compatible document editor), and the content will look as shown in the following extract:

Document ID: 08112a64-2be8-412b-87a2-47eb73f9bc9a\topic.xml
Data Type: xml

Id	en-US	ja-JP	Notes	System Data
TXT_Title	EX01: Changing your User Profile			
BUB210txt_DP_CP_DD_CD	In this exercise, you will learn how to update your *User Profile* in SAP, to change your date and time formats. You will also learn how to set default values for common input fields.			
IL462.tt	Version History			
F18.jip	Changing your user defaults			
BUB232txt_DP_CP_DD_CD	Click on the **System** menu...			
BUB233txt_DP_CP_DD_CD	...point to **User Profile**...			
BUB234txt_DP_CP_DD_CD	...and then select **Own Data**.			
BUB236txt_DP_CP_DD_CD	If you notice that your name is			

This document is extremely easy to understand. For each document exported, it contains two lines of code, and a table. The two lines of code at the top provide the unique UPK identifier for the document, and the type of document. Both of these are only for UPK's internal use, and allow UPK to import the translated text into the correct place. This is why it is extremely important that we take a copy of the content that we want to translate, and then export the copy—the *Document ID* is the identifier of the document into which the translation will be re-imported.

> You can check the *Document ID* shown in the document heading with the *Document ID* shown in the content object's Properties to confirm that you have indeed exported the copy and not the original of the content object.

The table is the thing that the translator needs to translate. It contains the following columns:

Column	Contents
Id	The identifier of the text that is to be translated. As with the two lines of code above the table, this is internal to UPK, and allows UPK to import the translated text into the correct place. This typically includes characters identifying the source of the text. This is all purely internal information, but for the curious, some of the more common indicators are: • `.txt`: Custom Bubble Text, or Web Page text • `.jip`: A jump-in-point • `.tt`: A ToolTip (typically, for a hyperlink) • `.dhl`: A Decision Frame lead-in sentence • `.dt`: A decision choice (path name) • `.iit`: Implicit text • `.trm`: Glossary term For Custom Bubble Text, the identifier includes a number of two-character pairs each preceded by an underscore (for example, **_DP,_CP,_DD,_CD** in the sample above). These determine the play mode in which the text will be used. The first character indictaes the playback mode, as follows: • **D**: Use in *See It!* and *Try It!* modes • **C**: Use in *Do It!* mode • **A**: Use in *Know It?* mode The second character indictaes the output type, as follows: • **P**: Use in the Player • **D**: Use in printed output (that is, documents)

Column	Contents
	So a code of **DP** indicates that the text is tagged for *See It!* and *Try It!* mode in the Player, and a code of **CD** indicates that the text is tagged for *Do It!* mode in printed output. As a single bubble text could have different portions tagged for different modes, you could have multiple rows in the translation table for the same bubble, but with different mode indicators. These need to be treated as separate translation units, despite any overlap in the texts. It is extremely important that the translator does not touch anything in this column, otherwise UPK will not be able to correctly re-import the file.
<Source Language>	This column contains the text in the source language. The translator should not change this text. If the translator is in the habit of overtyping the source-language text with the translated text then they should be advised to copy this column to the **<Target Language>** column, and overtype *that*, instead. Note that formatting is retained. This is useful for allowing the translator to match the format. Any formatting applied to the translated content will be retained when it is imported.
<Target Language>	This column is blank. The translator will enter the translation of the text in the **<Source Language>** column into this column. Note that the translator should format (bold, italics, and so on) the translated text to match the source text, as this text will be re-imported as formatted (and not as pure text).
Notes	You can enter any notes to the translator in this column (for example, telling them not to translate any screen elements!).
System Data	This column specifies other system-generated information required for translation (such as image properties). You will not normally need to change this information.

Enter any necessary notes, and then pass the Word document to the translator. Once you receive it back, you can proceed to *Importing a translated file*, below.

> In addition to Custom Text, the export file will also include all other related text that you have created yourself, such as role names, Parameter texts, and so on.

Translating via XLIFF

XLIFF is an industry-standard format for exchanging files to be translated. It separates content from formatting, so that the translator can concentrate only on the text that needs to be translated. XLIFF also has the advantage that the translator does not need to have a copy of the software application used to create the original source material (or even a copy of Microsoft Word)—they can use whatever XLIFF-compatible software they like.

> **Version Difference**
>
> XLIFF support was introduced in OnDemand version 9.1.

XLIFF also works well with machine translation, because the translation software will understand the format of the file (assuming that it is XLIFF-compatible, which all good machine translation software will be).

For completeness, an extract of the `.xlf` file for the same section of the Topic as shown in the Word document earlier is given below. For clarity, the text to be translated is shown in bold.

```
<?xml version="1.0" encoding="UTF-8"?>
<xliff version="1.1" xmlns="urn:oasis:names:tc:xliff:document:1.1">
  <file datatype="xml" original="08112a64-2be8-412b-87a2-
  47eb73f9bc9a/topic.xml" source-language="en-US" target-
  language="ja-JP">
    <body>
      <trans-unit id="TXT_Title">
        <source xml:lang="en-US">
          EX01: Changing your User Profile
        </source>
     </trans-unit>
     <trans-unit id="BUB210.txt_DP_CP_DD_CD">
       <source xml:lang="en-US"
          xmlns="urn:oasis:names:tc:xliff:document:1.1">
       <bpt id="1">&lt;p&gt;</bpt>
       <bpt id="2">&lt;fmt font="Arial;8"&gt;</bpt>
       In this exercise, you will learn how to update your
       <ept id="2">&lt;/fmt&gt;</ept><bpt id="3">&lt;fmt
         font="Arial;8" sty="i"&gt;</bpt>User Profile<ept id="3">&lt;
         /fmt&gt;</ept><bpt id="4">&lt;fmt font="Arial;8"&gt;</bpt>
       in SAP, to change your date and time formats. You will also
         learn how to set default values for common input fields.
       <ept id="4">&lt;/fmt&gt;</ept><ept id="1">&lt;/p&gt;</ept>
       </source>
    </trans-unit>
    <trans-unit id="IL462.tt">
```

```
      <source xml:lang="en-US">Version History</source>
    </trans-unit>
    <trans-unit id="F18.jip">
      <source xml:lang="en-US">Changing your user defaults</source>
    </trans-unit>
    <trans-unit id="BUB232.txt_DP_CP_DD_CD">
      <source xml:lang="en-US" xmlns="urn:oasis:names:tc:xliff:
        document:1.1">
      <bpt id="5">&lt;p&gt;</bpt>
      <bpt id="6">&lt;fmt font="Arial;8"&gt;</bpt>
      Click on the <ept id="6">&lt;/fmt&gt;</ept><bpt id="7">&lt;fmt
        font="Arial;8" sty="b"&gt;</bpt>System<ept id="7">&lt;/
        fmt&gt;</ept><bpt id="8">&lt;fmt font="Arial;8"&gt;</bpt>
        menu...<ept id="8">&lt;/fmt&gt;</ept><ept id="5">&lt;/p&gt;
      </ept></source>
    </trans-unit>
    <trans-unit id="BUB233.txt_DP_CP_DD_CD">
      <source xml:lang="en-US" xmlns="urn:oasis:names:tc:xliff:
        document:1.1">
      <bpt id="9">&lt;p&gt;</bpt>
      <bpt id="10">&lt;fmt font="Arial;8"&gt;</bpt>...point to
      <ept id="10">&lt;/fmt&gt;</ept><bpt id="11">&lt;fmt
         font="Arial;8" sty="b"&gt;</bpt>User Profile<ept
         id="11">&lt;/fmt&gt;</ept><bpt id="12">&lt;fmt
         font="Arial;8"&gt;</bpt>...<ept id="12">&lt;/fmt&gt;
      </ept><ept id="9">&lt;/p&gt;</ept></source>
   </trans-unit>
   <trans-unit id="BUB234.txt_DP_CP_DD_CD">
      <source xml:lang="en-US" xmlns="urn:oasis:names:tc:xliff:
        document:1.1">
      <bpt id="13">&lt;p&gt;</bpt>
      <bpt id="14">&lt;fmt font="Arial;8"&gt;</bpt>...and then select
      <ept id="14">&lt;/fmt&gt;</ept><bpt id="15">&lt;fmt
         font="Arial;8" sty="b"&gt;</bpt>Own Data<ept id="15">&lt;/
         fmt&gt;</ept><bpt id="16">&lt;fmt font="Arial;8"&gt;
      </bpt>.<ept id="16">&lt;/fmt&gt;</ept><ept id="13">&lt;/p&gt;
      </ept></source>
      <trans-unit id="BUB236.txt_DP_CP_DD_CD">
        <source xml:lang="en-US"
           xmlns="urn:oasis:names:tc:xliff:document:1.1">
        <bpt id="2">&lt;p&gt;&lt;fmt font="Arial;8"&gt;</bpt>
          If you notice that your name is incorrect, then you can
             change it onthis screen.
        <ept id="2">&lt;/fmt&gt;&lt;/p&gt;</ept><bpt
          id="3">&lt;p&gt;&lt;fmt font="Arial;8"&gt;</bpt><ept
          id="3">&lt;/fmt&gt;&lt;/p&gt;</ept></source>
      </trans-unit>
    </body>
  </file>
</xliff>
```

Again, all of this is purely internal (it's referred to as a "machine-readable" format for good reason) but for the adventurous reader, if you look into the code it's not really that difficult to follow. You can see the same identifiers as shown in the first column of the Word table in the `<trans-unit id>` tag, the source language is shown in the `<source>` tag, and so on. However, you shouldn't really need to interpret this file yourself. Just pass it to your translators, and when you receive it back, continue with *Importing a translated file*, next.

Importing a translated file

This section assumes that you have previously exported a Topic in Word format, that you sent this to your translator for translation, and have received the file back from translation. The same steps apply to XLIFF files. For reference, an extract of the Word file that we have received back for our example Topic is shown below:

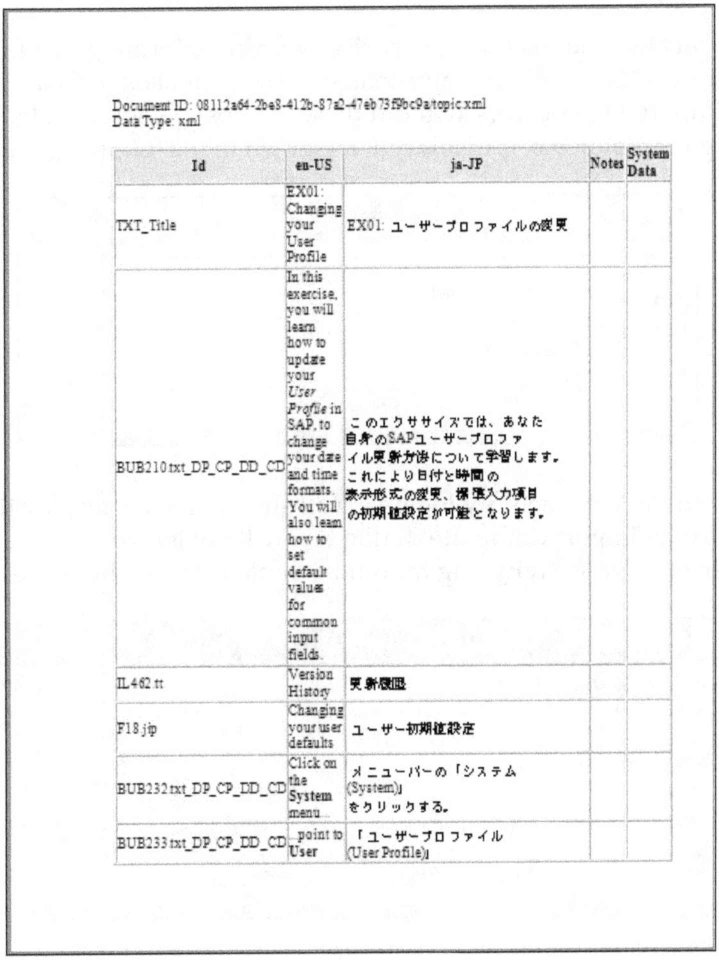

Document ID: 08112a64-2be8-412b-87a2-47eb73f9bc9a/topic.xml
Data Type: xml

Id	en-US	ja-JP	Notes	System Data
TXT_Title	EX01: Changing your User Profile	EX01: ユーザープロファイルの変更		
BUB210txt_DP_CP_DD_CD	In this exercise, you will learn how to update your *User Profile* in SAP, to change your date and time formats. You will also learn how to set default values for common input fields.	このエクササイズでは、あなた自身のSAPユーザープロファイル更新方法について学習します。これにより日付と時間の表示形式の変更、標準入力項目の初期値設定が可能となります。		
IL462.tt	Version History	更新履歴		
F18.jip	Changing your user defaults	ユーザー初期値設定		
BUB232txt_DP_CP_DD_CD	Click on the System menu	メニューバーの「システム(System)」をクリックする。		
BUB233txt_DP_CP_DD_CD	...point to User	「ユーザープロファイル(User Profile)」		

To import a file that has been translated, carry out the following steps:

1. From the Library, select menu option **Tools | Import | Localization**. You do not need to select the document that you originally exported – UPK will use the *Document ID* to locate the correct document(s) to import into. The **Import for Localization** dialog box is displayed.

2. In the **Translated content** field, navigate to and select the file containing the translated text.
3. Click on **OK**. You may see a **Security Warning** informing you that the `wordtoxliff.dot` file contains macros. If so, you need to **Enable Macros** (the import will not work without these macros). Eventually, the **Import Complete** dialog box is displayed, as shown in the following screenshot:

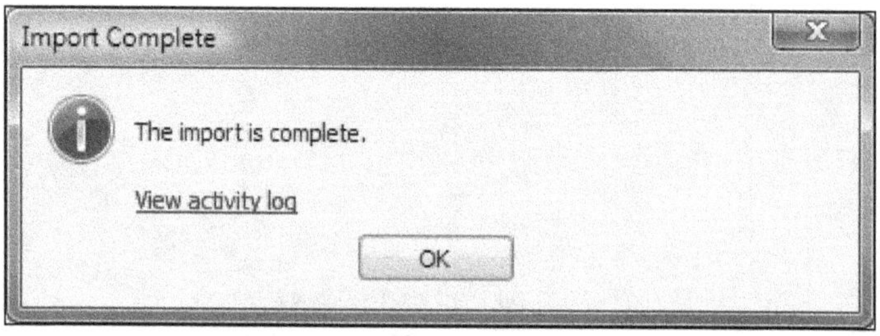

4. Click on the **View activity log** link. You should always display the **Activity Log**, as the **Import Complete dialog** box will not tell you if there have been any errors. The **Activity Log** for our example is shown in the next screenshot:

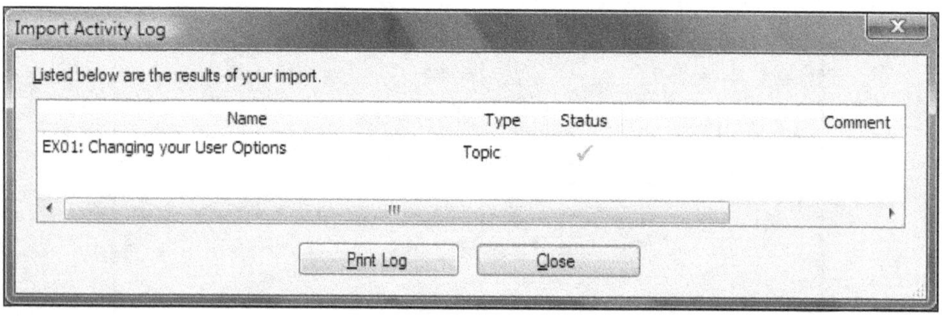

5. If the **Activity Log** indicates that any content objects were not imported, then the import file needs to be corrected and the import re-tried. Note that you can re-import a single file as often as necessary; each import will overwrite the previous version (and not create a new copy).
6. Click on **Close** to close the **Activity Log**, and then click on **OK** to close the **Import Complete** dialog box.

You will now see that the object in your Library appears in the local language, as shown in the following screenshot:

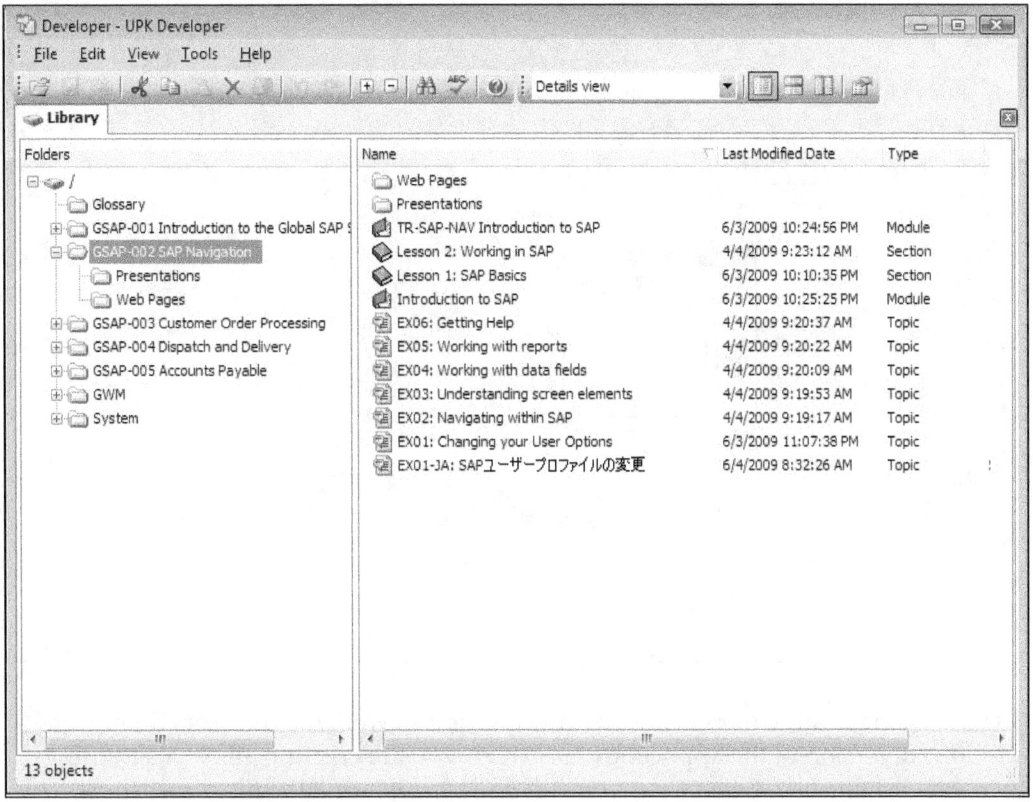

Note that this has *overwritten* the previous version (the *copy* of the original-language version, if you have followed this process correctly) of this content object. (Actually, it has overwritten only the text elements for this content object—the screenshots, Action, and any links to or from the content object are retained.) This is why it is extremely important to take a copy of the object that you want to translate, and then export/translate/import this copy.

If you now display the content object (either in the Player or in Preview mode), you will see the translated version. For our example, we have translated a single Topic. The following screenshot shows a sample Frame taken from this Topic (this is the same Frame as shown in the original English version at the start of this chapter, if you want to compare).

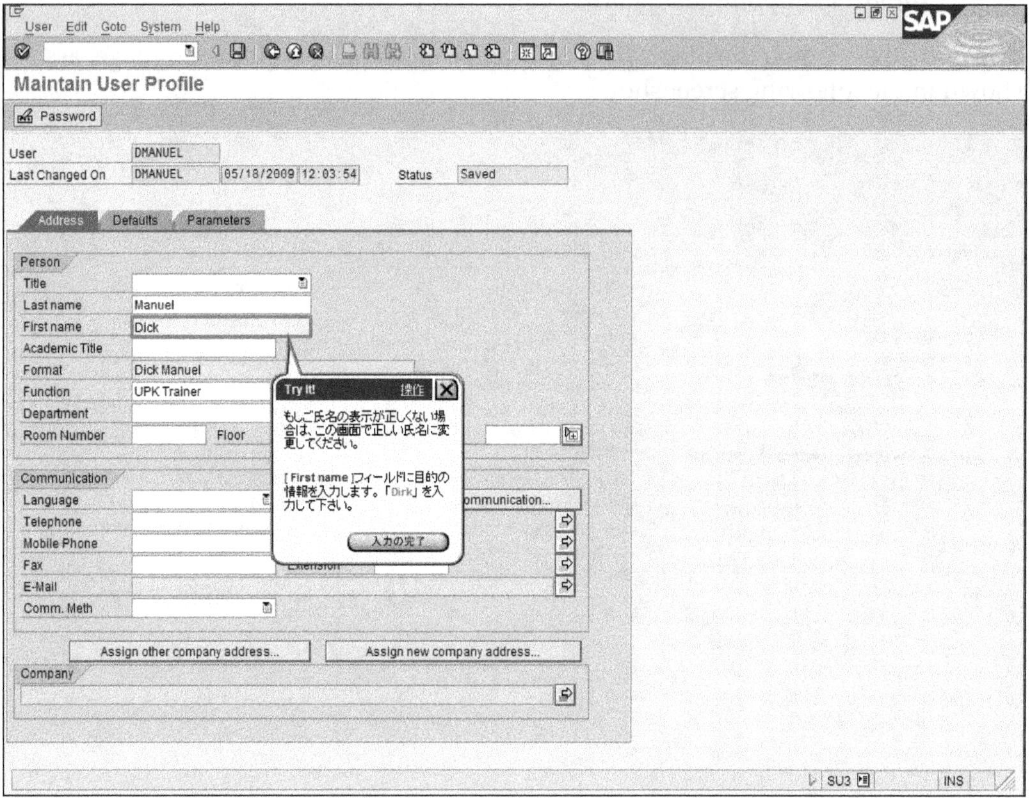

So now we have all of our Custom Text translated as well. If your users do not use a localized version of the application for which you are creating all of this training, then you are finished. Otherwise, you still need to replace all of the screenshots. This is the subject of our next section.

Replacing screenshots with localized versions

We are now using a foreign-language template for all Template Text, and have translated all of our Custom Text. However, there is one more thing that may need to be translated: the screens themselves. Many applications (including Windows and SAP applications) allow users to select their language, and have all of the screens displayed in that language. If you want your translated exercises to use screens for the relevant language (and in most cases you would—unless users are explicitly required to use English screens regardless of their native language) then you need to replace all of the screenshots in your simulation with the equivalent foreign-language versions. Although this may seem like a daunting prospect, UPK does provide a feature to simplify this re-recording of a topic.

When you re-record a topic, UPK will replace the screenshots in the recording with newly captured ones, and re-capture the Actions, but will leave all of the Custom Texts, and Explanation Frames intact. It will also retain any Alternative Paths and Branches, and any Alternative Actions recorded. So really, all you are doing is replacing the screenshots.

To re-record a Topic, carry out the following steps:

1. Start the application for which you want to replace the screens.
2. Flip to UPK, and open up the Topic in the Topic Editor.
3. Position yourself on the first frame for which you want to replace the screenshot (for translations, this will normally be the first frame in the recording).

4. From the menu bar, select menu option **Edit | Re-record Topic**. You are flipped back to the application, and the **Re-recorder** panel is displayed in the upper-right corner of the screen, as shown in the following screenshot:

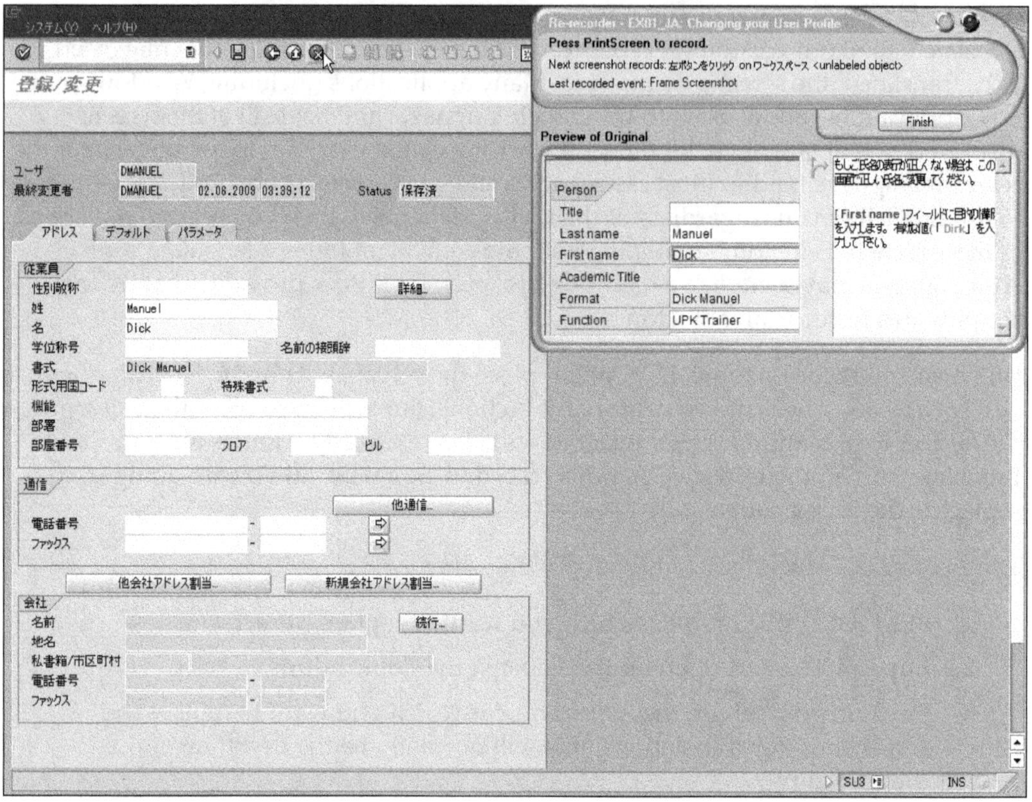

Note that the **Re-recorder** window contains a preview of the current (original language) screen (on the left) and the current (by now, translated) bubble text (on the right) so that you can confirm that you are capturing the correct screen.

5. Make sure that you are on the correct screen in the application, perform the required action, and then press the *Prt Scr* key. The screenshot and action will be recaptured, and the recorder will automatically move on to the next frame. Repeat this step for all remaining frames in the current path.

6. If there are Alternative Paths or Branches in your simulation, then click on the next path in the path list, and return to Step 5.

7. Once you have recaptured all screenshots for all paths, click the **Finish** button. The recorder closes, and you are passed back into Topic Editor.
6. Save your changes, and close the Topic Editor.

And that's it! Done! Our topic has now been completely translated, and appears in the Player as shown in the following screenshot:

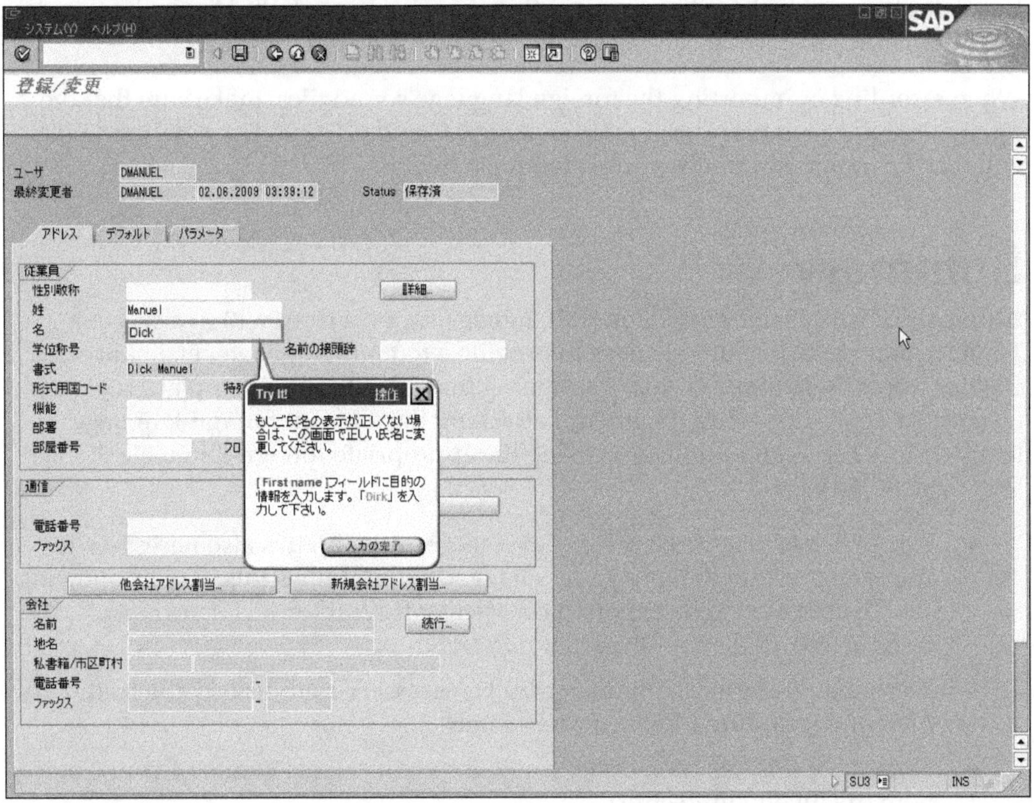

Nice job! Of course, the *difficult* part is making sure that you have the same data available in the local-language version of the system. You may also have to adjust action areas (as I had to in the previous example), where screen content shifts in size or position, to accommodate different font sets and/or word lengths.

Re-recording the sound files

If you make use of sound in your Topics, then you will need to re-record the sound files, in the local language. The simplest way to do this is to re-record the sound files from within UPK, as explained in Chapter 11, *Incorporating Sound into Your Topics.*

Alternatively, you may choose to export the existing sound files and pass these to the translator for re-recording, before importing them back into UPK. Again, how to do this is explained in Chapter 11, *Incorporating Sound into Your Topics.*

When recording or importing the foreign language sound files, make sure that the foreign-language template has first been assigned to the Topic. The new sound files will then be imported into the correct template folder.

Summary

Although UPK does not provide multi-language support from within a single Topic, it does make it relatively easy to provide a foreign-language version of an existing Topic. In its simplest form, assuming that you only use Template Texts and no Custom Texts, this is just a matter of attaching the relevant foreign-language template to a Topic, and publishing using the appropriate foreign-language Deployment Package.

- If your Topic includes Custom Text (and most will), it is also necessary to translate this into the foreign language. UPK simplifies this, too, by allowing the Custom Text to be exported (in Microsoft Word or XLIFF format), translated, and then re-imported into UPK.
- To round off the localization, it may be necessary to re-record any sound files, and recapture localized screenshots.
- Once all of this has been done, you will have localized copies of your Topics, with (relatively) little effort.

Afterword

Congratulations, you have made it through to the end of this book. You are now well-equipped to begin developing quality training simulations, using Oracle User Productivity Kit 3.5 (or OnDemand 9.1, which shares about 95% of UPK 3.5's functionality).

In this book you have learned not only what functionality UPK provides, but have also learned how to best make use of this functionality. You have seen practical examples of how to add value to your exercises, and how to get UPK to generate the content that you want your trainees to see, rather than the default, 'vanilla' content.

You should now have a firm appreciation of what can be done with just a little extra effort. And you will no doubt have come to realize that if you *do* make the extra effort, your users, and your managers or clients, will undoubtedly thank you for it.

Happy developing!

A
Installing UPK 3.5

This Appendix explains how to install UPK 3.5. Why is this information hidden away at the back of the book in an Appendix? Surely, installing UPK is the first thing that you'll want to do? Well, no, not normally. UPK is an expensive piece of software, and is therefore almost solely the preserve of large corporations. These corporations are more likely than not to either be running a client/server environment which is installed and administered by a central IT group, or to have a managed (and quite likely customized) installation process, possibly based on a *push* model, or automatic software base loading. In such cases, it is unlikely that a UPK developer will install UPK themselves, and almost certainly not as a "vanilla" install. In addition, even if you are installing UPK yourself, it is (hopefully!) a one-time activity, so there is no point in cluttering up the front of this book with information that you will use only once.

This Appendix explains how to install a stand-alone (single user) environment, or the client side of a client/server environment. (As mentioned above, in a multi-developer environment you are unlikely to be installing the server side yourself, and even if you are, that is beyond the scope of this book. Maybe the next one.) This Appendix assumes that you are in possession of the UPK installation files. If you are a paid-up license holder, you will know where to find these. If not, ask your company/client, or Oracle representative.

This Appendix also explains how to install the UPK Topic Player, which is required in order to be able to open Standalone Topic File deliverables. (See Chapter 6, *Publishing Content* for more information on this.) Note that developers must also install this Player if they want to open Standalone Topic Files—it is not "bundled" into the *UPK Developer* installation.

Installing the UPK developer environment

To install UPK, follow these steps:

1. Obtain the UPK installation pack, and then run the `Setup.exe` file. The following screen is displayed:

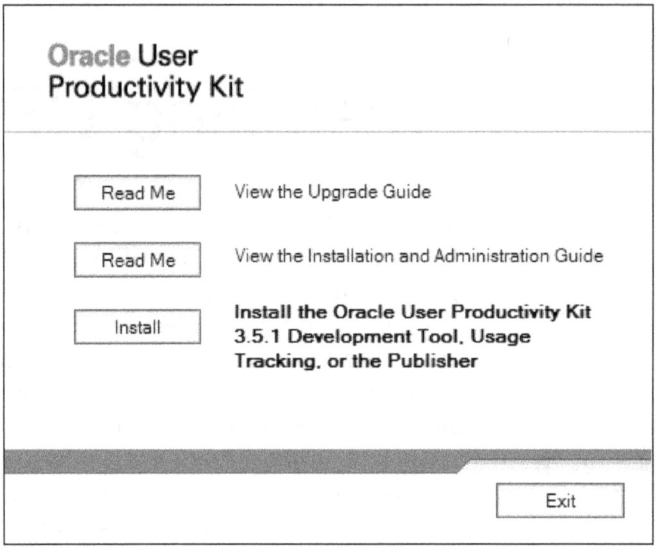

2. Click on **Install**. The following dialog box is displayed:

3. Select the language in which you want the installation instructions to be displayed, and then click on **OK**. The following screen is displayed:

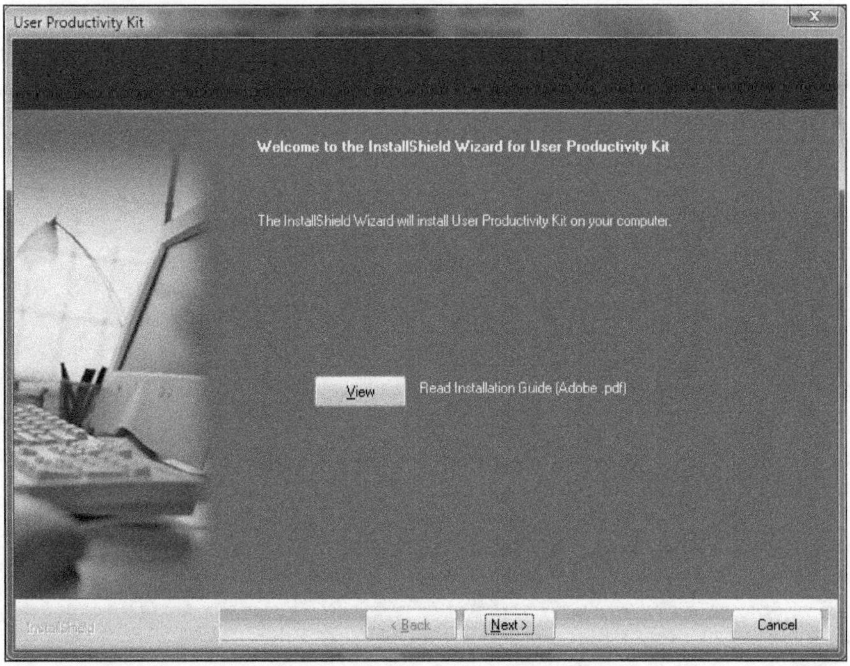

4. Click on **Next**. The following screen is displayed:

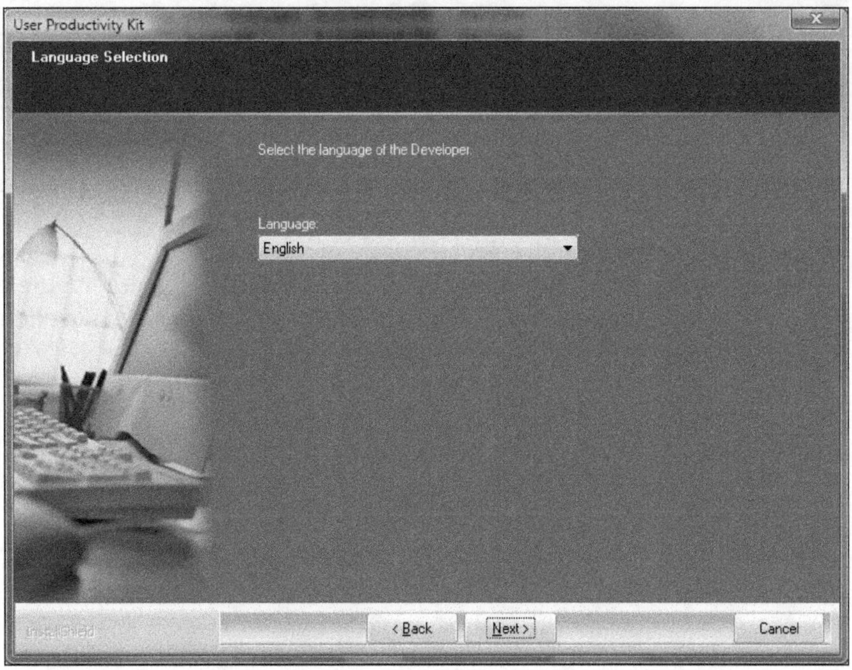

5. In the **Language** field, select the language in which you want UPK to be installed. This will affect what language the screens appear in. If you are reading this book in English, then I'm guessing that you want to select **English**.
6. Click **Next**. The following screen is displayed:

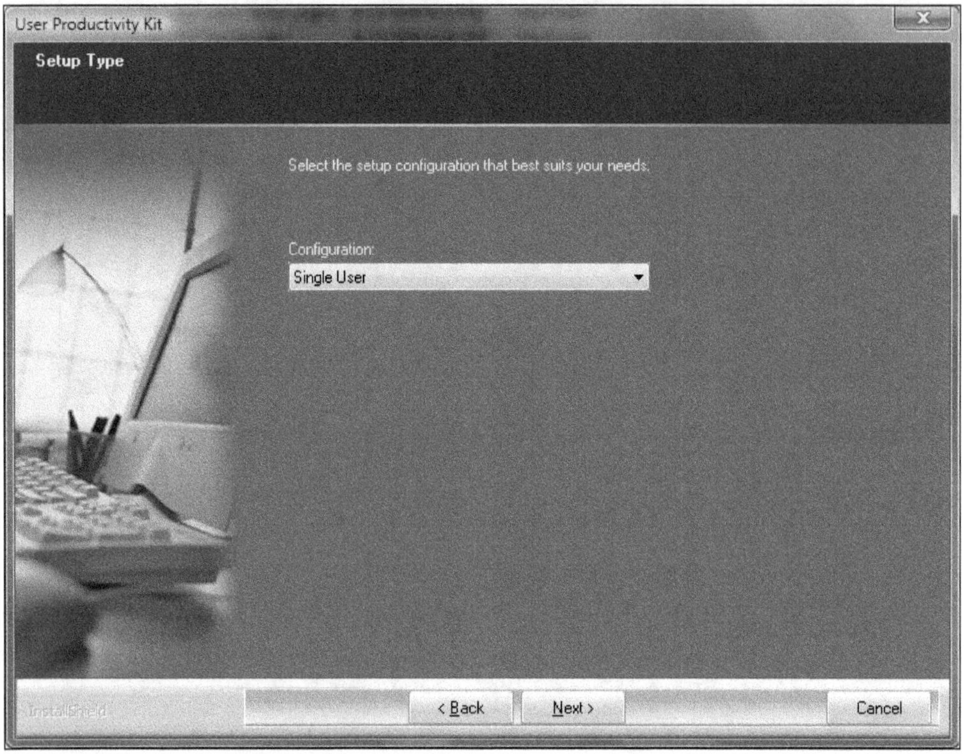

7. In the **Configuration** field, select the type of installation that you want to perform. For the purposes of this book, you should select either **Single User** for a single-user implementation, or **Client** for the client side of a client/server implementation.

8. Click **Next**. The following screen is displayed:

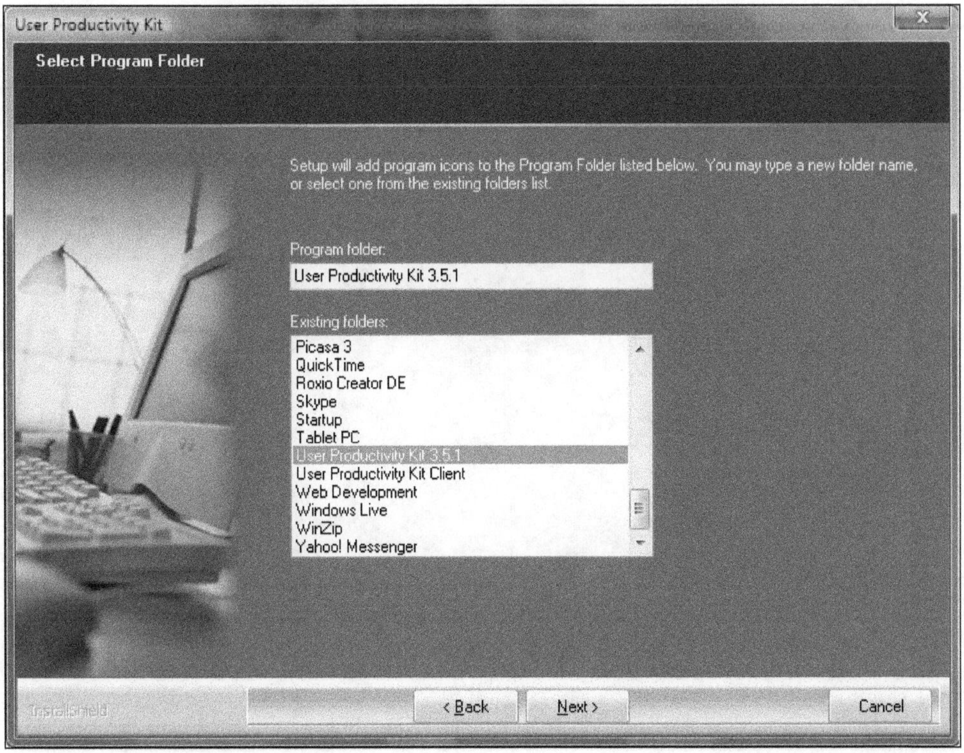

9. Select the program folder into which you want UPK to be installed. This is the "folder" in the Windows Start Menu in which the shortcut to the UPK programs will be placed. It is normally sufficient to accept the default of **User Productivity Kit 3.5.1**.

10. Click **Next**. The following screen is displayed:

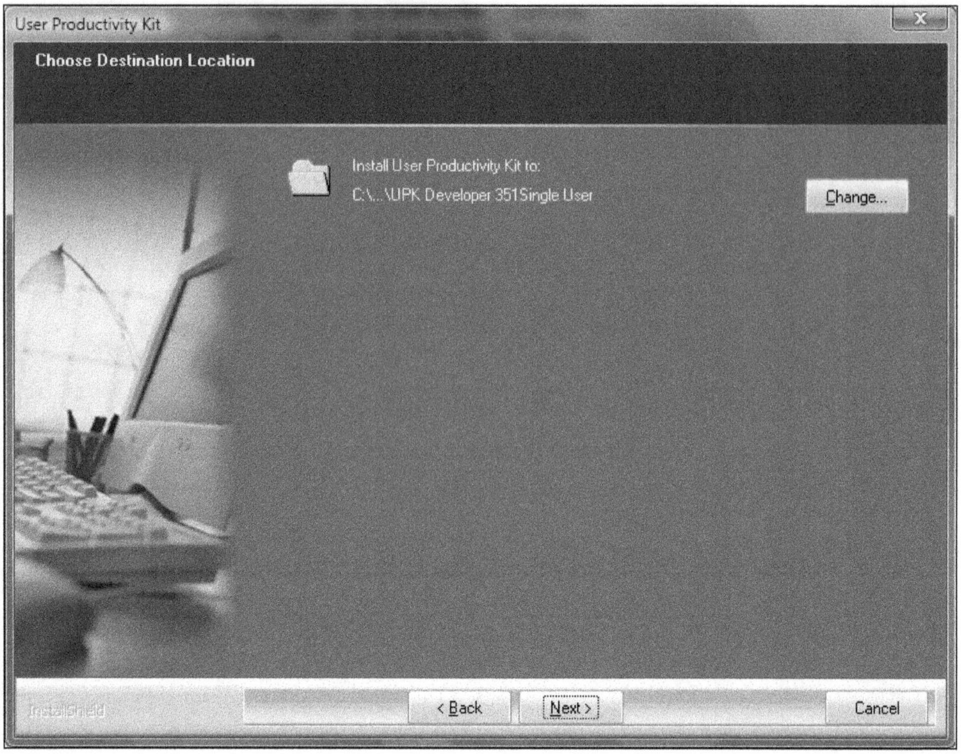

11. If necessary, use the **Change** button to change the location into which the UPK executables will be installed. Normally, the default location is acceptable. Click **Next**. The following screen is displayed:

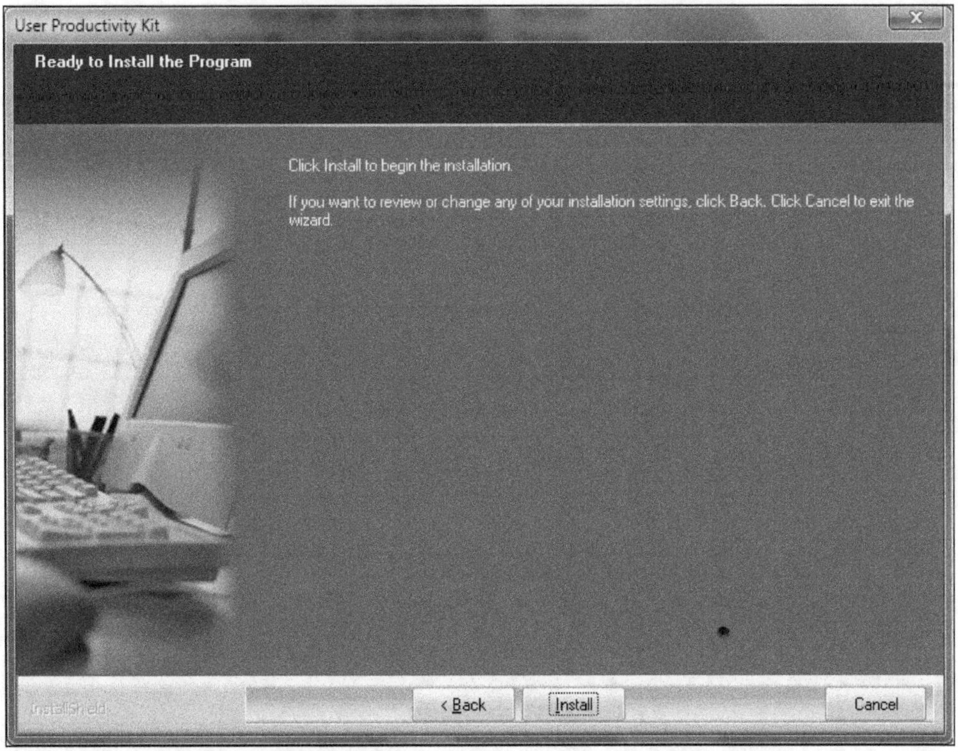

> **Version Difference**
>
> UPK 3.5.1 was the first release to ship with an integrated Oracle database. Prior to this version, the Firebird database needed to be installed separately.

12. Click on **Install**. UPK will progress through installing all of the required components. Depending on what is already installed on your workstation, one or more of the following messages may be displayed as the various components are installed:

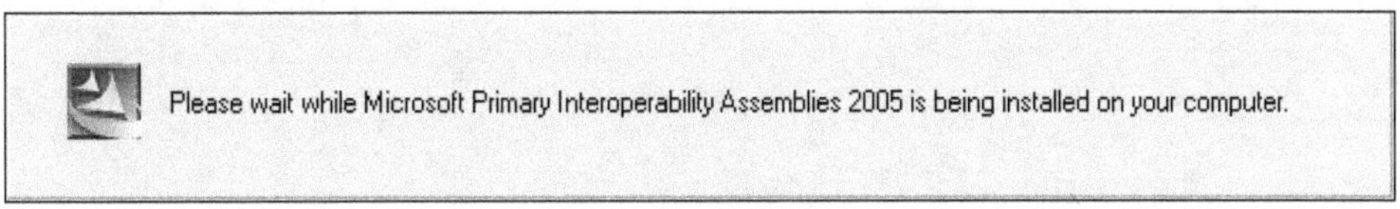

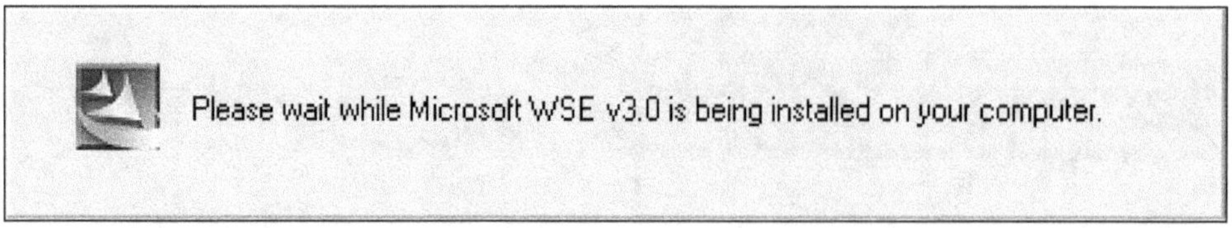

13. Once all of the required components have been installed, the InstallShield Wizard will install the actual UPK program files. During this installation, the following progress screen is displayed:

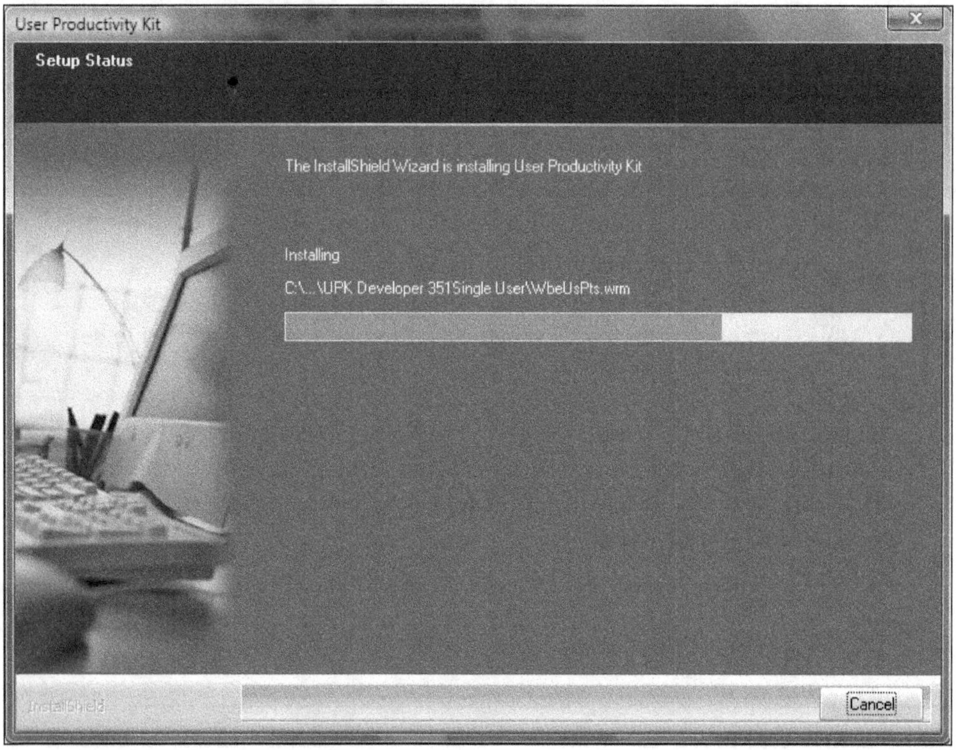

14. Finally, the following screen will be displayed, indicating that the installation is complete, and was successful:

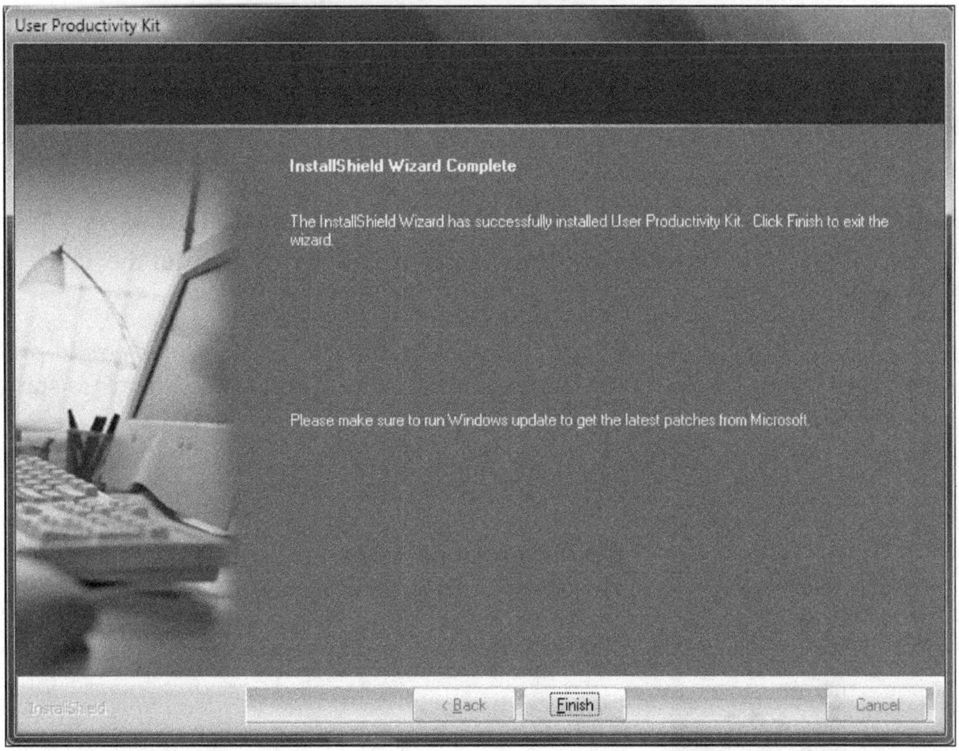

15. Click **Finish**. The following message is displayed, as UPK sets up the database.

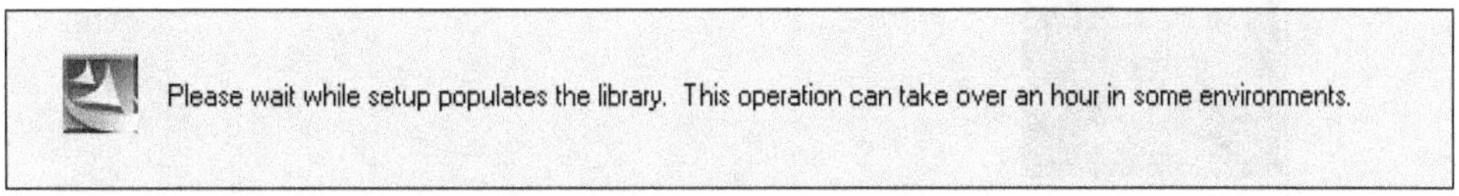

Eventually, this message will disappear, which indicates that installation and initialization is complete.

Congratulations! You have now installed UPK. A world of wonder now awaits you. But before you rush back to Chapter 2, *Organizing Your Library*, you should refer to the next section, *Accessing UPK for the first time*—you still need to set up your UPK profile (even in a stand-alone setup).

Accessing UPK for the first time

The first time that you access UPK, you will be prompted to specify some additional information. The exact information that you need to provide will vary depending on whether you are accessing a stand-alone version of UPK, or logging onto a UPK client. These options are discussed separately below; refer to the one section that applies to your environment.

Accessing a stand-alone installation

To access UPK for the first time in a stand-alone installation, carry out the following steps:

1. Start UPK, either by clicking on the shortcut on your Windows Desktop, or by selecting it from your Windows **Start** menu. The **Profile Wizard** is started, as shown in the following screenshot:

2. Click on **Next**. The **Profile name** dialog box is displayed.

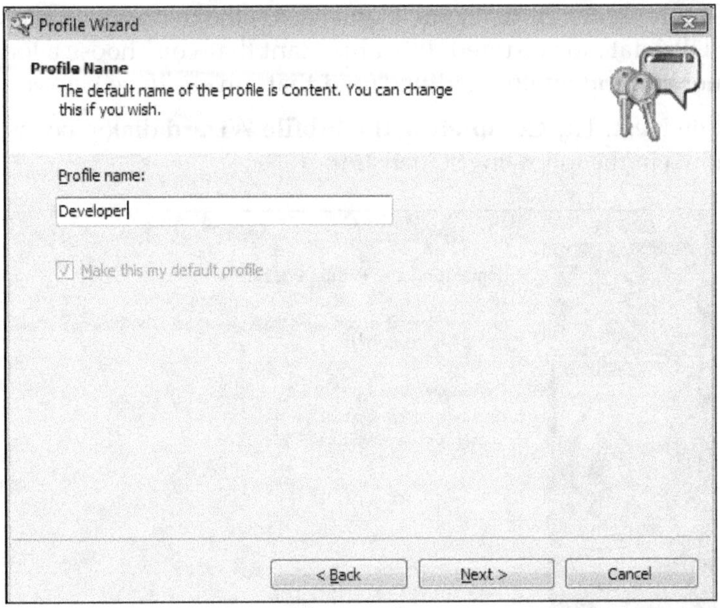

3. Enter a name for your profile. This is not particularly significant in a stand-alone installation.
4. Click on **Next**. The **Data Storage Location** dialog box is displayed:

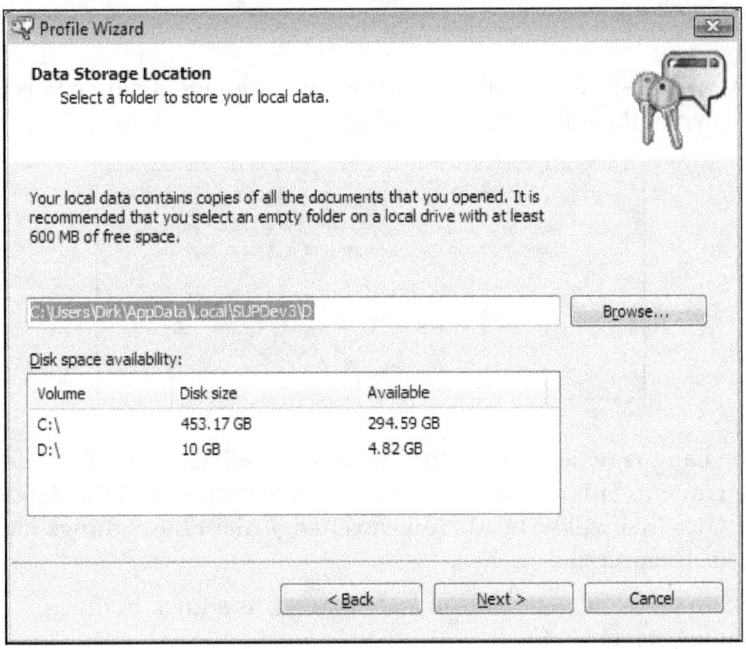

5. Confirm (or enter, or navigate to and select) the folder in which you want your UPK data to be stored. It is important that you choose a location that will not be accidentally modified, and that can easily be backed up.
6. Click on **Next**. The **Completing the Profile Wizard** dialog box is displayed, as shown in the following screenshot:

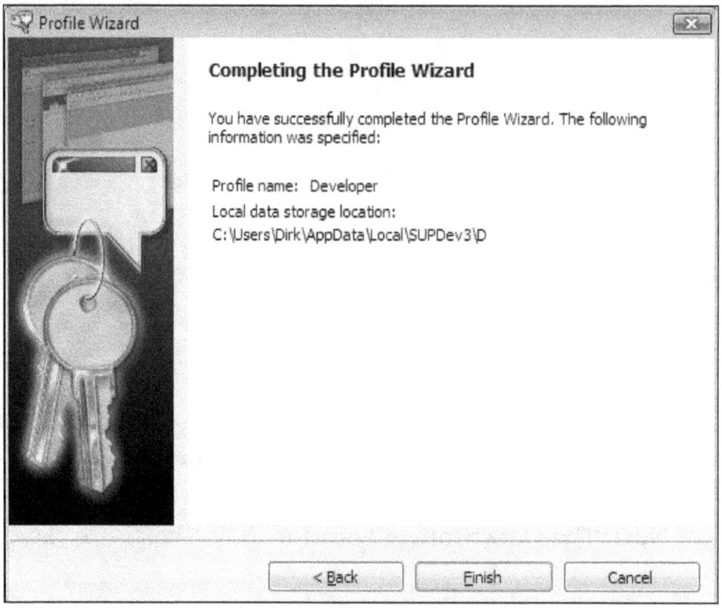

7. Click on **Finish**. The **Primary Authoring Language** dialog box is displayed, as shown in the following screenshot:

8. In the **Language** field, select the language in which you will be developing your content. This affects your default spellchecker, and the default templates that will be used. You can change all of these things for individual objects, if required.
9. Click on **OK**. The **Start Screen** is displayed, as shown in the following screenshot:

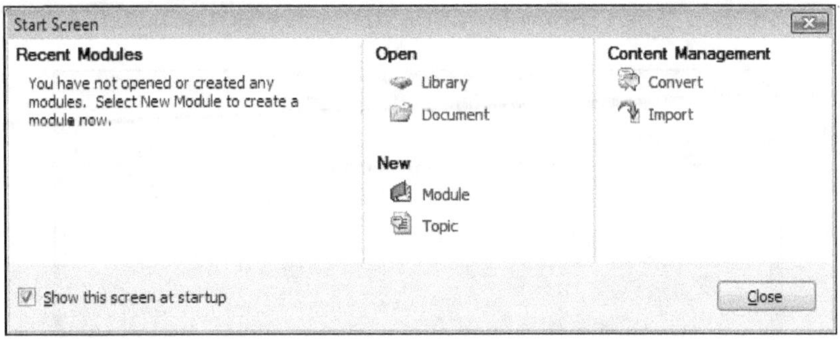

You have now set up your UPK profile, and successfully accessed UPK. Most of the steps above are a one-time setup; every subsequent time that you access UPK, you will start from the **Start Screen** shown above (unless you deselect the **Show this screen at startup** option).

Logging onto a UPK client

To access UPK in a client/server environment, carry out the steps described below:

1. Start UPK, either by clicking on the shortcut on your Windows Desktop, or by selecting it from your Windows Start menu. The **Profile Wizard** is started, as shown in the following screenshot:

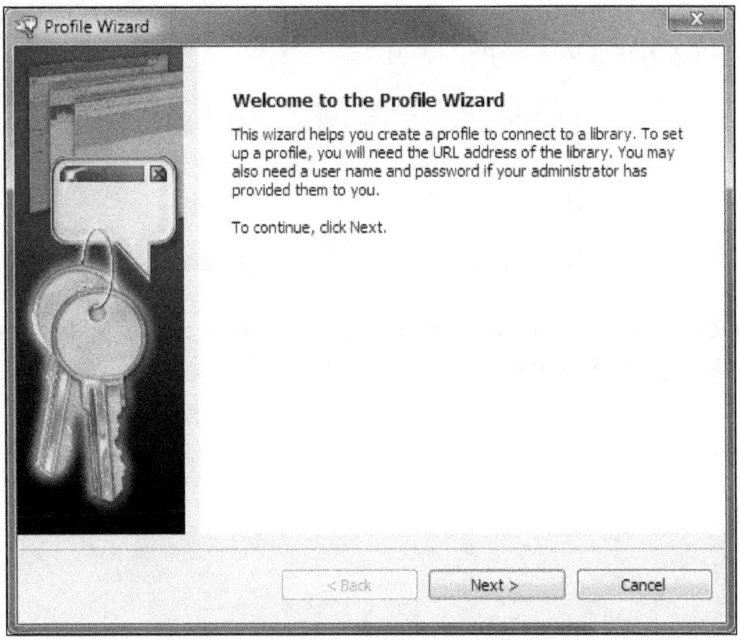

2. Click on **Next**. The **Library Location** dialog box is displayed:

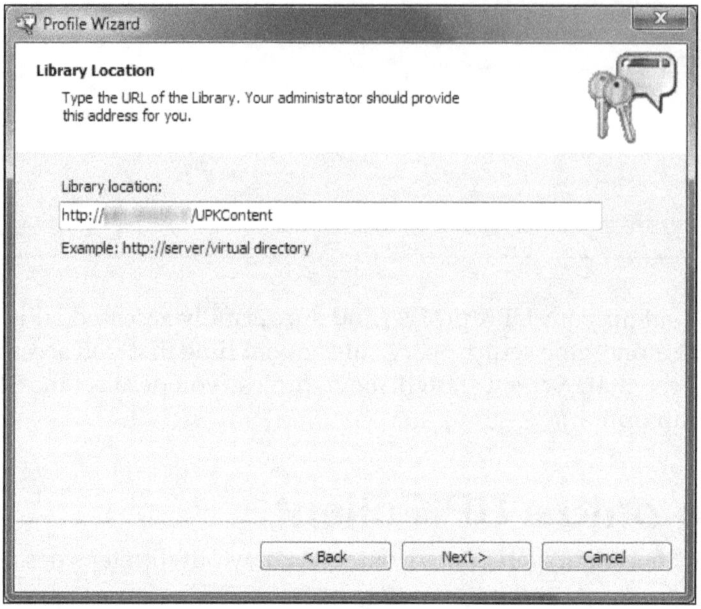

3. In the **Library Location** field, enter the URL of the UPK library to which you want to log on to (this is the "server side" of the client/server environment).
4. Click **Next**. UPK will attempt to connect to the server, during which time the following dialog box is displayed:

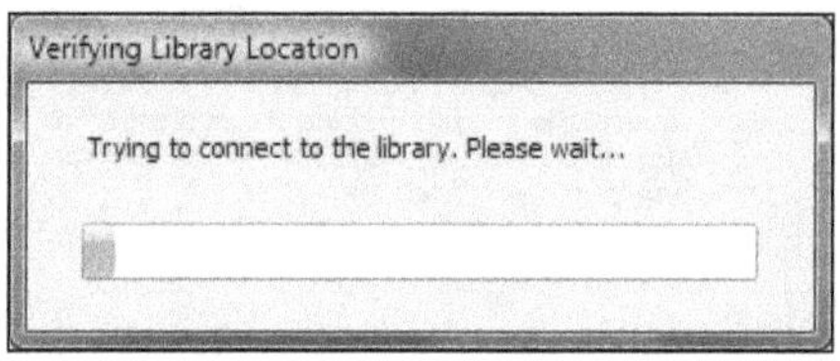

Once UPK has connected to the server, the above message disappears, and is replaced by the **Credentials** dialog box:

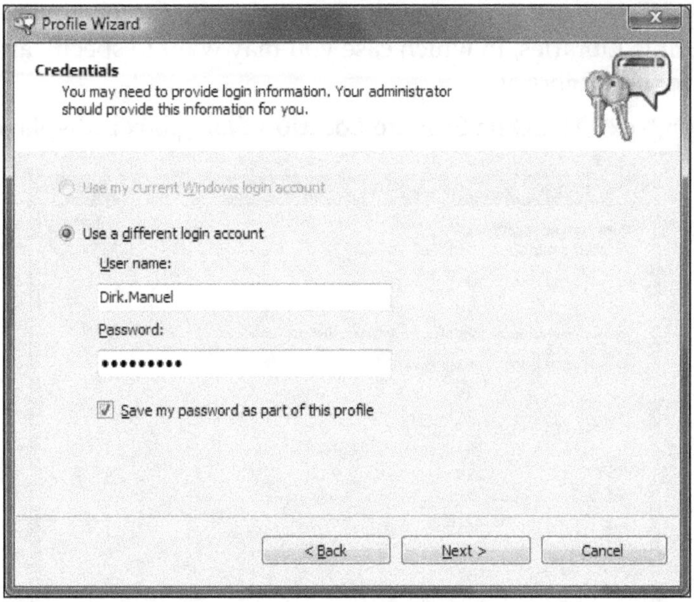

5. In the above screen, you need to select the type of authorization that is being used. UPK can either authenticate using your Windows credentials, or using its own internal user access tables. Which method is used is determined by the Administrator when the server side of UPK is installed.

   Select either **Use my current Windows login account**, or **Use a different login account** and specify your user name and password, as necessary.

6. Click **Next**. The **Profile Name** dialog box is displayed:

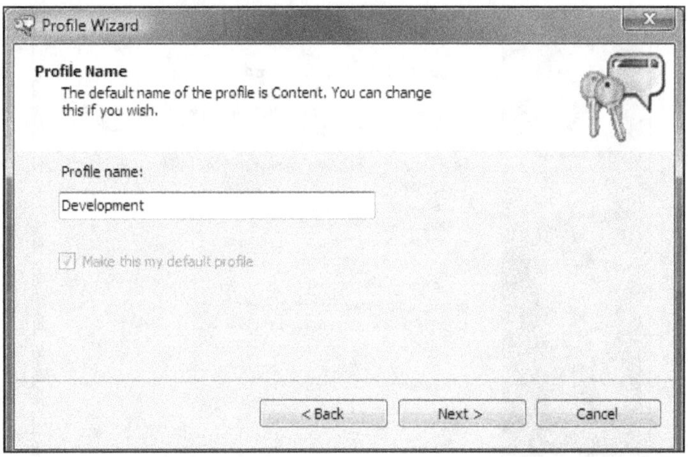

7. Enter a name for your profile. This is only really significant if you have access to multiple Libraries, in which case you may want to specify an appropriate name for each Library.
8. Click on **Next**. The **Data Storage Location** dialog box is displayed:

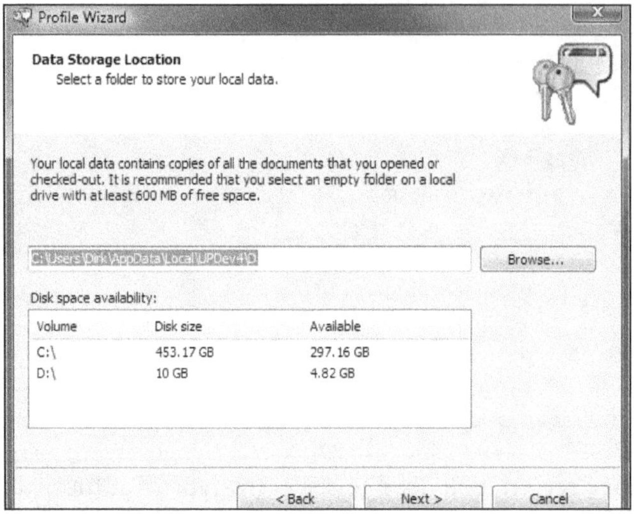

9. Confirm (or enter, or navigate to and select) the folder in which you want your local repository to be stored. It is important that you choose a location that will not be accidentally modified, and that can easily be backed up.
10. Click on **Next**. The **Completing the Profile Wizard** dialog box is displayed, as shown in the following screenshot:

11. Click on **Finish**. The **Primary Authoring Language** dialog box is displayed, as shown in the following screenshot:

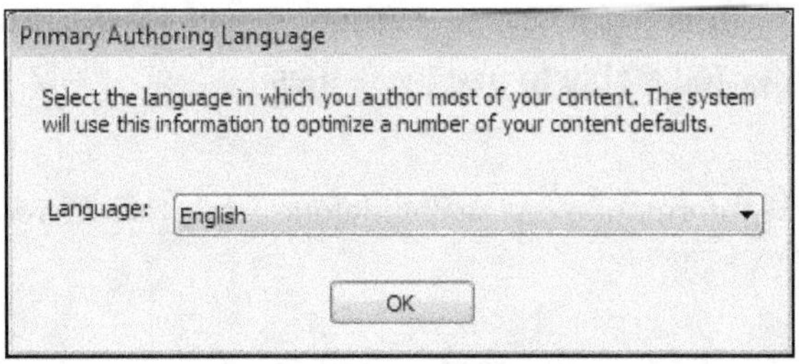

12. In the **Language** field, select the language in which you will be developing your content. This affects your default spellchecker, and the default templates that will be used. You can change all of these things for individual objects, if required.
13. Click on **OK**. The **Start Screen** is displayed, as shown in the following screenshot:

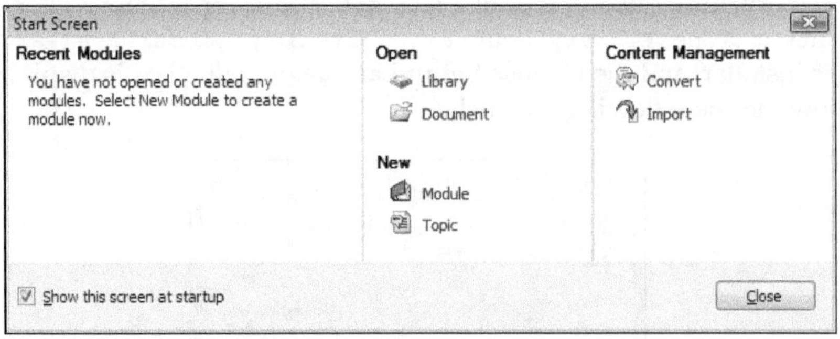

> If you have access to multiple Libraries, then you will initially be logged on to your default Library. You can change the Library that you are logged on to via menu option **Tools | Profile**.

You have now set up your UPK profile, and successfully accessed UPK. Most of the steps above are a one-time setup; every subsequent time that you access UPK, you will start from the **Start** screen shown above (unless you deselect the **Show this screen at startup** option).

Installing the Topic Player

One of the formats in which training content developed in UPK can be delivered is as Standalone Topic Files (file type `.odtpc`). Trainees will require a special player—the Topic Player—in order to be able to use these files.

> For more information on the Standalone Topic format, refer to Chapter 6, *Publishing Content*.

This Topic Player is available to all UPK users (who have a valid end user license!) but must be installed separately, by each trainee. This section explains how to install this Topic Player.

To install the Topic Player, carry out the following steps:

1. Locate the installer for the Topic Player. This is named `odweb.exe`, and can be found either in the same directory as the Standalone Topic Files that you have created (see Chapter 6, *Publishing Content*), or in your UPK installation directory, under `User Productivity Kit\{version}\LibraryDocuments\Content\IOne\Library\Neutral\Publishing Common\Data\Parts`. Run this installer, and the **Choose Setup Language** dialog box is displayed, as shown in the following screenshot:

2. Select your required installation language, and then click on **OK**. (Note that this selection influences the language in which the labels and buttons in the Topic Player are displayed. It does not affect the language in which the Topics are played.) The following screen is displayed:

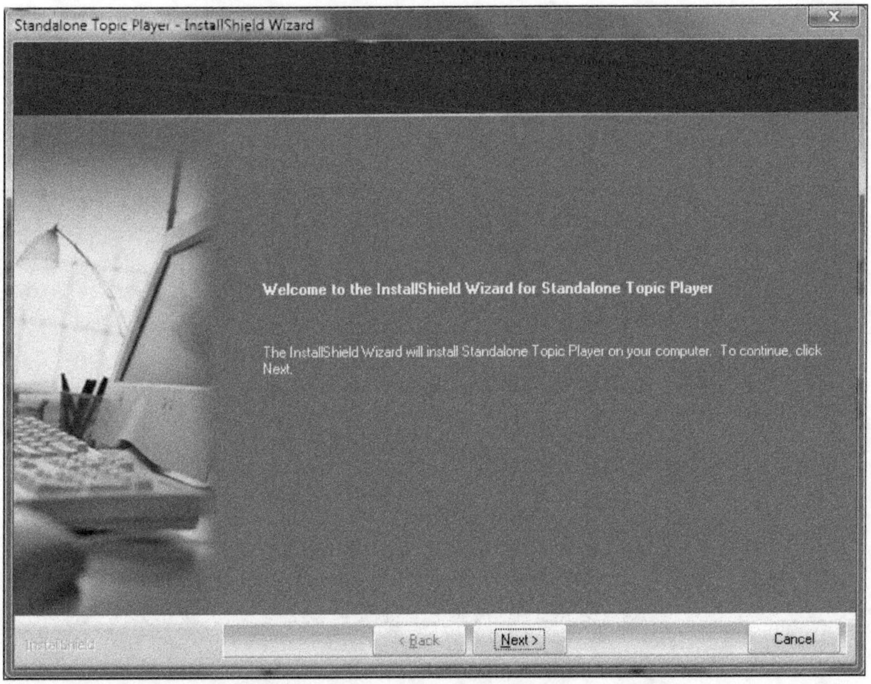

3. Click on **Next**. The following screen is displayed:

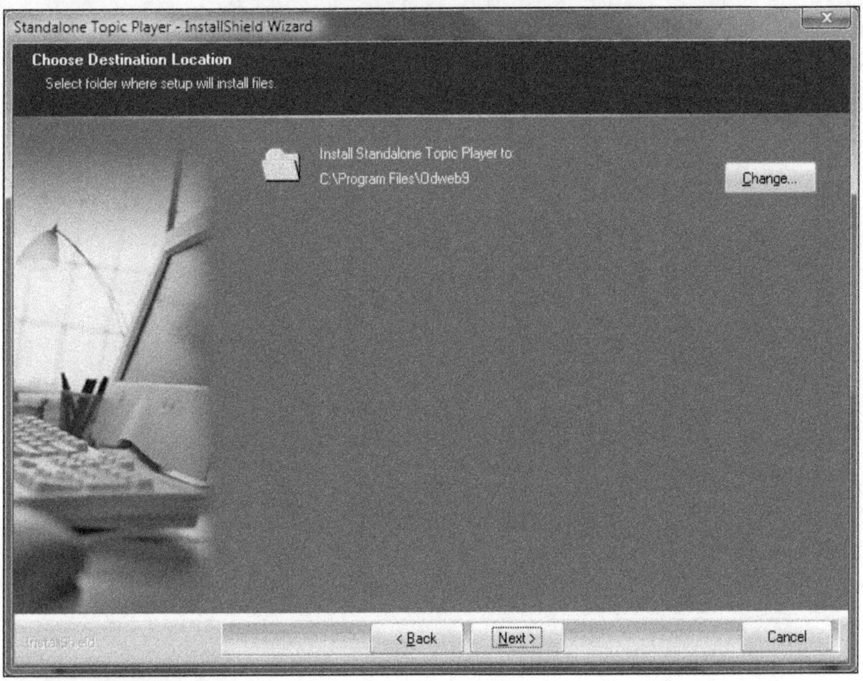

4. If necessary, use the **Change** button to change the location into which the UPK executables will be installed. Normally, the default location is acceptable.

5. Click on **Next**. The following screen is displayed:

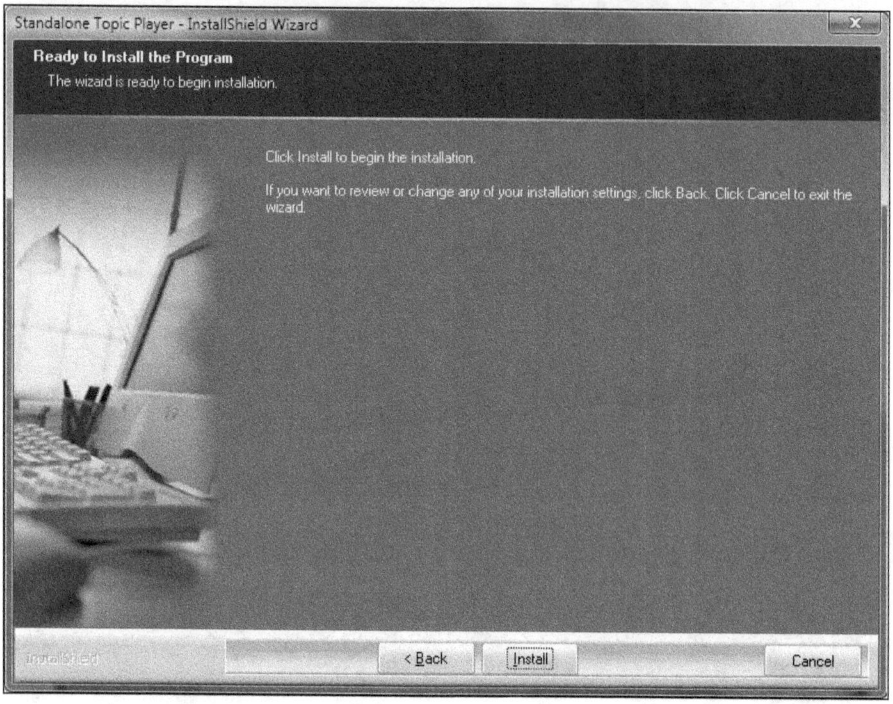

6. Click on **Install**. The following screen is displayed:

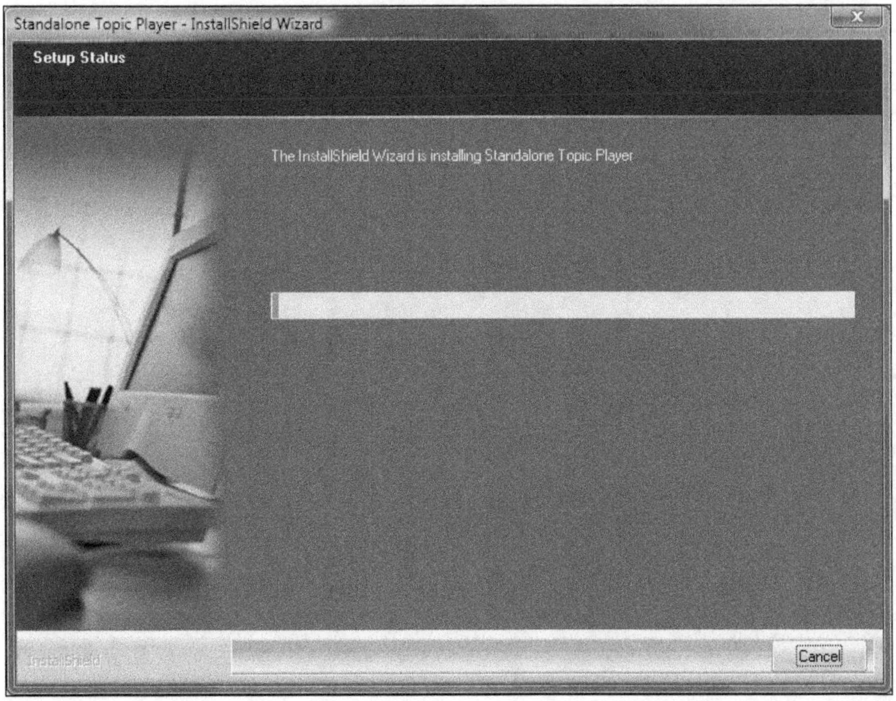

> You may see additional messages informing you that the *Microsoft Visual C++ 2008 Redistributable* is being installed, if it is not installed already.

When the installation is complete, the following confirmation screen is displayed:

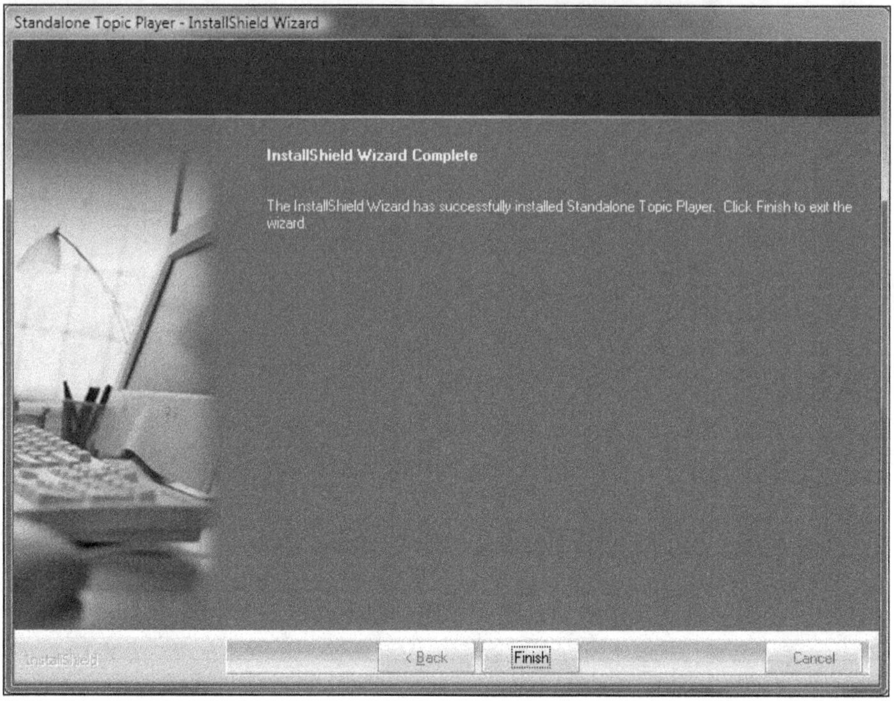

7. Click on **Finish**.

That's it. All done. Now, if you double-click on a Standalone Topic File (file type `.odtpc`) then the Topic Player will automatically be launched. Again, refer to Chapter 6, *Publishing Content*, for full details.

Summary

This Appendix has walked you through how to install the following:

- UPK 3.5 Developer
- UPK Topic Payer

Hopefully, you will never have to refer to this Appendix again.

B
Object Types

This chapter lists all of the Object Types that are recognized by UPK, and shows the Template Text that is generated for each type. The Template Text for both the **Standard** template and the **Microsoft** template are shown in the following table. Where the **Microsoft** Template text differs from the **Standard** Template Text, it is **highlighted**.

Object Type	Standard Template Text	Microsoft Template Text
`ActiveX`	Click the desired object.	Click the desired object.
`Alert`	Click the <ObjectName> alert.	Click the <ObjectName> alert.
`Animation`	Click the animation.	Click the animation.
`Application`	Click the <ObjectName> animation.	Click the <ObjectName> animation.
`Balloon`	Click the help balloon.	Click the help balloon.
`Border`	Click the <ObjectName> border.	Click the <ObjectName> border.
`Calendar`	Click the desired date.	Click the desired date.
`Caret`	Click the <ObjectName> caret.	Click the <ObjectName> caret.
`Cartooon graphic`	Click the <ObjectName> cartoon graphic.	Click the <ObjectName> cartoon graphic.
`Chart`	Click the <ObjectName> chart.	Click the <ObjectName> chart.
`Checkbox`	Click the <ObjectName> check box.	**Select the <ObjectName> option.**
`CheckListBox`	Select the desired item(s) in the <ObjectName> list.	Select the desired item(s) in the <ObjectName> list.
`CheckListBox Item`	Click the <ObjectName> list item.	Click the <ObjectName> list item.
`CheckListBox Item - Checkbox`	Select the box before the <ObjectName> item.	Select the check box before the <ObjectName> item.

Object Type	Standard Template Text	Microsoft Template Text
`Clock`	Click the <ObjectName> clock.	Click the <ObjectName> clock.
`Column`	Click an entry in the <ObjectName> column.	Click an entry in the <ObjectName> column.
`Column Header`	Click the <ObjectName> column header.	Click the <ObjectName> column header.
`Combobox`	Click the <ObjectName> list.	**Click the <ObjectName> box.**
`Combobox - Editbox`	Click in the edit field of the <ObjectName> combobox.	**Click the <ObjectName> box.**
`Date/Time box`	Click the <ObjectName> date/ time field.	**Click the <ObjectName> date/ time box.**
`Cursor`	Click the <ObjectName> cursor.	Click the <ObjectName> cursor.
`Date/Time box - Editbox`	Click in the <ObjectName> field.	**Click in the <ObjectName> box.**
`Date/Time box - DownSpinButton`	Click the <ObjectName> date/ time box.	Click the <ObjectName> date/ time box.
`Date/Time box - Spinbox`	Click the up or down arrow next to the <ObjectName> field.	Click the up or down arrow next to the <ObjectName> box.
`Date/Time box - UpSpinButton`	Click the <ObjectName> date/ time box.	Click the <ObjectName> date/ time box.
`Diagram`	Click the <ObjectName> diagram.	Click the <ObjectName> diagram.
`Dial box`	Click the <ObjectName> dial box.	Click the <ObjectName> dial box.
`DragListBox`	Click an entry in the list.	**Select an entry in the list.**
`DragListBox Item`	Click the <ObjectName> list item.	**Select the <ObjectName> list item.**
`Drop-down button`	Click the button to the right of the <ObjectName> field.	**Click the drop-down arrow to the right of the <ObjectName> box.**
`DropDown Grid Button`	Click the <ObjectName> button.	Click the <ObjectName> button.
`DropDown List`	Click an entry in the list.	Select an entry in the list.
`DropDown Menu Button`	Click the <ObjectName> dropdown button to activate the menu.	Click the <ObjectName> dropdown arrow to access the menu.
`Editfield`	Click in the <ObjectName> field.	**Click the <ObjectName> box.**
`Equation`	Click the <ObjectName> equation.	Click the <ObjectName> equation.

Object Type	Standard Template Text	Microsoft Template Text
`Graphics`	Click the <ObjectName> graphic.	Click the <ObjectName> graphic.
`Grip object`	Click the <ObjectName> grip.	Click the <ObjectName> grip.
`Hot key field`	Click the <ObjectName> hotkey field.	**Click the <ObjectName> keyboard shortcut box.**
`Hyperlink`	Click the <ObjectName> hyperlink.	**Click the <ObjectName> link.**
`IP Address box`	Click in the <ObjectName> ip address.	**Click in the <ObjectName> Internet Protocol address.**
`IP Address box - Editbox`	Click in the <ObjectName> ip address field.	**Click in the <ObjectName> Internet Protocol address box.**
`Listbox`	Click an entry in the list.	**Select an entry in the list.**
`Listbox item`	Click the <ObjectName> list item.	Select the <ObjectName> list item.
`Menu bar`	Click the <ObjectName> menu bar.	Click the <ObjectName> menu bar.
`Menu entry`	Click the <ObjectName> menu.	**Click the <ObjectName> command.**
`Object Group`	Click the <ObjectName> object group.	Click the <ObjectName> object group.
`Outline`	Click the <ObjectName> tree control.	**Click an entry the <ObjectName> tree control.**
`Outline item`	Click the <ObjectName> tree item.	Click the <ObjectName> tree item.
`Outline item button`	Click the + button before the <ObjectName> tree item.	Click the plus sign before the <ObjectName> tree item.
`Pager`	Click the <ObjectName> arrow.	Click the <ObjectName> arrow.
`Pager - Down Arrow`	Click the <ObjectName> arrow.	Click the <ObjectName> arrow.
`Pager - Horizontal`	Click the <ObjectName> arrow.	Click the <ObjectName> arrow.
`Pager - Left Arrow`	Click the <ObjectName> arrow.	Click the <ObjectName> arrow.
`Pager - Right Arrow`	Click the <ObjectName> arrow.	Click the <ObjectName> arrow.
`Pager - Up Arrow`	Click the <ObjectName> arrow.	Click the <ObjectName> arrow.
`Pager - Vertical`	Click the <ObjectName> arrow.	Click the <ObjectName> arrow.
`Pane`	Click the <ObjectName> pane.	Click the <ObjectName> pane.
`Pointer`	Click the <ObjectName> pointer.	Click the <ObjectName> pointer.

Object Type	**Standard Template Text**	**Microsoft Template Text**
`Popup menu`	Click the <ObjectName> menu.	**(Does not exist in Microsoft Template)**
`Progress bar`	Click the <ObjectName> progress bar.	Click the <ObjectName> progress bar.
`Property page`	Click the <ObjectName> property page.	Click the <ObjectName> property page.
`Pushbutton`	Click the <ObjectName> button.	Click the <ObjectName> button.
`Radiobutton`	Click the <ObjectName> option.	**Select the <ObjectName> option.**
`RichEdit`	Click the <ObjectName> field.	Click the <ObjectName> box.
`Row`	Click an entry in the <ObjectName> row.	Click an entry in the <ObjectName> row.
`Row header`	Click the <ObjectName> row header.	Click the <ObjectName> row header.
`Ruler`	Click the ruler.	Click the ruler.
`Ruler - Horizontal`	Click the horizontal ruler.	Click the horizontal ruler.
`Ruler - Vertical`	Click the vertical ruler.	Click the vertical ruler.
`Scrollbar`	Click the <ObjectName> scrollbar.	Click the <ObjectName> scrollbar.
`Scrollbar - Horizontal`	Click the <ObjectName> scrollbar.	Click the <ObjectName> scrollbar.
`Scrollbar - Vertical`	Click the <ObjectName> scrollbar.	Click the <ObjectName> scrollbar.
`Scrollbar box`	Click the <ObjectName> scrollbar.	Click the <ObjectName> scrollbar.
`Scrollbar box - Horizontal`	Click the <ObjectName> scrollbar.	Click the <ObjectName> scrollbar.
`Scrollbar box - vertical`	Click the <ObjectName> scrollbar.	Click the <ObjectName> scrollbar.
`Scrollbar button`	Click the <ObjectName> button of the scrollbar.	**Click the <ObjectName> scroll arrow of the scrollbar.**
`Scrollbar button - Down`	Click the <ObjectName> button of the scrollbar.	**Click the <ObjectName> scroll arrow of the scrollbar.**
`Scrollbar button - Horizontal`	Click the <ObjectName> button of the scrollbar.	**Click the <ObjectName> scroll arrow of the scrollbar.**
`Scrollbar button - Left`	Click the <ObjectName> button of the scrollbar.	**Click the <ObjectName> scroll arrow of the scrollbar.**

Object Type	Standard Template Text	Microsoft Template Text
`Scrollbar button - PageDown`	Click the <ObjectName> button of the scrollbar.	**Click the <ObjectName> scroll arrow of the scrollbar.**
`Scrollbar button - PageLeft`	Click the <ObjectName> button of the scrollbar.	**Click the <ObjectName> scroll arrow of the scrollbar.**
`Scrollbar button - PageRight`	Click the <ObjectName> button of the scrollbar.	**Click the <ObjectName> scroll arrow of the scrollbar.**
`Scrollbar button - PageUp`	Click the <ObjectName> button of the scrollbar.	**Click the <ObjectName> scroll arrow of the scrollbar.**
`Scrollbar button - Right`	Click the <ObjectName> button of the scrollbar.	**Click the <ObjectName> scroll arrow of the scrollbar.**
`Scrollbar button - Up`	Click the <ObjectName> button of the scrollbar.	**Click the <ObjectName> scroll arrow of the scrollbar.**
`Scrollbar button - Vertical`	Click the <ObjectName> button of the scrollbar.	**Click the <ObjectName> scroll arrow of the scrollbar.**
`Separator`	Click the <ObjectName> separator.	Click the <ObjectName> separator.
`Slider`	Click the <ObjectName> slider, and drag it to the desired level.	**Move the <ObjectName> slider to the desired level.**
`Slider - Track`	Click the <ObjectName> slider.	Click the <ObjectName> slider.
`Sound`	Click the <ObjectName> sound.	Click the <ObjectName> sound.
`Spin box`	Click the up or down arrow next to the <ObjectName> field.	**Click the up or down arrow next to the <ObjectName> box.**
`Spin box - Down button`	Click the down arrow next to the <ObjectName> field.	**Click the down arrow next to the <ObjectName> box.**
`Spin box - Up button`	Click the up arrow next to the <ObjectName> field.	**Click the up arrow next to the <ObjectName> box.**
`Static Text`	Click in the <ObjectName> field.	**Click the <ObjectName> box.**
`Statusbar`	Click the statusbar.	**Click the status bar.**
`Statusbar button`	Click the <ObjectName> button in the statusbar.	**Click the <ObjectName> button on the statusbar.**
`Tab`	Click the <ObjectName> tab.	Click the <ObjectName> tab.
`Tab - Horizontal`	Click the <ObjectName> horizontal tab.	Click the <ObjectName> horizontal tab.
`Tab - vertical`	Click the <ObjectName> vertical tab.	Click the <ObjectName> vertical tab.
`Tab list`	Click the <ObjectName> tab list.	Click the <ObjectName> tab list.
`Table`	Click the <ObjectName> table.	Click the <ObjectName> table.

Object Type	**Standard Template Text**	**Microsoft Template Text**
`Table cell`	Click the <ObjectName> cell.	Click the <ObjectName> cell.
`Titlebar`	Click the titlebar.	Click the title bar.
`Titlebar button`	Click the <ObjectName> button in the titlebar.	**Click the <ObjectName> button on the titlebar.**
`Toolbar`	Click the <ObjectName> toolbar.	Click the <ObjectName> toolbar.
`Toolbar button`	Click the <ObjectName> button.	Click the <ObjectName> button.
`Tooltip`	Click the <ObjectName> tooltip.	Click the <ObjectName> tooltip.
`Universal Object`	Click the <ObjectName> object.	Click the <ObjectName> object.
`Whitespace`	Click the <ObjectName> whitespace.	Click the <ObjectName> whitespace.
`Window`	Click the <ObjectName>.	Click the <ObjectName>.
`Workspace`	Click the desired object.	Click the desired object.

Index

Symbols

<Bubble text> sound file 367
<Classes> section, template file
<class> elements, attributes 391
about 390
DisplayName attribute 391
Gender attribute 391
ListName attribute 391
name attribute 391
<Defaults> section, template file
about 392
Defaults> element, Gender attribute 392
<Events> section, template file
about 388
Event Type 390
ShiftKeyPrefix 390
<Instructions> section, template file
<Template> elements, series 398
about 397
continue 398
decision_headline 400
knowit_confirmdemo 399
knowit_continue 399
knowit_dragwarning 399
knowit_explanation 398
knowit_finish_close 399
knowit_leadin 398
knowit_leadout 398
knowit_nextstep 398
knowit_warningL1 398
knowit_warningL2 398
knowit_warningL3_0 398
knowit_warningL3_H 399
knowit_warningL4 399
leadin 398
leadin_score 398
leadout 398
pauselink 398
scoring 399
scoring_NO 399
scoring_YES 399
strinp_anything_text 399
strinp_anything_text_noexample 400
strinp_formatter 400
strinp_nothing 400
strinp_or 400
strinp_something_text 399
strinp_something_text_noexample 399
strinp_suppress_example 399
typingcomplete 399
<Keynames> section, template file
<Key> element 396
about 395
<ShiftKeyPrefix> section, template file 397
<Styles> section, template file
about 388
bold attribute 388
color attribute 388
italics attribute 388
<Template> sections, template file
<ObjectName /> element 394
<ObjectType /> element 394
<Template> element 393
<Text> element 393
about 393
<XHTMLText> and </XHTMLText> tags 401

A

Action Area, Screenshot pane 81, 82
Action Area on/off button 91, 102

action areas
- Action Area on/off 91
- copying 91
- deleting 91
- modifying 91
- new action area, creating 91

Action Frames 83, 290, 291
Action Properties pane 86
- about 87

actions
- about 87
- action areas, adjusting 90, 91
- Action Properties pane 87
- bubble text, adjusting 92, 93, 94
- Drag 87
- keyboard action, working with 94, 95, 96, 97, 98
- Keyboard 87
- Left begin drag 87
- Left button down 87
- Left button up 87
- Left click 87
- Left double-click 87
- Left triple-click 87
- Middle begin drag 88
- Middle button down 88
- Middle button up 88
- Middle click 88
- Middle double-click 88
- mouse actions, working with 89, 90
- Point 88
- Right begin down 88
- Right begin drag 88
- Right begin up 88
- Right click 88
- Right double-click 88
- Right triple-click 88
- string input actions, working with 98-103
- Wheel 88

actions, capturing
- about 46
- problematic actions 46

ActiveX
- Microsoft Template Text 491
- Standard Template Text 491

Add 'anything' button 110
Add 'blank' button 110
Add 'something' button 110
additional roles 344
Add new text button 109
AICC 191
Alert
- Microsoft Template Text 491
- Standard Template Text 491

Alternative Actions
- adding 257-263
- Alternative icon 262, 263
- capturing, automatically 264
- default action 264
- Enter button 258
- Next action button 261, 264
- Previous action button 261, 264
- recording, for frame 259
- Set as default action button 264
- Template text is visible in Know It? mode button 259

Alternative icon 262
Alternative Paths
- about 265
- adding, to Topic 266-268
- Change end point button 269
- deleting 269
- end point, changing 269
- looping back 279
- Next alternative button 269
- Next Frame button 268
- Previous alternative button 269
- re-join point, changing 269
- user input, auto responding to 279, 280

Animation
- Microsoft Template Text 491
- Standard Template Text 491

Application
- Microsoft Template Text 491
- Standard Template Text 491

application-based structure 38
automatic, publishing
- /password:<password>, parameter 217
- /profile:<profile>, parameter 217
- /profilename:<profile>, parameter 217
- <settings>, parameter 217
- batch job, publishing via 218, 219
- command line command 216, 217
- CommandLinePublish.exe file 217

files, settings 216
Aviation Industry Computer-Based Training Committee. *See* **AICC**

B

Balloon
Microsoft Template Text 491
Standard Template Text 491
Bold button 123
Border
Microsoft Template Text 491
Standard Template Text 491
Branch
about 273
Decision Frames, in Know It! mode 278
Decision Frames, in See It! mode 277
decision path, deleting 277
inserting 273-276
Insert Path button 273
order of paths, changing in Decision Frame 276, 277
Broken Links pane, Developer screen 27
Bubble
Bubble Properties pane 115
custom text, adding 121
custom text, tagging for different nodes 124, 125
format, changing 116
icon, adding 118, 119
pointer, changing 116
redo function 127
repositioning 117
size, changing 118
string input Bubble text, standerized approach 125, 127
template text versus custom text 120
text, changing 119
text, formatting 123, 124
texts, selecting 122, 123
undo function 127
Bubble format
Bubble, repositioning 117
Bubble, size changing 118
Bubble pointer, changing 116
changing 116
icon, adding to Bubble 118, 119
Bubble icon button 119
Bubble Pointer button 116
Bubble Properties pane 86
about 115
Bubble text link button 312
Create link button 313
Create new web page button 313
Bubble text
adjusting 92, 93
Change end point button 94
changing 119
formatting 123
Ignore context button 94
template text versus custom text 120
Bubble text, formatting
Bold button 123
Custom Text Font button 123
Font Color button 123
Hyperlink button 124
Italics button 123
Non-breaking Text button 124
Template Text Font button 124
Underline button 123
Bubble Text options, content defaults
about 52
bubble pointer option 53
fill option 54
font option 54
icon option 53
Use Template Text option 54

C

Calendar
Microsoft Template Text 491
Standard Template Text 491
Cancel Check Out button 242
Caret
Microsoft Template Text 491
Standard Template Text 491
Cartooon graphic
Microsoft Template Text 491
Standard Template Text 491
Change end point button 269
Chart
Microsoft Template Text 491
Standard Template Text 491

Checkbox
Microsoft Template Text 491
Standard Template Text 491
Check In All button 235
Check In button 237
CheckListBox
Microsoft Template Text 491
Standard Template Text 491
CheckListBox Item
Microsoft Template Text 491
Standard Template Text 491
CheckListBox Item - Checkbox
Microsoft Template Text 491
Standard Template Text 491
Check Out button 241
Check Spelling button 162
Clear Search button 357
client/server environment
about 233
UPK, accessing in 481-485
Clock
Microsoft Template Text 492
Standard Template Text 492
CMS 180
Column
Microsoft Template Text 492
Standard Template Text 492
Column Header
Microsoft Template Text 492
Standard Template Text 492
Combobox
Microsoft Template Text 492
Standard Template Text 492
Combobox - Editbox
Microsoft Template Text 492
Standard Template Text 492
Concept pane
about 303
Create link button 311
Create new web page button 303
Web Page, attaching 306
Web Page, using 302-305
content
Content Conversion Wizard 253
converting, from OnDemand 252-256
converting, from previous version UPK 252-256
Document ID 455
Do It! mode 169
exporting 246, 247
exporting, for translation 451-455
importing 246, 247
Know It? mode 169
pre-publication checks 162
publishing 171
publishing, for online use 180
See It! mode 168
testing 168, 170
Try It! mode 169
content, publishing
for online use 180
generic approach 171-179
published, folder structure 179, 180
content, publishing for online use
HTML Web Site, creating 186
LMS Package, creating 191
Standalone Topic Files, creating 195
player, creating 180
content-based structure 38
content defaults
Bubble Text, options 52-54
general options 50, 51
Introduction/End Frames, options 55
setting 50
String Input, options 56, 57
Content Conversion Wizard
about 253
browse button 253
OnDemand.ini file 253
Title Selection dialog box 254
Content Management System. *See* **CMS**
content object
about 233
check-out, cancelling 242
checking in 234, 235
checking out 240
deleted document, restoring 245, 246
document versions, working with 242, 243
earlier version, displaying 243
earlier version, reverting to 243, 245
exporting 247-249
Glossary, assigning 331, 332
glossary links, updating 168
importing 249-252

previewing 170
Properties button 236
spell, checking 162-166
spelling options, changing 166, 167
content object, checking in
about 234, 235
change, specifying reason for 239, 240
check-in scope, confirming 237-239
content object, properties 236
content objects, selecting 237
local repository 234
Related Documents pane 238
UPK Workflow 235, 236
content object, checking out
cancelling 242
Check Out button 241
from server 240, 241
Copy Action Area button 91
course-based structure 38
Create link button, Concept pane 311
Create new Action Area button 91
Create new web page button, Concept pane 303
Cursor
Microsoft Template Text 492
Standard Template Text 492
custom template
assigning, to existing Topics 409, 410
creating 402
editing 403
template copy, taking 402
Template Text, customizing 404-406
using, as default template 408, 409
Custom Text
about 367
adding, to Bubble 121
content object, exporting for translation 451-456
tagging, for different nodes 124, 125
versus template text 120
Visible in Do It! button 125
Visible in Know It? button 125
Visible in Player button 125
Visible in Print button 125
Visible in See It!/Try It! button 125
translated file, importing 459-461
translating 451
using, in Topics 284
XLIFF, translating via 457, 459
Custom Text Font button 123
custom view
creating 36, 37

D

Date/Time box
Microsoft Template Text 492
Standard Template Text 492
Date/Time box - DownSpinButton
Microsoft Template Text 492
Standard Template Text 492
Date/Time box - Editbox
Microsoft Template Text 492
Standard Template Text 492
Date/Time box - Spinbox
Microsoft Template Text 492
Standard Template Text 492
Decision Frame
about 14
Delay time (s) field 277
Header 272
inserting 270-272
in Know It! mode 278
in See It! mode 277-278
order of paths, changing 276-277
Rename button 271
decision path
Delete Path button 277
deleting 277
Define custom colors button 105
Delay time (s) field 277
Delete Action Area button 91
Delete button 142
deleted document, content object
restoring 245
Delete entry button 114
Delete Path button 277
delivery formats
selecting 19, 20
deployment packages
customizing 414
deployment category, creating 417-419
deployment formats defining, area 415-417
logo, customizing 419-421

output style, customizing 422, 423
publishing category, setting 424, 425
Developer screen
Broken Links pane 27
Checked out by 32
Checked out hostname 32
Column Chooser dialog box 34
Creation date 32
Document ID 32
Frames 32
information displayed for objects, changing 32
Language 32
Last modified by 33
Last modified date 33
Link count 33
Name 33
Owner 32
panes, arranging on screen 28-31
Path 33
properties pane 26
Related Documents pane 28
screen layout 26
State 33
structure 25
Type 33
Version 33
views, working with 35
Diagram
Microsoft Template Text 492
Standard Template Text 492
Dial box
Microsoft Template Text 492
Standard Template Text 492
document
content, changing 434-440
documentation, output formats
HP Quality Center Test Script 18
instructor manual 18
job aid 18
System Process Document 18
Test Document 18
Training Guide 17
document formats
customizing 427
document's contents, changing 434-440
existing document format, copying 427
name, changing 428, 430
output format, publication options changing 430, 431
UPK settings, customizing 428-434
Document ID 455
documents, publishing
about 198, 199
automatic, publishing 216
HP Quality Center Test Script, publishing 211
Instructor Manual, publishing 205
Job Aid, publishing 207
System Process document, publishing 199
Test Document, publishing 209
Training Guide, publishing 214
document versions
earlier version, displaying 243
earlier version, reverting to 243-245
working with 242, 243
Do It! mode 16
drag-and-drop
about 66
Action area size in pixels option 68
Distance between screenshots in pixels option 68
Enable automatic recording option 67
recording, steps 68-77
DragListBox
Microsoft Template Text 492
Standard Template Text 492
DragListBox Item
Microsoft Template Text 492
Standard Template Text 492
Drop-down button
Microsoft Template Text 492
Standard Template Text 492
DropDown Grid Button
Microsoft Template Text 492
Standard Template Text 492
DropDown List
Microsoft Template Text 492
Standard Template Text 492
DropDown Menu Button
Microsoft Template Text 492
Standard Template Text 492

E

edit 47
Editfield
Microsoft Template Text 492
Standard Template Text 492
empty Topic
creating 58, 59
recording 59
Topic, recording 59, 60
Empty Topics icon 154
End Frame 83, 291, 292
end point button 94
Enter button 258
Equation
Microsoft Template Text 492
Standard Template Text 492
existing content objects
copy, taking 446
custom text, translating 451
foreign-language Deployment Package, using 448-451
foreign-language template, using 446-448
providing, in another language 445
screenshots, replacing with localized versions 463, 465
sound files, re-recording 466
Explanation Frames
about 84, 292
Explanation Frame button 294
Insert button 294
inserting 293-297
inserting, issues 297
viewing 298
Export function 247-249

F

file header, template file 387
First Frame 85
folders, library 40
Font Color button 123
foreign-language templates
about 441, 442
format 444, 445
supported languages 442, 443
Frame
Alternative Path, adding 266-269
copying 299, 300
deleting 141, 142, 143
missing Frames, adding 128, 130
No-context Frame, inserting 130, 131
pasting 301
sound options, setting up 367
sound properties, displaying 365-367
sound recorder specifying, steps 368, 369
Frame Delay 52
Frame Structure button 83
Frame Structure Pane, Topic Editor
about 82
Action Frame 83
Decision Frame 83
End Frame 83
Explanation Frame 84
First Frame 85
frames, numbering 85
Go To Frame 85
Last Frame 85
Next Frame 85
Previous Frame 85
standard toolbar, buttons 85
Start Frame 83

G

general options, content defaults
Frame delay 52
Know It? Required Percentage 52
language 51
Remediation options 52
screen resolution 52
template 51
GKS 8
Global Knowledge Software. *See* **GKS**
Glossary
about 326, 327
assigning, to content objects 331, 332
closing 330, 331
creating, in UPK 328
entries, creating from within glossary 328, 329
links, generating manually 335
links, regenerating 333
links, updating 333-335
saving 330

stand-alone Glossary, generating 336
Training Guide 336
Word-format Glossary, creating 336-338
Go To Frame 85
Graphics
Microsoft Template Text 493
Standard Template Text 493
Grip object
Microsoft Template Text 493
Standard Template Text 493

H

Hide action area button 280
Horizontal Layout button 156
Hot key field
Microsoft Template Text 493
Standard Template Text 493
HP Quality Center Test Script
about 18
publishing 212
HP Quality Center Test Script, publishing
document, properties 212
files, generated 213
Group actions by Context ID, option 213
options 212
output, example 213
Text mode, option 212
Use encoded folder and file names, option 212, 213
HTML Web Site
about 13
Concepts pane 188
Convert screenshots to 256 colors, option 186
creating 186
files, generated 186
Keyword Index link 188
Keyword Index page 188
output, example 187-191
publishing, options 186
Section 508c 186
Hyperlink
Microsoft Template Text 493
Standard Template Text 493
Hyperlink button 124

I

Ignore context button 94
image editing application
selecting 137, 138
Import function 249-252
Infoblocks 302
Insert Path button 273
Insert template text as custom text button 376
Insert template text as user text button 122
installing
Topic Player 486-490
UPK 3.5 470-477
UPK developer environment 470-477
instructor-led training, issues
additional administrative burden 10
additional capital costs 10
ongoing data refreshes 10
significant data set up 10
system instability, possibility 10
Instructor Manual
about 18
publishing 205
Instructor Manual, publishing
document, properties 205
files, generated 205
instructor note, property 205
options 205
output, example 206
Introduction/End Frames options, content defaults 55
Introduction frame 284, 285
IP Address box
Microsoft Template Text 493
Standard Template Text 493
IP Address box - Editbox
Microsoft Template Text 493
Standard Template Text 493
Italics button 123

J

Job Aid
about 18
publishing 207
Job Aid, publishing
about 207

document, properties 207
files, generated 207
Job Aid Revision, property 207
options 207
output, example 208
jump-in point
about 352
defining 353
selecting, in Player 354, 355
working 355

K

keyboard action
working with 94-98
Keyword Index page, HTML Web Site
about 188
Table of Contents link 189
Know It? mode 16
Decision Frames 278

L

Last Frame 85
Learning Management System. *See* **LMS**
Lessons 145
library
about 23
accessing 24
application-based structure 38
course-based structure 38
Developer screen 24, 25
folders, creating 40
module-based structure 38
security-based structure 38
structure, changing 40
structure, selecting 37
version-based structure 38
versus outline 145, 146
Link New Module button 151
Link New Topic button 153
Listbox
Microsoft Template Text 493
Standard Template Text 493
Listbox item
Microsoft Template Text 493
Standard Template Text 493
LMS
about 11, 191
creating 191
LMS Package
about 13
Convert screenshots to 256 colors, option 193
files, generated 194
Format for Print It! mode, option 193
Include sound files, option 192
output, example 194
Playback Modes, option 193
Prefix URL, option 193
publishing, options 192
SCORM Version, option 193

M

Menu bar
Microsoft Template Text 493
Standard Template Text 493
Menu entry
Microsoft Template Text 493
Standard Template Text 493
Mercury TestDirector. *See* **HP Quality Center Test Script**
Missing Frame(s)
about 128
option, inserting 129, 130
Modify Action Areas button 91
module-based structure 38
Modules
about 145, 146
and Section, differences 146
mouse actions
action areas, adjusting 90, 91
bubble text, adjusting 92-94
working with 89, 90
multi-user environment. *See* **client/server environment**

N

Next action button 261
Next alternative button 269
Next Frame 85
Next Frame button 268
No-context Frame, inserting 130, 131
Non-breaking Text button 118, 124

O

Object Group
Microsoft Template Text 493
Standard Template Text 493
Object name 100
object type
about 100
ActiveX 491
Alert 491
Animation 491
application 491
Balloon 491
Border 491
Calendar 491
Caret 491
Cartooon graphic 491
Chart 491
Checkbox 491
CheckListBox 491
CheckListBox Item 491
CheckListBox Item - Checkbox 491
Clock 492
Column 492
Column Header 492
Combobox 492
Combobox - Editbox 492
Cursor 492
Date/Time box 492
Date/Time box - DownSpinButton 492
Date/Time box - Editbox 492
Date/Time box - Spinbox 492
Date/Time box - UpSpinButton 492
defining 410-414
Diagram 492
Dial box 492
DragListBox 492
DragListBox Item 492
Drop-down button 492
DropDown Grid Button 492
DropDown List 492
DropDown Menu Button 492
Editfield 492
Equation 492
Graphics 493
Grip object 493
Hot key field 493
Hyperlink 493
IP Address box 493
IP Address box - Editbox 493
Listbox 493
Listbox item 493
Menu bar 493
Menu entry 493
Object Group 493
Outline 493
Outline item 493
Outline item button 493
Pager 493
Pager - Down Arrow 493
Pager - Horizontal 493
Pager - Left Arrow 493
Pager - Right Arrow 493
Pager - Up Arrow 493
Pager - Vertical 493
Pane 493
Pointer 493
Popup menu 494
Progress bar 494
Property page 494
Pushbutton 494
Radiobutton 494
RichEdit 494
Row 494
Row header 494
Ruler 494
Ruler - Horizontal 494
Ruler - Vertical 494
Scrollbar 494
Scrollbar - Horizontal 494
Scrollbar - Vertical 494
Scrollbar box 494
Scrollbar box - Horizontal 494
Scrollbar box - vertical 494
Scrollbar button 494
Scrollbar button - Down 494
Scrollbar button - Horizontal 494
Scrollbar button - Left 494
Scrollbar button - PageDown 495
Scrollbar button - PageLeft 495
Scrollbar button - PageRight 495
Scrollbar button - PageUp 495
Scrollbar button - Right 495
Scrollbar button - Up 495

Scrollbar button - Vertical 495
Separator 495
Slider 495
Slider - Track 495
Sound 495
Spin box 495
Spin box - Down button 495
Spin box - Up button 495
Static Text 495
Statusbar 495
Statusbar button 495
Tab 495
Tab - Horizontal 495
Tab - vertical 495
Table 495
Table cell 496
Tab list 495
Titlebar 496
Titlebar button 496
Toolbar 496
Toolbar button 496
Tooltip 496
Universal Object 496
Whitespace 496
window 496
Workspace 496
Object type Editfield 101
OnDemand
about 8
version, differences 249, 252
version 9.1 8
version 9.1.7 8
OnDemand.ini file 254
OnDemand 6.x 253
OnDemand 7.x 253
OnDemand 8.7 23, 145, 252
OnDemand 8.x 252
OnDemand 9.1 23, 145, 146
OnDemand 9.x 146, 252
online delivery, output formats
Do It! mode 16
HTML Web Site 13
Know It? mode 16
LMS package 13
Player format 13
Print It! mode 17
See It! mode 15
Try It! mode 16
online use
content, publishing for 180
Open the Topic Editor, recorder options 65
Outline
about 146
adjusting 154-160
building 148
creating 148
creating, steps 148-150
Glossary field 150
Language field 149
Location field 149
Microsoft Template Text 493
Name field 149
New Module dialog box 149
Outline Elements, inserting 151, 152
selecting, guidelines 147, 148
Standard Template Text 493
structure 147
Template field 149
Topic, inserting 152, 153
Topic placeholders, inserting 153, 154
versus library 145, 146
Outline Editor 150
Outline Elements
about 57, 148
inserting, in Outline 151, 152
Topics, inserting 152, 153
Outline item
Microsoft Template Text 493
Standard Template Text 493
Outline item button
Microsoft Template Text 493
Standard Template Text 493
outlines 23
output formats, UPK
about 12, 13
documentation 17
online delivery 13-15

P

Package
creating 317, 318
files, adding 318-320
linking, to content object 320-323

linking, to URL 323-326
used, for linking files 316
Pager
Microsoft Template Text 493
Standard Template Text 493
Pager - Down Arrow
Microsoft Template Text 493
Standard Template Text 493
Pager - Horizontal
Microsoft Template Text 493
Standard Template Text 493
Pager - Left Arrow
Microsoft Template Text 493
Standard Template Text 493
Pager - Right Arrow
Microsoft Template Text 493
Standard Template Text 493
Pager - Up Arrow
Microsoft Template Text 493
Standard Template Text 493
Pager - Vertical
Microsoft Template Text 493
Standard Template Text 493
Pane
Standard Template Text 493
Parameters page 132
plan 47
Player
creating 180
convert screenshots to 256 colors, option 182
create links for backward compatibility, option 182
Default playback mode, option 184
Enable Direct Do It!, option 184
Enable skipping in Try It! mode , option 183
Enable users to change their Player preferences, option 183
files, generated 184
Format for Print It! mode, option 182
include sound files, option 182
jump-in points, defining 354, 355
Key combination for advancing in Do It! mode , option 184
Marquee color , option 182
options changing, permissions assigning 359-361
output, example 185
Play audio , option 183
Preferences button 360
publishing, options 182
roles, selecting 345
Show introduction text, option 183
training, providing 361
training options 362
publishing, for online use 180
publishing, options 181
Player, training options
Player, training optionsUPK 363
Player, training optionsUPK Player, explaining 362
Player, training optionsUPK simulation creating, UPK Player used 363
Player format 13
Pointer
Microsoft Template Text 493
Standard Template Text 493
Popup menu
Microsoft Template Text 494
Standard Template Text 494
pre-publication checks, content 162
Preferences button 360
Previous action button 261
Previous alternative button 269
Previous Frame 85
Print It! mode 17
Progress bar
Microsoft Template Text 494
Standard Template Text 494
Properties button 236
Properties button, content object
Workflow category 236
Properties pane, Developer screen 26, 27
property editor pane, Topic Editor
Action Properties pane, Show/Hide 86
Bubble Properties pane, Show/Hide 86
buttons 86
Sound Properties pane, Show/Hide 86
Property page
Microsoft Template Text 494
Standard Template Text 494
publish 47
published content, integrating

Topic, integrating into presentation 219-223
UPK, integrating 223
Pushbutton
Microsoft Template Text 494
Standard Template Text 494

R

Radiobutton
Microsoft Template Text 494
Standard Template Text 494
Recapture action button 95
Recapture screenshot 133
record 47
Recorded Topics icon 154
recorder options
Open the Topic Editor 65
recorder screenshot key 65
screenshot capture 64
setting 64
Time (in seconds) to hide recorder window before screen capture 65
recorder screenshot key, recorder options 65
recorder window
about 60, 61
for automatic recording 62
recording
adjusting 128-130
empty Topic, creating 58-59
empty Topic, recording 59
Frames, deleting 141-143
image editing application, selecting 137-138
missing Frames, adjusting 128-130
No-context Frame, inserting 130-131
planning 47-50
recorder window 60-61
recorder window, for automatic recording 62
sample exercise 62, 63
screenshot, editing 64-68
screenshots, recapturing 132, 133
screenshots, replacing 131
time, deciding 21
Topic, recording 59, 60
Topic, re-recording 62, 63
recording, planning
guidelines 48-50
Related Documents pane, content object checking in 238, 239
Related Documents pane, Developer screen 28
Rename button 271
Replace text button 109
RichEdit
Microsoft Template Text 494
Standard Template Text 494
roles
about 339, 352
additional roles 344
assigning, to Topics 343, 344
defining 340, 342
issues 340
Publish button 349
publishing for 349-351
selecting, in player 345-348
trainee's selection 348
Row
Microsoft Template Text 494
Standard Template Text 494
Row header
Microsoft Template Text 494
Standard Template Text 494
Ruler
Microsoft Template Text 494
Standard Template Text 494
Ruler - Horizontal
Microsoft Template Text 494
Standard Template Text 494
Ruler - Vertical
Microsoft Template Text 494
Standard Template Text 494

S

Save button 154
SCORM 191
screen layout, Developer screen
Broken Links pane 27
horizontal layout 26
panes, arranging on screen 28-31
properties pane 26, 27
Related Documents pane 28
single view 26
vertical layout 26

view toolbar, buttons 26
screenshot
editing 136-140
image editing application, selecting 137, 138
recapturing 132, 133
replacing 131
Screenshot pane, Topic Editor
about 81, 82
Action Area 81, 82
Scrollbar
Microsoft Template Text 494
Standard Template Text 494
Scrollbar - Horizontal
Microsoft Template Text 494
Standard Template Text 494
Scrollbar - Vertical
Microsoft Template Text 494
Standard Template Text 494
Scrollbar box
Microsoft Template Text 494
Standard Template Text 494
Scrollbar box - Horizontal
Microsoft Template Text 494
Standard Template Text 494
Scrollbar box - vertical
Microsoft Template Text 494
Standard Template Text 494
Scrollbar button
Microsoft Template Text 494
Standard Template Text 494
Scrollbar button - Down
Microsoft Template Text 494
Standard Template Text 494
Scrollbar button - Horizontal
Microsoft Template Text 494
Standard Template Text 494
Scrollbar button - Left
Microsoft Template Text 494
Standard Template Text 494
Scrollbar button - PageDown
Microsoft Template Text 495
Standard Template Text 495
Scrollbar button - PageLeft
Microsoft Template Text 495
Standard Template Text 495
Scrollbar button - PageRight
Microsoft Template Text 495
Standard Template Text 495
Scrollbar button - PageUp
Microsoft Template Text 495
Standard Template Text 495
Scrollbar button - Right
Microsoft Template Text 495
Standard Template Text 495
Scrollbar button - Up
Microsoft Template Text 495
Standard Template Text 495
Scrollbar button - Vertical
Microsoft Template Text 495
Standard Template Text 495
Search button 356
search facility
search facilityabout 356, 357
search facilitykeywords, assigning to Topics 357-359
search facilitykeywords, using 357
Section
about 146
and Modules, differences 146
security-based structure
about 38
See It! mode
about 15
Decision Frames 277
self-paced learning 11
Separator
Microsoft Template Text 495
Standard Template Text 495
Set as password field button 115
Set to default button 114
Shareable Content Object Reference Model,. *See* **SCORM**
Show custom text first button 123, 367
simulations
about 8
recording 43-45
screen 9
single-user environment. *See* **stand-alone environment**
Single Layout button 158
Slider
Microsoft Template Text 495
Standard Template Text 495

Slider - Track
Microsoft Template Text 495
Standard Template Text 495
SmartHelp 229
SmartMatch 229
SME 45
Sound
Microsoft Template Text 495
Standard Template Text 495
sound
in player 382
publishing 380, 382
sound.wma 373
sound files
custom text sound files, recording 375, 376
deleting 379, 380
exporting 377, 378
importing 378, 379
locating, in library 372-374
re-recording 466
recording, for template text 369-372
sound properties
for Frame, displaying 365-367
Sound Properties button 366
Sound Properties pane 86
Play All button 371
Play button 371
Record button 154, 369
spelling options
Custom dictionary, option 167
Ignore words in UPPERCASE, option 167
Try to split compound words into two individual word, option 167
Spin box
Microsoft Template Text 495
Standard Template Text 495
Spin box - Up button
Microsoft Template Text 495
Standard Template Text 495
stand-alone environment 233
stand-alone installation
UPK, accessing in 478-481
Standalone Topic Files
about 13
Convert screenshots to 256 colors, option 196
files, generated 197
Format for Print It! mode, option 196
Include setup for topic player, option 196
Include sound files, option 196
output, example 197, 198
publishing, options 195, 196
Use encoded folder and file names, option 196
standard Details view 36
Start Frame 83, 284, 285
Static Text
Microsoft Template Text 495
Standard Template Text 495
Statusbar
Microsoft Template Text 495
Standard Template Text 495
Statusbar button
Microsoft Template Text 495
Standard Template Text 495
string input actions
<Something> option, removing 111
activity pane 100
Add 'anything' button 110
Add 'blank' button 110
Add 'something' button 110
application 100
background color, adjusting 105, 106
case sensitivity 114
Clear List option 113
delete entry, button 114
font, adjusting 107, 108
issues 103
new text, adding 109
object name 100
object type 100
Object type Editfield 101
passwords fields 114, 115
set as password field, button 115
set to default, button 114
string input action area, adjusting 104, 105
string input case sensitivity 115
String input options context menu 114
text, replacing 109
user entry, validating 108, 109
working with 98-103
String input background color button 105
String input case sensitivity button 115
String Input options, content defaults 56, 57

Subject Matter Expert. *See* **SME**
System Process Document 18
System Process document, publishing
additional information, property 200
BPD Revision, property 200
Convert screenshots to 256 characters, option 202
Department, property 200
document, properties 199, 200
files, generated 203
Include alternatives, option 202
Include images from packages, option 202
Include images in web pages, option 202
Last changed by, property 200
Microsoft file type, option 201
options 201
output, example 203, 204
Output, property 200
output format type, option 201
Paper size, option 202
Required Fields, property 200
Screenshots, option 202
Status, property 200
Text mode, option 202
Trigger, property 200
Use encoded folder and file names, option 202

T

Tab
Microsoft Template Text 495
Standard Template Text 495
Tab - Horizontal
Microsoft Template Text 495
Standard Template Text 495
Tab - vertical
Microsoft Template Text 495
Standard Template Text 495
Table cell
Microsoft Template Text 495
Standard Template Text 495
Tab list
Microsoft Template Text 495
Standard Template Text 495
template files, Template text
<Classes> section 390, 391
<Defaults> section 392
<Events> section 388-390
<Instructions> section 397-401
<Keynames> section 395-397
<ShiftKeyPrefix> section 397
<Styles> section 388
<Template> sections 392-395
about 386
creating 387
file header 387
languages 384, 385
Template Text
about 367
configuring 383
customizing 404-406
template files 384
versus custom text 120
Template Text Font button 124
Template text is visible in Know It? mode button 259
Template text visible in Know It? mode button 122
Test Document
about 18
publishing 209
Test Document, publishing
additional validation, property 209
document, properties 209
estimated time, property 209
files, generated 210
options 209, 210
output, example 210
purpose of test, property 209
Test Doc Revision, property 210
Test setup, property 210
Titlebar
Microsoft Template Text 496
Standard Template Text 496
Titlebar button
Microsoft Template Text 496
Standard Template Text 496
Toolbar
Microsoft Template Text 496
Standard Template Text 496
Toolbar button
Microsoft Template Text 496
Standard Template Text 496

Tooltip
Microsoft Template Text 496
Standard Template Text 496
Topic
about 23, 57, 145, 146
integrating, into presentation 219- 223
keywords, assigning 357, 358
organizing 146-148
previewing 170
re-recording 463-465
roles, assigning 343, 344
value, adding 283
Topic Editor
about 80
Frame Structure Pane 82-85
Property Editor pane 86
Screenshot pane 81, 82
Topic enhancing, Custom Text used
Action Frame 290
End Frame 291, 292
Explanation Frames 292
Explanation Frames, inserting 293-297
Explanation Frames, issues 297
Frames, copying 299, 300
Frames, pasting 300, 301
Introduction pane, version differences 286-289
Start Frame 284, 285
Topic placeholders
inserting 153, 154
Topic Player
installing, steps 486-490
training
trainingproviding, on Player 362
Training Guide 17
Training Guide, Glossary 336
Training Guide, publishing
document, properties 214
files, generated 214
options 214
output, example 214, 215
translated file
importing 460, 462
Try It! mode 16

U

Underline button 123
Undo button 127
Universal Object
Microsoft Template Text 496
Standard Template Text 496
UPK 363
about 7, 8
accessing, for first time 478
accessing, in client/server environment 481-485
accessing, in stand-alone installation 478-481
automatic recording 45
content, publishing 171
custom template, creating 402
custom text sound files, recording 375, 376
deployment packages, customizing 414
Developer screen 24
document formats, customizing 427, 428
employing 19
files, adding to Package 318-320
files linking, Package used 316
full-text search facility 356, 357
Glossary 326, 327
Glossary, creating 328
history 8
need for 8
new object type, defining 410-414
OnDemand 8
output formats 12, 13
Package, creating 317, 318
Package, linking to content object 320-323
role, in recording simulation 43-45
settings, customizing 428
Show this screen at startup option 24
simulations 8
simulations, screen 9
skipping enabling ability, removing 425, 427
sound, in player 382
sound, publishing 381, 382
sound file, existing 367
sound file, missing 367
sound files, attaching to Frame 367
sound files, deleting 379, 380
sound files, exporting 377, 378
sound files, importing 378, 379

sound files, locating in Library 372-375
sound files, recording for Template Text 369-371
sound properties, displaying for Frame 365-367
sound recorder, specifying 368, 369
Start Screen window 24
supported languages 442, 443
Template text, configuring 383, 384
Topic, previewing 170
Topic Player, installing 486-490
using, ways 19
version, differences 240
Web Page 301
working 11, 12
UPK, integrating into application
context, capturing 224-229
SmartHelp 229
SmartMatch 229
UPK, need for
instructor-led training 10
self-paced learning 11
simulations 8
UPK, supported languages
Danish (da) 442
Dutch (nl) 443
English (en) 443
Finnish (fi) 443
French (fr) 443
French Canadian (fr-ca) 443
German (de) 443
Hungarian (hu) 443
Italian (it) 443
Japanese (ja) 443
Korean (ko) 443
Mexican Spanish (es-mx) 443
Norwegian (no) 443
Polish (pl) 443
Portuguese (pt) 443
Russian (ru) 443
Simplified Chinese (zh-CHS) 443
Spanish (es) 443
Swedish (sv) 443
Traditional Chinese (zh-CHT) 443
Turkish (tr) 443
UPK, working
output formats 12, 13
UPK 2.x 252
UPK 3.1 8
UPK 3.5
about 146
automatic recording 45
installing 470-477
key changes 23
UPK 3.5.1
client/server edition 234
UPK 3.x 146
UPK developer environment
installing 470-477
UPK Player
Do It! mode 16
example 14
explaining, during classroom training 362
Know It? mode 16
modes 15
Print It! mode 17
See It! mode 15
Try It! mode 16
UPK simulation, creating 363
UPK simulation
creating, UPK Player used 363
UPK using, ways
delivery formats, selecting 19
recording 21, 22
recording time, deciding 21
standards 20
styles 20
UPK Workflow 235, 236
Up One Level button 152
User Productivity Kit. *See* **UPK**
Use templates button 122
Use Template Text button 120

V

version
differences 234-252
version-based structure 38
Vertical Layout button 156
views
all by owner 35
all by state 35
all checked out 35
checked out to me 35, 36

deleted documents 35
details view 35
lost documents 36
owned by me 35
standard Details view 36
working with 35
Visible in Do It! button 125
Visible in Know It? button 125
Visible in Player button 125
Visible in Print button 125
Visible in See It!/Try It! button 125

W

Web Page
attaching, in concept pane 306
Bubble text link button 312
creating 311
Editor 304
files, adding to Package 318-320
files linking, Packages used 316
image position, adjusting 309, 310
images, adding 306-308
images, using 306
image size, adjusting 309, 310
independent Web Pages, creating 311
linking, via hyperlink 312-314
linking, via icon 314, 315
Package, creating 317, 318
Package, linking to content object 320-323
Save button 304
using, in concept pane 302-305
using, in topics 311, 312
Whitespace
Microsoft Template Text 496
Standard Template Text 496
Window
Microsoft Template Text 496
Standard Template Text 496
Workflow category, Properties button
Assigned To 236
State 236
Workspace
Microsoft Template Text 496
Standard Template Text 496

X

XLIFF
used, for custom text translation 457, 459

Z

Z prefix 402
Zip files 316

Thank you for buying
Oracle User Productivity Kit 3.5

About Packt Publishing

Packt, pronounced 'packed', published its first book "*Mastering phpMyAdmin for Effective MySQL Management*" in April 2004 and subsequently continued to specialize in publishing highly focused books on specific technologies and solutions.

Our books and publications share the experiences of your fellow IT professionals in adapting and customizing today's systems, applications, and frameworks. Our solution based books give you the knowledge and power to customize the software and technologies you're using to get the job done. Packt books are more specific and less general than the IT books you have seen in the past. Our unique business model allows us to bring you more focused information, giving you more of what you need to know, and less of what you don't.

Packt is a modern, yet unique publishing company, which focuses on producing quality, cutting-edge books for communities of developers, administrators, and newbies alike. For more information, please visit our website: `www.packtpub.com`.

Writing for Packt

We welcome all inquiries from people who are interested in authoring. Book proposals should be sent to `author@packtpub.com`. If your book idea is still at an early stage and you would like to discuss it first before writing a formal book proposal, contact us; one of our commissioning editors will get in touch with you.

We're not just looking for published authors; if you have strong technical skills but no writing experience, our experienced editors can help you develop a writing career, or simply get some additional reward for your expertise.

www.ingramcontent.com/pod-product-compliance
Lightning Source LLC
LaVergne TN
LVHW082019200926
848481LV00010B/2888
* 9 7 8 1 8 4 9 6 8 0 1 6 5 *